Acclaim for ERIC HOBSBAWM's

The Age of Extremes

"An extraordinary book. . . . Hobsbawm's history of the twentieth century is . . . the history of a world which has both brought to full flowering the material and cultural potential of the nineteenth century and betrayed its promise. . . . [Written] in simple, clean prose, utterly free of jargon, pomposity, and pretension. . . . Hobsbawm has a unique range. . . . A challenging, often brilliant, and always cool and intelligent account of the world we have now inherited."
—Tony Judt, *The New York Review of Books*

"Having written a three-volume history of the 'long 19th century' (1789–1914), the great British historian Eric Hobsbawm has now turned to the 'short 20th century'. . . . What concerns him is . . . the great economic and social forces that constitute, for him, the warp and woof of history. . . . A bracing and magisterial work from a rich and acerbic mind."
—Stanley Hoffmann, *The New York Times Book Review*

"Few readers will come away unimpressed by the arguments with which he makes his case or by the breadth and depth of learning he brings to this massive task. . . . No one could write a genuinely comprehensive history of the 20th century, but Hobsbawm has come as close as anybody is likely to get. . . . A magnificent achievement of a very rare and remarkable kind."
—Walter Russell Mead, *Los Angeles Times Book Review*

"Eric Hobsbawm has laid down the lines on which the debate will proceed. . . . No future historian will be able to ignore it."
—*The Economist*

"A dazzling survey taking in everything from particle physics to post-modernist art, from collective farms to supermarket check-outs."
—*Financial Times*

"One of the most enthralling works of history that I have ever read. . . . Hobsbawm writes with a refreshing clarity which is delightfully pugnacious. He never hedges. One learns exactly what he thinks and why."
—Anthony Storr, *Literary Review*

"Remarkable. . . . Hobsbawm provides an interpretation of the recent past that makes mere retellings of events and profiles of famous leaders seem, in contrast, like so much potted journalism. . . . Deeply thoughtful and surprisingly new."
—Michael Kazin, *Washington Post Book World*

ERIC HOBSBAWM

The Age of Extremes

A History of the World, 1914–1991

VINTAGE BOOKS

A Division of Random House, Inc.   New York

FIRST VINTAGE BOOKS EDITION, FEBRUARY 1996

The Library of Congress has cataloged the Pantheon edition as follows:
Hobsbawm, E. J. (Eric J.), 1917–
The age of extremes, 1914–1991/Eric Hobsbawm.
p. cm.
Includes bibliographical references and index.
ISBN: 0-394-58575-5
1. History, Modern—20th century. I Title.
D421.H582 1995
909.82—dc20 94-28981
Vintage ISBN: 0-679-73005-2

Manufactured in the United States of America
B987

Contents

PART THREE: THE LANDSLIDE

Illustrations

(*Copyright holders are indicated in italics*)

Preface and Acknowledgements

Nobody can write the history of the twentieth century like that of any other era, if only because nobody can write about his or her lifetime as one can (and must) write about a period known only from outside, at second- or third-hand, from sources of the period or the works of later historians. My own lifetime coincides with most of the period with which this book deals, and for most of it, from early teen-age to the present, I have been conscious of public affairs, that is to say I have accumulated views and prejudices about it as a contemporary rather than as a scholar. This is one reason why under my professional hat as a historian I avoided working on the era since 1914 for most of my career, though not refraining from writing about it in other capacities. "My period," as they say in the trade, is the nineteenth century. I think it is now possible to see the Short Twentieth Century from 1914 to the end of the Soviet era in some historical perspective, but I come to it without the knowledge of the scholarly literature, let alone of all but a tiny sprinkle of archive sources, which historians of the twentieth century, of whom there is an enormous number, have accumulated.

It is, of course, utterly impossible for any single person to know the historiography of the present century, even that in any single major language, as, let us say, the historian of classical antiquity or of the Byzantine Empire knows what has been written in and about those long periods. Nevertheless, my own knowledge is casual and patchy even by the standards of historical erudition in the field of contemporary history. The most I have been able to do is to dip into the literature of particularly thorny and controverted questions—say, the history of the Cold War or that of the 1930s—far enough to satisfy myself that the views expressed in this book are tenable in the light of specialist research. Of course, I cannot have succeeded. There must be any number of questions on which I display ignorance as well as controversial views.

This book, therefore, rests on curiously uneven foundations. In addition to the wide and miscellaneous reading of a good many years, supplemented by what reading was necessary to give lecture courses on twentieth-century history to the graduate students of the New School for Social Research, I have drawn on the accumulated knowledge, memories and opinions of someone who has lived through the Short Twentieth Century, as what the social anthropologists call a "participant observer," or simply as an open-eyed traveller, or what my ancestors would have called a *kibbitzer,* in quite a lot of countries. The historical value of such experiences does not depend on being present on great historic occasions, or having known or even met prominent history-makers or statesmen. As a matter of fact, my experience as an occasional journalist enquiring into this or that country, chiefly in Latin America, has been that interviews with presidents or other decision-makers are usually unrewarding, for the obvious reason that most of what such people say is for the public record. The people from whom illumination comes are those who can, or want to, speak freely, preferably if they have no responsibility for great affairs. Nevertheless, though necessarily partial and misleading, to have known people and places has helped me enormously. It may be no more than the sight of the same city at an interval of thirty years—Valencia or Palermo—which alone brings home the speed and scale of social transformation in the third quarter of the present century. It may be simply a memory of something said in conversations long ago and stored away, sometimes for no clear reason, for future use. If the historian can make some sense of this century it is in large part because of watching and listening. I hope I have communicated to readers something of what I have learned through doing so.

The book also, and necessarily, rests on the information drawn from colleagues, students, and anyone else whom I buttonholed while I was working on it. In some cases the debt is systematic. The chapter on the sciences was submitted to my friends Alan Mackay FRS, who is not only a crystallographer but an encyclopedist, and John Maddox. Some of what I have written about economic development was read by my colleague at the New School, Lance Taylor, formerly of MIT, and much more was based on reading the papers, listening to the discussions and generally keeping my ears open during the conferences organized on various macro-economic problems at the World Institute for Development Economic Research of the U.N. University (UNU/WIDER) in Helsinki when it was transformed into a major international centre of research and discussion under the direction of Dr. Lal Jayawardena. In general, the summers I was able to spend at that admirable institution as a McDonnell Douglas visiting scholar were invaluable to me, not least through its proximity to, and intellectual concern with, the U.S.S.R. in its last years. I have not always accepted the advice of those I consulted, and, even when I have, the errors are strictly my own. I have derived much benefit from the conferences and colloquia at which academics spend much of their time meeting their colleagues largely for the purpose of picking each others' brains. I cannot possibly acknowledge all the colleagues from whom I have derived benefit or correction on formal or informal occasions, nor even all the information I have incidentally acquired from being lucky enough to teach a particularly international group of students at the New School. However, I think I must specifically acknowledge what I learned about the Turkish revolution and about the nature of Third World migration and social mobility from term papers produced by Ferdan Ergut and Alex Julca. I am also indebted to the doctoral dissertation of my pupil Margarita Giesecke on APRA and the Trujillo Rising of 1932.

As the historian of the twentieth century draws closer to the present he or she becomes increasingly dependent on two types of sources: the daily or periodical press and the periodic reports, economic and other surveys, statistical compilations and other publications by national governments and international institutions. My debt to such papers as the *London Guardian*, the *Financial Times* and the *New York Times* should be obvious. My debt to the invaluable publications of the United Nations and its various agencies, and the World Bank, is recorded in the bibliography. Nor should their predecessor, the League of Nations, be forgotten. Though an almost total failure in practice, its admirable economic enquiries and analyses, culminating in the pioneering *Industrialisation and World Trade* of 1945 deserve our gratitude. No history of economic social and cultural changes in this century could be written without such sources.

Most of what I have written in this book, except obvious personal judgments of the author, readers will have to take on trust. There is no point in overloading a book such as this with a vast apparatus of references or other signs of erudition. I have tried to confine my references to the source of actual quotations, to the source of statistics and other quantitative data—different sources sometimes give different figures—and to the occasional support for statements which readers may find unusual, unfamiliar or unexpected, and some points where the author's controversial view might require some backing. These references are in brackets in the text. The full title of the source is to be found at the end of the volume. This bibliography is no more than a full list of all the sources actually cited or referred to in the text. It is *not* a systematic guide to further reading. A brief pointer to further reading is printed separately. The apparatus of references, such as it is, is also quite separate from the footnotes, which merely amplify or qualify the text.

Nevertheless, it is only fair to point to some works on which I have relied quite a lot or to which I am particularly indebted. I would not want their authors to feel unappreciated. In general I owe much to the work of two friends: the economic historian and indefatigable compiler of quantitative data, Paul Bairoch, and Ivan Berend, formerly President of the Hungarian Academy of Sciences, to whom I owe the concept of the Short Twentieth Century. For the general political history of the world since the Second World War, P. Calvocoressi (*World Politics Since 1945*) has been a sound, and sometimes—understandably—tart guide. For the Second World War I owe much to Alan Milward's superb *War, Economy and Society 1939–45*, and for the post-1945 economy I have found Herman Van der Wee's *Prosperity and Upheaval: The World Economy 1945–1980* and also *Capitalism Since 1945* by Philip Armstrong, Andrew Glyn and John Harrison most useful. Martin Walker's *The Cold War* deserves far more appreciation than most of the lukewarm reviewers have given it. For the history of the Left since the Second World War I am greatly indebted to Dr. Donald Sassoon of Queen Mary and Westfield College, University of London, who has kindly let me read his so far uncompleted vast and perceptive study on this subject. For the history of the U.S.S.R. I am particularly indebted to the writings of Moshe Lewin, Alec Nove, R. W. Davies and Sheila Fitzpatrick; for China to those of Benjamin Schwartz and Stuart Schram; for the Islamic world to Ira Lapidus and Nikki Keddie. My views on the arts owe much to John Willett's works on Weimar culture (and to his conversation), and to Francis Haskell. In chapter 6 my debt to Lynn Garafola's *Diaghilev* should be obvious.

My special thanks go to those who have actually helped me to prepare this book. They are, first, my research assistants Joanna Bedford in London and Lise Grande in New York. I would particularly like to stress my debt to the exceptional Ms. Grande, without whom I could not possibly have filled the enormous gaps in my knowledge, and verified half-remembered facts and references. I am greatly indebted to Ruth Syers, who typed my drafts, and to Marlene Hobsbawm, who read the chapters from the point of view of the non-academic reader with a general interest in the modern world, to whom this book is addressed.

I have already indicated my debt to the students of the New School, who listened to the lectures in which I tried to formulate my ideas and interpretations. To them this book is dedicated.

Eric Hobsbawm
London–New York, 1993–94

The Century: A Bird's Eye View

TWELVE PEOPLE LOOK AT THE TWENTIETH CENTURY

Isaiah Berlin (philosopher, Britain): "I have lived through most of the twentieth century without, I must add, suffering personal hardship. I remember it only as the most terrible century in Western history."

Julio Caro Baroja (anthropologist, Spain): "There's a patent contradiction between one's own life experience—childhood, youth and old age passed quietly and without major adventures—and the facts of the twentieth century . . . the terrible events which humanity has lived through."

Primo Levi (writer, Italy): "We who survived the Camps are not true witnesses. This is an uncomfortable notion which I have gradually come to accept by reading what other survivors have written, including myself, when I re-read my writings after a lapse of years. We, the survivors, are not only a tiny but also an anomalous minority. We are those who, through prevarication, skill or luck, never touched bottom. Those who have, and who have seen the face of the Gorgon, did not return, or returned wordless."

René Dumont (agronomist, ecologist, France): "I see it only as a century of massacres and wars."

Rita Levi Montalcini (Nobel Laureate, science, Italy): "In spite of everything there have been revolutions for the better in this century . . . the rise of the fourth estate, and the emergence of women after centuries of repression."

William Golding (Nobel Laureate, writer, Britain): "I can't help thinking that this has been the most violent century in human history."

Ernst Gombrich (art historian, Britain): "The chief characteristic of the twentieth century is the terrible multiplication of the world's population. It is a catastrophe, a disaster. We don't know what to do about it."

Yehudi Menuhin (musician, Britain): "If I had to sum up the twentieth century, I would say that it raised the greatest hopes ever conceived by humanity, and destroyed all illusions and ideals."

Severo Ochoa (Nobel Laureate, science, Spain): "The most fundamental thing is the progress of science, which has been truly extraordinary . . . This is what characterizes our century."

Raymond Firth (anthropologist, Britain): "Technologically, I single out the development of electronics among the most significant developments of the twentieth century; in terms of ideas, the change from a relatively rational and scientific view of things to a non-rational and less scientific one."

Leo Valiani (historian, Italy): "Our century demonstrates that the victory of the ideals of justice and equality is always ephemeral, but also that, if we manage to preserve liberty, we can always start all over again . . . There is no need to despair, even in the most desperate situations."

Franco Venturi (historian, Italy): "Historians can't answer this question. For me the twentieth century is only the ever-renewed effort to understand it."

(Agosti and Borgese, 1992, pp. 42, 210, 154, 76, 4, 8, 204, 2, 62, 80, 140, 160.)

I

On the 28 June 1992 President Mitterrand of France made a sudden, unannounced and unexpected appearance in Sarajevo, already the centre of a Balkan war that was to cost many thousands of lives during the remainder of the year. His object was to remind world opinion of the seriousness of the Bosnian crisis. Indeed, the presence of a distinguished, elderly and visibly frail statesman under small-arms and artillery fire was much remarked on and admired. However, one aspect of M. Mitterrand's visit passed virtually without comment, even though it was plainly central to it: the date. Why had the President of France chosen to go to Sarajevo on that particular day? Because the 28 June was the anniversary of the assassination, in Sarajevo, in 1914, of the Archduke Franz Ferdinand of Austria-Hungary, which led, within a matter of weeks, to the outbreak of the First World War. For any educated European of Mitterrand's age, the connection between date, place and the reminder of a historic catastrophe precipitated by political error and miscalculation leaped to the eye. How better to dramatize the potential implications of the Bosnian crisis than by choosing so symbolic a date? But hardly anyone caught the allusion except a few professional historians and very senior citizens. The historical memory was no longer alive.

The destruction of the past, or rather of the social mechanisms that link one's contemporary experience to that of earlier generations, is one of the most characteristic and eerie phenomena of the late twentieth century. Most young men and women at the century's end grow up in a sort of permanent present lacking any organic relation to the public past of the times they live in. This makes historians, whose business it is to remember what others forget, more essential at the end of the second millennium than ever before. But for that very reason they must be more than simply chroniclers, remembrancers and compilers, though this is also the historians' necessary function. In 1989 all governments, and especially all Foreign Ministries, in the world would have benefited from a seminar on the peace settlements after the two world wars, which most of them had apparently forgotten.

However, it is not the purpose of this book to tell the story of the period which is its subject, the Short Twentieth Century from 1914 to 1991, although no one who has been asked by an intelligent American student whether the phrase "Second World War" meant that there had been a "First World War" is unaware that knowledge of even the basic facts of the century cannot be taken for granted. My object is to understand and explain *why* things turned out the way they did, and how they hang together. For anyone of my age-group who has lived through all or most of the Short Twentieth Century this is inevitably also an autobiographical endeavour. We are talking about, amplifying (and correcting) our own memories. And we are talking as men and women of a particular time and place, involved, in various ways, in its history as actors in its dramas—however insignificant our parts—as observers of our times and, not least, as people whose views of the century have been formed by what we have come to see as its crucial events. We are part of this century. It is part of us. Readers who belong to another era, for instance the student entering university at the time this is written, for whom even the Vietnam War is prehistory, should not forget this.

For historians of my generation and background, the past is indestructible, not only because we belong to the generation when streets and public places were still called after public men and events (the Wilson station in pre-war Prague, the Metro Stalingrad in Paris), when peace treaties were still signed and therefore had to be identified (Treaty of Versailles) and war memorials recalled yesterdays, but because public events are part of the texture of our lives. They are not merely markers in our private lives, but what has formed our lives, private and public. For this author the 30 January 1933 is not simply an otherwise arbitrary date when Hitler became Chancellor of Germany, but a winter afternoon in Berlin when a fifteen-year-old and his younger sister were on the way home from their neighbouring schools in Wilmersdorf to Halensee and, somewhere on the way, saw the headline. I can see it still, as in a dream.

But not only one old historian has the past as part of his permanent present. Over huge stretches of the globe everybody over a certain age, irrespective of his personal background and life-story, has passed through the same central experiences. These have marked us all, to some extent in the same ways. The world that went to pieces at the end of the 1980s was the world shaped by the impact of the Russian Revolution of 1917. We have all been marked by it, for instance, inasmuch as we got used to thinking of the modern industrial economy in terms of binary opposites, "capitalism" and "socialism" as alternatives mutually excluding one another, the one being identified with economies organized on the model of the U.S.S.R., the other with all the rest. It should now be becoming clear that this was an arbitrary and to some extent artificial construction, which can only be understood as part of a particular historical context. And yet, even as I write, it is not easy to envisage, even in retrospect, other principles of classification which might have been more realistic than that which placed the U.S.A., Japan, Sweden, Brazil, the German Federal Republic and South Korea in a single pigeon-hole, and the state economies and systems of the Soviet region which collapsed after the 1980s in the same compartment as those in East and Southeast Asia which demonstrably did not collapse.

Again, even the world which has survived the end of the October Revolution is one whose institutions and assumptions were shaped by those who were on the winning side of the Second World War. Those who were on the losing side or associated with it were not only silent and silenced, but virtually written out of history and intellectual life except in the role of "the enemy" in the moral world drama of Good versus Evil. (This may now also be happening to the losers in the Cold War of the second half of the century, though probably not to quite the same extent or for so long.) This is one of the penalties of living through a century of religious wars. Intolerance is their chief characteristic. Even those who advertised the pluralism of their own non-ideologies did not think the world was big enough for permanent coexistence with rival secular religions. Religious or ideological confrontations, such as those which have filled this century, build barricades in the way of the historian, whose major task is not to judge but to understand even what we can least comprehend. Yet what stands in the way of understanding is not only our passionate convictions, but the historical experience that has formed them. The first is easier to overcome, for there is no truth in the familiar but mistaken French phrase *tout comprendre c'est tout pardonner* (to understand all is to forgive all). To understand the Nazi era in German history and to fit it into its historical context is not to forgive the genocide. In any case, no one who has lived through this extraordinary century is likely to abstain from judgement. It is understanding that comes hard.

II

How are we to make sense of the Short Twentieth Century, that is to say of the years from the outbreak of the First World War to the collapse of the U.S.S.R. which, as we can now see in retrospect, forms a coherent historical period that has now ended? We do not know what will come next, and what the third millennium will be like, even though we can be certain that the Short Twentieth Century will have shaped it. However, there can be no serious doubt that in the late 1980s and early 1990s an era in world history ended and a new one began. That is the essential information for historians of the century, for though they can speculate about the future in the light of their understanding of the past, their business is not that of the racing tipster. The only horse-races they can claim to report and analyse are those already won or lost. In any case, the record of forecasters in the past thirty or forty years, whatever their professional qualification as prophets, has been so spectacularly bad that only governments and economic research institutes still have, or pretend to have, much confidence in it. It is even possible that it has got worse since the Second World War.

In this book the structure of the Short Twentieth Century appears like a sort of triptych or historical sandwich. An Age of Catastrophe from 1914 to the aftermath of the Second World War was followed by some twenty-five or thirty years of extraordinary economic growth and social transformation, which probably changed human society more profoundly than any other period of comparable brevity. In retrospect it can be seen as a sort of Golden Age, and was so seen almost immediately it had come to an end in the early 1970s. The last part of the century was a new era of decomposition, uncertainty and crisis—and indeed, for large parts of the world such as Africa, the former U.S.S.R. and the formerly socialist parts of Europe, of catastrophe. As the 1980s gave way to the 1990s, the mood of those who reflected on the century's past and future was a growing *fin-de-siècle* gloom. From the vantage-point of the 1990s, the Short Twentieth Century passed through a brief Golden Age, on the way from one era of crisis to another, into an unknown and problematic but not necessarily apocalyptic future. However, as historians may wish to remind metaphysical speculators about "The End of History," there will be a future. The only completely certain generalization about history is that, so long as there is a human race, it will go on.

The argument of this book is organized accordingly. It begins with the First World War, which marked the breakdown of the (western) civilization of the nineteenth century. This civilization was capitalist in its economy; liberal in its legal and constitutional structure; bourgeois in the image of its characteristic hegemonic class; glorying in the advance of science, knowledge and education, material and moral progress; and profoundly convinced of the centrality of Europe, birthplace of the revolutions of the sciences, arts, politics and industry, whose economy had penetrated, and whose soldiers had conquered and subjugated most of the world; whose populations had grown until (including the vast and growing outflow of European emigrants and their descendants) they had risen to form a third of the human race; and whose major states constituted the system of world politics.*

The decades from the outbreak of the First World War to the

---

*I have tried to describe and explain the rise of this civilization in a three-volume history of the "long nineteenth century" (from the 1780s to 1914) and tried to analyse the reasons for its breakdown. The present text will refer back to these volumes, *The Age of Revolution, 1789–1848*, *The Age of Capital, 1848–1875* and *The Age of Empire 1875–1914*, from time to time, where this seems useful.

aftermath of the Second, was an Age of Catastrophe for this society. For forty years it stumbled from one calamity to another. There were times when even intelligent conservatives would not take bets on its survival. It was shaken by two world wars, followed by two waves of global rebellion and revolution, which brought to power a system that claimed to be the historically predestined' alternative to bourgeois and capitalist society, first over one sixth of the world's land surface, and after the Second World War over one third of the globe's population. The huge colonial empires, built up before and during the Age of Empire, were shaken and crumbled into dust. The entire history of modern imperialism, so firm and self-confident when Queen Victoria of Great Britain died, had lasted no longer than a single lifetime—say, that of Winston Churchill (1874–1965).

More than this: a world economic crisis of unprecedented depth brought even the strongest capitalist economies to their knees and seemed to reverse the creation of a single universal world economy, which had been so remarkable an achievement of nineteenth-century liberal capitalism. Even the U.S.A., safe from war and revolution, seemed close to collapse. While the economy tottered, the institutions of liberal democracy virtually disappeared between 1917 and 1942 from all but a fringe of Europe and parts of North America and Australasia, as fascism and its satellite authoritarian movements and regimes advanced.

Only the temporary and bizarre alliance of liberal capitalism and communism in self-defence against this challenger saved democracy, for the victory over Hitler's Germany was essentially won, and could only have been won, by the Red Army. In many ways this period of capitalist–communist alliance against fascism—essentially the 1930s and 1940s—forms the hinge of twentieth-century history and its decisive moment. In many ways it is a moment of historical paradox in the relations of capitalism and communism, placed, for most of the century—except for the brief period of antifascism—in a posture of irreconcilable antagonism. The victory of the Soviet Union over Hitler was the achievement of the regime installed there by the October Revolution, as a comparison of the performance of the Russian Tsarist economy in the First World War and the Soviet economy in the Second World War demonstrates (Gatrell/ Harrison, 1993). Without it the Western world today would probably consist (outside the U.S.A.) of a set of variations on authoritarian and fascist themes rather than a set of variations on liberal parliamentary ones. It is one of the ironies of this strange century that the most lasting results of the October revolution, whose object was the global overthrow of capitalism, was to save its antagonist, both in war and in peace—that is to say, by providing it with the incentive, fear, to reform itself after the Second World War, and, by establishing the popularity of economic planning, furnishing it with some of the procedures for its reform.

Still, even when liberal capitalism had—and only just—survived the triple challenge of slump, fascism and war, it still seemed to face the global advance of revolution, which could now rally round the U.S.S.R., which had emerged from the Second World War as a superpower.

And yet, as we can now see in retrospect, the strength of the global socialist challenge to capitalism was that of the weakness of its opponent. Without the breakdown of nineteenth-century bourgeois society in the Age of Catastrophe, there would have been no October revolution and no U.S.S.R.. The economic system improvised in the ruined rural Eurasian hulk of the former Tsarist Empire under the name of socialism would not have considered itself, nor been considered elsewhere, as a realistic global alternative to the capitalist economy. It was the Great Slump of the 1930s that made it look as though it was so, as it was the challenge of fascism which made the U.S.S.R. into the indispensable instrument of Hitler's defeat, and therefore into one of the two superpowers whose confrontations dominated and terrified the second half of the Short Twentieth Century, while—as we can also now see—in many respects stabilizing its political structure. The U.S.S.R. would not have found itself, for a decade-and-a-half in the middle of the century, at the head of a "socialist camp" comprising a third of the human race, and an economy that briefly looked as though it might out-race capitalist economic growth.

Just how and why capitalism after the Second World War found itself, to everyone's surprise including its own, surging forward into the unprecedented and possibly anomalous Golden Age of 1947–73, is perhaps the major question which faces historians of the twentieth century. There is as yet no agreement on an answer, nor can I claim to provide a persuasive one. Probably a more convincing analysis will have to wait until the entire "long wave" of the second half of the twentieth century can be seen in perspective, but, although we can now look back on the Golden Age as a whole, the Crisis Decades through which the world has lived since then are not yet complete at the time this is written. However, what can already be assessed with great confidence is the extraordinary scale and impact of the consequent economic, social and cultural transformation, the greatest, most rapid and most fundamental in recorded history. Various aspects of it are discussed in the second part of this book. Historians of the twentieth century in the third millennium will probably see the century's major impact on history as the one made by and in this astonishing period. For the changes in human life it brought about all over the globe were as profound as they were irreversible. Moreover, they are still continuing. The journalists and philosophical essayists who detected "the end of history" in the fall of the Soviet Empire were wrong. A better case can be made for saying that the third quarter of the century marked the end of the seven or eight millennia of human history that began with the invention of agriculture in the stone age, if only because it ended the long era when the overwhelming majority of the human race lived by growing food and herding animals.

Compared to this, the history of the confrontation between "capitalism" and "socialism," with or without the intervention of states and governments such as the U.S.A. and the U.S.S.R. claiming to represent one or the other, will probably seem of more limited historical interest—comparable, in the long rn, to the sixteenth and seventeenth-century wars of religion or the Crusades. For those who lived through any part of the Short Twentieth Century they naturally bulked large, and so they do in this book, since it is written by a twentieth-century writer for late-twentieth-century readers. Social revolutions, the Cold War, the nature, limits and fatal flaws of "really existing socialism" and its breakdown, are discussed at length. Nevertheless, it is important to remember that the major and lasting impact of the regimes inspired by the October revolution was as a powerful accelerator of the modernization of backward agrarian countries. As it happened, its major achievements in this respect coincided with the capitalist Golden Age. How effective, or even how consciously held, the rival strategies for burying the world of our forefathers were, need not be considered here. As we shall see, until the early 1960s, they seemed at least evenly matched, a view which seems preposterous in the light of the collapse of Soviet socialism, though a British prime minister, conversing with an American president, could then still see the U.S.S.R. as a state whose "buoyant economy . . . will soon outmatch capitalist society in the race for material wealth" (Horne, 1989, p. 303). However, the point to note is simply that, in the 1980s, socialist Bulgaria and non-socialist Ecuador had more in common than either had with the Bulgaria or Ecuador of 1939.

Although the collapse of Soviet socialism and its enormous and still not fully calculable, but mainly negative, consequences were the most dramatic incident in the Crisis Decades which followed the Golden Age, these were to be decades of *universal* or global crisis. The crisis affected the various parts of the world in different ways and degrees, but it affected all, irrespective of their political, social and economic configurations, because the Golden Age had, for the first time in history, created a single, increasingly integrated and universal world economy largely operating across state frontiers ("transnationally"), and therefore also increasingly across the frontiers of state ideology. Consequently the accepted ideas of institutions of all regimes and systems were undermined. Initially the troubles of the 1970s were seen only as a hopefully, temporary pause in the Great Leap Forward of the world economy, and countries of all economic and political types and patterns looked for temporary solutions. Increasingly it became clear that this was an era of long-term difficulties, for which capitalist countries sought radical solutions, often by following secular theologians of the unrestricted free market who rejected the policies that had served the world economy so well in the Golden Age, but now seemed to be failing. The ultras of *laissez-faire* were no more successful than anyone else. In the 1980s and early 1990s the capitalist world found itself once again staggering under the burdens of the inter-war years, which the Golden Age appeared to have removed: mass unemployment, severe cyclical slumps, the ever-more spectacular confrontation of homeless beggars and luxurious plenty, between limited state revenues and limitless state expenditures. Socialist countries, with their now flagging and vulnerable economies, were driven towards equally or even more radical breaks with their past, and, as we know, towards breakdown. That breakdown can stand as the marker for the end of the Short Twentieth Century, as the First World War can stand as the marker for its beginning. At this point my history concludes.

It concludes—as any book completed in the early 1990s must—with a view into obscurity. The collapse of one part of the world revealed the malaise of the rest. As the 1980s passed into the 1990s it became evident that the world crisis was not only general in an economic sense, but equally general in politics. The collapse of the communist regimes between Istria and Vladivostok not only produced an enormous zone of political uncertainty, instability, chaos and civil war, but also destroyed the international system that had stabilized international relations for some forty years. It also revealed the precariousness of the domestic political systems that had essentially rested on that stability. The tensions of troubled economies undermined the political systems of liberal democracy, parliamentary or presidential, which had functioned so well in the developed capitalist countries since the Second World War. They also undermined whatever political systems operated in the Third World. The basic units of politics themselves, the territorial, sovereign and independent "nation-states," including the oldest and stablest, found themselves pulled apart by the forces of a supranational or transnational economy, and by the infranational forces of secessionist regions and ethnic groups. Some of these—such is the irony of history—demanded the outdated and unreal status of miniature sovereign "nation-states" for themselves. The future of politics was obscure, but its crisis at the end of the Short Twentieth Century was patent.

Even more obvious than the uncertainties of world economics and world politics was the social and moral crisis, reflecting the post-1950 upheavals in human life, which also found widespread if confused expression in these Crisis Decades. It was a crisis of the beliefs and assumptions on which modern society had been founded since the Moderns won their famous battle against the Ancients in the early eighteenth century—of the rationalist and humanist assumptions, shared by liberal capitalism and communism, and which made possible their brief but decisive alliance against fascism, which rejected them. A conservative German observer, Michael Sturmer, rightly observed in 1993 that the beliefs of both East and West were at issue:

> There is a strange parallelism between East and West. In the East state doctrine insisted that humanity was the master of its destiny. However, even we believed in a less official and less extreme version of the same slogan: mankind was on the way to becoming master of its destinies. The claim to omnipotence has disappeared absolutely in the East, only relatively *chez nous*—but both sides have suffered shipwreck (Bergedorf, 98, p. 95).

Paradoxically, an era whose only claim to have benefited humanity rested on the enormous triumphs of a material progress based on science and technology ended in a rejection of these by substantial bodies of public opinion and people claiming to be thinkers in the West.

However, the moral crisis was not only one of the assumptions of modern civilization, but also one of the historic structures of human relations which modern society inherited from a pre-industrial and pre-capitalist past, and which, as we can now see, had enabled it to function. It was not a crisis of one form of organizing societies, but of all forms. The strange calls for an otherwise unidentified "civil society," for "community" were the voice of lost and drifting generations. They were heard in an age when such words, having lost their traditional meanings, became vapid phrases. There was no other way left to define group identity, except by defining the outsiders who were not in it.

For the poet T. S. Eliot "this is the way the world ends—not with a bang but a whimper." The Short Twentieth century ended with both.

III

How did the world of the 1990s compare with the world of 1914? It contained five or six billion human beings, perhaps three times as many people as at the outbreak of the First World War, and this in spite of the fact that during the Short Century more human beings had been killed or allowed to die by human decision than ever before in history. A recent estimate of the century's "megadeaths" is 187 millions (Brzezinski, 1993), which is the equivalent of more than one in ten of the total world population in 1900. Most people in the 1990s were taller and heavier than their parents, better fed, and far longer-lived, though the catastrophes of the 1980s and 1990s in Africa, Latin America and the ex-U.S.S.R. may make this difficult to believe. The world was incomparably richer than ever before in its capacity to produce goods and services and in their endless variety. It could not have managed otherwise to maintain a global population several times larger than ever before in the world's history. Most people until the 1980s lived better than their parents, and, in the advanced economies, better than they had ever expected to live or even imagined it possible to live. For some decades in the middle of the century it even looked as though ways had been found of distributing at least some of this enormous wealth with a degree of fairness to the working people of the richer countries, but at the end of the century inequality had once again the upper hand. It had also made a massive entry into the former "socialist" countries where a certain equality of poverty had previously reigned. Humanity was far better educated than in 1914. Indeed, probably for the first time in history most human beings could be described as literate, at least in official statistics, though the significance of this achievement was far less clear at the end of the century than it would have been in 1914, given the enormous and probably growing gap between the minimum of competence officially accepted as literacy, often shading into "functional illiteracy," and the command of reading and writing still expected at elite levels.

The world was filled with a revolutionary and constantly advancing technology, based on triumphs of natural science which could be anticipated in 1914, but had then barely begun to be pioneered. Perhaps the most dramatic practical consequence of these was a revolution in transport and communications which virtually annihilated time and distance. It was a world which could bring more information and entertainment than had been available to emperors in 1914, daily, hourly, into every household. It let people speak to one another across oceans and continents at the touch of a few buttons, and, for most practical purposes, abolished the cultural advantages of city over countryside.

Why, then, did the century end, not with a celebration of this unparalleled and marvellous progress, but in a mood of uneasiness? Why, as the epigraphs to this chapter show, did so many reflective minds look back upon it without satisfaction, and certainly without confidence in the future? Not only because it was without doubt the most murderous century of which we have record, both by the scale, frequency and length of the warfare which filled it, barely ceasing for a moment in the 1920s, but also by the unparalleled scale of the human catastrophes it produced, from the greatest famines in history to systematic genocide. Unlike the "long nineteenth century," which seemed, and actually was, a period of almost unbroken material, intellectual *and moral* progress, that is to say of improvement in the conditions of civilized life, there has, since 1914, been a marked regression from the standards then regarded as normal in the developed countries and in the milieus of the middle classes and which were confidently believed to be spreading to the more backward regions and the less enlightened strata of the population.

Since this century has taught us, and continues to teach us, that human beings can learn to live under the most brutalized and theoretically intolerable conditions, it is not easy to grasp the extent of the, unfortunately accelerating, return to what our nineteenth-century ancestors would have called the standards of barbarism. We forget that the old revolutionary Frederick Engels was horrified at the explosion of an Irish Republican bomb in Westminster Hall, because, as an old soldier, he held that war was waged against combatants and not non-combatants. We forget that the pogroms in Tsarist Russia which (justifiably) outraged world opinion and drove Russian Jews across the Atlantic in their millions between 1881 and 1914, were small, almost negligible, by the standards of modern massacre: the dead were counted in dozens, not hundreds, let alone millions. We forget that an international Convention once provided that hostilities in war "must not commence without previous and explicit warning in the form of a reasoned declaration of war or of an ultimatum with conditional declaration of war," for when was the last war that began with such an explicit or implicit declaration? Or one that ended with a formal treaty of peace negotiated between the belligerent states? In the course of the twentieth century, wars have been increasingly waged against the economy and infrastructure of states and against their civilian populations. Since the First World War the number of civilian casualties in war has been far greater than that of military casualties in all belligerent countries except the U.S.A. How many of us recall that it was taken for granted in 1914 that:

Civilized warfare, the textbooks tell us, is confined, as far as possible, to disablement of the armed forces of the enemy; otherwise war would continue till one of the parties was exterminated. "It is with good reason . . . that this practice has grown into a custom with the nations of Europe." (*Encyclopedia Britannica*, XI ed., 1911, art: War.)

We do not quite overlook the revival of torture or even murder as a normal part of the operations of public security in modern states, but we probably fail to appreciate quite how dramatic a reversal this constitutes of the long era of legal development, from the first formal abolition of torture in a Western country in the 1780s to 1914.

And yet, the world at the end of the Short Twentieth Century cannot be compared with the world at its beginning in the terms of the historical accountancy of "more" and "less." It was a qualitatively different world in at least three respects.

First, it was no longer Eurocentric. It had brought the decline and fall of Europe, still the unquestioned centre of power, wealth, intellect and "Western civilization" when the century began. Europeans and their descendants were now reduced from perhaps a third of humanity to at most one sixth, a diminishing minority living in countries which barely, if at all, reproduced their populations, surrounded by, and in most cases—with some shining exceptions such as the U.S.A. (until the 1990s)—barricading themselves against the pressure of immigration from the regions of the poor. The industries Europe had pioneered were migrating elsewhere. The countries which had once looked across the oceans to Europe looked elsewhere. Australia, New Zealand, even the bi-oceanic U.S.A., saw the future in the Pacific, whatever exactly this meant.

The "great powers" of 1914, all of them European, had disappeared, like the U.S.S.R., inheritor of Tsarist Russia, or were reduced to regional or provincial status, with the possible exception of Germany. The very effort to create a single supranational "European Community" and to invent a sense of European identity to correspond to it, replacing the old loyalties to historic nations and states, demonstrated the depth of this decline.

Was this a change of major significance, except for political historians? Perhaps not, since it reflected only minor changes in the economic, intellectual and cultural configuration of the world. Even in 1914 the U.S.A. had been the major industrial economy, and the major pioneer, model and propulsive force of the mass production and mass culture which conquered the globe during the Short Twentieth Century, and the U.S.A., in spite of its many peculiarities, was the overseas extension of

Europe, and bracketed itself with the old continent under the heading "western civilization." Whatever its future prospects, the U.S.A. looked back from the 1990s on "The American Century," an age of its rise and triumph. The ensemble of the countries of nineteenth-century industrialization remained, collectively, by far the greatest concentration of wealth, economic and scientific-technological power on the globe, as well as the one whose peoples enjoyed by far the highest standard of living. At the end of the century this still more than compensated for deindustrialization and the shift of production to other continents. To this extent the impression of an old Eurocentric or "Western" world in full decline was superficial.

The second transformation was more significant. Between 1914 and the early 1990s the globe has become far more of a single operational unit, as it was not, and could not have been in 1914. In fact, for many purposes, notably in economic affairs, the globe is now the primary operational unit and older units such as the "national economies," defined by the politics of territorial states, are reduced to complications of transnational activities. The stage reached by the 1990s in the construction of the "global village"—the phrase was coined in the 1960s (McLuhan, 1962)—will not seem very advanced to observers in the mid-twenty-first century, but it had already transformed not only certain economic and technical activities, and the operations of science, but important aspects of private life, mainly by the unimaginable acceleration of communication and transport. Perhaps the most striking characteristic of the end of the twentieth century is the tension between this accelerating process of globalization and the inability of both public institutions and the collective behaviour of human beings to come to terms with it. Curiously enough, private human behaviour has had less trouble in adjusting to the world of satellite television, E-mail, holidays in the Seychelles and transoceanic commuting.

The third transformation, and in some ways the most disturbing, is the disintegration of the old patterns of human social relationships, and with it, incidentally, the snapping of the links between generations, that is to say, between past and present. This has been particularly evident in the most developed countries of the western version of capitalism, in which the values of an absolute a-social individualism have been dominant, both in official and unofficial ideologies, though those who hold them often deplore their social consequences. Nevertheless, the tendencies were to be found elsewhere, reinforced by the erosion of traditional societies and religions, as well as by the destruction, or autodestruction, of the societies of "real socialism."

Such a society consisting of an otherwise unconnected assemblage of self-centred individuals pursuing only their own gratification (whether this is called profit, pleasure or by some other name) was always implicit in the theory of the capitalist economy. Ever since the Age of Revolution, observers of all ideological colours predicted the consequent disintegration of the old social bonds in practice and monitored its progress. The Communist Manifesto's eloquent tribute to the revolutionary role of capitalism is familiar ("The bourgeoisie . . . has pitilessly torn asunder the motley feudal ties that bound man to his 'natural superiors' and has left remaining no other nexus between man and man than naked self-interest"). But that is not quite how the new and revolutionary capitalist society had worked in practice.

In practice, the new society operated not by the wholesale destruction of all that it had inherited from the old society, but by selectively adapting the heritage of the past for its own use. There is no "sociological puzzle" about the readiness of bourgeois society to introduce "a radical individualism in economics and . . . to tear up all traditional social relations in the process" (i.e. where they got in its way), while fearing "radical experimental individualism" in culture (or in the field of behaviour and morality) (Daniel Bell, 1976, p. 18). The most effective way to build an industrial economy based on private enterprise was to combine it with motivations which had nothing to do with the logic of the free market—for instance with the Protestant ethic; with the abstention from immediate gratification; with the ethic of hard work; with family duty and trust; but certainly not with the antinomian rebellion of individuals.

Yet Marx and the other prophets of the disintegration of old values and social relationships were right. Capitalism was a permanent and continuous revolutionizing force. Logically, it would end by disintegrating even those parts of the pre-capitalist past which it had found convenient, nay perhaps essential, for its own development. It would end by sawing off at least one of the branches on which it sat. Since the middle of the century this has been happening. Under the impact of the extraordinary economic explosion of the Golden Age and after, with its consequent social and cultural changes, the most profound revolution in society since the stone age, the branch began to crack and break. At the end of this century it has for the first time become possible to see what a world may be like in which the past, including the past in the present, has lost its role, in which the old maps and charts which guided human beings, singly and collectively, through life no longer represent the landscape through which we move, the sea on which we sail. In which we do not know where our journey is taking us, or even ought to take us.

This is the situation with which a part of humanity must already come to terms at the end of the century, and more will have to in the new millennium. However, by then it may have become clearer where humanity is going than it is today. We can look backward over the road that brought us here, and this is what I have tried to do in this book. We do not know what will shape the future, although I have not resisted the temptation to reflect on some of its problems, insofar as they arise from the debris of the period that has just come to an end. Let us hope it will be a better, juster and more viable world. The old century has not ended well.

The Age of Catastrophe

CHAPTER ONE

The Age of Total War

> Lines of grey muttering faces, masked with fear,
> They leave their trenches, going over the top,
> While time ticks blank and busy on their wrists,
> And hope, with furtive eyes and grappling fists,
> Flounders in mud. O Jesus, make it stop!
>
> —Siegfried Sassoon (1947, p. 71)

It may be thought better, in view of the allegations of "barbarity" of air attacks, to preserve appearances by formulating milder rules and by still nominally confining bombardment to targets which are strictly military in character . . . to avoid emphasizing the truth that air warfare has made such restrictions obsolete and impossible. It my be some time until another war occurs and meanwhile the public may become educated as to the meaning of air power.

—Rules as to Bombardment by Aircraft, 1921 (Townshend, 1986, p. 161)

(Sarajevo, 1946.) Here as in Belgrade, I see in the streets a considerable number of young women whose hair is greying, or completely grey. Their faces are tormented, but still young, while the form of their bodies betrays their youth even more clearly. It seems to me that I see how the hand of this last war has passed over the heads of these frail beings . . .

This sight cannot be preserved for the future; these heads will soon become even greyer and disappear. That is a pity. Nothing could speak more clearly to future generations about our times than these youthful grey heads, from which the nonchalance of youth has been stolen.

Let them at least have a memorial in this little note.

—Signs by the Roadside (Andrić, 1992, p. 50)

I

"The lamps are going out all over Europe," said Edward Grey, Foreign Secretary of Great Britain, as he watched the lights of Whitehall on the night when Britain and Germany went to war in 1914. "We shall not see them lit again in our lifetime." In Vienna the great satirist Karl Kraus prepared to document and denounce that war in an extraordinary reportage-drama of 792 pages to which he gave the title *The Last Days of Humanity*. Both saw the world war as the end of a world, and they were not alone. It was not the end of humanity, although there were moments, in the course of the thirty-one years of world conflict between the Austrian declaration of war on Serbia on 28 July 1914 and the unconditional surrender of Japan on 14 August 1945—four days after the explosion of the first nuclear bomb—when the end of a considerable proportion of the human race did not look far off. There were surely times when the god or gods, whom pious humans believed to have created the world and all in it, might have been expected to regret having done so.

Mankind survived. Nevertheless, the great edifice of nineteenth-century civilization crumpled in the flames of world war, as its pillars collapsed. There is no understanding the Short Twentieth Century without it. It was marked by war. It lived and thought in terms of world war, even when the guns were silent and the bombs were not exploding. Its history and, more specifically, the history of its initial age of breakdown and catastrophe, must begin with that of the thirty-one years' world war.

For those who had grown up before 1914 the contrast was so dramatic that many of them—including the generation of this historian's parents, or, at any rate, its central European members, refused to see any continuity with the past. "Peace" meant "before 1914": after that came something that no longer deserved the name. This was understandable. In 1914 there had been no major war for a century, that is to say, a war in which all, or even a majority of, major powers had been involved, the major players in the international game at that time being the six European "great powers" (Britain, France, Russia, Austria-Hungary, Prussia—after 1871 enlarged into Germany—and, after it was unified, Italy), the U.S.A. and Japan. There had been only one brief war in which more than two of the major powers had been in battle, the Crimean War (1854–56) between Russian on one side, Britain and France on the other. Moreover, most wars involving major powers at all had been comparatively quick. Much the longest of them was not an international conflict but a civil war within the U.S.A. (1861–65). The length of war was measured in months or even (like the 1866 war between Prussia and Austria) in weeks. Between 1871 and 1914 there had been no wars in Europe at all in which the armies of major powers crossed any hostile frontier, although in the Far East Japan fought, and beat, Russia in 1904–5, thus hastening the Russian revolution.

There had been no *world* wars at all. In the eighteenth century France and Britain had contended in a series of wars whose battlefields ranged from India through Europe to North America, and across the world's oceans. Between 1815 and 1914 no major power fought another outside its immediate region, although aggressive expeditions of imperial or would-be imperial powers against weaker overseas enemies were, of course, common. Most of these were spectacularly one-sided fights, such as the U.S. wars against Mexico (1846–48) and Spain (1898) and the various campaigns to extend the British and French colonial empires, although the worm turned once or twice, as when the French had to withdraw from Mexico in the 1860s, the Italians from Ethiopia in 1896. Even the most formidable opponents of modern states, their arsenals increasingly filled with an overwhelmingly superior technology of death, could only hope, at best, to postpone the inevitable retreat. Such exotic conflicts were the stuff of adventure literature or the reports of that mid-nineteenth-century innovation the war correspondent, rather than matters of direct relevance to most inhabitants of the states which waged and won them.

All this changed in 1914. The First World War involved *all* major powers and indeed all European states except Spain, the Netherlands, the three Scandinavian countries and Switzerland. What is more, troops from the world overseas were, often for the first time, sent to fight and work outside their own regions. Canadians fought in France, Australians and New Zealanders forged their national consciousness on a peninsula in the Aegean—"Gallipoli" became their national myth—and, more significantly, the United States rejected George Washington's warning against "European entanglements" and sent its men to fight there, thus determining the shape of twentieth-century history. Indians were sent to Europe and the Middle East, Chinese labour battalions came to the West, Africans fought in the French army. Though military action outside Europe was not very significant, except in the Middle East, the naval war was once again global: its first battle was fought in 1914 off the Falkland Islands, its decisive campaigns, by German submarines and Allied convoys, on and under the seas of the North and mid-Atlantic.

That the Second World War was literally global hardly needs to be demonstrated. Virtually all independent states of the world were involved, willingly or unwillingly, although the republics of Latin America participated only in the most nominal manner. The colonies of imperial powers had no choice in the matter. Except for the future Irish Republic, Sweden, Switzerland, Portugal, Turkey and Spain in Europe, and possibly Afghanistan outside Europe, virtually the whole globe was belligerent or occupied or both. As for the battlefields, the names of Melanesian islands and of settlements in the North African deserts, in Burma and the Philippines became as familiar to newspaper readers and radio listeners—and this was quintessentially the war of the radio news bulletins—as the names of Arctic and Caucasian battles, of Normandy, Stalingrad and Kursk. The Second World War was a lesson in world geography.

Local, regional or global, the wars of the twentieth century were to be on an altogether vaster scale than anything previously experienced. Among seventy-four international wars between 1816 and 1965, which American specialists, who like to do that kind of thing, have ranked by the number of people they killed, the top four occurred in the twentieth century: the two world wars, the Japanese war against China in 1937–39, and the Korean war. They killed upwards of one million persons in battle. The largest documented international war of the post-Napoleonic nineteenth century, that between Prussia/Germany and France in 1870–71, killed perhaps 150,000, an order of magnitude roughly comparable to the deaths in the Chaco war of 1932–35 between Bolivia (pop. *c.* 3 million) and Paraguay (pop. *c.* 1.4 million). In short, 1914 opens the age of massacre (Singer, 1972, pp. 66, 131).

There is not space in this book to discuss the origins of the First World War, which the present author has tried to sketch in *The Age of Empire*. It began as an essentially European war between the triple alliance of France, Britain and Russia on one side, the so-called "central powers" of Germany and Austria-Hungary on the other, Serbia and Belgium being immediately drawn in by the Austrian attack on one (which actually set off the war) and the German attack on the other (which was part of the German strategic war plan). Turkey and Bulgaria soon joined the central powers, while on the other side the Triple Alliance gradually built up into a very large coalition. Italy was bribed in; Greece, Rumania and (much more nominally) Portugal were also involved. More to the point, Japan joined in almost immediately in order to take over German positions in the Far East and Western Pacific, but took no interest in anything outside its own region, and—more significantly—the U.S.A. entered in 1917. In fact, its intervention was to be decisive.

The Germans, then as in the Second World War, were faced with a possible war on two fronts, quite apart from the Balkans into which they were drawn by their alliance with Austria-Hungary. (However, since three of the four Central Powers were in that region—Turkey and Bulgaria as well as Austria—the strategic problem there was not so urgent.) The German plan was to knock out France quickly in the West and then move with equal rapidity to knock out Russia in the East, before the Tsar's empire could bring the full weight of its enormous military manpower into effective action. Then, as later, Germany planned for a lightning campaign (what would in the Second World War be called a *blitzkrieg*) because it had to. The plan almost succeeded, but not quite. The German army advanced into France, among other places through neutral Belgium, and was only halted a few dozen miles east of Paris on the river Marne five to six weeks after war had been declared. (In 1940 the plan was to succeed.) They then withdraw a little, and both sides—the French now supplemented by what remained of the Belgians and by a British land force which was soon to grow enormously—improvised parallel lines of defensive trenches and fortifications which soon stretched without a break from the Channel coast in Flanders to the Swiss frontier, leaving a good deal of eastern France and Belgium in German occupation. They did not shift significantly for the next three-and-a-half years.

This was the "Western Front," which became a machine for massacre such as had probably never before been seen in the history of warfare. Millions of men faced each other across the sandbagged parapets of the trenches under which they lived like, and with, rats and lice. From time to time their generals would seek to break out of the deadlock. Days, even weeks of unceasing artillery bombardment—what a German writer later called "hurricanes of steel" (Ernst Jünger, 1921)—were to "soften up" the enemy and drive him underground, until at the right moment waves of men climbed over the parapet, usually protected by coils and webs of barbed wire, into "no-man's land," a chaos of waterlogged shell-craters, ruined tree-stumps, mud and abandoned corpses, to advance into the machine-guns that mowed them down. As they knew they would. The attempt of the Germans to break through at Verdun in 1916 (February–July) was a battle of two millions, with one million casualties. It failed. The British offensive on the Somme, designed to force the Germans to break off the Verdun offensive cost Britain 420,000 dead—60,000 on the first day of the attack. It is not surprising that in the memory of the British and the French, who fought most of the First World War on the western front, it remained the "Great War," more terrible and traumatic in memory than the Second World War. The French lost almost 20 per cent of their men of military age, and if we include the prisoners of war, the wounded and the permanently disabled and disfigured—those *"gueules casseés"* ("smashed faces") which became so vivid a part of the after-image of the war—not much more than one in three French soldiers came through the war without harm. The chances of the five million or so British soldiers surviving the war unharmed were just about evens. The British lost a generation—half a million men under the age of thirty (Winter, 1986 p. 83)—notably among their upper classes, whose young men, destined as gentlemen to be officers who set an example, marched into battle at the head of their men and were consequently mown down first. One quarter of the Oxford and Cambridge students under the age of twenty-five who served in the British army in 1914 were killed (Winter, 1986, p. 98). The Germans, though the number of their dead was even greater than the French, lost only a smaller proportion of their much larger military age-groups—13 per cent. Even the apparently modest losses of the U.S.A. (116,000, against the 1.6 millions of French, the almost 800,000 of British, the 1.8 millions of Germans) actually demonstrate the murderous nature of the Western front, the only one where they fought. For while the U.S.A. lost between 2.5 and 3 times as many in the Second World War as in the First, the American forces in 1917–18 were in action for barely a year-and-a-half, compared to the three-and-a-half years of the Second World War, and on only a single narrow sector and not world-wide.

The horrors of warfare on the Western Front were to have even darker consequences. The experience itself naturally helped to brutalize both warfare and politics: if one could be conducted without counting the human or any other costs, why not the other? Most men who served in the First World War—overwhelmingly as conscripts—came out of it as convinced haters of war. However, those ex-soldiers who had passed through this kind of war without being turned against it sometimes drew from the shared experience of living with death and courage a sense of incommunicable and savage superiority, not least to women and those who had not fought, which was to fill the early ranks of the post-war ultra-right. Adolf Hitler was only one of such men for whom having been a *frontsoldat* was the formative experience of their lives. However, the opposite reaction had equally negative consequences. After the war it became quite evident to politicians, at least in democratic countries, that bloodbaths like 1914–18 would no longer be tolerated by the voters. The post-1918 strategy of Britain and France, like the post-Vietnam strategy of the U.S.A., was based on this assumption. In the short run this helped the Germans to win the Second World War in the West in 1940 against a France committed to crouch behind its incomplete fortifications and, once these had been breached, simply unwilling to fight on; and a Britain desperate to avoid committing itself to the sort of massive land war that had decimated its people in 1914–18. In the longer run democratic governments failed to resist the temptation of saving their own citizens' lives by treating those of enemy countries as totally expendable. The dropping of the atom bomb on Hiroshima and Nagasaki in 1945 was not justified as indispensable for victory, which was by then absolutely certain, but as a means of saving American soldiers' lives. But perhaps the thought that it would prevent America's ally the U.S.S.R. from establishing a claim to a major part in Japan's defeat was not absent from the minds of the U.S. government either.

While the Western Front settled into bloody stalemate, the Eastern Front remained in movement. The Germans pulverised a clumsy Russian invasion force at the battle of Tannenberg in the first month of war and thereafter, with the intermittently effective help of the Austrians, pushed Russia out of Poland. In spite of occasional Russian counter-offensives, it was clear that the Central Powers had the upper hand, and Russia was fighting a defensive rearguard action against the German advance. In the Balkans the Central Powers were in control, in spite of an uneven military performance by the rocky Habsburg empire. The local belligerents, Serbia and Romania, incidentally, suffered by far the greatest proportional military losses. The Allies, in spite of occupying Greece, made no headway until the collapse of the Central Powers after the summer of 1918. The plan by Italy to open another front against Austria-Hungary in the Alps failed, mainly because many Italian soldiers saw no reason to fight for the government of a state they did not consider theirs, and whose language few of them could speak. After a major military debacle at Caporetto in 1917, which left a literary memory in Ernest Hemingway's novel *A Farewell to Arms*, the Italians had even to be stiffened by transfers from other Allied armies. Meanwhile France, Britain and Germany bled each other to death on the Western Front, Russia was increasingly destabilized by the war she was patently losing, and the Austro-Hungarian empire increasingly tottered towards its break-up, which its local nationalist movements longed for, and to which the Allied foreign ministries resigned themselves without enthusiasm, rightly foreseeing an unstable Europe.

How to break the stalemate on the Western Front was the crucial problem for both sides, for without victory in the West neither could win the war, all the more so since the naval war was also deadlocked. Except for some isolated raiders, the Allies controlled the oceans, but the British and German battle-fleets faced and immobilized each other on the North Sea. Their only attempt to engage in battle (1916) ended indecisively, but since it confined the German fleet to its bases, on balance it was to the Allies' advantage.

Both sides tried to do it by technology. The Germans—always strong in chemistry—brought poison gas onto the battlefield, where it proved both barbarous and ineffective, leaving behind the only genuine case of government humanitarian revulsion against a means of conducting warfare, the Geneva Convention of 1925, by which the world pledged itself not to use chemical warfare. And indeed, though all governments continued to prepare for it and expected the enemy to use it, it was not used by either side in the Second World War though humanitarian feelings did not prevent the Italians from gassing colonial people. (The steep decline in the values of civilization after the Second World War eventually brought poison gas back. During the Iran–Iraq war of the 1980s Iraq, then enthusiastically supported by the Western states, used it freely against both soldiers and civilians.) The British pioneered the caterpillared armoured vehicle, still known by its then code-name of *tank*, but their far from impressive generals had not yet discovered how to use it. Both sides used the new and still frail airplanes, as well as (by Germany) the curious cigar-shaped hydrogen-filled airships, experimenting with aerial bombardment, fortunately not to much effect. Air warfare also came into its own, notably as a means of terrorizing civilians, in the Second World War.

The only technological weapon which had a major effect on warfare in 1914–18 was the submarine, for both sides, unable to defeat each other's soldiers, resorted to starving the other's civilians. Since all Britain's supplies were seaborne, it seemed feasible to strangle the British Isles by increasingly ruthless submarine warfare against shipping. The campaign came close to success in 1917, before effective ways to counter it were found, but it did more than anything else to draw the U.S.A. into the war. The British, in turn, did their best to blockade supplies to Germany, i.e. to starve both the German war economy and the German population. They were more effective than they ought to have been, since, as we shall see, the German war economy was not run with the efficiency and rationality on which the Germans prided themselves. Unlike the German military machine, which, in the First as in the Second World War, was strikingly superior to any other. This sheer superiority of the German army as a military force might just have proved decisive, had the Allies not been able to call on the practically unlimited resources of the U.S.A. from 1917. As it was, Germany, even hobbled by the alliance with

Austria, secured total victory in the East, driving Russia out of the war, into revolution and out of a large part of her European territories in 1917–18. Shortly after imposing the penal peace of Brest-Litowsk (March 1918) the German army, now free to concentrate in the West, actually broke through the Western Front and advanced on Paris again. Thanks to the flood of American reinforcements and equipment, the Allies recovered, but for a while it looked a close thing. However, it was the last throw of an exhausted Germany, which knew itself to be close to defeat. Once the Allies began to advance in the summer of 1918, the end was only a few weeks away. The Central Powers not only admitted defeat but collapsed. Revolution swept across central and south-eastern Europe in the autumn of 1918, as it had swept across Russia in 1917 (see next chapter). No old government was left standing between the borders of France and the Sea of Japan. Even the belligerents on the victorious side were shaken, although it is difficult to believe that Britain and France would not have survived even defeat as stable political entities; but not Italy. Certainly none of the defeated countries escaped revolution.

If one of the great ministers or diplomats of the past—the ones on whom aspiring members of their countries' foreign services were still told to model themselves, a Talleyrand or a Bismarck—had risen from their graves to observe the First World War, they would certainly have wondered why sensible statesmen had not decided to settle the war by some compromise before it destroyed the world of 1914. We must also wonder. Most non-revolutionary and non-ideological wars of the past had not been waged as struggles to death or total exhaustion. In 1914 ideology was certainly not what divided the belligerents, except insofar as the war had to be fought on both sides by mobilizing public opinion, i.e. by claiming some profound challenge to accepted national values, such as Russian barbarism against German culture, French and British democracy against German absolutism, or the like. Moreover there were statesmen who recommended some kind of compromise settlement even outside Russia and Austria-Hungary which lobbied their Allies in this sense with increasing desperation as defeat drew near. Why, then, was the First World War waged by the leading powers on both sides as a zero-sum game, i.e. as a war which could only be totally won or totally lost?

The reason was that this war, unlike earlier wars, which were typically waged for limited and specifiable objects, was waged for unlimited ends. In the Age of Empire, politics and economics had fused. International political rivalry was modelled on economic growth and competition, but the characteristic feature of this was precisely that it had no limit. "The 'natural frontiers' of Standard Oil, the Deutsche Bank or the De Beers Diamond Corporation were at the end of the universe, or rather at the limits of their capacity to expand" (Hobsbawm, 1987, p. 318). More concretely, for the two main contestants, Germany and Britain, the sky had to be the limit, since Germany wanted a global political and maritime position like that now occupied by Britain, and which therefore would automatically relegate an already declining Britain to inferior status. It was either/or. For France, then as later, the stakes were less global but equally urgent: to compensate for its increasing, and apparently inevitable, demographic and economic inferiority to Germany. Here also the issue was the future of France as a great power. In both cases compromise would merely have meant postponement. Germany itself, one might have supposed, could wait until its growing size and superiority established the position German governments felt to be their country's due, which would happen sooner or later. Indeed, the dominant position of a twice defeated Germany with no claims to independent military power in Europe was more unchallenged in the early 1990s than the claims of militarist Germany ever were before 1945. Yet that is because Britain and France, as we shall see, were forced after the Second World War, however reluctantly, to accept their relegation to second-rank status, just as Federal Germany, with all its economic strength, recognized that in the post-1945 world supremacy as a single state was, and would have to remain, beyond its power. In the 1900s, at the peak of the imperial and imperialist era, both the German claim to unique global status ("The German spirit will regenerate the world," as the phrase went) and the resistance of Britain and France, still undeniable "great powers" in a Euro-centred world, were as yet intact. On paper no doubt compromise was possible on this or that point of the almost megalomaniac "war aims" which both sides formulated as soon as war had broken out, but in practice the only war aim that counted was total victory: what in the Second World War came to be called "unconditional surrender."

It was an absurd and self-defeating aim which ruined both victors and vanquished. It drove the defeated into revolution, and the victors into bankruptcy and physical exhaustion. In 1940 France was overrun by inferior German forces with ridiculous ease and speed, and accepted subordination to Hitler without hesitation, because the country had almost bled to death in 1914–18. Britain was never the same again after 1918 because the country had ruined its economy by waging a war substantially beyond its resources. Moreover, total victory, ratified by a penal, dictated peace, ruined what little chances there were of restoring something even faintly like a stable, liberal, bourgeois Europe, as the economist John Maynard Keynes immediately recognized. If Germany was not reintegrated into the European economy, i.e. if the country's economic weight within that economy was not recognized and accepted, there could be no stability. But this was the last consideration in the minds of those who had fought to eliminate Germany.

The peace-settlement, imposed by the major surviving victorious powers (U.S.A., Britain, France, Italy) and usually, if inaccurately, known as the Treaty of Versailles,* was dominated by five considerations. The most immediate was the breakdown of so many regimes in Europe, and the emergence in Russia of an alternative revolutionary Bolshevik regime dedicated to universal subversion, and a magnet for revolutionary forces everywhere else (see chapter 2). Second, there was the need to control Germany which had, after all, almost defeated the entire Allied coalition singlehanded. For obvious reasons this was, and has ever since remained, the major concern of France. Third, the map of Europe had to be re-divided and re-drawn, both to weaken Germany and to fill the large empty spaces left in Europe and the Middle East by the simultaneous defeat and collapse of the Russian, Habsburg and Ottoman empires. The main claimants to the succession, at least in Europe, were various nationalist movements which the victors tended to encourage insofar as they were adequately anti-Bolshevik. In fact, in Europe the basic principle of re-ordering the map was to create ethnic-linguistic nation states, according to the belief that nations had the "right to self-determination." President Wilson of the U.S.A., whose opinions were seen as expressing those of the power without whom the war would have been lost, was passionately committed to this belief, which was (and is) more easily held by those far from the ethnic and linguistic realities of the regions which were to be divided into neat nation-states. The attempt was a disaster, as can still be seen in the Europe of the 1990s. The national conflicts tearing the continent apart in the 1990s were the old chickens of Versailles once again coming home to roost.† The remapping of the Middle East was

---

*Technically the Treaty of Versailles only made peace with Germany. Various parks and royal chateaux in the neighbourhood of Paris gave their names to the other treaties: Saint Germain with Austria; Trianon with Hungary; Sèvres with Turkey; Neuilly with Bulgaria.

†The Yugoslav civil war, the secessionist agitation in Slovakia, the secession of the Baltic states from the former U.S.S.R., the conflicts between Hungarians and Romanians over Transylvania, the separatism of Moldova (Moldavia, formerly Bessarabia), and for that matter Transcaucasian nationalism, are among the explosive problems which either did not exist or could not have existed before 1914.

along conventional imperialist lines—division between Britain and France—except for Palestine, where the British government, anxious for international Jewish support during the war, had incautiously and ambiguously promised to establish "a national home" for the Jews. This was to be another problematic and unforgotten relic of the First World War.

The fourth set of considerations were those of domestic politics within the victor countries—which meant, in practice, Britain, France and the U.S.A.—and frictions between them. The most important consequence of such internal politicking was that the U.S. Congress refused to ratify a peace settlement largely written by or for its President, and the U.S.A. consequently withdrew from it, with far-reaching results.

 Finally, the victor powers desperately searched for the kind of peace settlement which would make impossible another war like the one that had just devastated the world, and whose after-effects were all around them. They failed in the most spectacular manner. Within twenty years the world was once again at war.

Making the world safe from Bolshevism and re-mapping Europe overlapped, since the most immediate way to deal with revolutionary Russia, if by any chance it survived—this was by no means certain in 1919—was to isolate it behind a "quarantine belt" (*cordon sanitaire*, in the contemporary language of diplomacy) of anti-communist states. Since the territory of these was largely or wholly carved out of the formerly Russian lands, their hostility to Moscow could be guaranteed. Going from north to south, these were: Finland, an autonomous region that had been allowed to secede by Lenin; three new little Baltic republics (Estonia, Latvia, Lithuania), for which there was no historical precedent; Poland, restored to independent statehood after 120 years, and an enormously enlarged Romania, its size doubled by accessions from the Hungarian and Austrian parts of the Habsburg empire and ex-Russian Bessarabia. Most of these territories had actually been detached from Russia by Germany and, but for the Bolshevik Revolution, would certainly have been returned to that state. The attempt to continue this isolation belt into the Caucasus, failed, essentially because revolutionary Russia came to terms with non-communist but revolutionary Turkey, which had no fondness for the British and French imperialists. Hence the briefly independent Armenian and Georgian states, set up after Brest Litowsk, and attempts under the British to detach oil-rich Azerbaijan, did not survive the victory of the Bolsheviks in the Civil War of 1918–20 and the Soviet–Turkish treaty of 1921. In short, in the East the Allies accepted the frontiers imposed by Germany on revolutionary Russia, insofar as these were not made inoperative by forces beyond their control.

This still left large parts, mainly of formerly Austro-Hungarian Europe, to be re-mapped. Austria and Hungary were reduced to German and Magyar rumps, Serbia was expanded into a large new Yugoslavia by a merger with the (formerly Austrian) Slovenia and the (formerly Hungarian) Croatia, as well as with the formerly independent small tribal kingdom of herdsmen and raiders, Montenegro, a bleak mass of mountains whose inhabitants reacted to the unprecedented loss of independence by converting en masse to communism, which, they felt, appreciated the heroic virtue. It was also associated with orthodox Russia, whose faith the unconquered men of the Black Mountain had defended against the Turkish unbelievers for so many centuries. A new Czechoslovakia was also formed by joining the former industrial core of the Habsburg empire, the Czech lands, to the areas of Slovak and Ruthenian country people once belonging to Hungary. Romania was enlarged into a multinational conglomerate, while Poland and Italy also benefited. There was absolutely no historical precedent for or logic in the Yugoslav and Czechoslovak combinations, which were constructs of a nationalist ideology which believed in both the force of common ethnicity and the undesirability of excessively small nation-states. All the southern slavs (=Yugoslavs) belonged to one state, as did the western slavs of the Czech and Slovak lands. As might have been expected, these shotgun political marriages did not prove very firm. Incidentally, except for rump Austria and rump Hungary, shorn of most—but in practice not entirely of all—their minorities, the new succession states, whether carved out of Russia or the Habsburg Empire, were no less multinational than their predecessors.

A penal peace, justified by the argument that the state was uniquely responsible for the war and all its consequences (the "war guilt" clause) was imposed on Germany to keep her permanently enfeebled. This was achieved not so much by territorial losses, though Alsace-Lorraine went back to France, a substantial region in the east to a restored Poland (the "Polish Corridor" which separated East Prussia from the rest of Germany), and some lesser adjustments to the German borders; rather it was to be ensured by depriving Germany of an effective navy and any air force; limiting its army to 100,000 men; imposing theoretically indefinite "reparations" (payments for the costs of the war incurred by the victors); by the military occupation of part of western Germany; and, not least, by depriving Germany of all her former overseas colonies. (These were redistributed among the British and their dominions, the French and, to a lesser extent, the Japanese, but, in deference to the growing unpopularity of imperialism, they were no longer called "colonies" but "mandates" to ensure the progress of backward peoples, handed over by humanity to imperial powers who would not dream of exploiting them for any other purpose.) Except for the territorial clauses, nothing was left of the Treaty of Versailles by the middle 1930s.

As for the mechanism for preventing another world war, it was evident that the consortium of European "great powers" which had been supposed to secure this before 1914 had utterly broken down. The alternative, urged on hard-nosed European politicos by President Wilson with all the liberal fervour of a Princeton political scientist, was to set up an all-embracing "League of Nations" (i.e. independent states) which would settle problems peacefully and democratically before they had got out of hand, preferably by public negotiation ("open covenants openly arrived at"), for the war had also made the habitual and sensible processes of international negotiation suspect as "secret diplomacy." This was largely a reaction against the secret treaties arranged among the Allies during the war, in which they carved up post-war Europe and the Middle East with a startling lack of concern for the wishes, or even the interests, of the inhabitants of these regions. The Bolsheviks, discovering these sensitive documents in the Tsarist archives, had promptly published them for the world to read, and an exercise of damage limitation was therefore called for. The League of Nations was indeed set up as part of the peace settlement, and proved an almost total failure, except as an institution for collecting statistics. It did, however, in its early days, settle one or two minor disputes which did not put world peace at much risk, such as that between Finland and Sweden over the Åland Islands.* The refusal of the U.S.A. to join the League of Nations deprived it of any real meaning.

It is not necessary to go into the details of interwar history to see that the Versailles settlement could not possibly be the basis of a stable peace. It was doomed from the start, and another war was therefore practically certain. As we have already noted, the U.S.A. almost immediately contracted out, and in a world no longer Euro-centred and Euro-determined,

---

*The Åland Islands, situated between Finland and Sweden, and part of Finland, were and are inhabited exclusively by a Swedish-speaking population, whereas the newly independent Finland was aggressively committed to the dominance of the Finnish language. As an alternative to secession to nearby Sweden, the League devised a scheme which guaranteed the exclusive use of Swedish on the islands, and safeguarded them against unwanted immigration from the Finnish mainland.

no settlement not underwritten by what was now a major world power could hold. As we shall see, this was true of the world's economic affairs as well as of its politics. Two major European, and indeed world, powers, were temporarily not only eliminated from the international game, but assumed not to exist as independent players—Germany and Soviet Russia. As soon as either or both these re-entered the scene, a peace settlement based on Britain and France alone—for Italy also remained dissatisfied—could not last. And, sooner or later Germany, or Russia, or both, would inevitably reappear as major players.

What little chance the peace had, was torpedoed by the refusal of the victor powers to reintegrate the losers. It is true that the total repression of Germany and the total outlawing of Soviet Russia soon proved impossible, but adjustment to reality was slow and reluctant. The French, in particular, only abandoned the hope of keeping Germany feeble and impotent unwillingly. (The British were not haunted by the memory of defeat and invasion.) As for the U.S.S.R., the victor states would have preferred it not to exist, and, having backed the armies of counter-revolution in the Russian Civil War, and sent military forces to support them, showed no enthusiasm about recognizing its survival. Their businessmen even dismissed the offers of the most far-reaching concessions to foreign investors made by Lenin, desperate for any way to re-start an economy almost destroyed by war, revolution and civil war. Soviet Russia was forced into developing in isolation, even though for political purposes the two outlaw states of Europe, Soviet Russia and Germany, drew together in the early 1920s.

Perhaps the next war might have been avoided, or at least postponed, if the pre-war economy had been restored again as a global system of prosperous growth and expansion. However, after a few years in the middle 1920s when it seemed to have put the war and post-war disruptions behind it, the world economy plunged into the greatest and most dramatic crisis it had known since the industrial revolution (see chapter 3). And this then brought to power, both in Germany and in Japan, the political forces of militarism and the extreme right committed to a deliberate break with the status quo by confrontation, if necessary military, rather than by gradually negotiated change. From then on a new world war was not only predictable, but routinely predicted. Those who became adults in the 1930s expected it. The image of fleets of airplanes dropping bombs on cities and of nightmare figures in gasmasks tapping their way like blind people through the fog of poison gas, haunted my generation: prophetically in one case, mistakenly in the other.

II

The origins of the Second World War have produced an incomparably smaller historical literature than the causes of the First, and for an obvious reason. With the rarest exceptions, no serious historian has ever doubted that Germany, Japan and (more hesitantly) Italy were the aggressors. The states drawn into the war against these three, whether capitalist or socialist, did not want a war, and most of them did what they could to avoid one. In the simplest terms the question who or what caused the Second World War can be answered in two words: Adolf Hitler.

Answers to historical questions are not, of course, so simple. As we have seen, the world situation created by the First World War was inherently unstable, especially in Europe, but also in the Far East, and peace was therefore not expected to last. Dissatisfaction with the status quo was not confined to the defeated states, although these, and notably Germany, felt they had plenty of cause for resentment, as indeed was the case. Every party in Germany, from the Communists on the extreme left to Hitler's National Socialists on the extreme right, concurred in condemning the Versailles Treaty as unjust and unacceptable. Paradoxically, a genuine German revolution might have produced an internationally less explosive Germany. The two defeated countries which were really revolutionized, Russia and Turkey, were too concerned with their own affairs, including the defence of their frontiers, to destabilize the international situation. They were forces for stability in the 1930s, and indeed Turkey remained neutral in the Second World War. However, both Japan and Italy, though on the winning side in the war, also felt dissatisfied, the Japanese with somewhat greater realism than the Italians, whose imperial appetites greatly exceeded their state's independent power to satisfy them. In any case, Italy had come out of the war with considerable territorial gains in the Alps, on the Adriatic and even in the Aegean Sea, even if not quite with all the booty promised to the state by the Allies in return for joining their side in 1915. However, the triumph of fascism, a counter-revolutionary and therefore ultra-nationalist and imperialist movement, underlined Italian dissatisfaction (see chapter 5). As for Japan, its very considerable military and naval force made it into much the most formidable power in the Far East, especially since Russia was out of the picture, and this was to some extent recognized internationally by the Washington Naval Agreement of 1922, which finally ended British naval supremacy by establishing a formula of 5 : 5 : 3 for the strength of the U.S., British and Japanese navies respectively. Yet Japan, whose industrialization was advancing at express speed—even though in absolute size the economy was still quite modest—2.5 per cent of world industrial production in the late 1920s—undoubtedly felt that it deserved a rather larger slice of the Far Eastern cake than the white imperial powers granted it. Moreover, Japan was acutely conscious of the vulnerability of a country that lacked virtually all natural resources needed for a modern industrial economy, whose imports were at the mercy of disruption by foreign navies, and whose exports were at the mercy of the U.S. market. Military pressure for the creation of a nearby land empire in China, it was argued, would shorten the Japanese lines of communication and thus make them less vulnerable.

Nevertheless, whatever the instability of the post-1918 peace and the probability of its breakdown, it is quite undeniable that what caused the Second World War concretely was aggression by the three malcontent powers, bound together by various treaties from the middle 1930s. The milestones on the road to war were the Japanese invasion of Manchuria in 1931; the Italian invasion of Ethiopia in 1935; the German and Italian intervention in the Spanish Civil War of 1936–39; the German invasion of Austria in early 1938; the German crippling of Czechoslovakia later in the same year; the German occupation of what remained of Czechoslovakia in March 1939 (followed by the Italian occupation of Albania); and the German demands on Poland which actually led to the outbreak of war. Alternatively, we can count these milestones negatively: the failure of the League to act against Japan; the failure to take effective measures against Italy in 1935; the failure of Britain and France to respond to the unilateral German denunciation of the Treaty of Versailles, and notably its military reoccupation of the Rhineland in 1936; their refusal to intervene in the Spanish Civil War ("non-intervention"); their failure to respond to the occupation of Austria; their retreat before German blackmail over Czechoslovakia (the "Munich Ageement" of 1938); and the refusal of the U.S.S.R. to continue opposing Hitler in 1939 (the Hitler–Stalin pact of August 1939).

And yet, if one side clearly did not want war and did everything possible to avoid it, and the other side glorified it and, in the case of Hitler, certainly actively desired it, none of the aggressors wanted the war they got, at the time they got it, and against at least some of the enemies they found themselves fighting. Japan, in spite of the military influence on its politics, would certainly have preferred to achieve its objectives—essentially the creation of an East Asian empire—without a *general* war, into which they only became involved because the U.S.A. was involved in one. What kind of war Germany wanted, when and against whom, are still matters of argument, since Hitler was not a man who documented his decisions, but two things are clear. A war against Poland (backed by Britain and France) in 1939 was not in his game plan, and the war in which he finally found himself, against both the U.S.S.R. and the U.S.A., was every German general's and diplomat's nightmare.

Germany (and later Japan) needed a rapid offensive war for the same reasons that had made it necessary in 1914. The joint resources of the potential enemies of each, once united and co-ordinated, were overwhelmingly greater than their own. Neither even planned effectively for a lengthy war, nor relied on armaments that had a long gestation period. (By contrast the British, accepting inferiority on land, put their money from the start into the most expensive and technologically sophisticated forms of armament and planned for a long war in which they and their allies would outproduce the other side.) The Japanese were more successful than the Germans in avoiding the coalition of their enemies, since they kept out of both Germany's war against Britain and France in 1939–40 and the war against Russia after 1941. Unlike all the other powers, they had actually been up against the Red Army in an unofficial but substantial war on the Siberian–Chinese border in 1939 and had been badly mauled. Japan only entered the war against Britain and the U.S.A., but not the U.S.S.R., in December 1941. Unfortunately for Japan, the only power it had to fight, the U.S.A., was so vastly superior in its resources to Japan, that it was virtually bound to win.

Germany seemed luckier for a while. In the 1930s, as war drew nearer, Britain and France failed to join with Soviet Russia, and eventually Soviet Russia preferred to come to terms with Hitler, while local politics prevented President Roosevelt from giving more than paper backing to the side he passionately supported. The war therefore began in 1939 as a purely European war, and indeed, after Germany marched into Poland, which was defeated and partitioned with the now neutral U.S.S.R. in three weeks, a purely west European war of Germany against Britain and France. In the spring of 1940, Germany overran Norway, Denmark, the Netherlands, Belgium and France with ridiculous ease, occupying the first four countries, and dividing France into a zone directly occupied and administered by the victorious Germans and a satellite French "state" (its rulers, drawn from the various branches of French reaction, no longer liked to call it a republic) with its capital in a provincial health resort, Vichy. Only Britain was left at war with Germany, under a coalition of all national forces, headed by Winston Churchill, based on a total refusal to come to any kind of terms with Hitler. It was at this moment that fascist Italy mistakenly chose to slide off the fence of neutrality, on which its government had cautiously been sitting, on to the German side.

For practical purposes, the war in Europe was over. Even if Germany could not invade Britain because of the dual obstacle of the sea and the Royal Air Force, there was no foreseeable war in which Britain could return to the Continent, let alone defeat Germany. The months of 1940–41, when Britain stood alone, are a marvellous moment in the history of the British people, or at any rate those who were lucky enough to live through it, but the country's chances were slim. The U.S.A.'s "Hemispheric Defense" re-armament programme of June 1940 virtually assumed that further arms for Britain would be useless and, even after Britain's survival was accepted, the United Kingdom was still seen chiefly as an outlying defence base for America. Meanwhile the map of Europe was re-drawn. The U.S.S.R., by agreement, occupied those European parts of the Tsarist empire lost in 1918 (except for the parts of Poland taken over by Germany) and Finland, against which Stalin had fought a clumsy winter war in 1939–40, which pushed the Russian frontiers a little further away from Leningrad. Hitler presided over a revision of the Versailles settlement in the former Habsburg territories that proved shortlived. British attempts to extend the war in the Balkans led to the expected conquest of the entire peninsula by Germany, including the Greek islands.

Indeed, Germany actually crossed the Mediterranean into Africa when its ally Italy, even more disappointing as a military power in the Second World War than Austria-Hungary had been in the First World War, looked like being thrown entirely out of its African empire by the British, fighting from their main base in Egypt. The German Afrika Korps, under one of the most talented generals, Erwin Rommel, threatened the entire British position in the Middle East.

The war was revived by Hitler's invasion of the U.S.S.R. on 22 June 1941, the decisive date in the Second World War; an invasion so senseless—for it committed Germany to a war on two fronts—that Stalin simply would not believe that Hitler could contemplate it. But for Hitler the conquest of a vast eastern land-empire, rich in resources and slave labour, was the logical next step, and, like all other military experts except the Japanese, he spectacularly underestimated the Soviet capacity to resist. Not, however, without some plausibility, given the disorganization of the Red Army by the purges of the 1930s (see chapter 13), the apparent state of the country, the general effects of the terror, and Stalin's own extraordinarily inept interventions into military strategy. In fact, the initial advances of the German armies were as swift and seemed as decisive as the campaigns in the West. By early October they were on the outskirts of Moscow, and there is evidence that, for a few days, Stalin himself was demoralized and contemplated making peace. But the moment passed, and the sheer size of the reserves of space, manpower, Russian physical toughness and patriotism, and a ruthless war effort, defeated the Germans and gave the U.S.S.R. time to organize effectively, not least by allowing the very talented military leaders (some of them recently released from gulags) to do what they thought best. The years of 1942–45 was the only time when Stalin paused in his terror.

Once the Russian war had not been decided within three months, as Hitler had expected, Germany was lost, since it was neither equipped for nor could sustain a long war. In spite of its triumphs, it had, and produced, far fewer aircraft and tanks than even Britain and Russia without the U.S.A. A new German offensive in 1942, after the gruelling winter, seemed as brilliantly successful as all the others, and pushed the German armies deep into the Caucasus and into the lower Volga valley, but it could no longer decide the war. The German armies were held, ground down and eventually surrounded and forced to surrender at Stalingrad (summer 1942–March 1943). After that the Russians in turn began the advance which only brought them into Berlin, Prague and Vienna by the end of the war. From Stalingrad on everyone knew that the defeat of Germany was only a question of time.

Meanwhile the war, still basically European, had become truly global. This was partly due to the stirrings of anti-imperialism among the subjects and dependents of Britain, still the geatest of world-wide empires, though they could still be suppressed without difficulty. The Hitler sympathisers among the Boers in South Africa could be interned—they reemerged after the war as the architects of the Apartheid regime of 1948—and Rashid Ali's seizure of power in Iraq in the spring of 1941 was quickly put down. Much more significant was that the triumph of Hitler in Europe left a partial imperial vacuum in Southeast Asia into which Japan now moved, by asserting a protectorate over the helpless relics of the French in Indochina. The U.S.A. regarded this extension of Axis power into Southeast Asia as intolerable, and put severe economic pressure on Japan, whose trade and supplies depended entirely on maritime communications. It was this conflict that led to war between the two countries. The Japanese attack on Pearl Harbor on 7 December 1941 made the war worldwide. Within a few months the Japanese had overrun all of Southeast Asia, continental and insular, threatening to invade India from Burma in the west, and the empty north of Australia from New Guinea.

Probably Japan could not have avoided war with the U.S.A. unless the country had given up the aim of establishing a powerful economic empire (euphemistically described as a "Greater East Asian Co-Prosperity Sphere"), which was the very essence of its policy. However, having watched the consequences of the European powers' failure to resist Hitler and Mussolini, and its results, F. D. Roosevelt's U.S.A. could not be expected to react to Japanese expansion as Britain and France had reacted to German expansion. In any case, U.S. public opinion regarded the Pacific (unlike Europe) as a normal field for U.S. action, rather like Latin America. American "isolationism" merely wanted to keep out of Europe. In fact, it was the Western (i.e. American) embargo on Japanese trade and freezing of Japanese assets, which forced Japan to take action, if the Japanese economy, which depended entirely on oceanic imports, was not to be strangled in short order. The gamble it took was dangerous, and proved suicidal. Japan would seize perhaps its only opportunity to establish its southern empire quickly; but since it calculated that this required the immobilization of the American navy, the only force that could intervene, it also meant that the U.S.A. with its overwhelmingly superior forces and resources would *immediately* be drawn into war. There was no way that Japan could win such a war.

The mystery is, why Hitler, already fully stretched in Russia, gratuitously declared war on the U.S.A., thus giving Roosevelt's government the chance to enter the European war on the British side without meeting overwhelming political resistance at home. For there was very little doubt in Washington's mind that Nazi Germany constituted a much more serious, or, at any rate, a much more global danger to the U.S. position—and the world—than Japan. The U.S. therefore deliberately chose to concentrate on winning the war against Germany before that against Japan, and to concentrate its resources accordingly. The calculation was correct. It took another three-and-a-half years to defeat Germany, after which Japan was brought to its knees in three months. There is no adequate explanation of Hitler's folly, though we know him to have persistently, and dramatically, underestimated the capacity for action, not to mention the economic and technological potential, of the U.S.A. because he thought democracies incapable of action. The only democracy he took seriously was the British, which he rightly regarded as not entirely democratic.

The decisions to invade Russia and to declare war against the U.S.A. decided the result of the Second World War. This did not seem immediately obvious, since the Axis powers reached the peak of their success in mid-1942, and did not entirely lose the military initiative until 1943. Moreover, the Western Allies did not effectively re-enter the European

Continent until 1944, for, while they successfully drove the Axis out of North Africa and crossed into Italy, they were successfully held at bay by the German army. In the meantime the Western Allies' only major weapon against Germany was airpower, and this, as subsequent research has shown, was spectacularly ineffective, except in killing civilians and destroying cities. Only the Soviet armies continued to advance, and only in the Balkans—mainly in Yugoslavia, Albania and Greece—did a largely communist-inspired armed resistance movement cause Germany, and even more Italy, serious military problems. Nevertheless, Winston Churchill was right when he confidently claimed after Pearl Harbor that victory by "the proper application of overwhelming force" was certain (Kennedy, p. 347). From the end of 1942 on nobody doubted that the Grand Alliance against the Axis would win. The Allies began to concentrate on what to do with their foreseeable victory.

We need not follow the course of military events further, except to note that, in the West, German resistance proved very hard to overcome even after the Allies re-entered the Continent in force in June 1944, and that, unlike 1918, there was no sign of any German revolution against Hitler. Only the German generals, the heart of traditional Prussian military power and efficiency, plotted Hitler's downfall in July 1944, since they were rational patriots rather than enthusiasts for a Wagnerian *Götterdämmerung* in which Germany would be totally destroyed. They had no mass support, failed and were killed *en masse* by Hitler's loyalists. In the East there was even less sign of a crack in Japan's determination to fight to the end, which is why nuclear arms were dropped on Hiroshima and Nagasaki to ensure a rapid Japanese surrender. Victory in 1945 was total, surrender unconditional. The defeated enemy states were totally occupied by the victors. No formal peace was made, since no authorities independent of the occupying forces were recognized, at least in Germany and Japan. The nearest thing to peace negotiations were the series of conferences between 1943 and 1945 in which the main allied powers—the U.S.A., the U.S.S.R. and Great Britain—decided the division of the spoils of victory and (not too successfully) tried to determine their postwar relations with each other: in Teheran in 1943; in Moscow in the autumn of 1944; in Yalta in the Crimea in early 1945; and at Potsdam in occupied Germany in August 1945. More successfully, a series of interallied negotiations between 1943 and 1945 set up a more general framework for political and economic relations between states, including the establishment of the United Nations. These matters belong to another chapter (see chapter 9).

Even more than the Great War, the Second World War was therefore fought to a finish, without serious thought of compromise on either side, except by Italy, which changed sides and political regimes in 1943 and was not treated entirely as an occupied territory, but as a defeated country with a recognized government. (It was helped by the fact that the Allies failed to drive the Germans, and a Fascist "Social Republic" under Mussolini dependent on them, out of half of Italy for almost two years.) Unlike the First World War, this intransigence on both sides requires no special explanation. This was a war of religion, or, in modern terms, of ideologies, on both sides. It was also, and demonstrably, a fight for life for most of the countries concerned. The price of defeat by the German National Socialist regime, as demonstrated in Poland and the occupied parts of the U.S.S.R., and by the fate of the Jews, whose systematic extermination gradually became known to an incredulous world, was enslavement and death. Hence the war was waged without limit. The Second World War escalated mass war into total war.

Its losses are literally incalculable, and even approximate estimates are impossible, since the war (unlike the First World War) killed civilians as readily as people in uniform, and much of the worst killing took place in regions, or at times, when nobody was in a position to count, or cared to. Deaths directly caused by this war have been estimated at between three and five times the (estimated) figure for the First World War (Milward, 270; Petersen, 1986), and, in other terms, at between 10 and 20 per cent of the *total* population in the U.S.S.R., Poland and Yugoslavia; and between 4 and 6 per cent of Germany, Italy, Austria, Hungary, Japan and China. Casualties in Britain and France were far lower than in the First World War—about 1 per cent, but in the U.S.A. somewhat higher. Nevertheless, these are guesses. Soviet casualties have been estimated at various times, even officially, at seven millions, eleven millions, or of the order of twenty or even fifty millions. In any case, what does statistical exactitude mean, where the orders of magnitude are so astronomic? Would the horror of the holocaust be any less if historians concluded that it exterminated not six millions (the rough and almost certainly exaggerated original estimate) but five or even four? What if the nine hundred days of the German siege of Leningrad (1941–44) killed a million or only three quarters or half a million by starvation and exhaustion? Indeed, can we really *grasp* figures beyond the reality open to physical intuition? What does it mean to the average reader of this page that out of 5.7 million Russian prisoners of war in Germany 3.3 million died (Hirschfeld, 1986)? The only certain fact about the casualties of the war is that, on the whole, they killed more men than women. In 1959 there were still, in the U.S.S.R., seven women between the ages of thirty-five and fifty for every four men (Milward, 1979, p. 212). Buildings could more easily be rebuilt after this war than surviving lives.

III

We take it for granted that modern warfare involves all citizens and mobilizes most of them; that it is waged with armaments which require a diversion of the entire economy to produce them, and which are used in unimaginable quantities; that it produces untold destruction and utterly dominates and transforms the life of the countries involved in it. Yet all these phenomena belong to the wars only of the twentieth century. There were, indeed, tragically destructive wars earlier, and even wars anticipating modern total war efforts, as in France during the Revolution. To this day the Civil War of 1861–65 remains the bloodiest conflict in U.S. history, which killed as many men as all the later wars of the U.S.A. put together, including both world wars, Korea and Vietnam. Nevertheless, before the twentieth-century, wars embracing all society were exceptional. Jane Austen wrote her novels during the Napoleonic wars, but no reader who did not know this already would guess it, for the wars do not appear in her pages, even though a number of the young gentlemen who pass through them undoubtedly took part in them. It is inconceivable that any novelist could write about Britain in the twentieth-century wars in this manner.

The monster of twentieth-century total war was not born full-sized. Nevertheless, from 1914 on, wars were unmistakably mass wars. Even in the First World War Britain mobilized 12.5 per cent of its men for the forces, Germany 15.4 per cent, France almost 17 per cent. In the Second World War the percentage of the total active labour force that went into the armed forces was pretty generally in the neighborhood of 20 per cent (Milward, 1979, p. 216). We may note in passing that such a level of mass mobilization, lasting for a matter of years, cannot be maintained except by a modern high-productivity industrialized economy, and—or alternatively—an economy largely in the hands of the non-combatant parts of the population. Traditional agrarian economies cannot usually mobilize so large a proportion of their labour force except seasonally, at least in the temperate zone, for there are times in the agricultural year when all hands are needed (for instance to get in the harvest). Even in industrial societies so great a manpower mobilization puts enormous strains on the labour force, which is why modern mass wars both strengthened the powers of organized labour and produced a revolution in the employment of women outside the household: temporarily in the First World War, permanently in the Second World War.

Again, twentieth-century wars were mass wars in the sense that they used, and destroyed, hitherto inconceivable quantities of products in the course of fighting. Hence the German phrase *Materialschlacht* to describe the western battles of 1914–18—battles of materials. Napoleon, luckily for the extremely restricted industrial capacity of France in his day, could win the battle of Jena in 1806 and thus destroy the power of Prussia with no more than 1,500 rounds of artillery. Yet even before the First World War France planned for a munitions output of 10–12,000 shells *a day*, and in the end its industry had to produce 200,000 shells *a day*. Even Tsarist Russia found that it produced 150,000 shells a day, or at the rate of four-and-a-half millions a month. No wonder that the processes of mechanical engineering factories were revolutionized. As for the less destructive implements of war, let us recall that during the Second World War the U.S. army ordered over 519 million pairs of socks and over 219 million pairs of pants, whereas the German forces, true to bureaucratic tradition, in a single year (1943) ordered 4.4 million pairs of scissors and 6.2 million pads for the stamps of military offices (Milward, 1979, p. 68). Mass war required mass production.

But production also required organization and management—even if its object was the rationalized destruction of human lives in the most efficient manner, as in the German extermination camps. Speaking in the most general terms, total war was the largest enterprise hitherto known to man, which had to be consciously organized and managed.

This also raised novel problems. Military affairs had always been the special concern of governments, since these took over the running of permanent ("standing") armies in the seventeenth century, rather than subcontracting them from military entrepreneurs. In fact, armies and war soon became far larger "industries" or complexes of economic activity than anything in private business, which is why in the nineteenth century they so often provided the expertise and the management skills for the vast private enterprises which developed in the industrial era, for instance railway projects or port installations. Moreover, almost all governments were in the business of manufacturing armaments and war material, although in the late nineteenth century a sort of symbiosis developed between government and specialized private armaments producers, especially in the high-tech sectors such as artillery and the navy, which anticipated what we now know as the "military-industrial complex" (see *Age of Empire*, chapter 13). Nevertheless, the basic assumption between the era of the French revolution and the First World War was that the economy would, so far as possible, continue to operate in wartime as it had in peacetime ("business as usual"), though of course certain industries would clearly feel its impact—for instance the clothing industry, which would be required to produce military garments far beyond any conceivable peacetime capacity.

The governments' main problem, as they saw it, was fiscal: how to pay for wars. Should it be through loans, through direct taxation, and, in either case, on what precise terms? Consequently it was Treasuries or Ministries of Finance which were seen as the commanders of the war economy. The First World War, which lasted so much longer than governments had anticipated, and used up so many more men and armaments, made "business as usual" and, with it, the domination of Ministries of Finance, impossible, even though Treasury officials (like the young Maynard Keynes in Britain) still shook their heads over the politicians' readiness to pursue victory without counting the financial costs. They were, of course, right. Britain waged both world wars far beyond its means, with lasting and negative consequences for its economy. Yet if war was to be waged at all on the modern scale, not only its costs had to be counted but its production—and in the end the entire economy—had to be managed and planned.

Governments only learned this by experience in the course of the First World War. In the Second World War they knew it from the outset, thanks largely to the experience of the First World War, the lessons of which their officials had studied intensively. Nevertheless, it only gradually became clear how completely governments had to take over the economy, and how essential physical planning and the allocation of resources (other than by the usual economic mechanisms) now were. At the outset of the Second World War only two states, the U.S.S.R. and, to a lesser extent, Nazi Germany, had any mechanism for physically controlling the economy, which is not surprising, since Soviet ideas of planning were originally inspired by, and to some extent based on, what the Bolsheviks knew of the German planned war economy of 1914–17 (see chapter 13). Some states, notably Britain and the U.S.A., had not even the rudiments of such mechanisms.

It is, therefore, a strange paradox that among the government-run planned war economies of both wars, and in total wars that meant *all* war economies those of the Western democratic states—Britain and France in the First World War; Britain and even the U.S.A. in the Second—proved far superior to Germany with its tradition and theories of rational-bureaucratic administration. (For Soviet planning, see chapter 13.) We can only guess at the reasons, but there is no doubt about the facts. The German war economy was less systematic and effective in mobilizing all resources for war—of course, until after the strategy of lightning strikes failed, it did not have to—and it certainly took less care of the German civilian population. Inhabitants of Britain and France who survived the First World War unharmed were likely to be somewhat healthier than before the war, even when they were poorer, and their workers' real income had risen. Germans were hungrier, and their workers' real wages had fallen. Comparisons in the Second World War are more difficult, if only because France was soon eliminated, the U.S.A. was richer and under much less pressure, the U.S.S.R. poorer and under much more. The German war economy had virtually all Europe to exploit but ended the war with far greater physical destruction than Western belligerents. Still, on the whole a poorer Britain, whose civilian consumption fell by over 20 per cent by 1943, ended the war with a slightly better-fed and healthier population, thanks to a war-planned economy systematically slanted towards equality and fairness of sacrifice, and social justice. The German system was, of course, inequitable on principle. Germany exploited both the resources and the manpower of occupied Europe, and treated the non-German populations as inferior, and, in extreme cases—Poles, but especially Russians and Jews—virtually as expendable slave-labour which did not even have to be kept alive. Foreign labour rose to form about one fifth of the labour force in Germany by 1944—30 per cent in the armaments industries. Even so, the most that can be claimed for Germany's own workers is that their real earnings stayed the same as in 1938. British child mortality and sickness rates fell progressively during the war. In occupied and dominated France, a country proverbially rich in food and out of the war after 1940, the average weight and fitness of the population at all ages declined.

Total war undoubtedly revolutionized management. How far did it revolutionize technology and production? Or, to put it another way, did it advance or retard economic development? It plainly advanced technology, since the conflict between advanced belligerents was not only one of armies but of competing technologies for providing them with effective weapons, and other essential services. But for the Second World War, and the fear that Nazi Germany might also exploit the discoveries of nuclear physics, the atom bomb would certainly not have been made, nor would the quite enormous expenditures needed to produce any kind of nuclear energy have been undertaken in the twentieth century. Other technological advances made, in the first instance, for purposes of war, have proved considerably more readily applicable in peace—one thinks of aeronautics and computers—but this does not alter the fact that war or the preparation for war has been a major device for accelerating technical progress by "carrying" the development costs of technological innovations which would almost certainly not have been undertaken by anyone making peacetime cost-benefit calculations, or which would have been made more slowly and hesitantly (see chapter 9).

Still, the technological bent of war was not new. Moreover, the modern industrial economy was built on constant technological innovation, which would certainly have taken place, probably at an accelerating rate, even without wars (if we can make this unrealistic assumption for the sake of argument). Wars, especially the Second World War, greatly helped to diffuse technical expertise, and they certainly had a major impact on industrial organization and methods of mass production, but what they achieved was, by and large, an acceleration of change rather than a transformation.

Did war advance economic growth? In one sense it plainly did not. The losses of productive resources were heavy, quite apart from the fall in the working population. Twenty-five per cent of pre-war capital assets were destroyed in the U.S.S.R. during the Second World War, 13 per cent in Germany, 8 per cent in Italy, 7 per cent in France, though only 3 per cent in Britain (but this must be offset by new wartime constructions). In the extreme case of the U.S.S.R., the net economic effect of the war was entirely negative. In 1945 the country's agriculture lay in ruins, as did the industrialization of the pre-war Five-Year Plans. All that remained was a vast and quite inadaptable armaments industry, a starving and decimated people and massive physical destruction.

On the other hand wars were clearly good to the U.S. economy. Its rate of growth in both wars was quite extraordinary, especially in the Second World War when it grew at the rate of roughly 10 per cent per annum, faster than ever before or since. In both wars the U.S.A. benefited from being both remote from the fighting, and the main arsenal of its allies, and from the capacity of its economy to organize the expansion of production more effectively than any other. Probably the most lasting economic effect of both world wars was to give the U.S. economy a global preponderance during the whole of the Short Twentieth Century, which only slowly began to fade towards the end of the century (see chapter 9). In 1914 it was already the largest industrial economy, but not yet the dominant economy. The wars, which strengthened it while, relatively or absolutely, weakening its competitors, transformed its economic situation.

If the U.S.A. (in both wars) and Russia (especially in the Second

World War) represent the two extremes of the wars' economic effects, the rest of the world is situated somewhere between these extremes; but on the whole closer to the Russian than to the American end of the curve.

IV

It remains to assess the human impact of the era of wars, and its human costs. The sheer mass of casualties, to which we have already referred, are only one part of these. Curiously enough, except, for understandable reasons, in the U.S.S.R., the much smaller figures of the First World War were to make a much greater impact than the vast quantities of the Second World War, as witness the much greater prominence of memorials and the cult of the fallen of the First World War. The Second World War produced no equivalent to the monuments to "the unknown soldier," and after it the celebration of "armistice day" (the anniversary of 11 November 1918) gradually lost its inter-war solemnity. Perhaps ten million dead hit those who had never expected such sacrifice more brutally than fifty-four million hit those who had already once experienced war as massacre.

Certainly both the totality of the war efforts and the determination on both sides to wage war without limit and at whatever cost, made its mark. Without it, the growing brutality and inhumanity of the twentieth century is difficult to explain. About this rising curve of barbarism after 1914 there is, unfortunately, no serious doubt. By the early twentieth century, torture had officially been ended throughout Western Europe. Since 1945 we have once again accustomed ourselves, without much revulsion, to its use in at least one third of the member-states of the United Nations, including some of the oldest and most civilized (Peters, 1985).

The growth of brutalization was due not so much to the release of the latent potential for cruelty and violence in the human being, which war naturally legitimizes, although this certainly emerged after the First World War among a certain type of ex-servicemen (veterans), especially in the strong-arm or killer squads and "Free Corps" on the nationalist ultra-Right. Why should men who had killed and seen their friends killed and mangled, hesitate to kill and brutalize the enemies of a good cause?

One major reason was the strange democratisation of war. Total conflicts turned into "people's wars," both because civilians and civilian life became the proper, and sometimes the main, targets of strategy, and because in democratic wars, as in democratic politics, adversaries are naturally demonized in order to make them properly hateful or at least despicable. Wars conducted on both sides by professionals, or specialists, especially those of similar social standing, do not exclude mutual respect and acceptance of rules, or even chivalry. Violence has its rules. This was still evident among fighter pilots in air forces in both wars, as witness Jean Renoir's pacifist film about the First World War, *La Grande Illusion*. Professionals of politics and diplomacy, when untrammeled by the demands of votes or newspapers, can declare war or negotiate peace with no hard feelings about the other side, like boxers who shake hands before they come out fighting, and drink with each other after the fight. But the total wars of our century were far removed from the Bismarckian or eighteenth-century pattern. No war in which mass national feelings are mobilized can be as limited as aristocratic wars. And, it must be said, in the Second World War the nature of Hitler's regime and the behaviour of the Germans, including the old non-Nazi German army, in Eastern Europe, was such as to justify a good deal of demonization.

Another reason, however, was the new impersonality of warfare, which turned killing and maiming into the remote consequence of pushing a button or moving a lever. Technology made its victims invisible, as people eviscerated by bayonets, or seen through the sights of firearms could not be. Opposite the permanently fixed guns of the western front were not men but statistics—not even real, but hypothetical statistics, as the "body-counts" of enemy casualties during the U.S. Vietnam War showed. Far below the aerial bombers were not people about to be burned and eviscerated, but targets. Mild young men, who would certainly not have wished to plunge a bayonet in the belly of any pregnant village girl, could far more easily drop high explosives on London or Berlin, or nuclear bombs on Nagasaki. Hard-working German bureaucrats who would certainly have found it repugnant to drive starving Jews into abattoirs themselves, could work out the railway timetables for a regular supply of death-trains to Polish extermination camps with less sense of personal involvement. The greatest cruelties of our century have been the impersonal cruelties of remote decision, of system and routine, especially when they could be justified as regrettable operational necessities.

So the world accustomed itself to the compulsory expulsion and killing on an astronomic scale, phenomena so unfamiliar that new words had to be invented for them: "stateless" ("apatride") or "genocide." The First World War led to the killing of an uncounted number of Armenians by Turkey—the most usual figure is 1.5 millions—which can count as the first modern attempt to eliminate an entire population. It was later followed by the better-known Nazi mass-killing of about five million Jews—the numbers remain in dispute. (Hilberg, 1985). The First World War and the Russian revolution forced millions to move as refugees, or by compulsory "exchanges of populations" between states, which amounted to the same. A total of 1.3 million Greeks were repatriated to Greece, mainly from Turkey; 400,000 Turks were decanted into the state which claimed them; some 200,000 Bulgarians moved into the diminished territory bearing their national name; while 1.5 or perhaps 2 million Russian nationals, escaping from the Russian revolution or on the losing side of the Russian civil war, found themselves homeless. It was mainly for these rather than the 320,000 Armenians fleeing genocide, that a new document was invented for those who, in an increasingly bureaucratized world, had no bureaucratic existence in any state: the so-called Nansen passport of the League of Nations, named after the great Norwegian arctic explorer who made himself a second career as a friend to the friendless. At a rough guess the years 1914–22 generated between four and five million refugees.

This first flood of human jetsam was as nothing to that which followed the Second World War, or to the inhumanity with which they were treated. It has been estimated that by May 1945 there were perhaps 40.5 million uprooted people in Europe, excluding non-German forced labourers and Germans who fled before the advancing Soviet armies (Kulischer, 1948, pp. 253–73). About thirteen million Germans were expelled from the parts of Germany annexed by Poland and the U.S.S.R., from Czechoslovakia and parts of south-eastern Europe where they had long been settled (Holborn, p. 363). They were taken in by the new German Federal Republic, which offered a home and citizenship to any German who returned there, as the new state of Israel offered a "right of return" to any Jew. When, but in an epoch of mass flight, could such offers by states have been seriously made? Of the 11,332,700 "displaced persons" of various nationalities found in Germany by the victorious armies in 1945, ten millions soon returned to their homelands—but half of these were compelled to do so against their will (Jacobmeyer, 1986).

These were only the refugees of Europe. The decolonization of India in 1947 created fifteen million of them, forced to cross the new frontiers between India and Pakistan (in both directions), without counting the two millions killed in the accompanying civil strife. The Korean War, another by-product of The Second World War, produced perhaps five million displaced Koreans. After the establishment of Israel—yet another of the war's after-effects—about 1.3 million Palestinians were registered with the United Nations Relief and Work Agency (UNRWA); conversely by the early 1960s 1.2 million Jews had migrated to Israel, the majority of these also as refugees. In short, the global human catastrophe unleashed by the Second World War is almost certainly the largest in human history. Not the least tragic aspect of this catastrophe is that humanity has learned to live in a world in which killing, torture and mass exile have become everyday experiences which we no longer notice.

Looking back on the thirty-one years from the assassination of the Austrian Archduke in Sarajevo to the unconditional surrender of Japan, they must be seen as an era of havoc comparable to the Thirty Years' War of the seventeenth century in German history. And Sarajevo—the first Sarajevo—certainly marked the beginning of a general age of catastrophe and crisis in the affairs of the world, which is the subject of this and the next four chapters. Nevertheless, in the memory of the generations after 1945, the Thirty-one Years' War did not leave behind the same sort of memory as its more localised seventeenth-century predecessor.

This is partly because it formed a single era of war only in the historian's perspective. For those who lived through it, it was experienced as two distinct though connected wars, separated by an "inter-war" period without overt hostilities, ranging from thirteen years for Japan (whose second war began in Manchuria in 1931) to twenty-three years for the U.S.A. (which did not enter the Second World War until December 1941). However, it is also because each of these wars had its own historical character and profile. Both were episodes of carnage without parallel, leaving behind the technological nightmare images that haunted the nights and days of the next generation: poison gas and aerial bombardment after 1918, the mushroom cloud of nuclear destruction after 1945. Both ended in breakdown and—as we shall see in the next chapter—social revolution over large regions of Europe and Asia. Both left the belligerents exhausted and enfeebled, except for the U.S.A., which emerged from both undamaged and enriched, as the economic lord of the world. And yet, how striking the differences! The First World War solved nothing. Such hopes as it generated—of a peaceful and democratic world of nation-states under the League of Nations; of a return to the world economy of 1913; even (among those who hailed the Russian Revolution) of world capitalism overthrown within years or months by a rising of the oppressed, were soon disappointed. The past was beyond reach, the future postponed, the present bitter, except for a few fleeting years in the mid-1920s. The Second World War actually produced solutions, at least for decades. The dramatic social and economic problems of capitalism in its Age of Catastrophe seemed to disappear. The Western world economy entered its Golden Age; Western political democracy, backed by an extraordinary improvement in material life, was stable; war was banished to the Third World. On the other side, even revolution appeared to have found its way forward. The old colonial empires vanished or were shortly destined to go. A consortium of communist states, organized around the Soviet Union, now transformed into a superpower, seemed ready to compete in the race for economic growth with the West. This proved to be an illusion, but not until the 1960s did it begin to vanish. As we can now see, even the international scene was stabilized, though it did not seem so. Unlike after the Great War, the former enemies—Germany and Japan—reintegrated into the (Western) world economy, and the new enemies—the U.S.A. and the U.S.S.R.—never actually came to blows.

Even the revolutions which ended both wars were quite different. Those after the First World War were, as we shall see, rooted in a revulsion against what most people who lived through it, had increasingly seen as a pointless slaughter. They were revolutions against the war. The revolutions after the Second World War grew out of the popular participation in a world struggle against enemies—Germany, Japan, more generally imperialism—which, however terrible, those who took part in it felt to be just. And yet, like the two World Wars, the two sorts of postwar revolution can be seen in the historian's perspective as a single process. To this we must now turn.

CHAPTER TWO

The World Revolution

At the same time [Bukharin] added, "I do think we have entered upon a period of revolution which may last fifty years before the revolution is at last victorious in all Europe and finally in all the world."

—Arthur Ransome, *Six Weeks in Russia in 1919*
(Ransome, 1919, p. 54)

How terrible to read Shelley's poem (not to mention the Egyptian peasant songs of 3,000 years ago), denouncing oppression and exploitation. Will they be read in a future still filled with oppression and exploitation, and will people say: "Even in those days . . ."

—Bertolt Brecht on reading Shelley's "The Masque of Anarchy"
in 1938 (Brecht, 1964)

Since the French Revolution there has arisen in Europe a Russian revolution, and this has once again taught the world that even the strongest of invaders can be repelled, once the fate of the Fatherland is truly entrusted to the poor, the humble, the proletarians, the labouring people.

From the wall newspaper of the *19 Brigata Eusebio Giambone* of the
Italian Partisans, 1944 (Pavone, 1991, p. 406)

Revolution was the child of twentieth-century war: specifically the Russian revolution of 1917 which created the Soviet Union, transformed into a superpower by the second phase of the Thirty-one Years' War, but, more generally, revolution as a global constant in the century's history. War alone does not necessarily lead to crisis, breakdown and revolution in belligerent countries. In fact, before 1914 the opposite assumption held the field, at least about established regimes with traditional legitimacy. Napoleon I had complained bitterly that the Emperor of Austria could happily survive a hundred lost battles, as the king of Prussia survived military disaster and the loss of half his lands, whereas he himself, child of the French revolution, would be at risk after a single defeat. Yet the strains of twentieth-century total war on the states and peoples involved in it were so overwhelming and unprecedented that they were almost bound to stretch both to their limits, and, as like as not, to breaking-point. Only the U.S.A. came out of the world wars very much as it had gone into them, only rather stronger. For all others the end of wars meant upheaval.

It seemed obvious that the old world was doomed. The old society, the old economy, the old political systems had, as the Chinese phrase put it, "lost the mandate of heaven." Humanity was waiting for an alternative. Such an alternative was familiar in 1914. Socialist parties, resting on the support of the expanding working classes of their countries and inspired by a belief in the historic inevitability of their victory, represented this alternative in most countries of Europe (see *Age of Empire*, chapter 5). It looked as though only a signal was needed for the peoples to rise, to replace capitalism by socialism, and thus to transform the meaningless sufferings of world war into something more positive: the bloody birth-pains and convulsions of a new world. The Russian Revolution or, more precisely, the Bolshevik revolution of October 1917, set out to give the world this signal. It therefore became an event as central to the history of this century as the French revolution of 1789 was to the nineteenth. Indeed, it is not an accident that the history of the Short Twentieth Century, as defined in this book, virtually coincides with the lifetime of the state born of the October revolution.

However, the October revolution had far more profound and global repercussions than its ancestor. For, if the ideas of the French revolution have, as is now evident, outlasted Bolshevism, the practical consequences of 1917 were far greater and more lasting than those of 1789. The October revolution produced by far the most formidable organized revolutionary movement in modern history. Its global expansion has no parallel since the conquests of Islam in its first century. A mere thirty to forty years after Lenin's arrival at the Finland Station in Petrograd, one third of humanity found itself living under regimes directly derived from the "Ten Days That Shook the World" (Reed, 1919), and Lenin's organizational model, the Communist Party. Most of them followed the U.S.S.R. in a second wave of revolutions which emerged from the second phase of the long world war of 1914–45. The present chapter is about this two-part revolution, although it naturally concentrates on the original and formative revolution of 1917 and the special house-style it imposed on its successors.

In any case, it largely dominated these.

I

For a large part of the Short Twentieth Century, Soviet communism claimed to be an alternative and superior system to capitalism, and one destined by history to triumph over it. For much of this period even many of those who rejected its claims to superiority were far from convinced that it might not triumph. And—with the significant exception of the years from 1933 to 1945 (see chapter 5), the international politics of the entire Short Twentieth Century since the October revolution can best be understood as a secular struggle by the forces of the old order against social revolution, believed to be embodied in, allied with, or dependent on the fortunes of the Soviet Union and international communism.

As the Short Twentieth Century advanced, this image of world politics as a duel between the forces of two rival social systems (each, after 1945, mobilized behind a superpower wielding weapons of global destruction), became increasingly unrealistic. By the 1980s it had as little relevance to international politics as the Crusades. Yet we can understand how it came into being. For, more completely and uncompromisingly even than the French revolution in its Jacobin days, the October revolution saw itself less as a national than as an ecumenical event. It was made not to bring freedom and socialism to Russia, but to bring about the world proletarian revolution. In the minds of Lenin and his comrades, the victory of Bolshevism in Russia was primarily a battle in the campaign to win the victory of Bolshevism on a wider global scale, and barely justifiable except as such.

That Tsarist Russia was ripe for revolution, richly deserved a revolution, and indeed that such a revolution would certainly overthrow Tsarism, had been accepted by every sensible observer of the world scene since the 1870s (see *Age of Empire*, chapter 12). After 1905–6, when Tsarism had actually been brought to its knees by revolution, nobody seriously doubted it. There are some historians who, in retrospect, argue that Tsarist Russia, but for the accident of the First World War and the Bolshevik revolution, would have evolved into a flourishing liberal-capitalist industrial society, and was on the way to doing so, but one would need a microscope to detect prophesies to this effect made before 1914.

Indeed, the Tsarist regime had barely recovered from the 1905 revolution when, indecisive and incompetent as always, it found itself once again lashed by a rapidly rising wave of social discontent. But for the solid loyalty of the army, police and civil service in the last months before the outbreak of war, the country seemed once again on the verge of an eruption. Indeed, as in so many of the belligerent countries, mass enthusiasm and patriotism after the outbreak of war defused the political situation—though, in the case of Russia, not for long. By 1915 the problems of the Tsar's government once again seemed insurmountable. Nothing seemed less surprising and unexpected than the revolution of March 1917* which overthrew the Russian monarchy and which was universally hailed by all Western political opinion other than the most rock-ribbed traditionalist reactionaries.

And yet, with the exception of those romantics who saw a straight road leading from the collective practices of the Russian village community to a socialist future, it was equally taken for granted by all that a Russian revolution could not and would not be socialist. The conditions for such a transformation were simply not present in a peasant country that was a by-word for poverty, ignorance and backwardness and where the industrial proletariat, Marx's predestined gravedigger of capitalism, was only a minuscule, though strategically localized, minority. The Russian Marxist revolutionaries themselves shared this view. Taken by itself, the overthrow of Tsarism and the landlord system would, and could only be expected to, produce a "bourgeois revolution." The class struggle between bourgeoisie and proletariat (which, according to Marx, could have only one outcome), would then continue under the new political conditions. Of course, Russia did not exist in isolation, and a revolution in that enormous country, stretching from the borders of Japan to those of Germany, and whose government was one of the handful of "great powers" that dominated the world situation, could not but have major international consequences. Karl Marx himself, at the end of his life, had hoped that a Russian revolution might act as a sort of detonator, setting off the proletarian revolution in the industrially more developed Western

---

*Since Russia still operated by the Julian calendar, which was thirteen days behind the Gregorian calendar adopted everywhere else in the Christian or Westernized world, the February revolution actually occurred in March, the October revolution on 7 November. It was the October revolution which reformed the Russian calendar, as it reformed Russian orthography, thus demonstrating the profundity of its impact. For it is well known that such small changes usually require socio-political earthquakes to bring them about. The most lasting and universal consequence of the French revolution is the metric system.

countries, where the conditions for a proletarian socialist revolution were present. As we shall see, towards the end of the First World War, it looked as though this was exactly what was going to happen.

There was only one complication. If Russia was not ready for the Marxists' proletarian socialist revolution, it was not ready for their liberal "bourgeois revolution" either. Even those who wished to achieve no more than this, had to find a way of doing so which did not rely on the small and feeble forces of the Russian Liberal middle class, a tiny minority population lacking both moral standing, public support and an institutional tradition of representative government into which it could fit. The Kadets, the party of bourgeois liberalism, had less than 2.5 per cent of the deputies in the freely elected (and soon dissolved) Constitutional Assembly of 1917–18. Either a bourgeois-liberal Russia had to be won by the rising of peasants and workers who did not know or care what it was, under the leadership of revolutionary parties who wanted something else, or, and this was more likely, the forces making the revolution would go beyond its bourgeois-liberal stage to a more radical one ("permanent revolution," to use the phrase adopted by Marx and revived during the 1905 Revolution by the young Trotsky). In 1917 Lenin, whose hopes had not gone much beyond a bourgeois-democratic Russia in 1905, also concluded from the start that the liberal horse was not a runner in the Russian revolutionary race. This was a realistic assessment. However, in 1917 it was as clear to him as to all other Russian and non-Russian Marxists that the conditions for a *socialist* revolution were simply not present in Russia. For Marxist revolutionaries in Russia, their revolution *had* to spread elsewhere.

But nothing seemed more likely than that it would, because the Great War ended in widespread political breakdown and revolutionary crisis, particularly in the defeated belligerent states. In 1918 all the four rulers of the defeated powers (Germany, Austria-Hungary, Turkey and Bulgaria) lost their thrones, plus the Tsar of Russia, defeated by Germany, who had already gone in 1917. Moreover, social unrest, amounting almost to revolution in Italy, shook even the European belligerents on the winning side.

As we have seen, the societies of belligerent Europe began to buckle under the extraordinary pressures of mass war. The initial surge of patriotism that had followed the outbreak of war had subsided. By 1916 war-weariness was turning into sullen and silent hostility to an apparently endless and indecisive slaughter that nobody seemed willing to end. While the adversaries of the war in 1914 had felt helpless and isolated, by 1916 they could feel that they spoke for the majority. How dramatically the situation had changed was demonstrated when, on 28 October 1916, Friedrich Adler, son of the leader and founder of the Austrian socialist party, deliberately and in cold blood assassinated the Austrian prime minister, Count Stürgkh, in a Vienna café—this was the age of innocence before the security men—as a public gesture against the war.

Anti-war sentiment naturally raised the political profile of the socialists, who increasingly reverted to their movements' pre-1914 opposition to war. Indeed, some parties (e.g. in Russia, Serbia and Britain—the Independent Labour Party) never ceased to oppose it, and, even where socialist parties supported the war, its most vocal enemies were to be found in their ranks.* At the same time, and in all major belligerent countries, the organized labour movement in the vast armaments industries, became a centre of both industrial and anti-war militancy. The lower-echelon union activists in these factories, skilled men in a strong bargaining position ("shop stewards" in Britain; "*Betriebsobleute*" in Germany) became by-words for radicalism. The artificers and mechanics in the new high-tech navies, little different from floating factories, moved in the same direction. Both in Russia and in Germany the chief naval bases (Kronstadt, Kiel) were to become major centres of revolution, and later a French naval mutiny in the Black Sea was to halt French military intervention against the Bolsheviks in the Russian Civil War of 1918–20. Rebellion against the war thus acquired both focus and agency. No wonder the Austro-Hungarian censors, monitoring the correspondence of their troops, began to note a change in tone. "If only the good Lord would bring us peace" turned into "We've had enough" or even "They say the socialists are going to make peace."

It is, therefore, no surprise that, once again according to the Habsburg censors, the Russian revolution was the first political event since the outbreak of the war to echo in the letters even of peasants' and workers' wives. And no surprise that, especially after the October revolution brought Lenin's Bolsheviks to power, the desires for peace and social revolution merged: a third of the sample of censored letters between November 1917 and March 1918 expected to get peace from Russia, a third from revolution, and another 20 per cent from a combination of both. That a Russian revolution would have major international repercussions was always clear: even the first one, in 1905–6, had shaken

---

*In 1917 an important Independent Social Democratic Party of Germany (U.S.P.D.) formally split on this issue from the majority of the Socialists (S.P.D.) which continued to support the war.

the surviving ancient empires of its time, from Austria-Hungary via Turkey and Persia to China (see *Age of Empire*, chapter 12). By 1917 all Europe had become a pile of social explosives ready for ignition.

II

Russia, ripe for social revolution, war-weary and on the verge of defeat, was the first of the regimes of central and eastern Europe to collapse under the stresses and strains of the First World War. The explosion was expected, though nobody could predict the timing and occasion of the detonation. A few weeks before the February revolution, Lenin in his Swiss exile had still wondered whether he would live to see it. In fact, the Tsar's rule collapsed when a demonstration of working-class women (on the socialist movement's customary "Women's Day"—8 March) combined with an industrial lock-out in the notoriously militant Putilov metalworks to produce a general strike and an invasion of the centre of the capital across the frozen river, essentially to demand bread. The fragility of the regime was revealed when the Tsar's troops, even the always loyal Cossacks, hesitated, then refused to attack the crowds and began to fraternize with them. When, after four chaotic days, they mutinied, the Tsar abdicated, to be replaced by a liberal "provisional government," not without some sympathy or even assistance from Russia's Western allies, who were afraid that the desperate Tsar's regime might pull out of the war and sign a separate peace with Germany. Four spontaneous and leaderless days on the street put an end to an Empire.* More than this: so ready was Russia for social revolution that the masses of Petrograd immediately treated the fall of the Tsar as the proclamation of universal freedom, equality and direct democracy. Lenin's extraordinary achievement was to transform this uncontrollable anarchic popular surge into Bolshevik power.

So, instead of a liberal and constitutional Western-oriented Russia ready and willing to fight the Germans, what emerged was a revolutionary vacuum: a powerless "provisional government" on one side, and, on the other, a multitude of grassroots "councils" (Soviets) springing up

---

*The human cost, larger than the October revolution but relatively modest: 53 officers, 602 soldiers, 73 policemen and 587 citizens injured, wounded or killed (W. H. Chamberlin, 1965, vol. I, p. 85).

spontaneously everywhere like mushrooms after the rains.* These actually held power, or at least veto-power, locally, but they had no idea what to do with it or what could or ought be done. The various revolutionary parties and organizations—Bolshevik and Menshevik Social Democrats, Social Revolutionaries, and numerous lesser factions of the Left, emerging from illegality—attempted to establish themselves in these assemblies, to coordinate them and to convert them to their policies, though initially only Lenin saw them as the alternative to the government ("All power to the Soviets"). However, it is clear that, when the Tsar fell, relatively few among the Russian people knew what the revolutionary party labels represented or, if they knew, could distinguish between their rival appeals. What they knew was that they no longer accepted authority—not even the authority of revolutionaries who claimed to know better than they.

The basic demand of the city poor was for bread, and, of the workers among them, for better wages and shorter hours. The basic demand of the 80 per cent of Russians who lived by agriculture, was, as always, for land. Both agreed that they wanted an end to the war, though the mass of peasant-soldiers who formed the army was at first not against fighting as such but against harsh discipline and the mistreatment of other ranks. These slogans, "Bread, Peace, Land" won rapidly growing support for those who propagated them, notably Lenin's Bolsheviks, who grew from a small troop of a few thousands in March 1917 to a quarter of a million members by the early summer of that year. Contrary to the Cold War mythology, which saw Lenin essentially as an organizer of coups, the only real asset he and the Bolsheviks had was the ability to recognize what the masses wanted; to, as it were, lead by knowing how to follow. When, for instance, he recognized that, contrary to the socialist programme, the peasants wanted a division of the land into family farms, he did not hesitate for a moment to commit the Bolsheviks to this form of economic individualism.

Conversely, the Provisional Government and its supporters failed to recognize their inability to get Russia to obey its laws and decrees. When businessmen and managers tried to re-establish labour discipline, they merely radicalized the workers. When the Provisional Government insisted on launching the army into another military offensive in June 1917,

---

*Such "councils," presumably rooted in the experience of Russian self-governing village communities, emerged as political entities among factory workers during the 1905 revolution. Since assemblies of directly elected delegates were familiar to organized workers everywhere, and appealed to their built-in sense of democracy, the term "Soviet," sometimes but not always translated into the local languages (councils; rate) had a strong international appeal.

the army had had enough, and the peasant-soldiers went home to their villages to take part in dividing the land with their kin. Revolution spread along the lines of the railways that carried them back. The time was not yet ripe for an immediate fall of the Provisional Government, but from the summer on radicalization accelerated both in the army and in the main cities, increasingly to the benefit of the Bolsheviks. The peasantry gave overwhelming support to the heirs of the Narodniks (see *Age of Capital*, chapter 9), the Social Revolutionaries, though these developed a more radical left wing which drew closer to the Bolsheviks, and briefly joined them in government after the October revolution.

As the Bolsheviks—then essentially a workers' party—found itself the majority in the major Russian cities, and especially in the capital, Petrograd and in Moscow, and gained ground rapidly in the army, the Provisional Government's existence became increasingly shadowy; especially when it had to appeal to the revolutionary forces in the capital to defeat an attempted counter-revolutionary coup by a monarchist general in August. The radicalized groundswell of their followers pushed the Bolsheviks inevitably towards the seizure of power. In fact, when the moment came, power had not so much to be seized as to be picked up. It has been said that more people were injured in the making of Eisenstein's great film *October* (1927) than had been hurt during the actual taking of the Winter Palace on 7 November 1917. The Provisional Government, with no one left to defend it, merely dissolved into thin air.

From the moment that the fall of the Provisional Govenment became certain, to the present, the October revolution has been drenched in polemics. Most of them are misleading. The real issue is not whether, as anticommunist historians have argued, it was a putsch or coup by the fundamentally antidemocratic Lenin, but who or what should or could follow the fall of the Provisional Government. From early September Lenin tried to convince the hesitant elements in his party not only that power might easily escape them if not seized by planned action during the, possibly short, time when it was within their grasp, but—perhaps with equal urgency—to answer the question "Can the Bolsheviks Retain State Power?" if they did seize it. What, indeed, could *anybody* do who tried to govern the volcanic eruption of revolutionary Russia? No party, other than Lenin's Bolsheviks, was prepared to envisage this responsibility on its own—and Lenin's pamphlet suggests that not all Bolsheviks were as determined as he. Given the favourable political situation in Petrograd, Moscow and the northern armies, the purely short-term case for seizing power now, rather than waiting further on events, was indeed difficult to answer. The military counter-revolution had only begun. A desperate government, rather than giving way to the Soviet, might surrender Petrograd to the German army, already on the northern border of what is now Estonia, i.e. a few miles from the capital. Moreover, Lenin rarely hesitated to look the darkest facts in the face. If the Bolsheviks failed to seize the moment, "a wave of real anarchy may become *stronger than we are*." In the last analysis Lenin's argument could not but convince his party. If a revolutionary party did not seize power when the moment and the masses called for it, how did it differ from a non-revolutionary one?

It was the longer-term prospect that was problematic, even supposing that the power seized in Petrograd and Moscow could be extended to the rest of Russia and maintained there against anarchy and counter-revolution. Lenin's own programme of committing the new Soviet (i.e. primarily Bolshevik Party) government to the "socialist transformation of the Russian Republic" was essentially a gamble on the conversion of the Russian Revolution into the world, or at least the European, revolution. Who—he said so often enough—could imagine that the victory of socialism "can come about . . . except by the complete destruction of the Russian and European bourgeoisie?" In the meanwhile the primary, indeed the only, duty of the Bolsheviks was to hold on. The new regime did little about socialism except to declare that this was its object, to take over the banks and to declare "workers' control" over the existing managements, i.e., to put the official stamp on what they had been doing anyway since the revolution, while urging them to keep production going. It had nothing further to tell them.*

The new regime did hold on. It survived a penal peace imposed by Germany at Brest-Litowsk, some months before the Germans were themselves defeated, and which detached Poland, the Baltic provinces, Ukraine and substantial parts of south and west Russia as well as, *de facto*, Transcaucasia (Ukraine and Transcaucasia were recovered). The Allies saw no reason to be more generous to the centre of world subversion. Various counter-revolutionary ("White") armies and regimes rose against the Soviets, financed by the Allies, who sent British, French, American, Japanese, Polish, Serb, Greek and Rumanian troops on to Russian soil. At the worst moments of the brutal and chaotic 1918–20 Civil War, Soviet Russia was reduced to a landlocked hulk of territory in North and Central Russia somewhere between the Ural region and the

---

*"I said to them: do all you want to do, take all you want, we shall support you, but take care of production, see that production is useful. Take up useful work, you will make mistakes, but you will learn." (Lenin: *Report on the Activities of the Council of People's Commissars*, 11/24 January 1918, Lenin, 1970, p. 551.)

present Baltic States, but for the tiny exposed finger of Leningrad, pointing at the Gulf of Finland. The only major assets the new regime possessed, as it improvised an eventually victorious Red Army out of nothing, was the incompetence and division of the quarrelling "White" forces, their capacity to antagonize the Great Russian peasantry, and the well-founded suspicion among the Western powers that their mutinous soldiers and sailors could not be safely ordered to fight the Bolsheviks. By late 1920 the Bolsheviks had won.

So, against expectations, Soviet Russia survived. The Bolsheviks maintained, indeed extended, their power not only (as Lenin noted with pride and relief after two months and fifteen days) longer than the Paris Commune of 1871, but through years of unbroken crisis and catastrophe, German conquest and a penal peace, regional breakaways, counter-revolution, civil war, foreign armed intervention, hunger and economic collapse. It could have no strategy or perspective beyond choosing, day by day, between the decisions needed for immediate survival and the ones which risked immediate disaster. Who could afford to consider the possible long-term consequences for the revolution of decisions which had to be taken *now*, or else there would be an end to the revolution and no further consequences to consider? One by one the necessary steps were taken. When the new Soviet Republic emerged from its agony, they were found to have led in a direction far removed from the one in the mind of Lenin at the Finland Station.

Still, the revolution survived. It did so for three major reasons: First, it possessed a uniquely powerful, virtually a state-building, instrument in the 600,000-strong centralized and disciplined Communist Party. Whatever its role before the revolution, this organizational model, tirelessly propagated and defended by Lenin since 1902, came into its own after it. Virtually all revolutionary regimes of the Short Twentieth Century were to adopt some variant of it. Second, it was quite evidently the only government able and willing to hold Russia together as a state, and therefore enjoyed considerable support from otherwise politically hostile patriotic Russians such as the officers without whom the new Red Army could not have been built. For these, as for the retrospective historian, the choice in 1917–18 lay not between a liberal-democratic or a non-liberal Russia, but between Russia and the disintegration which was the fate of the other archaic and defeated empires, namely Austria-Hungary and Turkey. Unlike these, the Bolshevik revolution preserved most of the multinational territorial unity of the old Tsarist state at least for another seventy-four years. The third reason was that the revolution had allowed the peasantry to take the land. When it came to the point, the bulk of the

Great Russian peasants—core of the state as well as of its new army—thought their chances of keeping it were better under the Reds than if the gentry returned. This gave the Bolsheviks a decisive advantage in the civil war of 1918–20. As it turned out, the Russian peasants were too optimistic.

III

The world revolution, which justified Lenin's decision to commit Russia to socialism, did not take place, and with it Soviet Russia was committed to a generation of impoverished and backward isolation. The options for its future development were determined, or at least narrowly circumscribed (see chapters 13 and 16). Yet a wave of revolution swept across the globe in the two years after October, and the hopes of the embattled Bolsheviks did not seem unrealistic. *"Völker hört die Signale"* ("Peoples, hear the signals") was the first line of the refrain of the Internationale in German. The signals came, loud and clear, from Petrograd and, after their capital had been transferred to a safer location in 1918, Moscow;* they were heard wherever labour and socialist movements operated, irrespective of their ideology, and even beyond. "Soviets" were formed by the tobacco workers in Cuba where few knew where Russia was. The years from 1917–19 in Spain came to be known as "the Bolshevik biennium," though the local left was passionately anarchist, i.e. politically at the opposite pole from Lenin. Revolutionary student movements erupted in Peking (Beijing) in 1919 and Córdoba (Argentina) in 1918, soon to spread across Latin America and to generate local revolutionary Marxist leaders and parties. The Indian nationalist militant M.N. Roy immediately fell under its spell in Mexico, where the local revolution, entering its most radical phase in 1917, naturally recognized its affinity with revolutionary Russia: Marx and Lenin became its icons, together with Moctezuma, Emiliano Zapata and assorted labouring Indians, and can still be seen on the great murals of its official artists. Within a few

---

*The capital city of Tsarist Russia was St. Petersburg, which sounded too German in the First World War and was therefore changed to Petrograd. After Lenin's death it became Leningrad (1924), and during the fall of the U.S.S.R. it returned to its original name. The Soviet Union (followed by its more slavish satellites) was unusually given to political toponymy, often complicated by the twists and turns of party fortunes. Thus Tsaritsyn on the Volga became Stalingrad, scene of an epic battle of the Second World War, but, after Stalin's death, Volgograd. At the time of writing it still had that name.

months Roy was in Moscow to play a major role in forming the new Communist International's policy for colonial liberation. Partly through resident Dutch socialists like Henk Sneevliet, the October revolution immediately made its mark on the Indonesian national liberation movement's main mass organization, Sarekat Islam. "This action of the Russian people," wrote a provincial Turkish paper, "someday in the future will turn into a sun and illuminate all humanity." In the distant interior of Australia, tough (and largely Irish Catholic) sheep-shearers, with no discernible interest in political theory, cheered the Soviets as a workers' state. In the U.S.A. the Finns, long the most strongly socialist of immigrant communities, converted to communism en masse, filling the bleak mining settlements of Minnesota with meetings "where the mentioning of the name of Lenin made the heart throb . . . In mystic silence, almost in religious ecstasy, did we admire everything that came from Russia" (Koivisto, 1983). In short, the October revolution was universally recognized as a world-shaking event.

Even many of those who saw the revolution at close quarters, a process less conducive to religious ecstasy, were converted, from prisoners-of-war who returned to their countries as convinced Bolsheviks and future communist leaders of their countries, like the Croat mechanic Josip Broz (Tito), to visiting journalists like the *Manchester Guardian*'s Arthur Ransome, not a notably political figure, best known for putting his passion for sailing into enchanting children's books. An even less Bolshevik figure, the Czech writer Jaroslav Hašek—future author of that masterpiece *The Adventures of the Good Soldier Schwejk*—found himself, for the first time in his life, the militant of a cause and, it is claimed, even more astonishingly, sober. He took part in the civil war as a Red Army commissar, after which he returned to his more familiar role as a Prague anarcho-bohemian and drunk, on the grounds that post-revolutionary Soviet Russia wasn't his style. But the revolution had been.

However, the events of Russia inspired not only revolutionaries but, more important, revolutions. In January 1918, within weeks of the taking of the Winter Palace, and while the Bolsheviks desperately tried to negotiate peace at all costs with the advancing German army a wave of mass political strikes and anti-war demonstrations swept through central Europe, starting in Vienna, spreading via Budapest and the Czech regions to Germany, and culminating in the revolt of the Austro-Hungarian navy's sailors in the Adriatic. As the last doubts about the defeat of the Central Powers disappeared, their armies finally broke. In September the Bulgarian peasant soldiers went home, proclaimed a Republic and marched on Sofia, though they were still disarmed with German help. In

October the Habsburg monarchy fell apart after the last lost battles on the Italian front. Various new nation-states were proclaimed in the (justified) hope that the victorious Allies would prefer them to the dangers of Bolshevik revolution. And indeed, the first Western reaction to the Bolsheviks' appeal to the peoples to make peace—and their publication of the secret treaties in which the Allies had carved up Europe among themselves—had been President Wilson's Fourteen Points, which played the nationalist card against Lenin's international appeal. A zone of small nation-states was to form a sort of quarantine belt against the Red virus. In early November mutinous sailors and soldiers spread the German revolution from the naval base of Kiel throughout the country. A Republic was proclaimed and the emperor retired to the Netherlands, to be replaced by a social-democratic ex-saddler as the head of state.

The revolution, which thus swept away all regimes from Vladivostok to the Rhine, was a revolt against the war and, for the most part, the achievement of peace defused much of the explosive it contained. Its social content was in any case vague, except among the peasant soldiers of the Habsburg, Romanov and Ottoman Empires and the lesser states of south-eastern Europe, and their families. There it consisted of four items: land, and suspicion of cities, or strangers (especially Jews) and or governments. This made peasants revolutionary but not Bolshevik in large parts of central and eastern Europe, though not in Germany (except for some of Bavaria), Austria, and parts of Poland. They had to be conciliated by a measure of land reform even in some conservative, indeed counter-revolutionary countries like Romania and Finland. On the other hand, where they constituted the majority of the population, they practically guaranteed that socialists, let alone Bolshevik ones, would not win democratic general elections. This did not necessarily make peasant bastions of political conservatism, but it fatally handicapped democratic socialists; or else—as in Soviet Russia—pressed them into abolishing electoral democracy. For this reason the Bolsheviks, having demanded a Constituent Assembly (a familiar revolutionary tradition since 1789) dissolved it as soon as it met, a few weeks after October. And the establishment of new small nation-states along Wilsonian lines, though far from eliminating national conflicts in the zone of revolutions, also diminished the scope for Bolshevik revolution. That, indeed, had been the intention of the Allied peacemakers.

On the other hand, the impact of the Russian revolution on the European upheavals of 1918–19 was so patent, that there could hardly be much room in Moscow for scepticism about the prospect of a spreading revolution of the world proletariat. To the historian—even to some local revolutionaries—it seemed clear that imperial Germany was a state of considerable social and political stability, with a strong, but essentially moderate working-class movement, which would certainly not have experienced anything like armed revolution but for the war. Unlike Tsarist Russia or ramshackle Austria-Hungary; unlike Turkey, the proverbial "sick man of Europe"; unlike the wild, gun-toting inhabitants of the mountains of the continent's south-east, who were capable of anything, it was not a country where upheavals were to be expected. And, indeed, compared to the genuinely revolutionary situations in defeated Russia and Austria-Hungary, the bulk of German revolutionary soldiers, sailors and workers remained as moderate and law-abiding as the, possibly apocryphal, jokes of Russian revolutionaries had always made them out to be ("Where there is a notice forbidding the public to step on the grass, German insurrectionaries will naturally walk only on the paths").

Yet this was the country where the revolutionary sailors carried the banner of the Soviets through the country, where the executive of a Berlin workers' and soldiers' soviet appointed a socialist government of Germany, where February and October seemed to be one, as effective power in the capital already appeared to be in the hands of radical socialists from the moment the emperor abdicated. This was an illusion, due to the total, but temporary, paralysis of the old army, state and power-structure under the double shock of utter defeat and revolution. After a few days the republicanised old regime was soon back in the saddle again, and no longer seriously troubled by the socialists, who even failed to gain a majority at the first elections, though these were held a few weeks after the revolution.* They were even less troubled by the newly improvised Communist Party, whose leaders, Karl Liebknecht and Rosa Luxemburg, were quickly murdered by free-lance army gunmen.

Nevertheless, the German revolution of 1918 confirmed the hopes of the Russian Bolsheviks, all the more because a shortlived Socialist republic was actually proclaimed in Bavaria in 1918, and, in the spring of 1919, after the assassination of its leader, a brief Soviet Republic was set up in Munich, the capital of German art, intellectual counter-culture and (politically less subversive) of beer. It overlapped with another and more serious attempt to carry Bolshevism westwards, the Hungarian Soviet

---

*The moderate majority social-democrats gained just under 38 per cent of the vote—their all-time high—the revolutionary Independent Social Democrats about 7.5 per cent of the vote.

Republic of March–July 1919.* Both were, of course, suppressed with the expected brutality. Moreover, disappointment with the Social Democrats rapidly radicalized German workers, many of whom transferred their loyalties to the Independent Socialists, and after 1920, to the Communist Party, which therefore became the largest such party outside Soviet Russia. Could not a German October revolution be expected after all? Even though 1919, the peak year of Western social unrest, had brought defeat to the only attempts to spread the Bolshevik revolution; even though the revolutionary wave was rapidly and visibly subsiding in 1920, the Bolshevik leadership in Moscow did not abandon the hope of German revolution until late in 1923.

On the contrary. It was in 1920 that the Bolsheviks committed themselves to what in retrospect seems a major error, the permanent division of the international labour movement. They did so by structuring their new international communist movement on the pattern of the Leninist vanguard party of an elite of fulltime "professional revolutionaries." The October revolution, as we have seen, had won wide sympathies in the international socialist movements, virtually all of which emerged from the world war both radicalized and enormously strengthened. With rare exceptions the socialist and labour parties contained large bodies of opinion that favoured joining the new Third or Communist International, which the Bolsheviks founded to replace the Second International (1889–1914), discredited and broken by the world war it had failed to resist.† Indeed, several, such as the Socialist Parties of France, Italy, Austria and Norway, and the Independent Socialists of Germany actually voted to do so, leaving the unreconstructed opponents of Bolshevism in a minority. Yet what Lenin and the Bolsheviks wanted was not an international movement of socialist sympathisers with the October revolution, but a corps of utterly committed and disciplined activists, a sort of global striking-force for revolutionary conquest. Parties unwilling to adopt the Leninist structure were refused admittance to or expelled from the new International, which could only be weakened by accepting such fifth columns of opportunism and reformism, not to mention what Marx had once called "parliamentary cretinism." In the imminent battle there could be a place only for soldiers.

*Its defeat spread a diaspora of political and intellectal refugees across the world, some of them with unexpected future careers, like the film-tycoon Sir Alexander Korda and the actor Bela Lugosi, best known as the star of the original horror film *Dracula*.

†The so-called First International was Karl Marx's own International Workingmen's Association of 1864–72.

The argument made sense on only one condition: that the world revolution was still in progress, and its battles were in immediate prospect. Yet while the European situation was far from stabilized, it was clear in 1920 that Bolshevik revolution was not on the agenda in the West, though it was also clear that in Russia the Bolsheviks were permanently established. No doubt, as the International met there seemed to be a chance that the Red Army, victorious in the Civil War, and now sweeping towards Warsaw, would spread the revolution westwards by armed force, as the by-product of a brief Russo–Polish War, provoked by the territorial ambitions of Poland. Restored to statehood after a century-and-a-half of non-existence, Poland now demanded its eighteenth century frontiers. These lay deep in Belorussia, Lithuania and the Ukraine. The Soviet advance, which has left a marvellous literary monument in Isaac Babel's *Red Cavalry*, was hailed by an unusually wide assortment of contemporaries ranging from the Austrian novelist Joseph Roth, later the elegist of the Habsburgs, to Mustafa Kemal, the future leader of Turkey. Yet the Polish workers failed to rise, and the Red Army was turned back at the gates of Warsaw. Henceforth, in spite of appearances, all was to be quiet on the western front. Admittedly, the prospects of the revolution moved East into Asia, to which Lenin had always paid considerable attention. Indeed, from 1920 to 1927 the hopes of world revolution seemed to rest on the Chinese revolution, advancing under the Kuomintang, then the party of national liberation, whose leader Sun Yat-sen (1866–1925) welcomed both the Soviet model, Soviet military assistance and the new Chinese Communist Party as part of his movement. The Kuomintang-Communist alliance was to sweep north from its bases in South China in the great offensive of 1925–27, bringing most of China once again under the control of a single government for the first time since the fall of the Empire in 1911, before the leading Kuomintang general, Chiang Kai-shek, turned on the communists and slaughtered them. Yet even before this proof that even the East was not yet ripe for October, the promise of Asia could not conceal the failure of revolution in the West.

By 1921 this was undeniable. The revolution was in retreat in Soviet Russia, though politically Bolshevik power was unassailable (see p. 379). It was off the agenda in the West. The Third Congress of the Comintern recognized this without quite admitting it by calling for a "united front" with the very socialists whom the Second had expelled from the army of revolutionary progress. Just what this meant was to divide the revolutionaries for the next generations. However, in any case it was too late. The movement was permanently split, the majority of left socialists, individuals and parties drifted back into the social-democratic movement, overwhelmingly led by anti-communist moderates. The new communist parties remained minorities of the European Left, and generally—with a few exceptions such as Germany, France or Finland—rather small, if impassioned minorities. Their situation was not to change until the 1930s (see chapter 5).

IV

Yet the years of upheaval left behind not only a single, huge but backward country now governed by communists and committed to the building of an alternative society to capitalism, but also a government, a disciplined international movement, and, perhaps equally important, a generation of revolutionaries committed to the vision of world revolution under the flag raised in October and under the leadership of the movement which, inevitably, had its headquarters in Moscow. (For several years it had been hoped soon to transfer it to Berlin, and German, not Russian, remained the official language of the International between the wars.) The movement may not have known quite how the world revolution was to advance after stabilisation in Europe and defeat in Asia, and the communists' scattered attempts at independent armed insurrection (Bulgaria and Germany in 1923, Indonesia in 1926, China in 1927 and—late and anomalous—Brazil in 1935) were disasters. Still, as the Great Slump and the rise of Hitler were soon to prove, the state of the world between the wars was hardly such as to discourage apocalyptic expectations (see chapters 3 to 5). This does not explain the sudden switch of the Comintern into the rhetorical mode of ultra-revolutionism and sectarian leftism between 1928 and 1934 since, whatever the rhetoric, in practice the movement neither expected nor prepared for taking power anywhere. The change, which proved politically calamitous, is rather to be explained by the internal politics of the Soviet Communist Party, as Stalin took control of it, and perhaps also as an attempt to compensate for the increasingly evident divergence between the interests of the U.S.S.R., as a state which inevitably had to coexist with other states—it began to win international recognition as a regime from 1920—and the movement whose aim was to subvert and overthrow all other governments.

In the end the state interests of the Soviet Union prevailed over the world revolutionary interests of the Communist International, which Stalin reduced to an instrument of Soviet state policy under the strict control of the Soviet Communist Party, purging, dissolving and reforming its components at will. World revolution belonged to the rhetoric of the past, and indeed any revolution was tolerable only if a) it did not conflict with Soviet state interest and b) could be brought under direct Soviet control. Western governments who saw the advance of communist regimes after 1944 essentially as an extension of Soviet power certainly read Stalin's intentions correctly; but so did the unreconstructed revolutionaries who bitterly blamed Moscow for not wanting communists to take power and discouraged every attempt to do so, even those which proved successful, as in Yugoslavia and China (see chapter 5).

Nevertheless, until the end Soviet Russia remained, even in the eyes of many self-serving and corrupt members of its *nomenklatura*, something more than just another great power. Universal emancipation, the construction of a better alternative to capitalist society was, after all, its fundamental reason for existence. Why else should hard-faced Moscow bureaucrats have continued to finance and arm the guerrillas of the communist-allied African National Congress whose chances of overthrowing the *apartheid* system of South Africa seemed and were minimal for decades? (Curiously enough the Chinese Communist regime, though it criticised the U.S.S.R. for betraying revolutionary movements after the break between the two countries, has no comparable record of practical support for Third World liberation movements.) Humanity, the U.S.S.R. had learned long since, would not be transformed by Moscow-inspired world revolution. In the long twilight of the Brezhnev years even Nikita Khrushchev's sincerely held conviction that socialism would "bury" capitalism by dint of its economic superiority faded away. It may well be that the terminal erosion of this belief in the system's universal vocation explains why, in the end, it disintegrated without resistance (see chapter 16).

None of these hesitations troubled the first generation of those inspired by the shining light of October to devote their lives to the world revolution. Like the early Christians, most pre-1914 socialists were believers in the great apocalyptic change which would abolish all that was evil and bring about a society without unhappiness, oppression, inequality and injustice. Marxism offered the hope of the millennium the guarantee of science and historic inevitability; the October revolution now offered the proof that the great change had begun.

The total number of these soldiers in the necessarily ruthless and disciplined army of human emancipation was perhaps no larger than a few tens of thousands; the number of the professionals of the international movement, "changing countries more often than pairs of shoes" as Bertolt Brecht put it in a poem written in their honour, was perhaps no more than a few hundreds in all. They must not be confused with what the

Italians, in the days of their million-strong Communist Party, called "the communist people," the millions of supporters and rank-and-file members for whom the dream of a new and good society was also real, though in practice theirs was no more than the old socialist movement's daily activism, and whose commitment was in any case one of class and community rather than of personal dedication. Yet though their numbers were small, the twentieth century cannot be understood without them.

Without the Leninist "party of a new type" of "professional revolutionaries" of which they were the cadres, it is inconceivable that in barely more than thirty years after October, one third of the human race would have found itself living under Communist regimes. What their faith, and their unqualified loyalty to the headquarters of world revolution in Moscow, gave communists was the ability to see themselves (sociologically speaking) as parts of a universal church, not a sect. Moscow-oriented communist parties lost leaders by secession and purge, but until the heart had gone out of the movement after 1956 they did not split, unlike the fragmenting groups of the Marxist dissidents who followed Trotsky and the even more fissiparous "Marxist-Leninist" conventicles of post-1960 Maoism. However small—and when Mussolini was overthrown in Italy in 1943 the Italian Communist Party consisted of about 5,000 men and women, mostly emerging from jail or exile—they were what the Bolsheviks had been in February 1917, the nucleus of an army of millions, potential rulers of a people and a state.

For this generation, especially those who had, however young, lived through the years of upheaval, revolution was what happened in their lifetimes; the days of capitalism were inevitably numbered. Contemporary history was the antechamber of ultimate victory for those who lived to see it, which would include only some soldiers of the revolution ("the dead on leave of absence" as the Russian communist Leviné put it shortly before being executed by those who overthrew the Munich Soviet of 1919). If bourgeois society itself had so much reason to doubt its future, why should they be confident of its survival? Their own lives demonstrated its reality.

Let us take the case of two young Germans temporarily linked as lovers, who were mobilized for life by the Bavarian Soviet revolution of 1919: Olga Benario, daughter of a prosperous Munich lawyer, and Otto Braun, a school-teacher. Olga was to find herself organizing revolution in the western hemisphere, attached and eventually married to Luís Carlos Prestes, the leader of a long insurrectionary march through the Brazilian backwoods who had talked Moscow into backing a rising in Brazil in

1935. The rising failed, and Olga was delivered by the Brazilian government to Hitler's Germany, where she eventually died in a concentration
camp. Meanwhile Otto, more successfully, set out to revolutionize the
East as Comintern military expert in China and, as it turned out, the
only non-Chinese to take part in the famous "Long March" of the Chinese communists before returning to Moscow and eventually to the
G.D.R. (The experience left him sceptical of Mao.) When, except in the
first half of the twentieth century, could two intertwined lives have taken
these shapes?

So, in the generation after 1917, Bolshevism absorbed all other social-
revolutionary traditions, or pushed them on to the margin of radical
movements. Before 1914 anarchism had been far more of a driving
ideology of revolutionary activists than Marxism over large parts of the
world. Marx, outside Eastern Europe, was seen rather as the guru of
mass parties whose inevitable, but not explosive, advance to victory he
had demonstrated. By the 1930s anarchism had ceased to exist as a
significant political force outside Spain, even in Latin America, where
the black-and-red had traditionally inspired more militants than the red
flag. (Even in Spain the Civil War was to destroy anarchism, whereas it
made the fortunes of the communists, hitherto relatively insignificant.)
Indeed, such social-revolutionary groups as existed outside Moscow-
communism henceforth took Lenin and the October revolution as their
point of reference, and were almost invariably headed or inspired by
some dissident or expelled figure from the Comintern, which engaged in
an increasingly ruthless hunt for heretics, as Joseph Stalin established,
and later clamped, his grip on the Soviet Communist Party and the International. Few of these dissident Bolshevik centres amounted to much
politically. By far the most prestigious and famous of the heretics,
the exiled Leon Trotsky—co-leader of the October revolution and architect of the Red Army—utterly failed in his practical endeavours. His
"Fourth International" intended to compete with the Stalinized Third
International, was virtually invisible. When he was assassinated by order
of Stalin in his Mexican exile in 1940, his political significance was
negligible.

In short, to be a social revolutionary increasingly meant to be a follower
of Lenin and the October revolution, and increasingly a member or supporter of some Moscow-aligned Communist party; all the more so when,
after the triumph of Hitler in Germany, these parties adopted the policies
of anti-fascist union which allowed them to emerge from sectarian isolation and to win mass support among both workers and intellectuals (see
chapter 5). The young who thirsted to overthrow capitalism became

orthodox communists, and identified their cause with the Moscow-centred international movement; and Marxism, restored by October as the ideology of revolutionary change, now meant the Marxism of Moscow's Marx–Engels–Lenin Institute, which was now the global centre for the dissemination of the great classic texts. Nobody else within sight offered both to interpret the world and to change it, or looked better able to do so. This was to remain the case until after 1956, when the disintegration of both Stalinist orthodoxy in the U.S.S.R. and of the Moscow-centred international communist movement brought the hitherto marginalized thinkers, traditions and organizations of left heterodoxy into the public sphere. Even so, they still lived under the gigantic shadow of October. Though anyone with the slightest knowledge of ideological history could recognize the spirit of Bakunin, or even Nechaev, rather than Marx in the student radicals of 1968 and after, it led to no significant revival of anarchist theory or movements. On the contrary, 1968 produced an enormous intellectual vogue for Marxism in theory—generally in versions which would have surprised Marx—and for a variety of "Marxist–Leninist" sects and groups, united by the rejection of Moscow and the old communist parties as insufficiently revolutionary and Leninist.

Paradoxically, this virtually complete take-over of the social-revolutionary tradition occurred at a moment when the Comintern had plainly abandoned the original revolutionary strategies of 1917–23, or, rather, envisaged strategies for the transfer of power quite different from those of 1917 (see chapter 5). From 1935 on, the literature of the critical left was filled with accusations that Moscow's movements missed, rejected, nay betrayed the opportunities for revolution, because Moscow did not want it any more. Until the proudly "monolithic" Soviet-centred movement began to break up from within, these arguments had little effect. So long as the communist movement retained its unity, cohesion and its striking immunity to fission, it was, for most of the world's believers in the need for global revolution, the only game in town. Moreover, who could possibly deny that the countries which broke with capitalism in the second great wave of world social revolution, from 1944 to 1949, did so under the auspices of the orthodox, Soviet-oriented communist parties? Not until after 1956 did the revolutionary-minded have a real choice between several such movements with some real claim to political or insurrectionary effectiveness. Even these—various brands of Trotskyism, Maoism and groups inspired by the Cuban revolution of 1959 (see chapter 15)—were still more or less Leninist in derivation. The old communist parties still remained much the largest groups on the far left, but by this time the heart had gone out of the old communist movement.

V

The force of the movements for world revolution lay in the communist form of organization, Lenin's "party of a new type," a formidable innovation of twentieth-century social engineering, comparable to the invention of Christian monastic and other orders in the Middle Ages. It gave even small organizations disproportionate effectiveness, because the party could command extraordinary devotion and self-sacrifice from its members, more than military discipline and cohesiveness, and a total concentration on carrying out party decisions at all costs. This impressed even hostile observers profoundly. And yet, the relation between the "vanguard party" model and the great revolutions it had been designed to make, and occasionally succeeded in making, was far from clear, although nothing was more evident than that the model came into its own *after* successful revolutions, or during wars. For the Leninist parties were essentially constructed as elites (vanguards) of leaders or rather, before revolutions had been won, "counter-elites," and social revolutions, as 1917 showed, depend on what happens among the masses and in situations which neither elites nor counter-elites can fully control. As it happens, the Leninist model actually had considerable appeal for young members of the old elites, especially in the Third World, who joined such parties in disproportionate numbers, in spite of these parties' heroic, and relatively successful, efforts to promote true proletarians. The major expansion of Brazilian communism in the 1930s rested on the conversion of young intellectuals from families of the land-owning oligarchy and junior army officers (Martins Rodrigues, 1984, pp. 390–97).

On the other hand the feelings of the actual "masses" (sometimes including the active supporters of the "vanguards") was often at odds with their leaders' ideas, especially in times of genuine mass insurrection. Thus the rebellion of the Spanish generals against the Popular Front government in July 1936 immediately released social revolution in large regions of Spain. That the militants, especially the anarchist ones, should proceed to collectivise the means of production, was not surprising, though the Communist Party and the central government later opposed and where possible reversed this transformation, and its pros and cons continue to be discussed in the political and historical literature. However, the event also released the greatest of all the waves of iconoclasm and anticlerical homicide, since this form of activity first became part of Spanish popular agitations in 1835, when Barcelona citizens had reacted to an unsatisfactory bullfight by burning a number of churches. About seven thousand clerical persons—i.e. 12–13 per cent of the country's priests and monks, though only a negligible proportion of its nuns –were killed, while in a *single* diocese of Catalonia (Gerona) over six thousand images were destroyed (Hugh Thomas, 1977, pp. 270–71; M. Delgado, 1992, p. 56).

Two things are clear about this terrifying episode: it was denounced by the leaders or spokesmen of the Spanish revolutionary left, passionate anticlericals though they were, including the notoriously priest-hating anarchists; and for those who perpetrated it, as well as for many of those who watched it, *this* more than anything else, was what the revolution really meant: the reversal of the order of society and its values, not just for a brief symbolic moment, but for ever (M. Delgado, 1992, pp. 52–53). It was all very well for leaders to insist, as they always did, that the capitalist and not the priest was the principal enemy: in their bones the masses felt differently. (Whether popular politics in a less macho society than the Iberian would have been as murderously iconoclastic is a counterfactual question, but one on which serious research about women's attitudes might nevertheless throw some light.)

As it happens, the kind of revolution which sees the structure of political order and authority suddenly evaporate, leaving the man (and, so far as she was allowed, the woman) on the street to their own devices, proved to be rare in the twentieth century. Even the closest other example of a sudden collapse of established regimes, the Iranian revolution of 1979, was not quite so unstructured, in spite of the extraordinary unanimity of the Teheran mobilization of the masses against the Shah, much of which must have been spontaneous. Thanks to the structures of Iranian clericalism the new regime was already present in the ruin of the old, though it would not take its complete shape for a little while (see chapter 15).

In fact, the typical post-October revolution of the short Twentieth Century, leaving aside some localized explosions, was to be either initiated by an (almost always military) *coup*, capturing the capital, or as the final outcome of a lengthy and mostly rural armed struggle. Since junior officers—much more rarely non-commissioned officers—of radical and Left-wing sympathies were common in poor and backward countries, where the military life provided attractive career prospects for able and educated young men without family connections and wealth, such initiatives were typically found in countries like Egypt (the Free Officer revolution of 1952), and other countries in the Middle East (Iraq 1958, Syria at various times since the 1950s, and Libya in 1969). Military men are part of the fabric of Latin American revolutionary history, although they have rarely, or for very long, taken over national power for clearly

Left-wing causes. On the other hand, to most observers' surprise, in 1974 a military putsch by young officers disillusioned with and radicalized by long colonial rearguard wars, overthrew the oldest Right-wing regime then operating in the world: the "revolution of carnations" in Portugal. The alliance between them, a strong Communist Party emerging from underground, and various radical Marxist groups, was soon divided and by-passed, to the relief of the European Community, which Portugal joined soon after.

The social structure, ideological traditions and political functions of the armed forces in developed countries made military men with political interests in these countries choose the right. Coups in alliance with communists, or even socialists, were not in their line. Admittedly in the liberation movements of the French Empire former soldiers of the native forces raised by France in its colonies—they had rarely been officers—came to play a prominent part (notably in Algeria). Their experience in and after the Second World War had been unsatisfactory, not only because of the usual discrimination, but also because the largely colonial soldiers in the forces of de Gaulle's Free France were, like the largely non-Gallic members of the armed resistance within France, quickly pushed into the shadows.

The Free French armies in the official victory parades after liberation were a great deal "whiter" than the ones which had actually won the Gaullist battle honours. Nevertheless, on the whole the colonial armies of imperial powers, even when actually officered by natives of the colony, remained loyal, or rather unpolitical, even if we allow for the fifty thousand or so Indian soldiers who joined the Indian National Army under the Japanese (M. Echenberg, 1992, pp. 141–45; M. Barghava and A. Singh Gill, 1988, p. 10; T. R. Sareen, 1988, pp. 20–21).

VI

The road to revolution through long guerrilla war was discovered rather late by twentieth-century social revolutionaries; perhaps this was because historically this form of essentially rural activity had been overwhelmingly associated with movements of archaic ideologies easily confused by sceptical city observers with conservatism, or even with reaction and counter-revolution. After all, the powerful guerrilla wars of the French revolutionary and Napoleonic period had been invariably directed *against* and never *for* France and the cause of its revolution. The very word "guerrilla" did not form part of Marxist vocabulary until after the Cuban revolution of 1959. The Bolsheviks, who had waged irregular as well as regular warfare during the Civil War, used the term "partisan," which became standard in Soviet-inspired resistance movements during the Second World War. In retrospect it is surprising that guerrilla action played next to no part in the Spanish Civil War, though there should have been plenty of scope for it in republican areas occupied by the Franco forces. In fact, the communists organized some quite significant guerrilla nuclei from outside after the Second World War. Before that World War it was simply not part of the tool-kit of the prospective makers of revolutions.

Except in China, where the new strategy was pioneered by some (but by no means all) communist leaders—after the Kuomintang under Chiang Kai-shek turned on its former communist allies in 1927, and after the spectacular failure of communist insurrection in the cities (as in Canton, 1927). Mao Tse-tung, the chief champion of the new strategy—which was eventually to make him the leader of Communist China—not only recognized that, after more than fifteen years of revolution, large regions of China were outside the effective control of any central administration, but, as a devoted admirer of *The Water Margin*, the great classical novel of Chinese social banditry, that guerrilla tactics were a traditional part of Chinese social conflict. Indeed, no classically educated Chinese would miss the similarity between the establishment of Mao's first free guerrilla zone in the Kiangsi mountains in 1927, and the mountain fortress of the *Water Margin* heroes, whom the young Mao had called upon his fellow-students to imitate in 1917 (Schram, 1966, pp. 43–44).

The Chinese strategy, however heroic and inspiring, seemed unsuited to countries with functioning modern internal communications and governments in the habit of administering all their territory, however remote and physically difficult. As it happened, it did not prove successful in the short run even in China, where the national government, after several military campaigns, forced the communists in 1934 to give up their free soviet territories in the main regions of the country and to retreat, by means of the legendary Long March, to a remote and thinly-populated outlying border region of the north-west.

After the Brazilian rebel lieutenants like Luís Carlos Prestes moved from backwoods trekking to communism in the late 1920s, no Left-wing groups of importance chose the guerrilla road elsewhere, unless we count General César Augusto Sandino's fight against the American marines in Nicaragua (1927–33), which was to inspire the Sandinista revolution fifty years later. (Still, rather implausibly, the Communist International tried to present Lampião, the celebrated Brazilian social bandit and hero of a thousand chap-books, in this light.) Mao himself did not become the guiding star of revolutionaries until after the Cuban Revolution.

However, the Second World War produced a more immediate and general incentive to take the guerrilla road to revolution: the need to resist the occupation of most of continental Europe, including large parts of the European Soviet Union, by the armies of Hitler's Germany and its allies. Resistance, and especially armed resistance, developed on a substantial scale after Hitler's attack on the U.S.S.R. mobilized the various communist movements. When the German army was finally defeated, with varying contributions from the local resistance movements (see chapter 5), the regimes of occupied or fascist Europe disintegrated, and social-revolutionary regimes under communist control took over, or attempted to take over, in several countries where the armed resistance had been most effective (Yugoslavia, Albania and—but for the British, and eventually U.S.-backed military support—Greece). They could probably also have taken over, though not for long, in Italy north of the Apennines, but, for reasons still debated on what remains of the revolutionary left, they did not try. The communist regimes which were established in East and South-east Asia after 1945 (in China, part of Korea and French Indochina) should also be regarded as children of wartime resistance; for even in China the massive advance of Mao's Red armies towards power only began after the Japanese army set out to take over the main body of China in 1937. The second wave of world social revolution emerged out of the Second World War, as the first had emerged out of the First—though in an utterly different way. This time it was the waging of war and not the revulsion against it which brought revolution to power.

The nature and policies of the new revolutionary regimes is considered elsewhere (see chapters 5 and 13). Here we are concerned with the process of revolution itself. The revolutions of the mid-century, which came at the victorious end of long wars, differed from the classical 1789 or "October" scenario, or even from the slow-motion break-up of old regimes like imperial China and Porfirian Mexico (see *Age of Empire*, chapter 12) in two ways. First—and in this they resemble the result of successful military coups—there was no real doubt about who had made the revolution or exercised power: the political group(s) associated with the victorious armed forces of the U.S.S.R., since Germany, Japan and Italy would not have been defeated only by Resistance forces—not even in China. (The victorious Western armies were of course opposed to communist-dominated regimes.) There was no interregnum or power vacuum. Conversely, the only situations when strong Resistance forces failed to take over quickly after the collapse of the Axis powers, was where the Western Allies maintained a foothold in liberated countries (South Korea, Vietnam) or where the internal anti-Axis forces were themselves divided, as in China. There the communists after 1945 had still to establish themselves against a corrupt and rapidly weakening, but co-belligerent Kuomintang government; observed by a notably unenthusiastic U.S.S.R..

Second, the guerrilla road to power inevitably led out of the towns and industrial centres where the traditional force of socialist labour movements lay, and into the rural hinterland. More precisely, guerrilla war is most easily maintained in bush, mountains, forests and on similar terrains, into sparsely-peopled territory remote from the main populations. In Mao's words, the countryside would surround the city before conquering it. In European resistance terms, urban insurrection—the rising of Paris in the summer of 1944; of Milan in the spring of 1945—had to wait until the war was virtually over, at least in their region. What happened to Warsaw in 1944 was the penalty of premature city risings: they have only one shot in their magazine, though a big one. In short, for most of the population, even of a revolutionary country, the guerrilla road to revolution meant waiting for long periods for change to come from somewhere else without being able to do much. The actual effective resistance fighters, including all their infrastructure, were, inevitably, a fairly small minority.

On their territory, of course, the guerrillas could not function without mass backing; not least because in lengthy conflicts their forces would have to be largely recruited locally: thus (as in China) parties of industrial workers and intellectuals might be quietly transformed into armies of former peasants. Yet their relation to the masses was inevitably not as simple as is suggested by Mao's phrase about the guerrilla fish swimming in the people's water. In typical guerrilla country almost any harried group of outlaws which behaved itself, by local standards, was apt to enjoy widespread sympathy against invading foreign soldiers, or for that matter any agents of national government. However, the deep-rooted divisions within the countryside also meant that winning friends automatically risked acquiring enemies. The Chinese Communists who established their rural soviet areas in 1927–28 found, to their unjustified surprise, that converting one clan-dominated village helped to establish a network of "red villages" based on connected clans, but also involved them in war against their traditional enemies, who formed a similar network of "black villages." "In some cases," they complained, "the class struggle was transformed into the fight of one village against another. There are cases when our troops had to besiege and destroy entire villages" (Rate-China, 1973, pp. 45–46). Successful guerrilla revolutionaries learned how to navigate such treacherous waters, but—as Milovan Djilas' memoir of the Yugoslav Partisan war makes clear, liberation was far more complex than a simple unanimous uprising of an oppressed people against foreign conquerors.

VII

These were not reflections likely to tarnish the satisfaction of communists who now found themselves at the head of all governments between the river Elbe and the China Seas. The world revolution, which had inspired them, had visibly advanced. Instead of a single, weak and isolated U.S.S.R., something like a dozen states had emerged, or were emerging, from the second great wave of global revolution, headed by one of the two powers in the world which deserved the name (the term superpower is recorded as early as 1944). Nor was the impetus of global revolution exhausted, for the decolonization of the old imperialist overseas possessions was still in full progress. Could it not be expected to lead to further advances of the cause of communism? Did not the international bourgeoisie itself fear for the future of what remained of capitalism, at least in Europe? Did not the French industrialist relatives of the young historian Le Roy Ladurie ask themselves, as they rebuilt their factories, whether in the end nationalization, or quite simply the Red Army, would not provide a final solution for their problems: sentiments which, he was to recall as an elderly conservative, confirmed his decision to join the French Communist Party in 1949 (Le Roy Ladurie, 1982, p. 37)? Did not a U.S. Undersecretary of Commerce tell President Truman's administration in March 1947 that most European countries were standing on the very brink and may be pushed over at any time; others are gravely threatened (Loth, 1988, p. 137)?

Such was the state of mind of the men and women who came out of illegality, battle and resistance, jail, concentration camp, or exile, to take over the responsibility for the future of countries, most of which lay in ruins. Perhaps some of them observed that, once again, capitalism had proved far easier to overthrow where it was weak or barely existed, than in its heartlands. And yet, could anyone deny that the world had shifted dramatically to the left? If the new communist rulers or co-rulers of their transformed states worried about anything immediately after the war, it was not about the future of socialism. It was about how to rebuild impoverished, exhausted and ruined countries, amid sometimes hostile populations, and about the danger of a war launched by the capitalist powers against the socialist camp before the rebuilding had made it safe. Paradoxically, the same fears haunted the sleep of Western politicians and ideologists. As we shall see, the Cold War which settled on the world after the second wave of world revolution was a contest of nightmares. Whether the fears of either East or West were justified, they were part of the era of world revolution born in October 1917. But that era itself was about to end, though it took another forty years before it was possible to write its epitaph.

Nevertheless it has changed the world, though not in the way that Lenin, and those who were inspired by the October Revolution, expected. Outside the Western hemisphere, the fingers of two hands are enough to count the few states of the world that have not gone through some combination of revolution, civil war, resistance to and liberation from foreign occupation, or the prophylactic decolonisation by empires doomed in an era of world revolution. (Britain, Sweden, Switzerland and perhaps Iceland are the only European cases.) Even in the western hemisphere, omitting the many violent changes of government always locally described as "revolutions," major social revolutions—in Mexico, in Bolivia, the Cuban revolution and its successors—have transformed the Latin American scene.

The actual revolutions made in the name of communism have exhausted themselves, although it is too early for funeral orations about them, so long as the Chinese, one fifth of the human race, continue to live in a country governed by a Communist Party. Yet it is obvious that a return to the world of the *ancien régimes* of those countries is as impossible as it was in France after the revolutionary and Napoleonic era, or, for that matter, as the return of ex-colonies to pre-colonial life has proved to be. Even where the experience of communism has been reversed, the present of the ex-communist countries, and presumably their future, bear, and will continue to bear, the specific marks of the counter-revolution which replaced the revolution. There is no way in which the Soviet era can be written out of Russian or world history, as though it had not been. There is no way in which St. Petersburg can return to 1914.

However, the indirect consequences of the era of upheaval after 1917 have been as profound as the direct consequences. The years after the Russian revolution opened the process of colonial emancipation and decolonisation and introduced both the politics of savage counter-revolution (in the form of fascism and other such movements—see chapter 4) and the politics of social-democracy to Europe. It is often forgotten, that until 1917 all labour and socialist parties (outside somewhat peripheral Australasia) chose to be in permanent opposition until the moment for socialism had come. The first social-democratic governments or coalition governments outside the Pacific were formed in 1917–19 (Sweden, Finland, Germany, Austria, Belgium), to be followed, within a few years, by Britain, Denmark and Norway. We tend to forget that the very moderation of such parties was largely a reaction to Bolshevism, as was the readiness of the old political system to integrate them.

In short, the history of the Short Twentieth Century cannot be understood without the Russian revolution and its direct and indirect effects. Not least because it proved to be the saviour of liberal capitalism, both by enabling the West to win the Second World War against Hitler's Germany and by providing the incentive for capitalism to reform itself and—paradoxically—through the Soviet Union's apparent immunity to the Great Depression, the incentive to abandon the belief in free market orthodoxy. As we shall see in the next chapter.

CHAPTER THREE

Into the Economic Abyss

No Congress of the United States ever assembled, on surveying the state of the Union, has met with a more pleasing prospect than that which appears at the present time ... The great wealth created by our enterprise and industry, and saved by our economy, has had the widest distribution among our own people, and has gone out in a steady stream to serve the charity and the business of the world. The requirements of existence have passed beyond the standard of necessity into the region of luxury. Enlarging production is consumed by an increasing demand at home and an expanding commerce abroad. The country can regard the present with satisfaction and anticipate the future with optimism.

> President Calvin Coolidge, Message to Congress,
> 4 December 1928

Next to war, unemployment has been the most widespread, the most insidious, and the most corroding malady of our generation: it is the specific social disease of Western civilization in our time.

> *The Times*, 23 January 1943

I

Let us suppose the First World War had been merely a temporary, if catastrophic, disruption of an otherwise stable economy and civilization. The economy would then have returned, after removing the debris of war, to something like normal and carried on from there. Rather in the same way as Japan buried the 300,000 dead of the 1923 earthquake, cleared the ruins which had made two or three millions homeless, and rebuilt a city like the old one, but rather more earthquake-proof. What would the inter-war world have been like under such circumstances? We cannot know, and it is pointless to speculate about what did not happen, and almost certainly could not have happened. The question is not useless, however, for it helps us to grasp the profound effect on the history of the twentieth century of the world economic breakdown between the wars.

But for it, there would certainly have been no Hitler. There would almost certainly have been no Roosevelt. It is extremely unlikely that the Soviet system would have been regarded as a serious economic rival and alternative to world capitalism. The consequences of the economic crisis in the non-European or non-Western world, which are sketched elsewhere, were patently dramatic. In short, the world of the second half of the twentieth century is incomprehensible without understanding the impact of the economic collapse. It is the subject of this chapter.

The First World War devastated only parts of the old world, mainly those in Europe. World revolution, the most dramatic aspect of the breakdown of nineteenth century bourgeois civilization, spread more widely: from Mexico to China and, in the form of movements for colonial liberation, from the Maghreb to Indonesia. However, it would have been perfectly easy to find parts of the globe whose citizens were remote from both, notably the United States of America, as well as large regions of sub-Saharan colonial Africa. Yet the First World War was followed by one kind of breakdown that was genuinely worldwide, at least wherever men and women were enmeshed in, or operated by, impersonal market transactions. Indeed, the proud U.S.A. itself, so far from being a safe haven from the convulsions of less fortunate continents, became the epicentre of this, the largest global earthquake ever to be measured on the economic historians' Richter Scale—the Great Inter-war Depression. In a sentence: between the wars the capitalist world economy appeared to collapse. Nobody quite knew how it might recover.

The operations of a capitalist economy are never smooth, and fluctuations of various length, often very severe, are integral parts of this way of running the affairs of the world. The so-called "trade cycle" of boom and slump was familiar to all businessmen from the nineteenth century. It was expected to repeat itself, with variations, every seven to eleven years. A rather more lengthy periodicity had first begun to attract attention at the end of the nineteenth century, as observers looked back on the unexpected peripeties of the previous decades. A spectacular, record-breaking global boom from about 1850 to the early 1870s had been followed by twenty-odd years of economic uncertainties (economic writers, somewhat misleadingly, spoke of a Great Depression), and then another evidently secular forward surge of the world economy (see *Age of Capital, Age of Empire*, chapter 2). In the early 1920s a Russian economist, N. D. Kondratiev, later an early victim of Stalin, discerned a pattern of economic development since the late eighteenth century through a series of "long waves" of from fifty to sixty years, though neither he nor anyone else could give a satisfactory explanation of these movements, and indeed sceptical statisticians have even denied their existence. They have since been universally familiar in the specialist literature under his name. Kondratiev, by the way, concluded at the time that the long wave of the world economy was due for its downturn.* He was right.

In the past, waves and cycles, long, medium and short, had been accepted by businessmen and economists rather as farmers accept the weather, which also has its ups and downs. There was nothing to be done about them: they created opportunities or problems, they could lead to bonanzas or bankruptcy for individuals or industries, but only socialists who, with Karl Marx, believed that cycles were part of a process by which capitalism generated what would in the end prove insuperable internal contradictions, thought they put the existence of the economic system as such at risk. The world economy was expected to go on growing and advancing, as it had patently done, except for the sudden and short-lived catastrophes of cyclical slumps, for over a century. What was novel about the new situation was that, probably for the first, and so far the only, time in the history of capitalism, its fluctuations seemed to be genuinely system-endangering. What is more, in important respects the secular rise of its curve seemed to break.

The history of the world economy since the Industrial Revolution had been one of accelerating technological progress, of continuous but uneven economic growth, and of increasing "globalization," that is to say of an increasingly elaborate and intricate worldwide division of labour; an increasingly dense network of flows and exchanges that bound every part of the world economy to the global system. Technical progress continued and even accelerated in the Age of Catastrophe, both transforming, and being transformed by, the era of world wars. Although in the lives of most men and women the central economic experiences of the age were cataclysmic, culminating in the Great Slump of 1929–33, economic

---

*That good predictions have proved possible on the basis of Kondratiev Long Waves—this is not very common in economics—has convinced many historians and even some economists that there is something in them, even if we don't know what.

growth during these decades did not cease. It merely slowed down. In the largest and richest economy of the time, the U.S.A., the average rate of growth of the GNP per head of the population between 1913 and 1938 was only a modest 0.8 per cent per year. World industrial production grew by just over 80 per cent in the twenty-five years after 1913, or at about half the rate of the previous quarter-century (W. W. Rostow, 1978, p. 662). As we shall see (chapter 9) the contrast with the post-1945 era was to be even more spectacular. Still, if some Martian had been observing the curve of economic movements from sufficiently far off to overlook the jagged fluctuations which human beings experienced on the ground, he, she or it would have concluded that the world economy was unquestionably continuing to expand.

Yet in one respect it patently was not. The globalization of the economy, it seemed, had stopped advancing in the inter-war years. Any way we measure it, the integration of the world economy stagnated or regressed. The pre-war years had been the greatest period of mass migration in recorded history, but now these streams dried out, or rather, were dammed by the disruptions of wars and political restrictions. In the last fifteen years before 1914 almost fifteen millions had landed in the U.S.A. In the next fifteen years the flow shrunk to five-and-a-half millions; in the 1930s and the war years it came to an almost complete stop: less than three quarters of a million entered the U.S.A. (Historical Statistics I, p.105, Table C 89–101). Iberian migration, overwhelmingly to Latin America, fell from one-and-three-quarter millions in the decade 1911–20 to less than a quarter of a million in the 1930s. World trade recovered from the disruptions of war and post-war crisis to climb a little above 1913 in the late twenties, then fell during the slump, but at the end of the Age of Catastrophe (1948) it was not significantly higher in volume than before the First World War (W. W. Rostow, 1978, p. 669). Between the early 1890s and 1913 it had more than doubled. Between 1948 and 1971 it would quintuple. This stagnation is all the more surprising, when we remember that the First World War produced a substantial number of new states in Europe and the Middle East. So many more miles of state borders should have led us to expect an automatic increase in interstate trade, as commercial dealings that had once taken place within the same country (say, Austria-Hungary or Russia) were now classified as international. (World trade statistics only measure trade that crosses frontiers.) Just so the tragic flood of post-war and post-revolution refugees, whose numbers were already to be measured in millions (see chapter 11) should have led us to expect a growth rather than a shrinking of global migration. During the Great Slump even the international flow of capital seemed to dry up. Between 1927 and 1933 international lending dropped by over 90 per cent.

Why this stagnation? Various reasons have been suggested, for instance that the largest of the world's national economies, the U.S.A., was getting virtually self-sufficient, except in the supply of a few raw materials; it had never been particularly dependent on foreign trade. However, even countries which had been heavy traders, like Britain and the Scandinavian states, showed the same trend. Contemporaries focused on a more obvious cause for alarm, and they were almost certainly right. Each state now did its best to protect its economy against threats from outside, that is to say against a world economy that was visibly in major trouble.

Both businessmen and governments had originally expected that, after the temporary disruptions of the world war, somehow the world economy would return to the happy days before 1914, which they regarded as normal. And indeed the immediate post-war boom, at least in the countries not disrupted by revolution and civil war, looked promising, even though both business and governments shook their heads over the enormously strengthened power of labour and its unions, which looked like raising production costs via higher wages and shorter hours. Yet readjustment proved more difficult than expected. Prices and the boom collapsed in 1920. This undermined the power of labour—British unemployment never thereafter fell much below 10 per cent and the unions lost half their members over the next twelve years—thus once again tilting the balance firmly towards the employers, but prosperity remained elusive.

The Anglo-Saxon world, the wartime neutrals and Japan did what they could to deflate, i.e. to get their economies back to the old and firm principles of stable currencies guaranteed by sound finance and the gold standard, which had been unable to resist the strains of war. Indeed, they more or less succeeded in doing so between 1922 and 1926. However, the great zone of defeat and convulsion from Germany in the West to Soviet Russia in the East saw a spectacular collapse of the monetary system, comparable only to that in part of the post-communist world after 1989. In the extreme case—Germany in 1923—the currency unit was reduced to one million millionth of its 1913 value, that is to say in practice the value of money was reduced to zero. Even in less extreme cases, the consequences were drastic. The writer's grandfather, whose insurance policy matured during the Austrian inflation,* liked to tell the story of

---

*Over the nineteenth century, at the end of which prices were much lower than they had been at the beginning, people got so used to stable or falling prices, that the mere word *inflation* was enough to describe what we now call "hyper-inflation."

drawing this large sum in devalued currency, and finding it was just enough to buy himself a drink in his favourite café.

In short, private savings disappeared totally, thus creating an almost complete vacuum of working capital for business, which does much to explain the massive reliance of the German economy on foreign loans in the following years. This made it unusually vulnerable when the slump came. The situation in the U.S.S.R. was hardly better, though wiping out private savings in monetary form had neither the same economic nor the same political consequences there. When the great inflation was ended in 1922–23, essentially by the decision of governments to stop printing paper money in unlimited quantities and to change the currency, people in Germany who had relied on fixed incomes and savings were wiped out, although at least a tiny fraction of the value of money had been saved in Poland, Hungary and Austria. However, the traumatic effect of the experience on the local middle and lower-middle classes may be imagined. It made central Europe ready for fascism. Devices for getting populations used to long periods of pathological price inflation (e.g. by the "indexation" of wages and other incomes—the word was first used around 1960) were not invented until after the Second World War.*

By 1924 these post-war hurricanes had calmed down, and it seemed possible to look forward to a return to what an American president christened "normalcy." There was indeed something like a return to global growth, even though some of the producers of raw materials and foodstuffs, including notably North American farmers, were troubled because prices of primary products turned down again after a brief recovery. The roaring 1920s were not a golden age on the farms of the U.S.A. Moreover, unemployment in most of Western Europe remained astonishingly, and by pre-1914 standards, pathologically, high. It is hard to remember that even in the boom years of the 1920s (1924–29) it averaged between 10 and 12 per cent in Britain, Germany and Sweden, and no less than 17–18 per cent in Denmark and Norway. Only the U.S.A., with average unemployment of about 4 per cent, was an economy really under full steam. Both facts pointed to serious weaknesses in the economy. The sagging of primary prices (which were prevented from falling further by building up increasingly large stockpiles) simply demonstrated that the demand for them could not keep pace with the capacity to produce. Nor should we overlook the fact that the boom, such as it was, was largely fuelled by the enormous flows of international capital

---

*In the Balkans and the Baltic states governments never entirely lost control of inflation, though it was serious.

which swept across the industrial worlds in those years, and notably to Germany. That country alone, which took about half of all the world's capital exports in 1928, borrowed between 20,000 and 30,000 billion Marks, half of it probably on short term (Arndt, p. 47; Kindleberger, 1986). Once again this made the German economy highly vulnerable, as was proved when the American money was withdrawn after 1929.

It therefore came as no great surprise to anyone except the boosters of smalltown America, whose image became familiar to the Western world at this time through the American novelist Sinclair Lewis' *Babbitt* (1922), that the world economy was in trouble again a few years later. The Communist International had indeed predicted another economic crisis at the height of the boom, expecting it—or so its spokesmen believed or pretended to believe—to lead to a new round of revolutions. It actually produced the opposite at short notice. However, what nobody expected, probably not even the revolutionaries in their most sanguine moments, was the extraordinary universality and depth of the crisis which began, as even non-historians know, with the New York Stock Exchange crash of 29 October 1929. It amounted to something very close to the collapse of the capitalist world economy, which now seemed gripped in a vicious circle where every downward movement of the economic indices (other than unemployment, which moved to ever more astronomic heights) reinforced the decline in all the others.

As the admirable experts of the League of Nations observed, though nobody took much notice of them, a dramatic recession of the North American industrial economy, soon spread to the other industrial heartland, Germany (Ohlin, 1931). U.S. industrial production fell by about a third from 1929 to 1931, German production by about the same, but these are smoothing averages. Thus in the U.S.A., Westinghouse, the great electrical firm, lost two-thirds of its sales between 1929 and 1933, while its net income fell by 76 per cent in two years (Schatz, 1983, p. 60). There was a crisis in primary production, both of foodstuffs and raw materials, as their prices, no longer kept up by building stocks as before, went into free fall. The price of tea and wheat fell by two thirds, the price of raw silk by three quarters. This prostrated—to name but the countries listed by the League of Nations in 1931—Argentina, Australia, the Balkan countries, Bolivia, Brazil, (British) Malaya, Canada, Chile, Colombia, Cuba, Egypt, Ecuador, Finland, Hungary, India, Mexico, the Netherlands Indies (the present Indonesia), New Zealand, Paraguay, Peru, Uruguay and Venezuela, whose international trade depended heavily on a few primary commodities. In short, it made the Depression global in the literal sense.

The economies of Austria, Czechoslovakia, Greece, Japan, Poland and Great Britain, extremely sensitive to the seismic shocks coming from the West (or East), were equally shaken. The Japanese silk industry had tripled its output in fifteen years to supply the vast and growing U.S. market for silk stockings, which now disappeared temporarily—and so did the market for the 90 per cent of Japan's silk that then went to America. Meanwhile the price of the other great staple of Japanese agricultural production, rice, also plummeted, as it did in all the great rice-producing zones of South and East Asia. Since, as it happened, the wheat price collapsed even more completely than that of rice, and wheat was therefore cheaper, many Orientals are said to have switched from the one to the other. However, the boom in chapattis and noodles, if there was one, worsened the situation of farmers in rice-exporting countries like Burma, French Indochina and Siam (now Thailand) (Latham, 1981, p. 178). Farmers tried to compensate for falling prices by growing and selling more crops, and this made prices sink even further.

For farmers dependent on the market, especially the export market, this meant ruin, unless they could retreat to the traditional ultimate redoubt of the peasant, subsistence production. This was indeed still possible in much of the dependent world, and insofar as most Africans, South and East Asians and Latin Americans were still peasants, it undoubtedly cushioned them. Brazil became a byword for the waste of capitalism and the depth of the Depression, as its coffee-growers desperately tried to prevent the price-collapse by burning coffee instead of coal on their steam railroad engines. (Between two thirds and three quarters of the coffee sold on the world market came from that country.) Nevertheless the Great Slump was far more tolerable for the still overwhelmingly rural Brazilians than the economic cataclysms of the 1980s; especially since poor people's expectations of what they could get of an economy were still extremely modest.

Still, even in colonial peasant countries someone suffered, as is suggested by the drop of about two thirds in the importation of sugar, flour, canned fish and rice into the Gold Coast (now Ghana), where the bottom had fallen out of the (peasant-based) cocoa market, not to mention the 98 per cent drop in the imports of gin (Ohlin, 1931, p. 52).

For those who, by definition, had no control over or access to the means of production (unless they could go home to a peasant family in some village), namely the men and women hired for wages, the primary consequence of the Slump was unemployment on an unimagined and unprecedented scale, and for longer than anyone had ever expected. At the worst period of the Slump (1932–33) 22–23 per cent of the British and

Belgian labour force, 24 per cent of the Swedish, 27 per cent of the U.S., 29 per cent of the Austrian, 31 per cent of the Norwegian, 32 per cent of the Danish and no less than 44 per cent of the German workers were out of jobs. What is equally to the point, even the recovery after 1933 did not reduce the average unemployment of the 1930s below 16–17 per cent in Britain and Sweden or below 20 per cent in the rest of Scandinavia, Austria and the U.S.A. The only Western state which succeeded in eliminating unemployment was Nazi Germany between 1933 and 1938. There had been nothing like this economic catastrophe in the lives of working people for as long as anyone could remember.

What made it even more dramatic was that public provision for social security, including unemployment relief, was either non-existent, as in the U.S.A., or, by late twentieth-century standards, extremely meagre, especially for the long-term unemployed. That is why security had always been such a vital concern of working people: protection against the terrible uncertainties of employment (i.e. wages), sickness or accident and the terrible certainties of an old age without earnings. That is why working people dreamed of seeing their children in modestly paid, but secure and pensionable jobs. Even in the country most fully covered by Unemployment Insurance schemes before the Slump (Great Britain) less than 60 per cent of the labour force were covered by it—and that only because Britain since 1920 had already been forced to adjust to mass unemployment. Elsewhere in Europe (except for Germany, where it was above 40 per cent) the proportion of working people with claims for unemployment relief ranged from zero to about one quarter (Flora, 1983, p. 461). People who had been used to fluctuating employment or to passing spells of cyclical unemployment were desperate when no job turned up anywhere, after their small savings had gone and their credit at the local grocer's shop had been exhausted.

Hence the central, the traumatic, impact of mass unemployment on the politics of the industrialized countries, for that is what first and foremost, the Great Slump meant, to the bulk of their inhabitants. What did it matter to them that economic historians (and indeed logic) can demonstrate that the majority of the nation's labour force, which was in employment even at the worst moments, was actually getting significantly better off, since prices were falling throughout the inter-war years, and the price of foodstuffs fell more rapidly than any other in the worst depression years. The image which dominated at the time was that of soup kitchens, of unemployed "Hunger Marchers" from smokeless settlements where no steel or ships were made converging on capital cities to denounce those they held responsible. Nor did politicians fail to observe that up to 85 per cent of the membership of the German Communist Party, growing almost as fast as the Nazi Party in the slump years, and, in the last months before Hitler's accession to power, faster, were unemployed (Weber, I, p. 243).

Unemployment was conceived, not surprisingly, as a deep and potentially mortal wound in the body politic. "Next to war" wrote an editorialist in the London Times in the middle of the Second World War, "unemployment has been the most widespread, the most insidious, and the most corroding malady of our generation: it is the specific social disease of Western civilization in our time" (Arndt, 1944, p. 250). Never before in the history of industrialization could such a passage have been written. It explains more about post-war Western governments' policies than prolonged archival researches.

Curiously enough, the sense of catastrophe and disorientation caused by the Great Slump was perhaps greater among businessmen, economists and politicians than among the masses. Mass unemployment, the collapse of agrarian prices, hit them hard, but they had no doubt that some political solution for these unexpected injustices was available—on the left or on the right—in so far as poor people could ever expect their modest needs to be satisfied. It was precisely the absence of any solutions within the framework of the old liberal economy that made the predicament of the economic decision-makers so dramatic. To meet immediate, short-term crises, they had, as they saw it, to undermine the long-term basis of a flourishing world economy. At a time when world trade fell by 60 per cent in four years (1929–32), states found themselves building increasingly high barriers to protect their national markets and currencies against the world economic hurricanes, knowing quite well that this meant the dismantling of the world system of multilateral trade on which, they believed, world prosperity must rest. The keystone of such a system, the so-called "most favoured nation status" disappeared from almost 60 per cent of 510 commercial agreements signed between 1931 and 1939 and, where it remained, it was usually in a limited form (Snyder, 1940).* Where would it end? Was there an exit from the vicious circle?

We shall consider the immediate political consequences of this, the most traumatic episode in the history of capitalism, below. However, its most significant long-term implication must be mentioned immediately. In a single sentence: the Great Slump destroyed economic liberalism for

---

*The "most favoured nation" clause actually means the opposite of what it seems to mean, namely that the commercial partner will be treated on the same terms as the "most favoured nation"—i.e. *no* nation will be most favoured.

half a century. In 1931–32 Britain, Canada, all of Scandinavia and the U.S.A. abandoned the gold standard, always regarded as the foundation of stable international exchanges and by 1936 they had been joined even by those impassioned believers in bullion, the Belgians and Dutch, and finally the very French.* Almost symbolically, Great Britain in 1931 abandoned Free Trade, which had been as central to the British economic identity since the 1840s as the American Constitution is to U.S. political identity. Britain's retreat from the principles of free transactions in a single world economy dramatises the general rush into national self-protection at the time. More specifically, the Great Slump forced Western governments to give social considerations priority over economic ones in their state policies. The dangers of failing to do so—radicalization of the Left and, as Germany and other countries now proved, of the Right—were too menacing.

So governments no longer protected agriculture simply by tariffs against foreign competition, though, where they had done so before, they raised tariff barriers even higher. During the Depression they took to subsidising it by guaranteeing farm prices, buying up surpluses or paying farmers not to produce, as in the U.S.A. after 1933. The origins of the bizarre paradoxes of the European Community's "Common Agricultural Policy," through which in the 1970s and 1980s increasingly exiguous minorities of farmers threatened to bankrupt the Community through the subsidies they enjoyed, go back to the Great Slump.

As for the workers, after the war "full employment," i.e. the elimination of mass unemployment, became the keystone of economic policy in the countries of a reformed democratic capitalism, whose most celebrated prophet and pioneer, though not the only one, was the British economist John Maynard Keynes (1883–1946). The Keynesian argument for the benefits of eliminating permanent mass unemployment was economic as well as political. Keynesians held, correctly, that the demand which the incomes of fully employed workers must generate, would have the most stimulating effect on depressed economies. Nevertheless, the reason why this means of increasing demand was given such urgent priority—the British government committed itself to it even before the end of the Second World War—was that mass unemployment was believed to be politically and socially explosive, as indeed it had proved to be in the Slump. This belief was so powerful that, when many years later mass

---

*In the classical form a *gold standard* gives the unit of a currency, e g. a dollar bill, the value of a particular weight of gold, for which, if necessary, the bank will exchange it

unemployment returned, and especially during the serious depression of the early 1980s, obervers (including the present author) confidently expected social unrest to occur, and were surprised when it did not (see chapter 14).

This was, of course, largely due to another prophylactic measure taken during, after and as a consequence of the Great Slump: the installation of modern welfare systems. Who can be surprised that the U.S. passed its Social Security Act in 1935? We have become so used to the universal prevalence of ambitious welfare systems in developed states of industrial capitalism—with some exceptions, such as Japan, Switzerland and the U.S.A.—that we forget how few "welfare states" in the modern sense there were before the Second World War. Even the Scandinavian countries were only just beginning to develop them. Indeed, the very term welfare state did not come into use before the 1940s.

The trauma of the Great Slump was underlined by the fact that the one country that had clamorously broken with capitalism appeared to be immune to it: the Soviet Union. While the rest of the world, or at least liberal Western capitalism, stagnated, the U.S.S.R. was engaged in massive ultra-rapid industrialization under its new Five-Year Plans. From 1929 to 1940 Soviet industrial production tripled, at the very least. It rose from 5 per cent of the world's manufactured products in 1929 to 18 per cent in 1938, while during the same period the joint share of the U.S.A., Britain and France, fell from 59 per cent to 52 per cent of the world's total. What was more, there was no unemployment. These achievements impressed foreign observers of all ideologies, including a small but influential flow of socio-economic tourists to Moscow in 1930–35, more than the visible primitiveness and inefficiency of the Soviet economy, or the ruthlessness and brutality of Stalin's collectivisation and mass repression. For what they were trying to come to terms with was not the actual phenomenon of the U.S.S.R. but the breakdown of their own economic system, the depth of the failure of Western capitalism. What was the secret of the Soviet system? Could anything be learned from it? Echoing Russia's Five-Year Plans, "Plan" and "Planning" became buzz-words in politics. Social Democratic parties adopted "plans," as in Belgium and Norway. Sir Arthur Salter, a British civil servant of the utmost distinction and respectability, and a pillar of the Establishment, wrote a book, *Recovery*, to demonstrate that a planned society was essential, if the country and the world were to escape from the vicious cycle of the Great Slump. Other British middle-of-the-road civil servants and functionaries set up a nonpartisan think-tank called PEP (Political and Economic Planning). Young Conservative politicians like the future prime minister Harold Macmillan

(1894–1986) made themselves spokesmen for "planning." Even the very Nazis plagiarized the idea, as Hitler introduced a "Four-Year Plan" in 1933. (For reasons to be considered in the next chapter, the Nazis' own success in dealing with the Slump after 1933 had fewer international repercussions.)

II

Why did the capitalist economy between the wars fail to work? The situation of the U.S.A. is a central part of any answer to this question. For if the disruptions of war and post-war Europe, or at least the belligerent countries of Europe, could be made at least partly responsible for the economic troubles there, the U.S.A. had been far away from the war, though briefly, if decisively, involved in it. So far from disrupting its economy, the First World War, like the Second World War, benefited it spectacularly. By 1913 the U.S.A. had already become the largest economy in the world, producing over one third of its industrial output—just under the combined total for Gemany, Great Britain and France. In 1929 it produced over 42 per cent of the total world output, as against just under 28 per cent for the three European industrial powers (Hilgerdt, 1945, Table 1.14). This is a truly astonishing figure. Concretely, while U.S. steel production rose by about one quarter between 1913 and 1920, steel production in the rest of the world fell by about one third (Rostow, 1978, p. 194, Table III. 33). In short, after the end of the first World War the U.S.A. was in many ways as internationally dominant an economy as it once again became after the Second World War. It was the Great Slump which temporarily interrupted this ascendancy.

Moreover, the war had not only reinforced its position as the world's greatest industrial producer, but turned it into the world's greatest creditor. The British had lost about a quarter of their global investments during the war, mainly those in the U.S.A., which they had to sell to buy war supplies; the French lost about half of theirs, mainly through revolution and breakdown in Europe. Meanwhile the Americans, who had begun the war as a debtor country, ended it as the main international lender. Since the U.S.A. concentrated its operations in Europe and the western hemisphere (the British were still by far the biggest investors in Asia and Africa) their impact on Europe was decisive.

In short, there is no explanation of the world economic crisis without the U.S.A. It was, after all, both the premier exporting nation of the world in the 1920s and, after Great Britain, the premier importing nation. As for raw materials and foodstuffs, it imported almost 40 per cent of all the imports of the fifteen most commercial nations, a fact which goes a long way to explaining the disastrous impact of the slump on the producers of commodities like wheat, cotton, sugar, rubber, silk, copper, tin and coffee (Lary, pp. 28-29). By the same token, it was to become the principal victim of the Slump. If its imports fell by 70 per cent between 1929 and 1932, its exports fell at the same rate. World trade dipped by less than a third from 1929 to 1939, but U.S. exports crashed by almost half.

This is not to underestimate the strictly European roots of trouble, which were largely political in origin. At the Versailles peace conference (1919) vast but undefined payments had been imposed on Germany as "reparations" for the cost of the war and the damage done to the victorious powers. To justify these a clause had also been inserted into the peace treaty making Germany *solely* responsible for the war (the so-called "war-guilt" clause) which was both historically doubtful and proved to be a gift to German nationalism. The amount Germany was to pay remained vague, as a compromise between the position of the U.S.A., which proposed fixing Germany's payments according to the country's capacity to pay, and the other Allies—chiefly the French—who insisted on recovering the entire costs of the war. Their, or at least France's, real object was to keep Germany weak and to have a means of putting pressure on it. In 1921 the sum was fixed at 132 billion (thousand million) Gold Marks, i.e. $33 billions at the time, which everyone knew to be a fantasy.

"Reparations" led to endless debates, periodic crises and settlements under American auspices, since the U.S.A., to its former Allies' displeasure, wished to link the question of Germany's debts to them, to that of their own wartime debts to Washington. These were almost as crazy as the sums demanded of the Germans, which amounted to one and a half times the entire national income of the country in 1929; the British debts to the U.S. amounted to half the British national income; the French debts to two-thirds (Hill, 1988, pp. 15–16). A "Dawes Plan" in 1924 actually fixed a real sum for Germany to pay annually; a "Young Plan" in 1929 modified the repayment scheme and, incidentally, set up the Bank of International Settlements in Basel (Switzerland), the first of the international financial institutions which were to multiply after the Second World War. (At the time of writing it is still in business.) For practical purposes all payments, German and Allied, ceased in 1932. Only Finland ever paid its war debts to the U.S.A.

Without going into the details, two questions were at issue. *First*, there was the point made by the young John Maynard Keynes, who wrote a savage critique of the Versailles conference in which he took part as a junior member of the British delegation: *The Economic Consequences of the Peace* (1920). Without a restoration of the German economy, he argued, the restoration of a stable liberal civilization and economy in Europe would be impossible. The French policy of keeping Germany feeble for the sake of French "security" was counter-productive. In fact, the French were too weak to impose their policy, even when they briefly occupied the industrial heartland of West Germany in 1923 on the excuse that the Germans were refusing to pay. Eventually they had to tolerate a policy of German "fulfilment" after 1924 which strengthened the German economy. But, second, there was the question of how reparations were to be paid. Those who wanted to keep Germany weak wanted cash rather than (as was rational) goods out of current production, or at least out of the income from German exports, since this would have strengthened the German economy against its competitors. In effect they forced Germany into heavy borrowing, so that such reparations as were paid came out of the massive (American) loans of the mid-1920s. For Germany's rivals this seemed to have the additional advantage that Germany ran into deep debt rather than expanding its exports to achieve an external balance. In fact, German imports soared. However, the whole arrangement, as we have already seen, made both Germany and Europe highly sensitive to the decline in American lending which began even before the crisis and the shutting of the American loan-tap, which followed the Wall Street Crisis of 1929. The entire house of cards of reparations collapsed during the Slump. By then the end of these payments had no positive effects on Germany or the world economy, because this had broken down as an integrated system and so, in 1931–33, had all arrangements for international payments.

However, wartime and post-war disruptions and political complications in Europe can only partly explain the severity of the inter-war economic breakdown. Speaking economically, we can look at it in two ways.

The first will see chiefly a striking and growing imbalance in the international economy, due to the asymmetry in development between the U.S.A. and the rest of the world. The world system, it can be argued, did not work, because, unlike Great Britain, which had been its centre before 1914, the U.S.A. did not much need the rest of the world, and therefore, again unlike Great Britain, which knew that the world payments system rested on the Pound Sterling and saw to it that it remained stable, the U.S.A. did not bother to act as a global stabilizer. The U.S.A. did not need the world much, because after the First World War it needed to import less capital, labour and (relatively speaking) fewer commodities than ever—except for some raw materials. Its exports, though internationally important—Hollywood virtually monopolised the international movie market—made a far smaller contribution to the national income than in any other industrial country. How significant this, as it were, withdrawal of the U.S.A. from the world economy was, may be debated. However, it is quite clear that this explanation of the Slump was one which influenced U.S. economists and politicians in the 1940s, and helped to convince Washington in the war years to take over responsibility for the stability of the world economy after 1945 (Kindleberger, 1973).

The second perspective on the Depression fixes on the failure of the world economy to generate enough demand for a lasting expansion. The foundations of the prosperity of the 1920s, as we have seen, were weak, even in the U.S.A., where farming was virtually already in depression, and money wages, contrary to the myth of the great jazz age, were not rising dramatically, and actually stagnant in the last mad years of the boom (Historical Statistics of the U.S.A., I, p. 164, Table D722–727). What was happening, as often happens in free market booms, was that, with wages lagging, profits rose disproportionately and the prosperous got a larger slice of the national cake. But as mass demand could not keep pace with the rapidly increasing productivity of the industrial system in the heyday of Henry Ford, the result was over-production and speculation. This, in turn, triggered off the collapse. Once again, whatever the arguments among historians and economists, who still continue to debate the issue, contemporaries with a strong interest in government policies were deeply impressed with the weakness of demand; not least John Maynard Keynes.

When the collapse came, it was of course all the more drastic in the U.S.A. because in fact a lagging expansion of demand had been beefed up by means of an enormous expansion of consumer credit. (Readers who remember the later 1980s may find themselves on familiar territory.) Banks, already hurt by the speculative real-estate boom which, with the usual help of self-deluding optimists and mushrooming financial crookery,* had reached its peak some years before the Big Crash, loaded with bad debts, refused new housing loans or to refinance existing ones. This did not stop them from failing by the thousands,† while (in 1933) nearly half of all U.S. home mortgages were in default and a thousand

---

*Not for nothing were 1920s the decade of psychologist Emile Coué (1857–1926) who popularised optimistic auto-suggestion by means of the slogan, constantly to be repeated. "Every day in every way I am getting better and better "

†The U.S. banking system did not permit the European kind of giant bank with a nation-wide system of branches, and therefore consisted of relatively weak local or, best, state-wide banks.

properties a day were being foreclosed (Miles et al., 1991, p. 108). Automobile purchasers alone owed $1,400 million out of a total personal indebtedness of $6,500 million in short- and medium-term loans (Ziebura, p. 49). What made the economy so much more vulnerable to this credit boom was that customers did not use their loans to buy the traditional mass consumption goods which kept body and soul together, and were therefore pretty inelastic: food, clothing and the like. However poor one is, one can't reduce one's demand for groceries below a certain point; and that demand will not double if one's income doubles. Instead they bought the durable consumer goods of the modern consumer society which the U.S.A. was even then pioneering. But the purchase of cars and houses could be readily postponed, and, in any case, they had and have a very high income elasticity of demand.

So, unless a slump was expected to be brief, or was short, and confidence in the future was not undermined, the effect of such a crisis could be dramatic. Thus automobile production in the U.S.A. *halved* between 1929 and 1931 or, at a much lower level, the production of poor people's gramophone records ("race" records and jazz records addressed to a black public) virtually ceased for a while. In short, "unlike railroads or more efficient ships or the introduction of steel and machine tools—which cut costs—the new products and way of life required high and expanding levels of income and a high degree of confidence about the future, to be rapidly diffused" (Rostow, 1978, p. 219). But that is exactly what was collapsing.

The worst cyclical slump sooner or later comes to an end, and after 1932 there were increasingly clear signs that the worst was over. Indeed, some economies roared ahead. Japan and, on a more modest scale, Sweden, reached almost twice the pre-slump level of production by the end of the 1930s, and by 1938 the German (though not the Italian) economy was 25 per cent above 1929. Even sluggish economies like the British showed plenty of signs of dynamism. Yet somehow the expected upsurge did not return. The world remained in depression. This was most visible in the greatest of all the economies, the U.S.A., for the various experiments in stimulating the economy undertaken under President F. D. Roosevelt's "New Deal"—sometimes inconsistently—did not really live up to their economic promise. A strong upsurge was followed, in 1937–38, by another economic crash, though on a rather more modest scale than after 1929. The leading sector of American industry, automobile production, never regained its 1929 peak. In 1938 it was little more than it had been in 1920 (Historical Statistics, II, p. 716). Looking back from the 1990s we are struck by the pessimism of intelligent commentators. Able and brilliant economists saw the future of capitalism, left to itself, as one of stagnation. This view, anticipated in Keynes' pamphlet against the Versailles peace treaty, naturally became popular in the U.S.A. after the Slump. Must not any mature economy tend to become a stagnating one? As the proponent of another pessimistic prognosis for capitalism, the Austrian economist Schumpeter, put it, "In any prolonged period of economic malaise economists, falling in like other people with the humours of their time, proffer theories that pretend to show that depression has come to stay" (Schumpeter, 1954, p. 1172). Perhaps historians looking back on the period from 1973 to the end of the Short Twentieth Century from an equal distance, will be equally struck by the persistent reluctance of the 1970s and 1980s to envisage the possibility of a general depression of the world capitalist economy.

All this in spite of the fact that the 1930s were a decade of considerable technological innovation in industry, for instance, in the development of plastics. Indeed, in one field—entertainment and what later came to be called "the media"—the inter-war years saw the major breakthrough, at least in the Anglo-Saxon world, with the triumph of mass radio, and the Hollywood movie industry, not to mention the modern rotogravure illustrated press (see chapter 6). Perhaps it is not quite so surprising that the giant movie theatres rose like dream palaces in the grey cities of mass unemployment, for cinema tickets were remarkably cheap, the youngest, as well as the oldest, disproportionately hit by unemployment then as later, had time to kill, and, as the sociologists observed, during the depression husbands and wives were more likely to share joint leisure activities than before (Stouffer, Lazarsfeld, pp. 55, 92).

III

The Great Slump confirmed intellectuals, activists and ordinary citizens in the belief that something was fundamentally wrong with the world they lived in. Who knew what could be done about it? Certainly few of those in authority over their countries, and certainly not those who tried to steer a course by the traditional navigational instruments of secular liberalism or traditional faith, and by the charts of the nineteenth century seas which were plainly no longer to be trusted. How much confidence did economists deserve, however brilliant, who demonstrated, with great lucidity, that the Slump in which even they lived, could not happen in a properly conducted free-market society, since (according to an economic law named after an early nineteenth century Frenchman) no overproduction was possible which did not very soon correct itself? In 1933 it was not easy to believe, for instance, that where consumer demand, and therefore consumption, fell in a depression, the rate of interest would fall by just as much as was needed to stimulate investment, so that the increased investment demand would exactly fill the gap left by the smaller consumer demand. As unemployment soared, it did not seem plausible to believe (as the British Treasury apparently did) that public works would not increase employment at all, because the money spent on them would merely be diverted from the private sector, which would otherwise have generated just as much employment. Economists who simply advised leaving the economy alone, governments whose first instincts, apart from protecting the gold standard by deflationary policies, was to stick to financial orthodoxy, balance budgets and cut costs, were visibly not making the situation better. Indeed, as the depression continued, it was argued with considerable force not least by J. M. Keynes who consequently became the most influential economist of the next forty years—that they were making the depression worse. Those of us who lived through the years of the Great Slump still find it almost impossible to understand how the orthodoxies of the pure free market, then so obviously discredited, once again came to preside over a global period of depression in the late 1980s and 1990s, which, once again, they were equally unable to understand or to deal with. Still, this strange phenomenon should remind us of the major characteristic of history which it exemplifies: the incredible shortness of memory of both the theorists and practitioners of economics. It also provides a vivid illustration of society's need for historians, who are the professional remembrancers of what their fellow-citizens wish to forget.

In any case, what was a "free market economy" when an economy increasingly dominated by huge corporations made nonsense of the term "perfect competition" and economists critical of Karl Marx could observe that he had been proved right, not least in his prediction of the growing concentration of capital (Leontiev, 1977, p. 78)? One did not have to be a Marxist, or show an interest in Marx, to observe how unlike the economy of nineteenth century free competition inter-war capitalism was. Indeed, well before the Wall Street crash, an intelligent Swiss banker observed that the failure of economic liberalism (and, he added, pre-1917 socialism) to maintain themselves as universal programmes, explained the pressure towards autocratic economics—fascist, communist or under the auspices of large corporations independent of their shareholders (Somary, 1929, pp. 174, 193). And by the end of the 1930s the liberal orthodoxies of free-market competition were so far away that the world economy could be seen as a triple system composed of a market sector, an inter-governmental sector (within which planned or controlled economies such as Japan, Turkey, Germany and the Soviet Union conducted their transactions with each other) and a sector of international public or quasi-public authorities which regulated certain parts of the economy (e.g. by international commodity agreements) (Staley, 1939, p. 231).

It is therefore not surprising that the effects of the Great Slump on both politics and public thinking were dramatic and immediate. Unlucky the government which happened to be in office during the cataclysm, whether it was on the right, like Herbert Hoover's presidency in the U.S.A. (1928–32), or on the left, like Britain's and Australia's labour governments. The change was not always as immediate as in Latin America, where twelve countries changed government or regime in 1930–31, ten of them by military coup. Nevertheless, by the middle 1930s there were few states whose politics had not changed very substantially from what they had been before the Crash. In Europe and Japan there was a striking move to the right, except in Scandinavia, where Sweden entered its half-century of social-democratic rule in 1932, and in Spain, where the Bourbon monarchy gave way to an unhappy, and as it turned out shortlived, Republic in 1931. More of this in the next chapter, though it must be said immediately that the almost simultaneous victory of nationalist, warlike, and actively aggressive regimes in two major military powers—Japan (1931) and Germany (1933)—constituted the most far-reaching and sinister political consequence of the Great Depression. The gates to the Second World War were opened in 1931.

The strengthening of the radical Right was reinforced, at least during the worst period of the Slump, by the spectacular setbacks for the revolutionary Left. So far from initiating another round of social revolution, as the Communist International had expected, the Depression reduced the international communist movement outside the U.S.S.R. to a state of unprecedented feebleness. This was admittedly due in some measure to the suicidal policy of the Comintern, which not only grossly underestimated the danger of National Socialism in Germany, but pursued a policy of sectarian isolation that seems quite incredible in retrospect, by deciding that its main enemy was the organized mass labour movement of social-democratic and labour parties (described as "social-fascist").* Certainly by 1934, after Hitler had destroyed the German CP

---

*This went so far that in 1933 Moscow insisted that the Italian communist leader P. Togliatti withdraw the suggestion that, perhaps, social-democracy was not the primary danger, at least in Italy. By then Hitler had actually come to power. The Comintern did not change its line until 1934.

(KPD), once Moscow's hope of world revolution and still by far the largest and apparently most formidable and growing section of the International, when even the Chinese Communists, expelled from their rural guerrilla bases, were no more than a harried caravan on its Long March to some distant and safe refuge, very little seemed to be left of a significant organized international revolutionary movement, legal or even illegal. In the Europe of 1934 only the French Communist Party still had a genuine political presence. In Fascist Italy, ten years after the March on Rome and in the depth of the international slump, Mussolini felt sufficiently confident actually to release some imprisoned communists to celebrate that anniversary (Spriano, 1969, p. 397). All this was to change within a few years (see chapter 5). But the fact remains that the immediate result of the Slump, at all events in Europe, was the exact opposite of what social revolutionaries had expected.

Nor was this decline of the Left confined to the communist sector, for with Hitler's victory the German Social Democratic Party disappeared from sight, while a year later Austrian social democracy fell after a brief armed resistance. The British Labour Party had already become a victim of the Slump, or rather of its belief in nineteenth century economic orthodoxy, in 1931, and its trade unions, which had lost half their members since 1920, were weaker than they had been in 1913. Most of European socialism had its backs to the wall.

Outside Europe, however, the situation was different. The northern parts of the Americas moved quite markedly to the left, as the U.S.A., under its new President Franklin D. Roosevelt (1933–45), experimented with a more radical New Deal, and Mexico, under President Lázaro Cardenas (1934–40) revived the original dynamism of the early Mexican Revolution, especially in the matter of agrarian reform. Quite powerful social/political movements arose on the crisis-stricken prairies of Canada. *Social Credit* and the Cooperative Commonwealth Federation (today's *New Democratic Party*), both on the Left by 1930s criteria.

It is not so easy to characterize the political impact of the Slump on the remainder of Latin America, for if its governments or ruling parties fell like ninepins as the collapse in the world price of their export staples broke their finances, they did not all fall in the same direction. Still, more of them fell towards the Left than to the Right, even if only briefly. Argentina entered the era of military government after a lengthy period of civilian rule; and though fascist-minded leaders like General Uriburu (1930–32) were soon sidelined, it clearly moved to the Right, even if a traditionalist Right. Chile, on the other hand, used the Slump to overthrow one of its rare military president-dictators, before the era of General Pinochet, Carlos Ibañez (1927–31), and moved, in a stormy fashion, towards the Left. It actually passed through a momentary "Socialist Republic" in 1932, under the splendidly named Colonel Marmaduke Grove, and later developed a successful Popular Front on the European model (see chapter 5). In Brazil the Slump ended the oligarchic "old Republic" of 1889–1930 and brought to power Getulio Vargas, best described as a nationalist-populist (see page 135). He dominated his country's history for the next twenty years. The shift in Peru was much more clearly to the Left, though the most powerful of the new parties, the American Popular Revolutionary Alliance (APRA)—one of the few successful mass working-classed-based parties of the European type in the western hemisphere*—failed in its revolutionary ambitions (1930–32). The change in Colombia was even more clearly to the Left. The Liberals, under a reform-minded president much influenced by Roosevelt's New Deal took over after almost thirty years of Conservative rule. The radical shift was even more marked in Cuba, where Roosevelt's inauguration allowed the inhabitants of this offshore U.S. protectorate to overthrow a hated and, even by the then prevailing Cuban standards, unusually corrupt President.

In the vast colonial sector of the world, the Slump brought a marked increase in anti-imperialist activity, partly because of the collapse of the commodity prices on which colonial economies (or at least their public finances and middle classes) depended, partly because the metropolitan countries themselves rushed to protect their agriculture and employment, irrespective of the effects of such policies on their colonies. In short, European states whose economic decisions were being determined by domestic factors, could not in the long term keep together empires with an infinite complexity of producer interests (Holland, 1985, p. 13) (see chapter 7).

For this reason, in most of the colonial world the Slump marked the effective beginning of indigenous political and social discontent, which could not but be directed against the (colonial) government, even where political nationalist movements did not emerge until after the Second World War. In both (British) West Africa and the Caribbean social unrest now made its appearance. It grew directly out of the crisis of local export crops (cocoa and sugar). However, even in countries with already developed anti-colonial national movements, the depression years brought a sharpening of conflict, particularly where political agitation had reached

---

*The others were the Chilean and Cuban Communist Parties.

the masses. These, after all, were the years of the expansion of the Muslim Brotherhood in Egypt (founded 1928) and of the second mobilization of the Indian masses by Gandhi (1931) (see chapter 7). Perhaps the victory of the Republican ultras under De Valera in the Irish elections of 1932 should also be seen as a belated anti-colonial reaction to the economic breakdown.

Probably nothing demonstrates both the globality of the Great Slump and the profundity of its impact more than this rapid bird's eye view of the virtually universal political upheavals it produced within a period measured in months or single years, from Japan to Ireland, from Sweden to New Zealand, from Argentina to Egypt. Yet the depth of its impact is not to be judged only, or even mainly, by its short-term political effects, dramatic though these often were. It was a catastrophe which destroyed all hope of restoring the economy, and the society, of the long nineteenth century. The period 1929–33 was a canyon which henceforth made a return to 1913 not merely impossible, but unthinkable. Old-fashioned liberalism was dead or seemed doomed. Three options now competed for intellectual-political hegemony. Marxist communism was one. After all, Marx's own predictions seemed to be coming true, as the American Economic Association itself was told in 1938 and, even more impressively, the U.S.S.R. appeared to be immune to the catastrophe. A capitalism shorn of its belief in the optimality of free markets and reformed by a sort of unofficial marriage or permanent liaison with the moderate social-democracy of non-communist labour movements was the second, and, after the Second World War, proved to be the most effective. However, in the short run it was not so much a conscious programme or policy alternative as a sense that once the Slump was over, such a thing must never be allowed to happen again and, in the best of cases, a readiness to experiment stimulated by the evident failure of classical free-market liberalism. Thus the Swedish social-democratic policy after 1932 was a conscious reaction to the failures of the economic orthodoxy that had dominated the disastrous British Labour government of 1929–31, at all events in the opinion of one of its major architects, Gunnar Myrdal. An alternative theory to the bankrupt free market economics was only in the process of elaboration. J. M. Keynes' *General Theory of Employment, Interest and Money*, the most influential contribution to it, was not published until 1936. An alternative government practice, the macro-economic steering and management of the economy based on national income accounting did not develop until the Second World War and after, though, perhaps with an eye on the U.S.S.R., governments and other public entities in the 1930s increasingly took to seeing the national economy as a whole and estimating the size of its total product or income.*

The third option was fascism, which the Slump transformed into a world movement, and, more to the point, a world danger. Fascism in its German version (National Socialism) benefited both from the German intellectual tradition which (unlike the Austrian one) had been hostile to the neoclassical theories of economic liberalism that had become the international orthodoxy since the 1880s, and from a ruthless government determined to get rid of unemployment at all costs. It dealt with the Great Slump, it must be said, rapidly and more successfully than any other (the record of Italian fascism was less impressive). However, this was not its major appeal in a Europe that had largely lost its bearings. But as the tide of fascism rose with the Great Slump, it became increasingly clear that in the Age of Catastrophe not only peace, social stability and the economy, but also the political institutions and intellectual values of nineteenth century liberal bourgeois society, were in retreat or collapse. To this process we must now turn.

---

*The first governments to do so were the U.S.S.R. and Canada in 1925. By 1939 nine countries had official government statistics of national income, and the League of Nations had estimates for twenty-six in all. Immediately after the Second World War estimates were available for thirty-nine, in the middle 1950s for ninety-three, and since then national income figures, often with only the remotest connection with the realities of their people's livelihood, have become almost as standard for independent states as national flags.

CHAPTER FOUR

The Fall of Liberalism

In Nazism we have a phenomenon which seems scarcely capable of subjection to rational analysis. Under a leader who talked in apocalyptic tones of world power or destruction and a regime founded on an utterly repulsive ideology of race-hatred, one of the most culturally and economically advanced countries of Europe planned for war, launched a world conflagration which killed around 50 million people, and perpetrated atrocities—culminating in the mechanized mass murder of millions of Jews—of a nature and scale as to defy imagination. Faced with Auschwitz, the explanatory powers of the historian seem puny indeed.

> –Ian Kershaw (1993, pp. 3–4)

To die for the Fatherland, for the Idea! . . . No, that is a cop-out. Even at the front killing's the thing . . . Dying is nothing, it's non-existent. Nobody can imagine his own death. Killing's the thing. That's the frontier to be crossed. Yes, that is a concrete act of your will. Because there you make your will live in another man's.

> –From the letter of a young volunteer for the
> Fascist Social Republic of 1943–45 (Pavone, 1991, p.431)

I

Of all the developments in the Age of Catastrophe, survivors from the nineteenth century were perhaps most shocked by the collapse of the values and institutions of the liberal civilization whose progress their century had taken for granted, at any rate in "advanced" and "advancing" parts of the world. These values were a distrust of dictatorship and absolute rule; a commitment to constitutional government with or under freely elected governments and representative assemblies, which guaranteed the rule of law; and an accepted set of citizens' rights and liberties, including freedom of speech, publication and assembly. State and society should be informed by the values of reason, public debate, education, science and the improvability (though not necessarily the perfectibility) of the human condition. These values, it seemed clear, had made progress throughout the century, and were destined to advance further. After all, by 1914 even the two last autocracies of Europe, Russia and Turkey, had made concessions in the direction of constitutional government, and Iran had even borrowed a constitution from Belgium. Before 1914 these values had been challenged only by traditionalist forces like the Roman Catholic church, building defensive barricades of dogma against the superior forces of modernity; by a few intellectual rebels and prophets of doom, mainly from "good families" and established centres of culture, and thus somehow part of the civilization they challenged; and the forces of democracy, on the whole a new and troubling phenomenon (see *Age of Empire*). The ignorance and backwardness of these masses, their commitment to the overthrow of bourgeois society by social revolution, and the latent human irrationality so easily exploited by demagogues, were indeed a cause for alarm. However, the most immediately dangerous of these new democratic mass movements, the socialist labour movements, were actually, both in theory and in practice, as passionately committed to the values of reason, science, progress, education and individual freedom as anyone. The German Social Democratic Party's May Day medal showed Karl Marx on one side, the Statue of Liberty on the other. Their challenge was to the economy, not to constitutional government and civility. It would not be easy to regard a government headed by Victor Adler, August Bebel or Jean Jaurès as the end of "civilization as we know it." In any case such governments seemed, as yet, remote.

Politically, indeed, the institutions of liberal democracy had advanced, and the eruption of barbarism in 1914–18 had, it seemed, only hastened this advance. Except for Soviet Russia, all the regimes emerging from the First World War, old and new, were, basically, elected representative parliamentary regimes, even Turkey. Europe, west of the Soviet border, consisted entirely of such states in 1920. Indeed, the basic institution of liberal constitutional government, elections to representative assemblies and/or presidents, was almost universal in the world of independent states by this time, although we must remember that the sixty-five or so independent states of the inter-war period were primarily a European and American phenomenon: one third of the world's population lived under colonial rule. The only states which had no elections whatever in the period 1919–47 were isolated political fossils, namely Ethiopia, Mongolia, Nepal, Saudi Arabia and Yemen. Another five states had only *one* election during this period, which does not argue a strong inclination towards liberal democracy, namely Afghanistan, Kuomintang China, Guatemala, Paraguay and Thailand, then still known as Siam, but the very existence of elections is evidence of at least some penetration of liberal political ideas, at least in theory. One would not, of course, wish to suggest that the mere existence or frequency of elections proves more than this. Neither Iran, which had six elections after 1930, nor Iraq, which had three, could even then count as strongholds of democracy.

Still, representative electoral regimes were frequent enough. And yet the twenty years between Mussolini's so-called "March on Rome" and the peak of the Axis success in the Second World War saw an accelerating, increasingly catastrophic, retreat of liberal political institutions.

In 1918–20 legislative assemblies were dissolved or became ineffective in two European states, in the 1920s in six, the 1930s in nine, while German occupation destroyed constitutional power in another five during the Second World War. In short, the only European countries with adequately democratic political institutions that functioned without a break during the entire inter-war period were Britain, Finland (only just), the Irish Free State, Sweden and Switzerland.

In the Americas, the other region of independent states, the situation was more mixed, but hardly suggested a general advance of democratic institutions. The list of *consistently* constitutional and non-authoritarian states in the western hemisphere was short: Canada, Colombia, Costa Rica, the U.S.A. and that now forgotten "Switzerland of South America" and its only real democracy, Uruguay. The best we can say is that the movements between the end of the First World War and that of the Second World War were sometimes to the Left as well as to the Right. As for the rest of the globe, much of which consisted of colonies, and was thus non-liberal by definition, it plainly moved away from liberal constitutions, insofar as it had ever had them. In Japan a moderate Liberal regime gave way to a nationalist-militarist one in 1930/31. Thailand made some tentative steps towards constitutional government, and Turkey was taken over by the progressive military modernizer Kemal Atatürk in the early 1920s, not a man to let any elections stand in his way. In the three continents of Asia, Africa and Australasia only Australia and New Zealand were consistently democratic, for the majority of South Africans remained strictly outside the ambit of the white men's constitution.

In short, political liberalism was in full retreat throughout the Age of Catastrophe, a retreat which accelerated sharply after Adolf Hitler became Germany's chancellor in 1933. Taking the world as a whole, there had been perhaps thirty-five or more constitutional and elected governments in 1920 (depending on where we situate some Latin American republics). Until 1938 there were perhaps seventeen such states, in 1944 perhaps twelve out of the global total of sixty-four. The world trend seemed clear.

It may be worth reminding ourselves that in this period the threat to liberal institutions came exclusively from the political right, for between 1945 and 1989 it was assumed, almost as a matter of course, that it came essentially from communism. Until then the term "totalitarianism," originally invented as a description or self-description of Italian Fascism, was applied virtually only to such regimes. Soviet Russia (from 1923: the U.S.S.R.) was isolated and neither able nor, after the rise of Stalin, willing to extend communism. Social revolution under Leninist (or any) leadership ceased to spread after the initial post-war wave had ebbed. The (Marxist) social-democratic movements had turned into state-sustaining rather than subversive forces, and their commitment to democracy was unquestioned. In most countries' labour movements communists were minorities, and where they were strong, in most cases they were, or had been, or were about to be, suppressed. The fear of social revolution, and the communists' role in it, was realistic enough, as the second wave of revolution during and after the Second World War proved, but in the twenty years of liberal retreat not a single regime that could be reasonably called liberal-democratic had been overthrown from the Left.* The danger came exclusively from the Right. And that Right represented not merely a threat to constitutional and representative government, but an ideological threat to liberal civilization as such, and a potentially world-wide *movement*, for which the label "fascism" is both insufficient and not wholly irrelevant.

It is insufficient, because by no means all the forces overthrowing liberal regimes were fascist. It is relevant, because fascism, first in its original Italian form, later in its German form of National Socialism, both inspired other anti-liberal forces, supported them and lent the international Right a sense of historic confidence: in the 1930s it looked like the wave of the future. As has been said, by an expert in the field: "It is no accident that . . . the eastern European royal dictators, bureaucrats,

---

*The closest to such an overthrow is the annexation of Estonia by the U.S.S.R. in 1940, for at the time this small Baltic country, having passed through some authoritarian years, had again passed to a more democratic constitution.

and officers, and Franco (in Spain) should have mimicked fascism" (Linz, 1975, p. 206).

The forces overthrowing liberal-democratic regimes were of three kinds, omitting the more traditional form of military coups installing Latin American dictators or *caudillos* which had no particular political colouring *a priori*. All were against social revolution, and indeed a reaction against the subversion of the old social order in 1917–20 was at the root of all of them. All were authoritarian and hostile to liberal political institutions, though sometimes for pragmatic reasons rather than on principle. Old-fashioned reactionaries might ban some parties, notably the communist, but not all. After the overthrow of the shortlived Hungarian soviet republic of 1919, Admiral Horthy, head of what he maintained was the kingdom of Hungary, though it no longer had either king or navy, governed an authoritarian state which remained parliamentary, but not democratic, in the old eighteenth century oligarchic sense. All tended to favour the military and foster the police, or other bodies of men capable of exercising physical coercion, since these were the most immediate bulwarks against subversion. Indeed, their support was often essential for the Right to come to power. And all tended to be nationalist, partly because of resentment against foreign states, lost wars, or insufficient empires, partly because waving national flags was a way to both legitimacy and popularity. Nevertheless, there were differences.

Old-fashioned authoritarians or conservatives—Admiral Horthy, Marshal Mannerheim of Finland, winner of the civil war of white vs. red in newly independent Finland; Colonel, later Marshal, Pilsudski, the liberator of Poland; King Alexander, formerly of Serbia, now of the newly united Yugoslavia; and General Francisco Franco of Spain—had no particular ideological agenda, other than anti-communism and the prejudices traditional to their class. They might find themselves allied to Hitler's Germany and to fascist movements in their own countries, but only because in the inter-war conjuncture, the "natural" alliance was one of all sectors of the political Right. Of course national considerations might cut across this alliance. Winston Churchill, a strongly Right-wing Tory in this period, though an uncharacteristic one, expressed some sympathy for Mussolini's Italy, and could not bring himself to support the Spanish Republic against General Franco's forces, but Germany's threat to Britain made him into the champion of international anti-fascist union. On the other hand, such old reactionaries might also have to confront the opposition of genuinely fascist movements in their own countries, sometimes with substantial mass support.

A second strand of the Right produced what has been called "organic statism" (Linz, 1975, pp. 277, 306–13) or conservative regimes, not so much defending a traditional order, but deliberately recreating its principles as a way of resisting both Liberal individualism and the challenge of labour and socialism. Behind it stood an ideological nostalgia for an imagined Middle Ages or feudal society, in which the existence of classes or economic groups was recognized, but the awful prospect of class struggle was kept at bay by the willing acceptance of social hierarchy, by a recognition that each social group or "estate" had its part to play in an organic society composed of all, and should be recognized as a collective entity. This produced various brands of "corporativist" theories which replaced liberal democracy by the representation of economic and occupational interest groups. This was sometimes described as "organic" participation or democracy, and therefore better than the real kind, but in fact was invariably combined with authoritarian regimes and strong states ruled from above, largely by bureaucrats and technocrats. It invariably limited or abolished electoral democracy ("Democracy based on corporative correctives" in the phrase of the Hungarian premier Count Bethlen) (Ranki, 1971). The most complete examples of such corporate states were found in some Roman Catholic countries, notably the Portugal of Professor Oliveira Salazar, the longest-lived of all Europe's anti-liberal regimes of the right (1927–74), but also in Austria between the destruction of democracy and the invasion of Hitler (1934–38), and, to some extent, in Franco's Spain.

Yet if reactionary regimes of this kind had origins and inspirations both older than fascism, and sometimes very different from it, no clear line separated the two, because both shared the same enemies, if not the same goals. Thus the Roman Catholic Church, profoundly and unswervingly reactionary as it was in the version officially consecrated by the first Vatican Council of 1870, was not fascist. Indeed, by its hostility to essentially secular states with totalitarian pretensions, it had to be opposed to fascism. Yet the doctrine of the "corporate state," most fully exemplified in Catholic countries, had been largely elaborated in (Italian) fascist circles, though these, of course, drew on the Catholic tradition among others. Indeed, these regimes were sometimes actually called "clerical fascist." Fascists in Catholic countries might emerge directly out of integrist Catholicism, as in the *Rexist* movement of the Belgian Leon Degrelle. The ambiguity of the Church's attitude to Hitler's racism has been often noted; less often, the considerable help given after the war by persons within the Church, sometimes in important positions, to fugitive Nazis or fascists of various kinds, including many accused of horrifying war crimes. What linked the Church not only with old-fashioned reactionaries but with fascists, was a common hatred for the eighteenth century Enlightment, the French Revolution and all that in the Church's opinion derived from it: democracy, liberalism and, of course, most urgently, "godless communism."

In fact, the fascist era marked a turning-point in Catholic history largely because the Church's identification with a Right whose major international standard-bearers now were Hitler and Mussolini created substantial moral problems for socially-minded Catholics, not to mention, as fascism retreated towards inevitable defeat, substantial political problems for insufficiently anti-fascist hierarchies. Conversely, anti-fascism, or just patriotic resistance to the foreign conqueror, for the first time gave democratic Catholicism (Christian Democracy) legitimacy within the Church. Political parties mobilizing the Roman Catholic vote had come into existence, on pragmatic grounds, in countries where Catholics were a significant minority, normally to defend Church interests against secular states, as in Germany and the Netherlands. The Church resisted such concessions to the politics of democracy and liberalism in officially Catholic countries, although it was sufficiently worried by the rise of godless socialism to formulate—a radical innovation—a social policy in 1891, which stressed the need to give workers their due while maintaining the sacredness of family and private property, but *not* of capitalism as such.* This had provided a first foothold for social Catholics, or others prepared to organize such forms of worker defence as Catholic labour unions, also more inclined by such activities to the more liberal side of Catholicism. Except in Italy, where Pope Benedict XV (1914–22) briefly permitted a large (Catholic) Popular Party to emerge after the First World War, until fascism destroyed it, democratic and social Catholics remained politically marginal minorities. It was the advance of fascism in the 1930s which brought them into the open, even though the Catholics who declared their support for the Spanish Republic were a small, if intellectually distinguished band. The support of Catholics went overwhelmingly to Franco. It was the Resistance, which they could justify on grounds of patriotism rather than ideology, which gave them their chance, and victory which allowed them to take it. But the triumphs of political Christian Democracy in Europe, and some decades later in parts of Latin America, belong to a later period. In the period when liberalism fell, the Church, with rare exceptions, rejoiced at its fall.

---

*This was the Encyclical *Rerum Novarum*, supplemented forty years later, and not by chance in the depth of the Great Slump, by *Quadragesimo Anno*. It remains the cornerstone of the Church's social policy to this day, as witness Pope John Paul II's 1991 Encyclical *Centesimus Annus*, issued on the centenary of *Rerum Novarum*. However, the precise balance of condemnation has varied with political context.

II

There remain the movements which can be truly called fascist. The first of these was the Italian one which gave the phenomenon its name, the creation of a renegade socialist journalist, Benito Mussolini, whose first name, a tribute to the Mexican anti-clerical president Benito Juárez, symbolized the passionate anti-papalism of his native Romagna. Adolf Hitler himself acknowledged his debt to, and respect for, Mussolini, even when both Mussolini and fascist Italy had demonstrated their feebleness and incompetence in the Second World War. In return Mussolini took over from Hitler, rather late in the day, the anti-semitism which had been totally absent from his movement before 1938, and indeed from the history of Italy since its unification.* However, Italian Fascism alone did not exercise much international attraction, even though it tried to inspire and finance similar movements elsewhere, and showed some influence in unexpected quarters, as on Vladimir Jabotinsky, the founder of Zionist "Revisionism," which became the government of Israel under Menachem Begin in the 1970s.

Without the triumph of Hitler in Germany in early 1933, fascism would not have become a general movement. In fact, all the fascist movements outside Italy that amounted to anything were founded after his arrival in power, notably the Hungarian Arrow Cross which scored 25 per cent of votes in the first secret ballot ever held in Hungary (1939), and the Romanian Iron Guard, whose real support was even greater. Indeed, even movements virtually financed entirely by Mussolini, like the Croatian *Ustashi* terrorists of Ante Pavelich, did not gain much ground, and become ideologically fascisized until the 1930s, when part of them also looked for inspiration and finance to Germany. More than this, without Hitler's triumph in Germany, the idea of fascism as a *universal* movement, a sort of Right-wing equivalent of international communism with Berlin as its Moscow, would not have developed. This did not produce a serious movement, but only, during the second World War, ideologically motivated collaborators with the Germans in occupied Europe. It was on this point that, notably in France, many on the traditional ultra-Right, however savagely reactionary, refused to follow:

*It should be said, in honour of Mussolini's countrymen, that during the war the Italian army flatly refused to deliver Jews for extermination to the Germans or anyone else in the areas it occupied—mainly south-eastern France and parts of the Balkans. Though the Italian administration also showed a conspicuous lack of zeal in the matter, about half of the small Italian Jewish population perished; some however, as anti-fascist militants rather than mere victims (Steinberg, 1990; Hughes, 1983).

they were nationalists or they were nothing. Some even joined the Resistance. Moreover, without the international standing of Germany as an evidently successful and rising world power, fascism would have had no serious impact outside Europe, nor indeed would non-fascist reactionary rulers have bothered to dress up as fascist sympathisers, as when Portugal's Salazar claimed in 1940 that he and Hitler were "linked by the same ideology" (Delzell, 1970, p. 348).

What the various brands of fascism had in common, other than—after 1933—a general sense of Germany hegemony, is not so easy to discern. Theory was not the strong point of movements devoted to the inadequacies of reason and rationalism and the superiority of instinct and will. They attracted all kinds of reactionary theorists in countries with an active conservative intellectual life—Germany is an obvious case in point—but these were decorative rather than structural elements of fascism. Mussolini could have readily dispensed with his house philosopher, Giovanni Gentile, and Hitler probably neither knew nor cared about the support of the philosopher Heidegger. Fascism cannot be identified either with a particular form of state organization, such as the corporate state—Nazi Germany lost interest in such ideas rapidly, all the more since they conflicted with the idea of a single undivided and total *Volksgemeinschaft*, or People's Community. Even so apparently central an element as racism was initially absent from Italian fascism. Conversely, of course, as we have seen, fascism shared nationalism, anti-communism, anti-liberalism etc. with other non-fascist elements on the Right. Several of these, notably among the non-fascist French reactionary groups, also shared with it a preference for politics as street violence.

The major difference between the fascist and the non-fascist Right was that fascism existed by mobilizing masses from below. It belonged essentially to the era of democratic and popular politics which traditional reactionaries deplored and which the champions of the "organic state" tried to by-pass. Fascism gloried in the mobilization of masses, and maintained it symbolically in the form of public theatre—the Nuremberg rallies, the masses on the Piazza Venezia looking up to Mussolini's gestures on his balcony—even when it came to power; as also did Communist movements. Fascists were the revolutionaries of counter-revolution: in their rhetoric, in their appeal to those who considered themselves victims of society, in their call for a total transformation of society, even in their deliberate adaptation of the symbols and names of the social revolutionaries, which is so obvious in Hitler's "*National Socialist Workers Party*" with its (modified) red flag and its immediate institution of the Reds' First of May as an official holiday in 1933.

Similarly, though fascism also specialized in the rhetoric of return to the traditional past, and received much support from classes of people who would genuinely have preferred to wipe out the past century if they could, it was in no real sense a traditionalist movement like, say, the Carlists of Navarra, who formed one of the main bodies of Franco's support in the Civil War or Gandhi's campaigns for a return to hand-looms and village ideals. It stressed many traditional *values*, which is another matter. They denounced liberal emancipation—women should stay at home and bear a great many children—and they distrusted the corroding influence of modern culture, and especially of the modernist arts, which the German National Socialists described as "cultural bolshevism" and degenerate. Yet the central fascist movements—the Italian and the German—did not appeal to those historic guardians of the conservative order, Church and King, but on the contrary sought to supplant them by an entirely non-traditional leadership principle embodied in self-made men legitimized by their mass support, and by secular ideologies, and sometimes cults.

The past to which they appealed was an artefact. Their traditions were invented. Even Hitler's racism was not the pride in an unbroken and unmixed line of kinship descent which provides genealogists with commissions from Americans who hope to prove their descent from some sixteenth-century Suffolk yeoman, but a late nineteenth-century post-Darwinian farrago claiming (and, alas, in Germany often receiving) the support of the new science of genetics, or more precisely of that branch of applied genetics ("eugenics") which dreamed of creating a human super-race by selective breeding and the elimination of the unfit. The race destined through Hitler to dominate the world did not even have a name until 1898 when an anthropologist coined the term "Nordic." Hostile as it was on principle to the heritage of the eighteenth-century Enlightenment and the French revolution, fascism could not formally believe in modernity and progress, but it had no difficulty in combining a lunatic set of beliefs with technological modernity in practical matters, except where it crippled its basic scientific research on ideological grounds (see chapter 18). Fascism was triumphantly anti-liberal. It also provided the proof that men can, without difficulty, combine crack-brained beliefs about the world with a confident mastery of contemporary high technology. The late twentieth century, with its fundamentalist sects wielding the weapons of television and computer-programmed fund-raising, have made us more familiar with this phenomenon.

Nevertheless, the combination of conservative values, the techniques of mass democracy, and an innovative ideology of irrationalist savagery, essentially centered in nationalism, must be explained. Such non-traditional movements of the radical Right had emerged in several European countries in the late nineteenth century in reaction against both liberalism (i.e. the accelerating transformation of societies by capitalism) and the rising socialist working-class movements, and, more generally, against the tide of foreigners that was sweeping across the world in the greatest mass migration of history up to that date. Men and women migrated not only across oceans and international frontiers, but from country to city; from one region of the same state to another—in short from "home" to the land of strangers and, turning the coin round, as strangers into others' home. Almost fifteen out of every hundred Poles left their country for good plus half a million a year as seasonal migrants—overwhelmingly, as such migrants did, to join the working classes of the receiving countries. Anticipating the late twentieth century, the late nineteenth pioneered mass xenophobia, of which racism—the protection of the pure native stock against contamination, or even submersion, by the invading subhuman hordes—became the common expression. Its strength can be measured not only by the fear of Polish immigration which led the great German liberal sociologist Max Weber into temporary support for the Pangerman League, but by the increasingly febrile campaign against mass immigration in the U.S.A., which eventually, during and after the First World War, led the country of the Statue of Liberty to bar its frontiers to those whom the Statue had been erected to welcome.

The common cement of these movements was the resentment of little men in a society that crushed them between the rock of big business on one side and the hard place of rising mass labour movements on the other. Or which, at the very least, deprived them of the respectable position they had occupied in the social order, and believed to be their due, or the social status in a dynamic society to which they felt they had a right to aspire. These sentiments found their characteristic expression in anti-semitism, which began to develop specific political movements based on hostility to the Jews in the last quarter of the nineteenth century in several countries. Jews were almost universally present, and could readily symbolize all that was most hateful about an unfair world, not least its commitment to the ideas of the Enlightenment and the French revolution which had emancipated them, and in doing so had made them so much more visible. They could serve as symbols of the hated capitalist/financier; of the revolutionary agitator; of the corroding influence of "rootless intellectuals" and the new mass media; of the competition—how could it be otherwise than "unfair"?—that gave them a disproportionate share of jobs in certain professions requiring education; and of the foreigner and outsider as such. Not to mention the accepted view among old-fashioned Christians that they had killed Jesus Christ.

Dislike of Jews was indeed pervasive in the Western world, and their position in nineteenth-century society was indeed ambiguous. Yet the fact that striking workers were apt, even when members of non-racist labour movements, to attack Jewish shopkeepers, and to think of their employers as Jews (often enough correctly, in large zones of central and eastern Europe), should not lead us into seeing them as proto-National Socialists, any more than the matter-of-course anti-semitism of Edwardian British liberal intellectuals, such as the Bloomsbury Group, made them into sympathisers of *political* anti-semites of the radical Right. The peasant anti-semitism of east-central Europe, where for practical purposes the Jew was the point of contact between the livelihood of the villager and the outside economy on which it depended, was certainly more permanent and explosive, and became more so as Slav, Magyar or Romanian rural societies became increasingly convulsed by the incomprehensible earthquakes of the modern world. Among such dark people tales of Jews sacrificing Christian children could still be believed, and moments of social explosion would lead to *pogroms*, which reactionaries in the Tsar's Empire encouraged, especially after the assassination of Tsar Alexander II in 1881 by social revolutionaries. Here a straight road leads from original grassroots anti-semitism to the extermination of Jewry during the Second World War. Certainly grassroots anti-semitism gave such Eastern European Fascist movements as acquired a mass base—notably the Romanian Iron Guard and the Hungarian Arrow Cross—their foundation. At all events, in the former territories of Habsburg and Romanov this connection was much clearer than in the German Reich, where grassroots rural and provincial anti-semitism, though strong and deeply rooted, was also less violent: one might even say, more tolerant. Jews who escaped from newly occupied Vienna to Berlin in 1938 were astonished at the absence of street anti-semitism. Here violence came by decree from above, as in November 1938 (Kershaw, 1983). Yet even so, there is no comparison between the casual and intermittent savagery of the pogroms and what was to come a generation later. The handful of dead of 1881, the forty to fifty of the Kishinev pogrom of 1903, outraged the world—and justifiably—because in the days before the advance of barbarism, such a number of victims seemed intolerable to a world which expected civilization to advance. Even the much larger pogroms that accompanied the mass peasant risings of the 1905 Russian revolution had, by later standards, only modest casualties—perhaps eight hundred dead in all. This may be compared with the 3,800 Jews killed in Vilnius

(Vilna) by the Lithuanians in three days of 1941 as the Germans invaded the U.S.S.R., and before the systematic exterminations got under way.

The new movements in the radical Right which appealed to, but fundamentally transformed, these older traditions of intolerance, appealed particularly to the lower and middle groups of European societies, and were formulated as rhetoric and theory by nationalist intellectuals who emerged as a trend in the 1890s. The very term "nationalism" was coined in that decade to describe these new spokesmen of reaction. Middle and lower-middle-class militancy took a turn to the radical Right chiefly in countries where the ideologies of democracy and liberalism were not dominant, or among classes which did not identify with them, that is to say, chiefly in countries which had not undergone a French revolution or its equivalent. Indeed, in the core countries of Western Liberalism— Britain, France, and the U.S.A.—the general hegemony of the revolutionary tradition prevented the emergence of any mass fascist movements of importance. It is a mistake to confuse the racism of American Populists or the chauvinism of French Republicans with proto-Fascism: these were movements of the Left.

This did not mean that, once the hegemony of Liberty, Equality and Fraternity no longer stood in the way, old instincts might not attach themselves to new political slogans. There is little doubt that the activists of the Swastika in the Austrian Alps were to be largely recruited from the sort of provincial professionals—veterinary surgeons, surveyors and the like—who had once been the local Liberals, an educated and emancipated minority in an environment dominated by peasant clericalism. Just so, in the later twentieth century, the disintegration of the classical proletarian labour and socialist movements left the instinctive chauvinism and racism of so many manual workers free play. Hitherto, while far from immune to such sentiments, they had hesitated to express them in public out of loyalty to parties passionately hostile to such bigotry. Since the 1960s Western xenophobia and political racism is found mainly among the manual labouring strata. However, in the decades when fascism was incubated, it belonged to those who did not get their hands dirty at work.

The middle and lower-middle strata remained the backbone of such movements thoughout the era of the rise of fascism. This is not seriously denied even by historians anxious to revise the consensus of "virtually" every analysis of Nazi support produced between 1930 and 1980 (Childers, 1983; Childers, 1991, pp. 8, 14-15). To take merely one case among the many enquires into the membership and support of such movements in inter-war Austria. Of the National Socialists elected as district councillors in Vienna in 1932, 18 per cent were self-employed, 56 per cent were white-collar, office workers and public employees, and 14 per cent were blue-collar. Of the Nazis elected in five Austrian assemblies outside Vienna in the same year, 16 per cent were self-employed and farmers, fifty-one were office-workers etc. and 10 per cent were blue-collars (Larsen et al., 1978, pp. 766–67).

This does not mean that Fascist movements could not acquire genuine mass support among the labouring poor. Whatever the composition of its cadres, the Romanian Iron Guard's support came from the poor peasantry. The Hungarian Arrow Cross electorate was largely working-class (the Communist Party being illegal and the Social Democratic Party, always small, paying the price for its toleration by the Horthy regime) and, after the defeat of Austrian Social Democracy in 1934, there was a noticeable swing of workers to the Nazi Party, especially in the Austrian provinces. Moreover, once fascist governments with public legitimacy had established themselves, as in Italy and Germany, far more formerly socialist and communist workers than the Left tradition likes to dwell on, fell into line with the new regimes. Nevertheless, since fascist movements had trouble in appealing to the genuinely traditional elements in rural society (unless reinforced, as in Croatia, by organizations like the Roman Catholic Church), and were the sworn enemies of the ideologies and parties identified with the organised working classes, their core constituency was naturally to be found in the middle strata of society.

How far into the middle class the original appeal of fascism extended is a more open question. Certainly its appeal to middle-class youth was strong, especially to Continental European university students who, between the wars, were notoriously on the ultra-Right. Thirteen per cent of the members of the Italian Fascist movement in 1921 (i.e. before the "March on Rome") were students. In Germany between 5 and 10 per cent of all students were party members as early as 1930, when the great majority of future Nazis had not begun to take an interest in Hitler (Kater, 1985, p. 467; Noelle/Neumann, 1967, p. 196). As we shall see, the element of middle-class ex-officers was strongly represented: the sort for whom the Great War, with all its horrors, marked a mountain-peak of personal achievement, from which the view showed only the disappointing lowlands of their future civilian life. These were, of course, segments of the middle strata particularly receptive to the appeals of activism. Broadly speaking, the appeal of the radical Right was the stronger, the greater the threat to the standing, actual or conventionally expected, of a middle-class occupation, as the framework buckled and broke that was supposed to hold their social order in place. In Germany the double blow of the Great Inflation which reduced the value of money to zero, and the subsequent Great Slump, radicalized even strata of the middle class such as middle and higher civil servants, whose position seemed secure, and who would, under less traumatic circumstances, have been happy to continue as old-style conservative patriots, nostalgic for Kaiser William, but willing to do their duty to a Republic headed by Field Marshal Hindenburg, had it not been visibly collapsing under their feet. Most nonpolitical Germans between the wars looked back to William's empire. As late as the 1960s, when most West Germans had (understandably) concluded that the best times in German history were *now*, 42 per cent of those over sixty years old still thought that the time before 1914 was better than the present, as against 32 per cent who were converted by the *Wirtschafts-wunder* (Noelle/Neumann, 1967, p. 196). The voters of the bourgeois Centre and Right defected in massive numbers to the Nazi Party between 1930 and 1932. Yet these were not the builders of fascism.

Such conservative middle classes were, of course, potential supporters or even converts to fascism, because of the way the inter-war lines of political battle were drawn. The threat to liberal society and all its values seemed to come exclusively from the Right; the threat to the social order from the Left. Middle-class people chose their politics according to their fears. Traditional conservatives usually sympathized with the demagogues of fascism and were prepared to ally with them against the major enemy. Italian Fascism had a rather good press in the 1920s and even in the 1930s, except from Liberalism leftwards. "But for the bold experiment of fascism the decade has not been fruitful in constructive statesmanship," wrote John Buchan, the eminent British Conservative and thriller-writer. (A taste for writing thrillers has, alas, rarely gone with left-wing convictions.) (Graves/Hodge, 1941, p. 248.) Hitler was brought to power by a coalition of the traditional Right, which he subsequently swallowed. General Franco included the then not very significant Spanish *Falange* in his national front, because what he represented was the union of the entire Right against the spectres of 1789 and 1917, between which he did not make fine distinctions. He was lucky enough not actually to join in the Second World War on Hitler's side, but he sent a volunteer force, the "Blue Division," to fight the godless communists in Russia side by side with the Germans. Marshal Pétain was certainly not a fascist or Nazi sympathiser. One reason why it was so difficult after the war to distinguish between wholehearted French fascists and pro-German collaborators on one hand, and the main body of support for Marshal Pétain's Vichy regime on the other, was that there was in fact no clear line. Those whose fathers had hated Dreyfus, the Jews and the bitch-Republic—some Vichy figures were old enough to have done so themselves—shaded insensibly into the zealots for a Hitlerian Europe. In short, the "natural" alliance of the Right between the wars went from traditional conservatives via old-style reactionaries to the outer fringes of fascist pathology. The traditional forces of conservatism and counter-revolution were strong, but often inert. Fascism provided them both with a dynamic and, perhaps even more important, with the example of victory over the forces of disorder. (Was not the proverbial argument in favour of fascist Italy, that "Mussolini made the trains run on time"?) Just as the dynamism of the communists exercised an attraction on the disoriented and rudderless Left after 1933, so the successes of fascism, especially after the National Socialist takeover in Germany, made it look like the wave of the future. The very fact that at this time fascism made a prominent, if brief, entrance on—of all countries—the political scene of Conservative Great Britain, demonstrates the power of this "demonstration effect." That it converted one of the most prominent of the nation's politicians and won the support of one of its major press-lords is more significant than the fact that Sir Oswald Mosley's movement was quickly abandoned by respectable politicians and Lord Rothermere's *Daily Mail* soon dropped its support of the British Union of Fascists. For Britain was still universally and rightly seen as a model of political and social stability.

III

The rise of the radical Right after the First World War was undoubtedly a response to the danger, indeed to the reality, of social revolution and working-class power in general, to the October revolution and Leninism in particular. Without these, there would have been no fascism, for though the demagogic Right-wing Ultras had been politically vocal and aggressive in a number of European countries since the end of the nineteenth century, they had almost invariably been kept well under control before 1914. To this extent apologists for fascism are probably right in holding that Lenin engendered Mussolini and Hitler. However, it is entirely illegitimate to exculpate fascist barbarism by claiming that it was inspired by and imitated the allegedly earlier barbarities of the Russian Revolution, as some German historians came close to doing in the 1980s (Nolte, 1987).

However, two important qualifications must be made to the thesis that the Right backlash was essentially a response to the revolutionary Left. First, it underestimates the impact of the First World War on an important stratum of, largely middle and lower middle-class, nationalist soldiers or young men who, after November 1918, resented their missed chance of heroism. The so-called "front-line soldier" (*frontsoldat*) was to play a most important part in the mythology of radical-Right movements—Hitler was one himself—and it was to provide a substantial bloc of the first ultra-nationalist strong-arm squads, such as the officers who murdered the German communist leaders Karl Liebknecht and Rosa Luxemburg in early 1919, the Italian *squadristi* and German *freikorps.* Fifty-seven per cent of the early Italian fascists were ex-servicemen. As we have seen, the First World War was a machine for brutalizing the world, and these men gloried in the release of their latent brutality.

The strong commitment of the Left, from the liberals onwards, to anti-war and anti-militarist movements, the huge popular revulsion against the mass killing of the First World War, led many to under-estimate the emergence of a relatively small, but absolutely numerous, minority for whom the experience of fighting, even under the conditions of 1914–18, was central and inspirational; for whom uniform and discipline, sacrifice—of self and others—and blood, arms and power were what made masculine life worth living. They did not write many books about the war, though (especially in Germany) one or two did. These Rambos of their time were natural recruits for the radical Right.

The second qualification is that the Right-wing backlash responded not against Bolshevism as such, but against all movements, and notably the organized working class, which threatened the existing order of soci-ety or could be blamed for its breakdown. Lenin was the symbol of this threat rather than the actual reality, which, for most politicians, was rep-resented not so much by the socialist labour parties, whose leaders were moderate enough, but by the upsurge of working-class power, confidence and radicalism, which gave the old socialist parties a new political force and, in fact, made them the indispensable props of liberal states. It is no accident that in the immediate post-war years the central demand of so-cialist agitators since 1889 was conceded almost everywhere in Europe: the eight-hour day.

It was the threat implicit in the rise of labour's power which froze the blood of conservatives, rather than the mere transformation of labour union leaders and opposition orators into government ministers, though this was bitter enough. They belonged by definition to "the Left." In an era of social upheaval, no clear line divided them from the Bolsheviks. In-deed, many of the socialist parties would have happily joined the com-munists in the immediate post-war years, had these not rejected their affiliation. The man whom Mussolini had assassinated after his "March on Rome" was not a CP leader but the Socialist, Matteotti. The traditional Right may have seen godless Russia as the embodiment of all that was evil in the world, but the rising of the Generals in 1936 was not directed against the communists as such if only because these were the smallest part of the Popular Front (see chapter 5). It was directed against a popular upsurge which, until the Civil War, favoured Socialists and Anarchists. It is an ex post facto rationalization which makes Lenin and Stalin the excuse for fascism.

And yet, what must be explained is why the Right-wing backlash after the First World War won its crucial victories in the form of fascism. For extremist movements of the ultra-Right had existed before 1914—hysterically nationalist and xenophobic, idealising war and violence, intolerant and given to strong-arm coercion, passionately anti-liberal, anti-democratic, anti-proletarian, anti-socialist and anti-rationalist, dreaming of blood and soil and a return to the values which modernity was disrupting. They had some political influence, within the political Right, and in some intellectual circles, but nowhere did they dominate or control.

What gave them their chance after the First World War, was the collapse of the old regimes and, with them, of the old ruling classes and their machinery of power, influence and hegemony. Where these remained in good working order, there was no need for fascism. It made no progress in Britain, in spite of the brief flurry of nerves noted above. The traditional Conservative Right remained in control. It made no effective progress in France until after the defeat of 1940. Though the traditional French radical Right—the monarchist *Action Française* and Colonel La Rocque's *Croix de Feu* (Fiery Cross)—were ready enough to beat up Leftists, it was not strictly fascist. Indeed, some elements of it would even join the Resistance.

Again, fascism was not needed where a new nationalist ruling class or group could take over in newly independent countries. These men could be reactionary and might well opt for authoritarian government, for reasons to be considered below, but it was rhetoric that identified every turn to the antidemocratic Right in Europe between the wars with fascism. There were no fascist movements of importance in the new Poland, which was run by authoritarian militarists and in the Czech part of Czechoslovakia, which was democratic, nor in the (dominant) Serbian core of the new Yugoslavia. Where significant fascist or similar movements existed in countries whose rulers were old-fashioned Right-wingers or reactionaries—in Hungary, Romania, Finland, even in Franco's Spain, whose leader was not himself a fascist—they had little trouble in keeping them under control unless (as in Hungary in 1944) the Germans put the screws on them. This does not mean that minority nationalist movements in old or new states might not find fascism attractive, if only because they could expect financial and political support from Italy and, after 1933, from Germany. This was clearly so in (Belgian) Flanders, in Slovakia and in Croatia.

The optimal conditions for the triumph of the crazy ultra-Right were an old state and its ruling mechanisms which could no longer function; a mass of disenchanted, disoriented and discontented citizens who no longer knew where their loyalties lay; strong socialist movements threatening or appearing to threaten social revolution, but not actually in a position to achieve it; and a move of nationalist resentment against the peace treaties of 1918–20. These were the conditions in which helpless old ruling elites were tempted to have recourse to the ultra-radicals, as the Italian Liberals did to Mussolini's fascists in 1920–22 and as the German Conservatives did to Hitler's National Socialists in 1932–33. These, by the same token, were the conditions that turned movements of the radical Right into powerful organized and sometimes uniformed and paramilitary forces (*squadristi*; storm-troopers) or, as in Germany during the Great Slump, into massive electoral armies. However, in neither of the two fascist states did fascism "conquer power," though in both Italy and Germany it made much of the rhetoric of "capturing the street" and "marching on Rome." In both cases fascism came to power by the connivance of, indeed (as in Italy) on the initiative of, the old regime, that is to say in a "constitutional" fashion.

The novelty of fascism was that, once in power, it refused to play the old political games, and took over completely where it could. The total transfer of power, or the elimination of all rivals, took rather longer in Italy (1922–28) than in Germany (1933–34) but, once it was achieved, there were no further internal political limits on what became, characteristically, the untrammeled dictatorship of a supreme populist "leader" (*Duce; Führer*).

At this point we must briefly dismiss two equally inadequate theses about fascism, the one fascist, but taken over by many liberal historians, the other dear to orthodox Soviet Marxism. There was no "fascist revolution" and neither was fascism the expression of "monopoly capitalism" or big business.

Fascist movements had the elements of revolutionary movements, inasmuch as they contained people who wanted a fundamental transformation of society, often with a notably anti-capitalist and anti-oligarchic edge. However, the horse of revolutionary fascism failed either to start or to run. Hitler rapidly eliminated those who took the "socialist" component in the name of the National Socialist German Workers' Party seriously—as he certainly did not. The utopia of a return to some kind of little man's Middle Ages, full of hereditary peasant-proprietors, artisan craftsmen like Hans Sachs and girls in blonde plaits, was not a programme that could be realized in major twentieth-century states (except in the nightmare version of Himmler's plans for a racially purified people), least of all in regimes which, like Italian and German Fascism, were committed in their way to modernisation and technological advance.

What National Socialism certainly achieved was a radical purging of the old Imperial elites and institutional structures. After all, the only group which actually launched a revolt against Hitler—and was consequently decimated—was the old aristocratic Prussian army in July 1944. This destruction of the old elites and the old frameworks, reinforced after the war by the policies of the occupying Western armies, was eventually to make it possible to build the Federal Republic on a much sounder basis than the Weimar Republic of 1918–33, which had been little more than the defeated empire minus the Kaiser. Nazism certainly had, and partly achieved, a social programme for the masses: holidays; sports; the planned "people's car," which the world came to know after the Second World War as the *Volkswagen* "beetle." Its chief achievement, however, was to liquidate the Great Slump more effectively than any other government, for the anti-liberalism of the Nazis had the positive side that it did not commit them to an *a priori* belief in the free market. Nevertheless, Nazism was a revamped and revitalized old regime rather than a basically new and different one. Like the imperial and militarist Japan of the 1930s (which nobody would claim to have been a revolutionary system), it was a non-liberal capitalist economy which achieved a striking dynamization of its industrial system. The economic and other achievements of fascist Italy were considerably less impressive, as was demonstrated in the Second World War. Its war economy was unusually feeble. Talk of a "fascist revolution" was rhetoric, though no doubt for many Italian rank-and-file fascists sincere rhetoric. It was much more openly a regime in the interests of the old ruling classes, having come into existence as a defence against post-1918 revolutionary unrest rather than, like in Germany, as a reaction to the traumas of the Great Slump and the inability of Weimar governments to cope with them. Italian fascism, which in one sense carried on the process of Italian unification from the nineteenth century, thus producing a stronger and more centralized government, had some significant achievements to its credit. It was, for instance, the only Italian regime successfully to suppress the Sicilian

Mafia and the Neapolitan Camorra. Yet its historical significance lay, not in its aims and achievements, but in its role as the global pioneer of a new version of the triumphant counter-revolution. Mussolini inspired Hitler, and Hitler never failed to acknowledge Italian inspiration and priority. On the other hand Italian fascism was, and for a long time remained, an anomaly among radical Right-wing movements in its toleration of, even a certain taste for, artistic avantgarde "modernism," and in some other respects—notably, until Mussolini fell into line with Germany in 1938, a complete lack of interest in anti-semitic racism.

As for the "monopoly capitalist" thesis, the point about really big business is that it can come to terms with any regime that does not actually expropriate it, and any regime must come to terms with it. Fascism was no more "the expression of the interests of monopoly capital" than the American New Deal or British Labour governments, or the Weimar Republic. Big business in the early 1930s did not particularly want Hitler, and would have preferred more orthodox conservatism. It gave him little support until the Great Slump, and even then support was late and patchy. However, when he came to power, business collaborated wholeheartedly, up to the point of using slave labour and extermination camp labour for its operations during the Second World War. Large and small business, of course, benefited from the expropriation of the Jews.

It must nevertheless be said that fascism had some major advantages for business over other regimes. First, it eliminated or defeated Left-wing social revolution, and indeed seemed to be the main bulwark against it. Second, it eliminated labour unions and other limitations on the rights of management to manage its workforce. Indeed, the fascist "leadership principle" was what most bosses and business executives applied to their subordinates in their own businesses and fascism gave it authoritative justification. Third, the destruction of labour movements helped to secure an unduly favourable solution of the Depression for business. Whereas in the U.S.A. the top 5 per cent of consuming units between 1929 and 1941 saw their share of total (national) income fall by 20 per cent (there was a similar but more modest egalitarian trend in Britain and Scandinavia), in Germany the top 5 per cent gained 15 per cent during the comparable period (Kuznets, 1956). Finally, as already noted, fascism was good at dynamising and modernising industrial economies—although actually not as good at adventurous and long-term techno-scientific planning as the Western democracies.

IV

Would fascism have become very significant in world history but for the Great Slump? Probably not. Italy alone was not a promising base from which to shake the world. In the 1920s no other European movement of radical Right counter-revolution looked as though it had much of a future, for much the same reason as insurrectionary attempts at communist social revolution failed: the post-1917 revolutionary wave had ebbed, and the economy seemed to recover. In Germany the pillars of imperial society, generals, civil servants and the rest, had indeed given some backing to the free-lance paramilitaries and other wild men of the Right after the November revolution, though (understandably) putting their main effort in keeping the new republic conservative, anti-revolutionary and, above all, a state capable of maintaining some international room for manoeuvre. However, when forced to choose, as during the Right-wing Kapp Putsch of 1920 and the Munich revolt of 1923, in which Adolf Hitler first found himself in the headlines, they unhesitatingly backed the status quo. After the economic upturn of 1924, the National Socialist Workers' Party was reduced to a rump of 2.5–3 per cent of the electorate, scoring little more than half of even the small and civilised German Democratic Party, little more than a fifth of the communists and well under a tenth of the Social Democrats in the elections of 1928. Yet two years later it had risen to over 18 per cent of the electorate, the second-strongest party in German politics. Four years later, in the summer of 1932, it was by far the strongest, with over 37 per cent of the total vote, though it did not maintain this support while democratic elections lasted. It was patently the Great Slump which turned Hitler from a phenomenon of the political fringe into the potential, and eventually the actual, master of the country.

However, even the Great Slump would not have given fascism either the force or the influence it plainly exercised in the 1930s, if it had not brought a movement of this kind to power in Germany, a state destined by its size, economic and military potential, and, not least, geographical position, to play a major political role in Europe under any form of government. Utter defeat in two world wars has, after all, not prevented Germany from ending the twentieth century as the dominant state on that continent. Just as, on the Left, the victory of Marx in the largest state of the globe ("one sixth of the world's land surface," as communists liked to boast between the wars) gave communism a major international presence, even at times when its political force outside the U.S.S.R. was negligible, so the capture of Germany by Hitler appeared to confirm the success of Mussolini's Italy and to turn fascism into a powerful global political current. The successful policy of aggressive militarist expansionism by both states (see chapter 5)—reinforced by that of Japan—dominated the international politics of the decade. It was therefore natural that suitable states or movements should be attracted and influenced by fascism, should seek the support of Germany and Italy, and—given these countries' expansionism—should often receive it.

In Europe, for obvious reasons, such movements belonged overwhelmingly to the political Right. Thus within Zionism (which at this time was overwhelmingly a movement of Ashkenazic Jews living in Europe), that wing of the movement which looked towards Italian fascism, Vladimir Jabotinsky's "Revisionists," were clearly seen and classified themselves on the Right, against the (predominant) socialist and liberal Zionist bodies. Yet the influence of fascism in the 1930s could not but be to some extent global, if only because it was associated with two dynamic and active powers. Yet outside Europe the conditions which created fascist movements in the home continent hardly existed. Hence, where fascist, or plainly fascist-influenced movements emerged, their political location and function was far more problematic.

Of course certain characteristics of European fascism found an echo overseas. It would have been surprising if the Mufti of Jerusalem and other Arabs resisting Jewish colonization in Palestine (and the British who protected it) had not found Hitler's anti-semitism to their liking, though it bore no relation to the traditional modes of Islamic coexistence with unbelievers of various kinds. Some upper-caste Hindus in India were, like modern Sinhalese extremists in Sri Lanka, conscious of their superiority as certified—indeed as the original—"Aryans" to darker races on their own subcontinent. And the Boer militants who were interned as pro-Germans during the Second World War—some became their country's leaders in the era of apartheid after 1948—also had ideological affinities with Hitler, both as convinced racists and through the theological influence of elitist ultra-Right-wing Calvinist currents in the Netherlands. Yet this hardly qualifies the basic proposition that fascism, unlike communism, was non-existent in Asia and Africa (except perhaps among some local European settlers) because it appeared to have no bearing on the local political situations.

This is broadly true even of Japan, though that country was allied to Germany and Italy, fought on the same side in the Second World War, and its politics were dominated by the Right. The affinities between the dominant ideologies of the eastern and western ends of the "Axis" are indeed strong. The Japanese were second to none in their conviction of racial superiority and the need for racial purity in their belief in the military virtues of self-sacrifice, absolute obedience to orders, self-abnegation and stoicism. Every Samurai would have subscribed to the motto of Hitler's SS ("Meine Ehre ist Treue," best translated as "Honour means blind subordination"). Theirs was a society of rigid hierarchy, of the total dedication of the individual (if such a term had any local meaning in the Western sense at all) to the nation and its divine Emperor, and the utter rejection of Liberty, Equality and Fraternity. The Japanese had no trouble in understanding the Wagnerian brand of myths about barbarian gods, pure and heroic medieval knights and the specifically German nature of mountain and forest, both filled with German *voelkisch* dreams. They had the same capacity to combine barbaric behaviour with a sophisticated aesthetic sensibility: the concentration camp torturer's taste for playing Schubert quartets. Insofar as fascism could have been translated into Zen terms, the Japanese might well have welcomed it, though they had no need of it. And indeed, among the diplomats accredited to the European fascist powers, but especially among the ultra-nationalist terror groups given to assassinating insufficiently patriotic politicians, and in the Kwantung army which was conquering, holding and enslaving Manchuria and China, there were Japanese who recognized these affinities and campaigned for closer identification with the European fascist powers.

Yet European fascism could not be reduced to an oriental feudalism with an imperial national mission. It belonged essentially to the era of democracy and the common man, while the very concept of a "movement" of mass mobilization for novel, indeed for would-be revolutionary purposes, behind self-selected leaders, made no sense in Hirohito's Japan. The Prussian army and tradition, rather than Hitler, fitted their view of the world. In short, despite the similarities with German national socialism (the affinities with Italy were far less), Japan was not fascist.

As for the states and movements which looked for support from Germany and Italy, especially during the Second World War when the Axis looked very much like winning, ideology was not their major motive, though some of the minor nationalist regimes in Europe, whose position depended entirely on German backing, readily advertised themselves as more Nazi than the SS, notably the Croatian Ustashi state. Yet it would be absurd to think of the Irish Republican Army or the Berlin-based Indian nationalists as in any sense "fascist" because, in the Second World War as in the First, some of them negotiated for German support on the principle that "my enemy's enemy is my friend." Indeed, the Irish Republican leader Frank Ryan, who entered such negotiations, was ideologically so anti-fascist that he had actually joined the International Brigades to fight General Franco in the Spanish Civil War, before being captured by Franco's forces and sent to Germany. Such cases need not detain us.

However, there remains a continent on which the ideological impact of European fascism is undeniable: the Americas.

In North America men and movements inspired by Europe were not of great significance outside particular immigrant communities whose members brought the ideologies of the old country with them, as the Scandinavians and Jews had brought a proclivity towards socialism, or who retained some loyalty to the country of their origin. Thus the sentiments of German—and to a much smaller extent, Italian—Americans contributed to U.S. isolationism, though there is no good evidence that they became fascists in large numbers. The paraphernalia of militias, coloured shirts and arms raised in salutes to leaders did not belong to the native Right-wing and racist mobilizations, of which the Ku Klux Klan was the most familiar. Anti-semitism was certainly strong, though its contemporary Right-wing U.S. version—as in Father Coughlin's popular radio sermons out of Detroit—probably owed more to the Right-wing corporatism of European Catholic inspiration. It is characteristic of the U.S.A. in the 1930s that the most successful and possibly dangerous demagogic populism of the decade, Huey Long's conquest of Louisiana, came from what was, in American terms, a clearly radical and Left-wing tradition. It cut down democracy in the name of democracy and appealed, not to the resentments of a petty-bourgeoisie or the anti-revolutionary instincts of self-preservation of the rich, but to the egalitarianism of the poor. Nor was it racist. No movement whose slogan was "Every Man a King" could belong in the fascist tradition.

It was in Latin America that European fascist influence was to be open and acknowledged, both on individual politicians, like Colombia's Jorge Eliezer Gaitán (1898–1948) and Argentina's Juan Domingo Perón (1895–1974), and on regimes, like Getulio Vargas' *Estado Novo* (New State) of 1937–45 in Brazil. In fact, and in spite of baseless U.S. fears of Nazi encirclement from the south, the main effect of fascist influence in Latin America was domestic. Apart from Argentina, which clearly favoured the Axis—but did so before Perón took power in 1943 as well as after—the governments of the Western hemisphere joined the war on the U.S. side, at least nominally. It is, however, true that in some South American countries their military had been modelled on the German system or trained by German or even Nazi cadres.

Fascist influence south of the Rio Grande is easily explained. Seen from the south, the U.S. after 1914 no longer looked, as it had in the nineteenth century, like the ally of the domestic forces of progress and the diplomatic counterweight to the imperial or ex-imperial Spaniards, French and British. U.S. imperial conquests from Spain in 1898, the Mexican revolution, not to mention the rise of the oil and banana industries, introduced an anti-Yankee anti-imperialism into Latin American politics, and one which the obvious taste of Washington in the first third of the century for gunboat diplomacy and landing marines did nothing to discourage. Victor Raul Haya de la Torre, founder of the anti-imperialist APRA (American Popular Revolutionary Alliance) whose ambitions were pan-Latin American, even if APRA only established itself in his native Peru, planned to have his insurrectionaries trained by the cadres of the celebrated anti-Yankee rebel Sandino in Nicaragua. (Sandino's long guerrilla war against U.S. occupation after 1927 was to inspire the "Sandinista" revolution in Nicaragua in the 1980s.) Moreover, the U.S.A. of the 1930s, enfeebled by the Great Slump, did not look anything like as formidable and dominant as before. Franklin D. Roosevelt's abandonment of the gunboats and marines of his predecessors could be seen not only as a "good neighbour policy" but also (mistakenly) as a sign of weakness. Latin America in the 1930s was not inclined to look north.

But, seen from across the Atlantic, fascism undoubtedly looked like the success story of the decade. If there was a model in the world to be imitated by up-and-coming politicians of a continent that had always taken its inspiration from the culturally hegemonic regions, such potential leaders of countries always on the look-out for the recipe to become modern, rich and great, it was surely to be found in Berlin and Rome, since London and Paris no longer provided much political inspiration and Washington was out of action. (Moscow was still seen essentially as a model for social revolution, which restricted its political appeal.)

And yet, how different from their European models were the political activities and achievements of men who made no bones about their intellectual debt to Mussolini and Hitler! I still recall my shock at hearing the President of revolutionary Bolivia admitting it without hesitation in a private conversation. In Bolivia soldiers and politicians with their eye on Germany found themselves organizing the revolution of 1952 which nationalized the tin-mines and gave the Indian peasantry radical land reform. In Colombia the great people's tribune Jorge Eliezer Gaitán, so far from choosing the political Right, captured the leadership of the Liberal Party and would certainly as president have led it in a radical direction, had he not been assassinated in Bogotá on 9 April 1948, an event which provoked the *immediate* popular insurrection of the capital (including its police) and the proclamation of revolutionary communes in many a provincial municipality of the country. What Latin American leaders took from European fascism was its deification of populist leaders with a reputation for action. But the masses they wanted to mobilize, and found themselves mobilizing, were not those who feared for what they might lose, but those who had nothing to lose. And the enemies against whom they mobilized them were not foreigners and outgroups (even though the element of anti-semitism in Perónist, or other Argentine politics is undeniable), but "the oligarchy"—the rich, the local ruling class. Perón found his core support in the Argentine working class, and his basic political machine in something like a labour party built around the mass labour union movement he fostered. Getulio Vargas in Brazil made the same discovery. It was the army that overthrew him in 1945 and, again, forced him into suicide in 1954. It was the urban working class, to which he had given social protection in return for political support, which mourned him as the father of his people. European fascist regimes destroyed labour movements, the Latin American leaders they inspired created them. Whatever the intellectual filiation, historically, we cannot speak of the same kind of movement.

V

Yet these movements too must be seen as part of the decline and fall of liberalism in the Age of Catastrophe. For if the rise and triumph of fascism was the most dramatic expression of the liberal retreat, it is a mistake, even in the 1930s, to see this retreat exclusively in terms of fascism. So at the conclusion of this chapter we must ask how it is to be explained. However, a common confusion which identifies fascism and nationalism must first be cleared away.

That fascist movements tended to appeal to nationalist passions and prejudices is obvious, though the semi-fascist corporate states, like Portugal and Austria 1934–38, being largely under Catholic inspiration, had to reserve their unqualified hatred for peoples and nations of another religion or godless ones. Moreover, simple nationalism was difficult for local fascist movements in countries conquered and occupied by Germany or Italy, or whose fortunes depended on the victory of those states against their own national governments. In suitable cases (Flanders, the Netherlands, Scandinavia) they could identify themselves with the Germans as part of a greater Teutonic racial group, but a more convenient stance (strongly backed by Dr. Goebbels' propaganda during the war), was paradoxically *internationalist*. Germany was seen as the core and only guarantee of a future *European order*, with the usual appeals to Charlemagne and anti-communism; a phase in the development of the European idea on which historians of the post-war European Community do not much like to dwell. The non-German military units which fought under the German flag in the Second World War, mainly as part of the SS, usually stressed this transnational element.

On the other hand it ought to be equally obvious that not all nationalisms sympathized with fascism, and not only because the ambitions of Hitler, and to a lesser extent Mussolini, threatened a number of them— e.g. the Poles and the Czechs. Indeed, as we shall see (chapter 5) in a number of countries mobilisation against fascism was to produce a patriotism of the Left, especially during the war, when resistance to the Axis was conducted by "national fronts" or governments spanning the entire political spectrum, excluding only fascists and their collaborators. Broadly speaking, whether a local nationalism found itself on the side of fascism depended on whether it had more to gain than to lose by the advance of the Axis, and whether its hatred of communism or some other state, nationality or ethnic group (the Jews, the Serbs) was greater than its dislike of Germans or Italians. Thus the Poles, though strongly anti-Russian and anti-Jewish, did not significantly collaborate with Nazi Germany, whereas the Lithuanians and some of the Ukrainians (occupied by the U.S.S.R. from 1939–41) did.

Why did liberalism recede between the wars, even in states which did not accept fascism? Western radicals, socialists and communists who lived through this period were inclined to see the era of global crisis as the final agony of the capitalist system. Capitalism, they argued, could no longer afford the luxury of ruling through parliamentary democracy, and under liberal freedoms, which, incidentally, had provided the power-base for moderate, reformist labour movements. Faced with insoluble economic problems and/or an increasingly revolutionary working class, the bourgeoisie now had to fall back on force and coercion, that is to say, on something like fascism.

As both capitalism and liberal democracy were to make a triumphant comeback in 1945, it is easy to forget that there was a core of truth in this view, as well as rather too much agitational rhetoric. Democratic systems do not work unless there is a basic consensus among most citizens about the acceptability of their state and social system, or at least a readiness to bargain for compromise settlements. This, in turn, is much facilitated by prosperity. In most of Europe these conditions were simply not present between 1918 and the Second World War. Social cataclysm seemed to be impending or had happened. The fear of revolution was such that over most of eastern and south-eastern Europe as well as part of the Mediterranean, communist parties were barely ever allowed to emerge from illegality. The unbridgeable gap between the ideological Right and even the moderate Left wrecked Austrian democracy in 1930–34, though it has flourished in that country since 1945 under exactly the same two-party system of Catholics and Socialists (Seton Watson, 1962, p. 184). Spanish democracy broke under the same tensions in the 1930s. The contrast with the negotiated transition from the Franco dictatorship to a pluralist democracy in the 1970s is dramatic.

What chances of stability there were in such regimes could not survive the Great Depression. The Weimar Republic fell largely because the Great Slump made it impossible to keep the tacit bargain between state, employers and organized workers, which had kept it afloat. Industry and government felt they had no choice but to impose economic and social cuts and mass unemployment did the rest. In mid-1932 National Socialists and communists between them polled an absolute majority of all German votes, and the parties committed to the Republic were reduced to little more than a third. Conversely, it is undeniable that the stability of democratic regimes after the Second World War, not least that of the new German Federal Republic, rested on the economic miracles of those decades (see chapter 9). Where governments have enough to distribute to satisfy all claimants, and most citizens' standard of life is steadily rising in any case, the temperature of democratic politics rarely rises to fever-pitch. Compromise and consensus tended to prevail, as even the most impassioned believers in the overthrow of capitalism found the status quo less intolerable in practice than in theory, and even the most uncompromising champions of capitalism took social security systems and regular negotiations of wage rises and fringe benefits with labour unions for granted.

Yet, as the Great Slump itself showed, this is only part of the answer. A very similar situation—the refusal of the organized workers to accept Depression cuts—led to the collapse of parliamentary government and, eventually, to the nomination of Hitler as head of government in Germany, but in Britain merely to a sharp shift from a Labour to a (Conservative) "National Government" within a stable and quite unshaken parliamentary system.* The Depression did not automatically lead to the

---

*A Labour government in 1931 split over this issue, some Labour leaders and their Liberal supporters went over to the Conservatives, who won the subsequent election by a landslide and remained comfortably in power until May 1940.

suspension or abolition of representative democracy, as is also evident from the political consequences in the U.S.A. (Roosevelt's New Deal) and Scandinavia (the triumph of social democracy). Only in Latin America, where government finances depended, for the most part, on the exports of one or two primary products, whose price collapsed suddenly and dramatically (see chapter 3), did the Slump produce the almost immediate and automatic fall of whatever governments were in being, mainly by military coups. It should be added that political change in the opposite direction also took place then in Chile and Colombia.

At bottom liberal politics was vulnerable because its characteristic form of government, representative democracy, was rarely a convincing way of running states, and the conditions of the Age of Catastrophe rarely guaranteed the conditions that made it viable, let alone effective.

The first of these conditions was that it should enjoy general consent and legitimacy. Democracy itself rests on this consent, but does not create it, except that in well-established and stable democracies the very process of regular voting has tended to give citizens—even those in the minority—a sense that the electoral process legitimizes the governments it produces. But few of the inter-war democracies were well-established. Indeed, until the early twentieth century democracy had been rare outside the U.S.A. and France (see *Age of Empire*, chapter 4). Indeed, at least ten of Europe's states after the First World War were either entirely new or so changed from their predecessors as to have no special legitimacy for their inhabitants. Even fewer democracies were stable. The politics of states in the Age of Catastrophe were, more often than not, the politics of crisis.

The second condition was a degree of compatibility between the various components of "the people," whose sovereign vote was to determine the common government. The official theory of liberal bourgeois society did not recognize "the people" as a set of groups, communities and other collectivities with interests as such, although anthropologists, sociologists and all practising politicians did. Officially the people, a theoretical concept rather than a real body of human beings, consisted of an assembly of self-contained individuals whose votes added up to arithmetical majorities and minorities, which translated into elected assemblies as majority governments and minority oppositions. Where democratic voting crossed the lines between the divisions of the national population, or where it was possible to conciliate or defuse conflicts between them, democracy was viable. However, in an era of revolution and radical social tensions, class struggle translated into politics rather than class peace was the rule. Ideological and class intransigence could wreck democratic government. Moreover, the botched peace settlements after 1918 multiplied what we, at the end of the twentieth century, know to be the fatal virus of democracy, namely the division of the body of citizens exclusively along ethnic-national or religious lines (Glenny, 1992, pp. 146–48), as in ex-Yugoslavia and Northern Ireland. Three ethnic-religious communities voting as blocs, as in Bosnia; two irreconcilable communities, as in Ulster; sixty-two political parties each representing a tribe or clan, as in Somalia, cannot, as we know, provide the foundation for a democratic political system, but—unless one of the contending groups or some outside authority is strong enough to establish (non-democratic) dominance—only for instability and civil war. The fall of the three multinational empires of Austria-Hungary, Russia and Turkey replaced three supranational states whose governments were neutral as between the numerous nationalities over which they ruled, with a great many more multinational states, each identified with *one*, or at most with two or three, of the ethnic communities within their borders.

The third condition was that democratic governments did not have to do much governing. Parliaments had come into existence not so much to govern as to control the power of those who did, a function which is still obvious in the relations between the U.S. Congress and the U.S. presidency. They were devices designed as brakes which found themselves having to act as engines. Sovereign assemblies, elected on a restricted but expanding franchise, were, of course, increasingly common from the Age of Revolution on, but nineteenth-century bourgeois society assumed that the bulk of its citizens' lives would take place, not in the sphere of government, but in the self-regulating economy and in the world of private and unofficial associations ("civil society").* It side-stepped the difficulties of running governments through elected assemblies in two ways: by not expecting too much governing, or even legislation, from their parliaments, and by seeing that government—or rather administration—could be carried on regardless of their vagaries. As we have seen (see chapter 1) bodies of independent, permanently appointed public officials had become an essential device for the government of modern states. A parliamentary majority was essential only where major and controversial executive decisions had to be taken, or approved, and organizing or maintaining an adequate body of supporters was the major task of government leaders, since (except in the Americas) the executive in parliamentary regimes was

---

*The 1980s in West and East were to be full of nostalgic rhetoric seeking an entirely impracticable return to an idealized nineteenth-century constructed on these assumptions.

usually not directly elected. In states with a restricted suffrage (i.e. an electorate composed mainly of the wealthy, powerful or influential minority) this was made easier by a common consensus of what constituted their collective interest (the "national interest"), not to mention the resources of patronage.

The twentieth century multiplied the occasions when it became essential for governments to govern. The kind of state which confined itself to providing the ground rules for business and civil society, and the police, prisons and armed forces to keep internal and external danger at bay, the "nightwatchman state" of political wits, became as obsolete as the "nightwatchmen" who inspired the metaphor.

The fourth condition was wealth and prosperity. The democracies of the 1920s broke under the tension of revolution and counter-revolution (Hungary, Italy, Portugal) or of national conflict (Poland, Yugoslavia); those of the thirties, under the tensions of the Slump. One has only to compare the political atmosphere of Weimar Germany and 1920s Austria with that of Federal Germany and post-1945 Austria to be convinced. Even national conflicts were less unmanageable, so long as each minority's politicians could feed at the state's common trough. That was the strength of the Agrarian Party in east-central Europe's only genuine democracy, Czechoslovakia: it offered benefits across national lines. In the 1930s, even Czechoslovakia could no longer hold together the Czechs, Slovaks, Germans, Hungarians and Ukrainians.

Under these circumstances democracy was, more likely than not, a mechanism for formalizing divisions between irreconcilable groups. Very often even in the best circumstances, it produced no stable basis for democratic government at all, especially when the theory of democratic representation was applied in the most rigorous versions of proportional representation.* Where, in times of crisis, no parliamentary majority was available, as in Germany (as distinct from Britain)† the temptation to look elsewhere was overwhelming. Even in stable democracies the political divisions the system implies are seen by many citizens as costs rather than benefits of the system. The very rhetoric of politics advertises candidates and party as the representative of the national rather than the

---

*The endless permutations of democratic electoral systems—proportional or otherwise—are all attempts to ensure or maintain stable majorities permitting stable governments in political systems which, by their very nature, make this difficult.

†In Britain the refusal to entertain any form of proportional representation ("winner takes all") favoured a two-party system, and marginalized other parties—since the First World War the once dominant Liberal Party, though it continued to

narrow party interest. In times of crisis the costs of the system seemed unsustainable, its benefits uncertain.

Under these circumstances it is easy to understand that parliamentary democracy in the successor states to the old empires, as well as in most of the Mediterranean and in Latin America, was a feeble plant growing in stony soil. The strongest argument in its favour, that, bad as it is, it is better than any alternative system, is itself half-hearted. Between the wars it only rarely sounded realistic and convincing. Even its champions spoke with muted confidence. Its retreat seemed to be inevitable, as even in the United States serious, but needlessly gloomy observers noted that "It Can Happen Here" (Sinclair Lewis, 1935). Nobody seriously predicted or expected its post-war renaissance, still less its return, however brief, as the predominant form of government across the globe in the early 1990s. For those who looked back on the period between the wars at this time, the fall of liberal political systems seemed a brief interruption in their secular conquest of the globe. Unfortunately, as the new millennium approached, the uncertainties surrounding political democracy no longer seemed quite so remote. The world may be unhappily re-entering a period when its advantages no longer seem as obvious as they did between 1950 and 1990.

---

poll a steady 10 per cent of the national vote (this was still the case in 1992). In Germany the proportional system, though slightly favouring larger parties, produced none after 1920 with even one third of seats (except the Nazis in 1932) among five major and a dozen or so minor groupings. In the absence of a majority the constitution provided for (temporary) executive rule by emergency powers, i e., the suspension of democracy.

CHAPTER FIVE

Against the Common Enemy

Tomorrow for the young the poets exploding like bombs,
The walks by the lake, the weeks of perfect communion;
  Tomorrow the bicycle races
Through the suburbs on summer evenings. But to-day the
  struggle . . .

–W. H. Auden, "Spain," 1937

Dear Mum, Of all people I know you are the one that will feel it most, so my very last thoughts go to you. Don't blame anyone else for my death, because I myself chose my fate.

I don't know what to write to you, because, even though I have a clear head, I can't find the right words. I took my place in the Army of Liberation, and I die as the light of victory is already beginning to shine . . . I shall be shot very shortly with twenty three other comrades.

After the war you must claim your rights to a pension. They will let you have my things at the jail, only I am keeping Dad's under-vest, because I don't want the cold to make me shiver . . .

Once again I say goodbye. Courage!

Your son.
Spartaco

—Spartaco Fontanot, metalworker, twenty-two years old, member
  of the French resistance group of Misak Manouchian, 1944
  (Lettere, p. 306)

I

Public opinion research is the child of America in the 1930s, for the extension of the "sample survey" of the market researchers into politics essentially began with George Gallup in 1936. Among the early results of this new technique is one which would have amazed all U.S. presidents before Franklin D. Roosevelt, and will amaze all readers who have grown up since the Second World War. When asked in January 1939 who Americans wanted to win, if a war broke out between the Soviet Union and Germany, 83 per cent favoured a Soviet victory against 17 per cent who were for Germany (Miller, 1989, pp. 283–84). In a century dominated by the confrontation between the anti-capitalist communism of the October revolution, represented by the U.S.S.R. and anti-communist capitalism, of which the U.S.A. was the champion and chief exemplar, nothing looks more anomalous than this declaration of sympathy, or at least preference, for the home of world revolution over a strongly anti-communist country, whose economy was recognizably capitalist. All the more so as the Stalinist tyranny in the U.S.S.R. was at that time, by general consent, at its worst.

The historic situation was certainly exceptional and comparatively short-lived. It lasted, at a maximum, from 1933 (when the U.S.A. recognized the U.S.S.R. officially) until 1947 (when the two ideological camps confronted each other as enemies in the "Cold War"), but more realistically, for the years from 1935 to 1945. In other words, it was determined by the rise and fall of Hitler's Germany (1933–45) (see chapter 4), against which both the U.S.A. and the U.S.S.R. made common cause, because they saw it as a greater danger than each of the two saw the other.

The reasons why they did so go beyond the range of conventional international relations or power politics, and this is what makes the anomalous alignment of states and movements which eventually fought and won the Second World War so significant. What eventually forged the union against Germany was the fact that it was not just any nation-state with reasons to feel discontented with its situation, but one whose policy and ambitions were determined by its ideology. In short, that it was a fascist power. So long as this was left aside or not appreciated, the ordinary calculations of *Realpolitik* held good. Germany could be opposed or conciliated, counter-balanced or, if need be, fought, depending on the interests of a country's state policy and the general situation. In fact, at one time or another between 1933 and 1941 all other major players in the international game treated Germany accordingly. London and Paris appeased Berlin (i.e. offered concessions at someone else's expense), Moscow exchanged a stance of opposition for one of helpful neutrality in return for territorial gains, and even Italy and Japan, whose interests aligned them with Germany, found that these interests also told them, in 1939, to stay out of the first stages of the Second World War. As it happened, the logic of Hitler's war drew all of them as well as the U.S.A. into it eventually.

But as the 1930s advanced it became increasingly clear that more was at issue than the relative balance of power between the nation-states constituting the international (i.e. primarily the European) system. Indeed, the politics of the West—from the U.S.S.R. through Europe to the Americas—can be best understood, not through the contest of states, but as an international ideological civil war. (As we shall see, this is not the best way to understand the politics of Afroasia and the Far East, which were dominated by the fact of colonialism (see chapter 7). And, as it turned out, the crucial lines in this civil war were not drawn between capitalism as such and communist social revolution, but between ideological families: on the one hand the descendants of the eighteenth-century Enlightenment and the great revolutions including, obviously, the Russian revolution; on the other, its opponents. In short, the frontier ran not between capitalism and communism, but between what the nineteenth century would have called "progress" and "reaction"—only that these terms were no longer quite apposite.

It was an international war, because it raised essentially the same issues in most Western countries. It was a civil war, because the lines between the pro- and anti-fascist forces ran through each society. Never has there been a period when patriotism, in the sense of automatic loyalty to a citizen's national government, counted for less. When the Second World War ended, the governments of at least ten old European countries were headed by men who, at its beginning (or, in the case of Spain, at the start of the Civil War), had been rebels, political exiles or, at the very least, persons who had regarded their own government as immoral and illegitimate. Men and women, often from the heart of their countries' political classes, chose loyalty to communism (i.e. to the U.S.S.R.) over that to their own state. The "Cambridge spies" and, probably to greater practical effect, the Japanese members of the Sorge spy ring, were only two groups out of many.* On the other hand, the special term "quisling" was invented—based on the name of a Norwegian Nazi—to describe the political forces within states attacked by Hitler who chose, out of conviction rather than expediency, to join their country's enemy.

---

*It has been argued that Sorge's information, based on the most reliable sources, that Japan did *not* intend to attack the U.S.S.R. in late 1941, enabled Stalin to transfer vital reinforcements to the Western Front at a time when the Germans were on the outskirts of Moscow (Deakin and Storry, 1964, chapter 13; Andrew and Gordievsky, 1991, pp. 281–82).

This was true even of people moved by patriotism rather than global ideology. For even traditional patriotism was now divided. Strongly imperialist and anti-communist Conservatives like Winston Churchill, and men of reactionary Catholic background like de Gaulle, chose to fight Germany, not because of any special animus against fascism, but because of "*une certaine idée de la France*" or "a certain idea of England." Yet even for such as these, their commitment could be part of an international *civil* war, since their concept of patriotism was not necessarily their governments'. In going to London and declaring, on 18 June 1940, that under him "Free France" would continue to fight Germany, Charles de Gaulle was committing an act of rebellion against the legitimate government of France, which had constitutionally decided to end the war, and was almost certainly supported in its decision by the great majority of Frenchmen at the time. No doubt Churchill, in such a situation, would have reacted in the same manner. Had Germany won the war, he would have been treated by his government as a traitor, as the Russians who fought with the Germans against the U.S.S.R. were treated by their country after 1945. Just so Slovaks and Croats, whose countries acquired their first taste of (qualified) state independence as satellites of Hitler's Germany regarded the leaders of their wartime states retrospectively as patriotic heroes or fascist collaborators on ideological grounds: members of each people fought on both sides.*

What bonded all these national civil divisions into a single global war, both international and civil, was the rise of Hitler's Germany. Or, more precisely, between 1931 and 1941 the march to conquest and war of the combination of states—Germany, Italy and Japan, of which Hitler's Germany became the central pillar. And Hitler's Germany was both more ruthlessly and manifestly committed to the destruction of the values and institutions of the "Western civilisation" of the Age of Revolution, and capable of carrying out its barbaric project. Step by step the potential victims of Japan, Germany and Italy watched the states of what came to be called "the Axis" push their conquests forward, towards the war which, from 1931 on, seemed unavoidable. As the phrase went, "fascism means war." In 1931 Japan invaded Manchuria and set up a puppet state there. In 1932 Japan occupied China north of the Great Wall and landed in Shanghai. In 1933 Hitler came to power in Germany, with a programme which he made no attempt to conceal. In 1934 a brief civil war in Austria

---

*However, this should not be used to justify the atrocities committed by either side which, certainly in the case of the Croat state of 1942–45, probably in the case of the Slovak state, were greater than their opponents', and in any case indefensible.

eliminated democracy in Austria, and introduced a semi-fascist regime distinguished chiefly by resisting integration into Germany and (with Italian backing at the time) defeating a Nazi coup which murdered the Austrian premier. In 1935 Germany denounced the peace treaties and re-emerged as a major military and naval power, re-acquiring (by plebiscite) the Saar region on its western frontier and, contemptuously resigning from the League of Nations. In the same year Mussolini, with equal contempt for international opinion, invaded Ethiopia, which Italy proceeded to conquer and occupy as a colony in 1936–37, after which the state also tore up its membership of the League. In 1936, Germany recovered the Rhineland and, with open assistance and intervention from both Italy and Germany, a military coup in Spain initiated a major conflict, the Spanish Civil War, about which more will be said below. The two fascist powers entered a formal alignment, the Rome–Berlin Axis, while Germany and Japan concluded an "Anti-Comintern Pact." In 1937, not surprisingly, Japan invaded China and set out on a course of open warfare which did not cease until 1945. In 1938 Germany plainly also felt the time for conquest had come. Austria was invaded and annexed in March, without military resistance, and, after various threats, the Munich agreement of October broke up Czechoslovakia and transferred large parts of it to Hitler, again peacefully. The remainder was occupied in March 1939, encouraging Italy, which had not demonstrated imperial ambitions for a few months, to occupy Albania. Almost immediately a Polish crisis, which arose once again out of German territorial demands, paralysed Europe. Out of it came the European war of 1939–41, which grew into the Second World War.

However, another thing wove the threads of national politics into a single international web: the consistent and increasingly spectacular feebleness of liberal-democratic states (which happened also to be the victor states of the First World War); their inability or unwillingness to act, singly or in conjunction, to resist the advance of their enemies. As we have seen, it was this crisis of liberalism which strengthened both the arguments and the forces of fascism and authoritarian government (see chapter 4). The Munich agreement of 1938 perfectly demonstrated this combination of confident aggression on one side, fear and concession on the other, which is why for generations the very word "Munich" became a synonym, in Western political discourse, for craven retreat. The shame of Munich, which was felt almost immediately, even by those who signed the agreement, lay not simply in handing Hitler a cheap triumph, but in the palpable fear of war that preceded it, and the even more palpable sense of relief that it had been avoided at any cost. "*Bande de cons*" the

French premier Daladier is said to have muttered contemptuously when, having signed away the life of an ally of France, he expected to be hissed on his return to Paris, but met nothing but delirious cheers. The popularity of the U.S.S.R., and the reluctance to criticise what was happening there, was chiefly due to its consistent opposition to Nazi Germany, so different from the hesitations of the West. The shock of the pact with Germany in August 1939 was all the greater.

II

The mobilization of the full potential of support against fascism, i.e. against the German camp, therefore, was a triple call for union of all political forces which had a common interest in resisting the Axis advance; for an actual policy of resistance, and for governments prepared to carry out such a policy. In fact, it took more than eight years to achieve this mobilization—ten, if we date the start of the race to world war in 1931. For the response to all three calls was, inevitably, hesitant, muffled or mixed.

The call for anti-fascist unity was, in some ways, likely to win the most immediate response, since fascism publicly treated liberals of various kinds, socialists and communists, any kind of democratic regimes and soviet regimes as enemies to be equally destroyed. In the old English phrase, they had all to hang together if they did not want to hang separately. The communists, who hitherto had been the most divisive force on the Enlightenment Left, concentrating their fire (as is, alas, characteristic of political radicals) not against the obvious enemy but against the nearest potential competitor, above all the Social Democrats (see chapter 2) changed course within eighteen months of Hitler's accession to power and turned themselves into the most systematic and, as usual, the most efficient, champions of anti-fascist unity. This removed the major obstacle to unity on the Left, though not deeply rooted mutual suspicions.

Essentially the strategy put forward (in conjunction with Stalin) by the Communist International (which had chosen as its new General Secretary George Dimitrov, a Bulgarian whose brave public defiance of the Nazi authorities in the Reichstag fire trial of 1933 had electrified anti-fascists everywhere)* was one of concentric circles. The united forces of labour

*Within a month of Hitler's accession to power, the German parliament building in Berlin was mysteriously burned down. The Nazi government immediately accused the Communist Party and used the occasion to suppress it. The communists accused

(the "United Front") would form the foundation of a wider electoral and political alliance with democrats and liberals (the "Popular Front"). Beyond this, as the advance of Germany continued, the communists envisaged an even wider extension into a "National Front" of all who, irrespective of ideology and political beliefs, regarded fascism (or the Axis powers) as the primary danger. This extension of the anti-fascist alliance beyond the political Centre to the Right—the French communists' "hand stretched out to the Catholics," or the British ones' readiness to embrace the notoriously red-baiting Winston Churchill—met with more resistance, on the traditional Left until the logic of war finally imposed it. However, the union of Centre and Left made political sense, and "Popular Fronts" were established in France (which pioneered this device) and Spain, which pushed back local offensives of the Right, and won dramatic election victories in Spain (February 1936) and France (May 1936).

These victories dramatized the costs of past disunion, because the united electoral lists of Centre and Left won substantial parliamentary majorities—but though they showed a striking shift of opinion *within* the Left, notably in France, in favour of the Communist Party, they did not indicate any serious widening of political support for anti-fascism. In fact, the triumph of the French Popular Front, which produced the first French government ever headed by a Socialist, the intellectual Léon Blum (1872–1950), was achieved by an increase of barely one per cent of the united Radical-Socialist-Communist vote of 1932, and the electoral triumph of the Spanish Popular Front by a slightly larger shift, but one that still left the new government with almost half the voters against it (and a Right somewhat stronger than before). Still, these victories pumped hope, even euphoria, into the local labour and socialist movements; more than can be said for the British Labour Party, shattered by slump and political crisis in 1931—it was reduced to a rump of fifty—but which, four years later, had not quite recovered its pre-slump vote, or much more than half of its 1929 seats. Between 1931 and 1935 the Conservative vote merely fell from c. 61 per cent to c. 54 per cent. The so-called "National" government of Britain, headed from 1937 on by Neville

---

the Nazis of having organized the fire for this purpose. An unbalanced Dutch loner of revolutionary sympathies, Van der Lubbe, as well as the leader of the communist parliamentary group and three Bulgarians working in Berlin for the Communist International, were arrested and tried. Van der Lubbe was certainly involved in the arson, the four arrested communists certainly not, nor obviously was the KPD. Current historical scholarship does not support the suggestion of a Nazi provocation.

Chamberlain, who became the synonym for the "appeasement" of Hitler, rested on solid majority support. There is no reason to suppose that, had war not broken out in 1939 and had an election been held in 1940, as it would have had to have been, the Conservatives would not have won it again comfortably. Indeed, except for most of Scandinavia, where the Social Democrats gained ground strongly, there was no sign of any significant electoral shift to the Left in Western Europe in the 1930s, and some fairly massive shifts to the Right in those parts of eastern and southeastern Europe in which elections were still held. There is a sharp contrast between the old and new worlds. Nothing like the dramatic shift from Republicans to Democrats in 1932 (their presidential vote rose from between fifteen and sixteen to almost twenty-eight millions in four years) occurred anywhere in Europe, but it must be said that, in electoral terms, Franklin D. Roosevelt reached his peak in 1932, even though (to everyone's surprise except the people's) he barely fell short of it in 1936.

Anti-fascism, therefore, organized the traditional adversaries of the Right, but did not swell their numbers; it mobilized minorities more easily than majorities. Among these minorities, intellectuals and those concerned with the arts were particularly open to its appeal (except for an international current of literature inspired by the nationalist and antidemocratic Right—see chapter 6), because the arrogant and aggressive hostility of National Socialism to the values of civilization as hitherto conceived was instantly obvious in the fields that concerned them. Nazi racism immediately led to the mass exodus of Jewish and Left-wing scholars who scattered across the remaining world of toleration. Nazi hostility to intellectual freedom almost immediately purged the German universities of perhaps one third of their teachers. The attacks on "modernist" culture, the public burning of "Jewish" and other undesirable books, began virtually as soon as Hitler entered government. However, while ordinary citizens might disapprove of the more brutal barbarities of the system—the concentration camps and the reduction of the German Jews (which included all those with at least one Jewish grandparent) to a segregated underclass without rights—a surprisingly large number saw them, at worst, as limited aberrations. After all, concentration camps were still primarily deterrents for potential communist opposition and jails for the cadres of subversion, an object with which many conventional conservatives had some sympathy, and when war broke out there were no more than about 8,000 persons in all of them. (Their expansion into an *univers concentrationnaire* of terror, torture and death for hundreds of thousands, even millions, happened during the war.) And, until the war, Nazi policy, however barbarous the treatment of the Jews, still appeared to envisage the "final solution" of the "Jewish problem" as mass expulsion rather than mass extermination. Germany itself appeared to the non-political observer as a stable, indeed an economically flourishing country with a popular government, though with some unattractive characteristics. Those who read books, including the Führer's own *Mein Kampf,* were more likely to recognize, in the bloodthirsty rhetoric of racist agitators and the localized torture and murder of Dachau or Buchenwald, the threat of an entire world built on the deliberate reversal of civilization. Western intellectuals (though at this time only a fraction of students, then overwhelmingly a contingent of sons and future entrants of the "respectable" middle classes) were therefore the first social stratum mobilised en masse against fascism in the 1930s. It was still a rather small stratum, though an unusually influential one, not least because it included the journalists who, in the non-fascist countries of the West, played a crucial role in alerting even more conservative readers and decision-makers to the nature of National Socialism.

The actual policy of resistance to the rise of the fascist camp was, once again, simple and logical on paper. It was to unite all countries against the aggressors (the League of Nations provided a potential framework for this), to make no concessions to them, and, by the threat and, if necessary, the reality of common action, to deter or defeat them. The U.S.S.R.'s foreign commissar Maxim Litvinov (1876–1951) made himself the spokesman of this "Collective Security." Easier said than done. The major obstacle was that, then as now, even states which shared the fear and suspicion of the aggressors had other interests which divided them or could be used to divide them.

How far the most obvious division counted, that between the Soviet Union committed in theory to the overthrow of bourgeois regimes and the end of their empires everywhere, and the other states, now saw the U.S.S.R. as the inspirer and instigator of subversion, is not clear. While governments—all the main ones after 1933 recognized the U.S.S.R.—were always prepared to come to terms with it when it suited their purposes, some of their members and agencies continued to regard Bolshevism, at home and abroad, as the essential enemy, in the spirit of the post-1945 cold wars. The British Intelligence services were admittedly exceptional in concentrating against the Red menace to such an extent that they did not abandon it as their main target until the middle 1930s (Andrew, 1985, p. 530). Nevertheless many a good conservative felt, especially in Britain, that the best of all solutions would be a German–Soviet war, weakening, perhaps destroying, both enemies, and a defeat of Bolshevism by a weakened Germany would be no bad thing. The sheer reluctance of

Western governments to enter into effective negotiations with the Red state, even in 1938–39 when the urgency of an anti-Hitler alliance was no longer denied by anyone, is only too patent. Indeed, it was the fear of being left to confront Hitler alone which eventually drove Stalin, since 1934 the unswerving champion of an alliance with the West against him, into the Stalin–Ribbentrop Pact of August 1939, by which he hoped to keep the U.S.S.R. out of the war while Germany and the Western powers would weaken one another, to the benefit of his state which, by the secret clauses of the pact, acquired a large part of the western territories lost by Russia after the revolution. The calculation proved wrong, but, like the abortive attempts to create a common front against Hitler, they demonstrate the divisions between states which made possible the extraordinary and virtually unresisted rise of Nazi Germany between 1933 and 1939.

Moreover, geography, history and economics gave governments different perspectives on the world. The continent of Europe as such was of little or no interest to Japan and the U.S.A., whose policies were Pacific and American, and to Britain, still committed to a worldwide empire and a global maritime strategy, though too weak to maintain either. The countries of Eastern Europe were squeezed between Germany and Russia and this obviously determined their policies, especially when (as it turned out) the Western powers were unable to protect them. Several had acquired formerly Russian territories after 1917, and, though hostile to Germany, therefore resisted any anti-German alliance which would bring Russian forces back on their lands. And yet, as the Second World War was to demonstrate, the only effective anti-fascist alliance was one which included the U.S.S.R. As for economics, countries like Britain which knew they had waged a First World War beyond their financial capacities, recoiled from the costs of rearmament. In short, there was a wide gap between recognizing the Axis powers as a major danger and doing something about it.

Liberal democracy (which by definition did not exist on the fascist or authoritarian side) widened this gap. It slowed down or prevented political decision, notably in the U.S.A., and unquestionably made it difficult, and sometimes impossible, to pursue unpopular policies. No doubt some governments used this to justify their own torpor, but the example of the U.S.A. shows that even a strong and popular president like F. D. Roosevelt was unable to carry his anti-fascist foreign policy against the opinion of the electorate. But for Pearl Harbor, and Hitler's declaration of war, the U.S.A. would almost certainly have continued to stay out of the Second World War. It is not clear under what circumstances it could have come in.

Yet what weakened the resolution of the crucial European democracies, France and Great Britain, was not so much the political mechanisms of democracy, as the memory of the First World War. This was a wound whose pain was felt both by voters and governments, because the impact of that war had been both unprecedented and universal. For both France and Britain it was, in human (though not in material) terms, far greater than the impact of the Second World War proved to be (see chapter 1). Another such war had to be avoided at almost all costs. It was certainly the last of all resorts of politics.

A reluctance to go to war must not be confused with a refusal to fight, though the potential military morale of the French, who had suffered more than any other belligerent country, was certainly weakened by the trauma of 1914–18. Nobody went into the Second World War singing, not even the Germans. On the other hand unqualified (non-religious) pacifism, though quite popular in Britain in the 1930s, was never a mass movement and faded away in 1940. In spite of the extensive tolerance for "conscientious objectors" in the Second World War, the numbers who claimed the right to refuse to fight were small (Calvocoressi, 1987, p. 63).

On the non-communist Left, even more emotionally committed to hatred of war and militarism after 1918 than it had been (in theory) before 1914, peace at any price remained a minority position, even in France where it was strongest. In Britain George Lansbury, a pacifist who, by the accident of an electoral holocaust, found himself at the head of the Labour Party after 1931, was efficiently and brutally removed from leadership in 1935. Unlike the French socialist-headed Popular Front government of 1936–38, British Labour could be criticized, not for lack of firmness towards the fascist aggressors, but for refusing to support the necessary military measures to make resistance effective, such as rearmament and conscription. So, for the same reasons, could the communists, who were never tempted by pacifism.

The Left was indeed in a quandary. On the one hand the strength of anti-fascism was that it mobilized those who feared war, both the last and the unknown horrors of the next. That fascism meant war was a convincing reason for fighting it. On the other hand, resistance to fascism which did not envisage the use of arms could not succeed. What is more, the hope of bringing about the collapse of Nazi Germany, or even Mussolini's Italy, by collective but peaceable firmness, rested on illusions about Hitler and about the supposed forces of opposition within Germany. In any case we who lived through those times *knew* that there would be a war, even as we sketched out unconvincing scenarios for avoiding it. We— the historian may also appeal to his memory—*expected* to fight in the next war, and probably to die. And as anti-fascists we had no doubt that when it came to the point we had no choice but to fight.

Nevertheless, the political dilemma of the Left cannot be used to explain the failure of governments, if only because effective preparations for war did not depend on resolutions passed (or not passed) at party congresses; or even, for a period of several years, on the fear of elections. Yet governments, and in particular the French and the British, had also been indelibly scarred by the Great War. France had emerged from it bled white, and still potentially a smaller and a weaker power than a defeated Germany. France was nothing without allies against a revived Germany, and the only European countries which had an equal interest in allying with France, Poland and the Habsburg succession states, were plainly too weak for the purpose. The French put their money on a line of fortifications (the "Maginot Line," named after a soon-forgotten minister) which, they hoped, would deter the attacking Germans by the prospect of losses like those of Verdun (see chapter 1). Beyond this they could only look to Britain and, after 1933, the U.S.S.R.

The British governments were equally conscious of fundamental weakness. Financially they could not afford another war. Strategically, they no longer had a navy capable of simultaneously operating in the three great oceans and in the Mediterranean. At the same time, the problem that really worried them was not what happened in Europe, but how to hold together, with patently insufficient forces, a global empire geographically larger than ever before, but also visibly on the verge of decomposition.

Both states thus knew themselves to be too weak to defend a status quo largely established in 1919 to suit them. Both also knew that this status quo was unstable, and impossible to maintain. Neither had anything to gain from another war, and plenty to lose. The obvious and logical policy was to negotiate with a revived Germany in order to establish a more durable European pattern, and this, beyond any doubt, meant making concessions to Germany's growing power. Unfortunately the revived Germany was Adolf Hitler's.

The so-called policy of "appeasement" has had such a bad press since 1939 that we must remember how sensible it seemed to so many Western politicians who were not viscerally anti-German or passionately anti-fascist on principle, and especially in Britain, where changes on the continental map, especially in "far-off countries of which we know little" (Chamberlain on Czechoslovakia in 1938), did not raise the blood pressure. (The French were understandably far more nervous about *any* initiatives favouring Germany, which must sooner or later turn against themselves, but France was weak.) A Second World War, it could safely be predicted, would ruin the British economy, and disband large parts of the British Empire. Indeed, this is what happened. Though it was a price socialists, communists, colonial liberation movements and President F. D. Roosevelt were only too ready to pay for the defeat of fascism, let us not forget that it was excessive from the point of view of rational British imperialists.

Yet compromise and negotiation with Hitler's Germany were impossible, because the policy objectives of National Socialism were irrational and unlimited. Expansion and aggression were built into the system and, short of accepting German domination in advance, i.e. choosing not to resist the Nazi advance, war was unavoidable, sooner rather than later. Hence the central role of ideology in the formation of policy in the 1930s: if it determined the aims of Nazi Germany, it excluded *realpolitik* for the other side. Those who recognized that there could be no compromise with Hitler, which was a realistic assessment of the situation, did so for entirely unpragmatic reasons. They regarded fascism as intolerable on principle and *a priori*, or (as in the case of Winston Churchill) they were driven by an equally *a priori* idea of what their country and empire "stood for," and could not sacrifice. The paradox of Winston Churchill was that this great romantic, whose political judgment had been almost consistently wrong on every matter since 1914—including the assessment of military strategy on which he prided himself—was realistic on the one question of Germany.

Conversely, the political realists of appeasement were entirely unrealistic in their assessment of the situation, even when the impossibility of a negotiated settlement with Hitler became obvious to any reasonable observer in 1938–39. This was the reason for the black tragicomedy of March–September 1939, which ended in a war nobody wanted at a time and in a place nobody wanted it (not even Germany), and which actually left Britain and France without any idea of what, as belligerents, they were supposed to do, until the *blitzkrieg* of 1940 swept them aside. In the face of the evidence they themselves accepted, the appeasers in Britain and France still could not bring themselves to negotiate seriously for an alliance with the U.S.S.R., without which war could neither be postponed nor won, and without which the guarantees against German attack suddenly and heedlessly scattered around Eastern Europe by Neville Chamberlain—without, incredible as it may seem, consulting or even adequately *informing* the U.S.S.R.—were waste paper. London and Paris did not want to fight, but at most to deter by a show of strength. This did not look plausible for a moment to Hitler, or for that matter to Stalin, whose negotiators asked vainly for proposals for joint strategic operations in the Baltic. Even as the German armies marched into Poland, Neville Chamberlain's government was still prepared to do a deal with Hitler, as Hitler had calculated he would (Watt, 1989, p. 215).

Hitler miscalculated, and the Western states declared war, not because their statesmen wanted it, but because Hitler's own policy after Munich cut the ground from under the appeasers' feet. It was he who mobilized the hitherto uncommitted masses against fascism. Essentially the German occupation of Czechoslovakia in March 1939 converted British public opinion to resistance, and in doing so forced the hand of a reluctant government; which in turn forced the hand of a French government that had no other option except to go along with its only effective ally. For the first time the fight against Hitler's Germany united rather than divided the British, but—as yet—to no purpose. As the Germans quickly and ruthlessly destroyed Poland, and partitioned its remains with Stalin, who retreated into a doomed neutrality, a "phony war" succeeded an implausible peace in the West.

No kind of *realpolitik* can explain the appeasers' policy after Munich. Once a war seemed sufficiently likely—and who in 1939 doubted this?—the only thing to do was to prepare for it as effectively as possible, and this was not done. For Britain, even Chamberlain's Britain, was certainly not prepared to accept a Hitler-dominated Europe before it happened, even if after the collapse of France there was some serious support for a negotiated peace—i.e. for accepting defeat. Even in France, where pessimism verging on defeatism was far more common among politicians and military men, the government did not intend to give up the ghost, or do so, until the army had collapsed in June 1940. Their policy was half-hearted, because they neither dared follow the logic of power-politics, nor the *a priori* convictions of resisters, to whom *nothing* could be more important than fighting fascism (as fascism or as Hitler's Germany) or those of anti-communists, to whom "Hitler's defeat would mean the collapse of the authoritarian systems which constitute the principle rampart against communist revolution" (Thierry Maulnier, 1938 in Ory, 1976, p. 24). It is not easy to say what determined these statesmen's actions, since they were moved not only by intellect, but by prejudices, preconceptions, hopes and fears which silently skewed their vision. There were the memories of the First World War and the self-doubt of politicians who saw their liberal democratic political systems and economies in what might well be final retreat; a state of mind more typical of the Continent than of Britain. There was the genuine uncertainty about whether, under such circumstances, the unpredictable results of a successful policy of resistance could justify the prohibitive costs that it might entail. For, after all, for most British and French politicians the best that could be achieved was to preserve a not very satisfactory and probably unsustainable status quo. And behind all this there was the question whether, if the status quo was doomed anyway, fascism was not better than the alternative, social revolution and Bolshevism. If the only kind of fascism on offer had been the Italian kind, few conservative or moderate politicians would have hesitated. Even Winston Churchill was pro-Italian. The problem was, that they faced not Mussolini but Hitler. Still, it is not without significance that the main hope of so many governments and diplomats of the 1930s, was to stabilize Europe by coming to terms with Italy, or at least to detach Mussolini from the alliance with his disciple. It did not work, even though Mussolini himself was sufficiently realistic to keep some freedom of action until, in June 1940, he then concluded, mistakenly but not altogether unreasonably, that the Germans had won and declared war himself.

III

The issues of the 1930s, whether fought out within states or between them, were thus transnational. Nowhere was this more immediately evident than in the Spanish Civil War of 1936–39, which became the quintessential expression of this global confrontation.

In retrospect it may seem surprising that this conflict *instantly* mobilized the sympathies of both Left and Right in Europe and the Americas, and notably of the Western world's intellectuals. Spain was a peripheral part of Europe, and its history had been persistently out of phase with the rest of the continent from which it was divided by the wall of the Pyrenees. It had kept out of all European wars since Napoleon, and was to keep out of the Second World War. Since the early nineteenth century its affairs had been of no real concern to European governments, though the U.S.A. had provoked a brief war against it in 1898 in order to rob it of the last remaining parts of the old worldwide empire of the sixteenth century, Cuba, Puerto Rico and the Philippines.* In fact, and contrary to the beliefs of this author's generation, the Spanish Civil War was not the first phase of the Second World War, and the victory of General Franco

---

*Spain retained a foothold in Morocco, disputed by the warlike local Berber tribesmen, who also provided the Spanish army with formidable fighting units, and some African territories further south, forgotten by everyone.

who, as we have seen, cannot even be described as a fascist, had no significant global consequences. It merely kept Spain (and Portugal) isolated from the rest of world history for another thirty years.

Yet it was no accident that the domestic politics of that notoriously anomalous and self-contained country became the symbol of a global struggle in the 1930s. They raised the fundamental political issues of the time: on the one side, democracy and social revolution, Spain being the only country in Europe where it was ready to erupt; on the other, a uniquely uncompromising camp of counter-revolution or reaction, inspired by a Catholic Church which rejected everything that had happened in the world since Martin Luther. Curiously enough, neither the parties of Muscovite communism nor those inspired by fascism were of serious significance there before the Civil War, for Spain went its own eccentric way both on the anarchist ultra-Left and on the Carlist ultra-Right.*

The well-meaning liberals, anti-clerical and masonic in the nineteenth-century manner of Latin countries, who took over from the Bourbons by a peaceful revolution in 1931, could neither contain the social ferment of the Spanish poor, in both cities and countryside, nor defuse it by effective social (i.e. primarily agrarian) reforms. In 1933 they were pushed aside by conservative governments whose policy of repressing agitations and local insurrections, such as the rising of the Asturian miners in 1934, simply helped to build up the potential revolutionary pressure. At this stage the Spanish Left discovered the Comintern's Popular Front, which was being urged on it from neighbouring France. The idea that all parties should form a single electoral front against the Right made sense to a Left that did not quite know what to do. Even the Anarchists, in this their last mass stronghold in the world, were inclined to ask their supporters to practise the bourgeois vice of voting in an election, which they had hitherto rejected as unworthy of the real revolutionary, though no anarchists actually sullied themselves by standing for election. In February 1936 the Popular Front won a small, but by no means sweeping majority of votes and, thanks to its coordination, a substantial majority of seats in the Spanish Parliament or *Cortes*. This victory produced not so much an effective government of the Left as a fissure through which the accumulated lava of social discontent could begin to spurt. This became increasingly evident in the next months.

At this stage, orthodox Right-wing politics having failed, Spain reverted

---

*Carlism was a fiercely monarchist and ultra-traditionalist movement with strong peasant support, mainly in Navarre. The Carlist fought civil wars in the 1830s and 1870s in support of one branch of the Spanish royal family.

to a form of politics it had pioneered, and which had become characteristic of the Iberian world: the *pronunciamento*, or military coup. But just
as the Spanish Left found itself looking beyond national frontiers to Popular Frontism, so the Spanish Right was drawn to the fascist powers. This
was not so much through the modest local fascist movement, the Falange,
as through the Church and the monarchists, for whom there was little difference between the equally godless liberals and communists, and no possibility of compromise with either. Italy and Germany hoped to draw some
moral and perhaps political benefit from a Right-wing victory. The Spanish generals who began seriously to plot a coup after the election needed
financial support and practical help, which they negotiated with Italy.

However, moments of democratic victory and political mass mobilization are not ideal for military coups, which rely for success on the convention that civilians, not to mention uncommitted sections of the armed
forces, accept the signals, just as military putschists whose signals are not
accepted, quietly recognize their failure. The classic *pronunciamento* is a
game best played at times when the masses are in recess or governments
have lost legitimacy. These conditions were not present in Spain. The
generals' coup of 17 July 1936 succeeded in some towns, and was met
with passionate resistance from people and loyal forces in others. It failed
to capture the two main cities of Spain, including the capital, Madrid.
In parts of Spain it therefore precipitated the social revolution it had
been intended to pre-empt. In all of Spain it became a long-drawn-out
civil war between the legitimate and duly elected government of the Republic, now extended to include socialists, communists and even some anarchists, but uneasily cohabiting with the forces of mass rebellion which
had defeated the coup, and the insurgent generals who presented themselves as nationalist crusaders against communism. The youngest, and
most politically intelligent of the generals, Francisco Franco y Baha-
monde (1892–1975) found himself the leader of a new regime, which in
the course of the war became an authoritarian state, with a single party—
a Right-wing conglomerate ranging from fascism to old monarchists and
Carlist ultras, the absurdly named Spanish Traditionalist Falange. But
both sides in the Civil War needed support. Both appealed to their potential backers.

The reaction of anti-fascist opinion to the rising of the generals was
immediate and spontaneous, unlike the reaction of the non-fascist governments, which was distinctly more cautious, even when, like the U.S.S.R.
and the socialist-led Popular Front government that had just come to
power in France, they were strongly for the Republic. (Italy and Germany

immediately sent arms and men to their side.) France was anxious to help, and gave some (officially "deniable") assistance to the Republic until urged into an official policy of "non-intervention" by internal divisions of the British government, deeply hostile to what they saw as the advance of social revolution and bolshevism in the Iberian Peninsula. Middle-class and conservative opinion in the West generally shared this attitude, though (except for the Catholic Church and the pro-fascists) it did not passionately identify with the generals. Russia, though firmly on the Republican side, also joined the British-sponsored Non-Intervention Agreement, whose object, to prevent German and Italian help to the generals, nobody expected, or wanted, to achieve and which consequently "graduated from equivocation to hypocrisy" (Thomas, 1977, p. 395). From September 1936 on, Russia wholeheartedly, if not quite officially, sent men and materials to support the Republic. Non-intervention, which meant merely that Britain and France refused to do anything about the massive intervention of the Axis powers in Spain, and in doing so abandoned the Republic, confirmed both fascists and anti-fascists in their contempt for the non-interveners. It also enormously raised the prestige of the U.S.S.R., the only power that helped the legitimate government of Spain, and of the communists inside and outside that country, not only because they organized this help, internationally, but also because they soon established themselves as the backbone of the Republic's military effort.

Yet even before the Soviets mobilized their resources, all from the liberals to the outer reaches of the Left immediately recognized the Spanish struggle as their own. As the finest British poet of the decade, W. H. Auden, wrote

> On that arid square, that fragment nipped off from hot
> Africa, soldered so crudely to inventive Europe;
> On that table-land scored by rivers,
> Our thoughts have bodies; the menacing shapes of our fever
> Are precise and alive.

What is more: there, and only there, was the endless and demoralizing retreat of the Left being halted by men and women who fought the advance of the Right in arms. Even before the Communist International began to organize the International Brigades (whose first contingents arrived at their future base in mid-October), indeed before the first organized volunteer columns appeared at the front (those of the Italian liberal-socialist movement *Giustizia e Libertá*), foreign volunteers already fought for the Republic in some quantities. Eventually over forty thousand young foreigners from over fifty nations* went to fight and many to die in a country about which most of them probably knew no more than what it looked like in a school atlas. It is significant that no more than a thousand foreign volunteers fought on the Franco side (Thomas, 1977, p. 980). For the benefit of readers who have grown up in the moral milieu of the late twentieth century, it must be added that these were neither mercenaries, nor, except in a very few cases, adventurers. They went to fight for a cause.

What Spain meant to liberals and those on the Left who lived through the 1930s, is now difficult to remember, though for many of us the survivors, now all past the Biblical life-span, it remains the only political cause which, even in retrospect, appears as pure and compelling as it did in 1936. It now seems to belong to a prehistoric past, even in Spain. Yet at the time it seemed to those who fought fascism to be the central front of their battle, because it was the only one in which action never ceased for over two-and-a-half years, the only one where they could participate as individuals, if not in uniform, then by collecting money, by helping refugees, and by the never-ending campaigns to put pressure on our own chicken-hearted governments. And the gradual, but apparently irreversible advance of the nationalist side, the foreseeable defeat and death of the Republic, merely made the need to forge a union against world fascism more desperately urgent.

For the Spanish Republic, in spite of all our sympathies and the (insufficient) help it received, fought a rearguard action against defeat from the start. In retrospect, it is clear that this was due to its own weaknesses. By the standards of the people's wars of the twentieth century, won or lost, the Republican war of 1936–39, with all its heroism, rates poorly; in part because it made no serious use of that powerful weapon against superior conventional forces, guerrilla warfare—a strange omission in the country which gave this form of irregular warfare its name. Unlike the Nationalists, who enjoyed a single military and political direction, the Republic remained politically divided, and—in spite of the communists' contribution—did not acquire a single military will and

---

*They included perhaps 10,000 French, 5,000 Germans and Austrians, 5,000 Poles and Ukrainians, 3,350 Italians, 2,800 from the U.S.A., 2,000 British, 1,500 Yugoslavs, 1,500 Czechs, 1,000 Hungarians, 1,000 Scandinavians and a number of others. The 2–3,000 Russians can hardly be classed as volunteers. About 7,000 of these were said to be Jews (Thomas, 1977, p. 982–84; Paucker, 1991, p. 15).

strategic command, or not until it was too late. The best it could do was from time to time to throw back potentially fatal offensives by the other side, thus prolonging a war which might well have been effectively ended in November 1936 by the capture of Madrid.

At the time, the Spanish Civil War hardly looked like a good omen for the defeat of fascism. Internationally, it was a miniature version of a European war, fought between fascist and communist states, the latter notably more cautious and less determined than the former. The Western democracies remained sure about nothing except their non-involvement. Internally it was a war in which the mobilization of the Right proved far more effective than that of the Left. It ended in total defeat, several hundred thousand dead, several hundreds of thousands of refugees in such countries as would receive them, including most of the surviving intellectual and artistic talents of Spain, which had, with the rarest exceptions, rallied to the Republic. The Communist International had mobilized all its formidable talents for the Spanish Republic. The future Marshal Tito, liberator and leader of Communist Yugoslavia, organized the flow of recruits to the International Brigades from Paris; Palmiro Togliatti, the Italian Communist leader, in effect ran the inexperienced Spanish Communist Party, and was among the last to escape from the country in 1939. It also failed, and knew it was failing, as did the U.S.S.R. which detached some of its most impressive military minds for service in Spain (e.g. the future Marshals Konev, Malinovsky, Voronov and Rokossovsky and the future Commander of the Soviet navy, Admiral Kuznetsov).

IV

And yet, the Spanish Civil War anticipated and prepared the shape of the forces which were, within a few years of Franco's victory, to destroy fascism. It anticipated the politics of the Second World War, that unique alliance of national fronts ranging from patriotic conservatives to social revolutionaries, for the defeat of the national enemy, and simultaneously for social regeneration. For the Second World War was, for those on the winning side, not merely a struggle for military victory, but—even in Britain and the U.S.A.—for a better society. Nobody dreamed of a postwar return to 1939—or even to 1928 or to 1918, as statesmen after the First World War had dreamed of a return to the world of 1913. A British government under Winston Churchill committed itself, in the midst of a desperate war, to a comprehensive welfare state and full employment. It was no accident that the Beveridge Report, which recommended all these, came out in as black a year as any in Britain's desperate war: 1942. The post-war plans of the U.S.A. dealt only incidentally with the problem of how to make another Hitler impossible. The real intellectual efforts of the post-war planners were devoted to learning the lessons of the Great Slump and the 1930s, so that these could not recur. As for the resistance movements in the countries defeated and occupied by the Axis, the inseparability of liberation and social revolution or at least major transformation, went without saying. Moreover, throughout formerly occupied Europe, east and west, the same kinds of governments emerged from victory: administrations of national union based on all the forces that had opposed fascism, without ideological distinction. For the first, and only, time in history, communist ministers sat beside conservative, liberal or social-democratic ministers in most European states, admittedly a situation not destined to last long.

Even though a common threat drew them together, this astonishing unity of opposites, Roosevelt and Stalin, Churchill and the British socialists, de Gaulle and the French communists, would have been impossible without a certain slackening of hostilities and mutual suspicions between the champions and the adversaries of the October revolution. The Spanish Civil War made this a great deal easier. Even anti-revolutionary governments could not forget that the Spanish government, under a Liberal president and prime minister, had complete constitutional and moral legitimacy when it appealed for aid against its insurgent generals. Even those democratic statesmen who betrayed it, out of fear for their own skins, had a bad conscience. Both the Spanish government and, more to the point, the communists who were increasingly influential in its affairs, insisted that social revolution was not their object, and, indeed, visibly did what they could to control and reverse it, to the horror of revolutionary enthusiasts. Revolution, both insisted, was not the issue: the defence of democracy was.

The interesting point is that this was not mere opportunism or, as the purists on the ultra-Left thought, treason to the revolution. It reflected a deliberate shift from an insurrectionary to a gradualist, from a confrontational to a negotiating, even a parliamentary, way to power. In the light of the Spanish people's reaction to the coup, which was undoubtedly revolutionary,* communists could now see how an essentially defensive tactic, imposed by the desperate situation of their movement after Hitler's

---

*In the words of the Comintern, the Spanish revolution was "an integral part of the anti-fascist struggle which rests on the widest social base. It is a popular

accession to power, opened perspectives of advance, i.e. a "democracy of a new type," arising out of the imperatives of both wartime politics and economics. Landlords and capitalists who supported the rebels would lose their property; not as landlords and capitalists but as traitors. The government would have to plan and take over the economy; not for reasons for ideology but by the logic of war-economies. Consequently, if victorious, "such a democracy of a new type cannot but be the enemy of the conservative spirit . . . It provides a guarantee for the further economic and political conquests of the Spanish working people" (ibid., p. 176).

The Comintern pamphlet of October 1936 thus described with considerable accuracy the shape of politics in the anti-fascist war of 1939–45. This was to be a war waged in Europe by all-embracing "people's" or "national front" governments or resistance coalitions, which was waged by state-managed economies and ended, in the occupied territories, with massive advances in the public sector, due to the expropriation of capitalists, not as such but as Germans or collaborators with the Germans. In several countries of central and eastern Europe the road led directly from anti-fascism to a "new democracy" dominated, and eventually swallowed by, the communists, but until the outbreak of the Cold War, the object of these post-war regimes was, quite specifically, not the immediate conversion to socialist systems or the abolition of political pluralism and private property.* In Western countries the net social and economic consequences of war and liberation were not very different, though the political conjuncture was. Social and economic reforms were introduced, not (as after the First World War) in response to mass pressure and the fear of revolution, but by governments committed to them on principle—governments, partly of the old reformist kind, like the Democrats in the U.S.A., the Labour Party, now in government in Britain; partly by parties of reform and national revival directly emerging from the various anti-fascist resistance movements. In short, the logic of the anti-fascist war led towards the Left.

---

revolution. It is a national revolution. It is an anti-fascist revolution." (Ercoli, October 1936, cited in Hobsbawm, 1986, p. 175.)

*As late as the foundation conference of the new cold war Communist Information Bureau (Cominform), the Bulgarian delegate, Vlko Tchervenkov, still described the perspectives of his country firmly in these terms (Reale, 1954, pp. 66–67, 73–74).

V

In 1936 and even more in 1939 these implications of the Spanish war seemed remote, even unreal. After almost a decade of apparently total failure for the Comintern's line of anti-fascist unity, Stalin erased it from his agenda, at least for the time being, and not only came to terms with Hitler (though both sides knew that this could not last), but even instructed the international movement to abandon the anti-fascist strategy, a senseless decision perhaps best explained by his proverbial aversion to even the slightest risks.* Yet in 1941 the logic of the Comintern line came into its own. For as Germany invaded the U.S.S.R. and brought the U.S.A. into the war—in short, as the struggle against fascism finally became a global war—the war became political as much as military. Internationally, it became an alliance between the capitalism of the U.S.A. and the communism of the Soviet Union. Within each country of Europe—but not, at the time, the world dependent on Western imperialism—it hoped to unite all who were ready to resist Germany or Italy, i.e. to form a Resistance coalition ranging across the political spectrum. Since all of belligerent Europe except Great Britain was occupied by the Axis powers, this war of the resisters was essentially one of civilians, or armed forces of former civilians, not recognized as such by the German and Italian armies: a savage struggle of partisans, which imposed political choices on all.

The history of European Resistance movements is largely mythological, since (except to some extent in Germany itself) the legitimacy of post-war regimes and governments essentially rested on their Resistance record. France is the extreme case, because there the governments after Liberation lacked all real continuity with the French government of 1940, which had made peace and cooperated with the Germans, and because organized, let alone armed, resistance had been rather weak, at any rate until 1944, and popular support for it had been patchy. Post-war France was rebuilt by General de Gaulle on the basis of the myth that, essentially, the eternal France had never accepted defeat. As he himself put it, "Resistance was a bluff that came off" (Gillois, 1973, p. 164). It was an act of policy that the only fighters in the Second World War commemorated on French war memorials today are Resistance fighters, and those who joined de Gaulle's forces. However, France is by no means the only case of a state built on the Resistance mystique.

---

*Perhaps he was afraid that enthusiastic communist participation in a French or British anti-fascist war might be seen by Hitler as a sign of his secret bad faith, and thus an excuse to attack him.

Two things must be said about European Resistance movements. First, their military importance (with the possible exception of Russia) was negligible before Italy withdrew from the war in 1943, and not decisive anywhere except perhaps in parts of the Balkans. One must repeat that their major significance was political and moral. Thus Italian public life was transformed after over twenty years of fascism, which had enjoyed considerable support, even among intellectuals, by the unusually impressive and widespread mobilization of the Resistance in 1943–45, including an armed partisan movement in central and northern Italy of up to 100,000 combatants with forty-five thousand dead (Bocca, 1966, pp. 297–302, 385–89, 569–70; Pavone, 1991, p. 413). While Italians could thus put the memory of Mussolini's era behind them with a good conscience, Germans, who had remained solidly behind their government to the end, could not put a distance between themselves and the Nazi era of 1933–45. Their internal resisters, a minority of communist militants, Prussian military conservatives, with a scattering of religious and liberal dissenters, were dead or emerged from concentration camps. Conversely, of course, support for fascism or collaboration with the occupier virtually removed the people concerned from public life for a generation after 1945, though the Cold War against communism found plenty of employment for such persons in the underworld or half-world of Western military and intelligence operations.*

The second observation about the Resistance is that, for obvious reasons—though with one notable exception in Poland—its politics were skewed to the Left. In each country the fascist and radical Right and conservatives, the local rich and others whose main terror was social revolution, tended to sympathize, or at least not to oppose, the Germans; so did a number of regionalist or lesser nationalist movements; themselves traditionally on the ideological Right, some of which actually hoped to

---

*The secret anti-communist armed force known, after its existence was revealed by an Italian politician in 1990, as *Stay Behind* (in Italy *Gladio* or "the sword") was set up in 1949 to continue internal resistance in various European countries after a Soviet occupation, if such a situation arose. Its members were armed and paid by the U.S.A., trained by the CIA and British secret and special forces, and its existence was concealed from the governments in whose territories they operated, apart from selected individuals. In Italy, and perhaps elsewhere, it originally consisted of last-ditch fascists who had been left behind as nuclei of resistance by the defeated Axis, who subsequently acquired a new value as fanatical anti-communists. In the 1970s, when invasion by the Red Army no longer seemed plausible even to American secret service operatives, the Gladiators found a new field of activity as Right-wing terrorists, sometimes masquerading as Left-wing terrorists.

benefit from their collaboration, notably Flemish, Slovak and Croat nationalism. So, it should not be forgotten, did the profoundly and intransigently anti-communist elements in the Catholic Church, and its armies of the conventionally pious, though Church politics were far too complex to be simply classified as "collaborationist" anywhere. It follows that those from the political Right who chose resistance were inevitably uncharacteristic of their political constituency. Winston Churchill and General de Gaulle were not typical members of their ideological families, though it must be said that for more than one visceral Right-wing traditionalist of military instincts, a patriotism that did not defend the fatherland was unthinkable.

This explains, if any special explanation is needed, the extraordinary prominence of the communists in the resistance movements, and, consequently, their startling political advance during the war. The European communist movements reached the peak of their influence in 1945–47 for this reason, except in Germany, where they did not recover from the brutal decapitation of 1933, and the heroic but suicidal attempts at resistance in the next three years. Even in countries far from social revolution, like Belgium, Denmark and the Netherlands, communist parties scored 10–12 per cent of the vote—a multiple of what they had ever scored before, forming the third- or fourth-largest blocs in their countries' parliaments. In France they emerged as the largest party of all in the 1945 elections, larger, for the first time, than their old rivals the socialists. In Italy their record was even more startling. A small, harried and notoriously unsuccessful band of illegal cadres before the war—they were actually threatened with dissolution by the Comintern in 1938—they emerged from two years of resistance as a mass party of eight hundred thousand members, soon (1946) to reach almost two millions. As for the countries where the war against the Axis had been waged essentially by the armed internal resistance—Yugoslavia, Albania and Greece—the partisan forces had been dominated by the communists, so much so that the British government under Churchill, who lacked the slightest sympathy for communism, transferred its support and aid from the royalist Mihailović to the communist Tito, when it became clear that one was incomparably more dangerous to the Germans than the other.

The communists took to resistance, not only because Lenin's "vanguard party" structure was designed to produce a force of disciplined and selfless cadres whose very purpose was efficient action, but because extreme situations, such as illegality, repression and war, were precisely what these bodies of "professional revolutionaries" had been designed for. Indeed, they "alone had foreseen the possibility of resistance war" (M.R.D.

Foot, 1976, p. 84). In this they differed from the mass soci
which found it almost impossible to operate in the absence ı
ity—elections, public meetings and the rest—which defined ̲ ̲ ̲ ucter-
mined their activities. Faced with a fascist take-over or German occupation,
social-democratic parties tended to go into hibernation, from which, in
the best of cases they emerged, like the German and Austrian ones, at the
end of the dark era, with most of their old support and ready to resume
politics. While not absent from the resistance, they were, for structural
reasons, under-represented. In the extreme case of Denmark a Social Democratic government was actually in office when Germany occupied the
country *and remained in office* throughout the war, though presumably
lacking in sympathy for the Nazis. (It took some years to recover from
this episode.)

Two other characteristics helped the communists to prominence in the
resistance: their internationalism and the passionate, quasi-millennial
conviction with which they dedicated their lives to the cause (see chapter 2). The first allowed them to mobilize men and women more open to
the anti-fascist appeal than to any patriotic call, e.g. in France the Spanish Civil War refugees who provided most of the armed partisan resistance
in the south-west of that country—perhaps twelve thousand fighters
before D-Day (Pons Prades, 1975, p. 66)—and the other refugees and
working-class immigrants from seventeen nations who, under the acronym MOI (*Main d'Oeuvre Immigrée*), did some of the Party's most dangerous work, such as the Manouchian group (Armenians and Polish
Jews) which attacked German officers in Paris.* The second generated
that combination of bravery, self-sacrifice and ruthlessness which impressed even the adversaries, and which that work of marvellous honesty,
the Yugoslav Milovan Djilas' *Wartime* (Djilas, 1977), brings out so
vividly. The communists, in the opinion of a politically moderate historian, were "among the bravest of the brave" (Foot, 1976, p. 86), and
though their disciplined organization gave them the best survival chances
in prisons and concentration camps, their losses were heavy. Suspicion of
the French CP, whose leadership was disliked even among other communists, could not entirely deny its claim to be *le parti des fusillés*, which
had at least fifteen thousand of its militants executed by the enemy (Jean
Touchard, 1977, p. 258). Not surprisingly, they had a powerful appeal to

---

*One of the author's friends, who eventually became deputy commander of MOI
under the Czech Artur London, was an Austrian Jew of Polish origin, whose resistance task was to organize anti-Nazi propaganda among the German troops in
France.

brave men and women, especially the young, and perhaps especially in countries where mass support for the active resistance had been scarce, as in France or Czechoslovakia. They also appealed strongly to intellectuals, the group most readily mobilized under the banner of anti-fascism, and who formed the core of the non-party (but generically Left-wing) resistance organizations. The love affair of French intellectuals with Marxism, the domination of Italian culture by people associated with the Communist Party, both of which lasted for a generation, were products of the resistance. Whether the intellectuals themselves launched themselves into resistance, like the leading post-war publisher who notes with pride that *all* members of his firm took up arms as partisans, or became communist sympathisers because they or their families had *not* been actual resisters—they might even have been on the other side—they all felt the pull of the Party.

Except in their Balkan guerrilla strongholds, the communists made no attempt to establish revolutionary regimes. It is true that they were in no position to do so anywhere west of Trieste even had they wanted to make a bid for power, but also that the U.S.S.R., to which their parties were utterly loyal, strongly discouraged such unilateral bids for power. The communist revolutions actually made (Yugoslavia, Albania, later China) were made *against* Stalin's advice. The Soviet view was that, both internationally and within each country, post-war politics should continue within the framework of the all-embracing anti-fascist alliance, i.e. it looked forward to a long-term coexistence, or rather symbiosis, of capitalist and communist systems, and further social and political change, presumably occurring by shifts within the "democracies of a new type" which would emerge out of the wartime coalitions. This optimistic scenario soon disappeared into the night of Cold War, so completely that few remember that Stalin urged the Yugoslav communists to keep the monarchy or that in 1945 British communists were opposed to the break-up of the Churchill wartime coalition, i.e. to the electoral campaign which was to bring the Labour government to power. Nevertheless, there is no doubt that Stalin meant all this seriously, and tried to prove it by dissolving the Comintern in 1943, and the Communist Party of the U.S.A. in 1944.

Stalin's decision, expressed in the words of an American communist leader "that we will not raise the issue of socialism in such a form and manner as to endanger or weaken ... unity" (Browder, 1944, in J. Starobin, 1972, p. 57) made his intentions clear. For practical purposes, as dissident revolutionaries recognized, it was a permanent goodbye to world revolution. Socialism would be confined to the U.S.S.R. and the area assigned by diplomatic negotiation as its zone of influence, i.e. basically that occupied by the Red Army at the end of the war. Even within that zone of influence it would remain an undefined prospect for the future rather than an immediate programme for the new "people's democracies." History, which takes little notice of policy intentions, went another way—except in one respect. The division of the globe, or a large part of it, into two zones of influence, negotiated in 1944–45, remained stable. Neither side overstepped the line dividing them more than momentarily for thirty years. Both withdrew from open confrontation, thus guaranteeing that cold world wars never became hot ones.

VI

Stalin's brief dream of post-war U.S.–Soviet partnership did not actually strengthen the global alliance of liberal capitalism and communism against fascism. Rather it demonstrated its strength and width. It was, of course, an alliance against a military threat, and one which would never have come into existence but for the series of Nazi Germany's aggressions, culminating in the invasion of the U.S.S.R. and the declaration of war against the U.S. Nevertheless, the very nature of war confirmed the 1936 insights into the implications of the Spanish Civil War: the unity of military and civilian mobilization and social change. On the allied side—more than on the fascist side—it was a war of reformers, partly because not even the most confident capitalist power could hope to win a long war without abandoning "business as usual," partly because the very fact of the Second World War dramatized the failures of the inter-war years, of which the failure to unite against the aggressors was merely one minor symptom.

That victory and social hope went together is also clear from what we know of the development of public opinion in the belligerent or liberated countries in which there was freedom to express it except, curiously enough, in the U.S.A., where the years since 1936 saw a marginal erosion of the Democratic presidential vote, but a marked revival of the Republicans: this was a country dominated by its domestic concerns and far more remote from the sacrifices of war than any other. Where there were genuine elections, they showed a sharp shift to the Left. The most dramatic case was the British, where the elections of 1945 defeated the universally loved and admired war-leader, Winston Churchill, and brought to power the Labour Party with a 50 per cent increase in its vote. In the next five years it presided over a period of unprecedented social reforms. Both the major parties had been equally involved in the war effort. The electorate chose the one which promised both victory and social transformation. The phenomenon was general in warring Western Europe, though neither its scale nor its radicalism should be exaggerated, as its public image tended to be, by the temporary elimination of the former fascist or collaborationist Right.

The situation in the parts of Europe liberated by guerrilla revolution or the Red Army is more difficult to judge, if only because mass genocide, mass population displacement and mass expulsion or forced emigration make it impossible to compare the pre-war and post-war countries bearing their old names. Throughout this area the bulk of the inhabitants of the countries invaded by the Axis saw themselves as its victims, with the exception of the politically divided Slovaks and Croats, who acquired nominally independent states under German auspices; the majority peoples in Germany's allied states, Hungary and Romania; and, of course, the large German diaspora. This did not mean that they sympathised with communist-inspired resistance movements—except perhaps for the Jews, persecuted by everyone else—still less (except for traditionally Russophile Balkan Slavs) with Russia. The Poles were overwhelmingly both anti-German and anti-Russian, not to mention anti-semitic. The small Baltic peoples, occupied by the U.S.S.R. in 1940, were both anti-Russian, anti-semitic and pro-German, while they had the choice in 1941–45. Neither communists nor resistance were to be found in Romania, and little enough in Hungary. On the other hand, both communism and pro-Russian sentiment were strong in Bulgaria, though resistance had been patchy, and in Czechoslovakia the CP, always a mass party, emerged as the largest party by far in genuinely free elections. Soviet occupation soon made such political differences academic. Guerrilla victories are not plebiscites, but there is little doubt that most Yugoslavs welcomed the triumph of Tito's partisans, except the German minority, the supporters of the Croatian Ustashi regime, on whom the Serbs took savage revenge for earlier massacres, and a traditionalist core in Serbia, where Tito's movement, and consequently anti-German warfare, had never flourished.* Greece remained proverbially divided, in spite of the refusal of Stalin to assist the Greek communist and pro-red forces against the British who supported their opponents. Only experts in

---

*However, the Serbs in Croatia and Bosnia, as well as the Montenegrins (who provided 17 per cent of the officers for the Partisan army) were strongly for Tito, as were important sections of Croats—Tito's own people—and the Slovenes. Most of the fighting took place in Bosnia.

kinship studies would care to hazard a guess about the political sentiments of the Albanians after the communists triumphed. However, in all these countries an era of massive social transformation was about to begin.

Oddly enough, the U.S.S.R. was (with the U.S.A.) the only belligerent country in which the war brought no significant social and institutional change. It began and ended the conflict under Joseph Stalin (see chapter 13). However, it is clear that the war imposed enormous strains on the stability of the system, especially in the harshly repressed countryside. But for the ingrained belief of National Socialism in the Slavs as a race of sub-human helots, the German invaders could have won lasting support among many Soviet peoples. Conversely, the real foundation of Soviet victory was the patriotism of the majority nationality of the U.S.S.R., the Great Russians, always the core of the Red Army, to which the Soviet regime appealed in its moment of crisis. Indeed, the Second World War became officially known in the U.S.S.R. as "the Great Patriotic War," and rightly so.

VII

At this point the historian must make a major leap to avoid falling into the pit of a purely occidental analysis. For very little of what has been written in this chapter so far applies to the greater part of the globe. It is not quite irrelevant to the conflict between Japan and continental East Asia, since Japan, dominated by the politics of the ultra-nationalist Right, was allied with Nazi Germany, and the main forces of resistance in China were the communists. It applies to some extent in Latin America, a great importer of fashionable European ideologies like fascism or communism, and especially to Mexico, reviving its great revolution in the 1930s under President Lázaro Cardenas (1934–40) and passionately taking sides for the Spanish Republic in the Civil War. In fact, after its defeat Mexico remained the only state which continued to recognize the Republic as the legitimate government of Spain. However, for most of Asia, Africa and the Islamic world, fascism, whether as an ideology or as the policy of an aggressor state, was not and never became the main, let alone the only enemy. This was "imperialism" or "colonialism," and the imperialist powers were, overwhelmingly, the liberal democracies: Britain, France, the Netherlands, Belgium and the U.S.A. Moreover, all imperial powers, with the single exception of Japan, were white.

Logically the enemies of the imperial power were also potential allies in the fight for colonial liberation. Even Japan, which, as the Koreans,

Taiwanese, Chinese and others could tell, had its own ruthless brand of colonialism, could appeal to anti-colonial forces in South-east and South Asia as a champion of non-whites against whites. The anti-imperial struggle and the anti-fascist struggle, therefore, tended to pull in opposite directions. Thus Stalin's pact with the Germans in 1939, which disrupted the Western Left, allowed Indian or Vietnamese communists to concentrate happily on opposing the British and French; whereas the German invasion of the U.S.S.R. in 1941 forced them, as good communists, to put the defeat of the Axis first, i.e. to put the liberation of their own countries much lower on the agenda. This was not merely unpopular, but strategically senseless at a time when the colonial empires of the West were at their most vulnerable, if not actually collapsing. And, indeed, local leftists who did not feel bound by the iron hoops of Comintern loyalty exploited the opportunity. The Indian National Congress launched the Quit India movement in 1942, while the Bengali radical Subhas Bose recruited an Indian Liberation Army for the Japanese from among the Indian army prisoners of war taken during the lightning initial advances. Anti-colonial militants in Burma and Indonesia saw matters the same way. The *reductio ad absurdum* of this anti-colonialist logic was the attempt by an extremist Jewish fringe group in Palestine to negotiate with the *Germans* (via Damascus, then under the Vichy French) for help in liberating Palestine from the British, which they regarded as the top priority for Zionism. (A militant of the group involved in this mission eventually became prime minister of Israel: Yitzhak Shamir.) Such approaches evidently did not imply any ideological sympathy for fascism, though Nazi anti-semitism might appeal to Palestinian Arabs at odds with Zionist settlers, and some groups in South Asia might recognize themselves in the superior Aryans of Nazi mythology. But these were special cases (see chapters 12 and 15).

What needs explaining is why, after all, anti-imperialism and the colonial liberation movements inclined overwhelmingly to the Left, and thus found themselves, at least at the end of the war, converging with the global anti-fascist mobilization. The fundamental reason is that the Western Left was the nursery of anti-imperialist theory and policies, and that support for colonial liberation movements came overwhelmingly from the international Left, and especially (since the Bolsheviks' 1920 Congress of the Eastern Peoples in Baku) from the Comintern and the U.S.S.R. Moreover, the activists and future leaders of independence movements, who belonged chiefly to the Western-educated elites of their countries, found themselves more at ease in the non-racist and anti-colonial milieu of local liberals, democrats, socialists and communists than in any other, when they came to their metropoles. They were in any case almost all modernizers, whom the nostalgic medievalist myths, Nazi ideology and the racist exclusiveness of their theories, reminded of just those "communalist" and "tribalist" tendencies which, in their opinion, were symptoms of their countries' backwardness which were exploited by imperialism.

In short, an alliance with the Axis, on the principle that "my enemy's enemies are my friends," could only be tactical. Even in South-east Asia, where Japanese rule was less repressive than the old colonialists', and exercised by non-whites against whites, it could only have been short-lived, since Japan, quite apart from its pervasive racism, had no interest in liberating colonies as such. (In fact, it was short-lived, because Japan was soon defeated.) Fascism or the Axis nationalisms held no particular attraction. On the other hand a man like Jawaharlal Nehru who (unlike the communists) did not hesitate to launch himself into the Quit India rebellion in 1942, the crisis year of the British Empire, never ceased to believe that a free India would build a socialist society, and that the U.S.S.R. would be an ally in this endeavour, perhaps even—with all qualifications—an example.

That the leaders and spokesmen for colonial liberation were, so often, minorities untypical of the population they set out to emancipate actually made convergence with anti-fascism easier, for the bulk of the colonial populations were moved, or at least mobilizable, by feelings and ideas to which (but for its commitment to racial superiority) fascism might have made some appeal: traditionalism; religious and ethnic exclusiveness; a suspicion of the modern world. In fact, these sentiments were not yet mobilized to any substantial extent or, if mobilized, they did not yet become politically dominant. Islamic mass mobilization did develop very strongly in the Muslim world between 1918 and 1945. Thus Hassan al-Banna's Muslim Brotherhood (1928), a fundamentalist movement strongly hostile to liberalism and communism, became the main standard-bearer of Egyptian mass grievances in the 1940s, and its potential affinities with the Axis ideologies were more than tactical, especially given its hostility to Zionism. Yet the movements and politicians which actually came to the top in Islamic countries, sometimes carried on the backs of the fundamentalist masses, were secular and modernizing. The Egyptian colonels who were to make the revolution of 1952, were emancipated intellectuals, who had been in contact with the small Egyptian communist groups, whose leadership, incidentally, was largely Jewish (Perrault, 1987). On the Indian subcontinent, Pakistan (a child of the 1930s and 1940s) has been correctly described as "the program of secularized elites who were forced by the [territorial] disunity of the Muslim population and by competition with the Hindu majorities to call their political society 'Islamic' rather than nationally separatist" (Lapidus, 1988, p. 738). In Syria the running was made by the Ba'ath Party, founded in the 1940s by two Paris-educated schoolteachers who, with all their Arab mysticism, were ideologically anti-imperialist and socialist. The Syrian constitution contains no mention of Islam. Iraqi politics (until the Gulf War of 1991) was determined by various combinations of nationalist officers, communists and Ba'athists, all devoted to Arab unity and socialism (at least in theory), but distinctly not to the Law of the Koran. Both for local reasons and because the Algerian revolutionary movement had a wide mass base (not least among the large emigration of labourers to France) there was a strong Islamic element in the Algerian revolution. However, the revolutionaries specifically agreed (in 1956) that "theirs was a struggle to destroy an anachronistic colonization but not a war of religion" (Lapidus, 1988, p. 693) and proposed to form a social and democratic republic, which became constitutionally a one-party socialist republic. Indeed, the period of anti-fascism is the only one in which actual communist parties acquired substantial support and influence within some parts of the Islamic world, notably in Syria, Iraq and Iran. It was only much later that the secular and modernizing voices of political leadership were drowned and silenced by the mass politics of fundamentalist revival (see chapters 12 and 15).

In spite of their conflicts of interest, which were to re-emerge after the war, the anti-fascism of the developed Western countries and the anti-imperialism of their colonies found themselves converging towards what both envisaged as a post-war future of social transformation. The U.S.S.R. and local communism helped to bridge the gap, since they meant anti-imperialism to one world, total commitment to victory to the other. However, unlike the European theatres of war, the non-European ones did not bring the communists major political triumphs, except in the special cases where (as in Europe) anti-fascism and national/social liberation coincided: in China and Korea, where the colonialists were the Japanese, and in Indochina (Vietnam, Cambodia, Laos), where the immediate enemy of freedom remained the French, whose local administration had subordinated itself to the Japanese, when these overran South-east Asia. These were the countries where communism was destined to triumph in the post-war era, under Mao, Kim Il Sung and Ho Chi Minh. Elsewhere the leaders of the states about to be decolonised came from movements, generally of the Left, but less hampered in 1941–45 by the need to give the defeat of the Axis priority over all else. Still, even these could not but look at the world situation after the Axis defeat with some optimism. The two super-powers were no friends to the old colonialism, at least on paper. A known anti-colonialist party had come to power in the heart of the largest empire of all. The force and legitimacy of the old colonialism had been severely undermined. The chances for freedom seemed better than ever before. This proved to be the case, but not without some savage rearguard actions by the old empires.

VIII

So the defeat of the Axis—more precisely, of Germany and Japan—left little grief behind, except in Germany and Japan itself, whose people had fought, with stubborn loyalty and formidable efficiency, to the last day. In the end fascism had mobilized nothing outside its core countries except a scattering of ideological minorities of the radical right, most of whom would have remained on the political fringes in their own countries, a few nationalist groups who expected to achieve their objects by a German alliance, and a lot of the flotsam and jetsam of war and conquest, recruited into the savage auxiliary soldiery of the Nazi occupation. The Japanese mobilized nothing but, momentarily, a sympathy for yellow rather than white skins. The major appeal of European fascism, that it provided a safeguard against working-class movements, socialism, communism and the godless devil's headquarters in Moscow that inspired them all, had won it a good deal of support among the conservative rich, though big-business support was always pragmatic rather than principled. It was not an appeal that would outlive failure and defeat. In any case, the net effect of twelve years of National Socialism was that large parts of Europe now lay at the mercy of the Bolsheviks.

So fascism dissolved like a clump of earth thrown into a river, and virtually disappeared from the political scene for good except in Italy, where a modest neo-fascist movement (the *Movimento Sociale Italiano*) honouring Mussolini has a permanent presence in Italian politics. This was not due merely to the exclusion from politics of persons formerly prominent in fascist regimes, though by no means from the state services and from public life, and still less from economic life. It was not even due to the trauma of good Germans (and, in a different way, loyal Japanese) whose world collapsed in the physical and moral chaos of 1945, and for whom mere fidelity to their old beliefs was actually counterproductive. It stood in the way of adjusting themselves to a new, initially incomprehensible, life under the occupying powers who imposed their institutions and ways on them: who laid the rails along which their trains would henceforth necessarily have to roll. National Socialism had nothing to offer to the post-1945 German except memories. It is typical that in a strongly National Socialist part of Hitler's Germany, namely in Austria (which, by a twist of international diplomacy found itself classified among the innocent rather than the guilty), post-war politics soon reverted to exactly what it had been before democracy was abolished in 1933, with the exception of a slight shift to the Left (see Flora, 1983, p. 99). Fascism disappeared with the world crisis that had allowed it to emerge. It had never been, even in theory, a universal programme or political project.

On the other hand anti-fascism, however heterogeneous and impermanent its mobilization, succeeded in uniting an extraordinary range of forces. What is more, this unity was not negative but positive and, in certain respects, lasting. Ideologically, it was based on the shared values and aspirations of the Enlightenment and the Age of Revolution: progress by the application of reason and science; education and popular government; no inequalities based on birth or origin; societies looking to the future rather than the past. Some of these similarities existed purely on paper, though it is not entirely insignificant that political entities as remote from Western, or indeed any, democracy as Mengistu's Ethiopia, Somalia before the fall of Siad Barre, Kim Il Sung's North Korea, Algeria and communist East Germany chose to give themselves the official title of Democratic or People's (Popular) Democratic Republic. It is a label which inter-war fascist, authoritarian and even traditional conservative regimes between the wars would have rejected with contempt.

In other respects common aspirations were not so remote from common reality. Western constitutional capitalism, communist systems and the third world were equally committed to equal rights for all races and both sexes, i.e. they all fell short of the common target, but not in ways that systematically distinguished one lot from another.* They were all secular states. More to the point, after 1945 they were virtually all states which, deliberately and actively, rejected the supremacy of the market and believed in the active management and planning of the economy by the state. Difficult though it might be to recall in the age of neoliberal economic theology, between the early 1940s and the 1970s the most prestigious and formerly influential champions of complete market freedom, e.g. Friedrich von Hayek, saw themselves and their like as prophets

---

*Notably all forgot the major part played by women in war, resistance and liberation.

in the wilderness vainly warning a heedless Western capitalism that it was rushing along the "Road to Serfdom" (Hayek, 1944). In fact, it was advancing into an era of economic miracles (see chapter 9). Capitalist governments were convinced that only economic interventionism could prevent a return to the economic catastrophes between the wars, and avoid the political dangers of people radicalized to the point of choosing communism, as they had once chosen Hitler. Third-world countries believed only public action could lift their economies out of backwardness and dependency. In the decolonised world, following the inspiration of the Soviet Union, they were to see the way forward as socialism. The Soviet Union and its newly extended family believed in nothing but central planning. And all three regions of the world advanced into the post-war world with the conviction that victory over the Axis, achieved by political mobilization and revolutionary policies as well as by blood and iron, opened a new era of social transformation.

In a sense they were right. Never has the face of the globe and human life been so dramatically transformed as in the era which began under the mushroom clouds of Hiroshima and Nagasaki. But as always history took only marginal notice of human intentions, even those of the national decision-makers. The real social transformation was neither intended nor planned. And in any case, the first contingency they had to face was the almost immediate breakdown of the great anti-fascist alliance. As soon as there was no longer a fascism to unite against, capitalism and communism once again got ready to face each other as one another's mortal enemies.

CHAPTER SIX

The Arts 1914–1945

The surrealists' Paris, too, is a little "universe." . . . In the larger one, the cosmos, things look no different. There, too, are crossroads where ghostly signals flash from the traffic, and inconceivable analogies and connections between events are the order of the day. It is the region from which the lyric poetry of Surrealism reports.

—Walter Benjamin, "Surrealism," from *One Way Street* (1979, p. 231)

The New Architecture seems to be making little progress in the U.S.A. . . . The advocates of the new style are full of earnestness, and some of them carry on in the shrill pedagogical manner of believers in the Single Tax . . . but, save on the level of factory design, they do not seem to be making many converts.

—H. L. Mencken, 1931

I

Why brilliant fashion-designers, a notoriously non-analytic breed, sometimes succeed in anticipating the shape of things to come better than professional predictors, is one of the most obscure questions in history; and, for the historian of culture, one of the most central. It is certainly crucial to anyone who wants to understand the impact of the age of cataclysms on the world of high culture, the elite arts, and, above all, the avant-garde. For it is generally accepted that these arts anticipated the actual breakdown of liberal-bourgeois society by several years (see *Age of Empire*, chapter 9). By 1914 virtually everything that can take shelter under the broad and rather undefined canopy of "modernism" was already in place: cubism; expressionism; futurism; pure abstraction in painting;

functionalism and flight from ornament in architecture; the abandonment of tonality in music; the break with tradition in literature.

A large number of names who would be on most people's list of eminent "modernists" were all mature and productive or even famous in 1914.* Even T. S. Eliot, whose poetry was not published until 1917 and after, was by then clearly a part of the London avant-garde scene [as a contributor (with Pound) to Wyndham Lewis's *Blast*]. These children of, at the latest, the 1880s, remained icons of modernity forty years later. That a number of men and women who only began to emerge after the war would also make most high-culture shortlists of eminent "modernists" is less surprising than the domination of the older generation.† (Thus even Schönberg's successors—Alban Berg and Anton Webern—belong to the generation of the 1880s.)

In fact, the only formal innovations after 1914 in the world of the "established" avant-garde seem to have been two: *Dadaism*, which shaded over into or anticipated *surrealism* in the western half of Europe, and the Soviet-born *constructivism* in the East. Constructivism, an excursion into skeletal three-dimensional and preferably moving constructions which have their nearest real-life analogue in some fairground structures (giant wheels, big dippers, etc.), was soon absorbed into the main stream of architecture and industrial design, largely through the Bauhaus (of which more below). Its most ambitious projects, such as Tatlin's famous rotating leaning tower in honour of the Communist International, never got built, or else lived evanescent lives as the decor of early Soviet public ritual. Novel as it was, constructivism did little more than extend the repertoire of architectural modernism.

Dadaism took shape among a mixed group of exiles in Zurich (where another group of exiles under Lenin awaited the revolution) in 1916, as an anguished but ironic nihilist protest against world war and the society that had incubated it: including its art. Since it rejected all art, it had no formal characteristics, although it borrowed a few tricks from the pre-1914 cubist and futurist avant-gardes, including notably *collage*, or sticking together bits and pieces, including parts of pictures. Basically anything that might cause apoplexy among conventional bourgeois art-lovers was acceptable Dada. Scandal was its principle of cohesion. Thus

---

*Matisse and Picasso; Schonberg and Stravinsky; Gropius and Mies van der Rohe; Proust, James Joyce, Thomas Mann and Franz Kafka; Yeats, Ezra Pound, Alexander Blok and Anna Akhmatova.

†Among others, Isaac Babel (1894); Le Corbusier (1897); Ernest Hemingway (1899); Bertolt Brecht, Garcia Lorca and Hanns Eisler (all born 1898); Kurt Weill (1900); Jean Paul Sartre (1905); and W.H. Auden (1907).

Marcel Duchamp's (1887–1968) exhibition of a public urinal as "ready-made art" in New York in 1917 was entirely in the spirit of Dada, which he joined on his return from the U.S.A.; but his subsequent quiet refusal to have anything further to do with art—he preferred to play chess—was not. For there was nothing quiet about Dada.

Surrealism, while equally devoted to the rejection of art as hitherto known, equally given to public scandal and (as we shall see) even more attracted to social revolution, was more than a negative protest; as might be expected from a movement essentially centred in France, a country where every fashion requires a theory. Indeed, we can say that, as Dada foundered in the early 1920s with the era of war and revolution that had given it birth, surrealism emerged from it as what has been called "a plea for the revival of the imagination, based on the Unconscious as revealed by psychoanalysis, together with a new emphasis on magic, accident, irrationality, symbols and dreams" (Willett, 1978).

In some ways it was a romantic revival in twentieth-century costume (see *Age of Revolution*, chapter 14), but with more sense of absurdity and fun. Unlike the mainstream "modernist" avant-gardes, but like Dada, surrealism had no interest in formal innovation as such: whether the Unconscious expressed itself in a random stream of words ("automatic writing") or in the meticulous nineteenth-century academician's style in which Salvador Dali (1904–89) painted his deliquescent watches in desert landscapes, was of no interest. What counted was to recognize the capacity of the spontaneous imagination, unmediated by rational control systems, to produce cohesion out of the incoherent, an apparently necessary logic out of the plainly illogical or even impossible. René Magritte's (1898–1967) *Castle in the Pyrenees*, carefully painted in the manner of a picture-postcard, emerges from the top of a huge rock, as though it had grown there. Only the rock, like a giant egg, is floating through the sky above the sea, painted with equal realistic care.

Surrealism was a genuine addition to the repertoire of avant-garde arts, its novelty attested by the ability to produce shock, incomprehension, or what amounted to the same thing, a sometimes embarrassed laughter, even among the older avant-garde. This was my own, admittedly juvenile, reaction to the 1936 International Surrealist Exhibition in London, and later to a surrealist painter friend in Paris, whose insistence on producing the exact equivalent in oils of a photograph of human entrails I found hard to understand. Nevertheless, in retrospect it must be seen as a remarkably fertile movement, though chiefly in France and countries such as the Hispanic ones, where French influence was strong. It influenced first-rate poets in France (Eluard, Aragon); in Spain (García

Lorca); Eastern Europe and Latin America (César Vallejo in Peru, Pablo Neruda in Chile); and indeed some of it still echoes through "magical realist" writing in that continent much later. Its images and visions—Max Ernst (1891–1976), Magritte, Joan Miró (1893–1983), yes, even Salvador Dali—have become part of ours. And, unlike most earlier Western avant-gardes, it actually fertilized the central art of the twentieth century, that of the camera. It is no accident that the cinema is indebted to surrealism not only for Luis Buñuel (1900–83) but also for the central scriptwriter of the French cinema in this era, Jacques Prévert (1900–77), while photojournalism is indebted to it for Henri Cartier-Bresson (1908–).

Yet, taken all in all, these were amplifications of the avant-garde revolution in the high arts which had already taken place before the world whose collapse it expressed actually went to pieces. Three things can be noted about this revolution in the era of cataclysms: the avant-garde became, as it were, part of established culture; it became at least partly absorbed into the fabric of everyday life; and—perhaps above all—it became dramatically politicized, perhaps more so than the high arts in any period since the Age of Revolution. And yet, we must never forget that, throughout this period, it remained isolated from the tastes and concerns of the mass of even the Western public, though it now impinged on it more than that public generally recognized. Except for a somewhat larger minority than before 1914, it was not what most people actually and consciously enjoyed.

To say that the new avant-garde became central to the established arts is not to claim that it displaced the classic and the fashionable, but that it supplemented both, and became the proof of a serious interest in cultural matters. The international operatic repertoire remained essentially what it had been in the Age of Empire, with composers born in the early 1860s (Richard Strauss, Mascagni) or even earlier (Puccini, Leoncavallo, Janacek) at the outer limits of "modernity," as, broadly speaking, it still remains.*

Yet the traditional partner of opera, namely ballet, was transformed into a consciously avant-garde medium by the great Russian impresario Sergei Diaghilev (1872–1929) mainly during the First World War. After his 1917 Paris production of *Parade* (designs by Picasso, music by Satie, libretto by Jean Cocteau, programme notes by Guillaume Apollinaire),

---

*It is significant that, with comparatively rare exceptions—Alban Berg, Benjamin Britten—the major creations for the musical stage after 1918, for instance *The Threepenny Opera, Mahagonny, Porgy and Bess*—were not written for official opera houses.

décors by the likes of the cubists Georges Braque (1882–1963) and Juan Gris (1887–1927); music by, or rewritten by Stravinsky, de Falla, Milhaud and Poulenc became *de rigueur,* while both styles of dancing and choreography were modernized accordingly. Before 1914, at least in Britain, the "Post-Impressionist Exhibition" had been jeered by a philistine public, while Stravinsky caused scandal wherever he went, as did the Armory Show in New York and elsewhere. After the war, the philistines fell silent before the provocative displays of "modernism," deliberate declarations of independence from the discredited pre-war world, manifestos of cultural revolution. And, through the modernist ballet, exploiting its unique combination of snob appeal, the magnetism of vogue (plus the new *Vogue*) and elite artistic status, the avant-garde broke out of its stockade. Thanks to Diaghilev, wrote a characteristic figure in the British cultural journalism of the 1920s, "the crowd has positively enjoyed decorations by the best and most ridiculed living painters. He has given us Modern Music without tears and Modern Painting without laughter" (Mortimer, 1925).

Diaghilev's ballet was merely one medium for the diffusion of the avant-garde arts which, in any case, varied from one country to the next. Nor, indeed, was the same avant-garde diffused throughout the Western world for, in spite of the continued hegemony of Paris over large regions of elite culture, reinforced after 1918 by the influx of American expatriates (the generation of Hemingway and Scott Fitzgerald), there was actually no longer a unified high culture in the old world. In Europe Paris competed with the Moscow-Berlin axis, until the triumphs of Stalin and Hitler silenced or dispersed the Russian or German avant-gardes. The fragments of the former Habsburg and Ottoman Empires went their own way in literature, isolated by languages which nobody seriously or systematically attempted to translate until the era of the anti-fascist diaspora in the 1930s. The extraordinary flowering of poetry in the Spanish language on both sides of the Atlantic had next to no international impact until the Spanish Civil War of 1936–39 revealed it. Even the arts least hampered by the tower of Babel, those of sight and sound, were less international than might be supposed, as a comparison of the relative standing of, say, Hindemith in and outside Germany or of Poulenc in and outside France shows. Educated English art-lovers entirely familiar with even the lesser members of the inter-war École de Paris, might not even have heard the names of German expressionist painters as important as Nolde and Franz Marc.

There were really only two avant-garde arts which all flag-carriers of artistic novelty in all relevant countries could be guaranteed to admire, and both came out of the new world rather than the old: films and jazz. The cinema was co-opted by the avant-garde some time during the First World War, having previously been unaccountably neglected by it (see *Age of Empire*). It not merely became essential to admire this art, and notably its greatest personality, Charlie Chaplin (to whom few self-respecting modern poets failed to address a composition), but avant-garde artists themselves launched themselves into film-making, most notably in Weimar Germany and Soviet Russia, where they actually dominated production. The canon of "art-films" which the highbrow film-buffs were expected to admire in small specialized movie-temples during the age of cataclysms, from one side of the globe to the other, consisted essentially of such avant-garde creations: Sergei Eisenstein's (1898–1948) *Battleship Potemkin* of 1925 was generally regarded as the all-time masterpiece. The Odessa Steps sequence of this work, which no one who ever saw it—as I did in a Charing Cross avant-garde cinema in the 1930s—will ever forget, has been described as "the classic sequence of silent cinema and possibly the most influential six minutes in cinema history" (Manvell, 1944, pp. 47–48).

From the mid-1930s, intellectuals favoured the populist French cinema of René Clair; Jean Renoir (not uncharacteristically the painter's son); Marcel Carné; Prévert, the ex-surrealist; and Auric, the ex-member of the avant-garde musical cartel *"Les Six."* These, as non-intellectual critics liked to point out, were less enjoyable, though no doubt artistically more high-class than the great bulk of what the hundreds of millions (including the intellectuals) watched every week in increasingly gigantic and luxurious picture-palaces, namely the production of Hollywood. On the other hand the hard-headed showmen of Hollywood were almost as quick as Diaghilev to recognize the avant-garde contribution to profitability. "Uncle" Carl Laemmle, the boss of Universal Studios, perhaps the least intellectually ambitious of the Hollywood majors, took care to supply himself with the latest men and ideas on his annual visits to his native Germany, with the result that the characteristic product of his studios, the horror movie (Frankenstein, Dracula etc.) was sometimes a fairly close copy of German expressionist models. The flow of central-European directors, like Lang, Lubitsch and Wilder, across the Atlantic—and practically all of them can be regarded as highbrows in their native grounds—was to have a considerable impact on Hollywood itself, not to mention that of technicians like Karl Freund (1890–1969) or Eugen Schufftan (1893–1977). However, the course of the cinema and the popular arts will be considered below.

The "jazz" of the "Jazz Age," i.e. some kind of combination of American Negroes, syncopated rhythmic dance-music and an instrumentation which was unconventional by traditional standards, almost certainly aroused universal approval among the avant-garde, less for its own merits than as yet another symbol of modernity, the machine age, a break with the past—in short, another manifesto of cultural revolution. The staff of the Bauhaus had itself photographed with a saxophone. A genuine passion for the sort of jazz which is now recognized as the major contribution of the U.S.A. to twentieth-century music, remained rare among established intellectuals, avant-garde or not, until the second half of the century. Those who developed it, as I did after Duke Ellington's visit to London in 1933, were a small minority.

Whatever the local variant of modernism, between the wars it became the badge of those who wanted to prove that they were both cultured and up to date. Whether or not one actually liked, or even had read, seen or heard, works by the recognized OK names—say, among literary English schoolboys of the first half of the 1930s, T. S. Eliot, Ezra Pound, James Joyce and D.H. Lawrence—it was inconceivable not to talk knowledgeably about them. What is perhaps more interesting, each country's cultural vanguard rewrote or revalued the past to fit in with contemporary requirements. The English were firmly told to forget about Milton and Tennyson, but to admire John Donne. The most influential British critic of the period, F. R. Leavis of Cambridge, even devised a canon, or "great tradition," of English novels which was the exact opposite of a real tradition, since it omitted from the historical succession anything the critic did not like, such as all of Dickens, with the exception of one novel hitherto regarded as one of the master's minor works, *Hard Times*.*

For lovers of Spanish painting, Murillo was now out, but admiration for El Greco was compulsory. But above all, anything to do with the Age of Capital and the Age of Empire (other than its avant-garde art) was not only rejected: it became virtually invisible. This was not only demonstrated by the vertical fall in the prices of nineteenth-century academic painting (and the corresponding but still modest rise of the Impressionists and later modernists): they remained practically unsaleable until the 1960s. The very attempts to recognize any merit in Victorian building had about them an air of deliberate provocation of *real* good taste, associated with camp reactionaries. The present author, grown up among the great architectural monuments of the liberal bourgeoisie which encircle Vienna's old "inner city," learned, by a sort of cultural osmosis, that they were to be regarded as either inauthentic or pompous or both. Such

*To be fair, Dr. Leavis eventually, if somewhat grudgingly, found less inadequate words of appreciation for this great writer.

buildings were not actually torn down *en masse* until the 1950s and 1960s, the most disastrous decade in modern architecture, which is why a Victorian Society to protect buildings of the 1840–1914 period was not set up in Britain until 1958 (more than twenty years after a Georgian Group, to protect the less outcast eighteenth-century heritage).

The impact of the avant-garde on the commercial cinema already suggests that "modernism" began to make its mark on everyday life. It did so obliquely, through productions which the broad public did not consider to be "art," and consequently to be judged by *a priori* criteria of aesthetic value: primarily through publicity, industrial design, commercial print and graphics, and genuine objects. Thus among champions of modernity Marcel Breuer's (1902–81) famous tubular chair (1925–29) carried an enormous ideological and aesthetic charge (Giedion, 1948, pp. 488–95). Yet it was to make its way through the modern world not as a manifesto, but as the modest but universally useful movable stacking chair. But there can be no doubt at all that, within less than twenty years of the outbreak of the First World War, metropolitan life all over the Western world was visibly marked by modernism, even in countries like the U.S.A. and Great Britain, which appeared entirely unreceptive to it in the 1920s. Streamlining, which swept through the American design of both suitable and unsuitable products from the early 1930s, echoed Italian futurism. The Art Deco style (derived from the Paris Exposition of Decorative Arts of 1925) domesticated modernist angularity and abstraction. The modern paperback revolution in the 1930s (Penguin Books) carried the banner of the avant-garde typography of Jan Tschichold (1902–74). The direct assault of modernism was still deflected. Not until after the Second World War did the so-called International Style of modernist architecture transform the city scene, though its chief propagandists and practitioners—Gropius, Le Corbusier, Mies van der Rohe, Frank Lloyd Wright, etc.—had long been active. Some exceptions apart, the bulk of public building, including public housing projects by municipalities of the Left, which might have been expected to sympathize with the socially conscious new architecture, showed little sign of its influence except an apparent dislike for decoration. Most of the massive rebuilding of working-class "Red Vienna" in the 1920s was undertaken by architects who figure barely, if at all, in most histories of architecture. But the lesser equipment of everyday life was rapidly reshaped by modernity.

How far this was due to the heritage of the arts-and-crafts and *art nouveau* movements, in which vanguard art had committed itself to daily use; how far to the Russian constructivists, some of whom deliberately set out to revolutionize mass production design; how far to the genuine suitability of modernist purism for modern domestic technology (e.g. kitchen design) we must leave to art history to decide. The fact remains that a short-lived establishment, which began very much as a political and artistic avant-garde centre, came to set the tone of both architecture and the applied arts of two generations. This was the Bauhaus, or art and design school of Weimar and later Dessau in Central Germany (1919–33), whose existence coincided with the Weimar Republic—it was dissolved by the National Socialists shortly after Hitler took power. The list of names associated with the Bauhaus in one way or another reads like a *Who's Who* of the advanced arts between the Rhine and the Urals: Gropius and Mies van der Rohe; Lyonel Feininger, Paul Klee and Wassily Kandinsky; Malevich, El Lissitzky, Moholy-Nagy, etc. Its influence rested not only on these talents but—from 1921—on a deliberate turn away from the old arts-and-crafts and (avant-garde) fine arts tradition to designs for practical use and industrial production: car bodies (by Gropius), aircraft seats, advertising graphics (a passion of the Russian constructivist El Lissitzky), not forgetting the design of the one and two million Mark banknotes during the great German hyper-inflation of 1923.

The Bauhaus—as its problems with unsympathetic politicians show—was considered deeply subversive. And, indeed, political commitment of one kind or another dominates the "serious" arts in the Age of Catastrophe. In the 1930s it reached even Britain, still a haven of social and political stability amid European revolution, and the U.S.A., remote from war but not from the Great Slump. That political commitment was by no means only to the Left, though radical art-lovers found it hard, especially when young, to accept that creative genius and progressive opinions should not go together. Yet, especially in literature, deeply reactionary convictions, sometimes translated into fascist practice, were common enough in Western Europe. The poets T. S. Eliot and Ezra Pound in Britain and exile; William Butler Yeats (1865–1939) in Ireland; the novelists Knut Hamsun (1859–1952) in Norway, an impassioned collaborator of the Nazis, D. H. Lawrence (1859–1930) in Britain and Louis Ferdinand Céline in France (1894–1961) are obvious examples. The brilliant talents of the Russian emigration cannot, of course, be automatically classified as "reactionary," although some of them were, or became, so; for a refusal to accept Bolshevism united émigrés of widely different political views.

Nevertheless, it is probably safe to say that in the aftermath of world war and the October revolution, and even more in the era of anti-fascism of the 1930s and 1940s, it was the Left, often the revolutionary Left, that primarily attracted the avant-garde. Indeed, war and revolution politicized a number of notably non-political pre-war avant-garde movements in France and Russia. (Most of the Russian avant-garde, however, showed no initial enthusiasm for October.) As Lenin's influence brought Marxism back to the Western world as the only important theory and ideology of social revolution, so it assured the conversion of avant-gardes to what the National Socialists, not incorrectly, called "cultural Bolshevism" (*Kultur-bolschewismus*). Dada was for revolution. Its successor, surrealism, had difficulty only in deciding which brand of revolution it was for, the majority of the sect choosing Trotsky over Stalin. The Moscow–Berlin axis which shaped so much of Weimar culture rested on common political sympathies. Mies van der Rohe built a monument to the murdered Spartacist leaders Karl Liebknecht and Rosa Luxemburg for the German Communist Party. Gropius, Bruno Taut (1880–1938), Le Corbusier, Hannes Meyer and an entire "Bauhaus Brigade" accepted Soviet commissions—admittedly at a time when the Great Slump made the U.S.S.R. not merely ideologically but also professionally attractive to Western architects. Even the basically not very political German cinema was radicalized, as witness the wonderful director G. W. Pabst (1885–1967), a man visibly more interested in presenting women rather than public affairs, and later quite prepared to work under the Nazis. Yet in the last Weimar years he was the author of some of the most radical films, including Brecht-Weill's *Threepenny Opera*.

It was the tragedy of modernist artists, Left or Right, that the much more effective political commitment of their own mass movements and politicians—not to mention their adversaries—rejected them. With the partial exception of Futurist-influenced Italian fascism, the new authoritarian regimes of both Right and Left preferred old-fashioned and gigantic monumental buildings and vistas in architecture, inspirational representations in both painting and sculpture, elaborate performances of the classics on stage, and ideological acceptability in literature. Hitler, of course, was a frustrated artist who eventually found a competent young architect to realize his gigantic conceptions, Albert Speer. However, neither Mussolini nor Stalin nor General Franco, all of whom inspired their own architectural dinosaurs, began life with such personal ambitions. Neither the German nor the Russian avant-garde, therefore, survived the rise of Hitler and Stalin, and the two countries, spearhead of all that was advanced and distinguished in the arts of the 1920s, almost disappeared from the cultural scene.

In retrospect we can see better than contemporaries could what a cultural disaster the triumph of both Hitler and Stalin proved to be, that is to say, how much the avant-garde arts were rooted in the revolutionary soil of central and eastern Europe. The best wine of the arts seemed to grow on the lava-streaked slopes of volcanos. It was not merely that the cultural authorities of politically revolutionary regimes gave more official recognition, i.e. material backing, to artistic revolutionaries than the conservative ones they replaced, even if their political authorities showed no enthusiasm. Anatol Lunacharsky, the "Commissar for Enlightenment," encouraged the avant-garde, though Lenin's taste in the arts was quite conventional. The social-democratic government of Prussia, before it was expelled in 1932 from office (unresistingly) by the authorities of the more right-wing German Reich, encouraged the radical conductor Otto Klemperer to turn one of the Berlin opera houses into a showcase of all that was advanced in music between 1928 and 1931. However, in some undefinable way, it also seems that the times of cataclysm heightened the sensibilities, sharpened the passions of those who lived through them, in Central and Eastern Europe. Theirs was a harsh not a happy vision, and its very harshness and the tragic sense that infused it was what sometimes gave talents which were not in themselves outstanding a bitter denunciatory eloquence, for instance B. Traven, an insignificant anarchist bohemian emigrant once associated with the short-lived Munich Soviet Republic of 1919, who took to writing movingly about sailors and Mexico (Huston's *Treasure of the Sierra Madre* with Bogart is based on him). Without it he would have remained in deserved obscurity. Where such an artist lost the sense that the world was intolerable, as the savage German satirist George Grosz did on emigrating to the U.S.A. after 1933, nothing remained but technically competent sentimentality.

The central European avant-garde art of the Age of Cataclysm rarely articulated hope, even though its politically revolutionary members were committed to an upbeat vision of the future by their ideological convictions. Its most powerful achievements, most of them dating from the years before Hitler's and Stalin's supremacy—"I can't think what to say about Hitler,"* quipped the great Austrian satirist Karl Kraus, whom the First World War had left far from speechless (Kraus, 1922)—come out of apocalypse and tragedy: Alban Berg's opera *Wozzek* (first performed 1926); Brecht-Weill's *Threepenny Opera* (1928) and *Mahagonny* (1931); Brecht-Eisler's *Die Massnahme* (1930); Isaac Babel's stories *Red Cavalry* (1926); Eisenstein's film *Battleship Potemkin* (1925); or Alfred Döblin's *Berlin-Alexanderplatz* (1929). As for the collapse of the

---

*"*Mir fallt zu Hitler nichts ein.*" This did not prevent Kraus, after a lengthy silence, writing some hundred pages on the subject, which nevertheless exceeded his grasp.

Habsburg Empire, it produced an extraordinary outburst of literature, ranging from the denunciation of Karl Kraus's *The Last Days of Humanity* (1922) through the ambiguous buffoonery of Jaroslav Hašek's *Good Soldier Schwejk* (1921) to the melancholy threnody of Josef Roth's *Radetskymarsch* (1932) and the endless self-reflection of Robert Musil's *Man without Qualities* (1930). No set of political events in the twentieth century has had a comparably profound impact on the creative imagination, although in their own ways the Irish revolution and civil war (1916–22) through O'Casey and, in a more symbolic mode, through its muralists, the Mexican revolution (1910–20)—but not the Russian revolution—inspired the arts in their respective countries. An empire destined to collapse as a metaphor for a Western elite culture itself undermined and collapsing: these images had long haunted the dark corners of the Central European imagination. The end of order found expression in the great poet Rainer Maria Rilke's (1875–1926) *Duino Elegies* (1913–23). Another Prague writer in the German language presented an even more absolute sense of the incomprehensibility of the human predicament, both singular and collective: Franz Kafka (1883–1924), almost all of whose work was published posthumously.

This, then, was art created

> In the day when heaven was falling
> the hour when earth's foundation fled

to cite the classical scholar and poet A. E. Housman, who was far from the avant-garde (Housman, 1988, p. 138). This was art whose view was that of the "angel of history," whom the German-Jewish Marxist Walter Benjamin (1892–1940) claimed to recognize in Paul Klee's picture *Angelus Novus*:

> His face is turned towards the past. Where we see a chain of events before us, *he* sees a single catastrophe which keeps piling wreckage upon ruin till they reach his feet. If only he could stay to wake the dead and to piece together the fragments of what has been broken! But a storm blows from the direction of Paradise, catching his wings with such force that the Angel can no longer close them. This storm drives him irresistibly into the future, to which his back is turned, while the pile of debris at his feet grows into the sky. This storm is what we call progress (Benjamin, 1971, pp. 84–85).

West of the zone of collapse and revolution the sense of a tragic and ineluctable cataclysm was less, but the future seemed equally enigmatic. In spite of the trauma of the First World War, continuity with the past was not so obviously broken until the 1930s, the decade of the Great Slump, fascism and the steadily approaching war.* Even so, in retrospect the mood of the Western intellectuals seems less desperate and more hopeful than that of the central Europeans, now scattered and isolated from Moscow to Hollywood, or the captive East Europeans silenced by failure and terror. They still felt themselves to be defending values threatened, but not yet destroyed, to revitalize what was living in their society, if need be by transforming it. As we shall see (chapter 18), much of the Western blindness to the faults of the Stalinist Soviet Union was due to the conviction that, after all, it represented the values of the Enlightenment against the disintegration of reason; of "progress" in the old and simple sense, so much less problematic than Walter Benjamin's "wind blowing from Paradise." It was only among ultra-reactionaries that we find the sense of the world as an incomprehensible tragedy, or rather, as in the greatest British novelist of the period, Evelyn Waugh (1903–66), as a black comedy for stoics; or, as in the French novelist Louis Ferdinand Céline (1894–1961), a nightmare even for cynics. Though the finest and most intelligent of the young British avant-garde poets of the time, W. H. Auden (1907–73), had a sense of history as tragedy—*Spain, Palais des Beaux Arts*—the mood of the group of which he was the centre found the human predicament acceptable enough. The most impressive British artists of the avant-garde, the sculptor Henry Moore (1898–1986) and the composer Benjamin Britten (1913–76), give the impression that they would have been quite ready to let the world crisis pass them by, had it not intruded. But it did.

The avant-garde arts were still a concept confined to the culture of Europe and its outliers and dependencies, and even there the pioneers on the frontier of artistic revolution still often looked longingly at Paris and even—to a lesser but surprising extent—at London.† It did not yet look to New York. What this means is that the non-European avant-garde

---

*Indeed, the major literary echoes of the First World War only began to reverberate towards the end of the 1920s when Erich Maria Remarque's *All Quiet on the Western Front* (1929, Hollywood film 1930) sold two-and-a-half million copies in eighteen months in twenty-five languages.

†The Argentinian writer Jorge Luis Borges (1899–1986) was notoriously anglophile and anglo-oriented, the extraordinary Alexandrian Greek poet C. P. Cavafy (1863–1933) actually had English as his first language, as—at least for writing purposes—had Fernando Pessoa (1888–1935), the greatest Portuguese poet of the century. Kipling's influence on Bertolt Brecht is well known.

barely existed outside the western hemisphere, where it was firmly anchored to both artistic experiment and social revolution. Its best-known representatives at this time, the mural painters of the Mexican revolution, disagreed only about Stalin and Trotsky, but not about Zapata and Lenin, whom Diego Rivera (1886–1957) insisted on including in a fresco destined for the new Rockefeller Center in New York (a triumph of art-deco second only to the Chrysler Building) to the displeasure of the Rockefellers.

Yet for most artists in the non-Western world the basic problem was modernity not modernism. How were their writers to turn spoken vernaculars into flexible and comprehensive literary idioms for the contemporary world, as the Bengalis had done since the mid-nineteenth century in India? How were men (perhaps, in these new days, even women) to write poetry in Urdu, instead of the classical Persian hitherto obligatory for such purposes; in Turkish instead of in the classical Arabic which Atatürk's revolution threw into the dustbin of history with the *fez* and the woman's veil? What, in countries of ancient cultures, were they to do with or about their traditions; arts which, however attractive, did not belong to the twentieth century? To abandon the past was revolutionary enough to make the Western revolt of one phase of modernity against another appear irrelevant or even incomprehensible. All the more so when the modernizing artist was at the same time a political revolutionary, as was more than likely. Chekhov and Tolstoy might seem more apposite models than James Joyce for those who felt their task—and their inspiration—was to "go to the people" and to paint a realistic picture of their sufferings and to help them rise. Even the Japanese writers, who took to modernism from the 1920s (probably through contact with Italian Futurism), had a strong and from time to time dominant socialist or communist "proletarian" contingent (Keene, 1984, chapter 15). Indeed, the first great Chinese modern writer, Lu Hsün (1881–1936), deliberately rejected Western models and looked to Russian literature where "we can see the kindly soul of the oppressed, their sufferings and struggles" (Lu Hsün, 1975, p. 23).

For most of the creative talents of the non-European world who were neither confined within their traditions nor simple Westernizers, the major task seemed to be to discover, to lift the veil from, and to present the contemporary reality of their peoples. Realism was their movement.

II

In a way, this desire united the arts of East and West. For the twentieth century, it was increasingly clear, was the century of the common people, and dominated by the arts produced by and for them. And two linked instruments made the world of the common man visible as never before and capable of documentation: reportage and the camera. Neither was new (see *Age of Capital*, chapter 15; *Age of Empire*, chapter 9) but both entered a self-conscious golden age after 1914. Writers, especially in the U.S.A., not only saw themselves as recorders or reporters, but wrote for newspapers and indeed were or had been newspapermen: Ernest Hemingway (1899–1961), Theodore Dreiser (1871–1945), Sinclair Lewis (1885–1951). "Reportage"—the term first appears in French dictionaries in 1929 and in English ones in 1931—became an accepted genre of socially-critical literature and visual presentation in the 1920s, largely under the influence of the Russian revolutionary avant-garde who extolled fact against the pop entertainment which the European Left had always condemned as the people's opium. The Czech communist journalist Egon Erwin Kisch, who gloried in the name of "Reporter in a Rush" (*Der rasende Reporter*, 1925, was the title of the first of a series of his reportages), seems to have given the term currency in central Europe. It spread, mainly via the cinema, through the Western avant-garde. Its origins are clearly visible in the sections headed "Newsreel" and "the Camera Eye"—an allusion to the avant-garde film documentarist Dziga Vertov—with which the narrative is intercut in John Dos Passos' (1896–1970) trilogy *USA*, written in that novelist's Left-wing period. In the hands of the avant-garde Left "documentary film" became a self-conscious movement, but in the 1930s even the hard-headed professionals of the news and magazine business claimed a higher intellectual and creative status by upgrading some movie newsreels, usually undemanding space-fillers, into the more grandiose "March of Time" documentaries, and borrowing the technical innovations of the avant-garde photographers as pioneered in the communist AIZ of the 1920s to create a golden age of the picture-magazine: *Life* in the U.S.A., *Picture Post* in Britain, *Vu* in France. However, outside the Anglo-Saxon countries it only began to flourish massively after the Second World War.

The new photo-journalism owed its merits not only to the talented men—even some women—who discovered photography as a medium, to the illusory belief that "the camera cannot lie," i.e. that it somehow represented "real" truth, and to the technical improvements that made unposed pictures easy with the new miniature cameras (the Leica launched in 1924), but perhaps most of all to the universal dominance of the cinema. Men and women learned to see reality through camera lenses. For while there was growth in the circulation of the printed word (now also increasingly interwoven with rotogravure photos in the tabloid press), it lost ground to the film. The Age of Catastrophe was the age of the large cinema screen. In the late 1930s for every British person who bought a daily newspaper, two bought a cinema ticket (Stevenson, pp. 396, 403). Indeed, as depression deepened and the world was swept by war, Western cinema attendances reached their all-time peak.

In the new visual media, avant-garde and mass arts fertilized one another. Indeed, in the old Western countries the domination of the educated strata and a certain elitism penetrated even the mass medium of film, producing a golden age for the German silent film in the Weimar era, for the French sound film in the 1930s, and for the Italian film as soon as the blanket of fascism which covered its talents had been lifted. Of these perhaps the populist French cinema of the 1930s was most successful in combining what intellectuals wanted from culture with what the larger public wanted from entertainment. It was the only highbrow cinema which never forgot the importance of the story, especially about love and crime, and the only one capable of making good jokes. Where the avant-garde (political or artistic) had its own way entirely, as in the documentary movement or agitprop art, its work rarely reached beyond small minorities.

However, the avant-garde input is not what makes the mass arts of the period significant. It is their increasingly undeniable cultural hegemony even though, as we have seen, outside the U.S.A. they still had not quite escaped from the supervision of the educated. The arts (or rather entertainments) which became dominant were those aimed at the broadest masses rather than at the large, and growing, middle-class and lower-middle class public with traditional tastes. These still dominated the European "boulevard" or "West End" stage or its equivalents, at least until Hitler dispersed the manufacturers of such products, but their interest is slight. The most interesting development in this middlebrow region was the extraordinary, explosive growth of a genre that had shown some signs of life before 1914, but no hint of its subsequent triumphs: the detective puzzle story, now mainly written at book-length. The genre was primarily British—perhaps a tribute to A. Conan Doyle's Sherlock Holmes, who became internationally known in the 1890s—and, more surprisingly, largely female or academic. Its pioneer, Agatha Christie (1891–1976), remains a bestseller to this day. The international versions of this genre were still largely, and evidently, inspired by the British model, i.e. they were almost exclusively about murder treated as a parlour game requiring some ingenuity, rather like the high-class crossword puzzles with enigmatic clues which were an even more exclusively British speciality. The genre is best seen as a curious invocation to a social order threatened but not yet breached. Murder, which now became the central, almost the only crime to mobilize the detective, irrupts into a characteristically ordered environment—the country house, or some familiar professional milieu—and is traced to one of those rotten apples which confirm the soundness of the rest of the barrel. Order is restored through reason as applied to the problem by the detective who himself (he was still overwhelmingly male) represents the milieu. Hence perhaps the insistence on the *private* investigator, unless the policeman himself is, unlike most of his kind, a member of the upper and middle classes. It was a deeply conservative, though still self-confident genre, unlike the contemporary rise of the more hysterical secret agent thriller (also mainly British), a genre with a great future in the second half of the century. Its authors, men of modest literary merits, often found a suitable metier in their country's secret service.*

By 1914 mass media on the modern scale could already be taken for granted in a number of Western countries. Nevertheless, their growth in the age of cataclysms was spectacular. Newspaper circulation in the U.S.A. rose much faster than population, doubling between 1920 and 1950. By that time something between 300 and 350 papers were sold for every 1,000 men, women and children in the typical "developed" country, though the Scandinavians and Australians consumed even more newsprint, and the urbanized British, possibly because their press was national rather than localized, bought an astonishing six hundred copies per thousand of the population *(U.N. Statistical Yearbook*, 1948). The press appealed to the literate, although in countries of mass schooling it did its best to satisfy the incompletely literate by means of pictures and comic strips, not yet admired by the intellectuals, and by developing a highly-coloured, attention-grabbing, pseudo-demotic idiom avoiding words of too many syllables. Its influence on literature was not negligible. The cinema, on the other hand, made small demands on literacy, and after it learned to talk in the late 1920s, practically none on the English-speaking public.

---

*The literary ancestors of the modern "hard-boiled" thriller or "private eye" story were much more demotic. Dashiell Hammett (1894–1961) began as a Pinkerton operative and published in pulp magazines. For that matter the only writer to turn the detective story into genuine literature, the Belgian Georges Simenon (1903–89), was an autodidact hack writer.

However, unlike the press, which in most parts of the world interested only a small elite, films were almost from the start an international mass medium. The abandonment of the potentially universal language of the silent film with its tested codes for cross-cultural communication probably did much to make spoken English internationally familiar and thus helped to establish the language as the global pidgin of the later twentieth century. For, in the golden age of Hollywood, films were essentially American—except in Japan, where about as many full-size movies were made as in the U.S.A. As for the rest of the world, on the eve of the Second World War Hollywood produced about as many films as all other industries combined, even if we include India which already produced about 170 a year for an audience as large as Japan's and almost as large as the U.S.A.'s. In 1937 it turned out 567 films, or rather more than ten a week. The difference between the hegemonic capacity of capitalism and bureaucratized socialism is that between this figure and the forty-one films the U.S.S.R. claimed to have produced in 1938. Nevertheless, for obvious linguistic reasons, so extraordinary a global predominance of a single industry could not last. In any case it did not survive the disintegration of the "studio system" which reached its peak in this period as a machine for mass-producing dreams, but collapsed shortly after the Second World War.

The third of the mass media was entirely new: radio. Unlike the other two, it rested primarily on the private ownership of what was still a sophisticated piece of machinery, and was thus confined essentially to the comparatively prosperous "developed" countries. In Italy the number of radio sets did not exceed that of automobiles until 1931 (Isola, 1990). The greatest densities of radio-sets were to be found, on the eve of the Second World War, in the U.S.A., Scandinavia, New Zealand and Britain. However, in such countries it advanced at a spectacular rate, and even the poor could afford it. Of Britain's nine million sets in 1939, half had been bought by people earning between £2.5 and £4 per week—a modest income—and another two millions by people earning less than this (Briggs, II, p. 254). It is perhaps not surprising that the radio audience doubled in the years of the Great Slump, when its rate of growth was faster than before or later. For radio transformed the life of the poor, and especially of housebound poor women, as nothing else had ever done. It brought the world into their room. Henceforth the loneliest need never again be entirely alone. And the entire range of what could be said, sung, played or otherwise expressed in sound, was now at their disposal. Is it surprising that a medium unknown when the First World War ended had captured ten million households in the U.S.A. by the year of the stock exchange crash, over twenty-seven millions by 1939, over forty millions by 1950?

Unlike film, or even the revolutionized mass press, radio did not transform the human ways of perceiving reality in any profound way. It did not create new ways of seeing or establishing relations between sense impressions and ideas (see *Age of Empire*). It was merely the medium, not the message. But its capacity for speaking simultaneously to untold millions, each of whom felt addressed as an individual, made it an inconceivably powerful tool of mass information and, as both rulers and salesmen immediately recognized, for propaganda and advertisement. By the early 1930s the President of the U.S.A. had discovered the potential of the radio "fireside chat," and the king of Britain that of the royal Christmas broadcast (1932 and 1933 respectively). In the Second World War, with its endless demand for news, radio came into its own as a political instrument and as a medium of information. The number of radio sets in continental Europe increased substantially in all countries except some of the worst victims of battle (Briggs, III, Appendix C). In several cases it doubled or more than doubled. In most of the non-European countries the rise was even steeper. Commerce, though from the start it ruled the airwaves over the U.S.A., had a harder conquest elsewhere, since by tradition governments were reluctant to give up control over so powerful a medium for influencing citizens. The BBC maintained its public monopoly. Where commercial broadcasting was tolerated, it was nevertheless expected to defer to the official voice.

It is difficult to recognize the innovations of radio culture, since so much that it pioneered has become part of the furniture of everyday life—the sports commentary, the news bulletin, the celebrity guest show, the soap opera, or indeed the serial programme of any kind. The most profound change it brought was simultaneously to privatize and to structure life according to a rigorous timetable, which henceforth ruled not only the sphere of labour but that of leisure. Yet curiously this medium—and, until the rise of video and VCR, its successor, television—though essentially centered on individual and family, created its own public sphere. For the first time in history people unknown to each other who met knew what each had in all probability heard (or, later, seen) the night before: the big game, the favourite comedy show, Winston Churchill's speech, the contents of the news bulletin.

The art most significantly affected by radio was music, since it abolished the acoustic or mechanical limitations on the range of sounds. Music, the last of the arts to break out of the bodily prison that confines oral communication, had already entered the era of mechanical reproduction before 1914 with the gramophone, although this was hardly yet within reach of the masses. The years between the wars certainly brought both gramophones and records within the range of the masses, though the virtual collapse of the record-market for "race records," i.e. typical poor people's music during the American Slump, demonstrates the fragility of this expansion. Yet the record, though its technical quality improved after about 1930 had its limits, if only of length. Moreover, its range depended on its sales. Radio, for the first time, enabled music to be heard at a distance at more than five minutes' unbroken length, and by a theoretically limitless number of listeners. It thus became both a unique popularizer of minority music (including classical music) and by far the most powerful means for selling records, as indeed it still remains. Radio did not change music—it certainly affected it less than the theatre or the movies, which also soon learned to reproduce sound—but the role of music in contemporary life, not excluding its role as aural wallpaper for everyday living, is inconceivable without it.

The forces which dominated the popular arts were thus primarily technological and industrial: press, camera, film, record and radio. Yet since the later nineteenth century an authentic spring of autonomous creative innovation had been visibly welling up in the popular and entertainment quarters of some great cities (see *Age of Empire*). It was far from exhausted, and the media revolution carried its products far beyond their original milieus. Thus the Argentine tango formalized, and especially amplified from dance into song, probably reached its peak of achievement and influence in the 1920s and 1930s, and when its greatest star Carlos Gardel (1890–1935) died in an air crash in 1935, he was mourned all over Spanish America, and (thanks to records) turned into a permanent presence. The samba, destined to symbolize Brazil as the tango did Argentina, is the child of the democratization of the Rio carnival in the 1920s. However, the most impressive and, in the long run, influential development of this sort was the development of jazz in the U.S.A., largely under the impact of the migration of Negroes from the southern states to the big cities of the middle-west and north-east: an autonomous art music of professional (mainly black) entertainers.

The impact of some of these popular innovations or developments was as yet restricted outside their native milieus. It was also as yet less revolutionary than it became in the second half of the century, when—to take the obvious example—an idiom directly derived from the American Negro blues became, as rock-and-roll, a global language of youth culture. Nevertheless, though—with the exception of film—the impact both of mass media and popular creation was more modest than it became in the second half of the century (this will be considered below); it was already enormous in quantity and striking in quality, especially in the U.S.A. which began to exercise an unchallengeable hegemony in these fields, thanks to its extraordinary economic preponderance, its firm commitment to commerce and democracy and, after the Great Slump, the influence of Rooseveltian populism. In the field of popular culture the world was American or it was provincial. With one exception, no other national or regional model established itself globally, though some had substantial regional influence (for instance, Egyptian music within the Islamic world) and an occasional exotic touch entered global commercial popular culture from time to time, as in the Caribbean and Latin American components of dance-music. The unique exception was sport. In this branch of popular culture—and who, having seen the Brazilian team in its days of glory will deny it the claim to art?—U.S. influence remained confined to the area of Washington's political domination. As cricket is played as a mass sport only where once the Union Jack flew, so baseball made little impact except where U.S. marines had once landed. The sport the world made its own was association soccer, the child of Britain's global economic presence, which had introduced teams named after British firms or composed of expatriate Britons (like the Saõ Paulo Athletic Club) from the polar ice to the Equator. This simple and elegant game, unhampered by complex rules and equipment, and which could be practised on any more or less flat open space of the required size, made its way through the world entirely on its merits and, with the establishment of the World Cup in 1930 (won by Uruguay) became genuinely international.

And yet, by our standards, mass sports, though now global, remained extraordinarily primitive. Their practitioners had not yet been absorbed by the capitalist economy. The great stars were still amateurs, as in tennis (i.e. assimilated to traditional bourgeois status), or professionals paid a wage not all that much higher than a skilled industrial worker's, as in British football. They had still to be enjoyed face-to-face, for even radio could only translate the actual sight of the game or race into the rising decibels of a commentator's voice. The age of television and sportsmen paid like filmstars was still a few years away. But, as we shall see (chapters 9–11) not all that many.

CHAPTER SEVEN

End of Empires

He became a terrorist revolutionary in 1918. His guru was present at his wedding night and he never lived with his wife for ten years till her death in 1928. It was an iron rule for the revolutionaries that they should keep aloof from women ... He used to tell me how India would become free by fighting the way the Irish fought. It was when I was with him that I read Dan Breen's *My Fight for Irish Freedom*. Dan Breen was Masterda's ideal. He named his organisa- tion the Indian "Republican Army, Chittagong branch" after the Irish Republican Army.

—Kalpana Dutt (1945, pp. 16–17)

The heaven-born breed of colonial administrators tolerated and even encouraged the bribery-corruption system because it provided a cheap machinery for the exercise of control over restless and often dissident populations. For what it means in effect is that what a man wants (e.g. to win his lawsuit, to get a government contract, to be given a birthday honour or to get an official job) can be achieved by doing a favour to the man with power to give or with-hold. The "favour" done need not be a gift of money (that is crude and few Europeans in India soiled their hands that way). It could be a gift of friendship and respect, lavish hospitality, or the gift of funds to a "good cause," but above all, loyalty to the Raj.

—M. Carritt (1985, pp. 63–64)

In the course of the nineteenth century a few countries—mostly those bordering on the northern Atlantic—conquered the rest of the non-

European globe with ridiculous ease. Insofar as they did not bother to occupy and rule it, the countries of the West established an even more unchallenged superiority by means of their economic and social system and its organization and technology. Capitalism and bourgeois society transformed and ruled the world and provided the model—until 1917 the only model—for those who did not want to be devoured or swept aside by the juggernaut of history. After 1917 Soviet communism provided an alternative model, but essentially a model of the same type, except that it dispensed with private enterprise and liberal institutions. The twentieth-century history of the non-Western or more exactly non-north-Western world is therefore essentially determined by its relations with the countries which had established themselves in the nineteenth century as the lords of human kind.

To this extent the history of the Short Twentieth Century remains geographically skewed, and can only be written as such, by the historian who wants to concentrate on the dynamics of global transformation. This does not mean that one shares the condescending and only too often ethnocentric or even racist sense of superiority, and the entirely unjustified self-satisfaction which is still common in the favoured countries. Indeed, this historian is passionately opposed to what E. P. Thompson has called "the enormous condescension" towards the world's backward and poor. Nevertheless, the fact remains that the dynamics of the greater part of the world's history in the Short Twentieth Century are derived, not original. They consist essentially in the attempts by the elites of non-bourgeois societies to imitate the model pioneered in the West, which was essentially seen as that of societies generating progress, the form of wealth, power and culture, by economic and techno-scientific "development" in a capitalist or socialist variant.* There was no operational model other than "westernisation" or "modernisation" or whatever one chose to call it. Conversely, only political euphemism separates the various synonyms of "backwardness" (as Lenin had no hesitation in describing the situation of his own country and "the colonial and backward countries") which international diplomacy has scattered round

---

*It is worth observing that the simple dichotomy "capitalist"/"socialist" is political rather than analytical It reflects the emergence of mass political labour movements whose socialist ideology was, in practice, little more than the concept of the present society ("capitalism") turned inside out. This was reinforced, after October 1917, by the long Red/anti-Red Cold War of the Short Twentieth Century. Instead of classifying the economic systems of, say, the U.S.A., South Korea, Austria, Hong Kong, West Germany and Mexico under the same heading of "capitalism," it would be perfectly possible to classify them under several

a decolonized world ("under-developed," "developing" etc.).

The operational model of "development" could be combined with various other sets of beliefs and ideologies, so long as these did not interfere with it, i.e. so long as the country concerned did not, say, ban the construction of airports on the grounds that they had not been authorised by Koran or Bible, or conflicted with the inspiring tradition of medieval knighthood, or were incompatible with the depth of the Slav soul. On the other hand, where such sets of belief were opposed to the process of "development" *in practice* and not merely in theory they guaranteed failure and defeat. However strong and sincere the belief that magic would turn machine-gun bullets aside, it worked too rarely to make much difference. Telephone and telegraph were better means of communication than the holy man's telepathy.

This is not to dismiss the traditions, beliefs or ideologies, unchanging or modified, by which societies coming into contact with the new world of "development" judged it. Both traditionalism and socialism concurred in detecting the empty moral space at the centre of triumphant economic—and political—capitalist liberalism, as it destroyed all bonds between individuals except those based on Adam Smith's "propensity to barter" and to pursue their personal satisfactions and interests. As a moral system, a way of ordering the place of human beings in the world, as a way of recognizing what and how much "development" and "progress" destroyed, the pre- or non-capitalist ideologies and value-systems were often superior to the beliefs that gunboats, merchants, missionaries and colonial administrators brought with them. As a means of mobilizing the masses in traditional societies against modernization, either capitalist or socialist, or more precisely against the outsiders who imported it, they could under some circumstances be quite effective, although in fact none of the successful movements of liberation in the backward world before the 1970s was inspired or achieved by traditional or neo-traditional ideologies. This is in spite of the fact that one such movement, the short-lived Khilafat agitation in British India (1920–21), which demanded the preservation of the Turkish Sultan as Caliph of all the faithful, the maintenance of the Ottoman Empire in its 1914 frontiers, and of Moslem control over the Holy Places of Islam (including Palestine), probably forced mass non-cooperation and civil disobedience on a hesitant Indian National Congress (Minault, 1982). The most characteristic mass mobilizations under the auspices of religion—"Church" retained its hold over the common people better than "King"—were rearguard actions, though sometimes stubborn and heroic ones like the peasant resistance to the secularising Mexican revolution under the banner of "Christ the King"

(1926–32), described by its chief historian in epic terms as "the Christiad" (Meyer, 1973–79). Fundamentalist religion as a major force of successful mass mobilization belongs to the last decades of the twentieth century, which have even witnessed a bizarre return to fashion among some intellectuals of what their educated grandfathers would have described as superstition and barbarism.

Conversely, the ideologies, the programmes, even the methods and forms of political organization which inspired the emancipation of dependent countries from dependency, backward ones from backwardness, were Western: liberal; socialist; communist and/or nationalist; secularist and suspicious of clericalism; using the devices developed for the purposes of public life in bourgeois societies—press, public meetings, parties, mass campaigns, even when the discourse adopted was, and had to be, in the religious vocabulary used by the masses. What this meant was that the history of the makers of the Third World transformations of this century is the history of elite minorities, and sometimes relatively minute ones, for—quite apart from the absence of the institutions of democratic politics almost everywhere—only a tiny stratum possessed the requisite knowledge, education or even elementary literacy. After all, before independence, over 90 per cent of the population of the Indian subcontinent was illiterate. The number of those literate in a Western language (i.e. English) was even more exiguous—say half a million out of three hundred millions or so before 1914, or one in six hundred.* Even the by far most education-hungry region (West Bengal) at the time of independence (1949–50) had only 272 college students to every 100,000 of the population, five times as high as in the North Indian heartland. The role played by these numerically insignificant minorities was enormous. The thirty-eight thousand Parsi men of Bombay Presidency, one of the main administrative divisions of British India, at the end of the nineteenth century, more than one quarter of whom were literate *in English,* not surprisingly became the elite of traders, industrialists and financiers throughout the subcontinent. The 100 advocates to the High Court of Bombay admitted between 1890 and 1900 contained two major national leaders of independent India (Mohandas Karamchand Gandhi and Vallabhai Patel) and the future founder of Pakistan, Muhammad Ali Jinnah (Seal, 1968, p. 884; Misra, 1961, p. 328). The all-purpose function of such Western-educated elites may be illustrated by one Indian family of this writer's acquaintance. The father, a landowner and prosperous lawyer

---

*Based on the data for those undergoing Western-type secondary schooling (Anil Seal, 1971, pp. 21–22).

and social figure under the British, became a diplomat and eventually state governor after 1947. The mother was the first woman minister in the Indian National Congress provincial governments of 1937. Of the four children (all educated in Britain), three joined the Communist Party, one became Commander-in-Chief of the Indian army; another eventually became a member of the Assembly for the party; a third—after chequered political fortunes—a minister in Mrs. Gandhi's government; while the fourth made his way into business.

None of this means that the Westernizing elites necessarily accepted all the values of the states and cultures they took as their models. Their personal views might range from 100 per cent assimilationism to a deep distrust of the West, combined with the conviction that only by adopting its innovations could the specific values of the native civilization be preserved or restored. The object of the most wholehearted and successful project of "modernization," Japan since the Meiji Restoration, was not to Westernize, but on the contrary to make traditional Japan viable. In the same way, what Third-World activists read into the ideologies and programmes they made their own was not so much the ostensible text as their own subtext. Thus in the period of independence, socialism (i.e. the Soviet communist version) appealed to decolonized governments, not only because the cause of anti-imperialism had always belonged to the metropolitan Left, but even more because they saw the U.S.S.R. as the model for overcoming backwardness by means of planned industrialization, a matter of far more urgent concern to them than the emancipation of whatever could be described in their countries as "the proletariat" (see pp. 350 and 376). Similarly while the Brazilian Communist Party never wavered in its commitment to Marxism, a particular kind of developmental nationalism became "a fundamental ingredient" in Party policy from the early 1930s, even when it conflicted with labour interests considered separately from others' (Martins Rodrigues, p. 437). Nevertheless, whatever the conscious or unconscious objectives of those who shaped the history of the backward world, modernization, that is to say, the imitation of Western-derived models, was the necessary and indispensable way to achieve them.

This was all the more obvious, since the perspectives of the Third World elites and those of the mass of their populations differed very substantially, except insofar as white (i.e. North Atlantic) racism provided a common bond of resentment which could be shared by maharajahs and sweepers. Even so, it might well be less felt by men, and especially women, who were used to inferior status within any society, irrespective of its members' skin-colour. Outside the Islamic world, the case where a common religion provided such a bond—in this case of immutable superiority to the unbelievers—was unusual.

II

The world economy of capitalism in the Age of Empire penetrated and transformed virtually all parts of the globe, even if, after the October Revolution, it temporarily stopped at the frontiers of the U.S.S.R. That is why the Great Slump of 1929–33 was to be such a landmark in the history of anti-imperialism and Third World liberation movements. Whatever the economy, the wealth, the cultures and political systems of countries had been before they came within reach of the North Atlantic octopus, they were all sucked into the world market, insofar as they were not dismissed by Western businessmen and governments as economically uninteresting, even if colourful, like the Bedouin of the great deserts before the discovery of oil or natural gas in their inhospitable habitat. Their value to the world market was essentially as suppliers of primary products—the raw materials for industry and energy and the products of farming and livestock rearing—and as an outlet for northern capital investment, mainly in government loans and the infrastructures of transport, communications and cities, without which the resources of dependent countries could not be effectively exploited. In 1913 over three quarters of all British overseas investment—and the British exported more capital than the rest of the world put together—was in government stocks, railways, ports and shipping (Brown, 1963, p. 153).

The industrialization of the dependent world was still part of no one's game-plan, even in countries like those of the southern cone of Latin America, where it seemed logical to process such locally produced foodstuffs as meat into more easily transportable form as tins of corned beef. After all, canning sardines and bottling port wine had not industrialized Portugal, nor was it intended that it should. In fact, the basic pattern in the minds of most northern governments and entrepreneurs was one in which the dependent world paid for its imports of their manufactures by the sale of its primaries. This had been the foundation of the British dominated world economy in the pre-1914 period (*Age of Empire*, chapter 2), although, with the exception of the countries of so-called "settler capitalism," the dependent world was not a particularly rewarding export market for manufacturers. The three hundred million inhabitants of the Indian subcontinent, the four hundred million Chinese, were too poor and supplied too many of their everyday needs locally to buy much from anyone. Fortunately for the British in their age of economic hegemony, their seven hundred million penniesworth added up to enough to keep the Lancashire cotton industry in business. Its interest, like that of all northern producers, was obviously to make the dependent market, such as it was, completely dependent on their production, i.e. to agrarianize it.

Whether or not they had this object, they could not succeed, partly because the local markets created by the very absorption of economies into a world market society, a society of buying and selling, stimulated local consumer-goods production, which it was cheaper to set up locally, and partly because many of the economies in the dependent regions, especially in Asia, were highly complex structures with long histories of manufacturing, considerable sophistication and impressive technical and human resources and potential. So the giant entrepôt port cities which came to be the characteristic links between the North and the dependent world—from Buenos Aires and Sydney to Bombay, Shanghai and Saigon—developed local industry in the shelter of their temporary protection from imports, even if that was not the intention of their rulers. It would hardly take much to make local textile producers in Ahmedabad or Shanghai, whether native or agents for some foreign firm, supply the Indian or Chinese market close by, with the cotton goods hitherto imported from distant and high-cost Lancashire. In fact, this is what happened in the aftermath of the First World War, and it broke the neck of the British cotton industry.

And yet, when we consider how logical Marx's prediction of the eventual spread of the industrial revolution to the rest of the world seemed, it is astonishing how little industry had left the world of developed capitalism before the end of the era of empires, and indeed before the 1970s. In the late 1930s the only major change in the world map of industralization was that due to the Soviet Five-Year Plans (see chapter 2). As late as 1960 the old heartlands of industrialization in Western Europe and North America produced over 70 per cent of gross world output and almost 80 per cent of the world's "value added in manufacturing," i.e. industrial output (Harris, 1987, pp. 102–3). The really dramatic shift away from the old West—including the major rise of the Japanese industry, which in 1960 turned out only something like 4 per cent of world industrial production—came in the last third of the century. Not until the 1970s did economists begin to write books on "the new international division of labour," i.e. the beginning of the deindustrialization of the old heartlands.

Evidently imperialism, the old "international division of labour," had a built-in tendency to reinforce the industrial monopoly of the old core countries. To this extent the inter-war Marxists, joined later by the post-1945 "dependency theorists" of various brands, had clear grounds for their attacks on imperialism as a mode of ensuring the continued backwardness of the backward countries. Yet paradoxically it was the relative immaturity of the development of the capitalist world economy, and, more exactly, of the technology of transport and communication, which kept industry located in its original homelands. There was nothing in the logic of profit-making enterprise and capital accumulation to keep the manufacture of steel in Pennsylvania or the Ruhr for ever, although it is no cause for surprise that governments of industrial countries, especially if inclined to protectionism or with large colonial empires, should do their best to stop potential competitors from harming the homeland's industry. But even imperial governments could have reasons to industralize their colonies, even though the only case where they did so systematically was Japan, which developed heavy industries in Korea (annexed in 1911) and, after 1931, in Manchuria and Taiwan because these resource-rich colonies were sufficiently close to the exiguous and notoriously raw-material-poor homeland to serve Japanese national industrialization directly. Yet even in the greatest of colonies, the discovery, during the First World War, that India had not been in a position to manufacture enough for industrial self-sufficiency and military defence led to a policy of government protection and direct participation in the country's industrial development (Misra, 1961, pp. 239, 256). If war brought the drawbacks of insufficient colonial industry home even to imperial administrators, the Slump of 1929–33 put them under financial pressure. As agricultural revenues fell, the income of colonial government had to be shored up by higher duties on manufactured goods, including the home country's own, British, French or Dutch. For the first time Western firms, which had hitherto imported freely, had a strong incentive to set up local production facilities in these marginal markets (Holland, 1985, p. 13). Still, even allowing for war and slump, the dependent world in the first half of the Short Twentieth Century remained overwhelmingly agrarian and rural. That is why the "great leap forward" of the world economy in the third quarter of the century was to prove so dramatic a turning-point in its fortunes.

III

Practically all parts of Asia, Africa and Latin/Caribbean America were and felt themselves to be dependent on what happened in a few states of the northern hemisphere, but (outside the Americas) most of them were also owned, administered or otherwise dominated and commanded by them. This applied even to those left with their own native authorities (e.g. as "protectorates" or princely states), for it was well understood that the "advice" of the British or French representative at the court of the local emir, bey, rajah, king or sultan, was compelling. It was true even in formally independent states like China, where foreigners enjoyed extra-territorial rights and supervision over some of the central functions of sovereign states, such as revenue collection. In these areas the problem of getting rid of foreign rule was bound to arise. This was not so in Central and South America, which consisted almost wholly of sovereign states, even though the U.S.A.—but no one else—was inclined to treat the smaller Central American ones as *de facto* protectorates, especially in the first and last thirds of the century.

The colonial world has been so completely transformed into a collection of nominally sovereign states since 1945 that it must seem, in retrospect, that this was not only inevitable but what the colonial peoples had always wanted. This is almost certainly true in those countries which looked back on a long history as political entities, the great Asian empires—China, Persia, the Ottomans—and perhaps one or two other countries like Egypt; especially when they were built round a substantial *"staatsvolk"* or "state people" like the Han Chinese or the believers in Shiite Islam as virtually the national religion of Iran. In such countries popular sentiment against foreigners could be easily politicized. It is no accident that China, Turkey and Iran have all three been the scene of important autochthonous revolutions. However, such cases were exceptional. More often, the very concept of a permanent territorial political entity, with fixed frontiers separating it from other such entities, and subject exclusively to one permanent authority, i.e. the idea of the independent sovereign state which we take for granted, was meaningless to people, at least (even in areas of permanent and fixed agriculture) above the village level. Indeed, even where a clearly self-described or recognized "people" existed, which Europeans liked to describe as a "tribe," the idea that it could be territorially separated from other people with whom it coexisted and intermingled and divided functions was difficult to grasp, because it made little sense. In such regions the only foundation for such independent states of the twentieth-century type were the territories into which imperial conquest and rivalry had divided them, usually without any reference to local structures. The post-colonial world is thus almost entirely divided by the frontiers of imperialism.

Moreover, those inhabitants of the Third World who most resented the Westerners (whether as unbelievers, as bringers of all manner of disruptive and godless modern innovations, or simply out of resistance to any change in ordinary people's ways of life, which they, not unjustifiably, supposed would be for the worse), were equally opposed to the elites' justified conviction that modernization was indispensable. This made a common front against the imperialists difficult, even in colonial countries where all members of the subject people bore the common burden of the colonialists' contempt for the inferior race.

The major task of middle-class nationalist movements in such countries was how to acquire the support of the essentially traditionalist and anti-modern masses without jeopardizing their own modernizing project. The dynamic Bal Ganghadar Tilak (1856–1920), in the early days of Indian nationalism, was right in supposing that the best way to win mass support, even among the lower middle classes—and not only in his native part of western India—was by defending the sanctity of cows and the marriage of ten-year-old girls, and asserting the spiritual superiority of the ancient Hindu or "Aryan" civilization and its religion to modern "Western" civilization and its native admirers. The first important phase of Indian nationalist militancy, from 1905 to 1910, was largely conducted in such "nativist" terms, not least among the young terrorists of Bengal. Eventually Mohandas Karamchand Gandhi (1869–1948) was to succeed in mobilizing the villages and bazaars of India in their tens of millions by very much the same appeal to nationalism as Hindu spirituality, though taking care not to break the common front with the modernizers (of whom, in a real sense, he was one—see *Age of Empire*, chapter 13), and to avoid the antagonism to Mohammedan India, which was always implicit in a militantly Hindu approach to nationalism. He invented the politician as saint, revolution by the collective act of passivity ("non-violent non-cooperation"), and even social modernization, such as the rejection of the caste system, by exploiting the reforming potential contained within the endlessly changing and all-embracing ambiguities of an evolving Hinduism. He succeeded beyond anyone's wildest hopes (or fears). And yet, as he himself recognized at the end of his life, before being assassinated by a militant in the Tilak tradition of Hindu exclusiveness, he had failed in his fundamental endeavour. In the long run it was impossible to reconcile what moved the masses and what had to be done. In the end, free India was to be governed by those who "did not look back to a revival in India of ancient times," who "had no sympathy or understanding of them . . . looked to the West and felt greatly attracted by Western progress" (Nehru, 1936, pp. 23–24). Yet, at the time this book is written, the tradition of Tilak's anti-modernism, now represented by the militant BJP Party, remained as the major focus of popular opposition, and—then as now—it is the major divisive force in India, not only among the masses, but also among the intellectuals. Mahatma Gandhi's brief attempt at a Hinduism both populist and progressive has sunk from sight.

A similar pattern emerged in the Muslim world, although there (except after successful revolutions) all modernizers always had to pay their respects to universal popular piety, whatever their private beliefs. However, unlike India, the attempts to read a reforming or modernizing message into Islam were not designed to mobilize the masses and did not do so. The disciples of Jamal al-Din al Afghani (1839–97) in Iran, Egypt and Turkey; of his follower Mohammed Abduh (1849–1905) in Egypt; of the Algerian Abdul Hamid Ben Badis (1889–1940) were not to be found in the villages but in schools and colleges, where the message of resistance to the European powers would in any case have found sympathetic audiences.* Nevertheless, the real revolutionaries of the Islamic world, and those who came to the top there were, as we have seen (chapter 5), non-Islamic secular modernizers: men like Kemal Atatürk, who substituted the bowler hat for the Turkish fez (itself a nineteenth-century innovation), roman letters for the Islam-tainted Arabic script and, in fact, broke the links between Islam, State and Law. Nevertheless, as recent history again confirms, mass mobilization was most easily achieved on the basis of anti-modern mass piety ("Islamic fundamentalism"). In short, a profound conflict separated the modernizers, who were also the nationalists (an entirely untraditional concept), and the common people of the Third World.

Anti-imperialist and anti-colonial movements before 1914 were, therefore, less prominent than one might think in the light of almost total liquidation of the Western and Japanese colonial empires within half a century of the outbreak of the First World War. Even in Latin America hostility to economic dependency in general and to the U.S.A. in particular, the only imperial state which insisted on a military presence in the region, was not then an important asset in local politics. The only empire that faced serious problems in some areas—i.e.

---

*In French North Africa rural piety was dominated by various Sufi holy men ("Marabouts") who were the particular target of the reformers' denunciation.

problems which could not be handled by police operations—was the British. By 1914 it had already conceded internal autonomy to the colonies of mass white settlement, known from 1907 as "dominions" (Canada, Australia, New Zealand, South Africa) and it was committed to autonomy ("Home Rule") for ever-troublesome Ireland. In India and Egypt it was already clear that imperial interests and local demands for autonomy, even for independence, might require political solutions. After 1905 one could even speak of some element of mass support for the nationalist movement in India and Egypt.

However, the First World War was the first set of events which seriously shook the structure of world colonialism, as well as destroying two empires (the German and the Ottoman, whose former possessions were divided, mainly between the British and the French) and temporarily knocking out a third, Russia (which recovered its Asian dependencies within a few years). The strains of the war on the dependencies, whose resources Britain needed to mobilize, generated unrest. The impact of the October Revolution and the general collapse of old regimes, followed by *de facto* Irish independence for the twenty-six Southern Counties (1921), made foreign empires look mortal for the first time. At the end of the war an Egyptian party, Said Zaghlul's *Wafd* ("delegation"), inspired by President Wilson's rhetoric, for the first time demanded complete independence. Three years of struggle (1919–22) forced the British to transform their protectorate into a semi-independent Egypt under British control, a formula which Britain also found convenient for the management of all but one of the Asian areas it took over from the Turkish Empire: Iraq and Transjordan. (The exception was Palestine, which they administered directly, vainly trying to reconcile the promises made during the war both to Zionist Jews, in return for support against Germany, and Arabs, in return for support against the Turks.)

It was less easy for Britain to find a simple formula for maintaining control over the largest colony of all, India, where the slogan of "self-rule" (*Swaraj*), adopted by the Indian National Congress for the first time in 1906, now edged increasingly towards complete independence. The revolutionary years 1918–22 transformed mass nationalist politics in the subcontinent, partly by turning the Muslim masses against the British, partly by the lapse into bloodthirsty hysteria of a British general in the turbulent year 1919, who massacred an unarmed crowd in an exitless enclosure, killing several hundreds (the "Amritsar Massacre"), but chiefly by the combination of a wave of workers' strikes combined with the mass civil disobedience called for by Gandhi and a radicalized Congress. For a moment an almost millennial mood seized the liberation movement: Gandhi announced that *Swaraj* would be won by the end of 1921. The government did "not seek to minimise in any way the fact that great anxiety is caused by the situation," as the towns were paralysed by non-cooperation, the countryside in large areas of North India, Bengal, Orissa and Assam was in uproar and "a large proportion of the Mohammedan population throughout the country are embittered and sullen" (Cmd 1586, 1922, p. 13). From now on India became intermittently ungovernable. Probably it was only the hesitation of most Congress leaders, including Gandhi, to plunge their country into the savage darkness of an uncontrollable insurrection by the masses, their own lack of confidence, and the conviction of most nationalist leaders, shaken but not utterly destroyed, that the British were genuinely committed to Indian reform that saved the British Raj. After Gandhi called off the campaign of civil disobedience early in 1922, on the grounds that it had led to the massacre of policemen in one village, it can reasonably be claimed that British rule in India depended on his moderation—far more than on police and army.

The conviction was not unjustified. While there was a powerful bloc of diehard imperialism in Britain, of which Winston Churchill made himself the spokesman, the effective view of the British ruling class after 1919 was that some form of Indian self-rule similar to "dominion status" was ultimately unavoidable, and the future of Britain in India depended on coming to terms with the Indian elite, including the nationalists. An end to unilateral British rule in India was henceforth only a question of time. Since India was the core of the entire British Empire, the future of that Empire as a whole, therefore, now seemed uncertain, except in Africa and the scattered islands of the Caribbean and Pacific, where paternalism still ruled unchallenged. Never had a larger area of the globe been under the formal or informal control of Britain than between the two world wars, but never before had the rulers of Britain felt less confident about maintaining their old imperial supremacy. This was one major reason why, when the position became unsustainable after the Second World War, the British, by and large, did not resist decolonisation. It is perhaps also the reason why other empires, notably the French—but also the Dutch— fought with arms to maintain their colonial positions after 1945. Their empires had not been shaken by the First World War. The only major headache of the French was that they had not yet completed their conquest of Morocco, but the warlike Berber clansmen of the Atlas mountains were essentially a military rather than a political problem and, in fact, a rather greater one for Spain's Moroccan colony, where a local highland intellectual, Abd-el-Krim, proclaimed a Rif Republic in 1923. Enthusiastically backed by French communists and others on the Left, Abd-el-Krim was defeated in 1926 with French help, after which the mountain Berbers returned to their habitual pursuits of fighting in the French and Spanish colonial armies abroad, and resisting any kind of central government at home. A modernizing anti-colonial movement in the French Islamic colonies and in French Indochina did not develop until well after the First World War, except for modest anticipations in Tunisia.

IV

The years of revolution had shaken primarily the British Empire, but the Great Slump of 1929–33 shook the entire dependent world. For practically all of it the era of imperialism had been one of almost continuous growth, unbroken even by the world war from which most of them remained remote. Of course, many of its inhabitants were not yet much involved in the expanding world economy, or did not feel themselves to be involved in any very novel way, for what did it matter to poor men and women who had dug and carried loads since the beginning of time in what exact global context they did so? Still, the imperialist economy brought substantial changes to the lives of ordinary people, especially in the regions of export-oriented primary production. Sometimes these changes had already surfaced in the sort of politics native or foreign rulers recognized. Thus, as the Peruvian *haciendas* were transformed, between 1900 and 1930, into coastal sugar factories and highland commercial sheep ranches, and the trickle of Indian labour migration to coast and city became a flow, new ideas seeped into the traditional hinterlands. By the early 1930s Huasicancha, an "especially remote" community some 3,700 metres up the inaccessible Andean slopes, was already debating which of two national radical parties would best represent its interests (Smith, 1989, esp. p. 175). Yet far more often nobody except the locals as yet knew or cared much how they changed.

What, for instance, did it mean for economies which had hardly used money, or had used it only for a limited range of purposes, to move into an economy where it was the universal means of exchange, as happened in the Indo-Pacific seas? The meaning of goods, services and transactions between people was transformed, and so consequently were the moral values of the society, and, indeed, its form of social distribution. Among the matrilineal rice-growing peasants of Negri Sembilan (Malaysia) the

1. Sarajevo: the Archduke Franz Ferdinand of Austria and his wife leaving the Town Hall of Sarajevo on their way to their assassination, which sparked off the First World War (28 June 1914).

2. The killing fields of France, seen by the dying: Canadian soldiers among shell-craters, 1918.

3. The killing fields of France, seen by the survivors: war cemetery, Chalons-sur-Marne.

4. Russia, 1917: soldiers with revolutionary banners ('Workers of all lands, unite!').

5. October revolution: image of Lenin ('great leader of the proletariat'). The workers' banner reads 'All power to the Soviets'.

6. World revolution, as seen on a Soviet May Day Poster, *c.* 1920. The red flag circling the globe is inscribed 'workers of all lands unite!'.

7. The traumatic post-war inflation, whose memory still haunts Germany: A German banknote for twenty million marks (July 1923).

8. Gateway to the Great Depression: the Wall Street crash of 1929.

9. Men without work: British unemployed in the 1930s.

10. The two leaders of fascism: Adolf Hitler (1889–1945) and Benito Mussolini (1883–1945) had much to smile about in 1938.

11. The Duce: young Italian fascists marching past Mussolini.

12. The Führer: Nazi rally at Nuremberg.

13. Spanish Civil war 1936–39: anarchist militia in Barcelona, 1936, on an improvised armoured vehicle.

14. Fascism triumphant? Adolf Hitler, conqueror of Europe, 1940–41, in occupied Paris.

15. Second World War: the bombs. US Boeing 'Flying Fortresses' raid Berlin.

16. Second World War: the tanks. Soviet armoured vehicles attacking in the greatest tank battle of history, Kursk 1943.

17. War of the non-combatants: London burning, 1940.

18. War of the non-combatants: Dresden burned, 1945.

19. War of the non-combatants: Hiroshima after the atom bomb, 1945.

20. War of the resisters: Josip Broz (Marshal Tito), 1892–1980, during the partisan struggle for the liberation of Yugoslavia.

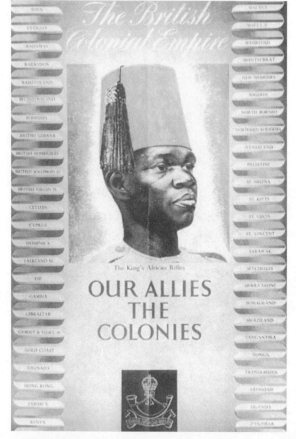

21. Empire before the fall: a British wartime poster.

22. Empire falling: Algiers about to win independence from France, 1961.

23. After Empire: Premier Indira Gandhi (1917–1984) heading the annual Independence Day parade in New Delhi.

24. (*left*) US Cruise missile.

25. (*below*) A silo for the Soviet SS missiles.

26. Two worlds divided: the Berlin Wall (1961–89), separating capitalism and 'real socialism', near the Brandenburg Gate.

27. Third World in ferment: Fidel Castro's rebel army enters liberated Santa Clara before taking power in Cuba on 1 January 1959.

28. The *guerrilleros*: insurrectionaries in El Salvador in the 1980s, preparing hand grenades.

29. From Third World guerrillas to First World students: demonstration against the US war in Vietnam, Grosvenor Square, London, 1968.

30. Social revolution in the name of God: Iran 1979, the first major twentieth-century social upheaval rejecting both the traditions of 1789 and 1917.

31. Cold War ended: the man who ended it. Mikhail Sergeyevich Gorbachev, General Secretary of the Communist Party of the Soviet Union (1985–91).

32. Cold War ended: the Berlin Wall falls, 1989.

33. Fall of European Communism: Stalin removed in Prague.

ancestral lands, cultivated mainly by the women, could only be inherited by or through women, but the new plots cleared in the jungle by the men, and on which supplementary crops were grown, such as fruit and vegetables, could be transmitted directly to men. But with the rise of rubber, a far more profitable crop than rice, the balance between the sexes changed, as inheritance from male to male gained ground. And this in turn strengthened the patriarchally-minded leaders of orthodox Islam, who were in any case trying to super-impose orthodoxy on local customary law, not to mention the local ruler and his kinfolk, another island of patrilineal descent in the local matrilineal lake (Firth, 1954). The dependent world was full of such changes and transformations in communities of people whose direct contact with the wider world was minimal—perhaps in this instance, only through a Chinese trader, himself in most cases originally a peasant or artisan emigrant from Fukien, whose culture had accustomed him to consistent effort, but above all to sophistication in matters of money, but otherwise equally far from the world of Henry Ford and General Motors (Freedman, 1959).

And yet, the world economy as such seemed remote, because its immediate, recognizable impact was not cataclysmic, except perhaps in the rapidly-growing cheap-labour industrial enclaves of such regions as India and China, where labour conflict, even labour organization on the Western models, spread from 1917, and in the gigantic port and industrial cities through which the dependent world communicated with the world economy that determined their fortunes: Bombay, Shanghai (whose population grew from 200,000 in the mid-nineteenth century to three-and-a-half millions in the 1930s), Buenos Aires or, on a smaller scale, Casablanca, whose population reached 250,000, less than thirty years after it opened as a modern port (Bairoch, 1985, pp. 517, 525).

The Great Slump changed all this. For the first time the interests of dependent and metropolitan economies clashed visibly, if only because the prices of primary products, on which the Third World depended, collapsed so much more dramatically than those of the manufactured goods which they bought from the West (chapter 3). For the first time colonialism and dependency became unacceptable even to those who had hitherto benefited from it. "Students rioted in Cairo, Rangoon and Djakarta (Batavia), not because they felt that some political millennium was in striking distance, but because depression had suddenly knocked away the supports which had made colonialism so acceptable to the generation of their parents" (Holland 1985, p. 12). More than this: for the first time (other than during wars) the lives of ordinary people were shaken by earthquakes plainly not of natural origin, and which called for protest rather than prayer. A mass basis for political mobilization came into existence, especially where peasants had come to be heavily involved in the world-market cash-crop economy, as on the West African coast and in South-east Asia. At the same time the Slump destabilized both the national and international politics of the dependent world.

The 1930s were, therefore, a crucial decade for the Third World, not so much because the Slump led to political radicalization but rather because it established contact between the politicized minorities and the common people of their countries. This was so even in countries like India, where the nationalist movement already had mobilized mass support. A second wave of mass non-cooperation in the early 1930s, a new compromise constitution conceded by the British, and the first nation-wide provincial elections in 1937 demonstrated the nationwide support of Congress, its members in the Ganges heartland rising from about sixty thousand in 1935 to one-and-a-half millions at the end of the 1930s (Tomlinson, 1976, p. 86). It was even more obvious in hitherto less mobilized countries. The outlines of the mass politics of the future began to emerge, dimly or clearly: Latin American populism based on authoritarian leaders seeking the support of urban workers; political mobilization by labour union leaders with a future as party leaders, as in the British Caribbean; a revolutionary movement with a strong base among labour migrants to and returners from, France, as in Algeria; a communist-based national resistance with strong agrarian links, as in Vietnam. At the very least, as in Malaya, the depression years fractured the bonds between colonial authorities and peasant masses, leaving a space for the rise of future politics.

By the end of the 1930s the crisis of colonialism had spread to other empires, although two of them, the Italian (which had just conquered Ethiopia) and the Japanese (which was trying to conquer China), were still expanding, though not for long. In India the new Constitution of 1935, an unhappy compromise with the rising forces of Indian nationalism, proved to be a major concession to it through the almost nationwide electoral triumph of Congress. In French North Africa serious political movements emerged for the first time in Tunisia, in Algeria—there were even some stirrings in Morocco—whilst mass agitation under communist leadership, orthodox and dissident, became substantial for the first time in French Indochina. The Dutch managed to keep control in Indonesia, a region which "feels the movements in the East as not many other countries do" (Van Asbeck, 1939), not because it was quiet, but mainly because the forces of opposition—Islamic, communist and secular nationalist—were divided among themselves and against each other. Even in what colonial ministries regarded as the somnolent Caribbean, a series of strikes in the oil fields of Trinidad and the plantations and cities of Jamaica between 1935 and 1938 turned into riots and island-wide clashes, revealing a hitherto unrecognized mass disaffection.

Only sub-Saharan Africa still remained quiescent, although even there the Slump years brought the first mass labour strikes after 1935, starting on the central African copper-belt, and London began to urge colonial governments to create labour departments, take steps to improve workers' conditions and stabilize labour forces, recognizing the current system of rural men's migration from village to mine as socially and politically destabilizing. The strike-wave of 1935–40 was Africa-wide. But it was not yet political in an anti-colonial sense, unless we count as political the spread of black-oriented African churches and prophets and of such rejectors of wordly governments as the (American-derived) millennial Watchtower movement on the Copper-belt. For the first time colonial governments began to reflect on the destabilizing effect of economic change on rural African society—which was actually passing through a notable era of prosperity—and to encourage research on this topic by social anthropologists.

However, politically, danger seemed remote. In the countryside this was the golden age of the white administrator, with or without the compliant "chief," sometimes created for this purpose where colonial administration was "indirect." In the cities a dissatisfied class of educated urban Africans was already sufficiently large in the mid-1930s to maintain a flourishing political press, such as the *African Morning Post* on the Gold Coast (Ghana), the *West African Pilot* in Nigeria, and the *Éclaireur de la Côte d'Ivoire* on the Ivory Coast ("it led a campaign against senior chiefs and the police; it demanded measures of social reconstruction; it urged the cause of the unemployed and of the African farmers hit by the economic crisis") (Hodgkin, 1961, p. 32). The leaders of local political nationalism were already emerging, influenced by ideas from the Black movement in the U.S.A., from the France of the Popular Front era, the ideas circulating in the West African Students Union in London, even from the communist movement.* Some of the future presidents of the future African republics were already on the scene—Kenya's Jomo Kenyatta (1889–1978); Dr. Namdi Azikiwe, later president of Nigeria.

---

*However, not a single leading African figure became, or remained, communist.

None of this as yet caused sleepless nights in European colonial ministries.

Did the universal end of colonial empires, though probable, actually seem imminent in 1939? Not if the present writer's memory of a "school" for British and "colonial" student communists in that year is any guide. And nobody was likely to have higher expectations at that time than impassioned and hopeful young Marxist militants. What transformed the situation was the Second World War. Though it was far more than this, it was unquestionably an inter-imperialist war, and, until 1943, the great colonial empires were on the losing side. France collapsed ignominiously, and many of its dependencies survived by permission of the Axis powers. The Japanese overran what there was of the British, Dutch, and other Western colonies in South-east Asia and the western Pacific. Even in North Africa the Germans occupied what they chose to control up to a few score miles west of Alexandria. At one point the British seriously considered withdrawing from Egypt. Only Africa south of the deserts remained under firm Western control, and indeed the British managed to liquidate the Italian Empire in the Horn of Africa with little trouble.

What fatally damaged the old colonialists was the proof that white men and their states could be defeated, shamefully and dishonourably, and the the old colonial powers were patently too weak, even after a victorious war, to restore their old positions. The test of the British Raj in India was not the major rebellion organized by Congress in 1942 under the slogan "Quit India," for they suppressed it without serious difficulty. It was that, for the first time, up to fifty-five thousand Indian soldiers defected to the enemy to form an "Indian National Army" under a Left-wing Congress leader, Subhas Chandra Bose, who had decided to seek Japanese support for Indian independence (Bhargava/Singh Gill, 1988, p. 10; Sareen, 1988, pp. 20–21). Japanese policy, possibly under the influence of the navy, more sophisticated than the soldiers, exploited the skin-colour of its people to claim merit as a liberator of colonies, with substantial success (except among the overseas Chinese and in Vietnam, where it maintained the French administration). An "Assembly of Greater East Asiatic Nations"* was even organized in Tokyo in 1943, attended by the "presidents" or "prime ministers" of Japanese-sponsored China, India, Thailand, Burma and Manchuria (but not Indonesia, which was offered even Japanese "independence" only when the war was lost). The colonial

---

*The term "Asian" only came into currency after the Second World War, for reasons which are obscure.

nationalists were too realistic to be pro-Japanese, though they appreciated the support from Japan, especially when this was substantial, as in Indonesia. When the Japanese were about to lose, they turned against them, but they never forgot how weak the old Western empires had proved to be. Nor did they overlook the fact that the two powers which had actually defeated the Axis, Roosevelt's U.S.A. and Stalin's U.S.S.R., were both, for different reasons, hostile to the old colonialism, even though American anti-communism soon made Washington the defender of conservatism in the Third World.

V

Not surprisingly, the old colonial systems first broke in Asia. Syria and Lebanon (formerly French) became independent in 1945; India and Pakistan in 1947; Burma, Ceylon (Sri Lanka), Palestine (Israel) and the Dutch East Indies (Indonesia) in 1948. In 1946 the U.S.A. had granted formal status of independence to the Philippines, which it had occupied since 1898. The Japanese Empire had, of course, disappeared in 1945. Islamic North Africa was already shaking, but still held. Most of sub-Saharan Africa and the islands of the Caribbean and Pacific remained relatively quiet. Only in parts of South-east Asia was this political decolonization seriously resisted, notably in French Indochina (the present Vietnam, Cambodia and Laos) where the communist resistance had declared independence after liberation under the leadership of the noble Ho Chi Minh. The French, supported by the British and later the U.S.A., conducted a desperate rearguard action to reconquer and hold a country against the victorious revolution. They were defeated and forced to withdraw in 1954, but the U.S.A. prevented the unification of the country and maintained a satellite regime in the southern part of a divided Vietnam. After this in turn looked like collapsing, the U.S.A. waged ten years of major war in Vietnam itself, until it was finally defeated and forced to withdraw in 1975, having dropped more high explosives on the unhappy country than had been used in the whole of the Second World War.

Resistance in the rest of South-east Asia was patchier. The Dutch (who turned out to be rather better than the British in decolonizing their Indian empire without partitioning it) were too weak to maintain adequate military power in the huge Indonesian archipelago, most of whose islands would have been quite prepared to keep them as counterweight to the predominance of the fifty-five million-strong Japanese. They gave up when they discovered that the U.S.A. did not consider Indonesia an essential front against world communism, unlike Vietnam. Indeed, so far from being under communist leadership, the new Indonesian nationalists had just put down an insurrection by the local Communist Party in 1948, an event which convinced the U.S.A. that Dutch military power would be better employed in Europe against the supposed Soviet threat than to maintain their empire. So the Dutch gave up, only maintaining a colonial foothold in the western half of the great Melanesian island of New Guinea, until this also was transferred to Indonesia in the 1960s. The British in Malaya found themselves caught between the traditional sultans who had done well out of empire and two different and mutually suspicious bodies of inhabitants, the Malays and the Chinese, each radicalized in different ways; the Chinese by the Communist Party which had gained much influence as the only body of resisters to the Japanese. Once the Cold War had broken out no question of allowing communists, let alone Chinese ones, into power or office in an ex-colony could arise, but after 1948 it took the British twelve years, fifty thousand troops, sixty thousand police and a home guard of two hundred thousand to defeat a primarily Chinese guerrilla insurrection and war. It may well be asked whether Britain would have paid the costs of these operations so willingly if Malaya's tin and rubber had not been such reliable dollar earners, thus guaranteeing the stability of sterling. However, the decolonization of Malaya would in any case have been a rather complex affair and was not achieved to the satisfaction of Malay conservatives and Chinese millionaires until 1957. In 1965 the mainly Chinese island of Singapore broke away to constitute itself an independent, and very rich, city state.

Unlike the French and the Dutch, Britain had learned by long experience in India that once a serious nationalist movement existed the only way to hold on to the advantages of empire was to let go of formal power. The British withdrew from the Indian subcontinent in 1947 before their inability to control it became patent, and without the slightest resistance. Ceylon (renamed Sri Lanka in 1972) and Burma were also given their independence, the former to its welcome surprise, the latter with more hesitation, since the Burmese nationalists, though led by an Anti-fascist People's Freedom League, had also cooperated with the Japanese. Indeed they were so hostile to Britain that, alone of all decolonized British possessions, Burma immediately refused to join the British Commonwealth, the non-committal association by which London tried to maintain at least the memory of the British Empire. In this it anticipated even Ireland, which declared itself a Republic outside the Commonwealth in the same year. All the same, while the rapid and peaceful retreat of Britain from the largest bloc of humanity ever subdued and administered by a foreign conqueror was a credit to the British Labour government which came to power at the end of the Second World War, it was far from an unqualified success. It was achieved at the cost of a bloodstained partition of India into a Muslim Pakistan and a non-denominational, but overwhelmingly Hindu India, in the course of which perhaps several hundred thousand people were massacred by religious opponents and several more millions were driven from their ancestral homes into what was now a foreign country. This had not been part of the plan of either Indian nationalism or Muslim movements or of the imperial rulers.

How the idea of a separate "Pakistan," whose very concept and name was only invented by some students in 1932–33, became reality by 1947 is a question that continues to haunt both scholars and dreamers about the "if onlys" of history. Since, as we can see with the wisdom of hindsight, the partition of India along religious lines established a sinister precedent for the world's future, it needs some explanation. In a sense it was nobody's or everybody's fault. In the elections under the 1935 Constitution, Congress had triumphed, even in most Muslim areas, and the national party claiming to represent the minority community, the Muslim League, had done rather poorly. The rise of a secular and nonsectarian, Indian National Congress naturally made many Muslims, most of them (like most Hindus) still non-voters, nervous of Hindu power, since the majority of the Congress leaders in a predominantly Hindu country were likely to be Hindus. Instead of recognizing these fears and giving Muslims special representation, the elections seemed to strengthen Congress claims to be the *only* national party, representing both Hindus and Muslims. This is what caused the Muslim League under its formidable leader, Muhammad Ali Jinnah, to break with Congress and to set out on what became the road to potential separatism. However, not until 1940 did Jinnah drop his opposition to a separate Muslim state.

It was the war that broke India in two. In one sense it was the last great triumph of the British Raj—and at the same time its last exhausted gasp. For the last time the Raj mobilized the men and the economy of India for a British war, on an even greater scale than in 1914–18, this time against the opposition of the masses now behind a party of national liberation, and—unlike the First World War—against imminent military invasion from Japan. The achievement was astonishing, but the costs were high. Congress opposition to the war kept its leaders out of politics

and, after 1942, in jail. The strains of the war economy alienated important bodies of the Raj's political supporters among the Muslims, notably
in the Punjab, and thus sent them to the Muslim League, which now became a mass force at the very moment when the government in Delhi,
fearing the Congress's ability to sabotage the war effort, deliberately and
systematically exploited Hindu–Muslim rivalry to immobilize the national movement. This time it can be truly said that Britain "divided to
rule." In its last desperate effort to win the war, the Raj destroyed not
only itself but its moral legitimation: the achievement of a single Indian
subcontinent in which all its multiple communities could coexist in relative peace under a single impartial administration and law. When the war
ended, the engine of communal politics could no longer be put into reverse.

By 1950 Asian decolonization was complete, except in Indochina.
Meanwhile the region of western Islam, from Persia (Iran) to Morocco,
was transformed by a series of popular movements, revolutionary coups
and insurrections, starting with the nationalization of the Western oil
companies in Iran (1951) and the swing to populism of that country
under Dr. Muhammad Mussadiq (1880–1967) supported by the then
powerful Tudeh (Communist) Party. (Not surprisingly communist parties
in the Middle East acquired some influence in the aftermath of the great
Soviet victory.) Mussadiq was to be overthrown by an Anglo-American
secret service coup in 1953. The revolution of the Free Officers in Egypt
(1952) led by Gamal Abdel Nasser (1918–70) and the subsequent overthrow of Western client regimes in Iraq (1958) and Syria could not be so
reversed, though the British and French, combining with the new anti-
Arab state of Israel, tried their best to overthrow Nasser in the Suez War
of 1956 (see p. 359). However, the French bitterly resisted the rising for
national independence in Algeria (1954–62), one of those territories, like
South Africa and—in a different manner—Israel, where the coexistence
of an indigenous population with a large body of European settlers made
the problem of decolonization particularly intractable. The Algerian war
was thus a conflict of peculiar brutality which helped to institutionalize
torture in the armies, police and security forces of countries that purported to be civilized. It popularized the subsequently widespread and
infamous use of torture by electric shocks applied to tongues, nipples and
genitalia, and led to the overthrow of the Fourth Republic (1958) and almost to that of the Fifth (1961), before Algeria won the independence
which General de Gaulle had long recognized as inevitable. Meanwhile
the French government had quietly negotiated the autonomy and (1956)
independence of the two other North African protectorates, Tunisia

(which became a republic) and Morocco (which remained a monarchy). In the same year the British quietly let go of the Sudan, which had become untenable when they lost control over Egypt.

It is not clear when the old empires realized that the Age of Empire was definitely at an end. Certainly, in retrospect, the attempt by Britain and France to reassert themselves as global imperial powers in the Suez adventure of 1956 seems more doomed than it evidently did to the governments of London and Paris, who planned a military operation to overthrow the revolutionary Egyptian government of Colonel Nasser, in conjunction with Israel. The episode was a catastrophic failure (except from the point of view of Israel), all the more ridiculous for the combination of indecision, hesitation and unconvincing disingenuousness by the British prime minister, Anthony Eden. The operation, barely launched, was called off under the pressure of the U.S.A., pushed Egypt towards the U.S.S.R., and ended for good what has been called "Britain's Moment in the Middle East," the epoch of unquestioned British hegemony in that region since 1918.

At all events, by the late 1950s it had become clear to the surviving old empires that formal colonialism had to be liquidated. Only Portugal continued to resist its dissolution since its backward, politically isolated and marginalized metropolitan economy could not afford neo-colonialism. It needed to exploit its African resources and, since its economy was uncompetitive, could do so only through direct control. South Africa and Southern Rhodesia, the African states with substantial white-settler populations (except for Kenya) also refused to go along with policies which would inevitably produce African-dominated regimes, and Southern Rhodesia even declared white-settler independence (1965) from Britain to avoid this fate. However, Paris, London and Brussels (the Belgian Congo) decided that the voluntary grant of formal independence with economic and cultural dependence was preferable to lengthy struggles likely to end in independence under Left-wing regimes. Only in Kenya was there a substantial popular insurrection and guerrilla war, though one largely confined to sections of one local people, the Kikuyu (the so-called Mau Mau movement, 1952–56). Elsewhere the policy of prophylactic decolonization was pursued successfully, except in the Belgian Congo, where it almost immediately collapsed into anarchy, civil war and international power politics. In British Africa the Gold Coast (now Ghana), which already had a mass party under a talented African politician and pan-African intellectual, Kwame Nkrumah, was granted independence in 1957. In French Africa Guinea was pitchforked into an early and impoverished independence in 1958 when its leader, Sekou Touré, refused to join a "French Community" offered by de Gaulle, which combined autonomy with strict dependence on the French economy, and was therefore—first among black African leaders—forced to look for help to Moscow. Almost all the remaining British, French and Belgian colonies in Africa were turned loose in 1960–62, the rest shortly after. Only Portugal and the independent settler states resisted the trend.

The larger British Caribbean colonies were quietly decolonized in the 1960s, the smaller islands at intervals between then and 1981, the Indian and Pacific islands in the late 1960s and 1970s. In fact, by 1970 no territories of any significant size remained under direct administration by the former colonialist powers or their settler regimes, except in Central and Southern Africa—and, of course, in embattled Vietnam. The imperial era was at an end. Less than three quarters of a century earlier, it had seemed indestructible. Even thirty years earlier, it covered most of the peoples of the globe. An irrecoverable part of the past, it became part of the sentimentalised literary and cinematic memories of the former imperial states, as a new generation of indigenous writers from formerly colonial countries began to produce a literature which began with the age of independence.

PART TWO

The Golden Age

CHAPTER EIGHT

Cold War

Although Soviet Russia intends to spread her influence by all possible means, world revolution is no longer part of her programme and there is nothing in the internal conditions within the Union which might encourage a return to the old revolutionary traditions. Any comparison between the German menace before the war and a Soviet menace today, must allow for ... fundamental differences ... There is, therefore, infinitely less danger of a sudden catastrophe with the Russians than with the Germans.

—Frank Roberts, British Embassy, Moscow, to Foreign Office, London, 1946 (Jensen, 1991, p. 56)

The war economy provides comfortable niches for tens of thousands of bureaucrats in and out of military uniform who go to the office every day to build nuclear weapons or to plan nuclear war; millions of workers whose jobs depend on the system of nuclear terrorism; scientists and engineers hired to look for that final "technological breakthrough" that can provide total security; contractors unwilling to give up easy profits; warrior intellectuals who sell threats and bless wars.

—Richard Barnet (1981, p. 97)

I

The forty-five years from the dropping of the atom bombs to the end of the Soviet Union do not form a single homogeneous period in world history. As we shall see in the following chapters, they fall into two halves, the decades on either side of the watershed of the early 1970s (see chapters 9 and 14). Nevertheless, the history of the entire period was welded into a single pattern by the peculiar international situation which dominated it until the fall of the U.S.S.R.: the constant confrontation of the two superpowers which emerged from the Second World War, the so-called "Cold War."

The Second World War had barely ended when humanity plunged into what can reasonably be regarded as a Third World War, though a very peculiar one. For, as the great philosopher Thomas Hobbes observed, "War consisteth not in battle only, or the act of fighting: but in a tract of time, wherein the will to contend by battle is sufficiently known" (Hobbes, chapter 13). The Cold War between the two camps of the U.S.A. and the U.S.S.R., which utterly dominated the international scene in the second half of the Short Twentieth Century, was unquestionably such a tract of time. Entire generations grew up under the shadow of global nuclear battles which, it was widely believed, could break out at any moment, and devastate humanity. Indeed, even those who did not believe that either side intended to attack the other found it hard not to be pessimistic, since Murphy's Law is one of the most powerful generalizations about human affairs ("If it can go wrong, sooner or later it will"). As time went on, more and more things were there which could go wrong, both politically and technologically, in a permanent nuclear confrontation based on the assumption that only the fear of "mutually assured destruction" (correctly concentrated into the acronym MAD) would prevent one side or the other from giving the ever-ready signal for the planned suicide of civilization. It did not happen, but for some forty years it looked a daily possibility.

The peculiarity of the Cold War was that, speaking objectively, no imminent danger of world war existed. More than this: in spite of the apocalyptic rhetoric on both sides, but especially on the American side, the governments of both the superpowers accepted the global distribution of force at the end of the Second World War, which amounted to a highly uneven but essentially unchallenged balance of power. The U.S.S.R. controlled, or exercised predominant influence in one part of the globe—the zone occupied by the Red Army and/or other communist armed forces at the end of the war, and did not attempt to extend its range of influence further by military force. The U.S.A. exercised control and predominance over the rest of the capitalist world as well as the western hemisphere and the oceans, taking over what remained of the old imperial hegemony of the former colonial powers. In return, it did not intervene in the zone of accepted Soviet hegemony.

In Europe the demarcation lines had been drawn in 1943–45, both by agreement at various summit meetings between Roosevelt, Churchill and Stalin, and by virtue of the fact that only the Red Army could actually defeat Germany. There were a few uncertainties, notably about Germany and Austria, which were solved by the partition of Germany along the lines of the Eastern and Western occupation forces, and the withdrawal of all ex-belligerents from Austria. The latter became a sort of second Switzerland—a small country committed to neutrality, envied for its persistent prosperity and therefore described (correctly) as "boring." The U.S.S.R. accepted West Berlin as a Western enclave inside its German territory with reluctance, but was not prepared to fight the issue.

The situation outside Europe was less clear-cut, except for Japan, where the U.S.A. from the start established a completely unilateral occupation that excluded not only the U.S.S.R. but any other co-belligerent. The problem was that the end of the old colonial empires was predictable, and indeed in 1945 plainly imminent on the Asian continent, but the future orientation of the new post colonial states was by no means clear. As we shall see (chapters 12 and 15) this was the zone in which the two superpowers continued, throughout the Cold War, to compete for support and influence, and hence the major zone of friction between them, and indeed the one where armed conflict was most likely, and actually broke out. Unlike Europe, not even the limits of the area under future communist control could be predicted, let alone agreed by negotiation in advance, however provisionally and ambiguously. Thus the U.S.S.R. did not much want a communist take over in China,* but it took place nevertheless.

However, even in what soon came to be called the "Third World," the conditions for international stability began to emerge within a few years, as it became clear that most of the new post-colonial states, however unsympathetic to the U.S.A. and its camp, were non-communist, indeed mostly anti-communist in their domestic politics, and "non-aligned" (i.e. outside the Soviet military bloc) in international affairs. In short, the "communist camp" showed no sign of significant expansion between the

---

*There was a spectacular lack of reference—in any context—to China in Zhdanov's report on the world situation which opened the founding conference of the Communist Information Bureau (Cominform) in September 1947, though Indonesia and Vietnam were classified as "joining the anti-imperialist camp" and India, Egypt and Syria as "sympathising" with it (Spriano, 1983, 286). As late as April 1949, when Chiang-Kai-shek abandoned his capital in Nanking, the Soviet ambassador—*alone* among the diplomatic corps—joined him in his retreat to Canton. Six months later Mao proclaimed the People's Republic (Walker, 1993, p. 63).

Chinese revolution and the 1970s, by which time Communist China was no longer in it (see chapter 16).

In effect, the world situation became reasonably stable soon after the war and remained so until the middle 1970s, when the international system and its component units entered another period of lengthy political and economic crisis. Until then both the superpowers accepted the uneven division of the world, made every effort to settle demarcation disputes without an open clash between their armed forces that might lead to a war between them, and, contrary to ideology and Cold War rhetoric, worked on the assumption that long-term peaceful coexistence between them was possible. Indeed, when it came to the point, both trusted one another's moderation, even at times when they were officially on the brink of, or even engaged in, war. Thus during the Korean War of 1950–53, in which the Americans were officially involved, but not the Russians, Washington knew perfectly well that up to 150 Chinese planes were actually Soviet planes flown by Soviet pilots (Walker, 1993, pp. 75–77). The information was kept dark, because it was correctly assumed that the last thing Moscow wanted was war. During the Cuban missile crisis of 1962, as we now know (Ball, 1992; Ball 1993), the main concern on both sides was how to prevent warlike gestures from being misinterpreted as actual moves to war.

Until the 1970s this tacit agreement to treat the Cold War as a Cold Peace held good. The U.S.S.R. knew (or rather learned) as early as 1953 that the U.S. calls to "roll back" communism were mere radio histrionics, when Soviet tanks were quietly allowed to re-establish communist control against a serious working-class revolt in East Germany. From then on, as the Hungarian revolution of 1956 confirmed, the West would keep out of the region of Soviet domination. The Cold War that actually tried to live up to its own rhetoric of a struggle for supremacy or annihilation was not the one in which basic decisions were taken by governments, but the shadowy contest between their various acknowledged and unacknowledged secret services, which in the West produced that most characteristic spin-off of the international tension, the fiction of espionage and covert killing. In this genre the British, through Ian Fleming's James Bond and John le Carré's sour-sweet heroes—both had served their time in the British secret services—maintained a steady superiority, thus compensating for their country's decline in the world of real power. However, except in some of the weaker countries of the Third World, the operations of KGB, CIA and their like were trivial in terms of real power politics, though often dramatic.

Was there, under these circumstances, a real danger of world war at any time during this long period of tension—except, of course, by the sort of accident which inevitably threatens those who skate long enough on sufficiently thin ice? It is hard to say. Probably the most explosive period was that between the formal enunciation of the "Truman Doctrine" in March 1947 ("I believe that it must be the policy of the United States to support free peoples who are resisting attempted subjugation by armed minorities or by outside pressures") and April 1951, when the same U.S. president dismissed General Douglas MacArthur, commander of the U.S. forces in the Korean War (1950–53), who pushed military ambition too far. This was the period when the American fear of social disintegration or revolution within the non-Soviet parts of Eurasia were not wholly fantastic—after all, in 1949 the communists took over China. Conversely, the U.S.S.R. found itself faced with a U.S. which enjoyed the monopoly of nuclear arms and multiplied militant and threatening declarations of anti-communism, while the first cracks appeared in the solidity of the Soviet bloc as Tito's Yugoslavia broke away (1948). Moreover, from 1949 on China was under a government which did not merely plunge readily into a major war in Korea, but—unlike all other governments—was willing to envisage actually fighting and surviving a nuclear holocaust.* Anything might happen.

Once the U.S.S.R. acquired nuclear weapons—four years after Hiroshima in the case of the atom bomb (1949), nine months after the U.S.A. in the case of the hydrogen bomb (1953)—both superpowers plainly abandoned war as an instrument of policy against one another, since it was the equivalent of a suicide pact. Whether they seriously envisaged nuclear action against third parties—the U.S.A. in Korea in 1951, and to save the French in Vietnam in 1954; the U.S.S.R. against China in 1969—is not quite clear, but in any case the weapons were not used. However, both used the nuclear threat, almost certainly without intending to carry it out, on some occasions: the U.S.A. to speed peace negotiations in Korea and Vietnam (1953, 1954), the U.S.S.R. to force Britain and France to withdraw from Suez in 1956. Unfortunately, the very certainty that neither superpower would actually *want* to press the nuclear button tempted both sides into using nuclear gesticulation for purposes of negotiation or (in the U.S.A.) for domestic politics, confident that the

---

*Mao is reported to have told the Italian leader Togliatti: "Who told you that Italy must survive? Three hundred million Chinese will be left, and that will be enough for the human race to continue." "Mao's blithe readiness to accept the inevitability of a nuclear war and its possible utility as a way to bring about the final defeat of capitalism, stunned his comrades from other countries" in 1957 (Walker, 1993, p. 126).

other did not want war either. This confidence proved justified, but at the cost of racking the nerves of generations. The Cuban missile crisis of 1962, an entirely unnecessary exercise of this kind, almost plunged the world into an unnecessary war for a few days, and actually frightened even the top decision-makers into rationality for a while.*

II

How then are we to explain the forty years of an armed and mobilized confrontation, based on the always implausible, and in this case plainly baseless, assumption that the globe was so unstable that a world war might break out at any moment, and was held at bay only by unceasing mutual deterrence? In the first instance, the Cold War was based on a Western belief, absurd in retrospect but natural enough in the aftermath of the Second World War, that the Age of Catastrophe was by no means at an end; that the future of world capitalism and liberal society was far from assured. Most observers expected a serious post-war economic crisis, even in the U.S.A., on the analogy of what had happened after the First World War. A future Nobel prize economist in 1943 spoke of the possibility, in the U.S.A., of "the greatest period of unemployment and industrial dislocation which any economy has ever faced" (Samuelson, 1943, p. 51). Indeed, the post-war plans of the U.S. government were far more concretely concerned with preventing another Great Slump than with preventing another war, a matter to which Washington gave only divided and provisional attention before victory (Kolko, 1969, pp. 244–46).

If Washington expected "the great post-war troubles" which undermined "stability—social, political and economic—in the world" (Dean Acheson, cited in Kolko, 1969, p. 485), it was because at the end of the war the belligerent countries, with the exception of the U.S.A., were a field of ruins inhabited by what seemed to Americans hungry, desperate, and probably radicalized peoples, only too ready to listen to the appeal of social revolution and economic policies incompatible with the inter-

---

*The Soviet leader N. S. Khrushchev decided to place Soviet missiles in Cuba to offset the American missiles already in place across the Soviet border in Turkey. (Burlatsky, 1992). The U.S.A. forced him to withdraw them by the threat of war, but also withdrew its missiles from Turkey The Soviet missiles, as President Kennedy was told at the time, made no difference to the strategic balance, though a considerable difference to presidential public relations (Ball, 1992, p. 18; Walker, 1988). The U.S. missiles withdrawn were described as "obsolescent."

national system of free enterprise, free trade and investment by which the U.S.A. and the world were to be saved. Moreover, the pre-war international system had collapsed, leaving the U.S.A. facing an enormously strengthened Communist U.S.S.R. across large stretches of Europe and even vaster stretches of the non-European world, whose political future seemed quite uncertain—except that in this explosive and unstable world anything that happened was more likely than not to weaken both capitalism and the U.S.A., and to strengthen the power which had come into existence by and for revolution.

The immediate post-war situation in many of the liberated and occupied countries seemed to undermine the situation of moderate politicians, with little to support them except the Western allies, and beset within and outside their governments by the communists, who emerged from the war everywhere far stronger than at any time in the past, and sometimes as the largest parties and electoral forces of their countries. The (socialist) premier of France came to Washington to warn that, without economic support, he was likely to fall to the communists. The terrible harvest of 1946, followed by the appalling winter of 1946–47, made both European politicians and American presidential advisers even more nervous.

Under the circumstances it is not surprising that the wartime alliance between the major capitalist and the socialist power now at the head of its own zone of influence should have broken down, as even less heterogeneous coalitions so often do at the end of wars. However, this is clearly not enough to explain why U.S. policy—Washington's allies and clients, with the possible exception of Britain, were considerably less overheated—should have been based, at least in its public statements, on a nightmare scenario of the Muscovite super-power poised for the immediate conquest of the globe, and directing a godless "communist world conspiracy" ever ready to overthrow the realms of freedom. It is even more inadequate to explain the campaign rhetoric of a J. F. Kennedy in 1960, at a time when what the British premier Harold Macmillan called "our modern free society—the new form of capitalism" (Horne, 1989, vol. II, p. 283) could not conceivably have been said to be in any immediate trouble.*

Why could the outlook of "the State Department professionals" in the aftermath of the war be described as "apocalyptic"? (Hughes, 1969, p. 28).

---

*"The enemy is the communist system itself—implacable, insatiable, unceasing in its drive for world domination . . . This is not a struggle for supremacy of arms alone. It is also a struggle for supremacy between two conflicting ideologies: freedom under God versus ruthless, godless tyranny" (Walker, 1993, p. 132).

Why did even the calm British diplomat who rejected any comparison of the U.S.S.R. with Nazi Germany then report from Moscow that the world was "now faced with the danger of a modern equivalent of the religious wars of the sixteenth century, in which Soviet communism will struggle with Western social democracy and the American version of capitalism for domination of the world"? (Jensen, 1991, pp. 41, 53–54; Roberts, 1991.) For it is now evident, and was reasonably probable even in 1945–47 that the U.S.S.R. was neither expansionist—still less aggressive—nor counting on any further extension of the communist advance beyond what is assumed had been agreed at the summits of 1943–45. Indeed, where Moscow controlled its client regimes and communist movements, these were specifically committed to *not* building states on the model of the U.S.S.R., but mixed economies under multi-party parliamentary democracies, which were specifically distinguished from "the dictatorship of the proletariat," and "still more" of a single party. These were described in inner-party documents as "neither useful nor necessary" (Spriano, 1983, p. 265). (The only communist regimes that refused to follow this line were those whose revolutions, actively discouraged by Stalin, escaped from Moscow's control, e.g. Yugoslavia.) Moreover, though this has not been much noticed, the Soviet Union demobilized its troops—its major military asset—almost as fast as the U.S.A., reducing the Red Army from a 1945 peak strength of almost twelve millions to three millions by late 1948 (*New York Times*, 24/10/1946; 24/10/1948).

On any rational assessment, the U.S.S.R. presented no immediate danger to anyone outside the reach of the Red Army's occupation forces. It emerged from war in ruins, drained and exhausted, its peacetime economy in shreds, its government distrustful of a population much of which, outside Great Russia, had shown a distinct and understandable lack of commitment to the regime. On its western fringe, it continued to have trouble with Ukrainian and other nationalist guerrillas for some years. It was ruled by a dictator who had demonstrated that he was as risk-averse outside the territory he controlled directly as he was ruthless within it: J. V. Stalin (see chapter 13). It needed all the economic aid it could get, and, therefore, had no short-term interest in antagonising the only power that could give it, the U.S.A. No doubt Stalin, as a communist, believed that capitalism would inevitably be replaced by communism, and to this extent any coexistence of the two systems would not be permanent. However, Soviet planners did not see capitalism as such in crisis at the end of the Second World War. They had no doubt that it would continue for a long time under the hegemony of the U.S.A., whose enormously increased wealth and power was only too obvious (Loth, 1988, pp. 36–

37). That, in fact, is what the U.S.S.R. suspected and was afraid of.* Its basic posture after the war was not aggressive but defensive.

However, a policy of confrontation on both sides arose out of their situation. The U.S.S.R., conscious of the precariousness and insecurity of its position, faced the world power of the U.S.A., conscious of the precariousness and insecurity of central and western Europe, and the uncertain future of much of Asia. Confrontation would probably have developed even without ideology. George Kennan, the American diplomat who in early 1946 formulated the "containment" policy which Washington adopted with enthusiasm, did not believe that Russia was crusading for communism, and—as his subsequent career proved—was far from an ideological crusader (except possibly against democratic politics, of which he had a low opinion). He was merely an able Russian expert of the old school of diplomatic power-politics—there were many such in European foreign offices—who saw Russia, Tsarist or Bolshevik, as a backward and barbarous society ruled by men moved by a "traditional and instinctive Russian sense of insecurity," always cutting itself off from the outside world, always under autocrats, always seeking "security" only in patient and deadly struggle for total destruction of rival power, never in compacts and compromises with it; always, consequently, responding only to "the logic of force," never to reason. Communism, of course, in his opinion made the old Russia more dangerous by reinforcing the most brutal of great powers with the most ruthless of utopian, i.e. world-conquering, ideologies. But the implication of the thesis was that the only "rival power" to Russia's, namely the U.S.A., would have had to "contain" its pressure by uncompromising resistance even if it had not been communist.

Conversely, from Moscow's point of view, the only rational strategy for defending and exploiting a vast but fragile new position of international power, was exactly the same: no compromise. Nobody knew better than Stalin how weak a hand he had to play. There could be no negotiation on the positions offered by Roosevelt and Churchill at the time when the Soviet effort was essential to defeat Hitler, and was still believed to be essential to defeat Japan. The U.S.S.R. might be ready to retreat from any exposed position beyond that fortified by what it considered to have been agreed at the summit meetings of 1943–45, and especially Yalta—for instance on the borders of Iran and Turkey in

---

*They would have been even more suspicious had they known that the U.S. joint chiefs of staff produced a plan to atom-bomb the twenty chief Soviet cities within ten weeks of the end of the war (Walker, 1993, pp. 26–27).

1945–46—but any attempt to re-open Yalta could only be met by a flat refusal. Indeed, the "No" of Stalin's foreign minister Molotov at all international meetings after Yalta became notorious. The Americans had the power; though only just. Until December 1947 there were no planes to transport the twelve available atom bombs or military capable of assembling them (Moisi, 1981, pp. 78–79). The U.S.S.R. had not. Washington would give nothing away except against concessions, but these were precisely what Moscow could not afford to make, even in return for desperately needed economic aid, which in any case the Americans did not want to give them, claiming to have "mislaid" the Soviet request for a post-war loan, made before Yalta.

In short, while the U.S.A. was worried about the danger of a possible Soviet world supremacy some time in the future, Moscow was worried about the actual hegemony of the U.S.A. now, over all parts of the globe not occupied by the Red Army. It would not take much to turn an exhausted and impoverished U.S.S.R. into yet another client region of the U.S. economy, stronger at the time than all the rest of the world put together. Intransigence was the logical tactic. Let them call Moscow's bluff.

Yet the politics of mutual intransigence, even of permanent power-rivalry, do not imply the daily danger of war. Nineteenth-century British foreign secretaries, who took it for granted that the expansionist urges of Tsarist Russia must be continuously "contained" in the Kennanite manner, knew perfectly well that moments of open confrontation were rare, and war crises even rarer. Still less does mutual intransigence imply the politics of life-or-death struggle or religious war. However, two elements in the situation helped to move confrontation from the realm of reason to that of emotion. Like the U.S.S.R., the U.S.A. was a power representing an ideology, which most Americans sincerely believed to be the model for the world. Unlike the U.S.S.R., the U.S.A. was a democracy. Unfortunately it must be said that the second of these was probably the more dangerous.

For the Soviet government, though it also demonized the global antagonist, did not have to bother about winning votes in Congress, or in presidential and congressional elections. The U.S. government did. For both purposes an apocalyptic anti-communism was useful, and therefore tempting, even for politicians who were not sincerely convinced of their own rhetoric, or, like President Truman's Secretary of Defense, James Forrestal (1882–1949) clinically mad enough to commit suicide because he saw the Russians coming from his window in the hospital. An external enemy who threatened the U.S.A. was convenient for American governments which had concluded, correctly, that the U.S.A. was now a world power—in fact, the greatest world power by far—and which still saw "isolationism" or a defensive protectionism as its major domestic obstacle. If America itself was not safe, then there could be no withdrawal from the responsibilities—and rewards—of world leadership, as after the First World War. More concretely, public hysteria made it easier for presidents to raise the vast sums required for American policy from a citizenry notorious for its disinclination to pay taxes. And anti-communism was genuinely and viscerally popular in a country built on individualism and private enterprise where the nation itself was defined in exclusively ideological terms ("Americanism") which could be virtually defined as the polar opposite of communism. (Nor should we forget the votes of immigrants from Sovietised Eastern Europe.) It was not the American government which initiated the squalid and irrational frenzy of the anti-Red witch-hunt, but otherwise insignificant demagogues—some of them, like the notorious Senator Joseph McCarthy, not even particularly anti-communist—who discovered the political potential of wholesale denunciation of the enemy within.* The bureaucratic potential had long since been discovered by J. Edgar Hoover (1895–1972), the virtually irremoveable chief of the Federal Bureau of Investigations (FBI). What one of the main architects of the Cold War called "the attack of the Primitives" (Acheson, 1970, p. 462) both facilitated and constrained Washington policy by pushing it to extremes, especially in the years following the victory of the communists in China, for which Moscow was naturally blamed.

At the same time the schizoid demand of the vote-sensitive politicians for a policy that should both roll back the tide of "communist aggression," save money and interfere as little as possible with Americans' comfort, committed Washington, and with it the rest of the alliance, not only to an essentially nuclear strategy of bombs rather than men, but to the ominous strategy of "massive retaliation," announced in 1954. The potential aggressor was to be threatened with nuclear weapons even in the case of a limited conventional attack. In short, the U.S.A. found itself committed to an aggressive stance, with minimal tactical flexibility.

Both sides thus found themselves committed to an insane arms race to mutual destruction, and to the sort of nuclear generals and nuclear intellectuals whose profession required them not to notice this insanity.

*The only politician of real substance who emerged from the underworld of the witch-hunters was Richard Nixon, the most unpleasant individual among post-war American presidents (1968–74).

Both also found themselves committed to what the retiring President Eisenhower, a moderate military man of the old school who found himself presiding over this descent into lunacy, without being quite infected by it, called "the military-industrial complex," i.e. the increasingly vast agglomeration of men and resources which lived by the preparation of war. It was a larger vested interest than ever before in times of stable peace between the powers. As might be expected, both military-industrial complexes were encouraged by their governments to use their excess capacity to attract and arm allies and clients, and, not least, to win profitable export markets, while keeping their most up-to-date armaments to themselves; and, of course, their nuclear weapons. For in practice the superpowers retained their nuclear monopoly. The British acquired bombs of their own in 1952, ironically with the object of lessening their dependence on the U.S.A.; the French (whose nuclear arsenal was actually independent of the U.S.A.) and the Chinese in the 1960s. While the Cold War lasted, none of these counted. In the course of the 1970s and 1980s some other countries acquired the capacity to make nuclear weapons, notably Israel, South Africa, and probably India, but such nuclear proliferation did not become a serious international problem until after the end of the bi-polar superpower world order in 1989.

So who was responsible for the Cold War? Since the debate on this question was for long an ideological tennis-match between those who put the blame exclusively on the U.S.S.R. and the (mainly, it must be said, American) dissidents who said it was primarily the fault of the U.S.A., it is tempting to join the historical mediators who put it down to mutual fear escalating from confrontation until the two "armed camps began to mobilize under their two opposing banners" (Walker, 1993, p. 55). This is plainly true, but it is not the whole truth. It explains what has been called the "congealing" of the fronts in 1947–49; the step-by-step partition of Germany, from 1947 to the building of the Berlin Wall in 1961; the failure of the anti-communists on the Western side to avoid complete involvement in the U.S.-dominated military alliance (except for General de Gaulle in France); and the failure of those on the Eastern side of the divide to escape complete subordination to Moscow (except for Marshal Tito in Yugoslavia). But it does not explain the apocalyptic *tone* of the Cold War. That came from America. All Western European governments, with or without large communist parties, were without exception wholeheartedly anti-communist, and determined to protect themselves against possible Soviet military attack. None would have hesitated if asked to choose between the U.S.A. and the U.S.S.R., even those committed by history, policy or negotiation to neutrality. Yet the "communist world conspiracy" was not a serious part of the domestic politics of any of those who had some claim to being political democracies, at least after the immediate post-war years. Among democratic countries it was *only* in the U.S.A. that presidents were elected (like John F. Kennedy in 1960) against communism, which in terms of domestic politics was as insignificant in that country as Buddhism in Ireland. If anyone put the crusading element into the *realpolitik* of international power confrontation, and kept it there, it was Washington. In fact, as the rhetoric of J. F. Kennedy's electioneering demonstrates with the clarity of good oratory, the issue was not the academic threat of communist world domination, but the maintenance of a real U.S. supremacy.* It must, however, be added that the governments of the NATO alliance, though far from happy about American policy, were ready to accept American supremacy as the price of protection against the military power of an abhorrent political system, while that system continued in existence. They were as unprepared as Washington to trust the U.S.S.R. In short, "containment" was everyone's policy; the destruction of communism was not.

III

Though the most obvious face of the Cold War was military confrontation and an ever-more frenetic nuclear arms race in the West, this was not its major impact. The nuclear arms were not used. Nuclear powers engaged in three major wars (but not against each other). Shaken by the communist victory in China, the U.S. and its allies (disguised as the United Nations) intervened in Korea in 1950 to prevent the communist regime in the North of that divided country from spreading to the South. The result was a draw. They did so again with the same object in Vietnam, and lost. The U.S.S.R. withdrew in 1988 after eight years of providing military support for a friendly government in Afghanistan against American-backed and Pakistan-supplied guerrillas. In short, the expensive high-technology hardware of superpower competition proved indecisive. The constant threat of war produced international peace movements, essentially directed against nuclear arms, which from time to time became mass movements in parts of Europe and were regarded by the Cold War crusaders as secret weapons of the communists. The movements for

*"We will mould our strength and become first again. Not first if. Not first but. But first period. I want the world to wonder not what Mr. Khrushchev is doing. I want them to wonder what the United States is doing" (Beschloss, 1991, p. 28).

nuclear disarmament were not decisive either, although a specific anti-war movement, that of young Americans against being conscripted for the Vietnam War (1965–75), proved more effective. At the end of the Cold War these movements left behind a memory of good causes and some curious peripheral relics, such as the adoption of the anti-nuclear logo by the post-1968 counter-cultures and an ingrained prejudice among environmentalists against any kind of nuclear energy.

Much more obvious were the political consequences of the Cold War. Almost immediately it polarized the world controlled by the superpowers into two sharply divided "camps." The governments of national anti-fascist unity which had led all Europe out of the war (except, significantly, the three main belligerent states, U.S.S.R., U.S.A. and Britain), split into homogeneous pro-communist and anti-communist regimes in 1947–48. In the West the Communists disappeared from governments to become permanent political outcasts. The U.S.A. planned military intervention if they won the 1948 elections in Italy. The U.S.S.R. followed suit by eliminating the non-communists from their multi-party "people's democracies" which were henceforth re-classified as "dictatorships of the proletariat," i.e. of the Communist Parties. A curiously restricted and Eurocentric Communist International (the "Cominform" or Communist Information Bureau) was set up to confront the U.S.A., but quietly dissolved in 1956 when international temperatures had cooled. Direct Soviet control was firmly clamped on all of Eastern Europe except, oddly enough, Finland, which was at the Soviets' mercy and dropped its strong Communist Party from its government in 1948. Why Stalin refrained from installing a satellite government there remains obscure. Perhaps the high probability that the Finns would once again take up arms (as they had done in 1939–40 and 1941–44) dissuaded him, for he certainly did not want to run the risk of a war that might get out of hand. He tried but failed to impose Soviet control on Tito's Yugoslavia, which consequently broke with Moscow in 1948, without joining the other side.

The politics of the Communist bloc were henceforth predictably monolithic, although the brittleness of the monolith became increasingly obvious after 1956 (see chapter 16). The politics of the U.S.-aligned states of Europe were less monochromatic since virtually all local parties except the communists were united in their dislike of the Soviets. In terms of foreign policy it did not matter who was in office. However, the U.S.A. simplified matters in two ex-enemy countries, Japan and Italy, by creating what amounted to a permanent single-party system. In Tokyo it encouraged the foundation of the Liberal-Democratic Party (1955), and in Italy, by insisting on the total exclusion of the natural opposition party from power, because it happened to be communist, it handed the country over to the Christian Democrats, supplemented as occasion required by a selection of dwarf parties—Liberals, Republicans etc. From the early 1960s the only other party of substance, the socialists, joined the government coalition, having disengaged themselves from a long alliance with the communists after 1956. The consequence in both these countries was both to stabilize the communists (in Japan, the socialists) as the major party of opposition, and to install a government regime of institutional corruption on a scale so sensational that, when finally revealed in 1992–93, it shocked even the Italians and Japanese. Both government and opposition, thus frozen into immobility, collapsed with the super-power balance that had kept it in being.

Although the U.S.A. soon reversed the reforming anti-monopolist policies which its Rooseveltian advisers had initially imposed on occupied Germany and Japan, fortunately for the peace of mind of America's allies, the war had eliminated National Socialism, fascism, overt Japanese nationalism and much of the right-wing and nationalist sector of the political spectrum from the acceptable public scene. It was therefore impossible as yet to mobilize these unquestionably effective anti-communist elements for the struggle of the "free world" against "totalitarianism," as the restored German big business corporations and the Japanese *zaibatsu* could be.* The political base of Western Cold War governments therefore ranged from the pre-war social-democratic Left to the pre-war moderate non-nationalist Right. Here the parties linked to the Catholic Church proved particularly useful, since the anti-communist and conservative credentials of the Church were second to none, but its "Christian-Democratic" parties (see chapter 4) had both a solid anti-fascist record and a (non-socialist) social programme. These parties thus played a central role in Western politics after 1945, temporarily in France, more permanently in Germany, Italy, Belgium and Austria (see also p. 283).

However, the effect of the Cold War on the international politics of Europe was more striking than on the Continent's domestic politics. It created the "European Community" with all its problems; an entirely unprecedented form of political organization, namely a permanent (or at least a long-lasting) arrangement to integrate the economies, and to some extent the legal systems, of a number of independent nation-states. Initially (1957) formed by six states (France, the German Federal Republic, Italy, the Netherlands, Belgium and Luxemburg), by the end of the

---

*However, former fascists were systematically used from the start by intelligence services and in other functions not in the public view.

Short Twentieth Century, when the system began to totter, like all other products of the Cold War, it had been joined by another six (Britain, Ireland, Spain, Portugal, Denmark, Greece), and was in theory committed to even closer political, as well as economic integration. This was to lead to permanent federal or confederal political union for "Europe."

The "Community" was, like so many other things in post-1945 Europe, created both by and against the U.S.A. It illustrates both the power and ambiguity of that country and its limits; but it also illustrates the strength of the fears that held the anti-Soviet alliance together. These were not only fears of the U.S.S.R. So far as France was concerned, Germany remained the chief danger, and the fear of a revived giant power in Central Europe was shared, to a lesser extent, by the other ex-belligerent or occupied states of Europe, all of whom now found themselves locked into the NATO alliance with both the U.S.A. and an economically revived and re-armed Germany, though fortunately a truncated one. There were also, of course, fears of the U.S.A., an indispensable ally against the U.S.S.R., but a suspect and unreliable one, not to mention one which, not surprisingly, was apt to put the interests of the American world supremacy above all else—including those of America's allies. One must not forget that in all the calculations about the post-war world, and in all post-war decisions, "the premise of all policy makers was American economic pre-eminence" (Maier, 1987, p. 125).

Fortunately for America's allies, the Western European situation in 1946–47 seemed so tense that Washington felt that the development of a strong European, and a little later, a strong Japanese economy was the most urgent priority, and the Marshall Plan, a massive design for European recovery, was launched accordingly, in June 1947. Unlike earlier aid, which was clearly part of aggressive economic diplomacy, it mostly took the form of grants rather than loans. Again, fortunately for them, the original American plan for a post-war world economy of free trade, free convertibility and free markets, dominated by the U.S.A. proved quite unrealistic, if only because the desperate payments difficulties of Europe and Japan, thirsting for ever-scarcer dollars, meant that there was no immediate prospect for liberalizing trade and payments. Nor was the U.S. in a position to impose on the European states its ideal of a single European plan, preferably leading to a single Europe modelled on the U.S.A. in its political structure as well as in its flourishing free enterprise economy. Neither the British, who still saw themselves as a world power, nor the French, who dreamed of a strong France and a weak and partitioned Germany, liked it. However, for the Americans an effectively restored Europe, part of the anti-Soviet military alliance which was the logical complement of the Marshall Plan—the North Atlantic Treaty Organization (NATO) of 1949—had realistically to rest on a German economic strength reinforced by German re-armanent. The best the French could do was to so entangle West German and French affairs that conflict between the two old adversaries would be impossible. The French therefore proposed their own version of European union, the "European Coal and Steel Community" (1951), which developed into the "European Economic Community or Common Market" (1957), later simply the "European Community" and, from 1993, "European Union." Its headquarters were in Brussels, but Franco–German unity was its core. The European Community was established as an *alternative* to the U.S. plan for European integration. Once again, the end of the Cold War was to undermine the foundation on which the European Community and the Franco–German partnership had been built; not least by unbalancing both through the German reunification of 1990 and the unpredicted economic troubles it brought.

However, even though the U.S.A. was unable to impose its politico-economic plans on the Europeans in detail, it was strong enough to dominate their international behaviour. The policy of the alliance against the U.S.S.R. was the U.S.A.'s, and so were its military plans. Germany was re-armed, hankerings after European neutralism were firmly suppressed, and the only attempt by Western powers to engage in a world policy independent of the U.S.A.'s, namely the Anglo-French Suez war against Egypt of 1956, was aborted under American pressure. The most that an allied or client state could allow itself to do was to refuse complete integration into the military alliance without actually leaving it (like General de Gaulle).

And yet, as the Cold War era stretched out, there was a growing gap between the overwhelming military, and therefore political, domination of the alliance by Washington, and the U.S.A.'s gradually weakening economic predominance. The economic weight of the world economy was now shifting from the U.S.A. to the European and Japanese economies, which the U.S.A. felt it had rescued and rebuilt (see chapter 9). The dollars, so scarce in 1947, had flowed out of the U.S.A. in a growing torrent, accelerated—especially in the 1960s—by the American penchant for deficit financing of the enormous costs of their global military activities, notably the Vietnam War (after 1965), as well as the most ambitious social welfare programme in U.S. history. The dollar, keystone of the post-war world economy planned and guaranteed by the U.S.A., grew weaker. In theory backed by the bullion of Fort Knox, which had held almost three quarters of the world's gold reserves, in practice it consisted increasingly of floods of paper or book-entries—but since the stability of the dollar was guaranteed by its link to a given quantity of gold, cautious Europeans, headed by the ultra-cautious and bullion-minded French, preferred to exchange potentially devalued paper for solid ingots. Gold therefore poured out of Fort Knox, its price rising as the demand for it rose. For most of the sixties the stability of the dollar, and with it of the international payment system, was no longer based on the U.S.A.'s own reserves but on the willingness of European central banks—under U.S. pressure—not to cash in their dollars for gold, and to join in a "Gold Pool" to stabilize the price of gold in the market. It did not last. In 1968 the "Gold Pool," now drained, was dissolved. *De facto*, the convertibility of the dollar ended. It was formally abandoned in August 1971, and with it the stability of the international payments system, and its control by the U.S.A. or any other single national economy came to an end.

When the Cold War ended, so little was left of the U.S. economic hegemony that even the military hegemony could no longer be financed out of the country's own resources. The 1991 Gulf War against Iraq, an essentially U.S. military operation, was paid for, willingly or reluctantly, by other countries which supported Washington. This was one of the rare wars out of which a major power actually made a profit. Fortunately for everyone concerned, except the unhappy inhabitants of Iraq, it was over within a matter of days.

IV

Some time in the early 1960s the Cold War appeared to move a few tentative steps in the direction of sanity. The dangerous years from 1947 to the dramatic events of the Korean War (1950–53) had passed without a world explosion. So had the seismic upheavals which shook the Soviet bloc after Stalin's death (1953), especially in the middle fifties. So far from fighting off social crisis, the countries of western Europe began to notice that they were actually living through an era of unexpected and general prosperity, which will be discussed more fully in the next chapter. In the traditional jargon of old-style diplomats, slackening tension was "détente." The word now became familiar.

It had first surfaced in the last years of the 1950s, when N. S. Khrushchev established his supremacy in the U.S.S.R. after post-Stalinist alarums and excursions (1958–64). This admirable rough diamond, a believer in reform and peaceful coexistence, who incidentally emptied

Stalin's concentration camps, dominated the international scene in the next few years. He was also perhaps the only peasant boy ever to rule a major state. However, détente had first to survive what looked like an unusually tense spell of confrontations between Khrushchev's taste for bluff and impulsive decisions and the gesture politics of John F. Kennedy (1960–63), the most overrated U.S. president of the century. The two superpowers were thus led by two high-risk operators at a time when—it is hard to recall—the capitalist West felt itself to be losing ground to the communist economies, which had grown faster than its own in the 1950s. Had they not just demonstrated a (short-lived) technological superiority to the U.S.A. by the dramatic triumph of Soviet satellites and cosmonauts? Moreover, had not—to everyone's surprise—communism just triumphed in Cuba, a country only a few dozen miles from Florida (see chapter 15)?

Conversely, the U.S.S.R. was worried not only by Washington's ambiguous, but often only too bellicose rhetoric, but by the fundamental rupture with China, which now accused Moscow of going soft on capitalism, thus forcing the pacifically-minded Khrushchev into a more uncompromising public stance towards the West. At the same time the sudden acceleration of decolonization and Third World revolution (see chapters 7, 12 and 15) seemed to favour the Soviets. A nervous but confident U.S.A. thus confronted a confident but nervous U.S.S.R. over Berlin, over the Congo, over Cuba.

In fact, the net result of this phase of mutual threats and brinkmanship was a relatively stabilized international system, and a tacit agreement of the two superpowers not to frighten each other and the world, symbolized by the installation of the telephone "hot line" which now (1963) came to link the White House with the Kremlin. The Berlin Wall (1961) closed the last undefined border between East and West in Europe. The U.S.A. accepted a communist Cuba on its doorstep. The small flames of liberation and guerrilla war lit by the Cuban revolution in Latin America, and by the wave of decolonization in Africa, did not turn into forest fires, but seemed to flicker out (see chapter 15). Kennedy was assassinated in 1963; Khrushchev sent packing in 1964 by the Soviet Establishment, which preferred a less impetuous approach to politics. The sixties and early seventies actually saw some significant steps to control and limit nuclear arms: test-ban treaties, attempts to stop nuclear proliferation (accepted by those who already had nuclear weapons or never expected to have them, but not by those building their own new nuclear arsenals like China, France and Israel), a Strategic Arms Limitation Treaty (SALT) between, the U.S.A. and the U.S.S.R., even some agreement about each side's Anti-Ballistic Missiles (ABMs). More to the point, trade between the U.S.A. and the U.S.S.R., politically strangled by both sides for so long, began to flourish as the 1960s turned into the 1970s. The prospects looked good.

They were not. In the middle 1970s the world entered what has been called the Second Cold War (see chapter 15). It coincided with a major change in the world economy, the period of long-term crisis which was to characterize the two decades beginning in 1973, and reached a climax in the early 1980s (chapter 14). However, initially the change in the economic climate was not much noticed by the players in the superpower game, except for the sudden jump in energy prices brought about by the successful coup of the oil-producers cartel, OPEC, one of several developments which seemed to suggest a weakening of the international domination of the U.S.A. Both superpowers were reasonably happy about the soundness of their economies. The U.S.A. was plainly less affected by the new economic slow-down than Europe; the U.S.S.R.—whom the gods wish to destroy they first make complacent— felt that everything was going its way. Leonid Brezhnev, Khrushchev's successor, who presided over the twenty years of what Soviet reformers were to call "the era of stagnation," seemed to have some cause for optimism, not least because the oil crisis of 1973 had just quadrupled the international market value of the gigantic new deposits of oil and natural gas which had been discovered in the U.S.S.R. since the middle 1960s.

Yet, economics apart, two inter-related developments now seemed to shift the balance of the superpowers. The first was what looked like defeat and destabilisation in the U.S.A., as that country launched itself into a major war. The Vietnam war demoralized and divided the nation, amid televised scenes of riots and anti-war demonstrations; destroyed an American president; led to a universally predicted defeat and retreat after ten years (1965–75); and, what was even more to the point, demonstrated the isolation of the U.S.A. For not a single one of America's European allies sent even nominal contingents of troops to fight alongside the U.S. forces. Why the U.S.A. came to embroil itself in a doomed war, against which both its allies, neutrals, and even the U.S.S.R. had warned it,* is almost impossible to understand, except as part of that dense cloud of

---

*"If you want to, go ahead and fight in the jungles of Vietnam. The French fought there for seven years and still had to quit in the end. Perhaps the Americans will be able to stick it out for a little longer, but eventually they will have to quit too"— Krushchev to Dean Rusk in 1961 (Beschloss, 1991, p. 649).

incomprehension, confusion and paranoia through which the main actors in the Cold War tapped their way.

And, if Vietnam was not enough to demonstrate America's isolation, the 1973 Yom Kippur war between Israel, which the U.S. had allowed to become its closest ally in the Middle East, and the Soviet-supplied forces of Egypt and Syria, made it even more evident. For when a hard-pressed Israel, short of planes and ammunition, appealed to the U.S.A. to rush supplies, the European allies, with the single exception of that last hold-out of pre-war fascism, Portugal, refused even to allow U.S. planes to use the U.S. air bases on their soil for this purpose. (The supplies reached Israel via the Azores.) The U.S. believed—one does not quite see why—that its own vital interests were at stake. Indeed, the U.S. Secretary of State, Henry Kissinger (whose President, Richard Nixon, was otherwise engaged vainly trying to fend off impeachment), actually declared the first nuclear alert since the Cuban missile crisis, an action characteristic in its brutal insincerity of this able and cynical operator. It did not sway America's allies, who were far more concerned with their oil supplies from the Middle East than with supporting some regional ploy of the U.S.A. which Washington claimed unconvincingly to be essential to the global struggle against communism. For, through OPEC, the Arab states of the Middle East had done what they could to impede support for Israel by cutting oil supplies and threatening oil embargoes. In doing so they discovered their ability to multiply the world price of oil. And the foreign ministries of the world could not fail to notice that there was nothing the all-powerful U.S.A. did, or could immediately do, about that.

Vietnam and the Middle East weakened the U.S.A., though it did not in itself alter the global balance of superpower, or the nature of the confrontation in the various regional theatres of the Cold War. However, between 1974 and 1979 a new wave of revolutions surged across a large part of the globe (see chapter 15). This, the third round of such upheavals in the Short Twentieth Century, actually looked as though it might shift the superpower balance away from the U.S.A., since a number of regimes in Africa, Asia and even on the very soil of the Americas were attracted to the Soviet side and—more concretely—provided the U.S.S.R. with military, and especially naval, bases outside its landlocked heartlands. It was the coincidence of this third wave of world revolution with the moment of public American failure and defeat which produced the Second Cold War. But it was also the coincidence of both with the optimism and self-satisfaction of Brezhnev's U.S.S.R. in the 1970s, which made it certain. This phase of conflict was waged by a combination of local wars in the Third World, fought indirectly by the U.S.A., which now avoided the Vietnam error of committing its own troops, and by an extraordinary acceleration of the nuclear arms race; the former less evidently irrational than the latter.

Since the situation in Europe had been so clearly stabilized—not even the Portuguese revolution of 1974 nor the end of the Franco regime in Spain changed it—and the lines had been so clearly drawn, in effect both superpowers had shifted their competition to the Third World. Détente in Europe had given the U.S.A. under Nixon (1968–74) and Kissinger the opportunity to score two major successes: the expulsion of the Soviets from Egypt and, much more significant, the informal recruitment of China into the anti-Soviet alliance. The new wave of revolutions, all of which were likely to be against the conservative regimes of which the U.S.A had made itself the global defender, gave the U.S.S.R. the chance to recover the initiative. As the collapsing Portuguese African empire (Angola, Mozambique, Guinea-Cape Verde) came under communist rule and the revolution which overthrew the Ethiopian emperor turned eastwards; as the rapidly growing Soviet navy acquired major new bases on either side of the Indian Ocean; as the Shah of Iran fell, a mood close to hysteria gripped American public and private debate. How else (except, in part, by a staggering ignorance of Asian topography) are we to explain the American view, seriously put forward at the time, that the entry of Soviet troops into Afghanistan marked the first step of a Soviet advance that would soon reach the Indian Ocean and the Persian Gulf* (see p. 479).

The unjustified self-satisfaction of the Soviets encouraged such gloom. Long before American propagandists explained, ex post facto, how the U.S.A. had set out to win the Cold War by bankrupting its antagonist, the Brezhnev regime had begun to bankrupt itself by plunging into an armaments programme which raised defence expenditure by an annual average of 4–5 per cent (in real terms) for twenty years after 1964. The race had been pointless, though it gave the U.S.S.R. the satisfaction of being able to claim that it reached parity with the U.S. in missile launchers by 1971, 25 per cent superiority by 1976 (it remained far below America in the number of warheads). Even the small Soviet nuclear arsenal had deterred the U.S.A. during the Cuba crisis, and both sides had long been able to reduce one another to multiple layers of rubble. The systematic Soviet effort to build a navy with worldwide presence on—or,

---

*The suggestion that the Nicaraguan Sandinistas brought military danger to within a few days' truck-drive of the Texan frontier was another, and characteristic, piece of school-atlas geopolitics.

rather, since its main strength was in nuclear submarines, under—the oceans, was not much more sensible in strategic terms, but at least it was comprehensible as a political gesture by a global superpower, which claimed the right to the global showing of the flag. Yet the very fact that the U.S.S.R. no longer accepted its regional confinement struck American Cold warriors as plain proof that western supremacy would end, if not reasserted by a show of power. The increasing confidence which led Moscow to abandon the post-Khrushchev caution in international affairs confirmed them.

The hysteria in Washington was not, of course, based on realistic reasoning. In real terms U.S. power, as distinct from U.S. prestige, remained decisively greater than Soviet power. As for the economies and the technology of the two camps, Western (and Japanese) superiority was beyond calculation. The Soviets, crude and inflexible, might by titanic efforts have managed to build the best economy of the 1890s vintage anywhere in the world (to cite Jowitt, 1991, p. 78), but what did it help the U.S.S.R. that by the middle 1980s it produced 80 per cent more steel, twice as much pig-iron and five times as many tractors than the U.S.A., when it had failed to adapt to an economy that depended on silicone and software (see chapter 16)? There was absolutely no evidence, or likelihood, that the U.S.S.R. wanted a war (except perhaps against China), let alone that it was planning a military attack on the West. The feverish scenarios of nuclear attack which came from the mobilized Western cold warriors and government publicity in the early 1980s were self-generated. They actually had the effect of convincing the Soviets that a pre-emptive nuclear attack by the West on the U.S.S.R. was possible, or even—as at moments in 1983—impending (Walker, 1993, chapter 11), and of setting off the largest mass European anti-nuclear peace movement of the Cold War, the campaign against the deployment of a new range of missiles in Europe.

Historians of the twenty-first century, remote from the living memories of the 1970s and 1980s, will puzzle over the apparent insanity of this outburst of military fever, the rhetoric of apocalypse, and the often bizarre international behaviour of U.S. governments, especially in the early years of President Reagan (1980–88). They will have to appreciate the depth of the subjective traumas of defeat, impotence and public ignominy which had lacerated the U.S. political establishment in the 1970s, and which were made even more painful by the apparent disarray of the American presidency during the years when Richard Nixon (1968–74) had to resign over a sleazy scandal, followed by two negligible successors. They culminated in the humiliating episode of U.S. diplomats held hostage in revolutionary Iran, Red revolution in a couple of small central American states and a second international oil crisis, as OPEC once again raised their price to an all-time peak.

The policy of Ronald Reagan, elected to the presidency in 1980, can be understood only as an attempt to wipe out the stain of felt humiliation by demonstrating the unchallengeable supremacy and invulnerability of the U.S.A., if need be by gestures of military power against sitting targets, like the invasion of the small Caribbean island of Grenada (1983), the massive naval and air attack on Libya (1986) and the even more massive and pointless invasion of Panama (1989). Reagan, perhaps just because he was a run-of-the-mill Hollywood actor, understood the mood of his people and the depth of the wounds to its self-esteem. In the end the trauma was only healed by the final, unpredicted and unexpected collapse of the great antagonist, which left the U.S.A. alone as a global power. Even then, we may detect in the Gulf War of 1991 against Iraq a belated compensation for the awful moments in 1973 and 1979 when the greatest power on the earth could find no response to a consortium of feeble Third World states which threatened to strangle its oil supplies.

The crusade against the "Evil Empire" to which—at least in public—President Reagan's government devoted its energies, was thus designed as therapy for the U.S.A. rather than as a practical attempt to re-establish the world power balance. This had, in fact, been done quietly in the later 1970s, when NATO—under a Democratic U.S. president and Social-Democratic Labour governments in Germany and Britain—had begun its own rearmament, and the new Left-wing states in Africa had been kept in check from the beginning by U.S.-backed movements or states, fairly successfully in Central and Southern Africa, where the U.S. could act together with the formidable *apartheid* regime of the Republic of South Africa, less so in the Horn of Africa. (In both areas the Russians had the invaluable assistance of expeditionary forces from Cuba, testifying to Fidel Castro's commitment to Third World revolution as well as to his alliance with the U.S.S.R.) The Reaganite contribution to the Cold War was of a different kind.

It was not so much practical as ideological—part of the Western reaction to the troubles of the era of troubles and uncertainties into which the world had seemed to drift after the end of the Golden Age (see chapter 14). A lengthy period of centrist and moderately social-democratic rule ended, as the economic and social policies of the Golden Age seemed to fail. Governments of the ideological Right, committed to an extreme form of business egoism and *laissez-faire,* came to power in several countries around 1980. Among these Reagan and the confident and formidable Mrs. Thatcher in Britain (1979–90) were the most prominent. For this new Right the state-sponsored welfare capitalism of the 1950s and 1960s, no longer buttressed, since 1973, by economic success, had always looked like a sub-variety of that socialism ("the road to serfdom," as the economist and ideologue von Hayek called it) of which they saw the U.S.S.R. as the logical end-product. The Reaganite Cold War was directed not only against the "Evil Empire" abroad, but against the memory of Franklin D. Roosevelt at home: against the Welfare State as well as any other intrusive state. Its enemy was liberalism (the "L-word" used to good effect in presidential election campaigns) as much as communism.

Since the U.S.S.R. was to collapse just after the end of the Reagan era, American publicists were naturally to claim that it had been overthrown by a militant campaign to break and destroy it. The U.S.A. had waged and won the Cold War and utterly defeated its enemy. We need not take this crusaders' version of the 1980s seriously. There is no sign that the U.S. government expected or envisaged the impending collapse of the U.S.S.R. or was in any way prepared for it when it happened. While it certainly hoped to put the Soviet economy under pressure, it was informed (mistakenly) by its own intelligence that it was in good shape and capable of sustaining the arms race with the U.S.A. In the early 1980s the U.S.S.R. was still seen (also mistakenly) as engaged in a confident global offensive. In fact, President Reagan himself, whatever the rhetoric put before him by his speech writers, and whatever went on in his not always lucid mind, actually believed in the coexistence of the U.S.A. and the U.S.S.R., but one which should not be based on an abhorrent balance of mutual nuclear terror. What he dreamed of was a world entirely without nuclear arms. And so, as became clear at their strange and excited summit meeting in the sub-arctic gloom of autumnal Iceland in 1986, did the new General Secretary of the Communist Party of the Soviet Union, Mikhail Sergeyevich Gorbachev.

The Cold War ended when one or both the superpowers recognized the sinister absurdity of the nuclear arms race, and when one or both accepted the other's sincerity in wishing to end it. It was probably easier for a Soviet leader to take this initiative than for an American, because the Cold War had never been seen by Moscow in the crusading terms common in Washington, perhaps because an excited public opinion did not have to be considered. On the other hand, just for this reason, it would be harder for a Soviet leader to convince the West that he meant business. That is why the world owes so enormous a debt to Mikhail Gorbachev, who not only took this initiative but succeeded, singlehanded, in convincing the U.S. government and others in the West that he meant what he said. However, let us not underestimate the contribution of President Reagan whose simple-minded idealism broke through the unusually dense screen of ideologists, fanatics, careerists, desperados and professional warriors around him to let himself be convinced. For practical purposes the Cold War ended at the two summits of Reykjavik (1986) and Washington (1987).

Did the end of the Cold War entail the end of the Soviet system? The two phenomena are historically separable, though obviously connected. The Soviet type of socialism had claimed to be a global alternative to the capitalist world system. Since capitalism had not collapsed, or looked like collapsing—though one wonders what would have happened if all the socialist and Third World debtors had united in 1981 to default simultaneously on their Western loans—the prospects of socialism as a world alternative depended on its ability to compete with the world capitalist economy, as reformed after the Great Slump and the Second World War, and as transformed by the "post-industrial" revolution of communications and information technology in the 1970s. That socialism was falling behind at an accelerating rate was patent after 1960. It was no longer competitive. Insofar as this competition took the form of a confrontation of two political, military and ideological superpowers, the inferiority became ruinous.

Both superpowers overstretched and distorted their economies by a massive and enormously expensive competitive arms race, but the world capitalist system could absorb the three trillion dollars of debt—essentially for military spending—into which the 1980s plunged the U.S.A., till then the world's greatest creditor-state. There was nobody, at home or abroad, to take the equivalent strain on Soviet expenditure, which, in any case, represented a far higher proportion of Soviet production—perhaps a quarter—than the 7 per cent of the titanic U.S. GDP which went on war outlays in the mid-1980s. The U.S.A., by a combination of historical luck and policy, had seen its dependencies turn into economies so flourishing that they outweighed its own. By the end of the 1970s the European Community and Japan together were 60 per cent larger than the U.S. economy. On the other hand, the Soviets' allies and dependents never walked on their own feet. They remained a constant and vast annual drain of tens of billions of dollars on the U.S.S.R. Geographically and demographically, the backward countries of the world, whose revolutionary mobilizations, Moscow hoped, would one day outweigh the global predominance of capitalism, represented 80 per cent of the world. In economic terms, they were peripheral. As for technology, as Western superiority grew almost exponentially, there was no contest. In short, the Cold War, from the start, was a war of unequals.

But it was not the hostile confrontation with capitalism and its superpower that undermined socialism. It was rather the combination of its own increasingly evident and crippling economic defects and the accelerating invasion of the socialist economy by the far more dynamic, advanced and dominant capitalist world economy. Insofar as the rhetoric of the Cold War saw capitalism and socialism, "the free world" and "totalitarianism," as two sides of an unbridgeable canyon, and rejected any attempt to bridge it,* one might even say that, short of the mutual suicide of nuclear war, it guaranteed the survival of the weaker contestant. For, barricaded behind iron curtains, even the inefficient and slackening centrally planned command economy was viable—perhaps sagging slowly, but in no way likely to collapse in short order.† It was the interaction of Soviet-type economics with the capitalist world economy from the 1960s on which made socialism vulnerable. When socialist leaders in the 1970s chose to exploit the newly available resources of the world market (oil prices, easy loans, etc.) instead of facing the hard problem of reforming their economic system, they dug their own graves (see chapter 16). The paradox of the Cold War was that what defeated and in the end wrecked the U.S.S.R. was not confrontation but détente.

Yet in one sense the Washington Cold War ultras were not entirely wrong. The real Cold War, as we can easily see in retrospect, ended at the Washington summit of 1987, but it could not be universally *recognized* as being at an end until the U.S.S.R. had visibly ceased to be a superpower, or indeed any kind of power. Forty years of fear and suspicion, of the sowing and harvesting of military-industrial dragons' teeth, could not be so easily reversed. The wheels of the war-making machine services went on turning on both sides. Professionally paranoic secret services went on suspecting every move by the other side as an astute trick to disarm the enemy's vigilance, the better to defeat him. It was the collapse of the Soviet Empire in 1989, the disintegration and dissolution of the U.S.S.R. itself in 1989–91, which made it impossible to pretend, let alone to believe, that nothing had changed.

---

*Cf. the American use of the term "Finlandization" as a term of abuse.

†To take the extreme case, the little communist mountain republic of Albania was poor and backward, but viable during the thirty or so years when it virtually sealed itself off from the world. Only when the walls sheltering it from the world economy were razed did it collapse into a pile of economic rubble.

V

But what exactly had changed? The Cold War had transformed the international scene in three respects. First, it had entirely eliminated, or overshadowed, all but one of the rivalries and conflicts that shaped world politics before the Second World War. Some disappeared because the empires of the imperial era vanished, and with them the rivalries of colonial powers over dependent territories under their rule. Others went, because all the "Great Powers" except two that had been relegated to the second or third divisions of international politics, and their relations with each other were no longer autonomous, or indeed of more than local interest. France and (West) Germany buried the old hatchet after 1947 not because Franco–Germany conflict had become unthinkable—French governments thought about it all the time—but because their common membership of the U.S. camp and the hegemony of Washington over Western Europe would not allow Germany to get out of hand. Even so, it is astonishing how rapidly the major preoccupation of states after large wars disappeared from sight: namely the winners' worry about the recovery plans of the losers, and the losers' plans how to reverse their defeat. Few in the West were seriously preoccupied by the dramatic return to great-power status of West Germany and Japan, armed, though non-nuclear, so long as both were, in effect, subordinate members of the U.S. alliance. Even the U.S.S.R. and its allies, though denouncing the German danger, of which they had bitter experience, did so for propaganda rather than out of real fear. What Moscow was afraid of was not the German armed forces, but the NATO missiles on German soil. But after the Cold War other power conflicts could emerge.

Second, the Cold War had frozen the international situation, and in doing so had stabilized what was an essentially unfixed and provisional state of affairs. Germany was the most obvious example. For forty-six years it remained divided—*de facto* if not, for long periods, *de jure*—into four sectors: the West, which became the Federal Republic in 1949; the middle, which became the German Democratic Republic in 1954; and the East, beyond the Oder-Neisse line, which expelled most of its Germans and became part of Poland and the U.S.S.R. The end of the Cold War and the disintegration of the U.S.S.R. reunited the two western sectors and left the Soviet-annexed parts of East Prussia detached and isolated, separated from the rest of Russia by the now independent state of Lithuania. It left the Poles with German promises to accept the 1945 frontiers, which did not reassure them. Stabilization did not mean peace. Except in Europe, the Cold War was not an era when fighting was forgotten. There was hardly a year between 1948 and 1989 without a fairly serious armed conflict somewhere. Nevertheless, conflicts were controlled, or stifled, by the fear that they might provoke an open—i.e. a nuclear—war between the superpowers. Iraq's claims against Kuwait—the small, oil-rich British protectorate at the top of the Persian Gulf, independent since 1961—were old and constantly reasserted. They did not lead to war until the Persian Gulf had ceased to be an almost automatic flashpoint of superpower confrontation. Before 1989 it is certain that the U.S.S.R., which was the chief armourer of Iraq, would have strongly discouraged any Baghdad adventurism in this area.

The development of the domestic politics of states was not, of course, frozen in the same manner—except where such changes would shift, or look like shifting, the allegiance of a state to its dominant superpower. The U.S. was not more inclined to tolerate communists or philo-communists in office in Italy, Chile or Guatemala than the U.S.S.R. was prepared to abdicate its right to send troops into brother-states with dissident governments, like Hungary and Czechoslovakia. It is true that the U.S.S.R. tolerated far less variety in its friendly and satellite regimes, but on the other hand its capacity to assert itself within them was much less. Even before 1970 it had completely lost what control it ever had over Yugoslavia, Albania and China; it had to tolerate some very individualist behaviour from the leaders of Cuba and Romania; and, as for the Third World countries it supplied with arms, and which shared its hostility to American imperialism, community of interests apart, it had no real hold over them at all. Hardly any of them even tolerated the legal existence of local communist parties. Nevertheless, the combination of power, political influence, bribery and the logic of bi-polarity and anti-imperialism kept the divisions of the world more or less stable. Except for China, no important state really changed sides unless by a home-grown revolution, which the superpowers could neither bring about nor prevent, as the U.S.A. discovered in the 1970s. Even those U.S. allies which found their policies increasingly constrained by the alliance, like the German governments after 1969 in the matter of *Ostpolitik*, did not pull out of an increasingly troublesome alignment. Politically impotent, unstable and indefensible political entities incapable of survival in a real international jungle—the region between the Red Sea and Persian Gulf was full of them—somehow remained in being. The shadow of the mushroom cloud guaranteed the survival not of liberal democracies in Western Europe, but of regimes like Saudi Arabia and Kuwait. The Cold War was the best time in which to be a mini-state—as after the Cold War the difference between problems solved and problems shelved became obvious.

Third, the Cold War had filled the world with arms to a degree that beggars belief. This was the natural result of forty years when major industrial states had constantly competed to arm themselves against a war that might break out at any moment; forty years of super-powers competing to win friends and influence people by distributing arms all over the globe, not to mention forty years of constant "low intensity" warfare with occasional outbreaks of major conflict. Econo-mies largely militarized, and in any case with enormous and influential military-industrial complexes, had an economic interest in selling their products abroad, if only to comfort their governments with proof that they were not *only* swallowing the astronomic and economically unproductive military budgets which kept them going. The unprece-dented global fashion for military governments (see chapter 12) provided a grateful market, fed not only by superpower largesse, but—since the oil-price revolution—by local revenues multiplied beyond the imagi-nation of earlier Third World sultans and sheikhs. Everybody ex-ported arms. Socialist economies and some declining capitalist states like Britain had little else to export that was competitive on the world mar-ket. The trade in death was not only in the large chunks of hardware which governments alone could use. An age of guerrilla warfare and ter-rorism also developed a large demand for light, portable and adequately destructive and murderous devices, and the underworlds of the late twentieth-century cities could provide a further civilian market for such products. In such milieux the Uzi machine-gun (Israeli), the Kalash-nikov rifle (Russian) and Semtex explosive (Czech) became household names.

In this manner the Cold War perpetuated itself. The little wars that had once set clients of one superpower against those of the other contin-ued after the old conflict ended on a local basis, resisting those who had launched them and now wanted to end them. The UNITA rebels in An-gola remained in the field against the government, although the South Africans and the Cubans had withdrawn from the unhappy country and although the U.S.A. and the United Nations had disavowed them and recognized the other side. They would not run short of arms. Somalia, armed first by the Russians when the emperor of Ethiopia was on the side of the U.S., then by the U.S., when revolutionary Ethiopia turned to Moscow, entered the post Cold War world as a famine-stricken territory of anarchic clan warfare, short of everything except an almost unlimited supply of guns, ammunition, land-mines and military transport. The U.S. and the U.N. mobilized to bring food and peace. It proved harder than flooding the country with guns. In Afghanistan the U.S.A. had distributed the hand-held "Stinger" anti-aircraft missiles and launchers wholesale to the anti-communist tribal guerrillas, calculating, correctly, that these would offset the Soviet command of the air. When the Russians withdrew, the war continued as though nothing had changed, except that, in the absence of planes, the tribesmen could now themselves exploit the flourishing demand for Stingers, which they sold profitably on the international arms market. In despair the U.S. offered to buy them back itself at the rate of $100,000 a piece, with spectacular lack of success (*International Herald Tribune*, p. 24, 5/7/93; *Repubblica* 6/4/94). As Goethe's sorcerer's apprentice exclaimed: "*Die ich rief die Geister, werd' ich nun nicht los.*"

The end of the Cold War suddenly removed the props which had held up the international structure and, to an extent not yet appreciated, the structures of the world's domestic political systems. And what was left was a world in disarray and partial collapse, because there was nothing to replace them. The idea, briefly entertained by American spokesmen, that the old bi-polar order could be replaced by a "new world order" based on the single superpower which remained in being, and therefore looked stronger than ever, rapidly proved unrealistic. There could be no return to the world before the Cold War, because too much had changed, too much had disappeared. All landmarks were fallen, all maps had to be altered. Politicians and economists used to one kind of world even found it difficult or impossible to appreciate the nature of the problems of another kind. In 1947 the U.S.A. had recognized the need for an immediate and gigantic project to restore the West European economies, because the supposed danger to these economies—communism and the U.S.S.R.—was easily defined. The economic and political consequences of the collapse of the Soviet Union and Eastern Europe were even more dramatic than the troubles of Western Europe, and would prove even more far-reaching. They were predictable enough in the late 1980s and even visible—but none of the wealthy economies of capitalism treated this impending crisis as a global emergency requiring urgent and massive action because its *political* consequences were not so easily specified. With the possible exception of West Germany, they reacted sluggishly—and even the Germans totally misunderstood and understimated the nature of the problem, as their troubles with the annexation of the former German Democratic Republic were to demonstrate.

The consequences of the end of the Cold War would probably have been enormous in any case, even had it not coincided with a major crisis in the world economy of capitalism and with the final crisis of the Soviet Union and its system. Since the historian's world is what happened and not what might have happened if things had been different, we need not consider the possibility of other scenarios. The end of the Cold War proved to be not the end of an international conflict, but the end of an era: not only for the East, but for the entire world. There are historic moments which may be recognized, even by contemporaries, as marking the end of an age. The years around 1990 clearly were such a secular turning-point. But, while everyone could see that the old had ended, there was utter uncertainty about the nature and prospects of the new.

Only one thing seemed firm and irreversible amid these uncertainties: the extraordinary, unprecedented, fundamental changes which the world economy, and consequently human societies, had undergone in the period since the Cold War began. These will, or should, have a far larger place in the history books of the third millennium than the Korean war, the Berlin and Cuba crises, and the Cruise missiles. To these transformations we must now turn.

CHAPTER NINE

The Golden Years

It is in the past forty years that Modena has really seen the great leap forward. The era from Italian Unification until then had been a long age of waiting, or of slow and intermittent modifications, before transformation accelerated to the speed of lightning. People now came to enjoy a standard of living previously confined to a tiny elite.

—G. Muzzioli (1993, p. 323)

No hungry man who is also sober can be persuaded to use his last dollar for anything but food. But a well-fed, well-clad, well-sheltered and otherwise well-tended person can be persuaded as between an electric razor and an electric toothbrush. Along with prices and costs, consumer demand becomes subject to management.

—J. K. Galbraith, *The New Industrial State* (1967, p. 24)

I

Most human beings operate like historians: they only recognize the nature of their experience in retrospect. In the course of the 1950s many people, especially in the increasingly prosperous "developed" countries, became aware that times were indeed strikingly improved, especially if their memories reached back to the years before the Second World War. A British Conservative premier fought and won a general election in 1959 on the slogan "You've never had it so good," a statement that was undoubtedly correct. Yet it was not until the great boom was over, in the disturbed seventies, waiting for the traumatic eighties, that observers—mainly, to begin with, economists—began to realize that the world, particularly the world of developed capitalism, had passed through an altogether exceptional phase of its history; perhaps a unique one. They looked for names to describe it: the "thirty glorious years" of the French (*les trente glorieuses*); the quarter-century Golden Age of the Anglo-Americans (Marglin and Schor, 1990). The gold glowed more brightly against the dull or dark background of the subsequent decades of crisis.

There are several reasons why it took so long to recognize the exceptional nature of the era. For the U.S.A., which dominated the world economy after the Second World War, it was not all that revolutionary. It merely continued the expansion of the war years which, as we have seen, had been uniquely kind to that country. It had suffered no damage, increased its GNP by two thirds (Van der Wee, 1987, p. 30) and ended the war with almost two thirds of the world's industrial production. Moreover, just because of the size and advance of the U.S. economy, its actual performance during The Golden Years was not as impressive as the rate of growth of other countries, which started from a much smaller base. Between 1950 and 1973 it grew more slowly than any other industrial country except Britain and, what is more to the point, its growth was no higher than in the most dynamic earlier periods of its development. In all other industrial countries, including even sluggish Britain, the Golden Age broke all previous records (Maddison, 1987, p. 650). In fact, for the U.S.A. this was, economically and technologically, a time of relative dropping back rather than of advance. The gap in productivity per man-hour between it and other countries diminished, and if in 1950 it enjoyed a national wealth (GDP) per capita double that of France and Germany, over five times that of Japan, and more than half as large again as Britain, the other states were fast catching up and continued to do so in the 1970s and 1980s.

Recovering from the war was the overwhelming priority for the European countries and Japan, and for the first years after 1945 they measured their success simply by how close they had come to a target set by reference to the past, not the future. In the non-communist states recovery also meant putting the fear of social revolution and communist advance, heritage of war and resistance, behind them. While most countries (other than Germany and Japan) were back to their pre-war levels by 1950, the early Cold War and the persistence of powerful communist parties in France and Italy discouraged euphoria. In any case, the material benefits of growth took some time to make themselves felt. In Britain it was not until the middle 1950s that they became palpable. No politician before then could have won an election on Harold Macmillan's slogan. Even in so spectacularly prosperous a region as Italy's Emilia-

Romagna, the benefits of the "affluent society" did not become general until the 1960s (Francia, Muzzioli, 1984, pp. 327–29). Moreover, the secret weapon of a society of *popular* affluence, namely full employment, did not become general until the 1960s, when the average of West European unemployment stood at 1.5 per cent. In the 1950s Italy still had almost 8 per cent out of work. In short, not until the 1960s did Europe come to take its extraordinary prosperity for granted. By then, indeed, sophisticated observers began to assume that, somehow, everything in the economy would go onwards and upwards for ever. "There is no special reason to doubt that the underlying trends of growth in the early and middle 1970s will continue much as in the 1960s," wrote a United Nations report in 1972. "No special influence can now be foreseen which would at all drastically change the external environment of European economies." The club of advanced capitalist industrial economies, the OECD (Organization for Economic Cooperation and Development) revised its forecasts for future growth upwards as the 1960s advanced. By the early 1970s they were expected to be ("in the medium term") over 5 per cent (Glyn, Hughes, Lipietz, Singh, 1990, p. 39). It was not to be.

It is now evident that the Golden Age essentially belonged to the developed capitalist countries, which, throughout these decades, represented about three quarters of the world's production and over 80 per cent of its manufacturing exports (OECD, Impact, 1979 pp. 18–19). One further reason why this specificity of the era was only slowly recognized was that in the 1950s the economic upsurge seemed quite world-wide and independent of economic regimes. Indeed, initially it looked as though the newly expanded socialist part of the world had the advantage. The growth-rate of the U.S.S.R. in the 1950s was faster than any Western country's, and the economies of Eastern Europe grew almost as rapidly— faster in hitherto backward countries, slower in the already industrialized or partly industrialized ones. Communist East Germany, however, lagged behind non-communist Federal Germany. Even though the Eastern Bloc of Europe lost pace in the 1960s, its GDP per capita over the whole of the Golden Age still grew slightly faster (or, in the case of the U.S.S.R. just less) than that in the major capitalist industrial countries (IMF, 1990, p. 65). Still, in the 1960s it became clear that capitalism was forging ahead rather than socialism.

Nevertheless, the Golden Age was a worldwide phenomenon, even though general affluence never came within sight of the majority of the world's population—those who lived in countries for whose poverty and backwardness the experts of the UN tried to find diplomatic euphemisms. Though the population of the Third World grew at a spectacular rate—the numbers of Africans, East Asians and South Asians more than doubled in the thirty-five years after 1950, the number of Latin Americans rose even faster (World Resources, 1986, p. 11). The 1970s and 1980s once again grew familiar with mass famine, its classic image, the starving exotic child observed after supper on every Western TV screen. During the Golden decades there was no mass starvation, except as the product of wars and political madness, as in China (see pp. 466–7). Indeed, as population multiplied, life expectancy stretched out by an average of seven years—even by seventeen years if we compare the later 1930s with the later 1960s (Morawetz, 1977, p. 48). This means that food production rose faster than population, as it did both in the developed and in every major area of the non-industrial world. In the 1950s it rose by more than 1 per cent a year per capita in every region of the "developing world" except Latin America, and even there it grew per capita, though more modestly. In the 1960s it still rose in all parts of the non-industrial world, but (once again with the exception of Latin America, this time ahead of the rest), only very slightly. Nevertheless, the total food production of the poor world in both the 1950s and 1960s rose faster than in the developed world.

In the 1970s the disparities between different parts of the poor world make such global figures useless. By then some regions, such as the Far East and Latin America, were drawing well ahead of their population growth, whereas Africa was falling behind by more than 1 per cent a year. In the 1980s the poor world's food production per capita did not grow at all outside South and East Asia (but even here some countries produced less per head than in the 1970s—Bangladesh, Sri Lanka, the Philippines. Certain regions stayed well below their 1970 levels, or even continued to fall, notably Africa, Central America and the Asian Near East (Van der Wee, 1987, p. 106; FAO, *The State of Food,* 1989, Annex, Table 2, pp. 113–15).

Meanwhile the problem of the developed world was that it produced so much surplus food that it did not know what to do with it and, in the 1980s, decided to grow substantially less, or else (as in the European Community) to dump its "butter mountains" and "milk lakes" below cost, thus undercutting producers in the poor countries. It became cheaper to buy Dutch cheese on Caribbean islands than in the Netherlands. Curiously, the contrast between food surpluses on one side, hungry people on the other, which had so outraged the world during the Great Depression of the 1930s, caused less comment in the late twentieth century. It was an aspect of the growing divergence between the rich and the poor world which became increasingly evident from the 1960s.

The industrial world was, of course, expanding everywhere: in the capitalist and socialist regions and in the "Third World." In the old West there were dramatic examples of industrial revolution, such as Spain and Finland. In the world of "really existing socialism" (see chapter 13) purely agrarian countries like Bulgaria and Romania acquired massive industrial sectors. In the Third World the most spectacular development of the so-called "newly industrialising countries" (NICs) occurred after the Golden Age, but everywhere the number of countries depending primarily on agriculture, at least for financing their imports from the rest of the world, diminished sharply. By the later 1980s a mere fifteen states paid for half their imports or more from farm exports. With one exception (New Zealand), all were in sub-Saharan Africa and Latin America (FAO, *The State of Food*, 1989, Annex, Table 11, pp. 149–51).

The world economy was thus growing at an explosive rate. By the 1960s it was plain that there had never been anything like it. World output of manufactures quadrupled between the early 1950s and the early 1970s and, what is even more impressive, world trade in manufactured products grew tenfold. As we have seen, world agricultural output also shot up, if not so spectacularly. It did so not so much (as so often in the past) by bringing new land into cultivation, but rather by raising its productivity. Grain yields per hectare almost doubled between 1950–52 and 1980–82—and more than doubled in North America, Western Europe and East Asia. World fisheries meanwhile trebled their catches before falling again (World Resources, 1986, pp. 47, 142).

One by-product of this extraordinary explosion was as yet barely noticed, though in retrospect it already looked menacing: pollution and ecological deterioration. During the Golden Age it attracted little attention, except from wild life enthusiasts and other protectors of human and natural rarities, because the dominant ideology of progress took it for granted that the growing domination of nature by man was the very measure of humanity's advance. Industrialization in the socialist countries was for this reason particularly blind to the ecological consequences of its massive construction of a rather archaic industrial system based on iron and smoke. Even in the West, the old nineteenth century businessman's motto "Where there's muck, there's brass" (i.e. pollution means money), was still convincing, especially for road-builders and real-estate "developers" who rediscovered the unbelievable profits to be made in an era of secular boom from speculation which could not go wrong. All one had to do was to wait for the value of the right building site to rise into the stratosphere. A single well-sited building could now make a man a multimillionaire virtually without cost, since he could borrow on the security of his future construction and borrow further as its value (built or unbuilt, occupied or empty) continued to go up. Eventually, as usual, there was a crash—the Golden Age ended like earlier booms in a real-estate-cum-banking collapse—but until then city centres, large and small, were ripped out and "developed" across the world, incidentally destroying medieval cathedral cities like Worcester in Britain or Spanish colonial capitals like Lima in Peru. Since the authorities in both East and West also discovered that something like factory methods could be used to construct public housing quickly and cheaply, filling the outskirts of cities with blankly menacing high-rise apartment blocks, the 1960s will probably go down as the most disastrous decade in the history of human urbanization.

In fact, far from worrying about the environment, there seemed to be grounds for self-satisfaction, as the results of nineteenth century pollution yielded to twentieth century technology and ecological conscience. Did not the simple banning of coal fires in London from 1953 abolish, at one stroke, the impenetrable fog so familiar from Charles Dickens' novels, which had periodically blanketed the city? Were not, some years later, salmon once again swimming up the once dead river Thames? Cleaner, smaller, quieter factories distributed themselves around the countryside instead of the vast smoke-swathed plants that had previously signified "industry." Airports replaced railway stations as the quintessential buildings representing transport. As the countryside emptied, people, or at least middle-class people moving into abandoned villages and farmsteads, could feel themselves closer than ever to nature.

Yet there is no denying that the impact of human activities on nature, primarily urban and industrial but also, it was eventually realized, agricultural, increased steeply from the middle of the century. This was largely due to the enormous increase in the use of fossil fuels (coal, oil, natural gas, etc.), whose potential exhaustion had worried earlier gazers into the future from the mid-nineteenth century on. New sources were discovered faster than they could be used. That total energy consumption shot up—it actually tripled in the U.S.A. between 1950 and 1973 (Rostow, 1978, p. 256; Table III, p. 58) is far from surprising. One of the reasons why the Golden Age was golden was that the price of a barrel of Saudi oil averaged less than $2 throughout the entire period from 1950 to 1973, thus making energy ridiculously cheap, and getting cheaper all the time. Ironically, it was only after 1973, when the oil-producers' cartel OPEC finally decided to charge what the traffic would bear (see pp. 473–4), that ecology-watchers took serious note of the effects of the consequent explosion in petrol-driven traffic, which was already darkening the skies above the great cities in the motorized, and in particular the American, parts of the world. Smog was the immediate worry and understandably so. However, carbon dioxide emissions warming the atmosphere almost tripled between 1950 and 1973, that is to say the concentration of this gas in the atmosphere increased by a little less than 1 per cent a year (World Resources, Table 11.1, p. 318; 11.4, p. 319; V. Smil, 1990, p. 4, Fig. 2). The production of chlorofluorcarbons, chemicals which affect the ozone layer, rose almost vertically. At the end of the war they had barely been used, but by 1974 over 300,000 tons of one compound and over 400,000 tons of another were being released into the atmosphere each year (World Resources, Table 11.3, p. 319). The rich Western countries naturally generated the lion's share of this pollution, though the unusually filthy industrialization of the U.S.S.R. produced almost as much carbon dioxide as the U.S.A.; almost five times as much in 1985 as in 1950. (Per capita, of course, the U.S.A. remained a long way ahead.) Only Britain actually lowered the amount emitted per inhabitant over this period (Smil, 1990, Table I, p. 14).

II

Initially this astonishing explosion of the economy seemed merely a gigantic version of what had gone before; as it were, a globalization of the state of the pre-1945 U.S.A., taking that country as the model of a capitalist industrial society. So, to some extent, it was. The age of the automobile had long arrived in North America, but after the war it came to Europe and later more modestly to the socialist world and the Latin American middle classes, while cheap fuel made the truck and the bus the major means of transport over most of the globe's land-mass. If the rise of Western affluent society could be measured by the multiplication of private cars—from Italy's 469,000 in 1938 to the same country's fifteen millions in 1975 (Rostow, 1978, p. 212; *U.N. Statistical Yearbook*, 1982, Table 175, p. 960)—the economic development of many a Third-World country could be recognized by the rate at which the number of its trucks grew.

Much of the great world boom was thus a catching up, or in the U.S.A. a continuation of old trends. The model of Henry Ford's mass production spread across the oceans to new auto industries, while in the U.S.A. the Fordist principle was extended to new kinds of production, from house-building to junk food (McDonald's was a post-war success story). Goods and services previously confined to minorities were now produced for a mass market, as in the field of mass travel to sunny beaches. Before the war never had more than 150,000 North Americans travelled to Central America and the Caribbean in any year, but between 1950 and 1970 their numbers grew from three hundred thousands to seven millions (U.S. Historical Statistics I, p. 403). The European figures were, not surprisingly, even more spectacular. Spain, which had virtually no mass tourism until the later 1950s, welcomed over fifty-four millions of foreigners per year at the end of the 1980s, a number only slightly surpassed by Italy's fifty-five millions (Stat. Jahrbuch, 1990, p. 262). What had once been luxury, became the expected standard of comfort, at all events in the rich countries: the refrigerator, the private washing machine, the telephone. By 1971 there were over 270 million telephones in the world, i.e. overwhelmingly in North America and Western Europe, and their spread was accelerating. Ten years later their numbers had almost doubled. In the developed market economies there was more than one phone for every two inhabitants (U.N. World Situation, 1985, Table 19, p. 63). In short, it was now possible for the average citizen in those countries to live as only the very wealthy had lived in their parents' day—except, of course, that mechanization had now replaced personal servants.

However, what strikes us most about the period is the extent to which the economic surge seemed powered by technological revolution. To this extent it multiplied not only improved products of the old kind, but quite unprecedented ones, including many which had been virtually unimagined before the war. Some revolutionary products, such as the synthetic materials known as "plastics" had been developed between the wars or even begun to enter commercial production, like nylon (1935), polystyrene and polythene. Some, like television and recording on magnetic tape, were then barely out of the experimental stage. The war, with its demands on high technology, prepared a number of revolutionary processes for later civilian use, though rather more on the British side (subsequently taken up by the U.S.A.) than among the science-minded Germans: radar, the jet engine, and various ideas and techniques which prepared the ground for post-war electronics and information technology. Without them the transistor (invented 1947) and the first civilian digital computers (1946) would certainly have appeared considerably later. Perhaps fortunately, nuclear energy, first mobilized during the war for destruction, remained largely outside the civilian economy, except as a (so far) marginal contribution to the world's generation of electrical energy—about 5 per cent in 1975. Whether these innovations were based on inter-war or post-war science, on inter-war technical or even commercial pioneering or on the great post-1945 forward rush—the integrated circuits developed in the 1950s, the lasers of the 1960s, or the various spin-offs from space rocketry—hardly matters for our purpose. Except in one sense. More than any previous period, the Golden Age rested on the most advanced and often esoteric scientific research, which now found practical application within a few years. Industry and even agriculture for the first time moved decisively beyond the technology of the nineteenth century (see chapter 18).

Three things about this technological earthquake strike the observer. *First*, it utterly transformed everyday life in the rich world and even, to a lesser extent, in the poor world, where radio could now reach the remotest villages thanks to the transistor and the miniaturized long-life battery, where the "green revolution" transformed rice and wheat cultivation and plastic sandals replaced bare feet. Any European reader of this book who makes a quick inventory of his or her personal possessions, can verify this. Most of the contents of the refrigerator or freezer (neither of which most family homes would have owned in 1945) is novel: freeze-dried food, factory-farmed poultry produce, meat stuffed with enzymes and various chemicals to change its taste, or even constructed by the "simulation of boneless high-quality cuts" (Considine, 1982, pp. 1164 ff.) not to mention products imported fresh by air from halfway across the globe, as would then have been impossible.

Compared to 1950 the share of natural or traditional materials—wood, metal treated in old-fashioned ways, natural fibres or fillings, even ceramics—in our kitchens, household furnishings and personal clothing has gone down dramatically, although the hype surrounding everything produced by the personal hygiene and beauty industry was such that it obscured (by systematically exaggerating) the degree of novelty of its enormously increased and diversified output. For technological revolution entered consumer consciousness to such an extent that novelty became the main sales appeal for everything from synthetic detergents (which came into their own in the 1950s) to laptop computers. The assumption was that "new" equalled not just better, but utterly revolutionized.

As for the products visibly representing technological novelty, their list is endless, and needs no comment: television; vinyl records (LPs came in 1948); followed by tapes (tape cassettes came in the 1960s) and compact discs; small portable transistor radios—the present writer got his first as a present from a Japanese friend in the late 1950s—digital watches, pocket calculators, battery and then solar-powered; and then the rest of domestic electronics, photo and video equipment. Not the least significant thing about these innovations is the systematic process of miniaturisation of such products, i.e. *portability*, which vastly extended their potential range and market. However, the technological revolution was perhaps symbolized just as much by superficially unchanged products which had, since the Second World War, been transformed from top to bottom, such as pleasure sailing boats. Their masts and hulls, their sails and rigging, their navigational equipment had little or nothing in common with inter-war vessels except shape and function.

Second, the more complex the technology involved, the more complex was the road from discovery or invention to production, and the more elaborate and expensive the process of traversing it. "Research and Development" (R & D) became central to economic growth and, for this reason, the already enormous advantage of the "developed market economies" over the rest was reinforced. (As we shall see in chapter 16, technological innovation did not flourish in the socialist economies.) The typical "developed country" had upwards of a thousand scientists and engineers for every million of its population in the 1970s, but Brazil had about 250, India 130, Pakistan about sixty, Kenya and Nigeria about thirty, (UNESCO, 1985, Table 5.18). Moreover, the process of innovation became so continuous that the cost of developing new products became an increasingly large and indispensable share of the cost of production. In the extreme case of the armaments industries, where, admittedly, money was no object, new devices, had barely become fit for practical use before they were scrapped for even more advanced (and, of course, vastly more expensive) pieces of equipment, to the considerable financial benefit of the corporations concerned. In the more mass-market-oriented industries such as pharmaceutical chemicals, a new and genuinely needed drug, especially when protected from competition by patent rights, could make several fortunes, which were explained away by its producers as absolutely essential for further research. Less easily protected innovators had to clean up more quickly, for as soon as other products entered the market, the price dropped through the floor.

Third, the new technologies were, overwhelmingly, capital-intensive and (except for the highly skilled scientists and technicians) labour-saving, or even labour-replacing. The major characteristic of the Golden Age was that it needed constant and heavy investment and, increasingly, that it did not need people, except as consumers. However, the impetus and speed of the economic surge was such that, for a generation, this was not obvious. On the contrary, the economy grew so fast that, even in the industrial countries, the industrial working class maintained or even increased its share of the occupied population. In all advanced countries but the U.S.A., the reserve lakes of labour filled during pre-war depression and post-war demobilization were drained, new supplies of labour were sucked in from the native countryside and from foreign immigration, and married women, hitherto kept outside the labour market, entered it in growing numbers. Nevertheless, the ideal to which the Golden Age aspired, though it was only gradually realized, was production, or even service, without humans: automated robots assembling cars, silent voids filled with banks of computers controlling the output of power, trains without drivers. Human beings were essential to such an economy only in one respect: as buyers of goods and services. Here lay its central problem. In the Golden Age it still seemed unreal and remote, like the future death of the universe by entropy about which Victorian scientists had warned the human race.

On the contrary. All the problems which had haunted capitalism in its era of catastrophe appeared to dissolve and to disappear. The terrible and inevitable cycle of boom and slump, so murderous between the wars became a succession of mild fluctuations thanks to—or so the Keynesian economists who now advised governments were convinced—their intelligent macro-economic management. Mass unemployment? Where was it to be found in the developed world in the 1960s, when Europe averaged 1.5 per cent of its labour force out of work and Japan 1.3 per cent (Van der Wee, 1987, p. 77)? Only in North America was it not yet eliminated. Poverty? Of course most of humanity remained poor, but in the old heartlands of industrial labour what meaning could the *Internationale*'s "Arise, ye starvelings from your slumbers" have for workers who now expected to have their car and spend their annual paid vacation on the beaches of Spain? And, if they fell upon hard times, would not an increasingly universal and generous Welfare State provide them with protection, undreamed of before, against the hazards of ill-health, misfortune, even the dreaded old age of the poor? Their incomes rose year by year, almost automatically. Would they not go on rising for ever? The range of goods and services offered by the productive system, and available to them, made former luxuries part of everyday consumption. It widened year by year. What more, in material terms, could humanity want except to extend the benefits already enjoyed by the favoured peoples of some countries to the unhappy inhabitants of those parts of the world, admittedly still the majority of mankind, who had not yet entered upon "development" and "modernization"?

What problems remained to be solved? An extremely intelligent and prominent British socialist politician wrote in 1956:

Traditionally socialist thought has been dominated by the economic problems posed by capitalism, poverty, mass unemployment, squalor, instability, and even the possibility of the collapse of the whole system . . . Capitalism had been reformed out of all recognition. Despite occasional minor recessions and balance of payments crises, full employment and at least a tolerable degree of stability are likely to be maintained. Automation can be expected steadily to solve any remaining problems of under-production. Looking ahead, our present rate of growth will give us a national output three times as high in fifty years (Crosland, 1957, p. 517).

III

How are we to explain this extraordinary and quite unexpected triumph of a system which, for half a lifetime, had seemed on the verge of ruin? What needs explaining, of course, is not the mere fact of a lengthy period of economic expansion and well-being, following on a similar period of economic and other troubles and disturbances. Such a succession of "long waves" of about half a century in length has formed the basic rhythm of the economic history of capitalism since the late eighteenth century. As we have seen (chapter 2), the Age of Catastrophe had drawn attention to this pattern of secular fluctuations, whose nature remains obscure. They are generally known by the name of the Russian economist Kondratiev. In the long perspective, the Golden Age was just another Kondratiev upswing, like the great Victorian boom of 1850–73—curiously the dates almost coincide at a century's distance—and the *belle époque* of the late Victorians and Edwardians. Like earlier such upswings, it was preceded and followed by "downswings." What needs explaining is not this, but the extraordinary scale and depth of this secular boom, which is a sort of pendant to the extraordinary scale and depth of the preceding era of crises and depressions.

There are no really satisfactory explanations for the sheer scale of this "Great Leap Forward" of the capitalist world economy, and consequently for its unprecedented social consequences. Of course other countries had enormous scope for catching up with the model economy of early twentieth-century industrial society, the U.S.A., a country devastated by neither war, defeat nor victory, though briefly shaken by the Great Slump. Other countries did indeed systematically try to imitate the U.S.A., a process which speeded up economic development, since it is always easier to adapt an existing technology than to invent a new one.

That, as the Japanese example was to show, could come later. However, there was clearly more to the Great Leap than this. There was a substantial restructuring and reform of capitalism and a quite spectacular advance in the globalization and internationalization of the economy.

The first produced a "mixed economy," which both made it easier for states to plan and manage economic modernization, and which also enormously increased demand. The great post-war economic success stories of capitalist countries, with the rarest exceptions (Hong Kong), are stories of industralization backed, supervised, steered, and sometimes planned and managed by governments: from France and Spain in Europe to Japan, Singapore and South Korea. At the same time the political commitment of governments to full employment and—to a lesser extent—to the lessening of economic inequality, i.e. a commitment to welfare and social security, for the first time provided a mass consumer market for luxury goods which could now become accepted as necessities. The poorer people are, the higher the proportion of their income they must spend on indispensable essentials such as food (a sensible observation known as "Engel's Law"). In the 1930s, even in the rich U.S.A. about a third of household expenditure still went on food, but by the early 1980s only 13 per cent. The rest was available for other expenditures. The Golden Age democratized the market.

The second multiplied the productive capacity of the world economy by making possible a far more elaborate and sophisticated international division of labour. Initially this was largely confined to the collective of the so-called "developed market economies," i.e. the countries in the U.S. camp. The socialist part of the world was largely separate (see chapter 13), and the most dynamic developers in the Third World in the 1950s opted for a segregated and planned industrialization by substituting their own production for imported manufactures. The core countries of Western capitalism, of course, traded with the overseas world, and very advantageously too, since the terms of trade favoured them—i.e. they could get their raw materials and foodstuffs more cheaply. Still, what really exploded was the trade in industrial products, mainly between the industrial core countries. World trade in manufactures multiplied over tenfold in the twenty years after 1953. Manufactures, which had formed a fairly constant share of world trade since the nineteenth century at a little less than half, now shot up to over 60 per cent (W. A. Lewis, 1981). The Golden Age remained anchored to the economies of the core capitalist countries—even in purely quantitative terms. In 1975 the Big Seven of capitalism alone (Canada, the U.S.A., Japan, France, Federal Germany, Italy and Great Britain) contained three quarters of all the passenger cars on the globe and almost as high a proportion of its telephones (*U.N. Statistical Yearbook*, 1982, pp. 955 ff., 1018 ff.). Nevertheless, the new industrial revolution could not be confined to any region.

The restructuring of capitalism and the advance in economic internationalisation were central. It is not so clear that technological revolution explains the Golden Age, though there was plenty of it. As has been shown, much of the new industrialization of these decades was the spread of old industrializations based on old technologies to new countries: the nineteenth-century industrialization of coal, iron and steel to the socialist agrarian countries; the twentieth-century American industries of oil and internal combustion engines to European ones. The impact of the high-research-generated technology on civilian industry probably did not become massive until the Crisis Decades after 1973, when the major breakthrough of information technology and genetic engineering took place, as well as a number of other leaps into the unknown. Perhaps the chief innovations which began to transform the world almost as soon as the war ended were chemical and pharmaceutical. Their impact on the demography of the Third World was immediate (see chapter 12). Their cultural effects were a little more delayed, but not much, for the Western sexual revolution of the 1960s and 1970s was made possible by antibiotics—unknown before the Second World War—which appeared to remove the major risks from sexual promiscuity by making venereal diseases easily curable, and by the birth-control pill which became widely available in the 1960s. (The risk was to return to sex in the 1980s with AIDS.)

All the same, an innovating high technology soon became so much part of the great boom that it must form part of any explanation, even if we do not regard it as decisive in its own right.

Post-war capitalism was unquestionably, as the Crosland quotation put it, a system "reformed out of all recognition" or, in the words of the British premier Harold Macmillian, a "new" version of the old system. What happened was far more than a return of the system from some avoidable inter-war "errors" to its "normal" record of "both . . . maintaining a high level of employment and . . . enjoying some non-negligible rate of economic growth" (H. G. Johnson, 1972, p. 6). Essentially it was a sort of marriage between economic liberalism and social democracy (or, in American terms, Rooseveltian New Deal policy), with substantial borrowings from the U.S.S.R., which had pioneered the idea of economic planning. That is why the reaction against it by the theological free marketeers was to be so impassioned in the 1970s and 1980s, when the policies based on this marriage were no longer protected by economic success. Men like the Austrian economist Friedrich von Hayek (1899–1992) had never been pragmatists, ready (if reluctant) to be persuaded that economic activities which interfered with *laissez-faire* worked; though of course they denied, with subtle arguments, that they could work. They were believers in the equation "Free Market = Freedom of the Individual" and consequently condemned any departure from it as, to quote the title of his 1944 book, *"The Road to Serfdom."* They had stood by the purity of the market in the Great Slump. They continued to condemn the policies which made the Golden Age golden, as the world grew richer and capitalism (plus political liberalism) flourished again on the basis of mixing markets and governments. But between the 1940s and the 1970s nobody listened to such Old Believers.

Nor can we doubt that capitalism was deliberately reformed, largely by the men who were in a position to do so in the U.S.A. and Britain, during the last war years. It is a mistake to suppose that people never learn from history. The inter-war experience, and especially the Great Slump, had been so catastrophic that nobody could possibly dream, as plenty of men in public life had done after the First World War, of returning as soon as possible to the time before the air-raid sirens had begun to sound. All the men (women were hardly yet accepted into the first division of public life) who sketched out what they hoped would be the post-war principles of the world economy and the future of the global economic order, had lived through the Great Slump. Some, like J. M. Keynes, had been in public life since before 1914. And if the economic memory of the 1930s was not enough to sharpen their appetite for reforming capitalism, the fatal political risks of not doing so were patent to all who had just fought Hitler's Germany, the child of the Great Slump, and were confronted with the prospect of communism and Soviet power advancing westwards across the ruins of capitalist economies that did not work.

Four things seemed clear to these decision-makers. The inter-war catastrophe, which must on no account be allowed to return, had been due largely to the breakdown of the global trading and financial system and the consequent fragmentation of the world into would-be autarchic national economies or empires. The global system had once been stabilized by the hegemony, or at least the centrality of the British economy and its currency, the pound sterling. Between the wars Britain and sterling were no longer strong enough to carry this load, which could now only be taken over by the U.S.A. and the dollar. (The conclusion, naturally, aroused more genuine enthusiasm in Washington than elsewhere.) Third, the Great Slump had been due to the failure of the unrestricted free market. Henceforth the market would have to be supplemented by, or to work within the framework of, public planning and economic management. Finally, for social and political reasons, mass unemployment must not be allowed to return.

Decision-makers outside the Anglo-Saxon countries could do little about the reconstruction of the world trading and financial system, but found the rejection of the old free market liberalism congenial enough. Strong state-guidance and state-planning in economic matters were not new in several countries, from France to Japan. Even the state ownership and management of industries was familiar enough, and had been widely extended in Western countries after 1945. It was in no sense a particular issue between socialists and anti-socialists, although the general leftward swing of wartime Resistance politics gave it more prominence than it would have had before the war, as for instance in the French and Italian Constitutions of 1946–47. Thus, even after fifteen years of socialist government, Norway in 1960 had a proportionately (and of course absolutely) smaller public sector than West Germany, which was not a country given to nationalization.

As for the socialist parties and labour movements which were so prominent in Europe after the war, they fitted in readily with the new reformed capitalism, because for practical purposes they had no economic policy of their own, except for the communists, whose policy consisted in gaining power and then following the model of the U.S.S.R. The pragmatic Scandinavians left their private sectors intact. The British Labour government of 1945 did not, but did nothing whatever to reform it, and showed a lack of interest in planning that was quite startling, especially when contrasted with the enthusiastic planned modernization of contemporary (and non-socialist) French governments. In effect, the Left concentrated on improving the conditions of their working-class constituencies and social reforms for this purpose. Since they had no alternative solutions except to call for the abolition of capitalism, which no social-democratic government knew how to, or tried to, abolish, they had to rely on a strong wealth-creating capitalist economy to finance their aims. In effect, a reformed capitalism which recognized the importance of labour and social-democratic aspirations suited them well enough.

In short, for a variety of reasons the politicians, officials and even many of the businessmen of the post-war West were convinced that a return to *laissez-faire* and the unreconstructed free market were out of the question. Certain policy objectives—full employment, the containment of communism, the modernization of lagging or declining or ruined economies—had absolute priority and justified the strongest government presence. Even regimes dedicated to economic and political liberalism now could, and had to, run their economies in ways which would once have been rejected as "socialist." After all, that is how Britain and even the U.S.A. had run their war-economies. The future lay with the "mixed economy." Though there were moments when the old orthodoxies of fiscal rectitude, stable currencies and stable prices still counted, even these were no longer absolutely compelling. Since 1933 the scarecrows of inflation and deficit finance no longer kept the birds away from the economic fields, but the crops still seemed to grow.

These were not minor changes. They led a U.S. stateman of ironclad capitalist credentials—Averell Harriman—in 1946 to tell his countrymen: "People in this country are no longer scared of such words as 'planning' . . . people have accepted the fact the government has got to plan as well as individuals in this country" (Maier, 1987, p. 129). They made it natural for a champion of economic liberalism and admirer of the U.S. economy, Jean Monnet (1888–1979) to become a passionate backer of French economic planning. They turned Lionel (Lord) Robbins, a free market economist who had once defended orthodoxy against Keynes and run a seminar jointly with Hayek at the London School of Economics, into a director of the semi-socialist British war economy. For thirty years or so there was a consensus among "Western" thinkers and decision-makers, notably in the U.S.A., which determined what other countries on the non-communist side could do, or rather what they could not do. All wanted a world of rising production, growing foreign trade, full employment, industrialization and modernization, and all were prepared to achieve it, if need be, through systematic government control and the management of mixed economies, and by co-operating with organized labour movements so long as they were not communist. The Golden Age of capitalism would have been impossible without this consensus that the economy of private enterprise ("free enterprise" was the preferred name)* needed to be saved from itself to survive.

However, though capitalism certainly reformed itself, we must make a clear distinction between the general readiness to do the hitherto unthinkable and the actual effectiveness of the specific new recipes which the chefs of the new economic restaurants were creating. This is hard to judge. Economists, like politicians, are always inclined to put down success to the sagacity of their policies, and, during the Golden Age,

---

*The word "capitalism," like "imperialism," was avoided in public discourse, since it had negative associations in the public mind. Not until the 1970s do we find politicians and publicists proudly declaring themselves "capitalist," slightly anticipated from 1965 in the motto of the business magazine *Forbes* which, reversing a jargon phrase of American communists, began to describe itself as a "capitalist tool."

when even weak economies like the British flourished and grew, there seemed plenty of scope for self-congratulation. Still, deliberate policy undoubtedly scored some striking successes. In 1945–46 France, for instance, set out quite consciously on a course of economic planning to modernize the French Industrial economy. This adaptation of Soviet ideas to a capitalist mixed economy must have had some effect, since between 1950 and 1979 France, hitherto a by-word for economic retardation, caught up more successfully than any other of the chief industrial countries with U.S. productivity, more so even than Germany (Maddison, 1982, p. 46). Nevertheless, we must leave the economists, a notably contentious tribe, to argue out the merits and demerits and the efficacy of the various policies of the various governments (mostly associated with the name of J. M. Keynes, who had died in 1946).

IV

The difference between broad intention and detailed application is particularly clear in the reconstruction of the international economy, for here the "lesson" of the Great Slump (the word constantly appears in the discourse of the 1940s) was at least partly translated into concrete institutional arrangements. U.S. supremacy was, of course, a fact. The political pressure for action came from Washington, even when many of the ideas and initiatives came from Britain, and where opinions differed, as between Keynes and the American spokesman Harry White,* over the new International Monetary Fund (IMF), the U.S. view prevailed. Yet the original plan for the new liberal economic world order envisaged it as part of a new international political order, also planned during the last war years as the United Nations, and it was not until the original model of the UN collapsed in the Cold War that the only two international institutions actually set up under the Bretton Woods Agreements of 1944, the World Bank ("International Bank for Reconstruction and Development") and the IMF, both still in existence, became *de facto* subordinated to U.S. policy. They were to foster long-term international investment and maintain exchange stability as well as dealing with balance-of-payments problems. Other points on the international programme did not generate special institutions (e.g. for controlling the price of primary commodities and for international measures to maintain full employment), or were

---

*Ironically, White later became a victim of the U.S. witch-hunt as an alleged secret Communist Party sympathiser.

only incompletely implemented. The proposed International Trade Organization ended up as the much more modest General Agreement on Tariffs and Trade (GATT), a framework for reducing trade barriers by periodic bargaining.

In short, insofar as the planners of the brave new world tried to construct a set of working institutions to give their projects reality, they failed. The world did not emerge from the war in the shape of a working international system of multilateral free trade and payments, and the American moves to establish it broke down within two years of victory. And yet, unlike the United Nations, the international system of trade and payments worked, though not in the way originally predicted or intended. In practice the Golden Age was the era of free trade, free capital movements and stable currencies that had been in the minds of the wartime planners. No doubt this was due primarily to the overwhelming economic dominance of the U.S.A. and of the dollar, which functioned all the better as a stabilizer because it was linked to a specific quantity of gold until the system broke down in the late 1960s and early 1970s. One must constantly bear in mind that in 1950 the U.S.A. alone contained 60 per cent or so of all the capital stock of all the advanced capitalist countries, produced 60 per cent or so of all their output, and even at the peak of the Golden Age (1970) still held over 50 per cent of the total capital stock of all these countries and produced almost half their output (Armstrong, Glyn, Harrison, 1991, p. 151).

It was also due to the fear of communism. For, contrary to American convictions, the chief obstacle to a free-trading international capitalist economy was not the protectionist instincts of foreigners, but the combination of traditional U.S. high tariffs at home and the drive for a vast expansion of American exports, which the war-time planners in Washington regarded as "essential to the attainment of full and effective employment in the U.S.A." (Kolko, 1969, p. 13). Aggressive expansion was plainly in the minds of American policy-makers as soon as the war was over. It was the Cold War which encouraged them to take a longer view, by persuading them that helping their future competitors to grow as rapidly as possible was politically urgent. It has even been argued that, in this manner, the Cold War was the major engine of the great global boom (Walker, 1993). This is probably an exaggeration, but the gigantic largesse of Marshall Aid (see pp. 240–1) certainly helped the modernization of such recipients as wanted to use it for this purpose—as Austria and France did systematically—and American aid was decisive in speeding up the transformation of West Germany and Japan. No doubt these two countries would have become great economic powers in any case. The mere fact that, as defeated states, they were not masters of their foreign policy gave them an advantage, since it did not tempt them into pouring more than a minimum of resources into the barren hole of military spending. Nevertheless, we have only to ask what would have happened to the German economy if its recovery had depended on the Europeans, who feared its revival. How fast would the Japanese economy have recovered, if the U.S.A. had not found itself building up Japan as the industrial base for the Korean War and again the Vietnam War after 1965? America funded the doubling of Japan's manufacturing output between 1949 and 1953, and it is no accident that 1966–70 were the years of peak Japanese growth—no less than 14.6 per cent per annum. The role of the Cold War is thus not to be underestimated, even if the long-term economic effect of the vast diversion of resources by states into competitive armaments was damaging. In the extreme case of the U.S.S.R. it was probably fatal. However, even the U.S.A. traded off military strength against growing economic weakness.

A capitalist world economy thus developed round the U.S.A. It raised fewer obstacles to the international movements of factors of production than any other since the mid-Victorian period, with one exception: international migration was slow to recover from inter-war strangulation. This was partly an optical illusion. The great Golden Age boom was fuelled not only by the labour of the formerly unemployed, but by vast flows of internal migration—from country to city, from farming (especially out of regions of poor upland soils), from poorer to richer regions. So Italian southerners flooded into the factories of Lombardy and Piedmont and four hundred thousand Tuscan share-croppers left their holdings in twenty years. The industrialization of Eastern Europe was essentially such a process of mass migration. Moreover, some of these internal migrants were actually international migrants, except that they had originally arrived in the receiving country, not as seekers for employment, but as part of the terrible mass exodus of refugees and expelled populations after 1945.

Nevertheless, it is notable that in an era of spectacular economic growth and increasing labour shortage, and in a Western world dedicated to free movements in the economy, governments resisted free immigration, and, when they found themselves actually permitting it (as in the case of the Caribbean and other inhabitants of the British Commonwealth, who had the right to settle because they were legally British), put a stop to it. In many cases such immigrants, mostly from the less developed Mediterranean countries, were only allowed conditional and temporary residence, so that they could be easily re-patriated, although the expansion of the European Economic Community to include several emigrant countries (Italy, Spain, Portugal, Greece) made this harder. Still, by the early 1970s about seven-and-a-half millions had migrated into the developed European countries (Potts, 1990, pp. 146–47). Even in the Golden Age immigration was a politically sensitive issue. In the difficult decades after 1973 it was to lead to a sharp rise in public xenophobia in Europe.

However, the world economy in the Golden Age remained *international* rather than *transnational*. Countries traded with each other to an ever greater extent. Even the U.S.A., which had been largely self-supplying before the Second World War, quadrupled its exports to the rest of the world between 1950 and 1970, but it also became a massive importer of consumer goods from the late 1950s on. In the late 1960s it even began to import automobiles (Block, 1977, p. 145). Yet, though the industrial economies increasingly bought and sold each others' production, the bulk of their economic activities remained home-centred. At the peak of the Golden Age the U.S.A. exported only just under 8 per cent of its GDP, and, more surprisingly, export-oriented Japan only a little more (Marglin and Schor, p. 43, Table 2.2).

Nevertheless, an increasingly *transnational* economy began to emerge, especially from the 1960s on, that is to say, a system of economic activities for which state territories and state frontiers are not the basic framework, but merely complicating factors. In the extreme case, a "world economy" comes into existence which actually has no specifiable territorial base or limits, and which determines, or rather sets limits to, what even the economies of very large and powerful states can do. Some time in the early 1970s such a transnational economy became an effective global force. It continued to grow, if anything more rapidly than before, during the Crisis Decades after 1973. Indeed its emergence largely created the problems of these decades. Of course it went hand in hand with a growing *internationalization*. Between 1965 and 1990 the percentage of the world's product which went in exports was to double (World Development, 1992, p. 235).

Three aspects of this transnationalization were particularly obvious: transnational firms (often known as "multinationals"), the new international division of labour and the rise of offshore finance. The last of these was not only one of the earliest forms of transnationalism to develop, but also the one which demonstrates most vividly the way in which the capitalist economy escaped from national, or any other, control.

The term "offshore" entered civilian public vocabulary some time in the 1960s to describe the practice of registering the legal seat of businesses in some, usually tiny and fiscally generous territory which permitted entrepreneurs to avoid the taxes and other constraints imposed on them by their own country. For every serious state or territory, however committed to the freedom of profit-making, had by the mid-century established certain controls and restrictions on the conduct of legitimate business in the interests of its people. A suitably complex and ingenious combination of the legal loopholes in the corporate and labour laws of kindly mini-territories—for instance Curaçao, the Virgin Islands and Liechtenstein—could do wonders for a firm's balance-sheet. For "the essence of offshoreness lies in turning an enormous number of loopholes into a viable but unregulated corporate structure" (Raw, Page and Hodgson, 1972, p. 83). For obvious reasons offshoreness lent itself particularly to financial transactions, although Panama and Liberia had long subsidized their politicians by the income from registering the merchant ships of other countries whose owners found their native labour and safety regulations too onerous.

Sometime in the 1960s a little ingenuity turned the old international financial centre, the City of London, into a major global offshore centre by the invention of "Eurocurrency" i.e. mainly "Eurodollars." Dollars held on deposit in non-U.S. banks and not repatriated, mainly to avoid the restrictions of U.S. banking law, became a negotiable financial instrument. These free-floating dollars, accumulating in huge quantities thanks to the growing American investments abroad and the enormous political and military expenditures of the U.S. government, became the foundation of an entirely uncontrolled global market, mainly in short-term loans. Its rise was quite dramatic. The net Eurocurrency market rose from perhaps fourteen billion dollars in 1964 to perhaps 160 billions in 1973 and almost five hundred billions five years later, when this market became the main mechanism for recycling the Klondike of oil-profits which the OPEC countries suddenly found themselves wondering how to spend and invest (see p. 473). The U.S.A. was the first country to find itself at the mercy of these vast, multiplying floods of unattached capital that washed round the globe from currency to currency, looking for quick profits. Eventually all governments were to be its victims, since they lost control over exchange rates and the world money supply. By the early 1990s even joint action by leading central banks proved impotent.

That firms based in one country, but operating in several, should expand their activities, was natural enough. Nor were such "multinationals" new. The U.S. corporations of this kind raised their foreign affiliates from about seven-and-a-half thousands in 1950 to over twenty-three thousands in 1966, mostly in western Europe and the western hemisphere (Spero, 1977, p. 92). However, increasingly other countries' firms followed. The German chemical corporation Hoechst, for instance, established or associated itself with 117 plants in forty-five countries, in all but six cases after 1950 (Fröbel, Heinrichs, Kreye, 1986, Tabelle IIIA, p. 281 ff.). The novelty lay rather in the sheer scale of operations of these transnational entities. By the early 1980s U.S. transnational corporations accounted for over three quarters of their country's exports and almost half its imports, and such corporations (both British and foreign) were responsible for over 80 per cent of British exports (U.N. Transnational, 1988, p. 90).

In one sense these are irrelevant figures, since the main function of such corporations was "to internalize markets across national frontiers," i.e. to make themselves independent of the state and its territory. Much of what the statistics (which are still basically collected country by country) show as imports or exports is in fact *internal* trade within a transnational entity such as General Motors, which operated in forty countries. The ability to operate in this manner naturally reinforced the tendency for capital to concentrate, familiar since Karl Marx. By 1960 it was already estimated that the sales of the two hundred largest firms in the (non-socialist) world were the equivalent of 17 per cent of the GNP of that sector of the world, and by 1984 they were said to amount to 26 per cent.* Most of such transnationals were based in substantial "developed" states. In fact, 85 per cent of the "big 200" were based in the U.S.A., Japan, Britain and Germany, with firms from eleven other countries making up the rest. Yet, even if the links of such super-giants with their native governments were likely to close, by the end of the Golden Age it is doubtful whether any of them, except the Japanese ones and some essentially military firms, could be confidently described as *identified* with their government's or nation's interests. It was no longer as clear as it had once seemed that, in the words of a Detroit tycoon who entered the U.S. government, "What's good for General Motors is good for the U.S.A." How could it be, when their operations in the home country were merely those in one market of the hundred in which, say, Mobil Oil was active, or the 170 in which Daimler-Benz was present? Business logic would force an international oil firm to calculate its strategy and policy towards its native country in exactly the same way as towards Saudi Arabia or Venezuela, namely in terms of profit and loss on the one hand, of the comparative power of company and government on the other.

The tendency for business transactions and business enterprises—and by no means only those of a few score of giants—to emancipate

---

*Such estimates are to be used with care, and are best treated simply as orders of magnitude.

themselves from the traditional nation state, became even more marked as industrial production began, slowly at first but with growing speed, to move out of the European and North American countries that had pioneered industralization and capitalist development. These countries remained the powerhouse of Golden Age growth. In the middle 1950s the industrial countries had sold about three-fifths of their manufactured exports to each other, in the early 1970s, three quarters. However, then things began to change. The developed world began to export somewhat more of its manufactures to the rest of the world, but—more significantly—the Third World began to export manufactures to the developed industrial countries on a substantial scale. As the traditional primary exports of backward regions lost ground (except, after the OPEC revolution, mineral fuels) they began, patchily but rapidly, to industralize. Between 1970 and 1983 the Third World's share of global industrial exports, hitherto stable at about 5 per cent, more than doubled (Fröbel et al, 1986, p. 200).

A new international division of labour therefore began to undermine the old one. The German firm Volkswagen set up car factories in Argentina, Brazil (three plants), Canada, Ecuador, Egypt, Mexico, Nigeria, Peru, South Africa and Yugoslavia—mainly after the mid-1960s. New Third-World industries supplied not only the swelling local markets, but also the world market. They could do this, both by exporting articles completely produced by local industry (such as textiles, most of which had by 1970 already emigrated from the old countries to the "developing" ones), and *by becoming part of a transnational process of manufacture.*

This was the decisive innovation of the Golden Age, though it did not fully come into its own until later. It could not have happened but for the revolution in transport and communication, which made it possible and economically feasible to split the production of a single article between, say, Houston, Singapore and Thailand, air-freighting the partly completed product between these centres and controlling the entire process centrally by modern information technology. Major electronics producers began to globalize themselves from the mid-1960s. The line of production now moved not through gigantic hangars on a single site, but across the globe. Some of them stopped in the extra-territorial "free production zones" or offshore plants which now began to spread, overwhelmingly in poor countries with cheap and mainly young women's labour, another and new device for escaping the control of a single state. Thus one of the earliest, Manaus, deep in the Amazonian jungle, manufactured textiles, toys, paper goods, electronics and digital watches for U.S., Dutch and Japanese firms.

All this produced a paradoxical change in the political structure of the world economy. As the globe became its real unit, the national economies of the large states found themselves giving way to such offshore centres, mostly situated in the small or tiny mini-states which had conveniently multiplied as the old colonial empires fell apart. At the end of the Short Twentieth Century the world, according to the World Bank, contained seventy-one economies with populations of less than two-and-a-half millions (eighteen of them with populations of less than 100,000), that is to say, two fifths of all the political units officially treated as "economies" (World Development, 1992). Until the Second World War such units had been regarded as economic jokes, and indeed not real states at all.* They were and are certainly incapable of defending their nominal independence in the international jungle, but in the Golden Age it became evident that they could flourish as well as, and sometimes better than, large national economies by providing services directly to the global economy. Hence the rise of new city states (Hong Kong, Singapore), a form of polity last seen to flourish in the Middle Ages; patches of Persian Gulf desert were transformed into major players on the global investment market (Kuwait), and of the many offshore refuges from state law.

This situation was to provide the multiplying ethnic movements of late twentieth century nationalism with unconvincing arguments for the viability of an independent Corsica or Canary Islands. Unconvincing, because the only independence achieved by secession was that of separation from the nation state with which such territories had previously been associated. Economically, separation would almost certainly make them more dependent on the transnational entities which increasingly determined such matters. The most convenient world for multinational giants is one populated by dwarf states or no states at all.

V

It was natural that industry should shift from high-cost to cheap labour locations as soon as this became technically possible and cost-effective, and the (hardly surprising) discovery that some non-white labour forces were at least as skilled and educated as white ones was to be an additional bonus for high-tech industries. Yet there was a particularly convincing reason why the Golden Age boom should lead to a shift away from the core countries of the old industralization. This was the peculiar "Keynes-

---

*Not until the early 1990s were the ancient statelets of Europe—Andorra, Liechtenstein, Monaco, San Marino—treated as potential members of the United Nations.

ian" combination of economic growth in a capitalist economy based on the mass consumption of a fully employed and increasingly well-paid and well-protected labour force.

This combination was, as we have seen, a political construct. It rested on an effective policy consensus between Right and Left in most "Western" countries, the extreme fascist-ultranationalist right having been eliminated from the political scene by the Second World War, the extreme communist left by the Cold War. It was also based on a tacit or explicit consensus between employers and labour organizations to keep labour demands within limits that did not eat into the profits, and the future prospects of profits high enough to justify the huge investments without which the spectacular growth of Golden Age labour productivity could not have taken place. Indeed, in the sixteen most industrial of the market economies investment grew at an annual rate of 4.5 per cent, about three times as fast as during the years from 1870 to 1913, even allowing for the rather less impressive rate in North America, which pushed the general average down (Maddison, 1982, Table 5.1, p. 96). *De facto*, the arrangement was triangular, with governments, formally or informally, presiding over the institutionalized negotiations between capital and labour, who were now habitually described, at least in Germany, as the "social partners." After the end of the Golden Age these arrangements were savagely assailed by the rising free-market theologians under the name of "corporatism," a word which had half-forgotten and entirely irrelevant associations with inter-war fascism (see p. 114).

This was a deal acceptable to all sides. Employers, who hardly minded high wages during a long boom with high profits, welcomed the predictability which made forward planning easier. Labour got regularly rising wages and fringe benefits, and a steadily extended and more generous Welfare State. Government got political stability, weakening communist parties (except in Italy) and predictable conditions for the macro-economic management which all states now practised. And the economies of the industrial capitalist countries did splendidly, if only because for the first time (outside North America and, perhaps Australasia) an economy of mass consumption came into existence on the basis of full employment and regularly rising real incomes, buttressed by social security, which in time was paid for by rising public revenues. Indeed, in the euphoric 1960s some incautious governments went so far as to guarantee the unemployed—who were then few—80 per cent of their former wage.

Until the late 1960s the politics of the Golden Age reflected this state of affairs. The war was followed everywhere by strongly reformist governments, Rooseveltian in the U.S.A., socialist-dominated or social-democratic in virtually all ex-belligerent Western Europe except in occupied West Germany (where there were neither independent institutions nor elections until 1949). Even the communists were in government until 1947 (see p. 238). The radicalism of the Resistance years affected even the emerging conservative parties—the West German Christian Democrats thought capitalism was bad for Germany as late as 1949 (Leaman, 1988)—or at least made it hard to swim against the tide. The British Conservative party claimed credit for the reforms of the Labour government of 1945.

Somewhat surprisingly, reformism soon retreated, though not the consensus. The great boom of the 1950s was presided over, almost everywhere, by governments of moderate conservatives. In the U.S.A. (from 1952) in Britain (from 1951), in France (except for brief episodes of coalition), West Germany, Italy and Japan, the Left was entirely out of power, though Scandinavia remained social democratic and socialist parties were in government coalitions in other small countries. There can be no doubt about the recession of the Left. This was not due to any massive loss of support by the socialists or even the communists in France and Italy where they were the major working-class party.* Nor, except perhaps in Germany, where the Social Democratic Party (SPD) was "unsound" on German unity, and in Italy where it remained allied to the communists, was it due to the Cold War. Everybody, except for the communists, was reliably anti-Russian. The mood of the booming decade was against the Left. This was not a time for change.

In the 1960s the centre of gravity of the consensus shifted towards the Left; perhaps partly due to the increasing retreat of economic liberalism before Keynesian management, even in anti-collectivist hold-outs like Belgium and West Germany, perhaps in part because the elderly gentlemen who had presided over the stabilization and revival of the capitalist system left the scene—Dwight Eisenhower (born 1890) in 1960, Konrad Adenauer (b. 1876) in 1965, Harold Macmillan (b. 1894) in 1964. Eventually (1969) even the great General de Gaulle (b. 1890) departed. A certain rejuvenation of politics took place. In fact, the peak years of the Golden Age seemed to be as congenial to the moderate Left, once again in government in many west European states, as the 1950s had been

---

*However, all Left parties were electoral minorities, though large ones The highest vote scored by such a party was 48.8 per cent by the British Labour Party in 1951, ironically in an election won by the Conservatives with a slightly smaller vote, thanks to the vagaries of the British electoral system

uncongenial. This drift to the Left was partly due to electoral shifts, as in West Germany, Austria and Sweden, and anticipated even more striking shifts in the 1970s and early 1980s, when both the French socialists and the Italian communists reached their all-time peaks, but essentially voting patterns remained stable. Electoral systems exaggerated relatively minor shifts.

However, there is a clear parallelism between the shift to the Left and the most significant public developments of the decade, namely the appearance of welfare states in the literal meaning of the word, that is to say states in which welfare expenditures—income maintenance, care, education, etc.—became the *greater part* of total public expenditure, and people engaged in welfare activities formed the largest body of all public employment, e.g. in the middle of the 1970s 40 per cent in Britain and 47 per cent in Sweden (Therborn, 1983). The first welfare states in this sense appeared round 1970. Of course the decline of military expenditure during the détente years automatically raised the proportion of spending under other headings, but the example of the U.S.A. shows that there was a real change. In 1970, while the Vietnam War was at its height, the number of school employees in the U.S.A. for the first time became significantly larger than the number of "military and civilian defense personnel" (Statistical History 1976, II, pp. 1102, 1104, 1141). By the end of the 1970s all advanced capitalist states had become such "welfare states," with six states spending more than 60 per cent of total public outlays for welfare (Australia, Belgium, France, West Germany, Italy, Netherlands). This was to produce considerable problems after the end of the Golden Age.

Meanwhile the politics of "developed market economies" seemed tranquil, if not somnolent. What was there to get impassioned about, except communism, the dangers of nuclear war and the crises imported into their affairs by imperial activities abroad, such as the Suez adventure of 1956 in Britain, the Algerian war in France (1954–61) and, after 1965, the Vietnam War in the U.S.A.? That was the reason why the sudden and almost worldwide spurt of student radicalism in and around 1968 took politicians and older intellectuals so much by surprise.

It was a sign that the Golden Age balance could not last. Economically this balance depended on a coordination between the growth of productivity and earnings which kept profits stable. A sag in the continuous rise of productivity and/or a disproportionate rise in wages would result in destabilization. It depended on what had been so dramatically absent between the wars, a balance between the growth of production and the ability of consumers to buy it. Wages had to rise fast enough to keep the market buoyant, but not fast enough to squeeze profits. But how to control wages in an era of labour shortage or, more generally, prices in a time of exceptionally booming demand? How, in other words, to control inflation, or at least keep it within bounds? Lastly, the Golden Age depended on the overwhelming political and economic dominance of the U.S.A. which acted—sometimes without meaning to—as the stabilizer and guarantor of the world economy.

In the course of the 1960s, all these showed signs of wear and tear. The hegemony of the U.S.A. declined and, as it slipped, the gold-dollar based world monetary system broke down. There were some signs of slow-down in labour productivity in several countries, and certainly signs that the great labour reservoir of internal migration which had fed the industrial boom was close to exhaustion. After twenty years, a new generation had become adult, for whom inter-war experience—mass unemployment, insecurity, stable or falling prices—were history and not part of experience. They had adjusted their expectations to the only experience of their age group, that of full employment and continuous inflation (Friedman, 1968, p. 11). Whatever the specific situation which triggered the "worldwide wage explosion" at the end of the 1960s—labour shortage, growing efforts by employers to hold down real wages or, as in France and Italy, the great student rebellions, all of them rested on the discovery by a generation of workers who had got used to having or finding work, that the regular and welcome rises so long negotiated by their unions were actually much less than could be screwed out of the market. Whether or not we detect a return to class struggle in this recognition of market realities (as many in the post-1968 "new Left" held), there is no doubt about the striking change of mood between the moderation and calm of wage negotiations before 1968 and the last years of the Golden Age.

Since it was directly relevant to the way the economy worked, the shift in labour's mood was far more significant than the great burst of student unrest in and around 1968, though the students provided more dramatic material for the media and far more food for the commentators. The student rebellion was a phenomenon outside economics and politics. It mobilized a particular minority sector of the population, as yet barely recognized as a special group in public life, and—since most of its members were still being educated—largely outside the economy, except as purchasers of rock records: the (middle-class) youth. Its cultural significance was far greater than its political significance, which was fleeting—unlike analogous movements in Third World and dictatorial countries (see pp 332 and 444). Yet it served as a warning, a sort of *memento mori* to a generation that half-believed it had solved the problems of Western society for good. The major texts of Golden Age reformism, Crosland's *The Future of Socialism;* J. K. Galbraith's *The Affluent Society;* Gunnar Myrdal's *Beyond the Welfare State;* and Daniel Bell's *The End of Ideology,* all written between 1956 and 1960, rested on the presumption of the growing internal harmony of a society that was now basically satisfactory, if improvable, that is to say, on confidence in the economy of organized social consensus. That consensus did not survive the 1960s.

So 1968 was neither an end nor a beginning, but only a signal. Unlike the wage explosion, the collapse of the Bretton Woods international financial system in 1971, the commodities boom of 1972–3 and the OPEC oil crisis of 1973, it does not figure much in the explanation of economic historians about the end of the Golden Age. Its end was not quite unexpected. The expansion of the economy in the early 1970s, accelerated by a rapidly rising inflation, by massive rises in the world's money supplies and the vast American deficit, became hectic. In the economists' jargon, the system became "overheated." In the twelve months from July 1972, the real GDP in the OECD countries rose by 7.5 per cent, and real industrial production by 10 per cent. Historians who had not forgotten the way the great mid-Victorian boom ended, might well have wondered whether the system was not riding for a fall. They would have been right, though I do not think anyone predicted the fall of 1974. Nor, perhaps, took it as seriously as it turned out to be, for, though the GNP of the advanced industrial countries actually *dropped* substantially—such a thing had not happened since the war—people still thought of economic crises in terms of 1929, and there was no sign of catastrophe. As usual, the immediate reaction of shocked contemporaries, was to look for special reasons for the collapse of the old boom, "an unusual bunching of unfortunate disturbances unlikely to be repeated on the same scale, the impact of which was compounded by some avoidable errors," to quote the OECD (McCracken, 1977, p. 14). The more simple-minded put it all down to the greed of the OPEC oil sheikhs. Any historian who puts major changes in the configuration of the world economy down to bad luck and avoidable accidents should think again. And this was a major change. The world economy did not recover its old stride after the crash. An era was at an end. The decades since 1973 were to be once again an age of crisis.

The Golden Age lost its gilt. Nevertheless, it had begun, indeed it had largely achieved the most dramatic, rapid and profound revolution in human affairs of which history has record. To this we must now turn.

CHAPTER TEN

The Social Revolution 1945–1990

LILY: My grandmother'd tell us things about the Depression.
          You can read about it too.

ROY: They're always tellin' us that we should be glad we got
          food and all that, 'cause back in the Thirties they used
          to tell us people were starving and got no jobs and all
          that stuff.

*   *   *

BUCKY: I never had a Depression, so it don't bother me really.
ROY: From what you hear, you'd hate to live in that time.
BUCKY: Well, I ain't livin' in that time.

—Studs Terkel, *Hard Times* (1970, pp. 22–23)

When [General de Gaulle] took power there were a million television sets in France . . . When he left there were ten million . . . The
state is always a show-biz affair. But yesterday's theatre-state was a
very different matter from the TV-state that exists today.

—Regis Debray (1994, p. 34)

I

When people face what nothing in their past has prepared them for they
grope for words to name the unknown, even when they can neither define
nor understand it. Some time in the third quarter of the century we can
see this process at work among the intellectuals of the West. The key-
word was the small preposition "after," generally used in its latinate form
"post" as a prefix to any of the numerous terms which had, for some
generations, been used to mark out the mental territory of twentieth-
century life. The world, or its relevant aspects, became post-industrial,

post-imperial, post-modern, post-structuralist, post-Marxist, post-Gutenberg, or whatever. Like funerals, these prefixes took official recognition of death without implying any consensus or indeed certainty about the nature of life after death. In this way the greatest and most dramatic, rapid and universal social transformation in human history entered the consciousness of reflective minds who lived through it. This transformation is the subject of the present chapter.

The novelty of this transformation lies both in its extraordinary speed and in its universality. True, the developed parts of the world, i.e. for practical purposes the central and western parts of Europe and North America, plus a thin layer of the cosmopolitan rich and mighty elsewhere, had long lived in a world of constant change, technological transformation and cultural innovation. For them the revolution of global society meant an acceleration or intensification of movement to which they were already accustomed in principle. After all, New Yorkers of the mid-1930s already looked up to a skyscraper, the Empire State Building (1934), whose height was not exceeded until the 1970s, and then only by a modest thirty metres or so. It took a while to notice, and even longer to take the measure of, the transformation of quantitative material growth into the qualitative upheavals of life, even in these parts of the world. But for most of the globe the changes were both sudden and seismic. For 80 per cent of humanity the Middle Ages ended suddenly in the 1950s; or perhaps better still, they were *felt* to end in the 1960s.

In many ways those who actually lived through these transformations on the spot did not grasp their full extent, since they experienced them incrementally, or as changes in the lives of individuals which, however dramatic, are not conceived as permanent revolutions. Why should the decision of country folk to look for work in the city imply in their minds any more lasting transformation than joining the armed forces or some branch of the war economy did for British or German men and women in the two world wars? They did not intend to change their way of life for good, even if it turned out that they did. It is those who see them from outside, re-visiting the scenes of such transformations at intervals, who recognize how much has changed. How utterly different, for instance, the Valencia of the early 1980s was from the same city and region in the early 1950s, when the present writer had last seen that part of Spain. How disoriented a Sicilian peasant Rip Van Winkle felt—actually, a local bandit absent in jail for a couple of decades from the mid-1950s—when he returned to the environs of Palermo which had in the meantime become unrecognizable by urban real-estate development. "Where once there were vineyards, now there are *palazzi*," he told me, head-shaking in disbelief. Indeed, the speed of change was such that historical time could be measured in even shorter intervals. Less than ten years (1962–71) separated a Cuzco where, outside the confines of the city, most Indian men still wore traditional costume from a Cuzco where a substantial proportion of them already wore *cholo*, i.e. European clothes. At the end of the 1970s stall holders in the food-market of a Mexican village already figured out their customers' costs on small Japanese pocket calculators, unknown there at the start of the decade.

There is no way in which readers not old and mobile enough to have seen history move in this manner since 1950, can expect to duplicate these experiences, although since the 1960s, when young Westerners discovered that travel to Third World countries was both feasible and fashionable, all it has taken to watch global transformation is an open pair of eyes. In any case, historians cannot remain content with images and anecdotes, however significant. They need to specify and to count.

The most dramatic and far-reaching social change of the second half of this century, and the one which cuts us off for ever from the world of the past, is the death of the peasantry. For since the neolithic era most human beings had lived off the land and its livestock or harvested the sea as fishers. With the exception of Britain, peasants and farmers remained a massive part of the occupied population even in industrialized countries until well into the twentieth century. So much so that in the present writer's student days, the 1930s, the refusal of the peasantry to fade away was still currently used as an argument against Karl Marx's prediction that they would. After all, on the eve of the Second World War, there was only one industrial country, in addition to Britain, where agriculture and fisheries employed less than 20 per cent of the population, namely Belgium. Even in Germany and the U.S.A., the greatest industrial economies, where the agricultural population had indeed been declining steadily, it still amounted to roughly a quarter; in France, Sweden and Austria it was still between 35 and 40 per cent. As for backward agrarian countries—say, in Europe, Bulgaria or Romania—something like four out of every five inhabitants worked on the land.

Yet consider what happened in the third quarter of the century. It is perhaps not too surprising that by the early 1980s less than three out of every 100 Britons or Belgians were in agriculture, so that the average Briton was far more likely in the course of everyday life to encounter a person who had once farmed in India or Bangladesh than one who actually farmed in the United Kingdom. The farming population of the U.S.A. had fallen to the same percentage, but, given its long-term steep decline, this was less astonishing than the fact that this tiny fraction of the labour force was in a position to flood the U.S.A. and the world with untold quantities of food. What few would have expected in the 1940s was that by the early 1980s *no* country west of the "Iron curtain" borders had more than 10 per cent of its population engaged in farming, except the Irish Republic (which was only a little above this figure), and the Iberian states. But the very fact that in Spain and Portugal people in agriculture, who had formed just under half the population in 1950, were reduced to 14.5 per cent and 17.6 per cent respectively thirty years later speaks for itself. The Spanish peasantry was halved in the twenty years after 1950, the Portuguese in the twenty years after 1960 (ILO, 1990, Table 2A; FAO, 1989).

These are spectacular figures. In Japan, for instance, farmers were reduced from 52.4 per cent of the people in 1947 to 9 per cent in 1985, i.e. between the time that a young soldier returned from the battles of the Second World War and the time he retired from his subsequent civilian career. In Finland—to take an actual life-history known to the writer—a girl born as a farmer's daughter and who became a farmer's working wife in her first marriage, could, before she had got far into middle age, have transformed herself into a cosmopolitan intellectual and political figure. But then, in 1940 when her father died in the winter war against Russia, leaving mother and infant on the family holding, 57 per cent of Finns were farmers and foresters. By the time she was forty-five less than 10 per cent were. What is more natural than that, under such circumstances, Finns should begin on farms and end in very different circumstances?

Yet if Marx's prediction that industrialization would eliminate the peasantry was at last evidently coming true in countries of headlong industrialization, the really extraordinary development was the decline of the farming population in countries whose obvious lack of such development the United Nations tried to disguise by a variety of euphemisms for the words "backward" and "poor." At the very moment when hopeful young leftists were quoting Mao Tse-tung's strategy for the triumph of revolution by mobilizing the countless rural millions against the encircled urban strongholds of the status quo, these millions were abandoning their villages and moving into the cities themselves. In Latin America the percentage of peasants halved in twenty years in Colombia (1951–73), in Mexico (1960–80) and—almost—in Brazil (1960–1980). It fell by two thirds, or almost two thirds, in the Dominican Republic (1960–81), Venezuela (1961–81) and Jamaica (1953–81). All these—except Venezuela —were countries in which at the end of the Second World War peasants had formed half, or an absolute majority of, the occupied population. But as early as the 1970s there was, in Latin America—outside the mini-states of the central American landstrip and Haiti—*no* country in which peasants were not a minority. The situation was similar in the countries of western Islam. Algeria slimmed its agriculturals from 75 per cent of the population to 20 per cent; Tunisia from 68 per cent to 23 per cent in just over thirty years; Morocco, less dramatically, lost its peasant majority in ten (1971–82). Syria and Iraq still had about half their people on the land in the mid-1950s. Within about twenty years the first had halved this percentage, the second reduced it to less than one third. Iran dropped from about 55 per cent of peasants in the mid-1950s to 29 per cent in the mid-1980s.

Meanwhile, of course, the peasants of agrarian Europe stopped tilling the land. By the 1980s even the ancient strongholds of peasant agriculture in the east and south-east of the continent had no more than a third or so of their labour force in farming (Romania, Poland, Yugoslavia, Greece), and some had considerably less, notably Bulgaria (16.5 per cent in 1985). Only one peasant stronghold remained in or around the neighbourhood of Europe and the Middle East—Turkey, where the peasantry declined, but, in the mid-1980s, still remained an absolute majority.

Only three regions of the globe remained essentially dominated by their villages and fields: sub-Saharan Africa, South and continental Southeast Asia, and China. In these regions alone was it still possible to find countries which the decline of the cultivators had apparently passed by— where those who grew crops and looked after animals remained throughout the stormy decades a steady proportion of the population—over 90 per cent in Nepal, about 70 per cent in Liberia, about 60 per cent in Ghana, or even—a somewhat surprising fact—70 per cent or so in India through the twenty-five years after independence, and barely less (66.4 per cent) even in 1981. Admittedly these regions of peasant dominance still represented half the human race at the end of our period. However, even they were crumbling at the edges under the pressures of economic development. The solid peasant bloc of India was surrounded by countries whose farming populations were visibly declining quite fast: Pakistan, Bangladesh and Sri Lanka, where peasants had long ceased to be a majority; as they had, by the 1980s, in Malaysia, the Philippines and Indonesia and, of course, in the new industrial states of East Asia, Taiwan and South Korea, which had more than 60 per cent of its people in the fields as recently as 1961. Moreover in Africa the peasant predominance of several southern countries was a Bantustan illusion. Farming, mostly conducted by the women, was the visible side of an economy which actually depended largely on the remittances of male migrant labour to the white cities and mines in the south.

The strange thing about this massive and silent exodus from the land in the greater part of the world's land mass and even more of its islands* is that it was only partly due to agricultural progress, at least in the former peasant areas. As we have seen (see chapter 9), the developed industrial countries with one or two exceptions, also transformed themselves into the major producers of agricultural goods for the world market, and they did so while reducing their actual farming population to a steadily diminishing, and sometimes an absurdly tiny percentage of their people. This was plainly achieved by an extraordinary spurt in capital-intensive productivity per head of the agriculturists. Its most immediately visible aspect was the sheer quantity of machinery which the farmer in rich and developed countries now had at his (or her) disposal and which realized the great dreams of plenty through mechanized agriculture that inspired all those symbolic bare-chested tractor-drivers in the propaganda photos of the young Soviet republic, and which Soviet agriculture so signally failed to live up to. Less visible, but equally significant, were the increasingly impressive achievements of agricultural chemistry, selective breeding and bio-technology. Under these conditions farming simply no longer needed the numbers of hands and arms without which, in pre-technological days, a harvest could not be got in, nor indeed the number of regular farm families and their permanent servants. And where they were needed, modern transport made it unnecessary to keep them in the country. Thus in the 1970s sheep farmers in Perthshire (Scotland) found it cost-effective to import expert specialist shearers from New Zealand for the (short) local shearing season which, naturally, did not coincide with that in the southern hemisphere.

In the poor regions of the world the agricultural revolution was not absent, though it was patchier. Indeed, but for irrigation and the input of *science* through the so-called "green revolution,"† controversial though the long-term consequences of both may be, large parts of South and South-east Asia would have been unable to feed a rapidly multiplying population. Yet, on the whole, the countries of the Third World, and parts of the (formerly or still socialist) Second World, no longer fed themselves, let alone produced the major exportable food surplus that might be expected from agrarian countries. At best they were encouraged to concentrate on specialized export crops for the market of the developed world, while

---

*About the three-fifths of the land area of the globe, omitting the uninhabited continent of Antarctica.

†The systematic introduction in parts of the Third World of new high-yielding crop varieties grown by methods specifically suited to them. Mainly since the 1960s.

their peasants, when not buying the dumped surpluses of export food from the North, went on hoeing and ploughing in the old, labour-intensive manner. There were no good reasons why they should have left an agriculture which needed their labour, except perhaps the population explosion which might make land scarcer. But the regions out of which the peasants flooded were often, as in Latin America, quite thinly settled and tended to have open frontiers to which a small proportion of the countrymen migrated as squatters and free settlers, often, as in Colombia and Peru, providing the political base for local guerrilla movements. Conversely, the Asian regions in which the peasantry maintained itself best was perhaps the most densely settled zone in the world with densities per square mile ranging from 250 to 2,000 (the average for South America is 41.5).

When the land empties the cities fill up. The world of the second half of the twentieth century became urbanized as never before. By the mid-1980s 42 per cent of its population were urban, and, but for the weight of the enormous rural populations of China and India, which kept three quarters of Asians countrymen, it would have been a majority (Population, 1984, p. 214). But even in the rural heartlands people shifted from country to city, and especially to the great city. Between 1960 and 1980 the urban population of Kenya doubled, though in 1980 it had only reached 14.2 per cent; but almost six out of every ten townsmen now lived in Nairobi, whereas twenty years earlier only four out of ten had done so. In Asia the multi-million city mushroomed, generally a capital. Seoul, Teheran, Karachi, Jakarta, Manila, New Delhi, Bangkok, all had between roughly 5 and 8.5 million inhabitants in 1980 and were expected to have between 10 and 13.5 million in the year 2000. In 1950 not one of them (except Jakarta) had more than about one-and-a-half millions each (World Resources, 1986). Indeed, by far the most gigantic urban agglomerations at the end of the 1980s were to be found in the Third World: Cairo, Mexico City, São Paulo and Shanghai, whose populations were counted in eight figures. For, paradoxically, while the developed world remained far more urbanized than the poor world (except for parts of Latin America and the Islamic zone), its own giant cities were dissolving. They had reached their peak in the early twentieth century, before the flight to suburbs and satellite out-of-town communities gained speed, and the old city centres became hollow shells at night when the workers, shoppers and seekers after entertainment had gone home. While Mexico City almost quintupled in the thirty years after 1950, New York, London and Paris slowly drifted out of, or to the lower edges of, the big league of cities.

Yet, in a curious way, both the old and the new worlds converged. The typical "great city" of the developed world became a region of linked urban settlements, generally focused on some central area or areas of business or administration recognizable from the air as a sort of mountain range of high-rise buildings and skyscrapers, except where (as in Paris) such building was not permitted.* Their interconnection, or perhaps the breakdown of private motor-traffic under the pressure of massive automobile ownership, was demonstrated, from the 1960s, by a new revolution in public transport. Never, since the first construction of urban street-car and underground railway systems in the late nineteenth century, had so many new subway and rapid suburban transit systems been built in so many places: from Vienna to San Francisco, from Seoul to Mexico. At the same time decentralization spread, as most component communities or suburban complexes developed their own shopping and leisure services, notably through the (American-pioneered) peripheral "shopping malls."

On the other hand the Third-World city, though also bound together by (usually obsolete and inadequate) public transport systems and a myriad of broken-down private buses and "collective taxis," could not but be scattered and unstructured, if only because there is no way in which agglomerations to ten to twenty million people cannot be so, especially if much of their component settlements have begun life as low-built shanty-towns, as like as not established by groups of squatters on some unused open space. The inhabitants of such cities may have to spend several hours a day travelling to and from employment (for regular work is precious), and they may be willing to make pilgrimages of equal length to places of public ritual like Rio de Janeiro's Maracanã Stadium (two hundred thousand seats), where Cariocas worship the divinities of *futebol*, but in fact, both Old and New World conurbations were increasingly collections of nominally—or, in the case of the West, often formally—autonomous communities, though in the rich West, at least on the outskirts, they contained far more green spaces than in the poor or overcrowded East and South. While in the slums and shanty-towns humans lived in symbiosis with the hardy rat and roach, the strange no-man's land between town and country that surrounded what was left of

---

*Such high-rise centres, the natural consequence of high land-prices in such districts, had been extremely unusual before 1950. New York was virtually unique. They became common from the 1960s, even low-slung, decentralized cities like Los Angeles, acquiring such a "downtown."

the "inner cities" of the developed world was colonized by the fauna of the wilds: weasel, fox and raccoon.

II

Almost as dramatic as the decline and fall of the peasantry, and much more universal, was the rise of the occupations which required secondary and higher education. Universal primary education, i.e. basic literacy, was indeed the aspiration of virtually all governments, so much so that by the late 1980s only the most honest or helpless states admitted to having as many as half their population illiterate, and only ten—all but Afghanistan and Africa—were prepared to concede that less than 20 per cent of their population could read and write. And literacy made striking progress, not least in the revolutionary countries under communist rule whose achievements in this respect were indeed most impressive, even when the claims to have "liquidated" illiteracy within some implausibly short spell of time were sometimes optimistic. Yet, whether or not mass literacy was general, the demand for places in secondary and especially in higher education multiplied at an extraordinary rate. And so did the numbers of people who had undergone it or were undergoing it.

This explosion of numbers was particularly dramatic in university education, hitherto so unusual as to be demographically negligible, except in the U.S.A. Before the Second World War even Germany, France and Britain, three of the largest, most developed, and educated countries with a total population of 150 millions, contained no more than 150,000 or so university students between them, or one tenth of one per cent of their joint populations. Yet by the late 1980s students were counted in millions in France, the Federal Republic of Germany, Italy, Spain and the U.S.S.R. (to name only European countries), not to mention Brazil, India, Mexico, the Philippines and, of course, the U.S.A., which had been the pioneer of mass college education. By this time in educationally ambitious countries, students formed upwards of 2.5 per cent of the *total* population—men, women and children—or even, in exceptional cases, above 3 per cent. It was not uncommon for 20 per cent of the twenty to twenty-four age-group to be in formal education. Even the academically most conservative countries—Britain and Switzerland—had risen to 1.5 per cent. Moreover some of the relatively largest student bodies were to be found in economically far from advanced countries: Ecuador (3.2 per cent), the Philippines (2.7 per cent) or Peru (2 per cent).

All this was not merely new, but quite sudden. "The most striking fact from the study of Latin American university students in the middle 1960s is that they were so few in number" (Liebman, Walker, Glazer, 1972, p. 35), U.S. scholars wrote during that decade, convinced that this echoed the basic elitist-European model of higher education south of the Rio Grande. And this in spite of the fact that their numbers had been growing by about 8 per cent a year. In fact, not until the 1960s was it undeniable that students had become, both socially and politically, a far more important force than ever before, for in 1968 the worldwide uprisings of student radicalism spoke louder than statistics. But these also became impossible to overlook. Between 1960 and 1980, to stick to well-schooled Europe, the number of students tripled or quadrupled in the most typical country, except where it multiplied by four to five, as in Federal Germany, Ireland and Greece; by five to seven, as in Finland, Iceland, Sweden and Italy; and seven to nine-fold, as in Spain and Norway (Burloiu, Unesco, 1983, pp. 62–63). At first sight it seems curious that, on the whole, the rush into the universities was less marked in the socialist countries, in spite of their pride in mass education, though the case of Mao's China is aberrant. The Great Helmsman virtually abolished all higher education during the Cultural Revolution (1966–76). As the troubles of the socialist systems grew in the 1970s and 1980s, they fell further behind the West. Hungary and Czechoslovakia had a smaller percentage of their populations in higher education than practically all other European states.

Does it seem quite as curious at second sight? Perhaps not. The extraordinary growth of higher education which, by the early 1980s, produced at least seven countries with more than 100,000 *teachers* at university level, was due to consumer pressure, to which socialist systems were not geared to respond. It was obvious to planners and governments that the modern economy required far more administrators, teachers and technical experts than in the past, who had to be trained somewhere—and universities or similar institutions of higher education had, by ancient tradition, functioned largely as training-schools for public service and the specialised professions. But while this, as well as a general democratic bias, justified a substantial expansion of higher education, the scale of the student explosion far exceeded what rational planning might have envisaged.

In fact, where families had the choice and the chance, they rushed their children into higher education, because it was by far the best way of winning them a better income, but, above all, higher social status. Of the Latin American students interviewed by U.S. investigators in the mid-1960s in various countries, between 79 and 95 per cent were convinced that study would put them into a higher social class within ten years. Only between 21 and 38 per cent felt that it would win them a much higher economic status than their family's (Liebman, Walker, Glazer, 1972). In fact, of course, it would almost certainly give them a higher income than non-graduates, and, in countries of small education, where the certificate of graduation guaranteed a place in the state machine, and therefore power, influence, and financial extortion, it could be the key to real wealth. Most students, of course, came from families that were better off than most—how otherwise could they have afforded to pay for some years' study by young adults of working age?— but not necessarily rich. Often the sacrifices their parents made were real. The Korean educational miracle, it was said, rested on the carcasses of cows sold by small farmers to push their children into the honoured and privileged ranks of scholars. (In eight years—1975–83—Korean students rose from 0.8 per cent to almost 3 per cent of the population.) No one who has the experience of being the first in his family to go to university full-time will have any difficulty in understanding their motivations. The great world boom made it possible for countless modest families—white-collar employees and public officials, shopkeepers and small businessmen, farmers, in the West, even prosperous skilled workers—to afford full-time study for their children. The Western welfare state, starting with the U.S. subsidies for ex-service students after 1945, provided substantial student aid in one way or another, though most students still expected a distinctly unluxurious life. In democratic and egalitarian countries, something like a right for graduates of secondary schools to move to higher things was often accepted, to the point where in France selective admission to a state university was still regarded as constitutionally impossible in 1991. (No such right existed in the socialist countries.) As young men and women surged into higher education, governments—for, outside the U.S.A., Japan and a few other countries, universities were overwhelmingly public rather than private institutions—multiplied new establishments to take them in, especially in the 1970s when the number of the world's universities more than doubled.* And, of course, the newly independent ex-colonies which multiplied during the 1960s insisted on their own institutions of higher education as a symbol of independence, as they insisted on a flag, an airline or an army.

---

*Here again, the socialist world was under smaller pressure.

These masses of young men and women and their teachers, counted in millions or at least in hundreds of thousands in all except the very smallest or the exceptionally backward states, increasingly concentrated in large and often isolated campuses or "university cities," were a novel factor in both culture and politics. They were transnational, moving and communicating ideas and experiences across frontiers with ease and speed, and were probably more at ease than governments with the technology of communications. As the 1960s revealed, they were not only politically radical and explosive, but uniquely effective in giving national, even international, expression to political and social discontent. In dictatorial countries they usually provided the *only* bodies of citizens capable of collective political action, and it is far from insignificant that, while other Latin American student populations swelled, their number in the military dictator Pinochet's Chile after 1973 was made to drop: from 1.5 to 1.1 per cent of the population. And if there was a single moment in the golden years after 1945 which corresponds to the world simultaneous upheaval of which the revolutionaries had dreamed after 1917, it was surely 1968, when students rebelled from the U.S.A. and Mexico in the West to socialist Poland, Czechoslovakia and Yugoslavia, largely stimulated by the extraordinary outbreak of May 1968 in Paris, epicentre of a Continent-wide student uprising. It was far from revolution, though it was considerably more than the "psychodrama" or "street theatre" which unsympathetic senior observers like Raymond Aron dismissed. After all, 1968 ended the era of General de Gaulle in France, the era of Democratic presidents in the U.S.A., the hopes of liberal communism in communist central Europe and (through the silent after-effects of the student massacre of Tlatelolco) it marked the beginning of a new era in Mexican politics.

The reason why 1968 (with its prolongation into 1969 and 1970) was not the revolution, and never looked as though it would or could be, was that students alone, however numerous and mobilizable, could not make one alone. Their political effectiveness rested on their ability to act as signals and detonators for larger but less easily combustible groups. Since the 1960s students have sometimes succeeded in doing so. They sparked off enormous working-class strike-waves in France and Italy in 1968–69, but, after twenty years of unparalleled improvement for wage-earners in economies of full employment, revolution was the last thing in the minds of the proletarian masses. Not until the 1980s—and then in non-democratic countries as widely different as China, South Korea and Czechoslovakia, did student rebellions look like realizing their potential for detonating revolution, or at least to force governments to treat them like a serious public danger by massacring them on a large scale, as in Tiananmen Square, Beijing. After the failure of the great dreams of 1968, some student radicals did indeed attempt to make revolution on their own by small-group terrorism, but, though such movements received a great deal of publicity (thus achieving at least one of their major objectives), they rarely had any serious political impact. Where they threatened to have, they were fairly rapidly suppressed once the authorities decided to act: in the 1970s with unexampled brutality and systematic torture in "dirty wars" in South America, with bribery and backstairs negotiations in Italy. The only significant survivors of these initiatives in the last decade of the century were the Basque nationalist terrorist ETA and the theoretically communist peasant guerrilla *Sendero Luminoso* in Peru, an undesired gift of the staff and students of the University of Ayacucho to their countrymen.

Nevertheless, this leaves us with a slightly puzzling question: why did the movement of this new social group of students, alone among the new or old social actors of the golden era, opt for a radicalism of the Left? For (if we leave aside rebels against the communist regimes) even nationalist student movements tended to stitch the red badge of Marx, Lenin or Mao somewhere on their banners until the 1980s.

In some ways this inevitably takes us well beyond social stratification, for the new student body was, by definition, also an age-group of youth, i.e. a temporary halting place on the human passage through life, and it also contained a rapidly growing, and disproportionately large, component of women, suspended between the impermanence of their age and the permanence of their sex. Later we shall consider the development of special youth cultures, which linked students to others of their generation, and the new women's consciousness, which also reached out beyond the universities. Youth groups, not yet settled in established adulthood, are the traditional locus for high spirits, riot and disorder, as even medieval university rectors knew, and revolutionary passions are more common at eighteen than at thirty-five, as generations of bourgeois parents in Europe had told generations of sceptical sons and (later) daughters. In fact, this belief was so ingrained in Western cultures that the Establishment in several countries—perhaps mostly Latin ones on either side of the Atlantic—entirely discounted student militancy, even to the point of armed guerrilla struggle, in the younger generation. If anything, it was a sign of a spirited rather than a torpid personality. Students from San Marcos in Lima (Peru), as the joke went, "did their revolutionary service" in some ultra-Maoist sect before settling down to a solid and unpolitical middle-class profession—while such a thing as normal life still continued in that unhappy country (Lynch, 1990). Mexican students soon learned *a.* that the state and party apparatus essentially recruited its cadres from the universities, and *b.* that the more revolutionary they were as students, the better the jobs they were likely to be offered after graduation. But even in respectable France, the ex-Maoist of the early 1970s who made a brilliant career in the state service became familiar.

Nevertheless, this does not explain why bodies of young people who were obviously on the way to a far better future than their parents, or, at any rate, than most non-students, should have—with rare exceptions—been attracted by political radicalism.* Indeed, a high proportion of them probably were not, preferring to concentrate on getting the degrees which guaranteed their future, though they were less noticeable than the smaller—but still numerically large—number of the politically active, especially when these dominated the visible parts of university life, by means of public demonstrations ranging from graffiti-and poster-filled walls to meetings, marches and pickets. Still, even this degree of Left-wing radicalization was new in the developed countries, though not in the backward and dependent ones. Before the Second World War, the great majority of students in central and western Europe and North America had been non-political or Right-wing.

The sheer explosion of student numbers suggests a possible answer. The number of French students at the end of the Second World War was less than 100,000. By 1960 it was over 200,000 and within the next ten years it tripled to 651,000 (Flora, p. 582; *Deux Ans*, 1990, p. 4). (During these ten years the number of students in the humanities multiplied by almost three-and-a-half, the number of students in the social sciences by four.) The most immediate and direct consequence was an inevitable tension between these masses of mainly first-generation students now suddenly pouring into universities, and institutions which were neither physically nor organizationally and intellectually prepared for such an influx. Moreover, as a growing proportion of the age-group had the chance to study—in France it was 4 per cent in 1950, 15½ per cent in 1970—going to university ceased to be an exceptional privilege which was

---

*Among these rare exceptions we note Russia where, unlike all the other communist countries of Eastern Europe and China, students as a group were neither prominent nor influential in the years of the break-up of communism. The democratic movement in Russia has been described as "a revolution of the forty-year-olds" watched by a de-politicized and demoralized youth (Riordan, 1991).

its own reward, and the constraints it imposed on young (and generally impecunious) adults were more resented. Resentment of one kind of authority, the university's, easily broadened out into resentment of any authority, and therefore (in the West) inclined students to the Left. It is not at all surprising that the 1960s became the decade of student unrest *par excellence*. Special reasons intensified it in this or that country—hostility to the Vietnam War in the U.S.A. (i.e. to military service), racial resentment in Peru (Lynch, 1990, pp. 32–37)—but the phenomenon was too general to need special ad hoc explanations.

And yet, in a more general, less definable, sense this new mass of students stood, as it were, at an awkward angle to the rest of society. Unlike other and older-established classes or social groupings, they had no established place in it or pattern of relations to it—for how could the new student armies be compared to the relatively tiny pre-war bodies (forty thousand in well-educated 1939 Germany)—who were merely a junior phase of middle-class life? In many ways the very existence of the new masses implied questions about the society that had engendered them; and from questions to criticism is but one step. How did they fit into it? What sort of society was it? The very youth of the student body, the very width of the generation gap between these children of the post-war world and the parents who remembered and compared, made their questions more urgent, their attitude more critical. For the discontents of the young were not blanketed by the consciousness of living through times of staggering improvement, far better times than their parents had ever expected to see. The new times were the only ones that young men and women who went to college knew. On the contrary, they felt things could be different and better, even when they did not quite know how. Their elders, used to, or at least remembering, times of hardship and unemployment, did not expect mass radical mobilizations at a time when, surely, the economic incentive for them in the developed countries was less than ever before. But the explosion of student unrest erupted at the very peak of the great global boom, because it was directed, however vaguely and blindly, against what they saw as characteristic of *this* society, not against the fact that the older society might not have improved quite enough. But, paradoxically, the fact that the impetus for the new radicalism came from groups unaffected by economic discontent, stimulated even the groups used to mobilize on an economic basis to discover that, after all, they could ask for far more from the new society than they had imagined. The most immediate effect of the European student rebellion was a wave of working-class strikes for higher wages and better conditions.

III

Unlike countryside and college populations, the industrial working classes experienced no demographic earthquakes, until in the 1980s they began to decline quite noticeably. This is surprising, considering how much talk there was, even from the 1950s on, about a "post-industrial society"; considering how revolutionary, indeed, were the technical transformations of production, most of which economized, by-passed or eliminated human labour; and considering how obviously the political parties and movements which based themselves on the working class were in crisis after 1970 or thereabouts. Yet the widespread impression that somehow the old industrial working class was dying out was statistically mistaken, at least on a global scale.

With the one major exception of the U.S.A., where the percentage of people employed in manufacturing began to decline from 1965, and very obviously after 1970, the industrial working classes remained pretty stable throughout the golden years even in the old industrial countries,* at about one third of the occupied population. In fact in eight out of twenty-one OECD countries—the club of the most developed—it continued to rise between 1960 and 1980. Naturally it rose in the newly industrialized parts of (non-communist) Europe, and then remained stable until 1980, while in Japan it increased dramatically, remaining fairly stable in the 1970s and 1980s. In the communist countries undergoing rapid industrialization, notably in Eastern Europe, proletarians multiplied faster than ever, as indeed they did in those parts of the Third World which entered on their own industrialization—Brazil, Mexico, India, Korea and others. In short, at the end of the golden years there were certainly far more workers in the world in absolute figures, and almost certainly a higher proportion of manufacturing employees in the global population, than ever before. With very few exceptions, such as Britain, Belgium and the U.S.A., in 1970 workers probably formed a larger proportion of the total occupied population than they had in the 1890s in all countries where vast mass socialist parties had suddenly emerged at the end of the nineteenth century on the basis of proletarian consciousness. Only in the 1980s and 1990s can we detect signs of a major contraction of the working class.

The illusion of a collapsing working class was due to the shifts within it, and within the process of production, rather than to demographic haemorrhage. The old industries of the nineteenth and early twentieth

---

*Belgium, (West) Germany, Britain, France, Sweden, Switzerland.

centuries declined, and their very visibility in the past, when they had often symbolized "industry" as a whole, made their decline particularly dramatic. Coal-miners, once counted in hundreds of thousands, in Britain even in millions, became less common than university graduates. The U.S. steel industry now employed fewer people than McDonald's hamburger restaurants. Even when such traditional industries did not disappear, they shifted from old to new industrial countries. Textiles, clothing and footwear migrated massively. The number of people employed in the textile and clothing industries within the German Federal Republic fell by more than half between 1960 and 1984, but in the early 1980s for every 100 German workers the German clothing industry employed thirty-four workers abroad. Even in 1966 it had been less than three. Iron and steel and ship-building virtually disappeared from the lands of early industrialization, but surfaced in Brazil and Korea, in Spain, Poland and Romania. Old industrial areas became "rustbelts"—a term invented in the U.S.A. in the 1970s—or even entire countries identified with an earlier phase of industry, such as Great Britain, were largely de-industrialized, turning into living or dying museums of a vanished past, which entrepreneurs exploited, with some success, as tourist attractions. As the last coal-mines disappeared from South Wales, where over 130,000 had earned their living as miners at the start of the Second World War, surviving elderly men descended into dead pits to demonstrate to tourist parties what they had once done down there in the eternal darkness.

And even when new industries replaced old ones, they were not the same industries, often enough not in the same places, and more likely than not, differently structured. The jargon of the 1980s which talked about "Post-Fordism" suggests as much.* The huge mass-production plant built around the conveyor belt, the city or region dominated by a single industry, as Detroit or Turin were by automobiles; the local working class united, welded together by residential segregation and workplace, into a multi-headed unity—these seemed to have been characteristics of the classic industrial era. It was an unrealistic image, but represented more than a symbolic truth. Where the old industrial structures flourished in the late twentieth century, as in newly industrializing Third World countries or socialist industrial economies, caught in their (deliberately) Fordist time-warp, the similarities to the inter-war, or

---

*The phrase, which emerged from attempts to rethink Left-wing analyses of industrial society, was popularized by Alain Lipietz, who took the term "Fordism" from the Italian Marxist thinker Gramsci.

even the pre-1914 Western industrial world were evident—even to the emergence of powerful labour organizations in great industrial centres based on big auto-works (as in São Paulo), or shipyards (as in Gdansk). Just so the United Auto Workers' and Steel Workers' unions had emerged from the great strikes of 1937 in what is now the rustbelt of the U.S. Middle West. Conversely, while the large mass-production firm and the large plant survived into the 1990s, though automated and altered, the new industries *were* very different. The classic "post-Fordist" industrial regions—for instance the Veneto, Emilia-Romagna and Tuscany in North and Central Italy—lacked the great industrial cities, the dominant firms, the huge plants. They were mosaics or networks of enterprises ranging from the cottage workshop to the modest (but high-tech) manufactory, spread across town and country. How would the city of Bologna like it, its mayor was asked by one of the largest firms in Europe, if one of its major factories were to be sited there? The mayor* politely fended off the suggestion. His city and region, prosperous, sophisticated and, as it happens, communist, knew how to handle the economic and social situation of the new agro-industrial economy: let Turin and Milan cope with the problems of their kinds of industrial city.

Of course eventually—and very plainly in the 1980s—the working classes visibly became the victims of the new technologies; especially the unskilled and semi-skilled men and women of the mass production lines, who could most easily be replaced by automated machinery. Or rather, as the great global boom decades of the 1950s and 1960s gave way to an era of world economic difficulties in the 1970s and 1980s, industry no longer expanded at the old rate which had swelled workforces even as production became more labour-saving (see chapter 14). The economic crises of the early 1980s recreated mass unemployment for the first time in forty years, at all events in Europe.

In some ill-advised countries the crisis produced a veritable industrial holocaust. Britain lost 25 per cent of its manufacturing industry in 1980–84. Between 1973 and the late 1980s the total number employed in manufacturing in the six old-industrial countries of Europe fell by seven millions, or about a quarter, about half of which was lost between 1979 and 1983. By the late 1980s, as the working classes in the old industrial countries eroded and the new ones rose, the workforce employed in manufactures settled down at about a quarter of all civilian employment in all western developed regions, except the U.S.A., where by that time it was well below 20 per cent (Bairoch, 1988). It was a long way from the

*He told me so himself.

old Marxist dream of populations gradually proletarianized by the development of industry until most people would be (manual) workers. Except in the rarest cases, of which Britain was the most notable, the industrial working class had always been a minority of the working population. Nevertheless, the apparent crisis of the working class and its movements, especially in the old industrial world, was patent long before there was— speaking globally—any question of a serious decline.

It was a crisis not of the class, but of its consciousness. At the end of the nineteenth century (see *Age of Empire*, chapter 5) the very miscellaneous and far from homogeneous populations who earned their living in the developed countries by selling their manual labour for wages learned to see themselves as a single working class, and to regard that fact as by far the most important thing about their situation as human beings in society. Or at least enough of them came to this conclusion to make parties and movements which appealed to them essentially as workers (as indicated by their very name—Labour Party, Parti Ouvrier, etc.) into huge political forces within a matter of a few years. They were, of course, united not only by wages and getting their hands dirty at work. They belonged, overwhelmingly, to the poor and the economically insecure, for, though the essential pillars of labour movements were far from destitution or pauperism, what they expected and got from life was modest, and well below what the middle classes expected. Indeed, the economy of consumer durables for the masses had passed them by everywhere before 1914, and everywhere except North America and Australasia between the wars. A British communist organizer sent to the arms factories of wartime Coventry, as militant as they were prosperous, came back open-mouthed: "Do you realize," he told his London friends, myself among them, "that up there the comrades have *cars?*"

They were united also by massive social segregation, by separate lifestyles or even clothing, and by the constriction of life-chances which separated them from the socially more mobile, if economically also hardpressed, white-collar strata. Workers' children did not expect to go, and rarely went, to university. Most of them did not expect to go to school at all after the minimum school-leaving age (usually fourteen). In the prewar Netherlands 4 per cent of the ten to nineteen-year-olds went to secondary schools beyond this age, and in democratic Sweden and Denmark an even smaller proportion. Workers lived differently from others, with different expectations of life, in different places. As one of the earliest of their (British) university-educated sons put it in the 1950s, when this segregation was still fairly obvious: "such people have their own recognizable styles of housing . . . their houses are usually rented, not owned" (Hoggart, 1958, p. 8).*

They were united, finally, by the central element of their life, collectivity: the domination of "us" over "I." What gave labour movements and parties their original strength was the justified conviction of workers that people such as they could not improve their lot by individual action, but only by collective action, preferably through organizations, whether by mutual aid, striking or voting. And, conversely, that the numbers and peculiar situation of manual wage-workers put collective action within their grasp. Where workers saw private escape-routes from their class, as in the U.S.A., their class-consciousness, though far from absent, was less of a uniquely defining characteristic of their identity. But "we" dominated "I," not only for instrumental reasons, but because—with the major, and often tragic exception of the married working-class housewife, imprisoned behind her four walls—working-class life had to be largely public, because the private space was so inadequate. And even the housewife shared in the public life of market, street, and neighbouring parks. Children had to play on streets or in parks. Young men and women had to dance and court outside. Men socialized in "public houses." Until the radio, which transformed the life of the housebound working-class woman between the wars—and then only in a few favoured countries—all forms of entertainment beyond the private party had to be public, and in poorer countries even television was, in its early years, something watched in some public space. From football match to political meeting or holiday outing, life was something experienced, for most pleasurable purposes, en masse.

In most respects this conscious working-class cohesiveness reached its peak, in older developed countries, at the end of the Second World War. During the golden decades almost all elements of it were undermined. The combination of secular boom, full employment and a society of genuine mass consumption utterly transformed the lives of working-class people in the developed countries, and continued to transform it. By the standards of their parents, and indeed, if old enough, by their own memories, they were no longer poor. Lives immeasurably more prosperous than any non-Americans or non-Australians had ever expected were privatised by both money technology and the logic of the market: television made it unnecessary to go to the football match, just as TV

---

*Cf also: "The predominance of industry, with its abrupt division between workers and management, tends to encourage the different classes to live apart, so that a particular district of a town becomes a reservation or ghetto" (Allen, 1968, pp. 32–33).

and videos have made it unnecessary to go to the cinema, or telephones to gossip with friends on the piazza or at the market. Trade unionists or party members who had once turned up for branch meetings or public political occasions because, among other things, they were also a form of diversion or entertainment, could now think of more attractive ways of spending their time, unless abnormally militant. (Conversely, face-to-face contact ceased to be an effective form of electoral campaigning, although it continued out of tradition and in order to cheer up the increasingly untypical party activists.) Prosperity and privatisation broke up what poverty and collectivity in the public place had welded together.

It was not that workers became unrecognizable as such, although, strangely, as we shall see, the new independent youth culture (see p. 324 ff.) from the late 1950s on took its fashions in both clothes and music from the working-class young. It was rather that some sort of affluence was now within the reach of most, and the difference between the owner of a Volkswagen Beetle and the owner of a Mercedes was far less than that between the owner of any car and the owner of no car, especially if the more expensive cars were (in theory) available on monthly instalments. Workers, especially in the last years of youth before marriage and household expenses dominated the budget, could now be luxury spenders, and the industrialization of the couture and beauty business from the 1960s on immediately responded. Between the top and the bottom end of the high-tech luxury markets which now developed—e.g. between the most expensive Hasselblad camera and the cheapest Olympus or Nikon that produced results while conferring status—there was only a difference of degree. In any case, starting with television, entertainments hitherto only available as personal services to millionaires were now in the most modest of living-rooms. In short, full employment and a consumer society aimed at a genuine mass market placed most of the working class in the old developed countries, at least for part of their lives, well above the threshold below which their fathers, or they themselves, had once lived: where income is primarily spent on basic necessities.

Moreover, several significant developments widened the cracks between different sections of the working classes, though this did not become evident until the end of full employment, during the economic crisis of the 1970s and 1980s, and until the pressure of neo-liberalism on the welfare policies and "corporatist" systems of industrial relations which had given substantial shelter to the weaker sections of the workers. For the top end of the working class—the skilled and supervisory—adjusted more easily to the era of modern high-tech production,* and their position was such that they could actually benefit from a free market, even as their less favoured brothers lost ground. Thus in Mrs. Thatcher's Britain, admittedly an extreme case, as government and union protection was dismantled, the bottom fifth of the workers actually became worse off compared to the rest of the workers than they had been a century earlier. And as the top 10 per cent of workers, with gross earnings three times as high as those in the bottom tenth, congratulated themselves on their improvement, they were increasingly likely to reflect that, as national and local tax-payers, they were subsidizing what came, in the 1980s, to be called by the sinister term "the underclass," who lived on the public welfare system which they themselves could, they hoped, do without except in emergencies. The old Victorian division between the "respectable" and the "unrespectable" poor revived, perhaps in a more embittered form, for in the glorious days of the global boom, when full employment seemed to take care of most of labour's material needs, welfare payments had been raised to generous levels which, in the new days of mass welfare demands, seemed to enable an army of the "unrespectable" to live far better on "welfare" than the old Victorian pauper "residuum." And far better than, in the opinion of hardworking tax-payers, they had a right to.

The skilled and respectable thus found themselves, perhaps for the first time, potential supporters of the political Right,† all the more since the traditional labour and socialist organizations naturally remained committed to redistribution and welfare, especially as the numbers of those needing public protection grew. The Thatcher governments in Britain relied for their success essentially on the secession of skilled workers from Labour. Desegregation, or rather a shift in segregation, promoted this crumbling of the labouring bloc. Thus the skilled and upwardly mobile moved out of the inner cities—especially as industries moved into periphery and country, leaving the old solid inner-city working-class districts, or "red belts," to be ghettoized or gentrified, while the new satellite towns or greenfield industries generated no single-class concentrations on the same scale. In the inner cities, public housing projects, once

---

*Thus in the U.S.A. "craftsmen and foremen" declined from 16 per cent of the total occupied population to 13 per cent between 1950 and 1990, whereas "laborers" declined from 31 per cent to 18 per cent in the same period.

†"The socialism of redistribution, of the Welfare State . . . was dealt a hard blow with the economic crisis of the seventies. Important sectors of the middle class as well as sectors of the better-paid workers, broke their links with the alternatives of democratic socialism and lent their votes to form new majorities for conservative governments" (Programma 2000, 1990).

built for the solid core of the working class, indeed with a natural bias towards those able to pay rent regularly, now turned into settlements of the marginal, the socially problematic and welfare-dependent.

At the same time mass migration brought a phenomenon hitherto confined, at least since the end of the Habsburg Empire, only to the U.S.A. and to a lesser extent France: ethnic and racial diversification of the working class and its consequence, conflicts within it. The problem lay not so much in ethnic diversity, even though the immigration of people of a different colour, or (like North Africans in France) likely to be classified as such, brought out an always latent racism even in countries that had been regarded as immune to it, such as Italy and Sweden. The weakening of traditional socialist labour movements made this easier, since these had been passionately opposed to such discrimination, and thus damped down the more anti-social expression of racist feelings within their constituency. However, leaving pure racism aside, traditionally—and even in the nineteenth century—labour migration had rarely led to that direct competition between different ethnic groups which divides working classes, since each particular group of migrants tended to find its own niche or niches in the economy, which it then colonized or even monopolized. Immigrant Jews in most Western countries moved en masse into the garment industry, but not into, say, motor manufacturing. To cite an even more specialized case, the staff of Indian restaurants in both London and New York, and no doubt wherever this form of Asian cultural expansion has reached outside the Indian subcontinent, was even in the 1990s primarily recruited from emigrants from one particular district of Bangladesh (Sylhet). Or else immigrant groups found themselves concentrated in particular districts or plants or workshops or grades of the same industry, leaving the rest to others. In such a "segmented labour market" (to use the jargon term), solidarity between different ethnic groups of workers was easier to develop and maintain, since the groups did not compete, and variations in their conditions could not—or only rarely—be ascribed to the self-interest of other groups of workers.*

For a variety of reasons, among them the fact that immigration in post-war Western Europe was largely a state-sponsored response to labour shortage, the new immigrants entered the same labour market as the natives, and with the same rights, except where they were officially

---

*Northern Ireland, where Catholics were systematically pushed out of the skilled industrial occupations which increasingly became Protestant monopolies, is an exception.

segregated from them as a class of temporary and therefore inferior "guest-workers." Both cases generated tension. Men and women with formally inferior rights hardly saw their interests as identical with people enjoying superior status. Conversely, French or British workers, even when they did not mind working side by side and on the same terms with Moroccans, West Indians, Portuguese or Turks, were by no means so ready to see foreigners promoted above them, especially those regarded as collectively inferior to the national-born. Moreover, and for similar reasons, there were tensions between different groups of immigrants, even when all resented the natives' treatment of outsiders.

In short, whereas in the period when classic labour parties and movements had been formed all sections of the workers (unless divided by unusually insuperable national or religious barriers) could reasonably assume that the same policies, strategies and institutional changes would benefit each, this was no longer automatically the case. At the same time both the changes in production, the emergence of the "two-thirds society" (see p. 340) and the changing, and increasingly fuzzy frontier between what was "manual" and what was "non-manual" work, diffused and dissolved the formerly clear outlines of "the proletariat."

IV

One major change which affected the working class, as well as most other parts of developed societies, was the strikingly greater part played in it by women; and notably—a new and revolutionary phenomenon—of married women. The change was indeed dramatic. In 1940 married women who lived with their husbands and worked for pay formed less than 14 per cent of the total female population of the U.S.A. In 1980 they formed over half: the percentage just about doubled between 1950 and 1970. That women entered the labour market in growing numbers was not, of course, new. From the end of the nineteenth century on, office work and shops and certain kinds of services, e.g. telephone exchanges and the caring professions, were powerfully feminized, and these tertiary occupations expanded and swelled at the (relative and eventually absolute) expense of both primary and secondary ones, that is to say, agriculture and industry. In fact this rise of the tertiary sector was one of the most striking tendencies of the twentieth century. It is less easy to generalize about women in manufacturing industries. In the old industrial countries the labour-intensive industries in which women had been characteristically concentrated, such as textiles and clothing, were on the decline; but so, in the new rustbelt regions and countries, were the heavy and mechanical industries with their overwhelmingly masculine, not to say macho composition—mines, iron and steel, shipbuilding, car and trucks manufacture. On the other hand, in newly developing countries, and in the enclaves of manufacture developing in the Third World, labour-intensive industries thirsty for female labour (which was traditionally less well-paid and less rebellious than male hands) flourished. The share of women in the local workforce therefore rose, though the case of Mauritius where it jumped from about 20 per cent in the early 1970s to over 60 per cent in the mid-1980s is rather extreme. Whether it grew (but less than the service sector) or remained stable in the developed industrial countries depended on national circumstances. In practice the distinction between women in manufacture and in the tertiary sector was not significant, since the bulk of them in both were in subaltern positions, and several of the feminized service occupations, notably those in the public and social services, were strongly unionized.

Women also, and in strikingly growing numbers, entered higher education, which was now the most obvious entrance gate to the (senior) professions. Immediately after the Second World War they constituted between 15 and 30 per cent of all students in most of the developed countries, except for Finland—a beacon of female emancipation—where they already formed almost 43 per cent. Even in 1960 nowhere in Europe and North America did they provide half of the students, though Bulgaria—another, and less widely advertised pro-feminine country—already almost reached that figure. (The socialist states were on the whole quicker to foster women's study—the GDR outdistanced the Federal Republic—but otherwise their feminist record was patchy.) However, in 1980 half or more than half of all students were women in the U.S.A., Canada and six socialist countries, headed by the GDR and Bulgaria, and in only four European countries did women by then constitute less than 40 per cent (Greece, Switzerland, Turkey and the U.K.). In a word, higher study was now as common among girls as among boys.

The mass entry of married women—i.e. largely mothers—into the labour market and the striking expansion of higher education formed the background, at least in the typical developed Western countries, to the impressive revival of feminist movements from the 1960s on. Indeed the women's movements are inexplicable without these developments. Since women in so many parts of Europe and North America had achieved the great aim of the vote and equal civic rights in the aftermath of the First World War and the Russian Revolution (*Age of Empire*, chapter 8), feminist movements had moved out of the sunlight into the shadows, even where the triumph of fascist and reactionary regimes had not destroyed them. They remained in the shadows, in spite of the victory of anti-fascism and (in Eastern Europe and parts of East Asia) revolution, which extended the rights won after 1917 to most countries that had not yet enjoyed them, most obviously by giving votes to the women of France and Italy in Western Europe, and indeed to women in all newly communist countries, in almost all former colonies and (in the first ten post-war years) in Latin America. Indeed, where elections were held at all, women everywhere in the world had acquired voting rights by the 1960s, except in some Islamic states and, rather curiously, in Switzerland.

Yet these changes were neither achieved by feminist pressures, nor did they have any immediate notable repercussion on the situation of women; even in the relatively few countries where voting had political effects. However, from the 1960s, starting in the U.S.A. but spreading rapidly through the rich Western countries and beyond into the elites of educated women in the dependent world—but not, initially, into the heartlands of the socialist world—we find a striking revival of feminism. While these movements belonged, essentially, to the educated middle-class milieu, it is likely that in the 1970s and especially the 1980s a politically and ideologically less specific form of women's consciousness spread among the masses of the sex (which ideologists now insisted should be called a "gender") far beyond anything achieved by the first wave of feminism. Indeed women as a group now became a major political force, as they had not done before. The first, and perhaps most striking example of this new gender-consciousness was the revolt of the traditionally faithful women in Roman Catholic countries against unpopular doctrines of the Church, as shown notably in the Italian referenda in favour of divorce (1974) and of more liberal abortion laws (1981); and later in the election to the presidency of pious Ireland of Mary Robinson, a woman lawyer very much associated with the liberalization of the Catholic moral code (1990). By the early 1990s a striking divergence of political opinions between the sexes was recorded in a number of countries by public opinion surveys. No wonder that politicians began to court this new women's consciousness, especially on the Left where the decline of working-class consciousness deprived parties of some of their older constituencies.

However, the very width of the new consciousness of femaleness and its interests makes simple explanations in terms of the changing role of women in the economy inadequate. In any case, what changed in the social revolution was not only the nature of women's own activities in society, but also the roles played by women or the conventional expectations of what those roles should be, and in particular the assumptions about the *public* roles of women and their public prominence. For while major changes, such as the massive entry of married women into the labour market might be expected to produce concomitant or consequential changes, they need not do so—as witness the U.S.S.R. where (after the initial utopian-revolutionary aspirations of the 1920s had been abandoned) married women generally found themselves carrying the double load of old household responsibilities and new wage-earning responsibilities without any change in relations between the sexes or in the public or private spheres. In any case the reasons why women in general, and especially married women, plunged into paid work had no necessary connection with their view of women's social position and rights. It might be due to poverty, to employers' preference for female over male workers as being cheaper and more biddable, or simply to the growing number—especially in the dependent world—of female-headed families. The mass labour migration of men, as from the countryside into the cities of South Africa, or from parts of Africa and Asia into the Persian Gulf states, inevitably left the women to head the family economy at home. Nor should we forget the appalling and sex-discriminating killings of the great wars, which left post-1945 Russia with five women for every three men.

None the less, the signs of significant, even revolutionary, changes in women's expectations about themselves and the world's expectations about their place in society, are undeniable. The new prominence of some women in politics was obvious, though it cannot be used in any way as a direct index of the situation of women as a whole in the countries concerned. After all, the percentage of women in the elected parliaments of macho Latin America (11 per cent) in the 1980s was considerably higher than the percentage of women in the equivalent assemblies of the demonstrably more "emancipated" North America. Again, a substantial proportion of the women who now, for the first time, found themselves heading states and governments in the dependent world did so through family inheritance: Indira Gandhi (India 1966–84) and Benazir Bhutto (Pakistan 1988–90; 1994) and Aung San Suu Kiy, who would have been chief of Burma but for the military veto, as daughters; Sirimavo Bandaranaike (Sri Lanka, 1960–65; 1970–77) and Corazon Acquino (Philippines, 1986–92) and Isabel Perón (Argentina, 1974–76) as widows. This was in itself no more revolutionary than the succession of Maria Theresa or Victoria to the throne of the Habsburg and British Empires long before. Indeed, the contrast between the female rulers of such countries as India, Pakistan and the Philippines, and the exceptionally depressed and oppressed state of women in their parts of the world underlines their untypicality.

And yet, before the Second World War, the succession of any woman to the leadership of any republic under *any* circumstances would have been regarded as politically unthinkable. After 1945 it became politically possible—Sirimavo Bandaranaike in Sri Lanka became the world's first woman premier in 1960—and by 1990 women were or had been heads of government in sixteen states (World's Women, p. 32). In the 1990s even the woman who had got to the top as a career politician was an accepted if uncommon part of the landscape: as prime minister in Israel (1969); Iceland (1980); Norway (1981); not least in Great Britain (1979); in Lithuania (1990); and France (1991); in the shape of Doi, accepted leader of the main (socialist) opposition party, in the far from feminist Japan (1986). The political world was indeed changing fast, even though the public recognition of women (if only as a political pressure group) still usually took the form, even in many of the most "advanced" countries, of symbolic or token representation on public bodies.

However, it makes little sense to generalize globally about the role of women in the public sphere, and the corresponding public aspirations of women's political movements. The dependent world, the developed world and the socialist or ex-socialist world are only marginally comparable. In the Third World, as in Tsarist Russia, the great mass of lower-class and poorly educated women remained outside the public sphere, in the modern "Western" sense, though some of these countries developed, and some already had, a small stratum of exceptionally emancipated and "advanced" women, mainly wives, daughters and other female kin of the established indigenous upper classes and bourgeoisies, analogous to the corresponding female intelligentsia and activists of Tsarist Russia. Such a stratum had existed in the Indian Empire even in colonial times, and seems to have emerged in several of the less rigorist Islamic countries—notably Egypt, Iran, Lebanon and the Maghreb—until the rise of Muslim fundamentalism pushed women into obscurity again. For these emancipated minorities a public space existed on the upper social levels of their own countries, where they could act and feel at home in much the same way as they (or their opposite numbers) could in Europe and North America, though probably they were slower to abandon the sexual conventions and traditional family obligations of their culture than Western women, or at least non-Catholic ones.* In this respect emancipated

---

*It can hardly be an accident that the rates of divorce and re-marriage in Italy, Ireland, Spain and Portugal were spectacularly lower in the 1980s than in the rest of

women in the "Westernized" dependent countries were far more favourably situated than their sisters in, say, the non-socialist Far East,
where the force of traditional roles and conventions to which even elite
women had to conform, was enormous and stifling. Educated Japanese or
Korean women who found themselves in the emancipated West for a few
years often dreaded the return to their own civilizations, and to an as yet
only marginally eroded sense of women's subordination.

In the socialist world the situation was paradoxical. Practically all
women were in the paid labour force in Eastern Europe—or at least it
contained almost as many women as men (90 per cent), a far higher proportion than anywhere else. Communism as an ideology had been passionately committed to women's equality and liberation, in every sense
including the erotic, in spite of Lenin's own dislike of casual sexual
promiscuity.* (However, both Krupskaya and Lenin were among the rare
revolutionaries who specifically favoured the sharing of housework between the sexes.) Moreover, the revolutionary movement, from the Narodniks through the Marxists, had welcomed women, especially intellectual
ones, with exceptional warmth, and had provided exceptional scope for
them, as was still evident in the 1970s when they were disproportionately
represented in some of the Left-wing terrorist movements. Yet, with
rather rare exceptions (Rosa Luxemburg, Ruth Fischer, Anna Pauker, La
Pasionaria, Federica Montseny) they were not prominent in the first political ranks of their parties, or indeed at all,† and in the new communist-
governed states they became even less visible. Indeed, women in leading
political functions virtually disappeared. As we have seen, one or two
countries, notably Bulgaria and the German Democratic Republic, clearly
gave their women unusually good chances of public prominence, as indeed of higher education, yet, on the whole, the public position of

---

the West European and North American zone. Divorce rates: 0.58 per 1,000 population, against 2.5 for a mean of nine other countries (Belgium, France, Federal Germany, Netherlands, Sweden, Switzerland, U.K., Canada, U.S.A.). Remarriages (per
cent of all marriages): 2.4 against 18.6 for a mean of nine countries.

*Thus the right to abortion, forbidden by the German Civil Code, was an im-
portant issue for agitation by the German Communist Party, which is why the German Democratic Republic was to enjoy a far more liberal abortion law than the
(Christian-Democrat-influenced) German Federal Republic, thus complicating the
legal problems of German unification in 1990.

†In the KPD, 1929, out of sixty-three members and candidate members of the
Central Committee there were six women. Out of 504 leading party members
1924–29, just 7 per cent were women.

women in communist countries was not notably different from that in developed capitalist ones, and, where it was, it did not necessarily bring advantages. When women streamed into a profession opened to them, as in the U.S.S.R., where the medical profession became largely feminized in consequence, it lost status and income. As against Western feminists, most married Soviet women, long used to a lifetime of paid work, dreamed of the luxury of staying at home and doing only one job.

Indeed, the original revolutionary dream of transforming the relations between the sexes and of altering the institutions and habits that embodied the old masculine domination generally ran into the sand, even where—as in the early years of the U.S.S.R., but not, in general, in the new European communist regimes after 1944—it was seriously pursued. In backward countries, and most communist regimes were established in such countries, it was blocked by the passive non-cooperation of traditional populations, who insisted that in practice, whatever the law said, women were treated as less than men. The heroic efforts at female emancipation were not, of course, in vain. To give women equal legal and political rights, to insist on their access to education and men's work and men's responsibilities, even to unveil them and allow them to come and go freely in public, are not small changes, as anyone can verify who compares women's predicament in countries where religious fundamentalism rules or is re-imposed. Moreover, even in those communist countries where female reality lagged rather far behind theory, even at times when governments imposed a virtual moral counter-revolution, seeking to re-install the family and women as basically child-bearers (as in the U.S.S.R. in the 1930s), the sheer freedom of personal choice available to them under the new system, including the freedom of sexual choice, was incomparably greater than it could have been before the new regime. Its real limits were not so much legal or conventional as material, like the shortage of devices for birth-control for which, as for other gynaecological needs, the planned economy made only the faintest provision.

Still, whatever the achievements and failures of the socialist world, it did not generate specifically feminist movements, and could indeed hardly have done so, given the virtual impossibility of any political initiatives not sponsored by state and party before the mid-1980s. However, it is unlikely that the issues which preoccupied feminist movements in the West would have found much echo in the communist states before then.

Initially these issues in the West, and notably in the U.S.A., which pioneered the revival of feminism, were mainly concerned with problems affecting middle-class women, or in the form which chiefly affected them. This is fairly evident if we look at the occupations in the U.S.A. where feminist pressure achieved its major breakthrough, and which, presumably, reflect the concentration of its efforts. By 1981 women had not only virtually eliminated men from office and white-collar occupations, most of which were indeed subaltern though respectable, but they formed almost 50 per cent of real-estate agents and brokers and almost 40 per cent of bank officers and financial managers, and they had established a substantial, though still inadequate presence in the intellectual professions, although the traditional professions of law and medicine still confined them to modest bridgeheads. But if 35 per cent of college and university teachers, over a quarter of computer specialists, and 22 per cent of those in the natural sciences were now women the masculine monopolies of manual labour, skilled and unskilled, remained virtually undented: only 2.7 per cent of truck-drivers, 1.6 per cent of electricians and 0.6 per cent of automobile mechanics were female. Their resistance to the female influx was certainly no weaker than that of doctors and lawyers, who had made way for 14 per cent of them; but it is not unreasonable to suppose that the pressure to conquer these bastions of masculinity was less.

Even a cursory reading of the American pioneers of the new feminism in the 1960s suggests a distinct class perspective on women's problems (Friedan, 1963; Degler, 1987). They were heavily concerned with the question "how a woman could combine career or job with marriage and family," one which was central only to those who have this choice, which did not then exist for most of the world's women and for all the poor ones. They were, with entire justification, concerned with *equality* between men and women, a concept that became the chief tool for the legal and institutional advance of Western women, since the word "sex" was inserted into the American Civil Rights Act of 1964, which was originally intended to prohibit only racial discrimination. But "equality" or rather "equal treatment" and "equal opportunity" assume that there are no significant differences between men and women, social or otherwise, and for most of the world's women, and especially the poor, it seemed obvious that part of the social inferiority of women was due to their difference as a sex from men and might therefore require sex-specific remedies— for instance special provisions for pregnancy and maternity or special protection against attacks by the physically stronger and more aggressive sex. U.S. feminism was slow to address such vital interests of working-class women as maternity leave. A later phase of feminism did indeed learn to insist on gender difference as well as gender inequality, even though the use of a liberal ideology of abstract individualism and the tool of "equal rights" law was not readily compatible with the recognition that women were not, and ought not necessarily to be, like men, and the other way round.*

Moreover, in the 1950s and 1960s the very demand to break out of the domestic sphere into the paid labour market had a strong ideological charge among the prosperous, educated middle-class married women which it did not have for others, for its motivations in these milieux were seldom economic. Among the poor, or those with tight budgets, married women went out to work after 1945 because, to put it crudely, children no longer did so. Child labour in the West had almost vanished, while on the contrary, the need to give children an education that would improve their prospects, put a greater financial burden on their parents for longer than in the past. In short, as has been said, "in the past children had worked so that their mothers could remain at home fulfilling domestic and reproductive responsibilities. Now when families needed additional income, mothers worked instead of children" (Tilly/Scott, 1987, p. 219). This could hardly have been possible without fewer children, even though a substantial mechanisation of household chores (notably by means of the domestic washing machines) and the rise of prepared and ready-cooked foods also made it easier. But for married middle-class women whose husbands earned an income suitable to their status, going out to work rarely made much of an addition to the family income, if only because women were paid so much less than men in the jobs then available for them. It might make no significant net contribution to the family when enough paid help to look after household and children had to be hired (in the form of cleaners and, in Europe, *au pair* girls) to enable the woman to earn an outside income.

If there was an incentive for married women to go outside the home in those circles, it was the demand for freedom and autonomy: for the

---

*Thus "affirmative action," i.e. giving a group *preferential* treatment in access to some social resource or activity, is consistent with equality only on the assumption that it is a temporary measure, to be phased out when equal access has been achieved on its own merits; i.e. that on the assumption that preferential treatment is merely the removal of an unfair handicap on entrants to the same race. This is obviously sometimes the case. But where we deal with permanent differences it cannot be to the point. It is absurd, even at first sight, to give men priority in entering courses on coloratura singing or to insist that it is theoretically desirable, on demographic grounds, that 50 per cent of army generals should be women. On the other hand it is entirely legitimate to give every man with the wish and potential qualification to sing *Norma*, and every woman with the wish and potential to lead an army, their chance to do so.

married woman to be a person in her own right and not an appendage of husband and household, someone judged by the world as an individual and not a member of a species ("just a housewife and mother"). Income came into it not because it was needed, but because it was something that a woman could spend or save without asking her husband first. Of course, as two-income middle-class households became more common, family budgets were increasingly calculated in terms of two incomes. Indeed, as higher education for middle-class children became almost universal, and parents might have to make financial contributions to their offspring into the late twenties or even later, paid work for middle-class married women ceased to be primarily a declaration of independence and became what it had long been for the poor, a way of making ends meet. Nevertheless, the consciously emancipatory element in it did not disappear, as the growth of "commuting marriages" showed. For the costs (and not only the financial ones) of marriages in which each spouse worked in often widely distant locations were high, though the revolution in transport and communications made it increasingly common in professions such as the academic, from the 1970s on. Yet where once middle-class wives (though not children above a certain age) had almost automatically followed wherever husbands' new jobs took them, it now became almost unthinkable, at least in middle-class intellectual circles, to disrupt the woman's own career, and her right to decide where she wanted to conduct it. At last, it seemed, men and women treated one another as equals in this respect.*

Nevertheless, in the developed countries of the world, middle-class feminism, or the movement of educated or intellectual women, broadened out into a sort of generic sense that the time for women's liberation, or at least women's self-assertion, had come. This was because the specific early middle-class feminism, though sometimes not directly relevant to the concerns of the rest of Western femininity, raised questions that concerned all: and these questions became urgent as the social upheaval we have sketched generated a profound, and in many ways sudden, moral and cultural revolution, a dramatic transformation of the conventions of social and personal behaviour. Women were crucial to this cultural revolution, since it pivoted on, and found expression in, changes in the traditional family and household of which they had always been the central element.

To this we must now turn.

---

*Though rarer, cases where the husband faced the problem of following where his wife's new job took her also became more frequent. Any academic of the 1990s could think of some examples within his or her personal acquaintance.

CHAPTER ELEVEN

Cultural Revolution

In the film, Carmen Maura plays a man who's had a transsexual operation and, due to an unhappy love-affair with his/her father, has given up men to have a lesbian (I guess) relationship with a woman, who is played by a famous Madrid transvestite.

—Film-review in the *Village Voice*, Paul Berman (1987, p. 572)

Successful demonstrations are not necessarily those which mobilize the greatest number of people, but those which attract the greatest interest among journalists. Exaggerating only slightly, one might say that fifty clever folk who can make a successful "happening" get five minutes on TV, can have as much political effect as half a million demonstrators.

—Pierre Bourdieu (1994)

I

The best approach to this cultural revolution is therefore through family and household, i.e. through the structure of relations between the sexes and generations. In most societies this had been impressively resistant to sudden change, though this does not mean that such structures were static. Moreover, in spite of appearances to the contrary, patterns were world-wide, or at least had basic similarities over very wide areas, although it has been suggested, on socio-economic and technological grounds, that there is a major difference between Eurasia (including both sides of the Mediterranean) on one hand, and the rest of Africa on the other (Goody, 1990, XVII). Thus polygamy, which is said to have been almost completely absent or had become so in Eurasia, except for specially privileged groups and in the Arab world, flourished in Africa, where more than a quarter of all marriages are said to be polygamous (Goody, 1990, p. 379).

Nevertheless, across all variations the vast majority of humanity shared a number of characteristics, such as the existence of formal marriage with privileged sex-relations for the spouses ("adultery" is universally treated as an offence); the superiority of husbands to wives ("patriarchy") and of parents to children, as well as of senior to junior generations; family households consisting of several people, and the like. Whatever the extent and complexity of the kinship network and the mutual rights and obligations within it, a nuclear residence—a couple plus children—was generally present somewhere, even when the co-resident or co-operating group or household was much larger. The idea that the nuclear family, which became the standard model in nineteenth and twentieth century Western society, had in some way evolved out of much larger family and kinship units, as part of the growth of bourgeois or any other individualism, rests on a historical misunderstanding, not least of the nature of social co-operation and its rationale in preindustrial societies. Even in so communist an institution as the Balkan Slavs' *zadruga* or joint family, "every woman works for her family in the narrow sense of the word, namely her husband and children, but also, when it is her turn, for the unmarried members of the community and the orphans" (Guidetti/Stahl, 1977, p. 58). The existence of such a family and household nucleus does not, of course, mean that the kin groups or communities within which it is to be found are in other respects similar.

Yet in the second half of the twentieth century these basic and long-lasting arrangements began to change with express speed, at all events in the "developed" Western countries, though unevenly, even within these regions. Thus in England and Wales—admittedly a rather dramatic example—in 1938 there was one divorce for every fifty-eight weddings (Mitchell, 1975, p. 30–32), but in the mid-1980s one for every 2.2 new weddings (*U.N. Statistical Yearbook*, 1987). Moreover, we can see the acceleration of this trend in the freewheeling 1960s. At the end of the 1970s there were more than ten divorces for every thousand married couples in England and Wales, or five times as many as in 1961 (*Social Trends*, 1980, p. 84).

This trend was by no means confined to Britain. Indeed, the spectacular change is most clearly seen in countries with strongly compelling traditional moralities such as Catholic ones. In Belgium, France and the Netherlands the crude divorce rate (annual number of divorces per thousand population) roughly trebled between 1970 and 1985. However, even in countries with a tradition of emancipation in these matters, like

Denmark and Norway, they could double or almost double in the same period. Clearly something unusual was happening to Western marriage. The women attending a gynaecological clinic in California in the 1970s showed "a substantial decrease in formal marriage, a reduction in the wish for children . . . and an attitudinal shift towards acceptance of a bisexual adaptation" (Esman, 1990, p. 67). It is unlikely that such a reaction from a cross-section of women would have been recorded anywhere, even in California, before that decade.

The number of people living alone (i.e. not as a member of any couple or larger family) also began to shoot up. In Britain they stayed much the same for the first third of the century at about 6 per cent of all households, drifting upwards fairly gently thereafter. Yet between 1960 and 1980 the percentage almost doubled from 12 per cent to 22 per cent of all households and by 1991 it was more than one-quarter (Abrams, Carr-Saunders, *Social Trends*, 1993, p. 26). In many Western big cities they formed about half of all households. Conversely, the classical Western nuclear family, the married couple with children, was in patent retreat. In the U.S.A. such families fell from 44 per cent of all households to 29 per cent in twenty years (1960–80); in Sweden, where almost half of all births in the mid-1980s were to unmarried women (World's Women, p. 16), from 37 per cent to 25 per cent. Even in the developed countries where they had still formed half or more than half of all households in 1960 (Canada, Federal Germany, Netherlands, Britain) the nuclear family was now a distinct minority.

In particular cases, it ceased to be even nominally typical. Thus in 1991 58 per cent of all black families in the U.S.A. were headed by a single woman and 70 per cent of all children were born to single mothers. In 1940 only 11.3 per cent of "non-white" families had been headed by single mothers, and even in cities, only 12.4 per cent (Franklin Frazier, 1957, p. 317). Even in 1970 the figure had only been 33 per cent (*New York Times*, 5/10/92).

The crisis of the family was linked with quite dramatic changes in the public standards governing sexual behaviour, partnership and procreation. These were both official and unofficial, and the major change in both is datable, and coincides with the 1960s and 1970s. Officially this was an extraordinary era of liberalization both for heterosexuals (i.e. mainly for women, who had enjoyed so much less freedom than men) and homosexuals, as well as for other forms of cultural-sexual dissidence. In Britain most homosexuality was de-criminalized in the second half of the 1960s, a few years later than the U.S.A., where the first state to make sodomy legal (Illinois) did so in 1961 (Johansson/Percy, p. 304, 1349). In the

Pope's own Italy divorce became legal in 1970, a right confirmed by referendum in 1974. The sale of contraceptives and birth-control information was legalized in 1971, and in 1975 a new family code replaced the old one which had survived from the fascist period. Finally, abortion became legal in 1978, confirmed by referendum in 1981.

Though permissive laws undoubtedly made hitherto forbidden acts easier, and gave far more publicity to these matters, the law recognized rather than created the new climate of sexual relaxation. That in the 1950s only 1 per cent of British women had cohabited for any length of time with their future husband before marriage was not due to legislation, and neither was the fact that in the early 1980s 21 per cent of them did so (Gillis, 1985, p. 307). Things now became permissible which had hitherto been prohibited, not only by law and religion, but also by customary morality, convention and neighbourhood opinion.

These tendencies did not, of course, affect all parts of the world evenly. While divorce increased in all countries where it was available (assuming, for the moment, that formal dissolution of mariage by official action had the same meaning in all of them), marriage had clearly become much less stable in some. In the 1980s it remained much more permanent in (non-communist) Roman Catholic countries. Divorce was far less common in the Iberian peninsula and in Italy and even rarer in Latin America; even in countries priding themselves on their sophistication: one divorce per twenty-two weddings in Mexico, per thirty-three in Brazil (but one per 2.5 in Cuba). South Korea remained unusually traditional for so fast-moving a country (one per eleven weddings), but in the early 1980s even Japan had a divorce rate less than one quarter of the French and far below the readily divorcing British and Americans. Even within the (then) socialist world there were variations, though smaller than in capitalism, except for the U.S.S.R. which was second only to the U.S.A. in its citizens' readiness to break up their marriages (U.N. World Social Situation, 1989, p. 36). Such variations cause no surprise. What was and is far more interesting is that, large or small, the same transformations can be traced across the entire "modernizing" globe. Nowhere was this more striking than in the field of popular, or more specifically of youth culture.

II

For if divorce, illegitimate births and the rise of the single-parent (i.e. overwhelmingly the single-mother) household indicated a crisis in the relation between the sexes, the rise of a specific, and extraordinarily powerful youth culture indicated a profound change in the relation between the generations. Youth, as a self-conscious group stretching from puberty—which in developed countries occurred several years earlier than in previous generations (Tanner, 1962, p. 153)—to the middle twenties, now became an independent social agent. The most dramatic political developments, particularly in the 1960s and 1970s, were the mobilizations of the age-band which, in less politicized countries, made the fortunes of the record industry, 75–80 per cent of whose output—namely rock music—was sold almost wholly to customers between the ages of fourteen and twenty-five (Hobsbawm, 1993, p. xxviii–xxix). The political radicalization of the 1960s, anticipated by smaller contingents of cultural dissidents and drop-outs under various labels, belonged to these young people, who rejected the status of children, or even adolescents (i.e. not-quite-mature adults), while denying full humanity to any generation above the age of thirty, except for the occasional guru.

Except in China, where the ancient Mao mobilized the youth levies to terrible effect (see chapter 16) the young radicals were led—insofar as they accepted leaders—by members of their peer-group. This was patently true of the world-wide student movements, but where these sparked off mass labour uprisings, as in France and Italy in 1968–69, the initiative there also came from young workers. Nobody with even minimal experience of the limitations of real life, i.e. no genuine adult, could have drafted the confident but patently absurd slogans of the Parisian May days of 1968 or the Italian "hot autumn" of 1969: "*tutto e subito,*" we want everything and we want it now (Albers/Goldschmidt/Oehlke, pp. 59, 184).

The new "autonomy" of youth as a separate social stratum was symbolized by a phenomenon which, on this scale, probably had no parallel since the romantic era of the early nineteenth century: the hero whose life and youth ended together. This figure, anticipated in the 1950s by the film star James Dean, was common, perhaps even ideal-typical, in what became the characteristic cultural expression of youth—rock music. Buddy Holly, Janis Joplin, Brian Jones of the Rolling Stones, Bob Marley, Jimi Hendrix and a number of other popular divinities fell victim to a life-style designed for early death. What made such deaths symbolic was that youth, which they represented, was impermanent by definition. To be an actor can be a lifetime career, but not to be a *jeune premier.*

Nevertheless, though the membership of youth is always changing—a student "generation" notoriously lasts a bare three or four years—its ranks are always being re-filled. The emergence of the adolescent as self-conscious social actor was increasingly recognized, enthusiastically by the manufacturers of consumer goods, sometimes less willingly by his or her seniors, as they found the space expanding between those who were willing to accept the label "child" and those who insisted on that of "adult." In the mid-sixties even Baden Powell's own movement, the English Boy Scouts, dropped the first part of their name as a concession to the mood of the times, and exchanged the old scout sombrero for the less obtrusive beret (Gillis, 1974, p. 197).

Age groups are nothing new in societies, and even in bourgeois civilization a stratum of those who are sexually mature but still engaged in physical and intellectual growth, and lack the experience of adult life, had been recognized. That this group was becoming younger in age as puberty began and maximum heights were reached earlier (Floud et al., 1990) did not in itself change the situation. It merely caused tension between the young and their parents and teachers who insisted on treating them as less grown-up than they felt themselves to be. Bourgeois milieux had expected that their young men—as distinct from their young women—passed through a period of turbulence and "sowing their wild oats" on the way to "settling down." The novelty of the new youth culture was threefold.

First, "youth" was seen not as a preparatory stage of adulthood but, in some sense, as the final stage of full human development. As in sport, the human activity in which youth is supreme, and which now defined the ambitions of more human beings than any other, life clearly went downhill after the age of thirty. At best, after that age it held little more of interest. That this did not, in fact, correspond to a social reality in which (except for sport, some forms of entertainment and perhaps pure mathematics) power, influence and achievement as well as wealth rose with age, was one more proof of the unsatisfactory way the world was organized. For, until the 1970s, the post-war world was actually governed by a gerontocracy to a greater extent than in most earlier periods, namely by men—hardly as yet by women—who had been adults at the end, or even at the beginning, of the First World War. This applied both to the capitalist world (Adenauer, de Gaulle, Franco, Churchill) and to the communist world (Stalin and Khrushchev, Mao, Ho-Chi-Minh, Tito), as well as to the large post-colonial states (Gandhi, Nehru, Sukarno). A leader below forty was a rarity even in revolutionary regimes emerging from military coups, a type of political change usually made by relatively junior officers because these have less to lose than senior ones. Hence much of the international impact of Fidel Castro, who captured power at the age of thirty-two.

Nevertheless, silent and perhaps not always conscious concessions to the juvenescence of society were made by the establishments of the old, and not least by the flourishing industries of cosmetics, hair-care and personal hygiene, which benefited disproportionately from the accumulating wealth of a few developed countries.* From the end of the 1960s there was a tendency to lower the voting age to eighteen—e.g. in the U.S.A., Britain, Germany and France—and also some sign of a lowering of the age of consent for (heterosexual) sexual intercourse. Paradoxically, as the expectation of life lengthened, the percentage of the old increased and, at least among the favoured upper and middle classes, senile decline was postponed, retirement was reached sooner and, in times of difficulty, "early retirement" became a favourite method of cutting labour costs. Business executives over forty who lost their jobs found it as hard as manual and white-collar workers to find new ones.

The second novelty of the youth culture follows from the first: it was or became dominant in the "developed market economies," partly because it now represented a concentrated mass of purchasing power, partly because each new generation of adults had been socialized as part of a self-conscious youth culture and bore the marks of this experience, and not least because the amazing speed of technological change actually gave youth a measurable advantage over more conservative, or at least more inadaptable age. Whatever the age-structure of the management of IBM or Hitachi, new computers were designed, new software devised, by people in their twenties. Even when such machines and programmes had been hopefully made idiot-proof, the generation that had not grown up with them was acutely aware of its inferiority to the generations that had. What children could learn from parents became less obvious than what parents did not know and children did. The role of generations was reversed. Blue jeans, the deliberately demotic wear pioneered on American college campuses by students who did *not* wish to look like their elders, came to appear, on weekdays and holidays, or even, in "creative" or other hip occupations at work, below many a grey head.

The third peculiarity of the new youth culture in urban societies was its astonishing internationalism. Blue jeans and rock music became the

---

*Of the global "personal products" market in 1990, 34 per cent was in non-communist Europe, 30 per cent in North America and 19 per cent in Japan. The remaining 85 per cent of the world's population divided 16–17 per cent among its (richer) members (*Financial Times*, 11/4/1991)

marks of "modern" youth, of the minorities destined to become majorities, in every country in which they were officially tolerated and in some where they were not, as in the U.S.S.R. from the 1960s on (Starr, 1990, chapters 12 to 13). The English language of rock lyrics was often not even translated. This reflected the overwhelming cultural hegemony of the U.S.A. in popular culture and life-styles, although it should be noted that the heartlands of Western youth culture themselves were the opposite of culturally chauvinist, especially in their musical tastes. They welcomed styles imported from the Caribbean, Latin America and, from the 1980s, increasingly Africa.

This cultural hegemony was not new, but its *modus operandi* had changed. Between the wars its chief vector had been the American film industry, the only one with a mass global distribution. It was seen by a public of hundreds of millions which reached its maximum size just after the Second World War. With the rise of television, of international film production and with the end of the Hollywood studio system, the American industry lost some of its predominance and more of its public. In 1960 it produced no more than one sixth of the world film output even without counting Japan and India (*U.N. Statistical Yearbook*, 1961), although eventually it was to recover much of its hegemony. The U.S.A. never managed to establish a comparable hold on the vast and linguistically more diversified markets of television. Its youth styles spread directly, or through amplification of their signals *via* the cultural halfway house of Britain, by a sort of informal osmosis. It spread through records and later tapes, whose major medium of promotion, then as before and since, was old-fashioned radio. It spread through the world distribution of images; through the personal contacts of international youth tourism, which distributed small but growing and influential streams of young men and women in jeans across the globe; through the world network of universities, whose capacity for rapid international communication became obvious in the 1960s. Not least, it spread through the force of fashion in the consumer society which now reached the masses, magnified by pressure within peer-groups. A global youth culture had come into being.

Could it have emerged in any earlier period? Almost certainly not. Its constituency would have been far smaller, relatively and absolutely, for the lengthening of full-time education, and especially the creation of vast populations of young men and women living together as an age-group in universities, dramatically expanded it. Moreover, even the adolescents who entered the full-time labour market at school-leaving age (between fourteen and sixteen in the typical "developed" country) had far more independent spending power than their predecessors, thanks to the prosperity and full employment of the Golden Age; and thanks to the greater prosperity of their parents, who had less need of their children's contribution to the family budget. It was the discovery of this youth market in the mid-1950s which revolutionized the pop music business and, in Europe, the mass-market end of the fashion industries. The British "teen-age boom" which began at this time, was based on the urban concentrations of relatively well-paid girls in the expanding offices and shops, often with more to spend than the boys, and in those days less committed to the traditional male patterns of expenditure on beer and cigarettes. The boom "first revealed its strength in fields where girls' purchases were pre-eminent, like blouses, skirts, cosmetics and pop records" (Allen, 1968, pp. 62–63), not to mention pop concerts, of which they were the most prominent and audible attenders. The power of young money may be measured by the sales of records in the U.S.A. which rose from $277 millions in 1955 when rock appeared, to six hundred millions in 1959 and two thousand millions in 1973 (Hobsbawm, 1993, p. xxix). Every member of the five to nineteen-year age-group in the U.S.A. spent at least five times as much on records in 1970 as in 1955. The richer the country, the greater the record business: youngsters in the U.S.A., Sweden, West Germany, the Netherlands and Britain spent between seven and ten times as much per head as those in poorer but rapidly developing countries like Italy and Spain.

Independent market power made it easier for youth to discover material or cultural symbols of identity. However, what sharpened the outlines of that identity was the enormous historical gap which separated the generations born before, say, 1925 from those born after, say, 1950; a gap far greater than that between parents and children in the past. Most parents with teen-age children became acutely aware of it in and after the 1960s. The young lived in societies sundered from their past, whether transformed by revolution, as in China, Yugoslavia or Egypt; by conquest and occupation, as in Germany and Japan; or by colonial liberation. They had no memory of the era before the deluge. Except perhaps through the shared experience of a great national war, such as bonded old and young together for a while in Russia and Britain, they had no way of understanding what their elders had experienced or felt—even when these were prepared to talk about the past, as most German, Japanese and French ones were reluctant to do. How could a young Indian, to whom Congress was a government or a political machine, understand one for whom it had been the expression of a nation struggling to be free? How, even, could the brilliant young Indian economists who swept the world's university departments understand their own teachers, for whom the height of ambition in the colonial period had been simply to become "as good as" their metropolitan models?

The Golden Age widened this gap, at least until the 1970s. How could boys and girls, growing up in an era of full employment, understand the experience of the 1930s, or, conversely, an older generation understand the young for whom a job was not a safe haven after stormy seas (especially a secure one with pension rights), but something that could be got at any time and abandoned any time a person felt like going to Nepal for a few months? This version of the generation gap was not confined to the industrial countries, for the dramatic decline of the peasantry created a similar chasm between rural and ex-rural, manual and mechanized generations. French history professors, brought up in a France where every child came from a farm or passed its vacations there, discovered they had to explain to students in the 1970s what milkmaids had done and what a farmyard with a dungheap looked like. What is more, this generation gap affected even those—the majority of the world's inhabitants—whom the great political events of the century had passed by or who had no particular opinions about them, except insofar as they affected their private lives.

But, of course, whether or not these events had passed them by, the majority of the world's population was now younger than ever. Over the greater part of the Third World where the demographic transition from high to low birthrates had not yet taken place, anything between two fifths and half the inhabitants at any moment of the second half of the century were likely to be less than fourteen years old. However strong their family ties, however powerful the web of tradition that enmeshed them, there could not but be a vast gap between their understanding of life, their experiences and expectations, and those of older generations. The South African political exiles who returned to their country in the early 1990s had a different understanding of what it meant to fight for the African National Congress from the youthful "comrades" who carried the same flag in the African townships. Conversely, what could the majority in Soweto, born long after Nelson Mandela entered jail, make of him other than as a symbol or an icon? In many ways in such countries the generation gap was even greater than in the West, where permanent institutions and political continuity bound old and young together.

III

Youth culture became the matrix of the cultural revolution in the wider sense of a revolution in manners and customs, in ways of spending leisure and in the commercial arts, which increasingly formed the atmosphere that urban men and women breathed. Two of its characteristics are therefore relevant. It was both demotic and antinomian, especially in matters of personal conduct. Everyone was to "do their own thing" with minimal outside restraint, although in practice peer pressure and fashion actually imposed as much uniformity as before, at least within peer-groups and subcultures.

That the upper social strata should let themselves be inspired by what they found among "the people" was not a novelty in itself. Even if we leave aside Queen Marie Antoinette playing at milkmaids, the romantics had adored rural folk culture, folk music and folk dance, their hippier intellectuals (Baudelaire) had fancied the urban *nostalgie de la boue* (the longing for the gutter), and many a Victorian had found that sex with someone from the lower orders, gender depending on taste, was unusually rewarding. (Such feelings were far from extinct in the late twentieth century.) In the Age of Empire cultural influences for the first time began to move systematically upward (see *Age of Empire*, chapter 9) both through the powerful impact of the newly developing plebeian arts and through the cinema, the mass market entertainment par excellence. Yet most of the popular and commercial entertainments between the wars remained in many ways under middle-class hegemony or were brought under its umbrella. The classic Hollywood movie industry was, above all, *respectable;* its social ideal that of the U.S. version of solid "family values," its ideology that of patriotic oratory. Whenever, in the pursuit of the box-office queue, it discovered a genre incompatible with the moral universe of the fifteen "Andy Hardy" films (1937–47) which won an Academy Award for "furthering the American way of life" (Halliwell, 1988, p. 321), as for instance in the early gangster movies which risked idealizing delinquents, the moral order was soon restored, insofar as it was not already in the safe hands of the Hollywood Production Code (1934–66), which limited the permissible time for screen kisses (with mouth shut) to a maximum of thirty seconds. The greatest triumphs of Hollywood—say, *Gone With the Wind*—were based on novels designed for middle-class middle-brow reading, and belonged to that cultural universe as firmly as Thackeray's *Vanity Fair* or Edmond Rostand's *Cyrano de Bergerac*. Only the anarchic and demotic genre of vaudeville and circus-born film comedy resisted gentrification for a while, although in the 1930s even it retreated under the pressure of a brilliant boulevard genre, the Hollywood "crazy comedy."

Again, the triumphant Broadway "musical" of the inter-war years, and the dance-tunes and ballads which studded it, were a bourgeois genre, though one unthinkable without the influence of jazz. They were written for a middle-class New York public with librettos and song-lyrics plainly addressed to an adult audience that saw itself as one of emancipated urban sophisticates. A rapid comparison of the lyrics of Cole Porter with those of the Rolling Stones will make the point. Like the golden age of Hollywood, the golden age of Broadway rested on a symbiosis of the plebeian and the respectable, but it was not demotic.

The novelty of the 1950s was that the upper- and middle-class young, at least in the Anglo-Saxon world which increasingly set the global tone, began to accept the music, the clothes, even the language of the urban lower classes, or what they took to be such, as their model. Rock music was the most startling example. In the mid-1950s it suddenly broke out of the ghetto of "Race" or "Rhythm and Blues" catalogues of American record companies, aimed at poor U.S. blacks, to become the universal idiom of the young, and notably of the *white* young. Young working-class dandies in the past had sometimes taken their styles from high fashion in the upper social strata or from such middle-class subcultures as the artistic boheme; working-class girls even more so. Now a curious reversal seemed to take place. The fashion market for the plebeian young established its independence and began to set the tone for the patrician market. As blue jeans (for both sexes) advanced, Paris *haute couture* retreated, or rather accepted defeat by using its prestigious names to sell mass-market products, directly or under licence. Nineteen sixty-five, by the way, was the first year when the French women's clothing industry produced more trousers than skirts (Veillon, p. 6). Young aristocrats began to shed the accents which, in Britain, had infallibly identified members of their class and began to talk an approximation to London working-class speech.* Respectable young men and, increasingly, young women, began to copy what had once been a strictly unrespectable macho fashion among manual workers, soldiers and the like, the casual use of obscenities in conversation. Literature kept pace: a brilliant theatrical critic brought the word "fuck" to the radio public. For the first time in the history of the fairy tale, Cinderella became the belle of the ball by *not* wearing splendid clothes.

This demotic turn in the tastes of the middle- and upper-class young in the Western world, which even had some parallels in the Third World

---

*The young men at Eton began to do so at the end of the 1950s, according to a vice-provost of that elite institution.

with the Brazilian intellectuals' championship of the *samba*,* may or may not have something to do with the rush of middle-class students into revolutionary politics and ideology a few years later. Fashion is often prophetic, nobody knows how. It was almost certainly reinforced among male youth by the public emergence, in the new climate of liberalism, of a homosexual subculture of singular importance as trend-setters in fashion and in the arts. However, perhaps it is not necessary to assume more than that the demotic style was a convenient way of rejecting the values of parental generations or, more precisely, a language in which the young could grope for ways of dealing with a world to which their seniors' rules and values no longer seemed relevant.

The essential antinomianism of the new youth culture came out most clearly at the moments when it found intellectual expression, as in the instantly famous posters of the Paris May days of 1968: "It is forbidden to forbid," and the American pop radical Jerry Rubin's maxim that one should never trust anyone who had not done time (in jail) (Wiener, 1984, p. 204). Contrary to first appearances, these were not political statements in the traditional sense—even in the narrow sense of aiming to abolish repressive laws. This was not their object. They were public announcements of private feelings and desires. As a slogan of May 1968 put it: "I take my desires for reality, for I believe in the reality of my desires" (Katsiaficas, 1987, p. 101). Even when such desires came together in public manifestations, groups and movements; even in what looked like, and sometimes had the effect of, mass rebellion, subjectivity was at their core. "The personal is political" became an important slogan of the new feminism, perhaps the most lasting result of the years of radicalization. It meant more than simply that political commitment had personal motivations and satisfactions, and that the criterion of political success was how it affected people. In some mouths it simply meant "I shall call anything that worries me, political," as in the title of a 1970s book, *Fat Is a Feminist Issue* (Orbach, 1978).

The May 1968 slogan "When I think of revolution I want to make love" would have puzzled not only Lenin, but also Ruth Fischer, the militant young Viennese communist whose championship of sexual promiscuity Lenin attacked (Zetkin, 1968, pp. 28ff.). Yet, conversely, even for the typically politically conscious neo-Marxist-Leninist radical of the 1960s and 1970s, Brecht's Comintern agent who, like the commercial

*Chico Buarque de Holanda, the major figure on the Brazilian pop music scene, was the son of an eminent progressive historian who had been a central figure in his country's intellectual-cultural revival in the 1930s.

traveller "made love with other things on his mind" ("*Der Liebe pflegte ich achtlos*"—Brecht, 1976, II, p. 722) would have been incomprehensible. For them the important thing was surely not what revolutionaries hoped to achieve by their actions, but what they did and how they felt while doing it. Making love and making revolution could not be clearly separated.

Personal liberation and social liberation thus went hand in hand; the most obvious ways of shattering the bonds of state, parental and neighbours' power, law and convention, being sex and drugs. The former, in all its manifold forms, did not have to be discovered. What the melancholy conservative poet meant by the line "Sexual intercourse began in 1963" (Larkin, 1988, p. 167) was not that this activity was uncommon before the 1960s or even that he had not practised it, but that it changed its public character with—his examples—the Lady Chatterley trial and "the Beatles' first LP." Where an activity had formerly been prohibited, such gestures against older ways were easy. Where it had previously been tolerated, officially or unofficially, as for instance lesbian relationships had, the fact that it was a gesture had to be specially established. A public commitment to the hitherto prohibited or unconventional ("coming out") therefore became important. Drugs, on the other hand, except for alcohol and tobacco, had hitherto been confined to small subcultures of high, low and marginal society, and did not benefit from permissive legislation. They spread not only as a gesture of rebellion, for the sensations they made possible could be sufficient attraction. Nevertheless, drug use was by legal definition an outlaw activity, and the very fact that the drug most popular among the Western young, marihuana, was probably more harmless than alcohol or tobacco, made smoking it (typically, a social activity) not merely an act of defiance but of superiority over those who banned it. On the wilder shores of the American 1960s, where rock fans and student radicals met, the line between getting stoned and building barricades often seemed hazy.

The newly extended field of publicly acceptable behaviour, including the sexual, probably increased experimentation and the frequency of behaviour hitherto considered unacceptable or deviant, and certainly increased its visibility. Thus in the U.S.A. the public emergence of an openly practised homosexual subculture, even in the two trend-setting cities of San Francisco and New York, which influenced one another, did not occur until well into the 1960s, its emergence as a political pressure group in these two cities not until the 1970s (Duberman et al., 1989, p. 460). However, the major significance of these changes was that, implicitly or explicitly, they rejected the long-established and historical ordering of human relations in society, which the social conventions and prohibitions expressed, sanctioned and symbolized.

What is even more significant is that this rejection was not in the name of some other pattern of ordering society, though the new libertarianism was given ideological justification by those who felt it needed such labels,* but in the name of the unlimited autonomy of individual desire. It assumed a world of self-regarding individualism pushed to its limits. Paradoxically the rebels against the conventions and restrictions shared the assumptions on which mass consumer society was built, or at least the psychological motivations which those who sold consumers goods and services found most effective in selling them.

The world was now tacitly assumed to consist of several billion human beings defined by their pursuit of individual desire, including desires hitherto prohibited or frowned on, but now permitted—not because they had now become morally acceptable but because so many egos had them. Thus until the 1990s official liberalization stopped short of legalizing drugs. These continued to be prohibited with varying degrees of severity and a high degree of inefficacy. For from the later 1960s an enormous market for cocaine developed with great rapidity, primarily among the prosperous middle classes of North America and, a little later, Western Europe. This, like the somewhat earlier and more plebeian growth in the market for heroin (also primarily North American) turned crime for the first time into genuinely big business (Arlacchi, 1983, pp. 215, 208).

IV

The cultural revolution of the later twentieth century can thus best be understood as the triumph of the individual over society, or rather, the breaking of the threads which in the past had woven human beings into social textures. For such textures had consisted not only of the actual relations between human beings and their forms of organization but also of the general models of such relations and the expected patterns of people's behaviour towards each other; their roles were prescribed, though not always written. Hence the often traumatic insecurity when

---

*However, there was next to no revival of the one ideology which believed that spontaneous, unorganized, anti-authoritarian and libertarian action would bring about a new, just and stateless society, namely Bakuninite or Kropotkinite *anarchism;* even though this corresponded far more closely to the actual ideas of most student rebels of the 1960s and 1970s than the then fashionable Marxism.

older conventions of behaviour were either overturned or lost their rationale, or the incomprehension between those who felt this loss and those too young to have known anything but anomic society.

Thus a Brazilian anthropologist in the 1980s described the tension of a middle-class male, raised in his country's Mediterranean culture of honour and shame, faced with the increasingly common contingency of a group of robbers who asked for his money and threatened to rape his girl-friend. Under such circumstances a gentleman had always been expected to defend the woman, if not the money, at the cost of his life; a lady, to prefer death to a fate proverbially "worse than death." Yet in the reality of late twentieth century big cities it was unlikely that resistance would save either the woman's "honour" or the money. The rational policy in such circumstances was to yield, so as to prevent the aggressors from losing their tempers and committing real mayhem or even murder. As for female honour, traditionally defined as virginity before marriage and total marital fidelity thereafter, what exactly was being defended in the light of the assumptions about, and the realities of, sexual behaviour by both men and women which were current among the educated and emancipated in the 1980s? And yet, as the anthropologist's enquiries showed, not surprisingly this did not make the predicament less traumatic. Less extreme situations could produce comparable insecurity and mental suffering—for instance ordinary sexual encounters. The alternative to an old convention, however unreasonable, might turn out to be not some new convention or rational behaviour, but no rules at all, or at least no consensus about what should be done.

Over most of the world the old social textures and conventions, though undermined by a quarter of a century of unparalleled social and economic transformation, were strained, but not yet in disintegration. This was fortunate for most of humanity, especially the poor, since the network of kin, community and neighbourhood was essential to economic survival and especially to success in a changing world. In much of the Third World it functioned as a combination of information service, labour exchange, a pool of labour and capital, a savings mechanism and a social security system. Indeed, without cohesive families the economic successes of some parts of the world—e.g. the Far East—are difficult to explain.

In the more traditional societies the strains would show chiefly inasmuch as the triumph of the business economy undermined the legitimacy of the hitherto accepted social order based on inequality, both because aspirations became more egalitarian and because the functional justifications of inequality were eroded. Thus the wealth and profligacy of Indian rajahs (like the known immunity to taxation of the British family's royal wealth, which was not challenged until the 1990s), had not been envied or resented by their subjects, as a neighbour's might have been. They belonged to, and were marks of, their special role in the social—perhaps even in the cosmic—order, which in some sense was believed to maintain, to stabilize and certainly to symbolize, their realm. In a somewhat different mode, the considerable privileges and luxuries of Japanese business tycoons were less unacceptable, so long as they were seen not as individually appropriated wealth, but essentially as adjuncts to their official positions in the economy, rather like the luxuries of British cabinet ministers—limousines, official residences, etc.—which are withdrawn within hours of their ceasing to occupy the post to which they are attached. The actual distribution of incomes in Japan, as we know, was considerably less unequal than in Western business societies. Yet anyone who observed the Japanese situation in the 1980s, even from afar, could hardly avoid the impression that during this boom decade the sheer accumulation of personal wealth and its public display made the contrast between the conditions under which the ordinary Japanese lived at home—so much more modestly than their Western homologues—and the condition of the Japanese rich far more visible. Perhaps for the first time they were no longer sufficiently protected by what had been seen as the legitimate privileges that go with service to state and society.

In the West, the decades of social revolution had created far greater havoc. The extremes of such breakdown are most easily visible in the public ideological discourse of the occidental *fin de siècle*, especially in the kind of public statements which, while laying no claim to analytical depth, were formulated in terms of widely held beliefs. One thinks of the argument, at one time common in some feminist circles, that women's domestic work should be calculated (and where necessary, paid) at a market rate, or the justification of abortion reform in terms of an abstract and unlimited "right to choose" of the individual (woman).* The pervasive influence of neo-classical economics, which in secular Western societies increasingly took the place of theology, and (via the cultural hegemony of the U.S.A.) the influence of the ultra-individualist American jurisprudence,

---

*The legitimacy of a claim must be distinguished clearly from the arguments used to justify it. The relation of husband, wife and children in a household has not the faintest resemblance to that of buyers and sellers in a market, however notional. Nor is the decision to have or not to have a child, even if taken unilaterally, one which concerns exclusively the individual who takes that decision. This statement of the obvious is perfectly compatible with the desire to transform women's household role or favour the right of abortion.

encouraged such rhetoric. It found political expression in the British premier Margaret Thatcher's: "There is no society, only individuals."

Yet, whatever the excesses of theory, practice was often equally extreme. Sometime in the 1970s, social reformers in the Anglo-Saxon countries, rightly shocked (as enquirers periodically were) by the effects of institutionalization on the mentally ill or impaired, successfully campaigned to have as many of them as possible let out of confinement "to be cared for in the community." But in the cities of the West there no longer was a community to care for them. There was no kin. Nobody knew them. There were only the streets of cities like New York filled with homeless beggars with plastic bags who gestured and talked to themselves. If they were lucky or unlucky (it depended on the point of view) they eventually moved from the hospitals that had expelled them to the jails which, in the U.S.A., became the main receptacle of the social problems of American society, especially its black part. In 1991 15 per cent of what was proportionately the largest prison population in the world—426 prisoners per 100,000 population—were said to be mentally ill (Walker, 1991; Human Development, 1991, p. 32, Fig. 2.10).

The institutions most severely undermined by the new moral individualism were the traditional family and traditional organized churches in the West, which collapsed dramatically in the last third of the century. The cement that had held the communities of Roman Catholics together crumbled with astonishing speed. In the course of the 1960s attendance at Mass in Quebec (Canada) fell from 80 to 20 per cent and the traditionally high French-Canadian birth-rate fell below the Canadian average (Bernier/Boily, 1986). Women's liberation, or more precisely women's demand for birth-control, including abortion and the right to divorce, drove perhaps the deepest wedge between the Church and what had in the nineteenth century become the basic stock of the faithful (see *Age of Capital*), as became increasingly evident in notoriously Catholic countries like Ireland and the Pope's own Italy, and even—after the fall of communism—in Poland. Vocations for the priesthood and other forms of the religious life fell steeply, as did the willingness to live lives of celibacy, real or official. In short, for good or ill, the Church's moral and material authority over the faithful disappeared into the black hole that opened between its rules of life and morality and the reality of late-twentieth-century behaviour. Western Churches with a less compelling hold over their members, including even some of the older Protestant sects, declined even more rapidly.

The material consequences of the loosening of traditional family ties were perhaps even more serious. For, as we have seen, the family was not

only what it had always been, a device for reproducing itself, but also a device for social cooperation. As such it had been essential for maintaining both the agrarian and the early industrial economies, the local and the global. This was partly because no adequate *impersonal* capitalist business structure had been developed before the concentration of capital and the rise of big business began to generate the modern corporate organization at the end of the nineteenth century, that "visible hand" (Chandler, 1977) which was to supplement Adam Smith's "invisible hand" of the market.*
But an even stronger reason was that the market by itself makes no provision for that central element in any system of private profit-seeking, namely trust; or, its legal equivalent, the performance of contracts. This required either state power (as the seventeenth-century political theorists of individualism knew well) or the ties of kin or community. Thus international trading, banking and finance, fields of sometimes physically remote activities, large rewards and great insecurity, had been most successfully conducted by kin-related bodies of entrepreneurs, preferably from groups with special religious solidarities like Jews, Quakers, or Huguenots. Indeed, even in the late twentieth century, such links were still indispensable in criminal business, which was not only against the law but outside its protection. In a situation where nothing else guaranteed contracts, only kin and the threat of death could do so. The most successful Calabrian *mafia* families therefore consisted of a substantial group of brothers (Ciconte, 1992, pp. 361–62).

Yet just these non-economic group bonds and solidarities were now being undermined, as were the moral systems that went with them. These had also been older than modern bourgeois industrial society, but they had also been adapted to form an essential part of it. The old moral vocabulary of rights and duties, mutual obligations, sin and virtue, sacrifice, conscience, rewards and penalties, could no longer be translated into the new language of desired gratification. Once such practices and institutions were no longer accepted as part of a way of ordering society that linked people to each other and ensured social cooperation and reproduction, most of their capacity to structure human social life vanished. They were reduced simply to expressions of individuals' preferences, and claims that the law should recognize the supremacy of these

---

*The operational model of really large enterprise before the era of corporate capitalism ("monopoly capitalism") was not drawn from private business experience, but from state or military bureaucracy—cf. the uniforms of railway employees. Often, indeed, it was, and had to be, directly conducted by the state or other non-profit-maximizing public authorities, like the postal and most telegraph and telephone services.

preferences.* Uncertainty and unpredictability impended. Compass needles no longer had a North, maps became useless. This is what became increasingly evident in the most developed countries from the 1960s on. It found ideological expression in a variety of theories, from extreme free-market liberalism to "postmodernism" and its like, which tried to sidestep the problem of judgment and values altogether, or rather to reduce them to the single denominator of the unrestricted freedom of the individual.

Initially, of course, the advantages of wholesale social liberalization had seemed enormous to all except ingrained reactionaries, and its costs minimal; nor did it seem to imply economic liberalization. The great tide of prosperity washing across the populations of the favoured regions of the world, reinforced by the increasingly comprehensive and generous public social security systems, appeared to remove the debris of social disintegration. Being a single parent (i.e. overwhelmingly a single mother) was still by far the best guarantee of a life of poverty, but in modern welfare states it also guaranteed a minimum of livelihood and shelter. Pensions, welfare services and, in the end, geriatric wards took care of the isolated old, whose sons and daughters could not, or no longer felt the obligation to, look after parents in their decline. It seemed natural to deal with other contingencies that had once been part of the family order in the same way, for instance by shifting the burden of caring for infants from mothers to public crèches and nurseries, as socialists, concerned with the needs of wage-earning mothers, had long demanded.

Both rational calculation and historical development seemed to point in the same direction as various kinds of progressive ideology, including all those which criticized the traditional family because it perpetuated the subordination of women or of children and adolescents, or on more general libertarian grounds. Materially, public provision was obviously superior to that which most families could provide for themselves, either because of poverty or for other reasons. That the children in democratic states emerged from the world wars actually healthier and better fed than before, proved the point. That welfare states survived in the richest countries at the end of the century, in spite of systematic attacks on them by free-market governments and ideologists, confirmed it. Moreover, it was a commonplace among sociologists and social anthropologists that in

---

*This is the difference between the language of (legal or constitutional) "rights," which became central to the society of uncontrolled individualism, at all events in the U.S.A., and the old moral idiom in which rights and obligations were the two sides of the same coin.

general the role of kinship "diminishes with the importance of governmental institutions." For better or worse, it declined with "the growth of economic and social individualism in industrial societies" (Goody, 1968, p. 402–3). In short, as had long been predicted, *Gemeinschaft* was giving way to *Gesellschaft;* communities to individuals linked in anonymous societies.

The material advantages of a life in a world in which community and family declined were, and remain, undeniable. What few realized was how much of modern industrial society up to the mid-twentieth century had relied on a symbiosis between old community and family values and the new society, and therefore how dramatic the effects of their spectacularly rapid disintegration were likely to be. This became evident in the era of neo-liberal ideology, when the macabre term "the underclass" entered, or re-entered the socio-political vocabulary around 1980.* These were the people who, in developed market societies after the end of full employment, could not manage or did not want to make a living for themselves and their families in the economy of the market (supplemented by the social security system), which seemed to work well enough for two thirds of most of the inhabitants of such countries, at all events until the 1990s (hence the phrase "the Two-Thirds Society" coined in that decade by a worried German Social-Democratic politician, Peter Glotz). The very word "underclass," like the old "underworld," implied an exclusion from "normal" society. Essentially such "underclasses" relied on public housing and public welfare, even when they supplemented their income by forays into the black or grey economy or into "crime," i.e. those parts of the economy not reached by the government's fiscal systems. However, since these were the strata where family cohesion had largely broken down, even their incursions into the informal economy, legal or illegal, were marginal and unstable. For, as the Third World and its new mass immigration to the Northern countries proved, even the unofficial economy of shanty-towns and illegal immigrants works well only with kinship networks.

The poor parts of the native-born urban Negro population in the U.S.A., that is to say, the majority of U.S. Negroes,† became the standard

---

*The late-nineteenth-century equivalent for this in Britain had been "the residuum."

†The description officially preferred at the time of writing is "African-American." However, these names change—in the author's lifetime there have been several such changes ("Coloured," "Negro," "Black")—and will go on changing. I use the term which probably had currency longer than any other among those who wished to show respect to the descendants of African slaves in the Americas.

example of such an "underclass," a body of citizens virtually excluded from official society, forming no real part of it or—in the case of many of its young males—of the labour market. Indeed, many of its young, especially the males, virtually considered themselves an outlaw society or antisociety. The phenomenon was not confined to people of any skin-colour. With the decline and fall of the labour-employing industries of the (nineteenth and early twentieth) century, such "underclasses" began to appear in a number of countries. Yet in the housing projects built by socially responsible public authorities for all who could not afford market rents or house purchases, but now inhabited by "the underclass," there was no community either, and little enough regular kin mutuality. Even "neighbourliness," the last relic of community, could hardly survive the universal fear, generally of wild adolescent males, now increasingly armed, that stalked these Hobbesian jungles.

Only in those parts of the world that had not yet entered the universe where human beings lived side by side but not as social beings did community survive to some extent, and with it a social order, though, for most human beings, a desperately poor one. Who could talk of a minority "underclass" in a country like Brazil where, in the mid-1980s, the top 20 per cent of the population received over 60 per cent of their country's income while the bottom 40 per cent received 10 per cent or even less? (U.N. World Social Situation, 1984, p. 84). It was generally a life of unequal status as well as income. Yet, for the most part, it still lacked the pervasive insecurity of urban life in the "developed" societies, their old guides to behaviour dismantled, and replaced by an uncertain void. The sad paradox of the twentieth century *fin de siècle* was that, by all the measurable criteria of social well-being and stability, living in socially retrograde but traditionally structured Northern Ireland, unemployed and after twenty unbroken years of something like civil war, was better, and actually safer, than living in most of the great cities of the United Kingdom.

The drama of collapsed traditions and values lay not so much in the material disadvantages of doing without the social and personal services once supplied by family and community. These could be replaced in the prosperous welfare states, although not in the poor parts of the world, where the great majority of humanity still had little to rely on except kin, patronage and mutual aid (for the socialist sector of the world, see chapters 13 and 16). It lay in the disintegration both of the old value systems and the customs and conventions which controlled human behaviour. This loss was felt. It was reflected in the rise of what came to be called (again in the U.S.A. where the phenomenon became noticeable from the end of the 1960s) "identity politics," generally ethnic/national or religious, and of militantly nostalgic movements seeking to recover a hypothetical past age of unproblematic order and security. Such movements were cries for help rather than carriers of programmes—calls for some "community" to belong to in an anomic world; some family to belong to in a world of social isolates; some refuge in the jungle. Every realistic observer and most governments knew that crime was not diminished or even controlled by executing criminals or by deterrence through long penal sentences, but every politician knew the enormous, emotionally loaded strength, rational or not, of the mass demand of ordinary citizens to *punish* the anti-social.

These were the political dangers of the fraying and snapping of the old social textures and value systems. However, as the 1980s advanced, generally under the banner of pure market sovereignty, it became increasingly obvious that it also constituted a danger to the triumphant capitalist economy.

For the capitalist system, even while built on the operations of the market, had relied on a number of proclivities which had no intrinsic connection with that pursuit of the individual's advantage which, according to Adam Smith, fuelled its engine. It relied on "the habit of labour," which Adam Smith assumed to be one of the fundamental motives of human behaviour, on the willingness of human beings to postpone immediate gratification for a long period, i.e. to save and invest for future rewards, on pride in achievement, on customs of mutual trust, and on other attitudes which were not implicit in the rational maximization of anyone's utilities. The family became an integral part of early capitalism because it supplied it with a number of these motivations. So did "the habit of labour," the habits of obedience and loyalty, including the loyalty of executives to their firm, and other forms of behaviour which could not readily be fitted into rational choice theory based on maximization. Capitalism could function in the absence of these, but, when it did, it became strange and problematic even for businessmen themselves. This happened during the fashion for piratical "take-overs" of business corporations and other financial speculations which swept the financial districts of ultra-free-market states like the U.S.A. and Britain in the 1980s, and which virtually broke all links between the pursuit of profit and the economy as a system of production. That is why capitalist countries which had not forgotten that growth is not achieved by profit maximization alone (Germany, Japan, France), made such raiding difficult or impossible.

Karl Polanyi, surveying the ruins of nineteenth-century civilization during the Second World War, pointed out how extraordinary and unprecedented were the assumptions on which it had been constructed: those of the self-regulating and universal system of markets. He argued that Adam Smith's "propensity to barter, truck and exchange one thing for another" had inspired "an industrial system . . . which practically and theoretically, implied that the human race was swayed in all its economic activities, if not also in its political, intellectual and spiritual pursuits, by that one particular propensity" (Polanyi, 1945, pp. 50–51). Yet Polanyi exaggerated the logic of capitalism in his time, just as Adam Smith had exaggerated the extent to which, taken by itself, the pursuit by all men of their economic advantage would automatically maximize the wealth of nations.

As we take for granted the air we breathe, and which makes possible all our activities, so capitalism took for granted the atmosphere in which it operated, and which it had inherited from the past. It only discovered how essential it had been, when the air became thin. In other words, capitalism had succeeded because it was not just capitalist. Profit maximization and accumulation were necessary conditions for its success but not sufficient ones. It was the cultural revolution of the last third of the century which began to erode the inherited historical assets of capitalism and to demonstrate the difficulties of operating without them. It was the historic irony of the neo-liberalism that became fashionable in the 1970s and 1980s, and looked down on the ruins of the communist regimes, that it triumphed at the very moment when it ceased to be as plausible as it had once seemed. The market claimed to triumph as its nakedness and inadequacy could no longer be concealed.

The main force of the cultural revolution was naturally felt in the urbanised "industrial market economies" of the old capitalist heartlands. However, as we shall see, the extraordinary economic and social forces released in later twentieth century also transformed what now came to be called the "Third World."

CHAPTER TWELVE

The Third World

[I suggested that], without books to read, life in the evenings on their [Egyptian] country estates must hang heavily, and that an easy chair and a good book on a cool veranda would make life much more agreeable. My friend said at once: "You don't think that a landlord in the district could sit out on a veranda after dinner with a bright light over his head, do you, and not get shot?" I might have thought of that myself.

—Russell Pasha, 1949

Whenever village conversation was steered to the subject of mutual help and the offer of cash loans as part of such help to fellow villagers, it rarely failed to raise statements bemoaning the decreasing cooperation between villagers... Such statements were always accompanied with reference to the fact that people in the village are becoming increasingly calculating in their approach to money matters. Villagers would then unfailingly hark back to what was termed as the "old days" when people were always ready to offer aid.

—M. b.Abdul Rahim, 1973
(in Scott, 1985, p. 188)

I

Decolonization and revolution dramatically transformed the political map of the globe. The number of internationally recognized independent states in Asia quintupled. In Africa, where there had been one in 1939, there were now about fifty. Even in the Americas, where early nineteenth-century decolonization had left behind twenty or so Latino republics, decolonization added another dozen. However, the important thing about them was not their number, but the enormous and growing demographic weight and pressure they represented collectively.

This was the consequence of an astonishing demographic explosion in the dependent world after the Second World War, which changed, and continues to change, the balance of world population. Since the first industrial revolution, possibly since the sixteenth century, this had been moving in favour of the "developed" world, i.e. of populations in or originating from Europe. From less than 20 per cent of the global population in 1750, these had risen to constitute about one third of humanity by 1900. The Age of Catastrophe froze the situation, but since the middle of the century, world population has grown at a rate beyond all precedent, and most of this has come from the regions once ruled by, or about to be conquered by, a handful of empires. If we take the membership of the rich countries in the OECD as representing the "developed world," their collective population at the end of the 1980s represented a mere 15 per cent of humanity; an inevitably declining share (but for immigration), since several of the "developed" countries were no longer giving birth to enough children to reproduce themselves.

This demographic explosion in the poor countries of the world, which first caused serious international worry at the end of the "Golden Age," is probably the most fundamental change in the Short Twentieth Century, even if we assume that global population will be eventually stabilized at ten billions (or whatever the current guess may be) some time in the twenty-first century.* A world population that doubled in the forty years since 1950, or a population like that of Africa which can expect to double in less than thirty years, is entirely without historical precedent, as are the practical problems it must raise. One has merely to consider the social and economic situation of a country 60 per cent of whose people are less than fifteen years old.

The demographic explosion in the poor world was so sensational because the basic birth-rates in these countries were usually far higher than those of the corresponding historical period in the "developed" countries, and because the enormous rates of mortality, which used to keep down the population, dropped like a stone since the 1940s—four or five times as fast as the corresponding drop in nineteenth-century Europe

---

*If the spectacular acceleration of growth we have experienced during this century were to continue, a catastrophe would seem to be unavoidable. Humanity reached its first billion about two hundred years ago. The next billion took 120 years to reach, the third thirty-five years, the fourth fifteen years. At the end of the 1980s it stood at 5.2 billions and was expected to exceed six billions by 2000.

(Kelley, 1988, p. 168). For, while in Europe this fall had to wait for the gradual improvement of living and environmental standards, modern technology swept through the world of the poor countries like a hurricane in the "Golden Age," in the form of modern drugs and the transport revolution. From the 1940s on, medical and pharmaceutical innovation for the first time was in a position to save lives on a massive scale (e.g. by DDT and antibiotics), which it had previously never been able to, except perhaps in the case of smallpox. So, as birth-rates stayed high, or even rose in times of prosperity, death-rates plummeted—in Mexico they dropped by more than half in the twenty-five years after 1944—and the population shot up, even though neither the economy nor its institutions had necessarily changed much. One incidental consequence of this was to widen the gap between the rich and poor, the advanced and backward countries, even when the economies of both regions grew at the same rate. To distribute a GDP twice as large as thirty years ago in a country whose population was stable is one thing; to distribute it among a population which (like Mexico) had doubled in thirty years is quite another.

It is important to begin any account of the Third World with some consideration of its demography, since the population explosion is the central fact of its existence. Past history in the developed countries suggests that, sooner or later it will also undergo what the experts call "the demographic transition," by stabilizing its population on the basis of a low birth-rate and a low death-rate, i.e. of giving up having more than one or two children. However, while there is indeed evidence that the "demographic transition" was in the process of taking place in several countries, notably in East Asia, at the end of the Short Twentieth Century the bulk of the poor countries had not advanced very far along that road, except in the ex-Soviet bloc. This was one reason for their continued poverty. Several countries with a giant population were so troubled about the tens of millions of additional mouths that asked to be fed every year that from time to time their governments engaged in ruthless coercion to impose birth control or some other kind of family limitation on their citizens (notably the sterilisation campaign in India in the 1970s and the "one-child" policy of China). It is unlikely that the population problem in any country will be solved by these means.

II

However, as they emerged into the post-war and post-colonial world, these were not the first concerns of the states of the poor world. What shape should they take?

Not surprisingly they adopted, or were urged into, political systems derived from their old imperial masters or those who had conquered them. The minority, emerging out of social revolution or (what amounted to the same thing) lengthy wars of liberation, were more likely to follow the model of the Soviet revolution. In theory, therefore, the world was increasingly filled with what purported to be parliamentary republics with contested elections, plus a minority of "people's democratic republics" under a single guiding party. (In theory everybody henceforth was democratic, though only the communist or social-revolutionary regimes insisted on being "popular" and/or "democratic" in their official title.*)

In practice these labels indicated at most where such new states wished to situate themselves internationally. They were in general as unrealistic as the official constitutions of the Latin American republics had long tended to be, and for the same reasons: in most cases they lacked the material and political conditions to live up to them. This was so even in the new states of the communist type, though their basically authoritarian structure and the device of a single "leading party" made them rather less unsuitable to states of a non-Western background than were liberal republics. Thus one of the few unshakeable and unshaken political principles of communist states was the supremacy of the (civilian) party over the military. Yet in the 1980s, among revolutionary-inspired states, Algeria, Benin, Burma, the Congo Republic, Ethiopia, Madagascar and Somalia—plus the somewhat eccentric Libya—were under the rule of soldiers who had come to power by coups, as were Syria and Iraq both under governments of the Ba'ath Socialist Party, though in rival versions.

Indeed, the prevalence of, or the tendency to lapse into, military regimes united Third World states of whatever constitutional and political affiliation. If we omit the main body of Third World communist regimes (North Korea, China, the Indochinese republics and Cuba), and the long-established regime sprung from the Mexican Revolution, it is difficult to think of any republics which have not known at least episodes of

---

*Before the collapse of communism the following states had the words "people's," "popular," "democratic" or "socialist" in their official names: Albania, Angola, Algeria, Bangladesh, Benin, Burma, Bulgaria, Cambodia, China, Congo, Czechoslovakia, Ethiopia, German Democratic Republic, Hungary, North Korea, Laos, Libya, Madagascar, Mongolia, Mozambique, Poland, Romania, Somalia, Sri Lanka, U.S.S.R., Vietnam, PDR Yemen, and Yugoslavia. Guyana announced itself as a "cooperative republic."

military regimes since 1945. (The few monarchies, with some exceptions [Thailand], seem to have been safer.) India, of course, remains at the time of writing by far the most impressive example of a Third World state that has both maintained unbroken civilian supremacy and an unbroken succession of government by regular and relatively honest popular election, though whether this justifies the label "the world's greatest democracy" depends on how precisely we define Lincoln's "government of the people, for the people, by the people."

We have become so accustomed to military coups and regimes in the world—even in Europe—that it is worth reminding ourselves that on the present scale they are a distinctly new phenomenon. In 1914 not a single internationally sovereign state had been under military rule, except in Latin America, where military *coups d'état* were part of tradition, and even there, at that time, the only major republic that was not under civilian rule was Mexico, which was in the middle of a revolution and civil war. There were plenty of militarist states, of states in which the military carried more than its share of political weight, and several states in which the bulk of the officer-corps was out of sympathy with its government— France being an obvious example. Nevertheless, the instinct and the habit of soldiers in properly conducted and stable states were to obey and keep out of politics; or, more precisely, to participate in politics only in the manner of another group of officially voiceless personages, ruling-class women, namely behind the scenes and by intrigue.

The politics of military coup were therefore the product of the new era of uncertain or illegitimate government. The first serious discussion of the subject, by an Italian journalist with memories of Machiavelli, Curzio Malaparte's *Coup d'État*, appeared in 1931, halfway through the years of catastrophe. In the second half of the century, while the superpower balance appeared to stabilize frontiers and, to a lesser extent, regimes, armed men became ever more commonly involved in politics, if only because the globe was now filled with up to two hundred states, most of which were new and therefore lacked any traditional legitimacy, and most of which were saddled with political systems more likely to produce political breakdown than effective government. In such situations the armed forces were often the only bodies capable of political or any other action on a state-wide basis. Moreover, since the international Cold War between the superpowers was largely conducted through the armed forces of client or allied states, these were subsidized and armed by the appropriate superpower or, in some cases, first by one and then by the other superpower, as in Somalia. There was more scope in politics for the men in tanks than ever before.

In the core countries of communism they were kept under control by the presumption of civilian supremacy through the party, although in his last lunatic years Mao Tse-tung came close to abandoning it at moments. In the core countries of the Western alliance the scope for military politics remained restricted by the absence of political instability or the effective mechanisms for keeping it under control. Thus after General Franco's death in Spain a transition to liberal democracy was negotiated efficiently under the aegis of the new king, and a putsch by the unreconstructed Francoist officers in 1981 was quickly stopped in its tracks by the king's refusal to accept it. In Italy, where the U.S.A. maintained a local coup potential against the possibility of participation in government by the large local Communist Party, civilian government remained in being, even though the 1970s produced various and still unexplained flurries of action in the obscure depth of the military, secret service and terrorist underworlds. Only where the traumas of decolonization (i.e. defeat by colonial insurrectionaries) proved intolerable, were Western officers tempted into military coups—as in France during the losing struggle to hold Indochina and Algeria in the 1950s, and (with Left-wing political orientation) in Portugal as the African empire collapsed in the 1970s. In both cases the armed forces were soon brought under civilian control again. The only military regime actually backed by the U.S.A. in Europe was that installed in 1967 (probably on local initiative) by a particularly witless group of ultra-Right-wing Greek colonels in a country where civil war between communists and their opponents (1944–49) had left bitter memories on both sides. The regime, distinguished by a taste for the systematic torture of its opponents, collapsed after seven years under the weight of its own political stupidity.

Conditions for military intervention in the Third World were far more inviting, especially in new, feeble and often tiny states where a few hundred armed men, reinforced or sometimes even replaced by foreigners, could carry decisive weight, and where inexperienced or incompetent governments were quite likely to produce recurrent states of chaos, corruption and confusion. The typical military ruler in most African countries was not an aspirant dictator, but someone genuinely trying to clear up such messes, hoping—too often in vain—that civilian government would soon take over again. Generally he failed in both endeavours, which is why few military chieftains lasted very long. In any case, the slightest hint that local government might fall into the hands of the communists virtually guaranteed American support.

In short, military politics, like military intelligence, tended to fill the void left by the absence of ordinary politics or intelligence. It was not any particular brand of politics, but a function of the surrounding instability and insecurity. However, it became increasingly pervasive in the Third World because virtually all the countries of the ex-colonial or dependent part of the globe were now committed, in one way or another, to policies which required them to have exactly those stable, functioning and efficient states which so few of them had. They were committed to economic independence and "development." In the aftermath of the second round of world war, world revolution and its consequence, global decolonization, it seemed that there was no future for the old programme of prosperity as primary-producers for the world market of the imperialist countries: the programme of the Argentine and Uruguayan *estancieros*, hopefully imitated by Mexico's Porfirio Díaz and Peru's Leguía. In any case it had ceased to look plausible since the Great Slump. Moreover, both nationalism and anti-imperialism called for policies less dependent on the old empires, and the example of the U.S.S.R. provided an alternative model of "development." Never did that example look more impressive than in the years after 1945.

The more ambitious states therefore called for an end to agrarian backwardness by systematic industrialization, whether on the centrally-planned Soviet model or by import substitution. Both, in different ways, rested on state action and state control. Even the less ambitious, who did not dream of a future of great tropical steelworks, powered by huge hydro-electric installations overshadowed by titanic dams, wanted to control and develop their own national resources themselves. Oil had been traditionally produced by private Western corporations, usually with the closest relations to imperial powers. Governments, following the example of Mexico in 1938, now took to nationalizing them and operating them as state enterprises. Those which refrained from nationalization discovered (especially after 1950 when ARAMCO offered Saudi Arabia the hitherto unimaginable deal of a 50/50 revenue split) that physical possession of oil and gas gave them the whip-hand in negotiations with the foreign corporations. In practice the Organization of Petrol Exporting Countries (OPEC), which eventually held the world to ransom in the 1970s, became possible because the ownership of the world's oil had shifted from companies to a relatively few producer-governments. In short, even those governments of decolonized or dependent states which were quite happy with relying on foreign capitalists old or new ("neo-colonialism" in contemporary Left-wing terminology), did so within a state-controlled economy. Probably the most successful of such states until the 1980s was the former French Ivory Coast.

Probably the least successful were new countries which underestimated the constraints of backwardness—lack of skilled and experienced experts, administrators and economic cadres; illiteracy; unfamiliarity or lack of sympathy with programmes of economic modernization—especially when their governments set themselves targets which even developed countries found difficult, such as centrally state-planned industrialization. Ghana, with Sudan the first sub-Saharan African state to be granted independence, thus threw away currency reserves of two hundred millions, accumulated thanks to high cocoa prices and wartime earnings—higher than the sterling balances of independent India—in an attempt to build an industrialized state-controlled economy, not to mention Kwame Nkrumah's plans for pan-African union. The results were disastrous, and made worse by the collapse of cocoa prices in the 1960s. By 1972 the great projects had failed, the domestic industries in the small country could survive only behind high tariff walls, price controls and import licences, which led to a flourishing black economy and generalized corruption that has remained ineradicable. Three quarters of all wage-earners were employed in the public sector, while subsistence agriculture (as in so many other African states) was neglected. After Nkrumah's overthrow by the usual military coup (1966) the country continued on its disillusioned way amid a succession of usually disappointed military, and occasionally civilian governments.

The dismal record of sub-Saharan Africa's new states should not lead us to underestimate the substantial achievements of better-placed ex-colonial or dependent countries, who chose the road of state-planned or state-sponsored economic development. What came to be known from the 1970s in international functionaries' jargon as the NICs (Newly Industrializing Countries) were all, with the exception of the city-state of Hong Kong, based on such policies. As anyone with the slightest knowledge of Brazil and Mexico will testify, they produced bureaucracy, spectacular corruption and much waste—but also a 7 per cent annual rate of growth in both countries for decades: in short, both achieved the desired transition to modern industrial economies. In fact, Brazil became for a time the eighth-largest industrial country of the non-communist world. Both countries had a sufficiently vast population to provide a substantial home market, so that industrialization by import substitution made sense, at least for quite a long time. Public spending and activities sustained high demand at home. At one time the Brazilian public sector handled about half the gross domestic product and represented nineteen out of the twenty largest companies, while in Mexico it employed a fifth of the total workforce and paid two fifths of the national wage-bill (Harris, 1987, pp. 84–85). State-planning in the Far East tended to rely less on direct public enterprise and more on favoured business groups dominated by government control of credit and investment, but the dependence of economic development on the state was the same. Planning and state initiative was the name of the game everywhere in the world in the 1950s and 1960s and in the NICs until the 1990s. Whether this form of economic development produced satisfactory or disappointing results depended on local conditions and human errors.

III

Development, state-controlled or not, was not of immediate interest to the great majority of the inhabitants of the Third World who lived by growing their own food; for even in countries or colonies whose public revenues relied on the income from one or two major export crops—coffee, bananas or cocoa—these were usually concentrated in a few restricted areas. In sub-Saharan Africa and most of South and Southeast Asia as well as in China, the mass of people continued to live by agriculture. Only in the western hemisphere and in the dry lands of western Islam did the countryside as yet drain into the giant cities, turning rural into urban societies in a couple of dramatic decades (see chapter 10). In fertile and not too densely populated regions, like much of black Africa, most people would have managed pretty well if left to themselves. Most of its inhabitants did not need their states, which were usually too weak to do much harm, and, if they grew too troublesome, could probably be by-passed by a retreat into village self-sufficiency. Few continents started the era of independence with greater advantages, which were soon to be thrown away. Most Asian and Islamic peasants were much poorer, or at least worse fed—sometimes, as in India, desperately and historically poor—and the pressure of men and women on limited lands was already more severe. Nevertheless, it seemed to a good many of them that the best solution to their problems was not to get involved with those who told them that economic development would bring untold wealth and prosperity, but to keep them at bay. Long experience had shown them and their ancestors before them, that no good came from outside. Generations of silent calculation had taught them that minimizing risks was a better policy than maximizing profits. This did not keep them entirely outside the ambit of a global economic revolution which reached even the more isolated among them in the form of plastic sandals, petrol-cans, ancient trucks and—of course—government offices with pieces of paper in them, but it tended to divide humanity in such areas into those who operated in and through the world of writing and offices and the rest. In most of the rural Third World the central distinction was between "coast" and "interior" or city and backwoods.*

The trouble was that, since modernity and government went together, "the interior" was governed by "the coast," the backwoods by the city, the illiterate by the educated. In the beginning was the word. The House of Assembly of what would shortly become the independent state of Ghana, included among its 104 members sixty-eight who had had some form of post-primary education. The 106 members of the Legislative Assembly for the Telengana (South India) contained ninety-seven with secondary or higher education, including fifty graduates. In both these regions the great majority of the inhabitants at the time were illiterate (Hodgkin, 1961, p. 29; Gray, 1970, p. 135). What is more, anyone wishing to be active in the *national* government of Third World states needed to be literate not only in the common language of the region (which was not necessarily that of his or her community) but in one of the small number of international languages (English, French, Spanish, Arabic, Mandarin Chinese), or at least the regional lingua franca which new governments tended to develop into written "national" languages (Swahili, Bahasa, Pidgin). The only exception was in those parts of Latin America where the written official languages (Spanish and Portuguese) coincided with the spoken language of the majority. Out of the candidates for public office in Hyderabad (India) in the general election of 1967 only three (out of thirty-four) spoke no English (Bernstorff, 1970, p. 146).

Even the more remote and backward people therefore increasingly recognized the advantages of superior education, even when they could not themselves share them; perhaps especially when they could not. In a literal sense, knowledge meant power, most obviously in countries where the state appeared to its subjects to be a machine that extracted their resources and then distributed these resources to state employees. Education meant a post, often a guaranteed post,† in the public service, with luck a career, which enabled men to extract bribes and commissions and to provide jobs for family and friends. A village in, say, Central Africa, which invested in the education of one of its young men, hoped for a

---

*Similar divisions were to be found in some of the backward regions of socialist states, e.g. in Soviet Kazakhstan, where the indigenous inhabitants showed no interest in abandoning farming and livestock, leaving industrialization and cities to a correspondingly large body of (Russian) immigrants.

†E.g. until the mid-1980s in Benin, Congo, Guinea, Somalia, Sudan, Mali, Rwanda and the Central African Republic (World Labour, 1989, p. 49).

return in the form of income and protection for the whole community from the government post which education would guarantee. In any case the successful civil servant was the best-paid man in the population. In a country like Uganda in the 1960s he could expect a (legal) salary 112 times the average per capita income of his countrymen (as against a comparable ratio of 10:1 in Great Britain) (U.N. World Social Situation, 1970, p. 66).

Where it seemed that poor people from the countryside might themselves share in the advantages of education, or provide them for their children (as in Latin America, the Third World region closest to modernity and most distant from colonialism), the desire to learn was virtually universal. "They all want to learn something," a Chilean communist organizer among the Mapuche Indians told the author in 1962. "I'm not an intellectual, and I can't teach them school knowledge, so I teach them how to play football." This thirst for knowledge explains much of the amazing mass migration from village to city which emptied the countryside of the South American continent from the 1950s on. For all enquiries concur that the attraction of the city lay not least in the better chances of education and training for the children. There they "could become something else." Schooling naturally opened the best prospects, but in backward agrarian regions even so simple a skill as being able to drive a motor vehicle could be the key to a better life. It was the first thing that an emigrant from a Quechua village in the Andes taught the cousins and nephews from home who joined him in the city, hoping to make their own way into the modern world, for had not his employment as an ambulance driver proved to be the foundation of his own family's success? (Julca, 1992).

Probably it was not until the 1960s or later that rural people outside parts of Latin America began systematically to see modernity as a promise rather than a threat. And yet there was one aspect of the policy of economic development which might have been expected to appeal to them since it directly affected the three fifths or more of human beings who lived by agriculture: land reform. This general slogan of politics in agrarian countries might cover anything from the break-up of large landholdings and their re-distribution to peasants and landless labourers to the abolition of feudal tenures or servitudes; rent reduction and tenancy reforms of various kinds to revolutionary land nationalization and collectivization.

There has probably never been more of it than in the decade after the end of the Second World War, for it was practised along the entire spectrum of politics. Between 1945 and 1950 almost half of the human race found themselves living in countries undergoing some kind of land reform—of the communist type in Eastern Europe and, after 1949 China, as a consequence of decolonization in the former British Indian empire and as a consequence of Japan's defeat, or rather American occupation policy, in Japan, Taiwan and Korea. The Egyptian revolution of 1952 extended its range to the western Islamic world: Iraq, Syria and Algeria followed the Cairo example. The Bolivian revolution of 1952 introduced it into South America, though Mexico since the revolution of 1910, or, more precisely, since its revival in the 1930s, had long championed *agrarismo*. Still, in spite of an increasing flood of political declarations and statistical enquiry on the subject, Latin America had too few revolutions, decolonizations or lost wars to have much actual land reform, until Fidel Castro's Cuban revolution (which introduced it on that island) put the matter on the political agenda.

For the modernizers the case for land reform was political (gaining peasant support for revolutionary regimes or for those which could preempt revolution or the like), ideological ("giving the land back to the toilers" etc.), and sometimes economic, although most revolutionaries or reformers did not expect too much from a mere distribution of land to a traditional peasantry and the landless or land-poor. Indeed, farm output fell drastically in Bolivia and Iraq immediately after these countries' respective land reforms in 1952 and 1958, though in fairness one should add that, where peasant skill and productivity were already high, land reform could quickly release a great deal of productive potential hitherto held in reserve by sceptical villagers, as in Egypt, Japan and, most strikingly, Taiwan (Land Reform, 1968, pp. 570–75). The case for maintaining a large peasantry in being was and is non-economic, since in the history of the modern world the enormous rise in agrarian output has gone together with an equally spectacular decline in the number and proportion of agriculturists; most dramatically so since the Second World War. Land reform could and did, however, demonstrate that peasant farming, especially by larger, modern-minded farmers, could be as efficient as, and more flexible than the traditional landed estate, the imperialist plantation, and, indeed, ill-judged modern attempts to conduct agriculture on a quasi-industrial basis, such as Soviet-type giant state farms and the British scheme for producing ground-nuts in Tanganyika (the present Tanzania) after 1945. Crops like coffee, or even sugar and rubber, once thought of as essentially plantation-produced, are so no longer, even if the plantation still maintains a clear advantage over small-scale and unskilled producers in some cases. Still, the major advances of Third World agriculture since the war, the "Green revolution" of new scientifically selected crops, have been achieved by business-minded farmers, as in the Punjab.

However, the strongest economic case for land reform rests not on productivity but on equality. On the whole economic development has tended, first to increase and later to diminish the inequality of national income distribution over the long haul, although economic decline and a theological belief in the free market have lately begun to reverse this here and there. Equality at the end of the Golden Age was greater in the developed Western countries than in the Third World. Yet while income inequality was at its highest in Latin America, followed by Africa, it was unusually low in a number of Asian countries, where a very radical land reform had been imposed under the auspices, or by, the American occupying forces: Japan, South Korea and Taiwan. (None, however, were as egalitarian as the socialist countries of Eastern Europe or, at the time, Australia.) (Kakwani, 1980.) Observers of the industrialising triumphs of these countries have naturally speculated how far they have been assisted by the social or economic advantages of this situation, just as observers of the much more fitful advance of the Brazilian economy, always on the verge of but never achieving its destiny as the U.S.A. of the southern hemisphere, have wondered how far it has been held back by the spectacular inequality of its income distribution—which inevitably restricts the domestic market for industry. Indeed, the striking social inequality of Latin America can hardly be unconnected with the equally striking absence of systematic agrarian reform from so many of its countries.

Land reform was undoubtedly welcomed by the peasantry of the Third World, at least until it was transformed into collective farming or cooperative production, as it usually was in communist countries. However, what the modernisers saw in it was not what it meant to the peasants, who were uninterested in macro-economic problems, who saw national politics in a different perspective from the city reformers, and whose demand for land was not based on general principle but on specific claims. Thus the radical land reform instituted by a government of reformist generals in Peru in 1969, which destroyed the country's system of large estates (*haciendas*) at one blow, failed for this reason. For the Indian highland communities, which had lived in unstable coexistence with the vast Andean livestock ranches to whom they supplied labour, reform simply meant the just return to the "native communities" of the common lands and pastures once alienated from them by the landlords, whose boundaries were accurately remembered over the centuries, and whose loss they had never accepted (Hobsbawm, 1974). They were not interested in the maintenance of the old enterprise as a productive unit (now under the ownership of the *comunidades* and its former workforce), in cooperative experiments, or in other agrarian novelties, other than the traditional mutual aid within the—far from egalitarian—community. After the reform the communities went back to "invading" the lands of the cooperativized estates (of which they were now co-proprietors), as though nothing had changed in the conflict between estate and community (and between communities in dispute about their lands) (Gómez Rodríguez, pp. 242–55). As far as they were concerned, nothing had changed. The land reform closest to the peasant ideal was probably the Mexican one of the 1930s, which gave the common land inalienably to village communities to organize as they wished (*ejidos*) and assumed peasants were engaged in subsistence agriculture. It was a huge political success, but economically irrelevant to subsequent Mexican agrarian development.

IV

It is not surprising that the dozens of post-colonial states which emerged after the Second World War, together with most of Latin America, which also plainly belonged to the regions dependent on the old imperial and industrial world, soon found themselves grouped together as the "Third World"—the term is said to have been coined in 1952 (Harris, 1987, p.18)—by contrast with the "First World" of the developed capitalist countries and the "Second World" of the communist ones. In spite of the evident absurdity of treating Egypt and Gabon, India and Papua-New Guinea as societies of the same kind, this was not wholly implausible, inasmuch as all were poor (compared to the "developed" world),* all were dependent, all had governments that wanted to "develop," and none believed, in the aftermath of the Great Slump and the Second World War, that the capitalist world market (i.e. the economists' doctrine of "comparative advantage") or spontaneous private enterprise at home would achieve this end. Moreover, as the iron grille of the Cold War was clamped across the globe, all who had any freedom of action wanted to avoid joining either of the two alliance systems, i.e. to keep out of the Third World War which everyone feared.

---

*With the rarest exceptions, notably Argentina, which though rich, never recovered from the decline and fall of the British Empire, which had given it prosperity as a food exporter until 1929.

This does not mean that the "non-aligned" were equally opposed to both sides in the Cold War. The inspirers and champions of the movement (usually called after its first international conference in 1955 at Bandung in Indonesia), were radical colonial ex-revolutionaries—Jawaharlal Nehru of India, Sukarno of Indonesia, Colonel Gamal Abdel Nasser of Egypt, and a dissident communist, President Tito of Yugoslavia. All these, like so many of the ex-colonial regimes, were or claimed to be socialist in their own (i.e. non-Soviet) way, including the Royal Buddhist socialism of Cambodia. All had some sympathies for the Soviet Union or were at least ready to accept economic and military help from it; not surprisingly, since the United States had abandoned its old anti-colonial traditions at a moment's notice after the world divided, and visibly looked for support among the most conservative elements of the Third World: Iraq (before the 1958 revolution), Turkey, Pakistan and the Shah's Iran, which formed the Central Treaty Organization (CENTO); Pakistan, the Philippines and Thailand in the South-east Asia Treaty Organization (SEATO), both designed to complete the anti-Soviet military system whose main pillar was NATO (neither amounted to much). When the essentially Afro-Asian non-aligned group became tri-continental after the Cuban revolution of 1959, its Latin American members not surprisingly came from the republics of the western hemisphere least sympathetic to the Big Brother of the North. Nevertheless, unlike the U.S. sympathisers in the Third World, who might actually join the western alliance system, the non-communist Bandung states had no intention of being involved in a global superpower confrontation, since, as the Korean and the Vietnam War and the Cuban missile crisis proved, they were the perpetual potential front line in such a conflict. The more the actual (European) border between the two camps was stabilized, the more likely, if the guns were to fire, the bombs to drop, it would be in some Asian mountains or African bush.

Yet though the superpower confrontation dominated, and to some extent stabilized, inter-state relations world-wide, it did not entirely control them. There were two regions in which indigenous Third World tensions, essentially unconnected with the Cold War, created permanent conditions for conflict which periodically erupted in war: the Middle East and the northern part of the Indian subcontinent. (Both, not by chance, were the heirs to imperial schemes of partition.) The latter conflict zone was more easily insulated from the global Cold War, in spite of Pakistan's attempts to involve the Americans, which failed until the Afghan War of the 1980s (see chapters 8 and 16). Hence the West heard little and remembers even less of the three regional wars: the Sino–Indian War of

1962 over the ill-defined border between the two countries, won by China; the Indo–Pakistan War of 1965 (handily won by India); and the second Indo–Pakistan conflict of 1971, arising out of the breakaway of East Pakistan (Bangladesh), which India supported. U.S.A. and U.S.S.R. tried to act as benevolent neutrals and mediators. The situation in the Middle East could not be so isolated, because several of America's allies were directly involved: Israel, Turkey and the Shah's Iran. Moreover, as the succession of local revolutions, military and civilian, proved—from Egypt in 1952 via Iraq and Syria in the 1950s and 1960s, South Arabia in the 1960s and 1970s, to Iran itself in 1979—the region was and remains socially unstable.

These regional conflicts had no essential connection with the Cold War: the U.S.S.R. had been among the first to recognize the new state of Israel, which later established itself as the main ally of the U.S.A., and the Arab or other Islamic states, Right or Left, were united in repressing communism within their frontiers. The main force of disruption was Israel, where the Jewish settlers built a larger Jewish state than had been envisaged under the British partition (driving out seven hundred thousand non-Jewish Palestinians, perhaps a larger number than the Jewish population in 1948) (Calvocoressi, 1989, p. 215), fighting one war per decade for the purpose (1948, 1956, 1967, 1973, 1982). In the course of these wars, which can best be compared with the wars fought by the Prussian king Frederick II in the eighteenth century to win recognition for his possession of Silesia, which he had robbed from his neighbour, Austria, Israel also turned itself into the most formidable military force in the region and acquired nuclear arms, but failed to establish a stable basis of relations with its neighbour states, let alone with the permanently embittered Palestinians within its extended frontiers or in the diaspora of the Middle East. The collapse of the U.S.S.R. removed the Middle East from the front line of the Cold War, but left it as explosive as before.

Three lesser centres of conflict helped to keep it so: the eastern Mediterranean, the Persian Gulf and the border region between Turkey, Iran, Iraq and Syria where the Kurds attempted vainly to win the national independence which President Wilson had incautiously urged them to demand in 1918. Unable to find a permanent backer among the powerful states, they disturbed the relations between all their neighbours, who massacred them by all available means, including in the 1980s poison gas, insofar as not resisted by the proverbial skill of the Kurds as mountain guerrilla fighters. The eastern Mediterranean remained relatively quiet, since both Greece and Turkey were members of NATO, even though the conflict between the two led to a Turkish invasion of Cyprus, which was partitioned in 1974. On the other hand the rivalry between the western powers, Iraq and Iran, for positions in the Persian Gulf was to lead to the savage eight-year war between Iraq and revolutionary Iran 1980–88 and, after the end of the Cold War, between the U.S.A. and its allies and Iraq in 1991.

One part of the Third World remained fairly remote from both global and local international conflicts until after the Cuban revolution: Latin America. Except for small patches on the mainland (the Guyanas, Belize—then known as British Honduras and the smaller islands of the Caribbean), it had been decolonized long ago. Culturally and linguistically its populations were Western, inasmuch as the great bulk of even its poor inhabitants were Roman Catholics and, but for some areas of the Andes and continental central America, spoke or understood a culture-language shared by Europeans. While the region had inherited an elaborate racial hierarchy from the Iberian conquerors, it also inherited from an overwhelmingly male conquest a tradition of massive miscegenation. There were few genuine whites, except in the southern cone of South America (Argentina, Uruguay, southern Brazil) populated by European mass immigration, where there were very few natives. In both cases achievement and social status cancelled out race. Mexico elected a recognizably Zapotec Indian, Benito Juárez, as president as early as 1861. At the time of writing Argentina has as president a Lebanese Muslim immigrant and Peru a Japanese immigrant. Both choices were still unthinkable in the U.S.A. To this day Latin America still remains outside the vicious circle of ethnic politics and ethnic nationalism which ravages the other continents.

Moreover, while most of the continent clearly recognized itself to be what was now called a "neocolonial" dependency on a single dominant imperial power, the U.S.A. was realistic enough not to send gunboats and marines into the larger states—it did not hesitate to use them against the small ones—and the Latin governments from the Rio Grande to Cape Horn knew perfectly well that the wise thing was to keep on the right side of Washington. The Organization of American States (OAS), founded in 1948, its headquarters in Washington, was not a body inclined to disagree with the U.S.A. When Cuba made its revolution, the OAS expelled it.

V

And yet, at the very moment when the Third World and the ideologies based on it were at their peak, the concept began to crumble. In the 1970s it became increasingly evident that no single name or label could adequately cover a set of increasingly divergent countries. The term was still convenient to distinguish poor countries of the world from the rich, and insofar as the gap between the two zones, often now called "the North" and "the South," was visibly widening, there was much point to the distinction. The gap in per capita GNP between the "developed" and the backward world (i.e. the OECD countries and the "low and middle economies")* continued to widen: the first group averaged 14.5 times the GNP per capita of the second in 1970 but over twenty-four times the poor countries' GNP per capita in 1990 (*World Tables,* 1991, Table 1). However, the Third World is demonstrably no longer a single entity.

What split it was primarily economic development. The triumph of OPEC in 1973 produced, for the first time, a body of Third World states, mostly backward by any criteria and hitherto poor, which now emerged as world-scale super-millionaires, especially when they consisted of smallish thinly inhabited stretches of sand or forest ruled by (usually Muslim) sheikhs or sultans. It was plainly impossible to class, say, the United Arab Emirates, each of whose half-million inhabitants (1975) had, in theory, a share of the GNP worth over $13,000—almost double the GNP per capita of the U.S.A. at this date (World Tables, 1991, pp. 596, 604)—in the same pigeon-hole as, say, Pakistan, which then enjoyed a GNP per capita of $130. Oil states with a large population did not do so well, but it nevertheless became evident that states dependent on the export of a single primary commodity, however disadvantaged in other respects, could become extremely rich, even if this easy money also, almost invariably, tempted them into throwing it out of the window.† By the early 1990s even Saudi Arabia had managed to run into debt.

In the second place, part of the Third World was visibly and rapidly becoming industrialized and joining the First World, even though it

*The OECD, which comprises most of the "developed" capitalist countries, includes Belgium, Denmark, the German Federal Republic, France, Great Britain, Ireland, Iceland, Italy, Luxemburg, Netherlands, Norway, Sweden, Switzerland, Canada and the U.S.A., Japan and Australia. For political reasons this organization, set up during the Cold War, also included Greece, Portugal, Spain and Turkey.

†This is not a Third World phenomenon. When informed of the wealth of the British North Sea oil fields, a cynical French politician is said to have remarked prophetically: "They will waste it and run into a crisis."

remained much poorer. South Korea, as spectacular an industrial success story as any in history, had a GNP per capita (1989) barely higher than that of Portugal, the poorest by far of the members of the European Community (World Bank Atlas, 1990, p. 7). Once again, qualitative differences apart, South Korea is no longer comparable with, say, Papua-New Guinea, although the GNP per capita of the two countries was exactly the same in 1969 and remained of the same order of magnitude until the middle of the 1970s: it is now about five times as large (World Tables, 1991, pp. 352, 456). As we have seen, a new category, the NICs, entered the international jargon. There was no precise definition, but practically all lists include the four "Pacific tigers" (Hong Kong, Singapore, Taiwan and South Korea), India, Brazil and Mexico, but the process of Third World industrialization is such that Malaya and the Philippines, Colombia, Pakistan and Thailand as well as some others have also been included. Actually, a category of new and rapid industrializers crosses the borders of the three worlds, for strictly it should also include such "industrialized market economies" (i.e. capitalist countries) as Spain and Finland, and most of the ex-socialist states of Eastern Europe; not to mention, since the late 1970s, Communist China.

In fact, in the 1970s observers began to draw attention to a "new international division of labour," i.e. a massive shift of industries producing for the world market from the first generation of industrial economies, which had previously monopolized them, to other parts of the world. This was partly due to the deliberate transfer by firms from the old industrial world of part or all of their production or supplies to the Second and Third Worlds, eventually followed by some transfers of even very sophisticated processes in high-tech industries, such as research and development. The revolution in modern transport and communications made genuinely worldwide production both possible and economic. It was also due to the deliberate efforts of Third World governments to industrialize by conquering export markets, if need be (but preferably not) at the expense of the old protection of home markets.

This economic globalization, which can be verified by anyone who checks the national origins of products sold in any North American shopping mall, developed slowly in the 1960s and accelerated strikingly during the decades of the world's economic troubles after 1973. How rapidly it advanced may once again be illustrated by South Korea which, at the end of the 1950s, still had almost 80 per cent of its working population in agriculture, from which it derived almost three quarters of its national income (Rado, 1962, pp. 740, 742–43). It inaugurated the first of its Five-Year development plans in 1962. By the late 1980s it got only

10 per cent of its GDP from agriculture and had become the eighth-largest industrial economy of the non-communist world.

In the third place, a number of countries emerged (or rather were sub-merged) at the bottom of the international statistics, which even international euphemism found it difficult to describe simply as "developing," since they were plainly both poor and increasingly lagging. A sub-group of low-income developing countries was tactfully established to distinguish the three billion human beings whose GNP per capita (had they received it) would have worked out at an average of $330 in 1989, from the five hundred luckier millions in less destitute countries, like the Dominican Republic, Ecuador and Guatemala, whose average GNP was about three times as high and the even more luxurious members of the next group (Brazil, Malaysia, Mexico and the like) which averaged about eight times as much. (The eight hundred or so millions in the most prosperous group enjoyed a theoretical GNP allocation per head of $18,280 or fifty-five times as much as the bottom three-fifths of humanity (World Bank Atlas, 1990, p. 10). In effect, as the world economy became genuinely global and, especially after the fall of the Soviet region, more purely capitalist and business-dominated, investors and entrepreneurs discovered that large parts of it were of no profitable interest to them, unless, perhaps, they could bribe its politicians and civil servants into wasting the money extracted from their unfortunate citizens on armaments or prestige projects.*

A disproportionately large number of these countries were to be found in the unhappy continent of Africa. The end of the Cold War deprived such states of the economic (i.e. largely military) aid which had turned some of them, like Somalia, into armed camps and eventual battlefields.

Moreover, as divisions among the poor increased, so globalization brought movements most obviously of human beings that crossed the dividing lines between regions and classifications. From the rich countries tourists flowed into the Third World as never before. In the middle of the 1980s (1985), to take only some Muslim countries, the sixteen millions of Malaysia received three million tourists per year; the seven million Tunisians two millions; the three million Jordanians two millions (Din, 1989, p. 545). From the poor countries the streams of labour migration into the rich swelled into huge torrents, insofar as they were

---

* "As a rule of thumb 5 per cent of $200,000 will win the help of a senior official below top rank. The same percentage of $2m and you are dealing with the permanent secretary. At $20m enter the minister and senior staff, while a cut from $200m 'justifies the serious attention of the head of state'" (Holman, 1993).

not dammed back by political barriers. By 1968 migrants from the Maghreb (Tunisia, Morocco and, above all, Algeria) already formed almost a quarter of all foreigners in France (in 1975 5.5 per cent of the Algerian population emigrated) and one third of all immigrants to the U.S.A. came from Latin America—at that time still overwhelmingly from Central America (Potts, 1990, pp. 145, 146, 150). Nor did this migration move only towards the old industrial countries. The number of foreign workers in the oil-producing states of the Middle East and Libya shot up from 1.8 to 2.8 millions in a mere five years (1975–80) (Population, 1984, p. 109). Most of them came from the region, but a large body came from South Asia and even further afield. Unfortunately in the grim 1970s and 1980s labour migration became increasingly hard to separate from the torrents of men, women and children who fled from, or were uprooted by, famine, political or ethnic persecution, war and civil war, thus facing the countries of the First World, equally committed (in theory) to helping refugees and (in practice) to preventing immigration from poor countries, with severe problems of political and legal casuistry. With the exception of the U.S.A., and to a lesser extent Canada and Australia, which encouraged or permitted mass immigration from the Third World, they opted to keep them out under the pressure of a growing xenophobia among their native populations.

VI

The astonishing "great leap forward" of the (capitalist) world economy, and its growing globalization not only divided and disrupted the concept of a Third World, it also brought virtually all its inhabitants consciously into the modern world. They did not necessarily like it. Indeed, many "fundamentalist" and other nominally traditionalist movements which now gained ground in several Third World countries, especially, but not exclusively, in the Islamic region, were specifically revolts against modernity, though this is certainly not true of all movements to which this imprecise label is attached.* But they knew themselves to be part of a world which was not like their fathers'. It came to them in the form of the dusty backroads bus or truck; the petrol pump; the battery-powered

---

* Thus conversion to "fundamentalist" Protestant sects, which is common in Latin America, is, if anything, a "modernist" reaction against the ancient status quo represented by local Catholicism. Other "fundamentalisms" are analogous to ethnic nationalism, e.g. in India.

transistor radio, which brought the world to them—perhaps even to the illiterates in their own unwritten dialect or language, though this was probably the privilege of the urban immigrant. But in a world where country people migrated to the cities in their millions, and even in rural Africa countries with urban populations of a third or more becoming common—Nigeria, Zaire, Tanzania, Senegal, Ghana, Ivory Coast, Chad, Central African Republic, Gabon, Benin, Zambia, Congo, Somalia, Liberia—almost everybody had worked in the city, or had a relative who lived there. Village and city were henceforth interwoven. Even the most remote now lived in a world of plastic sheeting, Coca-Cola bottles, cheap digital watches and artificial fibres. By a strange inversion of history the back country of the Third World even began to commercialize its skills in the First World. On city street-corners of Europe small groups of peripatetic Indians from the South American Andes played their melancholy flutes and on the pavements of New York, Paris and Rome black pedlars from West Africa sold trinkets to the natives as the natives' ancestors had done on their trading voyages to the Dark Continent.

Almost certainly the big city was the crucible of change, if only because it was modern by definition. "In Lima," as an upwardly mobile migrant from the Andes used to tell his children, "there's more progress, there's much more stimulation" (*más roce*) (Julca, 1992). However much the migrants used the tool-kit of traditional society to construct their urban existence, building and structuring the new shanty-towns like the old rural communities, too much in the city was novel and unprecedented, too many of its mores conflicted with those of the olden days. Nowhere was this more dramatic than in the expected behaviour of young women, whose break with tradition was deplored from Africa to Peru. In a traditional *huayno* song from Lima (*"La gringa"*) an immigrant boy complains:

> When you came from your homeland, you came as a country girl
> Now you are in Lima you comb your hair in a city way
> You even say, wait "please." I'm going to dance the twist
> . . .
> Don't be pretentious, be less proud
> . . .
> Between your hair and my hair, there is no difference.
> (Mangin, 1970, pp. 31–32.)*

*Or, from Nigeria in the image of a new type of African girl in the market literature of Onitsha: "The girls are no longer the traditional, quiet, modest playthings

Yet from the city the consciousness of modernity spread to the country-side (even where rural life was not itself transformed by new crops, new technology, and new forms of organization and marketing) through the dramatic "green revolution" of grain-crop farming by scientifically de-signed crop varieties in parts of Asia, which spread from the 1960s on, or, a little later, by the development of new export crops for the world mar-ket, made possible both by the mass air-freighting of perishables (tropical fruit, flowers) and new consumer tastes in the "developed" world (co-caine). The effect of such rural changes is not to be underestimated. Nowhere did the old ways and the new come into more frontal collision than on the Amazonian frontier of Colombia, which in the 1970s became a staging-post for the transport of Bolivian and Peruvian coca, and the lo-cation of the laboratories processing it into cocaine. This happened a few years after it had been settled by peasant frontier colonists escaping from the state and landlords, and who were defended by those recognized pro-tectors of the peasant way of life, the (communist) guerrillas of the FARC. Here the market, in its most ruthless form, clashed with those who lived by subsistence farming and what men could get with a gun, a dog and a fishing-net. How could a patch of yucca and bananas compete against the temptation to cultivate a crop commanding bonanza prices— even though unstable ones—and the old way of life against the airstrips and the boomtown settlements of the drug-makers and traffickers and their freewheeling gunmen, bars and brothels (Molano, 1988)?

The countryside was indeed being transformed, but even its transfor-mations depended on the city civilization and its industries, for often enough its very economy depended on the earnings of the emigrants, as in the so-called "black homelands" of apartheid South Africa, which gen-erated only 10-15 per cent of their inhabitants' income, the remainder com-ing from the earnings of migrant workers in the white territories (Ripken and Wellmer, 1978, pp. 196). Paradoxically, in the Third World as in parts of the First, the city could become the saviour of a rural economy which, but for its impact, might have been abandoned by people who had learned from migrant experience—their own or their neighbours'—that men and women had alternatives. They discovered that it was not in-evitable that they should slave a lifetime away scratching a wretched livelihood from marginal, exhausted and stony land, as their ancestors had done. Plenty of rural settlements across the globe, in romantic, and

---

of their parents. They write love letters. They are coy. They demand presents from their boy-friends and victims They even deceive men. They are no longer the dumb creatures to be won through their parents" (Nwoga, 1965, pp. 178–79).

therefore agriculturally marginal landscapes, were emptied of all except the elderly from the 1960s on. Yet a highland community whose emigrants discovered a niche in the economy of the big city which they could occupy—in this case selling fruit, or, more precisely, strawberries in Lima—could maintain or revitalize its pastoral character by a shift from farm-income to non-farm-income operating through a complicated symbiosis of migrant and resident households (Smith, 1989, chapter 4). It is perhaps significant that, in this particular case, which has been unusually well studied, the migrants rarely became workers. They chose to fit into the great network of the Third World "informal economy" as petty traders. For the major social change in the Third World was probably that carried by the new and growing middle and lower-middle classes of migrants engaged in some method, or more likely multiple methods, of earning money, and the major form of its economic life was—especially in the poorest countries—the informal economy which escaped official statistics.

So, some time in the last third of the century the wide trench that separated the small modernizing or Westernized ruling minorities of Third World countries from the mass of their peoples began to be filled by the general transformation of their societies. We do not yet know how or when this happened or what forms the new consciousness of this transformation took, for most of these countries still lacked even adequate government statistical services or the machinery of market and public opinion research, or the academic social science departments with research students to keep busy. In any case, what happens at the grassroots of societies is difficult to discover even in the best-documented countries, until it has happened, which is why the early stages of new social and cultural fashions among the young are unpredictable, unpredicted and often unrecognized even by those who live by making money out of them, like the popular culture industry, let alone by the parental generation. Yet clearly something was stirring in Third World cities below the level of elite consciousness, even in an apparently completely stagnant country like the Belgian Congo (now Zaire), for how else can we explain that the type of popular music developed there in the inert 1950s became the most influential in Africa in the 1960s and 1970s (Manuel, 1988, pp. 86, 97–101)? For that matter, how can we explain the rise of political consciousness which causes the Belgians to send the Congo off to independence in 1960 virtually at a moment's notice, though until then this colony, almost equally hostile to native education as to native political activity, looked, to most observers, as "likely to remain as shut off from the rest of the world as Japan before the Meiji restoration" (Calvocoressi, 1989, p. 377)?

Whatever the stirrings in the 1950s, by the 1960s and 1970s the signs of major social transformation were quite evident in the western hemisphere, and undeniable in the Islamic world and the major countries of South and South-east Asia. Paradoxically, they were probably least visible in the parts of the socialist world which corresponded to the Third World, e.g. in Soviet central Asia and the Caucasus. For it is not often recognized that communist revolution was an engine of conservation. While it set out to transform a specified number of aspects of life—state power, property relations, economic structure and the like—it froze others in their pre-revolutionary shapes, or at any rate protected them against the universal continuous subversion of change in capitalist societies. In any case its strongest weapon, sheer state power, was less effective at transforming human behaviour than either the positive rhetoric about "the new socialist man" or the negative rhetoric about "totalitarianism" liked to think. Uzbeks and Tadjiks who lived north of the Soviet–Afghan border were almost certainly more literate and more secularized and better-off than those who lived south of it, but they may not have differed as much in their mores as seventy years of socialism would have led one to expect. Blood-feud was probably not a major preoccupation of the authorities in the Caucasus since the 1930s (though during collectivisation the death of a man in a *kolkhoz* threshing-machine accident led to a feud which entered the annals of Soviet jurisprudence), but in the early 1990s observers warned of "the danger of national self-extermination [in Chechnia] since the majority of the Chechen families have been dragged into a vendetta type relationship" (Trofimov/Djangava, 1993).

The cultural consequences of this social transformation await the historian. They cannot be considered here, though it is clear that, even in very traditional societies, the network of mutual obligation and customs came under increasing strain. "The extended family in Ghana and across Africa" it was observed (Harden, 1990, p. 67) "functions under immense stress. Like a bridge that has borne too much high-speed traffic for too many years, its foundations are cracking . . . The rural old and the urban young are separated by hundreds of miles of bad roads and centuries of development."

Politically it is easier to assess the paradoxical consequences. For, with the entry of the masses of the population, or at least the young and city people, into a modern world, the monopoly of the small, Westernized elites who shaped the first generation of post-colonial history was being challenged. And with them, the programmes, the ideologies, the very vocabulary and syntax of the public discourse, on which the new states rested. For the new urban and urbanised masses, even the new massive

middle classes, however educated, were not, and by virtue of sheer numbers, could not be, the old elites, whose members could hold their own
with the colonialists or with their fellow-graduates from European or
American schools. Often—this was very obvious in South Asia—they resented them. In any case, the masses of the poor did not share the belief
in the Western nineteenth-century aspiration of secular progress. In the
western Islamic countries the conflict between the old secular leaders and
the new Islamic mass democracy became patent, and explosive. From Algeria to Turkey the values which, in the countries of Western liberalism,
are associated with constitutional government and the rule of law, as for
instance the rights of women, were being protected—insofar as they existed—against democracy by the military force of the liberators of their
nations, or their heirs.

The conflict was not confined to Islamic countries, nor the reaction
against the old values of progress to the masses of the poor. The Hindu
exclusivism of the BJP party in India had substantial support among the
new business and middle classes. The impassioned and savage ethno-
religious nationalism which in the 1980s turned peaceful Sri Lanka into a
killing field, comparable only to El Salvador, occurred, unexpectedly, in a
prosperous Buddhist country. It was rooted in two social transformations:
the profound identity crisis of villages whose social order had gone to
pieces, and the rise of a mass stratum of better-educated youth (Spencer,
1990). Villages transmuted by in- and out-migration, divided by the
widening differences between rich and poor that the cash economy
brought, racked with the instability brought by the unevenness of an
education-based social mobility, the fading of the physical and linguistic
markers of caste and status which separated people but also left no doubt
about their positions—these inevitably lived in anxiety about their community. This has been used to explain, among other things, the appearance of novel symbols and rituals of a togetherness which was itself
novel, such as the sudden development of congregational forms of Buddhist worship in the 1970s, replacing older private and household forms
of devotion; or the institution of school sports days opened with the national anthem played on borrowed tape cassettes.

These were the politics of a changing and inflammable world. What
made them less predictable was that in many countries of the Third
World nationwide politics in the sense invented and recognized in
the West since the French Revolution had never existed, or had not been
allowed to function. Where there was a long tradition of politics with
some kind of mass roots, or even a substantial acceptance among the passive citizens of the legitimacy of the "political classes" who conducted

their affairs, a degree of continuity could be maintained. Colombians, as readers of García Márquez know, continued to be born little liberals or little conservatives, as they had for more than a century, though they might change the content of the bottles with these labels. The Indian National Congress changed, split and reformed in the half-century since independence, but until the 1990s Indian general elections—with only fleeting exceptions—continued to be won by those who appealed to its historic aims and traditions. Though communism disintegrated elsewhere, the deep-rooted Left-wing tradition of Hindu (West) Bengal, as well as competent administration maintained the Communist Party (Marxist) in almost permanent government in the state where the national struggle against Britain had meant not Gandhi nor even Nehru, but the terrorists and Subhas Bose.

Moreover, structural change might itself lead politics in directions familiar in the history of the First World. "Newly industrializing countries" were likely to develop industrial working classes who demanded workers' rights and labour unions, as the record of Brazil and South Korea showed, as indeed did that of Eastern Europe. They did not have to develop political labour-cum-people's parties reminiscent of the mass social democratic movements of pre-1914 Europe, although it is not insignificant that Brazil generated just such a successful national party in the 1980s, the Workers' Party (PT). (But the tradition of the workers' movement in its home base, the automobile industry of São Paulo, was a combination of populist labour law and communist factory militants, and that of the intellectuals who flocked to support it was solidly Left, as was the ideology of the Catholic clergy, whose support helped to put it on its feet.)* Again, the rapid industrial growth tended to generate large and educated professional classes which, though far from subversive, would have welcomed the civic liberalization of authoritarian industrializing regimes. Such longings for liberalization were to be found, in the 1980s, in different contexts and with varying results, in Latin America and the Far-Eastern NICs (South Korea and Taiwan), as well as within the Soviet bloc.

Nevertheless, there were vast areas of the Third World where the political consequences of social transformation were indeed impossible to

*Except for the socialist orientation of the one, the anti-socialist ideology of the other, the similarities between the Brazilian Workers' Party and the contemporary Polish Solidarity movement were striking: a bona fide proletarian leader—a shipyard electrician and skilled auto-worker—a brains trust of intellectuals and strong Church backing. They are even greater if we remember that the PT sought to replace the communist organization, which opposed it.

foresee. All that was certain, was the instability and inflammability of that world, to which the half-century since the Second World War had borne witness.

We must now turn to that part of the world which, for most of the Third World after decolonization, appeared to provide a more suitable and encouraging model for progress than the West: the "Second World" of the socialist systems modelled on the Soviet Union.

CHAPTER THIRTEEN

"Real Socialism"

The October Revolution did not only produce a world-historical division by establishing the first post-capitalist state and society, but it also divided Marxism and socialist politics . . . After the October Revolution, socialist strategies and perspectives began to be based upon political example instead of upon analyses of capitalism.

—Göran Therborn (1985, p. 227)

Economists today . . . understand much better than before the real versus the formal modes of the economy's functioning. They know about the "second economy," maybe even a third one too, and about a welter of informal but widespread practices without which nothing works.

—Moshe Lewin in Kerblay (1983, p. xxii)

I

When the dust of the battles of war and civil war had settled in the early 1920s, and the blood of the corpses and wounds had congealed, most of what had before 1914 been the Orthodox Russian Empire of the Tsars emerged intact as an empire, but under the government of the Bolsheviks and dedicated to the construction of world socialism. It was the only one of the antique dynastic-cum-religious empires to survive the First World War, which shattered both the Ottoman Empire, whose sultan was khalif of all faithful Muslims, and the Habsburg Empire which maintained a special relationship with the Roman Church. Both broke up under the pressures of defeat. That Russia survived as a single multi-ethnic entity stretching from the Polish border in the west to the Japanese border in the east was almost certainly due to the October revolution, for the tensions which had broken up the earlier empires elsewhere emerged or re-emerged in the Soviet Union at the end of the 1980s, when the communist system that had held the union together since 1917 effectively abdicated. Whatever the future was to bring, what emerged in the early 1920s was a single state, desperately impoverished and backward—far more backward even than Tsarist Russia—but of enormous size: "one sixth of the world's surface," as communists liked to boast between the wars—dedicated to a society different from and opposed to capitalism.

In 1945 the borders of the region that seceded from world capitalism were dramatically extended. In Europe they now included the entire area east of a line running, roughly, from the river Elbe in Germany to the Adriatic sea, and the entire Balkan peninsula except Greece and the small part of Turkey that remained on that continent. Poland, Czechoslovakia, Hungary, Yugoslavia, Romania, Bulgaria and Albania now moved into the socialist zone, as well as that part of Germany occupied by the Red Army after the war and transformed into a "German Democratic Republic" in 1954. Most of the areas lost by Russia in the aftermath of war and revolution after 1917 and one or two territories previously belonging to the Habsburg Empire were also recuperated or acquired by the Soviet Union between 1939 and 1945. Meanwhile a vast new extension of the future socialist region took place in the Far East with the transfer of power to communist regimes in China (1949) and, partly, in Korea (1945) and what had been French Indochina (Vietnam, Laos, Cambodia) in the course of a thirty years' war (1945–75). There were a few further extensions of the communist region somewhat later, both in the western hemisphere—Cuba (1959) and in Africa in the 1970s—but substantially the socialist sector of the globe had taken shape by 1950. Thanks to the enormous numbers of the Chinese people, it now included about one third of the world's population, though the average size of the socialist states other than China, the U.S.S.R. and Vietnam (fifty-eight millions) was not particularly large. Their populations ranged from the 1.8 millions of Mongolia to the thirty-six millions of Poland.

This was the part of the world whose social systems some time in the 1960s came to be called, in the terminology of Soviet ideology, the countries of "really existing socialism"; an ambiguous term which implied or suggested that there might be other and better kinds of socialism, but in practice this was the only kind actually functioning. This was also the region whose social and economic systems as well as whose political regimes collapsed totally in Europe as the 1980s gave way to the 1990s.

In the East the political systems maintained themselves for the time being, though the actual economic restructuring they undertook in varying degrees amounted to a liquidation of socialism as hitherto understood by those regimes, notably in China. The scattered regimes elsewhere imitating or inspired by "really existing socialism" in other parts of the world had either collapsed or were probably not destined for a long life.

The first thing to observe about the socialist region of the globe was that for most of its existence it formed a separate and largely self-contained sub-universe both economically and politically. Its relations with the rest of the world economy, capitalist or dominated by the capitalism of the developed countries, were surprisingly scanty. Even at the height of the great boom in international trade during the Golden Years, only something like 4 per cent of the exports of the developed market economies went to the "centrally planned economies" and by the 1980s the share of Third World exports going to them was not much more. The socialist economies sent rather more of their modest exports to the rest of the world but even so two thirds of their international trade in the 1960s (1965) was within their own sector* (U.N. International Trade, 1983, vol. 1, p. 1046).

There was, for obvious reasons, little movement of people from the "first" to the "second" world, though some East European states began to encourage mass tourism from the 1960s. Emigration to non-socialist countries as well as temporary travel was strictly controlled, and at times virtually impossible. The political systems of the socialist world, essentially modelled on the Soviet system, had no real equivalent elsewhere. They were based on a strongly hierarchical and authoritarian single party which monopolized state power—in fact it sometimes virtually substituted itself for the state—operating a centrally planned command economy and (at least in theory) imposing a single mandatory Marxist-Leninist ideology on its country's inhabitants. The segregation or self-segregation of the "socialist camp" (as Soviet terminology came to call it from the late 1940s) gradually crumbled in the 1970s and 1980s. Nevertheless, the sheer degree of mutual ignorance and incomprehension that persisted between the two worlds was quite extraordinary, especially when we bear in mind that this was a period when both travel and communication of information were utterly revolutionized. For long periods very little information about these countries was allowed out and very little about other parts of the world was permitted to enter. In return, even non-expert educated

*The data refer strictly speaking, to the U.S.S.R. and its associated states, but it will serve as an order of magnitude.

and sophisticated citizens of the First World often found they could not make sense of what they saw or heard in countries whose past and present was so different from their own and whose languages were often beyond their reach.

The fundamental reason for the separation of the two "camps" was no doubt political. As we have seen, after the October revolution Soviet Russia saw world capitalism as the enemy to be overthrown as soon as practicable by world revolution. That revolution did not take place and Soviet Russia was isolated, surrounded by a capitalist world, many of whose most powerful governments wanted to prevent the establishment of this centre of global subversion, and, later, to eliminate it as soon as possible. The mere fact that the U.S.S.R. did not acquire official diplomatic recognition of its existence by the U.S.A. until 1933 demonstrates its initial outlaw status. Moreover, even when the always realistic Lenin was prepared, and indeed anxious, to make the most far-reaching concessions to foreign investors in return for their assistance in Russia's economic development, in practice he found no takers. Thus the young U.S.S.R. was necessarily launched on a course of self-contained development, in virtual isolation from the rest of the world economy. Paradoxically this was soon to provide it with its most powerful ideological argument. It seemed immune to the gigantic economic depression which devastated the capitalist economy after the Wall Street crash of 1929.

Politics once again helped to isolate the Soviet economy in the 1930s and, even more dramatically, the expanded Soviet sphere after 1945. The Cold War froze both the economic and the political relations between the two sides. For practical purposes all economic relations between them other than the most trivial (or the unavowable) had to pass through the state controls imposed by both. Trade between the blocs was a function of political relations. Not until the 1970s and 1980s were there signs that the separate economic universe of the "socialist camp" was being integrated into the wider world economy. In retrospect we can see that this was the beginning of the end for "really existing socialism." Yet there is no theoretical reason why the Soviet economy, as it emerged from revolution and civil war, could not have evolved in a far closer relationship with the rest of the world economy. Centrally planned and Western-type economies can be closely linked, as shown by the case of Finland, which at one point (1983) took over a quarter of its imports from the U.S.S.R. and sent a similar proportion of its exports there. However, the "socialist camp" that concerns the historian is the one which actually emerged, not what might have been.

The central fact of Soviet Russia was that its new rulers, the Bolshevik

Party, had never expected it to survive in isolation, let alone to become the nucleus of a self-contained collectivist economy ("socialism in one country"). None of the conditions which Marx or any of his followers had hitherto considered essential to the establishment of a socialist economy were present in this enormous hulk of a territory which was virtually a synonym for economic and social backwardness in Europe. The founders of Marxism assumed that the function of a Russian revolution could only be to spark off the revolutionary explosion in the more advanced industrial countries where the preconditions for the construction of socialism were present. As we have seen, this was exactly what looked like was happening in 1917–18, and it appeared to justify Lenin's highly controversial decision—at least among Marxists—to set the course of the Russian Bolsheviks for Soviet power and socialism. In Lenin's view, Moscow would only be the temporary headquarters of socialism until it could move to its permanent capital in Berlin. It is no accident that the official language of the Communist International, set up as the general staff of world revolution in 1919, was—and remained—not Russian but German.

When it became clear that Soviet Russia was to be, for the time being, which would certainly not be short, the only country in which proletarian revolution had triumphed, the logical, indeed the only persuasive policy for the Bolsheviks, was to transform it from a backward into an advanced economy and society as soon as possible. The most obvious known way to do this was to combine an all-out offensive against the cultural backwardness of the notoriously "dark," ignorant, illiterate and superstitious masses with an all-out drive for technological modernization and industrial revolution. A Soviet-based communism therefore became primarily a programme for transforming backward countries into advanced ones. This concentration on ultra-rapid economic growth was not without its appeal even in the developed capitalist world in its age of catastrophe, desperately seeking for a way to recover its economic dynamism. It was even more directly relevant to the problems of the world outside Western Europe and North America, most of which could recognize its own image in the agrarian backwardness of Soviet Russia. The Soviet recipe for economic development—centralized state economic planning aimed at the ultra-rapid construction of the basic industries and infrastructure essential to a modern industrial society—seemed designed for them. Moscow was not only a more attractive model than Detroit or Manchester because it stood for anti-imperialism, but it also seemed a more suitable model, especially for countries lacking both in private capital and a large body of private and profit-oriented industry. "Socialism" in this sense inspired a number of newly independent ex-colonial countries after the

Second World War whose governments rejected the communist political system (see chapter 12). Since the countries joining that system were also backward and agrarian, with the exception of Czechoslovakia, the future German Democratic Republic and, to a lesser extent, Hungary, the Soviet economic recipe also seemed to suit them, and their new rulers launched themselves into the task of economic construction with genuine enthusiasm. Moreover, the recipe seemed to be effective. Between the wars, and especially during the 1930s, the rate of growth of the Soviet economy outpaced all other countries except Japan, and in the first fifteen years after the Second World War the economies of the "socialist camp" grew considerably faster than those of the West, so much so that Soviet leaders like Nikita Khrushchev sincerely believed that, the curve of their growth continuing upwards at the same rate, socialism would outproduce capitalism within a foreseeable future; as indeed did the British premier Harold Macmillan. More than one economic observer in the 1950s wondered whether this might not happen.

Curiously enough no discussion of "planning," which was to be the central criterion of socialism, nor of rapid industrialization with priority for the heavy industries, was to be found in the writings of Marx and Engels, though planning is implicit in a socialized economy. But socialists, Marxist or otherwise, before 1917 had been too busy opposing capitalism to give much thought to the nature of the economy that would replace it, and after October Lenin himself, dipping, as he himself put it, one foot into the deep waters of socialism, made no attempt to dive into the unknown. It was the crisis of the Civil War that brought matters to a head. It led to the nationalization of all industries in mid-1918, and to the "War Communism" by means of which an embattled Bolshevik state organized its life-and-death struggle against counter-revolution and foreign intervention, and tried to raise the resources for it. All war economies, even in capitalist countries, involve planning and control by the state. In fact, the specific inspiration for Lenin's idea of planning was the German war economy of 1914–18 (which, as we have seen, was probably not the best model of its period and kind). Communist war economies were naturally inclined on grounds of principle to replace private by public property and management, and to dispense with the market and the price-mechanism, especially as none of these were of much use to improvise a national war effort at a moment's notice, and there were indeed communist idealists, like Nikolai Bukharin, who saw the civil war as the opportunity to establish the main structures of a Communist Utopia, and the grim economy of crisis, permanent and universal shortage, and the non-monetary allocation of rationed basic necessities to the people in kind—bread, clothes, bus-tickets—as a spartan pre-view of that social ideal. In fact, as the Soviet regime emerged victorious from the struggles of 1918–20 it was evident that War Communism, however necessary for the time being, could not continue, partly because the peasants would rebel against the military requisitioning of their grain, which had been its base, and the workers against its hardships, partly because it provided no effective means for restoring an economy which had been virtually destroyed: iron and steel production was down from 4.2 million tons in 1913 to two hundred thousand in 1920.

With his habitual realism Lenin introduced the New Economic Policy in 1921, which in effect reintroduced the market and, indeed, in his own words, retreated from War Communism to "State Capitalism." Yet it was at this very moment, when Russia's already retrograde economy had fallen to 10 per cent of its pre-war size (see chapter 2), that the need to industrialize massively, and to do so by government planning, became the obvious priority task for the Soviet government. And while the New Economic Policy dismantled War Communism, state control and compulsion remained as the only known model of an economy of socialized ownership and management. The first planning institution, the State Commission for the Electrification of Russia (GoElRo), in 1920 aimed, naturally enough, at modernizing technology, but the State Planning Commission set up in 1921 (Gosplan) had more universal objectives. It remained in being under that name until the end of the U.S.S.R. It became the ancestor and inspirer of all state institutions designed to plan, or even to exercise macro-economic supervision over, the economies of twentieth-century states.

The New Economic Policy (NEP) was the subject of impassioned debate in Russia in the 1920s and again in the early Gorbachev years of the 1980s, but for the opposite reasons. In the 1920s it was clearly recognized as a defeat for communism, or at least a diversion of the columns marching towards socialism from the main highway to which, in one way or another, the way back had to be found. Radicals, such as the followers of Trotsky, wanted a break with NEP as soon as possible and a massive drive for industrialization, which was the policy eventually adopted under Stalin. Moderates, headed by Bukharin, who had put the ultra-radicalism of the War Communist years behind him, were keenly aware of the political and economic constraints under which the Bolshevik government had to operate in a country more overwhelmingly dominated by peasant agriculture than before the revolution. They favoured a gradual transformation. Lenin's own views could not be adequately expressed after paralysis hit him in 1922—he survived only until early

1924—but, while he could express himself, he seems to have favoured gradualism. On the other hand, the debates of the 1980s were retrospective searches for an historical socialist alternative to the Stalinism which actually succeeded NEP: a different road to socialism from the one actually envisaged by the Bolshevik Right and Left in the 1920s. In retrospect Bukharin became a sort of proto-Gorbachev.

These debates are no longer relevant. Looking back we can see that the original justification for the decision to establish socialist power in Russia disappeared when "proletarian revolution" failed to conquer Germany. Worse than this, Russia survived the Civil War in ruins and far more backward than it had been under Tsarism. True, Tsar, nobility, gentry and bourgeoisie had gone. Two millions emigrated, incidentally depriving the Soviet state of a large section of its educated cadres. But so had the industrial development of the Tsarist era, and most of the industrial workers who provided the social and political base for the Bolshevik party. Revolution and civil war had killed or dispersed them or transferred them from factories into the offices of state and party. What remained was a Russia even more firmly anchored in the past, the immobile, unshiftable mass of peasants in the restored village communities, to whom the revolution had (against earlier Marxist judgment) given the land, or rather whose occupation and distribution of the land in 1917–18 it had accepted as the necessary price of victory and survival. In many ways NEP was a brief golden age of peasant Russia. Suspended above this mass was the Bolshevik Party no longer representing anyone. As Lenin recognized with his usual lucidity, all it had going for it was the fact that it was, and was likely to remain, the accepted and established government of the country. It had nothing else. Even so, what actually governed the country was an undergrowth of smaller and larger bureaucrats, on average even less educated and qualified than before.

What options had this regime, which was, moreover, isolated and boycotted by foreign governments and capitalists, mindful of the expropriation of Russian assets and investments by the Revolution? NEP was indeed brilliantly successful in restoring the Soviet economy from the ruin of 1920. By 1926 Soviet industrial production had more or less recovered its pre-war level, though this did not mean much. The U.S.S.R. remained as overwhelmingly rural as in 1913 (82 per cent of the population in both cases) (Bergson/Levine, 1983, p. 100; Nove, 1969), and indeed only 7.5 per cent were employed outside agriculture. What this mass of peasants wanted to sell to the cities; what it wanted to buy from them; how much of its income it wanted to save; and how many of the many millions who chose to feed themselves in the villages rather than

face city poverty wanted to leave the farms: this determined Russia's economic future, for, apart from the state's tax income, the country had no
other available source of investment and labour. Leaving aside all political
considerations, a continuation of NEP, modified or not, would at best
produce a modest rate of industrialization. Moreover, until there was a
great deal more industrial development, there was little that the peasants
could buy in the city to tempt them to sell their surplus rather than to
eat and drink it in the villages. This (known as the "scissors crisis") was
to be the noose that eventually strangled NEP. Sixty years later a similar
but proletarian "scissors" undermined Gorbachev's *perestroika*. Why, Soviet workers were to argue, should they raise their productivity to earn
higher wages unless the economy produced the consumer goods to buy
with these higher wages? But how were these goods to be produced unless Soviet workers raised their productivity?

It was therefore never very likely that NEP—i.e. balanced economic
growth based on a peasant market economy steered by the state which
controlled its commanding heights—would prove a lasting strategy. For a
regime committed to socialism the political arguments against it were in
any case overwhelming. Would it not put the small forces committed to
this new society at the mercy of petty commodity production and petty
enterprise which would regenerate the capitalism just overthrown? And
yet, what made the Bolshevik Party hesitate was the prospective cost of
the alternative. It meant industrialization by force: a second revolution,
but this time not rising from below but imposed by state power from
above.

Stalin, who presided over the ensuing iron age of the U.S.S.R., was an
autocrat of exceptional, some might say unique, ferocity, ruthlessness and
lack of scruple. Few men have manipulated terror on a more universal
scale. There is no doubt that under some other leader of the Bolshevik
Party the sufferings of the peoples of the U.S.S.R. would have been less,
the number of victims smaller. Nevertheless, any policy of rapid modernization in the U.S.S.R., under the circumstances of the time, was bound to
be ruthless and, because imposed against the bulk of the people and imposing serious sacrifices on them, to some extent coercive. And the centralized command economy which conducted this drive through its
"plans" was, equally inevitably, closer to a military operation than to an
economic enterprise. On the other hand, like military enterprises which
have genuine popular moral legitimacy, the breakneck industrialization of
the first Five-Year Plans (1929–41) generated support by the very "blood,
toil, tears and sweat" it imposed on the people. As Churchill knew, sacrifice itself can motivate. Difficult though it may be to believe, even

the Stalinist system, which once again turned peasants into serfs attached to the land and made important parts of the economy dependent on a prison labour force of between four and thirteen millions (the Gulags) (Van der Linden, 1993) almost certainly enjoyed substantial support, though clearly not among the peasantry (Fitzpatrick, 1994).

The "planned economy" of the Five-Year Plans which took the place of NEP in 1928 was necessarily a crude instrument—far cruder than the sophisticated calculations of the Gosplan's pioneer economists of the 1920s, which were in turn far cruder than the planning instruments available to governments and large corporations in the later twentieth century. Essentially its business was to create new industries rather than to run them, and it chose to give immediate priority to the basic heavy industries and energy-production which were the foundation of any large industrial economy: coal, iron and steel, electricity, oil, etc. The U.S.S.R.'s exceptional wealth in suitable raw materials made this choice both logical and convenient. As in a war economy—and the Soviet planned economy was a kind of war economy—targets for production can, and indeed often must, be set without considering cost and cost-effectiveness, the test being whether they can be met and when. As in all such life-or-death efforts, the most effective method of fulfilling targets and meeting deadlines is giving urgent orders which produce all-out rushes. Crisis is its form of management. The Soviet economy settled down as a set of routines broken by frequent, almost institutionalized "shock efforts" in response to orders from above. Nikita Krushchev was later desperately to look for a way of making the system work in some other way than as a response to "shouting" (Khruschev, 1990, p. 18). Stalin, earlier, had exploited "storming" by deliberately setting unrealistic targets which encouraged superhuman efforts.

Moreover, the targets once set had to be understood, and carried out down to the remotest outpost of production in inner Asia—by administrators, managers, technicians and workers who, at least in the first generation, were inexperienced, ill-educated and used to wooden ploughs rather than machines. (The cartoonist David Low, visiting the U.S.S.R. in the early 1930s, drew a sketch of a collective farm-girl "absent-mindedly trying to milk a tractor.") This eliminated the last elements of sophistication, except at the very top which, for that very reason, carried the responsibility of an increasingly total centralization. As Napoleon and his chief-of-staff had once had to compensate for the technical deficiencies of his marshals, essentially untrained fighting officers promoted from the ranks, so all decisions were increasingly concentrated at the apex of the Soviet system. Gosplan's overcentralization compensated for the shortage of managers. The drawback of this procedure was an enormous bureaucratization of the economic apparatus as well as of all other parts of the system.*

So long as the economy remained at the semi-subsistence level and had merely to lay the foundation for modern industry, this rough-and-ready system, developed mainly in the 1930s, worked. It even developed its own flexibility, in an equally crude manner. Setting one lot of targets did not necessarily get into the immediate way of setting other targets, as it would in the sophisticated labyrinth of a modern economy. In fact, for a backward and primitive country isolated from foreign help, command industrialization, with all its waste and inefficiencies, worked impressively. It turned the U.S.S.R. into a major industrial economy in a few years and one capable, as Tsarist Russia had not been, of surviving and winning the war against Germany in spite of the temporary loss of areas containing a third of her population and, in many industries, half the industrial plant. One must add that in few other regimes could or would the people have borne the unparalleled sacrifices of this war effort (see Milward, 1979, pp. 92–97), or, indeed, those of the 1930s. Yet, if the system kept the consumption of the population at rock-bottom—in 1940 the economy produced only a little over one pair of footwear in all for each inhabitant of the U.S.S.R.—it guaranteed them that social minimum. It gave them work, food, clothes and housing at controlled (i.e. subsidized) prices and rents, pensions, health care and a rough equality until the system of rewards by special privileges for the "*nomenklatura*" got out of hand after Stalin's death. Much more generously, it gave education. The transformation of a largely illiterate country into the modern U.S.S.R. was, by any standards, a towering achievement. And for millions from the villages to whom, even in the harshest of times, Soviet development meant the opening of new horizons, the escape from darkness and ignorance to the city, light and progress, not to mention personal advancement and careers, the case for the new society was entirely convincing. In any case, they knew no other.

However, this success story did not include agriculture and those who lived by it, for industrialization rested on the backs of an exploited peasantry. There is very little to be said in favour of the Soviets' peasant and agricultural policy except perhaps that the peasants were not the only ones to carry the burden of "socialist primitive accumulation" (the phrase

* "If sufficiently clear instructions are to be issued for every major product group and for every producing unit, and in the absence of multi-level planning, then the centre cannot but be saddled with a colossal burden of work" (Dyker, 1985, p. 9).

of a follower of Trotsky who favoured it)* as has been claimed. The workers also carried part of the burden of generating resources for investing in the future.

The peasants—the majority of the population—were not only legally and politically inferior in status, at least until the (entirely inoperative) 1936 Constitution; they were not only taxed more highly and received inferior security, but the basic agricultural policy that replaced NEP, namely compulsory collectivization in cooperative or state farms, was and remained disastrous. Its immediate effect was to lower grain output and almost halve livestock, thus producing a major famine in 1932–33. Collectivisation led to a drop in the already low productivity of Russian farming, which did not regain the NEP level until 1940 or, allowing for the further disasters of the Second World War, 1950 (Tuma, 1965, p. 102). The massive mechanizations which tried to compensate for this fall was also, and has remained, massively inefficient. After a promising postwar period when Soviet agriculture even produced a modest surplus of grain for export, though the U.S.S.R. never even looked like becoming a major exporter as Tsarist Russia had been, Soviet farming ceased to be able to feed the population. From the early 1970s on it relied, sometimes to the extent of a quarter of its needs, on the world grain market. But for the slight relaxation of the collective system, which allowed peasants to produce for the market from small private plots—they covered about 4 per cent of the farmed area in 1938—the Soviet consumer would have eaten little but black bread. In short, the U.S.S.R. exchanged an inefficient peasant agriculture for an inefficient collective agriculture at vast cost.

As so often, this reflected the social and political conditions of Soviet Russia, rather than the inherent nature of the Bolshevik project. Cooperation and collectivization, combined in varying degrees with private cultivation—or even, as in the Israeli *kibbuzim*, more communist than anything in the U.S.S.R.—can be successful, while pure peasant farming has often been better at extracting subsidies from governments than profits from the soil.† However, in the U.S.S.R. there is no doubt at all that the agrarian policy was a failure. And one only too often copied, at

*In Marx's terms, "primitive accumulation" by expropriation and pillage was necessary to enable capitalism to acquire the original capital which subsequently undertook its own endogenous accumulation.

†Thus in the first half of the 1980s, Hungary, with a largely collectivised farming, exported more agricultural products than France from an agricultural area little more than a quarter of the French, and about twice as much (in value) as Poland did from an agricultural area almost three times the size of the Hungarian. Polish farming, like French, was not collective (FAO Production, 1986, FAO Trade, vol. 40, 1986).

least initially, by subsequent socialist regimes.

The other aspect of Soviet development for which very little can be said is the enormous and overblown bureaucratization which a centralized command government engendered, and with which even Stalin was unable to cope. Indeed, it has been seriously suggested that the Great Terror of the later 1930s was Stalin's desperate method to "overcome the bureaucratic maze and its skilful dodging of most government controls or injunctions" (Lewin, 1991, p. 17), or at least to prevent it from taking over as an ossified ruling class, as was eventually to happen under Brezhnev. Every attempt to make the administration more flexible and efficient merely swelled it and made it more indispensable. In the last years of the 1930s it grew at two-and-a-half times the rate of employment in general. As war approached, there was more than one administrator for every two blue-collar workers (Lewin, 1991). Under Stalin the top layer of these leading cadres were, as has been said, "uniquely powerful slaves, always on the brink of catastrophe. Their power and privileges were shadowed by a constant *memento mori*." After Stalin, or rather after the last of the "great bosses," Nikita Khrushchev, was removed in 1964, there was nothing in the system to prevent stagnation.

The third drawback of the system, and the one which in the end sank it, was its inflexibility. It was geared to constant growth in the output of products whose character and quality had been predetermined, but it contained no built-in mechanism for varying either quantity (except upward) or quality, or for innovation. In fact, it did not know what to do about inventions, and did not use them in the civilian economy, as distinct from the military-industrial complex.* As for the consumers, they were provided for neither by a market, which would have indicated their preferences, nor by any bias in their favour within the economic or, as we shall see, the political system. On the contrary, the system's original bias towards maximum growth of capital goods was reproduced by the planning machine. The most that one might claim is that, as the economy grew, it provided more consumer goods even while industrial structure kept on favouring capital goods. Even so, the system of distribution was so bad, and, above all, the system of organizing services so non-existent, that the rising standard of living in the U.S.S.R.—and improvement from the 1940s to the 1970s was very striking—could function effectively only with the help of, or by means of, an extensive "second" or

---

* "As little as one-third of all inventions find an application in the economy and even in these cases their diffusion is rare" (Vernikov, 1989, p. 7). The data appear to refer to 1986.

"black" economy, which grew rapidly, particularly from the end of the 1960s. Since unofficial economies by definition escape from official documentation, we can only guess at its size—but in the late 1970s it was estimated that the Soviet urban population spent about twenty billion roubles on private consumer, medical and legal services, plus about another seven billions in "tips" to ensure service (Alexeev, 1990). This would at the time have been a sum comparable to the total of imports of the country.

In short, the Soviet system was designed to industrialize a very backward and undeveloped country as rapidly as possible, on the assumption that its people would be content with a standard of living guaranteeing a social minimum and a standard of material living somewhat above subsistence—how much depended on what trickled down from the general growth of an economy geared to further industrialization. Inefficient and wasteful though it was, it achieved these objects. In 1913 the Tsarist Empire, with 9.4 per cent of the world's population, produced 6 per cent of the world's total of "national incomes" and 3.6 per cent of its industrial output. In 1986 the U.S.S.R., with less than 6 per cent of the global population produced 14 per cent of the globe's "national income" and 14.6 per cent of its industrial output. (But it produced only a slightly higher share of the world's agricultural output.) (Bolotin, 1987, pp. 148–52.) Russia had been transformed into a major industrial power, and indeed its status as a superpower, maintained for almost half a century, rested on this success. However, and contrary to the expectations of the communists, the engine of Soviet economic development was so constructed as to slow down rather than speed up when, after the vehicle had advanced a certain distance, the driver stepped on the accelerator. Its dynamism contained the mechanism of its own exhaustion. This was the system which, after 1944, became the model for the economies under which a third of the human race lived.

However, the Soviet revolution also developed a very special political system. The European popular movements of the Left, including the Marxist labour and socialist movements to which the Bolshevik party belonged, drew on two political traditions: electoral, and sometimes even direct democracy, and the centralized action-oriented revolutionary efforts inherited from the Jacobin phase of the French Revolution. The mass labour and socialist movements which emerged almost everywhere in Europe at the end of the nineteenth century, whether as parties, labour unions, cooperatives or a combination of all these, were strongly democratic both in their internal structure and their political aspirations. In fact, where constitutions based on a wide franchise did not yet exist, they were the chief forces pressing for them and, unlike the anarchists, the Marxists were fundamentally committed to *political* action. The political system of the U.S.S.R., which was also later transferred to the socialist world, broke sharply with the democratic side of socialist movements, though maintaining an increasingly academic commitment to it in theory.* It even moved far beyond the Jacobin heritage, which, whatever its commitment to revolutionary rigour and ruthless action, did not favour individual dictatorship. In short, as the Soviet economy was a command economy, so Soviet politics was command politics.

This evolution reflected partly the history of the Bolshevik Party, partly the crises and urgent priorities of the young Soviet regime and partly the peculiarities of the drunkard cobbler's ex-seminarist son from Georgia who became the autocrat of the U.S.S.R. under the self-chosen political name "the man of steel," namely J. V. Stalin (1879–1953). Lenin's model of the "Vanguard Party," a uniquely efficient disciplined cadre of professional revolutionaries, geared to carrying out the tasks assigned to them by a central leadership, was potentially authoritarian, as numerous other equally revolutionary Russian Marxists had pointed out from the start. What was to stop "substitutism" of the party for the masses it claimed to lead? Of its (elected) committees for the members, or rather the regular congresses expressing their views? Of the actual operational leadership for the central committee, and eventually by the (in theory elected) unique leader who in practice replaced all of these? The danger, as it turned out, was no less real because Lenin neither wanted to nor was in a position to be a dictator, or because the Bolshevik Party, like all organizations of the ideological Left, behaved much less like a military staff and much more like an endless debating society. It became more immediate after the October Revolution, as the Bolsheviks turned from a body of a few thousand illegals into a mass party of hundreds of thousands, eventually of millions of professional mobilizers, administrators, executives and controllers, who swamped the "Old Bolsheviks" and other pre-1917 socialists who had joined them, such as Leon Trotsky. They shared none of the old political culture of the Left. All they knew was that the party was right and that decisions made by superior authority must be carried out if the revolution was to be saved.

*Thus the authoritarian centralism so characteristic of communist parties retained the official name of "democratic centralism," and the 1936 Soviet Constitution is, on paper, a typical democratic constitution, with as much room for multiparty elections as, say, the American constitution. Nor was this pure window-dressing, since much of it was drafted by Nikolai Bukharin, who, as an old pre-1917 Marxist revolutionary, undoubtedly believed that this type of constitution suited a socialist society.

Whatever the pre-revolutionary attitude of the Bolsheviks to democracy in and outside the party, to free speech, civil liberties and toleration, the circumstances of the years 1917–21 imposed an increasingly authoritarian mode of government on (and within) a party committed to any action that was (or seemed) necessary to maintain the fragile and struggling Soviet power. It had not actually begun as a one-party government, nor one rejecting opposition, but it won the Civil War as a single-party dictatorship buttressed by a powerful security apparatus, and using terror against counter-revolutionaries. Equally to the point, the party itself abandoned internal democracy, as the collective discussion of alternative policies was banned (in 1921). The "democratic centralism" which governed it in theory became mere centralism. It ceased to operate by its own party constitution. The annual meetings of party congresses became less regular, until under Stalin they became unpredictable and occasional. The NEP years relaxed the non-political atmosphere, but not the feeling that the party was a beleaguered minority which might have history on its side, but was working against the grain of the Russian masses and the Russian present. The decision to launch the industrial revolution from above, automatically committed the system to imposing authority, perhaps even more ruthlessly than in the Civil War years, because its machinery for exercising power continuously was now much greater. It was then that the last elements of a separation of powers, the modest even if diminishing room for manoeuvre of the Soviet government as distinct from the party, came to an end. The single political leadership of the party now concentrated absolute power in its hands, subordinating all else.

It was at this point that the system became an autocracy under Stalin, and one seeking to impose total control over all aspects of its citizens' lives and thoughts, all their existence being, so far as possible, subordinated to the achievement of the system's objectives, as defined and specified by the supreme authority. This was certainly not envisaged by Marx and Engels, nor did it develop in the second (Marxist) International and most of its parties. Thus Karl Liebknecht, who, with Rosa Luxemburg, became the leader of the German communists and was assassinated with her in 1919 by reactionary officers, did not even claim to be a Marxist, though he was the son of a founder of the German Social Democratic Party. The Austro-Marxists, though, as their name suggests, committed to Marx, made no bones about going their own various ways, and even when a man was branded an official heretic, as Eduard Bernstein was for his "revisionism," it was taken for granted that he was a legitimate social-democrat. Indeed, he continued as an official editor of the works of Marx and Engels. The idea that a socialist state should force every citizen to think the same, let alone to endow its leaders collectively with something like papal infallibility (that any single person should exercise this function was unthinkable), would not have crossed the mind of any leading socialist before 1917.

One might at most claim that Marxist socialism was for its adherents a passionate personal commitment, a system of hope and belief, which had some characteristics of a secular religion (though not more than the ideology of non-socialist crusading groups) and, perhaps more to the point, that, once it became a mass movement, subtle theory inevitably became at best a catechism; at worst, a symbol of identity and loyalty, like a flag, which must be saluted. Such mass movements, as intelligent central European socialists had long noted, also tended to admire, even to worship, leaders, though it must be said that the well-known tendency to argument and rivalry within Left-wing parties would usually keep this under some control. The construction of the Lenin mausoleum on the Red Square, where the preserved body of the great leader would for ever be visible to the faithful, did not derive from anything in even the Russian revolutionary tradition, but was an obvious attempt to mobilize the appeal of Christian saints and relics to a backward peasant people for the benefit of the Soviet regime. One might also claim that in the Bolshevik Party constructed by Lenin, orthodoxy and intolerance were to some extent implanted not as values in themselves but for pragmatic reasons. Like a good general—and Lenin was fundamentally a planner of action—he did not want arguments in the ranks which would prevent practical effectiveness. Moreover, like other practical geniuses, he was convinced that he knew best, and had little time for other opinions. In theory, he was an orthodox, even a fundamentalist, Marxist because it was clear to him that any monkeying with the text of a theory whose essence was revolution was likely to encourage compromisers and reformists. In practice, he unhesitatingly modified Marx's views and added to them freely, always defending his literal loyalty to the master. Since, for most of the years before 1917, he led, and represented an embattled minority on the Russian Left, and even within Russian social democracy, he acquired a reputation for intolerance of dissent, but he had as little hesitation in welcoming his opponents, once the situation had changed, as he had in denouncing them, and, even after October, he never relied on his authority within the party, but invariably on argument. Nor, as we have seen, did his positions ever make their way unchallenged. Had he lived, Lenin would no doubt have gone on denouncing opponents, and, as in the civil war, his pragmatic intolerance would know no limits. Yet there is no evidence that he envisaged, or would even have tolerated, the sort of secular version of a universal and compulsory state-cum-private religion which developed after his death. Stalin may not have founded it consciously. He may merely have gone with what he saw as the mainstream of a backward peasant Russia and its autocratic and orthodox tradition. But it is unlikely that, without him, it would have developed, and certain that it would not have been imposed on, or copied by other socialist regimes.

Yet one thing must be said. The possibility of dictatorship is implicit in any regime based on a single, irremovable party. In a party organized on the centralized hierarchical basis of Lenin's Bolsheviks, it becomes a probability. And irremovability was merely another name for the total conviction of the Bolsheviks that the Revolution must not be reversed, and that its fate was in their hands and in nobody else's. Bolsheviks argued that a bourgeois regime might safely envisage the defeat of a Conservative administration and the succession of a Liberal, since this would not change the bourgeois character of society, but it would and could not tolerate a communist regime, for the same reason that a communist one could not tolerate being overthrown by any force that would restore the old order. Revolutionaries, including revolutionary socialists, are not democrats in the electoral sense, however sincerely convinced of acting in the interests of "the people." Nevertheless, even if the assumption that the party was a political monopoly with a "leading role" made a democratic Soviet regime as unlikely as a democratic Catholic Church, it did not imply personal dictatorship. It was Joseph Stalin who turned communist political systems into non-hereditary monarchies.*

In many ways Stalin, tiny,† cautious, insecure, cruel, nocturnal and endlessly suspicious, seems a figure out of Suetonius' *Lives of the Caesars* rather than out of modern politics. Outwardly unimpressive and indeed forgettable, "a grey blur" as a contemporary observer called him in 1917 (Sukhanov), he conciliated and manoeuvred where he had to, until he reached the top; but, of course, his very considerable gifts had got him

---

*The similarity with monarchy is indicated by the tendency of some such states actually to move in the direction of hereditary succession, a development which would have seemed absurdly unthinkable to earlier socialists and communists. North Korea and Romania were two cases in point.

†The present writer, who saw Stalin's embalmed body in the Red Square mausoleum before it was removed in 1961 can remember the shock of seeing a man so tiny and yet so all-powerful. Significantly, all films and photographs concealed the fact that he was only 5 ft. 3 ins. tall.

close to the top even before the revolution. He was a member of the first government after the revolutionary government as Commissar for nationalities. When he finally became the unchallenged leader of the party and (in effect) of the state, he lacked the palpable sense of personal destiny, the charisma and self-confidence which made Hitler the founder and accepted master of his party and kept his entourage loyal to him without coercion. Stalin ruled his party, as everything else within reach of his personal power, by terror and fear.

In turning himself into something like a secular Tsar, defender of the secular Orthodox faith, the body of whose founder, transformed into a secular saint, awaited the pilgrims outside the Kremlin, Stalin showed a sound sense of public relations. For a collection of peasant and animal-herding peoples mentally living in the Western equivalent of the eleventh century, this was almost certainly the most effective way of establishing the legitimacy of the new regime, just as the simple, unqualified, dogmatic catechisms to which he reduced "Marxism-Leninism" were ideal for introducing ideas to the first generation of literates.* Nor can his terror simply be seen as the assertion of a tyrant's unlimited personal power. There is no doubt that he enjoyed that power, the fear that he inspired, the ability to give life or death, just as there is no doubt that he was quite indifferent to the material rewards that someone in his position could command. Yet, whatever his personal psychological kinks, Stalin's terror was, in theory, as rationally instrumental a tactic as was his caution where he lacked control. Both, in fact, were based on the principle of avoiding risks, which, in turn, reflected that very lack of confidence in his ability to assess situations ("to make a Marxist analysis," in the Bolshevik jargon) which had distinguished Lenin. His terrifying career makes no sense except as a stubborn, unbroken, pursuit of that utopian aim of a communist society to whose reassertion he devoted the last of his publications, a few months before his death (Stalin, 1952).

Power in the Soviet Union was all that the Bolsheviks had gained by the October Revolution. Power was the only tool they could wield to change society. This was beset by constant, and in one way or another, constantly renewed, difficulties. (This is the meaning of Stalin's otherwise absurd thesis that the class struggle would become more intense decades after "the proletariat had taken power.") Only the determination to use power consistently and ruthlessly to eliminate all possible obstacles to the process could guarantee eventual success.

*And not only these. The 1939 *Short History* of the Soviet Communist Party, whatever its lies and intellectual limitations, was pedagogically a masterly text.

Three things drove a policy based on this assumption towards a murderous absurdity.

First, Stalin's belief that in the last analysis only he knew the way forward and was sufficiently determined to pursue it. Plenty of politicians and generals have this sense of indispensability, but only those with absolute power are in a position to compel others to share this belief. Thus the great purges of the 1930s which, unlike earlier forms of terror, were directed against the party itself and especially its leadership, began after many hardened Bolsheviks, including those who had supported him against the various oppositions of the 1920s and genuinely backed the Great Leap Forward of Collectivization and Five-Year Plan, found the ruthless cruelties of the period and the sacrifices it imposed, more than they would willingly accept. No doubt many of them remembered Lenin's refusal to back Stalin as his successor because of his excessive brutality. The seventeenth Congress of the CPSU(b) revealed a substantial opposition to him. Whether it actually constituted a threat to his power we shall never know, for between 1934 and 1939 four or five million party members and officials were arrested on political grounds, four or five hundred thousand of them were executed without trial, and the next (eighteenth) Party Congress which met in the spring of 1939, contained a bare thirty-seven survivors of the 1827 delegates who had been present at the seventeenth in 1934 (Kerblay, 1983, p. 245).

What gave this terror an unprecedented inhumanity was that it recognized no conventional or other limits. It was not so much the belief that a great end justifies all the means necessary to achieve it (though it is possible that this was Mao Tse-tung's belief), or even the belief that the sacrifices imposed on the present generation, however large, are as nothing to the benefits which will be reaped by the endless generations of the future. It was the application of the principle of total war to all times. Leninism, perhaps because of the powerful strain of voluntarism which made other Marxists distrust Lenin as a "Blanquist" or "Jacobin," thought essentially in military terms, as his own admiration for Clausewitz would indicate, even if the entire vocabulary of Bolshevik politics did not bear witness to it. "Who whom?" was Lenin's basic maxim: the struggle as a zero-sum game in which the winner took, the loser lost, all. As we know, even the liberal states waged both world wars in this spirit, and recognized absolutely no limit on the suffering they were prepared to impose on the population of "the enemy," and, in the First World War, even on their own armed forces. Indeed, even the victimization of entire blocs of people, defined on *a priori* grounds, became part of warfare: such as the internment during the Second World War of all U.S. citizens of Japanese origin or of all resident Germans and Austrians in Britain on the grounds that they might contain some potential agents of the enemy. This was part of that relapse of nineteenth-century civil progress into a renaissance of barbarism, which runs like a dark thread through this book.

Fortunately, in constitutional and preferably democratic states under the rule of law and with a free press, there are some countervailing forces. In systems of absolute power there are none, even though eventually conventions of power-limitation may develop, if only for the sake of survival and because the use of total power may be self-defeating. Paranoia is its logical end-product. After Stalin's death a tacit understanding among his successors decided to put an end to the era of blood, although (until the Gorbachev era) it was left to dissidents within and scholars or publicists abroad to estimate the full human cost of the Stalin decades. Henceforth Soviet politicians died in their beds, and sometimes at an advanced age. As the Gulags emptied in the late 1950s, the U.S.S.R. remained a society which treated its citizens badly by Western standards, but it ceased to be a society which imprisoned and killed its citizens on a uniquely massive scale. Indeed, by the 1980s it had a distinctly smaller proportion of its inhabitants in jail than the U.S.A. (268 prisoners per 100,000 population against 426 per 100,000 in the U.S.A.) (Walker, 1991). Moreover, in the 1960s and 1970s the U.S.S.R. actually became a society in which the ordinary citizen probably ran a smaller risk of being deliberately killed by crime, civil conflict or the state than a substantial number of other countries in Asia, Africa and the Americas. Nevertheless, it remained a police state, an authoritarian society and, by any realistic standards, an unfree one. Only officially authorized or permitted information was available to the citizen—any other kind remained at least technically punishable by law until Gorbachev's policy of *glasnost* ("openness")—and freedom of travel and settlement depended on official permission, an increasingly nominal restriction within the U.S.S.R., but a very real one where frontiers had to be crossed even into another friendly "socialist" country. In all these respects the U.S.S.R. remained distinctly inferior to Tsarist Russia. Moreover, even though for most everyday purposes the rule of law operated, the powers of administrative, i.e. arbitrary, imprisonment or internal exile remained.

It will probably never be possible to calculate the human cost of Russia's iron decades adequately, since even such official statistics of execution and Gulag populations as exist or might become available cannot cover all the losses, and estimates vary enormously depending on the assumption made by the estimators. "By a sinister paradox" it has been said, "we are better informed as to losses to Soviet livestock in this period than about the number of the regime's opponents who were exterminated" (Kerblay, 1983, p. 26). The suppression of the 1937 census alone introduces almost insuperable obstacles. Still, whatever assumptions are made,* the number of direct and indirect victims must be measured in eight rather than seven digits. In these circumstances it does not much matter whether we opt for a "conservative" estimate nearer to ten than to twenty millions or a larger figure: none can be anything but shameful and beyond palliation, let alone justification. I add, without comment, that the total population of the U.S.S.R. in 1937 was said to have been 164 millions, or 16.7 millions less than the demographic forecasts of the Second Five-Year Plan (1933–38).

Brutal and dictatorial though it was, the Soviet system was not "totalitarian," a term which became popular among critics of communism after the Second World War, having been invented in the 1920s by Italian fascism to describe its objects. Hitherto it had been used almost exclusively to criticize both it and German National Socialism. It stood for an all-embracing centralized system which not only imposed total physical control over its population but, by means of its monopoly of propaganda and education, actually succeeded in getting its people to internalize its values. George Orwell's *1984* (published in 1949) gave this Western image of the totalitarian society its most powerful form: a society of brainwashed masses under the watchful eye of "Big Brother," from which only the occasional lonely individual dissented.

This is certainly what Stalin would have *wanted* to achieve, though it would have outraged Lenin and other Old Bolsheviks, not to mention Marx. Insofar as it aimed at the virtual deification of the leader (what was later shyly euphemized as "the cult of personality"), or at least at establishing him as a compendium of virtues, it had some success, which Orwell satirized. Paradoxically, this owed little to Stalin's absolute power. The communist militants outside the "socialist" countries who wept genuine tears as they learned of his death in 1953—and many did—were voluntary converts to the movement they believed him to have symbolized and inspired. Unlike most foreigners, all Russians knew well enough how much suffering had been, and still was, their lot. Yet in some sense by virtue merely of being a strong and legitimate ruler of the Russian lands and a modernizer of these lands, he represented something of themselves: most recently as their leader in a war which was, for Great Russians at least, a genuinely national struggle.

---

*For the uncertainties of such procedures see Kosinski, 1987, pp. 151–52.

Yet, in every other respect, the system was not "totalitarian," a fact which throws considerable doubt on the usefulness of the term. It did not exercise effective "thought control," let alone ensure "thought conversion," but in fact depoliticized the citizenry to an astonishing degree. The official doctrines of Marxism-Leninism left the bulk of the population virtually untouched, since it had no apparent relevance to them, unless they were interested in a career in which such esoteric knowledge was expected. After forty years of education in a country dedicated to Marxism, passers-by on Marx Square in Budapest were asked who Karl Marx was. They were told:

> He was a Soviet philosopher; Engels was his friend. Well, what else can I say? He died at an old age. (Another voice): Of course, a politician. And he was, you know, he was what's his name's—Lenin's, Lenin, Lenin's works—well he translated them into Hungarian (Garton Ash, 1990, p. 261).

For the majority of Soviet citizens most public statements about politics and ideology coming from on high were probably not consciously absorbed at all, unless they bore directly on their everyday problems—which they rarely did. Only the intellectuals were forced to take them seriously in a society built on and around an ideology that claimed to be rational and "scientific." Yet, paradoxically, the very fact that such systems needed intellectuals, and gave those who did not publicly dissent from it substantial privileges and advantages, created a social space outside the state's control. Only terror as ruthless as Stalin's could completely silence the unofficial intellect. In the U.S.S.R. it re-emerged as soon as the ice of fear began to thaw—*The Thaw* (1954) was the title of an influential *roman à thèse* by Ilya Ehrenburg (1891–1967), a talented survivor—in the 1950s. In the 1960s and 1970s dissent, both in the uncertainly tolerated form of communist reformers and in the form of total intellectual, political and cultural dissidence, dominated the Soviet scene, though officially the country remained "monolithic"—a favourite Bolshevik term. This was to become evident in the 1980s.

II

The communist states which came into being after the Second World War, i.e. all except the U.S.S.R., were controlled by communist parties formed or shaped in the Soviet, i.e. Stalinist, mould. This was true even to some extent of the Chinese Communist Party, which had established real autonomy from Moscow in the 1930s under Mao Tse-tung. It was, perhaps, less true of later recruits to the "socialist camp" from the Third World—Fidel Castro's Cuba, and various more shortlived African, Asian and Latin American regimes which arose in the 1970s, and which also tended to assimilate themselves officially to the established Soviet pattern. In all of them we find one-party political systems with highly centralized authority structures; officially promulgated cultural and intellectual truth determined by political authority; central state-planned economies; even, the most obvious relic of the Stalinist heritage, strongly profiled supreme leaders. Indeed, in the states directly occupied by the Soviet army, including the Soviet security services, local governments were compelled to follow the Soviet example, for instance by organizing show trials and purges of local communists on the Stalin model, a matter for which the native communist parties showed no spontaneous enthusiasm. In Poland and East Germany they even managed to avoid these caricatures of the judicial process altogether, and no leading communist was killed or handed over to the Soviet security services, although, in the aftermath of the break with Tito prominent local leaders in Bulgaria (Traicho Kostov) and Hungary (Laszlo Rajk) were executed and in Stalin's last year a particularly implausible mass trial of leading Czech communists, with a markedly anti-semitic tinge, decimated the old leadership of the local party. It may or may not have had some connection with the increasingly paranoiac behaviour of Stalin himself as he deteriorated both physically and mentally and planned to eliminate even his most loyal supporters.

The new regimes of the 1940s, though in Europe all were made possible by the victory of the Red Army, were only in four cases imposed exclusively by the force of that army: in Poland; the occupied part of Germany; Romania (where the local communist movement consisted at best of a few hundred people, most of them not ethnic Romanians); and, in substance, Hungary. In Yugoslavia and Albania it was very much home-grown, in Czechoslovakia the communist party's 40 per cent of the vote in 1947 almost certainly reflected genuine strength at the time, and in Bulgaria communist influence was reinforced by the Russophile sentiment so universal in that country. Communist power in China, Korea and former French Indochina—or rather, after the Cold War division, in the northern parts of those countries—owed nothing to Soviet arms, though after 1949 the smaller communist regimes benefited, for a while, from Chinese support. The subsequent additions to the "socialist camp," starting with Cuba, had made their own way there, although struggling guerrilla liberation movements in Africa could count on serious support from the Soviet bloc.

Yet, even in the states where communist power was imposed only by the Red Army, the new regime initially enjoyed a temporary legitimacy and, for a time, some genuine support. As we have seen (chapter 5), the idea of building a new world on what was so visibly the total ruin of the old, inspired many of the young and the intellectuals. However unpopular party and government, the very energy and determination which both brought to the task of post-war reconstruction commanded a broad, if reluctant, assent. Indeed, the success of the new regimes in this task was hard to deny. In the more backward agrarian states, as we have seen, the communist commitment to industrialization, that is, to progress and modernity, re-echoed far beyond the party's ranks. Who could doubt that countries like Bulgaria or Yugoslavia were advancing far more rapidly than had seemed likely, or even possible before the war? Only where a primitive and ruthless U.S.S.R. had occupied and forcibly absorbed less backward regions, or, at any rate, regions with developed cities, as in the areas transferred in 1939–40, and in the Soviet zone of Germany (after 1954 the German Democratic Republic), which continued for some time after 1945 to be pillaged by the U.S.S.R. for its own reconstruction, did the balance look entirely negative.

Politically, the communist states, home-grown or imposed, began by forming a single bloc under the leadership of the U.S.S.R., which, on grounds of anti-Western solidarity, was supported even by the communist regime which took full control of China in 1949, though Moscow's influence over the Chinese Communist Party had been tenuous ever since Mao Tse-tung became its unchallengeable leader in the middle 1930s. Mao went his own way amid professions of loyalty to the U.S.S.R., and Stalin, as a realist, was careful not to strain his relations with the effectively independent giant eastern brother-party. When in the later 1950s Nikita Khrushchev did strain them the result was an acrimonious breach, as China challenged Soviet leadership of the international communist movement, though not very successfully. Stalin's attitude to the states and communist parties in the parts of Europe occupied by the Soviet armies was less conciliatory, partly because his armies were still present in Eastern Europe, but also because he thought he could rely on the genuine local communist loyalty to Moscow, and to himself personally. He was almost certainly surprised in 1948 when the Yugoslav communist leadership, so loyalist that Belgrade had been made the headquarters of the reconstructed Cold War Communist International (the "Communist Information Bureau" or Cominform) only a few months earlier, pushed their resistance to Soviet directives to the point of an open breach, and when Moscow's appeal to the loyalty of good communists over the head of Tito met with next to no serious response in Yugoslavia. Characteristically his reaction was to extend purges and show-trials to the remaining satellite communist leaderships.

Nevertheless, the Yugoslav secession left the rest of the communist movement unaffected. The political crumbling of the Soviet bloc began with Stalin's death in 1953, but especially with the official attacks on the Stalinist era in general and, more cautiously, on Stalin himself, at the Twentieth Congress of the CPSU in 1956. Although aimed at a highly restricted domestic Soviet audience—foreign communists were excluded from Khrushchev's secret speech—the news soon got out that the Soviet monolith had split. The effects within the Soviet-dominated region of Europe was immediate. Within a few months a new, reforming communist leadership in Poland was peacefully accepted by Moscow (probably with the help of advice from the Chinese), and a revolution broke out in Hungary. Here the new government under another communist reformer, Imre Nagy, announced the end of one-party rule, which the Soviets might conceivably have tolerated—opinions among them were divided— but also the withdrawal of Hungary from the Warsaw Pact and its future neutrality, which they would not tolerate. The revolution was suppressed by the Russian army in November 1956.

That this major crisis within the Soviet bloc was not exploited by the Western alliance (except for purposes of propaganda) demonstrated the stability of East–West relations. Both sides tacitly accepted the boundaries of each other's zones of influence, and during the 1950s and 1960s no indigenous revolutionary changes appeared on the globe to disturb this balance, except in Cuba.*

In regimes where politics was so obviously in control, no sharp line between political and economic developments can be drawn. Thus the governments of Poland and Hungary could not but make economic concessions to peoples who had so clearly demonstrated their lack of enthusiasm for communism. In Poland agriculture was de-collectivized, though this did not make it notably more efficient, and, more to the point, the political force of a working class, much strengthened by the

---

*The revolutions of the 1950s in the Middle East, Egypt in 1952, and Iraq in 1958, contrary to Western fears, did not change the balance, in spite of providing much scope for U.S.S.R. diplomatic success, chiefly because the local regimes eliminated their own communists ruthlessly, where they were influential, as in Syria and Iraq.

rush into heavy industrialization, was henceforth tacitly acknowledged. After all, it was an industrial movement in Poznan which had initiated the events of 1956. From then until the triumph of Solidarity at the end of the 1980s, Polish politics and economics were dominated by the confrontation of irresistible mass, the regime, and an immovable object, the working class, which, initially without organization, was eventually organized into a classical labour movement, allied as usual with intellectuals, and eventually formed a political movement, just as Marx had predicted. Only the ideology of this movement, as Marxists had to note with melancholy, was not anti-capitalist but anti-socialist. Typically these confrontations were about the periodic attempts of Polish governments to cut down the heavy subsidies on basic living-costs by raising prices. These then led to strikes, followed typically (after a crisis in the government) by retreat. In Hungary the leadership imposed by the Soviets after the defeat of the 1956 revolution was more genuinely reformist and effective. It set out under János Kádár (1912–89) systematically (and possibly with tacit support from influential quarters in the U.S.S.R.) to liberalize the regime, conciliate the opposition and, in effect, to achieve the objectives of 1956 within the limits of what the U.S.S.R. would regard as acceptable. In this it was notably successful until the 1980s.

This was not the case in Czechoslovakia, politically inert since the ruthless purges of the early 1950s, but cautiously and tentatively beginning to de-Stalinize. For two reasons this process snowballed in the second half of the 1960s. The Slovaks (including the Slovak component of the CP), never entirely at ease in the bi-national state, provided backing for potential opposition in the party. It is no accident that the man elected to the general secretaryship in a party coup in 1968 was a Slovak, Alexander Dubček.

However, quite separately, pressure to reform the economy, and introduce some rationality and flexibility into the Soviet-type command system, became increasingly hard to resist in the 1960s. As we shall see, it was by then felt throughout the communist bloc. Economic decentralization, which was not in itself politically explosive, became so when combined with the demand for intellectual and, even more, for political liberalization. In Czechoslovakia this demand was all the stronger, not only because Stalinism had been particularly harsh and long-lasting, but also because so many of its communists (especially intellectuals, sprung from a party with genuine mass support both before and after the Nazi occupation) were profoundly shocked by the contrast between the communist hopes they still retained and the reality of the regime. As so often in Nazi-occupied Europe, where the party became the heart of the resistance movement, it attracted young idealists whose commitment at such a time was a guarantee of selflessness. What, other than hope and possible torture and death, could someone expect who, like a friend of the present writer, joined the party in Prague in 1941?

As always—as was indeed inevitable, given the structure of communist states—reform came from above, i.e. from within the party. The "Prague Spring" of 1968, preceded and accompanied by politico-cultural ferment and agitation, coincided with the general outburst of global student radicalism which is discussed elsewhere (see chapter 10): one of the rare movements which crossed oceans and the borders of social systems, and produced simultaneous social movements, mainly student-centred, from California and Mexico to Poland and Yugoslavia. The "Action Programme" of the Czechoslovak CP might or might not have been—just—acceptable to the Soviets, though it moved the one-party dictatorship rather dangerously towards a pluralist democracy. However, the cohesion, perhaps the very existence of the East European Soviet bloc seemed to be at stake, as the "Prague Spring" revealed, and increased, the cracks within it. On the one side hard-line regimes without mass support, such as Poland and East Germany, feared internal destabilization from the Czech example, which they criticized bitterly; on the other, the Czechs were supported enthusiastically by most European communist parties, by the reforming Hungarians and, from outside the bloc, by the independent communist regime of Tito in Yugoslavia, as well as by Romania which, since 1965, had begun to mark its distance from Moscow on nationalist grounds under a new leader, Nicolae Ceauşescu (1918–89). (In internal matters Ceauşescu was anything but a communist reformer.) Both Tito and Ceauşescu visited Prague and received hero's welcomes from the public. Hence Moscow, though not without divisions and hesitation, decided to overthrow the Prague regime by military force. This proved to be the virtual end of the Moscow-centred international communist movement, already cracked by the 1956 crisis. However, it held the Soviet bloc together for another twenty years, but henceforth only by the threat of Soviet military intervention. In the last twenty years of the Soviet bloc, even the leadership of the ruling communist parties appear to have lost any real belief in what they were doing.

Meanwhile, and quite independently of politics, the need to reform or change the economic system of Soviet-type central planning became increasingly urgent. On the one hand, the developed non-socialist economies grew and flourished as never before (see chapter 9), widening the already considerable gap between the two systems. This was particularly obvious in Germany, where both systems coexisted in different parts of the same country. On the other hand, the rate of growth of the socialist economies, which had surpassed the Western economies up to the latter part of the 1950s, began visibly to slacken off. The Soviet GNP, which grew at a rate of 5.7 per cent per annum in the 1950s (almost as fast as in the first twelve years of industrialization, 1928–40), fell to 5.2 per cent in the 1960s, 3.7 per cent in the first half of the 1970s, 2.6 per cent in the second half of that decade and 2 per cent in the last five years before Gorbachev (1980–85) (Ofer, 1987, p. 1778). The record of Eastern Europe was similar. Attempts to make the system more flexible, essentially by decentralization, were made in the 1960s almost everywhere in the Soviet bloc, not least in the U.S.S.R. itself under premier Kosygin in the 1960s. With the exception of the Hungarian reforms, they were not notably successful, and, in several cases, they hardly got off the ground or (as in Czechoslovakia) were not allowed to for political reasons. A somewhat eccentric member of the family of socialist systems, Yugoslavia, was not notably more successful when, out of hostility to Stalinism, it replaced the centrally planned state economy with a system of autonomous cooperative enterprises. As the world economy entered a new period of uncertainties in the 1970s, nobody in East or West any longer expected the "really existing" socialist economies to overtake and surpass, or even to keep pace with the non-socialist ones. However, though more problematic than before, their future did not seem a cause for immediate worry. This was soon to change.

PART THREE

The Landslide

CHAPTER FOURTEEN

The Crisis Decades

> I was asked the other day about United States competitiveness and I replied that I don't think about it at all. We at NCR think of ourselves as a globally competitive company that happens to be head-quartered in the United States.
>
> —Jonathan Schell, *N.Y. Newsday*, 1993

> At a particularly neuralgic level, one of the results (of mass unemployment) could be the progressive alienation from the rest of society of the young who, according to contemporary surveys, still *want* jobs, however difficult they may be to obtain, and still *hope* for meaningful careers. More broadly, there must be some danger that the coming decade will be a society in which not merely are "we" progressively divided from "they" (the two divisions representing, very roughly, the labour force and management), but in which the majority groups are increasingly splintered, with the young and the relatively unprotected at odds with the better protected and more experienced members of the work force.
>
> —The Secretary-General of OECD (Investing, 1983, p. 15)

I

The history of the twenty years after 1973 is that of a world which lost its bearings and slid into instability and crisis. And yet, until the 1980s it was not clear how irretrievably the foundations of the Golden Age had crumbled. Until after one part of the world—the U.S.S.R. and the Eastern Europe of "real socialism"—had collapsed entirely, the global nature of the crisis was not recognized, let alone admitted in the developed non-communist regions. Even so, for many years economic troubles were still "recessions." The half-century's taboo on the use of the terms "depression" or "slump," that reminder of the Age of Catastrophe, was not completely broken. Simply to use the word might conjure up the thing, even if the "recessions" of the 1980s were "the most serious for fifty years"—a phrase which carefully avoided specifying the actual period, the 1930s. The civilization that had elevated the word-magic of the advertisers into a basic principle of the economy, was caught in its own mechanism of delusion. Not until the early 1990s do we find admissions—as, for instance, in Finland—that the economic troubles of the present were actually worse than those of the 1930s.

In many ways this was puzzling. Why should the world economy have become less stable? As economists observed, the elements stabilizing the economy were now actually stronger than before, even though free-market governments, like those of Presidents Reagan and Bush in the U.S.A., Mrs. Thatcher and her successor in Britain, tried to weaken some of them (World Economic Survey, 1989, pp. 10–11). Computerized inventory control, better communications and quicker transport reduced the importance of the volatile "inventory cycle" of the old mass production which produced enormous stocks "just in case" they were needed at times of expansion, and then stopped dead while stocks were sold off in times of contraction. The new method, pioneered by the Japanese, and made possible by the technologies of the 1970s was to carry far smaller inventories, produce enough to supply dealers "just in time," and in any case with a far greater capacity to vary output at short notice to meet changing demands. This was the age not of Henry Ford but of Benetton. At the same time the sheer weight of government consumption and of that part of private income which came from government ("transfer payments" such as social security and welfare) also stabilized the economy. Between them they amounted to about a third of GDP. If anything both increased in the crisis era, if only because the cost of unemployment, pensions and health care rose. As this era was still continuing at the end of the Short Twentieth Century, we may have to wait for some years before the economists are able to use the historians' ultimate weapon, hindsight, to find a persuasive explanation.

Of course the comparison of the economic troubles of the 1970s–90s with those between the wars is flawed, even though the fear of another Great Slump haunted these decades. "Can it happen again?" was a question asked by many, especially after a new, dramatic American (and global) stock exchange crash in 1987 and a major international exchange crisis in 1992 (Temin, 1993, p. 99). The Crisis Decades after 1973 were no more a

A CHANGING WORLD

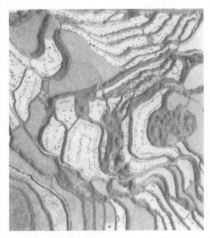

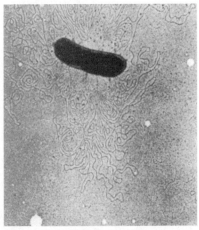

34. The pattern of the old: agricultural terracing in the Liping valley, Guizhou, China.

35. The pattern of the new: Electron micrograph of an intestinal bacterium spewing forth its chromosomes (x 55,000 magnification).

FROM THE OLD TO THE NEW

36. The world that ended after 8,000 years: Chinese peasant, ploughing.

37. The ancient world meets the new: Turkish immigrant couple in West Berlin.

38. The emigrants: West Indians, arriving hopefully in 1950s London.

39. Refugees: Africa at the end of the century.

40. City Life: the old – Ahmedabad (India).

41. (*left*) City Life: the new – Chicago.

43. (*opposite above left*) Transport: rail, the nineteenth-century heritage – Augsburg, Germany.

44. (*opposite above right*) Transport: the internal combustion engine triumphed in the twentieth century. Motorways, cars, and pollution in Houston, Texas.

42. City Life – underground: rush hour in Shinjuku, Tokyo.

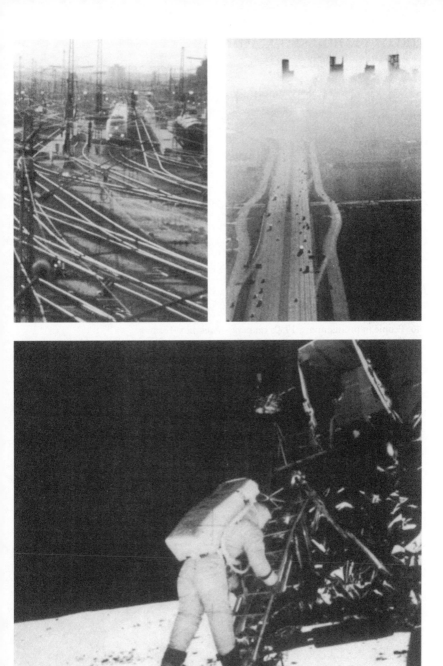

45. Transport beyond the earth. The first moon landing, 1969.

FROM PEOPLE TO MACHINES

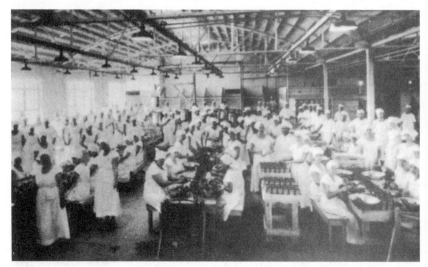

46. People in production: a 1930s cannery – Amarillo, Texas.

47. Production without people: Dungeness nuclear power station.

48. Where people once produced: de-industrialization in North England (Middlesbrough).

DAILY LIFE TRANSFORMED

49. Revolution in the kitchen: the refrigerator.

50. Revolution in the living room: the television set.

53. Old regime – civilian version: Neville Chamberlain (1869–1940),
British premier 1937–40, fishing.

54. (*left*) Old regime – uniformed
version: Louis (Francis Albert Victor
Nicholas), 1st Earl Mountbatten of
Burma (1900–79), last Viceroy of
India.

51. (*opposite below left*) Shopping
transformed: the supermarket.

52. (*opposite below right*) Leisure
transformed: miniaturization and
mobility – the portable radio-cassette
player.

55. New regime – the leader as revolutionary: Lenın speaking from the back of a truck, 1917.

56. New regime – the leader as revolutionary: Gandhi leaving an East End settlement in 1931 to negotiate with the British government.

57. (*left*) Stalin (Josif Vissarionovich Djugashvili, 1879–1953).

58. (*below*) Hitler's birthday parade, 1939.

59. (*left*) 'Chairman Mao' of China: Mao Tse-tung (1893–1976), as seen by Andy Warhol.

60. (*below*) The corpse of Ayatollah Khomeini, (1900–89), leader of revolutionary Iran, lies in state in Teheran.

61. (*left*) The artist as rebel after 1917. George Grosz (1893–1959) savages the German ruling class.

62. (*below*) The 1930s – the proletariat: British shipyard workers march on London.

63. The 1960s – the students: Demonstration against the Vietnam War, Berkeley, California. Note the prominence of women.

LOOKING FORWARD

64. End of the century: claims to world conquest.

65. After the Gulf War, 1991.

66. After the Free Market: homeless.

67. Before freedom: waiting to vote in South Africa, 1994.

68. Sarajevo eighty years after 1914.

"Great Depression" in the sense of the 1930s than the decades after 1873 had been, even though they were also given that name at the time. The global economy did not break down, even momentarily, although the Golden Age ended in 1973–75 with something very like a classical cyclical slump, which reduced industrial production in the "developed market economies" by 10 per cent in one year and international trade by 13 per cent (Armstrong, Glyn, 1991, p. 225). Economic growth in the developed capitalist world continued, though at a distinctly slower pace than during the Golden Age, except for some of the (mainly Asian) "newly industrializing countries" or NICs (see chapter 12), whose industrial revolutions had only begun in the 1960s. The growth of the collective GDP of the advanced economies until 1991 was barely interrupted by short periods of stagnation in the recession years 1973–75 and 1981–83 (OECD, 1993, pp. 18–19). International trade in the products of industry, the motor of world growth, continued, and in the boom years of the 1980s even accelerated to a rate comparable with the Golden Age. At the end of the Short Twentieth Century the countries of the developed capitalist world were, taken as a whole, far richer and more productive than in the early 1970s, and the global economy of which they still formed the central element was vastly more dynamic.

On the other hand, the situation in particular regions of the globe was considerably less rosy. In Africa, in Western Asia and in Latin America the growth of GDP per capita ceased. Most people actually became poorer in the 1980s and output fell for most years of the decade in the first two of these regions, for some years in the last (World Economic Survey, 1989, pp. 8, 26). Nobody seriously doubted that for these parts of the world the 1980s were an era of severe depression. As for the former area of Western "real socialism," after 1989 their economies, which had continued in modest growth during the 1980s, collapsed utterly. In this region the comparison of the crisis after 1989, with the Great Slump was perfectly apposite, although it underestimated the devastation of the early 1990s. Russia's GDP fell by 17 per cent in 1990–91, by 19 per cent in 1991–92 and by 11 per cent in 1992–93. Though some stabilization began in the early 1990s, Poland had lost over 21 per cent of its GDP in 1988–92, Czechoslovakia almost 20 per cent, Romania and Bulgaria 30 per cent or more. Their industrial production in mid-1992 was between half and two thirds that of 1989 (*Financial Times*, 24/2/94; EIB papers, November 1992, p. 10).

This was not the case in the East. Nothing was more striking than the contrast between the disintegration of the economies of the Soviet region and the spectacular growth of the Chinese economy in the same period.

In that country, and indeed in much of South-east and East Asia, which emerged in the 1970s as the most dynamic economic region of the world economy, the term "Depression" had no meaning—except, curiously enough, in the Japan of the early 1990s. However, though the capitalist world economy flourished, it was not at ease. The problems which had dominated the critique of capitalism before the war, and which the Golden Age had largely eliminated for a generation—"poverty, mass unemployment, squalor, instability" (see p. 268)—reappeared after 1973. Growth was, once again, interrupted by severe slumps, as distinct from "minor recessions," in 1974–75, 1980–82 and at the end of the 1980s. Unemployment in Western Europe rose from an average of 1.5 per cent in the 1960s to 4.2 per cent in the 1970s (Van der Wee, p. 77). At the peak of the boom in the late 1980s it averaged 9.2 per cent in the European Community, in 1993, 11 per cent. Half of the unemployed (1986–87) had been out of work for more than a year, one third for more than two years (Human Development, 1991, p. 184). Since the potential working population was no longer being swelled, as in the Golden Age, by the flood of growing post-war babies, and since young people, in good times and bad, tended to have much higher unemployment rates than older workers, one would have expected permanent unemployment to shrink, if anything.*

As for poverty and squalor, in the 1980s even many of the richest and most developed countries found themselves, once again, getting used to the everyday sight of beggars on the streets, and the even more shocking spectacle of the homeless sheltering in doorways in cardboard boxes, insofar as they were not removed from visibility by the police. On any night of 1993 in New York twenty-three thousand men and women slept on the street or in public shelters, a small part of the 3 per cent of the population of the city which had, at one time or another in the five years before then, no roof over their heads (*New York Times*, 16/11/93). In the United Kingdom (1989) 400,000 people were officially classed as "homeless" (Human Development, 1992, p. 31). Who, in the 1950s, or even the early 1970s, would have expected this?

The re-appearance of homeless paupers was part of the striking growth

---

*Between 1960 and 1975 the population aged fifteen to twenty-four rose by some twenty-nine millions in the "developed market economies," but between 1970 and 1990 only about six millions. Incidentally, the rates of youth unemployment in the Europe of the 1980s were startlingly high, except in social-democratic Sweden and West Germany. They ranged (1982–88) from over 20 per cent for Britain to over 40 per cent for Spain and 46 per cent for Norway (U.N. World Survey, 1989, pp. 15–16).

of social and economic inequality in the new era. By world standards the rich "developed market economies" were not—or not yet—particularly unfair in the distribution of their income. In the most inegalitarian among them—Australia, New Zealand, the U.S.A., Switzerland—the top 20 per cent of the households enjoyed an income, on average, between eight and ten times that of the bottom fifth, and the top 10 per cent usually took home between 20 and 25 per cent of their country's total income; only the top Swiss, New Zealanders, and the rich of Singapore and Hong Kong took home much more. This was as nothing compared to the inequality of countries like the Philippines, Malaysia, Peru, Jamaica or Venezuela, where they received over a third of their country's total income, let alone Guatemala, Mexico, Sri Lanka and Botswana, where they took home over 40 per cent, not to mention the world contender for the championship of economic inequality, Brazil.* In that monument to social injustice the lowest 20 per cent of the population divided 2½ per cent of the nation's total income among themselves, while the top 20 per cent enjoyed almost two-thirds of it. The top 10 per cent alone appropriated almost half (World Development, 1992, pp. 276–77; Human Development, 1991, pp. 152–53, 186).†

Nevertheless, during the Crisis Decades inequality unquestionably increased in the "developed market economies," and all the more so since the almost automatic rise in real incomes to which the working classes had got used in the Golden Age had now come to an end. The extremes of poverty and wealth both grew, as did the range of income distribution in between. Between 1967 and 1990 the number of American Negroes earning less than $5,000 (1990) and the number of those earning more than $50,000 both grew at the expense of the intermediate incomes (*New York Times*, 25/9/92). Since the rich capitalist countries were far richer than ever before, and their people, on the whole, were now cushioned by the generous welfare and social security systems of the Golden Age (see p. 284), there was less social unrest than might have been expected, but government finances found themselves squeezed between enormous social welfare payments, which climbed faster than state revenues in

---

*The actual champions, i.e. those with a Gini coefficient of more than 0.6 were some much smaller countries, also in the Americas. The Gini co-efficient, a convenient measure of inequality, measures inequality of a scale from 0.0—an equal distribution of income—to 1.0—maximum inequality. The coefficient for Honduras in 1967–85 was 0.62, for Jamaica 0.66 (Human Development, 1990, pp. 158–59).

†Comparable data for some of the most inegalitarian countries are not available. The list would certainly also include several other African and Latin American states and, in Asia, Turkey and Nepal.

economies growing more slowly than before 1973. In spite of substantial efforts, hardly any national governments in the rich—and mainly democratic—countries, and certainly not those most hostile to public social welfare, managed to reduce the vast proportion of their expenditure for these purposes, or even to keep it in check.*

Nobody in 1970 had expected, let alone intended, all this to happen. By the early 1990s a mood of insecurity and resentment had begun to spread even through much of the rich countries. As we shall see, it contributed to the breakdown of traditional political patterns in them. Between 1990 and 1993 few attempts were made to deny that even the developed capitalist world was in depression. Nobody seriously claimed to know what to do about it, other than to hope it would pass. Nevertheless, the central fact about the Crisis Decades is not that capitalism no longer worked as well as it had done in the Golden Age, but that its operations had become uncontrollable. Nobody knew what to do about the vagaries of the world economy or possessed instruments to manage them. The major instrument for doing so in the Golden Age, government policy, national or internationally coordinated, no longer worked. The crisis decades were the era when the national state lost its economic powers.

This was not immediately obvious, because—as usual—most politicians, economists and businessmen failed to recognize the permanence of the shift in the economic conjuncture. The policies of most governments in the 1970s, and the politics of most states, assumed that the troubles of the 1970s were only temporary. A year or two would bring a return to the old prosperity and the old growth. There was no need to change the policies that had served so well for a generation. Essentially the story of that decade was one of governments buying time—in the case of third-world and socialist states often by going heavily into what they hoped was short-term debt—and applying the old recipes of Keynesian economic management. As it happened, in most advanced capitalist countries social-democratic governments were in office in much of the 1970s, or returned to office after unsuccessful conservative interludes (as in Britain in 1974 and the U.S.A. in 1976). These were not likely to abandon the policies of the Golden Age.

---

*In 1972 fourteen such states spent a mean of 48 per cent of their central government expenditure on housing, social security, welfare and health. In 1990 they spent a mean of 51 per cent. The states concerned are: Australia and New Zealand, the U.S. and Canada, Austria, Belgium, Britain, Denmark, Finland, (Federal) Germany, Italy, the Netherlands, Norway and Sweden (calculated from World Development, 1992, Table 11).

The only alternative offered was that propagated by the minority of ultra-liberal economic theologians. Even before the crash, the long-isolated minority of believers in the unrestricted free market had begun their attack on the domination of the Keynesians and other champions of the managed mixed economy and full employment. The ideological zeal of the old champions of individualism was now reinforced by the apparent impotence and failure of conventional economic policies, especially after 1973. The newly created (1969) Nobel Prize for economics backed the neo-liberal trend after 1974 by awarding it to Friedrich von Hayek (see p. 271) in 1974, and, two years later, to an equally militant champion of economic ultra-liberalism, Milton Friedman.* After 1974 the free marketeers were on the offensive, although they did not come to dominate government policies until the 1980s, with the exception of Chile, where a terrorist military dictatorship allowed U.S. advisers to install an unrestricted free market economy, after the overthrow of a popular government in 1973 thus, incidentally, demonstrating that there was no intrinsic connection between the free market and political democracy. (To be fair to Professor von Hayek, unlike the run-of-the-mill Cold War propagandists of the West, he did not claim that there was.)

The battle between Keynesians and neo-liberals was neither a purely technical confrontation between professional economists, nor a search for ways of dealing with novel and troubling economic problems. (Who, for instance, had so much as considered the unpredicted combination of economic stagnation and rapidly rising prices, for which the jargon term "stagflation" had to be invented in the 1970s?) It was a war of incompatible ideologies. Both sides put forward economic arguments. The Keynesians claimed that high wages, full employment and the Welfare State created the consumer demand that had fuelled expansion, and that pumping more demand into the economy was the best way to deal with economic depressions. The neo-liberals argued that Golden Age economics and politics prevented the control of inflation and the cutting of costs in both government and private business, thus allowing profits, the real motor of economic growth in a capitalist economy, to rise. In any case, they held, that Adam Smith's "hidden hand" of the free market was bound to produce the greatest growth of the "Wealth of Nations" and the best sustainable distribution of wealth and income within it; a claim which the Keynesians denied. Yet economics in both cases rationalized an ideological

---

* The prize was instituted in 1969 and before 1974 had been awarded to men distinctly not associated with *laissez-faire* economics.

commitment, an *a priori* view of human society. Neo-liberals distrusted and disliked social-democratic Sweden, a spectacular economic success-story of the twentieth century, not because it was to run into trouble in the Crisis Decades—as did other types of economy—but because it was based on "the famed Swedish economic model with its collectivist values of equality and solidarity" (*Financial Times*, 11/11/90). Conversely, Mrs. Thatcher's government in Britain was unpopular on the Left, even during its years of economic success, because it was based on an a-social, indeed an anti-social egoism.

These were positions barely accessible to argument. Suppose, for instance, it could be shown that the supply of blood for medical use was best obtained by buying it off anyone willing to sell a pint of his or her blood at the market price. Would this have weakened the argument for the British system of unpaid voluntary donors, so eloquently and powerfully put forward by R. M. Titmuss in *"The Gift Relationship"* (Titmuss, 1970)? Surely not, although Titmuss had also shown that the British way of giving blood was as efficient and safer than the commercial way.* Other things being equal, for many of us a society in which citizens are prepared to give selfless help to unknown fellow-humans, however symbolically, is better than one in which they won't. In the early 1990s the Italian political system was shattered by a voters' rebellion against its endemic corruption, not because many Italians had actually suffered from it—a large number of them, perhaps a majority had benefited from it—but on moral grounds. The only political parties not swept away by the moral avalanche were those not involved in the system. Champions of absolute individual freedom were unmoved by the evident social injustices of unrestricted market capitalism, even when (as in Brazil for most of the 1980s) it did not produce economic growth. Conversely, believers in equality and social fairness (like the present author) welcomed the chance to argue that even capitalist economic success might rest most firmly on a relatively egalitarian distribution of income, as in Japan (see p. 356).†

---

*This was confirmed in the early 1990s when the blood-transfusion services of some countries, but not Britain, discovered that patients had been infected by commercially acquired blood contaminated by the HIV/Aids virus.

†The richest 20 per cent of the population in the 1980s had 4.3 times the total income of the poorest 20 per cent, which was less than the figure in any other (capitalist) industrial country, even Sweden. The average for the eight most industrialized countries of the European Community was 6, the figure for the U.S.A. 8.9 (Kidron/Segal, 1991, pp. 36–37). To put it another way: the U.S.A in 1990 had ninety-three dollar billionaires, the European Community fifty-nine, not counting the thirty-three domiciled in Switzerland and Lichtenstein. Japan had nine (ibid.).

That each side also translated its fundamental beliefs into pragmatic arguments, e.g. about whether the allocation of resources through free-market pricing was or was not optimal, was secondary. But, of course, both sides had to produce policies to deal with the economic slow-down.

In this respect the supporters of Golden Age economics were not very successful. This was partly because they were constrained by their polit-ical and ideological commitment to full employment, welfare states and the post-war consensus politics. Or rather, they were squeezed between the demands of capital and labour, when Golden Age growth no longer allowed both profits and non-business incomes to rise without getting in each other's way. In the 1970s and 1980s Sweden, the social-democratic state *par excellence*, maintained full employment with remarkable success by industrial subsidies, work-spreading and expanding state and public employment dramatically, thus making possible a notable extension of the welfare system. Even so, the policy could only be maintained by holding down the living standards of employed workers, penal tax-rates on high incomes and heavy deficits. In the absence of a return to the days of the Great Leap Forward, these could only be temporary measures, and from the mid-1980s on they were reversed. At the end of the Short Twentieth Century the "Swedish Model" was in retreat even in its own country.

However, the model was also, and perhaps even more fundamentally, undermined by the globalization of the economy after 1970, which put the governments of all states—except perhaps the U.S.A., with its enor-mous economy—at the mercy of an uncontrollable "world market." (Moreover, it was an undeniable fact that "the market" was very much more likely to distrust Left governments than conservative ones.) In the early 1980s even a country as large and wealthy as France, then under a socialist government, found it impossible to pump up its economy unilat-erally. Within two years of President Mitterand's triumphant election France faced a balance-of-payments crisis, was forced to devalue its cur-rency, and to replace Keynesian demand stimulation by "austerity with a human face."

On the other hand, the neo-liberals were also at a loss, as was to be-come obvious at the end of the 1980s. They had little trouble attacking the rigidities, inefficiencies and economic wastages so often sheltering under Golden Age government policies once these were no longer kept afloat by the ever-rising tide of Golden Age prosperity, employment and government revenues. There was considerable scope for applying the neo-liberal cleansing-agent to the encrusted hull of many a good ship

"Mixed Economy" with beneficial results. Even the British Left was eventually to admit that some of the ruthless shocks imposed on the British economy by Mrs. Thatcher had probably been necessary. There were good grounds for some of the disillusion with state-managed industries and public administration that became so common in the 1980s.

Nevertheless, the mere belief that business was good and government bad (in President Reagan's words "government was not the solution but the problem") was not an alternative economic policy. Nor, indeed, could it be for a world in which, even in the Reaganite U.S.A., central government expenditure amounted to about a quarter of the Gross National Product, and, indeed, in the developed countries of the European Community, averaged over 40 per cent of GNP (World Development, 1992, p. 239). Such enormous chunks of the economy could be managed in a businesslike manner and with a due sense of costs and benefits (as was not always the case), but they did not and could not operate like markets even when ideologists made them pretend to. In any case most neo-liberal governments were obliged to manage and steer their economies, while claiming that they were only encouraging market forces. Moreover, there was no way in which the weight of the state could be reduced. After fourteen years in power the most ideological of free-market regimes, Thatcherite Britain, actually taxed its citizens somewhat more heavily than they had been taxed under Labour.

In fact, there was no single or specific neo-liberal economic policy, except after 1989 in the former socialist states of the Soviet region, where some predictably disastrous attempts were made, on the advice of Western economic whiz-kids, to transfer the operations of the economy to the free market from one day to the next. The greatest of neo-liberal regimes, President Reagan's U.S.A., though officially devoted to fiscal conservatism (i.e. balanced budgets), and Milton Friedman's "monetarism," in fact used Keynesian methods to spend its way out of the depression of 1979–82 by running a gigantic deficit and engaging in an equally gigantic armaments build-up. So far from leaving the value of the dollar entirely to monetary rectitude and the market, Washington after 1984 returned to deliberate management through diplomatic pressure (Kuttner, 1991, pp. 88–94). As it happened, the regimes most deeply committed to *laissez-faire* economics were also sometimes, and notably in the case of Reagan's U.S.A. and Thatcher's Britain, profoundly and viscerally nationalist and distrustful of the outside world. The historian cannot but note that the two attitudes are contradictory. In any case, neo-liberal triumphalism did not survive the world economic setbacks of the early 1990s, nor perhaps the unexpected discovery that the most dynamic and rapidly growing economy of the globe after the fall of Soviet communism, was that of Communist China, leading Western business-school lectures and the authors of management manuals, a flourishing genre of literature, to scan the teachings of Confucius for the secrets of entrepreneurial success.

What made the economic problems of the Crisis Decades unusually troubling, and socially subversive, was that conjunctural fluctuations coincided with structural upheavals. The world economy facing the problems of the 1970s and 1980s was no longer that of the Golden Age, although it was, as we have seen, the predictable product of that era. Its system of production had been transformed by technological revolution and it had been globalized or "transnationalized" to an extraordinary extent, and with dramatic consequences. Moreover, by the 1970s it became impossible to overlook the revolutionary social and cultural consequences of the Golden Age, discussed in earlier chapters, as well as its potential ecological consequences.

The best way to illustrate these is through work and unemployment. The general tendency of industrialization has been to replace human skill with the skill of machines, human labour with mechanical forces, thus throwing people out of work. It was assumed, correctly, that the vast growth of the economy made possible by this constant industrial revolution would automatically create more than enough new jobs to replace the lost old ones, although opinions differed about how large a body of unemployed workers was necessary for the efficient operation of such an economy. The Golden Age had apparently confirmed this optimism. As we have seen (see chapter 10), the growth of industry was so great that the number and proportion of industrial workers even in the most industrialized countries did not seriously drop. Yet the Crisis Decades began to shed labour at a spectacular rate, even in plainly expanding industries. Between 1950 and 1970 the number of long-distance telephone operators in the U.S.A. dropped by 12 per cent, as the number of calls grew fivefold; but between 1970 and 1980 it fell by 40 per cent while calls tripled (Technology, 1986, p. 328). The number of workers diminished, relatively, absolutely and, in any case, rapidly. The rising unemployment of these decades was not merely cyclical but structural. The jobs lost in bad times would not come back when times improved: they would never come back.

This was not only because the new international division of labour transferred industries from old regional countries and continents to new ones, turning the old centres of industry into "rust-belts," or, in some ways, even more spectrally, into urban landscapes like face-lifts from which all trace of former industry had been removed. The rise of new industrial countries is indeed striking. In the mid-1980s seven of such countries in the Third World alone already consumed 24 per cent of the world's steel and produced 15 per cent of it—still as good an index of industrialization as any.* Moreover, in a world of free economic flows across state borders—except, characteristically, of migrants seeking work—labour-intensive industries naturally migrated from high-wage to low-wage countries, that is to say, from the rich core countries of capitalism like the U.S.A. to countries on the periphery. Every worker employed at Texan rates in El Paso was an economic luxury, if a worker, even an inferior one, was available at one tenth of the wage across the river in Mexican Juárez.

Yet even the pre-industrial and the new early industrial countries, were governed by the iron logic of mechanization, which sooner or later made even the cheapest human being more expensive than a machine capable of his or her work, and by the equally iron logic of genuine world-wide free-trading competition. Cheap as labour was in Brazil, compared to Detroit and Wolfsburg, the São Paulo automobile industry faced the same problems of increasing labour redundancy through mechanization as in Michigan and Lower Saxony; or so the author was told by its trade union leaders in 1992. The performance and productivity of machinery could be constantly, and for practical purposes, endlessly raised by technological progress, and its cost could be dramatically reduced. Not so that of human beings, as a comparison of the improvements in the speed of air transport and the 100-metre world record demonstrates. In any case the cost of human labour cannot, for any length of time, be reduced below the cost of keeping human beings alive at the minimum level regarded as acceptable in their society, or indeed at any level. Human beings are not efficiently designed for a capitalist system of production. The higher the technology, the more expensive the human component of production compared to the mechanical.

The historic tragedy of the Crisis Decades was that production now visibly shed human beings faster than the market economy generated new jobs for them. Moreover, this process was accelerated by global competition, by the financial squeeze on governments, which—directly or indirectly—were the largest single employers, and, not least, after 1980, by the then prevailing free-market theology which pressed for the transfer of employment to profit-maximizing forms of enterprise, especially to private firms which, by definition, considered no interest but their own

---

*China, South Korea, India, Mexico, Venezuela, Brazil and Argentina (Piel, 1992, pp. 286–89).

pecuniary one. This meant, among other things, that governments and other public entities ceased to be what has been called "the employer of last resort" (World Labour, 1989, p. 48). The decline of trade unions, weakened both by economic depression and by the hostility of neo-liberal governments, accelerated this process, since the protection of jobs was one of their most cherished functions. The world economy was expanding, but the automatic mechanism by which its expansion generated jobs for men and women who entered the labour market without special qualifications was visibly breaking down.

To put the matter another way. The peasantry, which had formed the majority of the human race throughout recorded history, had been made redundant by agricultural revolution, but the millions no longer needed on the land had in the past been readily absorbed by labour-hungry occupations elsewhere, which required only a willingness to work, the adaptation of country skills, like digging and building walls, or the capacity to learn on the job. What would happen to the workers in those occupations when they in turn become unnecessary? Even if some could be re-trained for the high-grade jobs of the information age which continued to expand (most of which increasingly demanded a higher education), there were not enough of these to compensate (Technology, 1986, pp. 7–9, 335). What, for that matter, would happen to the peasants of the Third World who still flooded out of their villages?

In the rich countries of capitalism, they now had welfare systems to fall back on, although those who became permanently welfare-dependent were both resented and despised by those who thought of themselves as earning a living by work. In the poor countries they joined the large and obscure "informal" or "parallel" economy in which men, women and children lived, nobody quite knew how, by a combination of small jobs, services, expedients, buying, selling and taking. In the rich countries they began to form or re-form an increasingly separate and segregated "underclass" whose problems were *de facto* regarded as insoluble, but secondary, since they formed only a permanent minority. The ghetto society of the native Negro population in the U.S.A.* became the textbook example of such a social underworld. Not that the "black economy" was absent in the First World. Researchers were surprised to discover that in the early 1990s the twenty-two million households of Britain between them held

---

*Black immigrants into the U.S.A from the Caribbean and Hispanic America behaved, essentially, like other immigrant communities, and did not allow themselves to be excluded from the labour market to anything like the same extent.

over £10 billions in cash, or an average of £460 per household, a figure said to be so high because the "black economy deals largely in cash" (*Financial Times*, 18/10/93).

II

The combination of depression and a massively restructured economy designed to expel human labour created a sullen tension that penetrated the politics of the Crisis Decades. A generation had got accustomed to full employment or the confidence that the sort of work a person wanted was sure to be available somewhere soon. While the Slump of the early 1980s had already brought insecurity back into the lives of workers in manufacturing industries, it was not until the Slump of the early 1990s that large sections of the white-collar and professional classes in countries like Great Britain felt that neither their jobs nor their futures were safe: almost half of all people in the most prosperous parts of the country thought they might lose theirs. These were times when people, their old ways of life already undermined and crumbling in any case (see chapter 10 and 11), were likely to lose their bearings. Was it an accident that "of the ten largest mass murders in American history . . . eight have occurred since 1980," typically the acts of middle-aged white men in their thirties and forties, "after a prolonged period of being lonely, frustrated and full of rage," and often precipitated by a catastrophe in their lives such as losing their job or divorce?* Was even "the growing culture of hate in the United States," which may have encouraged them, an accident (Butterfield, 1991)? This hate certainly became audible in the lyrics of popular music in the 1980s, and evident in the growingly overt cruelty of film and TV programmes.

This sense of disorientation and insecurity produced significant tectonic cracks and shifts in the politics of the developed countries, even before the end of the Cold War destroyed the international balance on which the stability of several Western parliamentary democracies had rested. In times of economic troubles voters are notoriously inclined to blame whatever party or regime is in power, but the novelty of the Crisis Decades was that the reaction against governments did not necessarily benefit the established forces of opposition. The major losers were the

---

* "This is especially true . . for some of the millions of people who have picked up in mid-life and moved. They get there and if they lose their job there, they really have no one to turn to."

social-democratic or labour parties of the West, whose main instrument of satisfying their supporters—economic and social action by national governments—lost its force, while the central bloc of these supporters, the working class, broke into fragments (see chapter 10). In the new transnational economy, domestic wages were far more directly exposed to foreign competition than before, and the ability of governments to shelter them was far less. At the same time in a period of depression the interests of various parts of the traditional social-democratic constituency diverged: those whose jobs were (relatively) safe; those who were insecure; those in the old and unionised regions and industries; those in the less threatened new industries in new and non-union areas; and the universally unpopular victims of bad times who sank into the "underclass." Moreover, since the 1970s a number of (mainly young and/or middle-class) supporters abandoned the main parties of the Left for more specialized campaigning movements—notably "the environment," women's movements and other so-called "new social movements"—thus weakening them. In the early 1990s labour and social-democratic governments became as uncommon as they had been in the 1950s, for even administrations nominally headed by socialists abandoned their traditional policies, willingly or not.

The new political forces which stepped into this void were a mixed assortment, ranging from the xenophobic and racist on the right, via secessionist parties (mainly, but not only ethnic/nationalist) to the various "Green" parties and other "new social movements" which claimed a place on the Left. Several of these established a significant presence in their country's politics, sometimes a regional dominance, though by the end of the Short Twentieth Century none had actually replaced the old political establishments. The support of others fluctuated wildly. Most of the influential ones rejected the universalism of democratic and citizen politics for the politics of some group identity, and consequently shared a visceral hostility to foreigners and outsiders, and to the all-inclusive nation-state of the American and French revolutionary tradition. We shall consider the rise of the new "identity politics" below.

However, the importance of these movements lay not so much in their positive content, as in their rejection of the "old politics." Several of the most formidable rested essentially on this negative claim, for instance the separatist Northern League in Italy, the 20 per cent of the U.S. electorate which supported a wealthy Texan maverick for President in 1992, or, for that matter, the electors of Brazil and Peru who actually elected men to the presidency in 1989 and 1990 on the grounds that they must be trustworthy as they had never heard of them before. In Britain only the systematically unrepresentative electoral system prevented the emergence of a massive third party at various times since the early 1970s, when the Liberals, alone or in combination or after fusion with a moderate Social Democratic breakaway from the Labour Party, gained almost as much support as—or even more support than—one or other of the two major parties. Since the early 1930s, another depression period, there had been nothing like the dramatic collapse of electoral support in the late 1980s and early 1990s for established parties with long records in government— the Socialist Party in France (1990), the Conservative Party in Canada (1993), the Italian government parties (1993). In short, during the Crisis Decades the hitherto stable structures of politics in the democratic capi- talist countries began to fall apart. What is more, the new political forces which showed the greatest potential for growth were those which com- bined populist demagogy, highly visible personal leadership and hostility to foreigners. Survivors from the inter-war era had reasons for feeling discouraged.

III

It was not much noticed that, again from around 1970, a similar crisis had begun to undermine the "Second World" of the "centrally planned economies." It was first concealed, later underlined, by the inflexibility of their political systems, so that the change, when it came, was sudden, as in the late 1970s, after the death of Mao in China, and in 1983–85, after the death of Brezhnev in the U.S.S.R. (see chapter 16). Economically, it was clear from the middle 1960s that centrally state-planned socialism badly needed reform. From the 1970s on there were strong signs of actual regression. This was the very moment when these economies were exposed, like every- one else—even if perhaps not to the same extent—to the uncontrollable movements and unpredictable fluctuations of the transnational world econ- omy. The massive entry of the U.S.S.R. on the international grain market, and the impact of the oil crises of the 1970s dramatized the ending of the "socialist camp" as a virtually self-contained regional economy protected from the vagaries of the world economy (see pp. 374).

East and West were curiously bonded together not only by the transnational economy, which neither could control, but by the strange interdependence of the Cold War power system. This, as we have seen (see chapter 8), stabilized both superpowers and the world between them, and was in turn to throw both into disorder when it collapsed. The dis- order was not merely political, but economic. For, with the sudden collapse of the Soviet political system, the inter-regional division of labour and the network of mutual dependence which had developed in the Soviet sphere also collapsed, forcing countries and regions that were geared to it to come to terms singly with a world market for which they were not equipped. But the West was equally unprepared to integrate the remains of the old communist "parallel world system" into its own world market, even when it wanted to, as the European Community did not.* Finland, one of the spectacular economic success stories of post-war Europe, was plunged into a major slump by the collapse of the Soviet economy. Germany, the greatest economic power of Europe, was to impose tremendous strains on its own economy, and on Europe as a whole, simply because its government (against warnings by its bankers, it must be said) completely underestimated the difficulty and costs of absorbing a relatively tiny part of the socialist economy, the sixteen-million-strong German Democratic Republic. These, however, were unpredicted consequences of the Soviet break-up, which almost nobody expected until it actually happened.

Nevertheless, in the meantime, as in the West, unthinkable thoughts became thinkable in the East; invisible problems became visible. Thus in both East and West the defence of the environment became an important campaigning issue in the 1970s, whether the issue was the defence of whales or the preservation of Lake Baikal in Siberia. Given the restrictions on public debate, we cannot exactly trace the development of critical thoughts in these societies, but by 1980 first-class and formerly reforming communist economists within the regime, like János Kornai in Hungary, were publishing notably negative analyses of the socialist economic systems, and the ruthless probes into the defects of the Soviet social system, which became known in the mid-eighties, had clearly been long gestating among the academics of Novosibirsk and elsewhere. When leading communists actually gave up their belief in socialism is even harder to establish, for after 1989–91 such people had some interest in retrospectively ante-dating their conversion. What was true in economics was even more patently true in politics, as Gorbachev's *perestroika* was to show, at any rate in the Western socialist countries. With all their historic admiration for and attachment to Lenin, there is little doubt that many reform communists would have wanted to abandon much of

---

* I recall the cry of anguish of a Bulgarian at an international colloquium in 1993: "What do you want us to do? We lost our markets in the former socialist countries. The European Community does not want to take our exports. As loyal members of the U.N. we can't even sell to Serbia now, because of the Bosnian blockade. Where do we go?"

the political heritage of Leninism, though few (outside the Italian Communist Party, to which reformers in the East felt attracted) were prepared to say so.

What most reformers in the socialist world would have wanted, was to transform communism into something like Western social democracy. Stockholm was their model rather than Los Angeles. There is no sign that Hayek and Friedman had many secret admirers in Moscow or Budapest. It was their bad luck that the crisis of the communist systems coincided with the crisis of Golden Age capitalism, which was also the crisis of social democratic systems. It was their even worse luck that the sudden collapse of communism made a programme of gradual transformation appear both undesirable and impractical, and that it occurred when the root-and-branch radicalism of the pure free-market ideologists was (briefly) triumphant in the capitalist West. This therefore became the theoretical inspiration of post-communist regimes, though in practice it proved as unrealisable there as anywhere else.

However, though in many ways the crises in East and West ran parallel and were linked into a single global crisis by both politics and economics, they differed in two major respects. For the communist system, which at least in the Soviet sphere, was inflexible and inferior, it was a matter of life and death, which it did not survive. Survival of the economic system was never at issue in the developed countries of capitalism, and, in spite of the crumbling of their political systems, neither, as yet, was the viability of these systems. This may explain, though it cannot justify, the implausible claim by an American writer that, with the end of communism, the future history of humanity would be that of liberal democracy. Only in one vital respect were these systems at risk: their future existence as single territorial states was no longer guaranteed. However, in the early 1990s, not a single one of the Western nation-states threatened with secessionist movements had actually broken up.

During the Age of Catastrophe, the end of capitalism had seemed near. The Great Slump could be described, like the title of a contemporary book, as *This Final Crisis* (Hutt, 1935). Few were seriously apocalyptic about the immediate future of developed capitalism, although a French historian and art dealer firmly predicted the end of Western civilization in 1976 on the not untenable ground that the momentum of the U.S. economy, which had carried the rest of the capitalist world forward in the past, was now a spent force (Gimpel, 1992). He therefore expected the current depression to "continue well into the next millennium." It is only fair to add that, until the middle or even late 1980s, few were apocalyptic about the prospects of the U.S.S.R. either.

However, precisely because of the greater and more uncontrollable dynamism of the capitalist economy, the social texture of Western societies had been far more profoundly undermined than that of socialist ones, and consequently in this respect the crisis of the West was more severe. The social fabric of the U.S.S.R. and Eastern Europe went to pieces as a result of the system's collapse and not as a precondition of it. Where comparisons were possible, as between West and East Germany, it seemed that the values and habits of traditional Germany had been better preserved under the lid of communism than in the Western region of economic miracles. The Jewish emigrants from the U.S.S.R. to Israel revived the classical music scene there, since they came from a country where going to live concerts was still a normal part of cultured behaviour, at any rate for Jews. The concert public had not yet been reduced, in effect, to a small and mainly middle-aged or elderly minority.* The inhabitants of Moscow and Warsaw were less worried by what troubled those of New York or London: a visibly rising crime rate, public insecurity, and the unpredictable violence of anomic youths. There was, obviously, little public flaunting of the kind of behaviour which outraged the socially conservative or conventional, even in the West, who saw it as evidence of the breakdown of civilization, and darkly muttered "Weimar."

How much of this difference between East and West was due to the greater wealth of Western societies and the far more rigid control of the state in the East is difficult to establish. In some respects East and West had evolved in the same direction. In both, families became smaller, marriages broke up more freely than elsewhere, the populations of states—or, at any rate, of their more urbanized and industrialized regions—reproduced themselves barely if at all. In both, so far as we can tell, the hold of traditional Western religions was drastically weakened, although it was claimed by religious enquirers that there was a revival of religious belief in post-Soviet Russia, though not in religious attendance. As events after 1989 showed, Polish women became as reluctant to let the Catholic Church dictate their mating habits as Italian women, although in the communist era Poles had shown a passionate attachment to the Church on nationalist and anti-Soviet grounds. Plainly the communist regimes provided less social space for subcultures, countercultures and underworlds of all kinds, and repressed dissidence. Moreover, peoples which had passed through the periods of genuinely ruthless and wholesale

---

*In New York, one of the world's two major musical centres, the concert public for classical music was said in the early 1990s to rest on twenty to thirty thousand people out of a population of ten millions.

terror, which studded the history of most such states, were likely to keep their heads down even when the exercise of power became gentler. Nevertheless, the relative tranquility of socialist life was not due to fear. The system insulated its citizens from the full impact of the Western social transformations because it insulated them from the full impact of Western capitalism. What change they underwent, came through the state or through their response to the state. What the state did not set out to change stayed much as it had been before. The paradox of communism in power was that it was conservative.

IV

About the vast area of the Third World (including those parts of it which were now industrializing) it is hardly possible to generalize. Insofar as its problems can be surveyed as a whole, I have tried to do so in chapters 7 and 12. The Crisis Decades, as we have seen, affected its regions in very different ways. How are we to compare South Korea, where the ownership of television sets went from 6.4 per cent of the population to 99.1 per cent in the fifteen years from 1970 to 1985 (Jon, 1993), with a country like Peru, where over half the population was below the poverty line—more than in 1972—and the per capita consumption was falling (Anuario, 1989), let alone with the ravaged countries of sub-Saharan Africa? The tensions within a subcontinent like India were those of a growing economy and a society in transformation. Those in areas like Somalia, Angola and Liberia were those of countries in dissolution, in a continent about whose future few were optimistic.

Only one generalization was fairly safe: since 1970 almost all the countries in this region had plunged deeply into debt. In 1990 they ranged from the three giants of international debt ($60 to 110 billions)—Brazil, Mexico and Argentina—through the other twenty-eight who owed over $10 billions each, down to the minnows who owed a billion or two. The World Bank (which had reason to know) counted only seven among the ninety-six "low-" and "middle-income" economies it monitored who had external debts substantially below a billion dollars—countries like Lesotho and Chad—and even these were many times as large as they had been twenty years earlier. In 1970 there had been only twelve countries with a debt over $1 billion, and none with debts over $10 billions. In more realistic terms, by 1980 six countries had a debt virtually as large as their entire GNP, or bigger; 1990 twenty-four countries owed more than they produced, including, taking the region as a whole, *all* of sub-Saharan Africa. The relatively most heavily indebted countries were not surprisingly to be found in Africa (Mozambique, Tanzania, Somalia, Zambia, Congo, the Ivory Coast), some disrupted by war, some by the collapse of the price of their exports. However, the countries which had to bear the heaviest cost of servicing these vast debts, that is to say, where this amounted to a quarter or more of the country's total exports, were more evenly spread. Indeed, among the regions of the world, sub-Saharan Africa was rather below this figure, better off in this respect than South Asia, Latin America and the Caribbean, and the Middle East.

Practically none of this money was ever likely to be repaid, but so long as the banks continued to earn interest on it—an average of 9.6 per cent in 1982 (UNCTAD)—they did not mind. There was a moment of genuine panic in the early 1980s when, starting with Mexico, the major Latin American debtors could no longer pay, and the Western banking system was on the verge of collapse, since several of the largest banks had lent their money with such abandon in the 1970s (when the petro-dollars flooded in, clamouring for investment) that they would now be technically bankrupt. Fortunately for the economy of the rich countries, the three Latin giants of debt failed to act together, separate arrangements for re-scheduling the debts were made and the banks, supported by governments and international agencies, had time in which gradually to write off their lost assets and to maintain technical solvency. The debt crisis remained, but was no longer potentially fatal. This was probably the most dangerous moment for the capitalist world economy since 1929. Its full story has not yet been written.

While their debts mounted, the assets or potential assets of the poor states did not. The capitalist world economy, which judges exclusively by profit or potential profit, clearly decided to write off a large part of the Third World in the Crisis Decades. Of the forty-two "low-income economies" in 1970, nineteen had zero net foreign investments. In 1990 direct foreign investors had lost total interest in twenty-six. Indeed there was substantial investment (more than $500 million) in only fourteen out of almost 100 low- and middle-income countries outside Europe, and massive investment (from about one billion or so upwards) in only eight, of which four were in East and South-east Asia (China, Thailand, Malaysia, Indonesia), and three in Latin America (Argentina, Mexico, Brazil).* The increasingly integrated transnational world economy did not entirely overlook the outcast regions. The smaller and more scenic among them

*The other investment attractor was, somewhat surprisingly, Egypt.

had potential as tourist paradises and offshore refuges from government control, and the discovery of some suitable resource on some hitherto uninteresting territory might well change the situation. However, on the whole a large part of the world was dropping out of the world economy. After the collapse of the Soviet bloc, this also looked like being the case with the area between Trieste and Vladivostok. In 1990 the only former socialist states of Eastern Europe which attracted any net foreign investment were Poland and Czechoslovakia (World Development, 1992, Tables 21, 23, 24). Within the vast area of the former U.S.S.R. there were clearly resource-rich districts or republics which attracted serious money, and zones which were left to their own miserable devices. One way or another, most of the former Second World was being assimilated to Third World status.

The main effect of the Crisis Decades was thus to widen the gap between rich and poor countries. The real GDP per capita of sub-Saharan Africa declined from 14 per cent of that of the industrial countries to 8 per cent between 1960 and 1987, that of the "least developed" countries (which included both African and non-African countries) from 9 per cent to 5 per cent.* (Human Development, 1991, Table 6.)

V

As the transnational economy established its grip over the world, it undermined a major, and since 1945, virtually universal, institution: the territorial nation-state, since such a state could no longer control more than a diminishing part of its affairs. Organizations whose field of action was effectively bounded by the frontiers of their territory, like trade unions, parliaments and national public broadcasting systems, therefore lost, as organizations not so bounded, like transnational firms, the international currency market and the globalized media and communications of the satellite era, gained. The disappearance of the superpowers, which could at any rate control their satellite states, was to reinforce this tendency. Even the most irreplaceable function nation-states had developed during the century, that of redistributing their income among their

---

* The "least developed nations" is a category established by the U.N. Mostly they have less than $300 per annum GNP per head. "Real GDP per capita" is a way of expressing this figure in terms of what it could purchase locally, instead of simply in terms of official exchange rates, according to a scale of "international purchasing power parities."

populations through the "transfer payments" of the welfare, educational and health services and other fund allocations, could no longer be territorially self-contained in theory, though most of it had to remain so in practice, except where supra-national entities like the European Community or Union supplemented it in some respects. During the heyday of the free-market theologians, the state was further undermined by the tendency to dismantle activities hitherto conducted by public bodies on principle, leaving them to "the market."

Paradoxically, but perhaps not surprisingly, this weakening of the nation-state went with a new fashion for cutting up the old territorial nation-states into what claimed to be (smaller) new ones, mostly based on the demand of some group to ethnic-linguistic monopoly. To begin with, the rise of such autonomist and separatist movements, mainly after 1970, was primarily a Western phenomenon, observable in Britain, Spain, Canada, Belgium, even in Switzerland and Denmark, but also, from the early 1970s, in the least centralized of socialist states, Yugoslavia. The crisis of communism spread it to the East, where more new and nominally national states were to be formed after 1991 than at any other time during the twentieth century. Until the 1990s it left the western hemisphere south of the Canadian border virtually unaffected. In the areas where the 1980s and 1990s brought the collapse and disintegration of states, as in Afghanistan and parts of Africa, the alternative to the old state was not so much a partition into new states as anarchy.

The development was paradoxical, since it was perfectly plain that the new mini-nation-states suffered from precisely the same drawbacks as the older ones, only, being smaller, more so. It was less surprising than it seemed, simply because the only actual state model available in the late twentieth century, was that of the bounded territory with its own autonomous institutions—in short the nation-state model of the Age of Revolution. Moreover, since 1918 all regimes had been committed to the principle of "national self-determination," which had been increasingly defined in ethnic-linguistic terms. In this respect Lenin and President Wilson were at one. Both the Europe of the Versailles peace treaties and what became the U.S.S.R. were conceived of as collections of such nation-states. In the case of the U.S.S.R. (and Yugoslavia, which later followed its example) these were unions of such states which, however, in theory—though not in practice—retained their right to secession.* When such

---

*In this they differed from the states of the U.S.A. which, since the end of the American Civil War in 1865, have not had the right to secession, except possibly for Texas.

unions broke up, it would naturally be along the pre-determined fracture lines.

However, in fact the new separatist nationalism of the Crisis Decades was quite a different phenomenon from the nation-state creation of the nineteenth and early twentieth century. It was indeed, a combination of three phenomena. One was the resistance of existing nation-states against their demotion. This became increasingly clear in the 1980s with the attempts by members or potential members of the European Community, sometimes of widely differing political complexions, like Norway and Mrs. Thatcher's Britain, to retain their regional autonomy within the all-European standardization in matters which they thought important. However, it was significant that the main traditional prop of nation-state self-defence, namely protectionism, was incomparably weaker in the Crisis Decades than it had been in the Age of Catastrophe. Global free trade remained the ideal and, to a surprising extent, the reality—more so than ever after the fall of the state-command economies—even though several states developed unacknowledged methods for protecting themselves against foreign competition. The Japanese and the French were said to be expert at this, but probably the Italians' success in keeping a lion's share of their home market for automobiles in Italian hands (i.e. Fiat) was the most striking. Nevertheless, these were rearguard actions, though increasingly hard-fought and sometimes successful ones. They were probably contested most bitterly where the issue was not simply economic but one of cultural identity. The French, and to a lesser extent the Germans, fought to maintain the vast subsidies for their peasants, not only because farmers had vital votes, but also because they genuinely felt that the destruction of peasant farming, however inefficient or uncompetitive, would mean the destruction of a landscape, a tradition, a part of the nation's character. The French, supported by the other Europeans, resisted the U.S. demand for free trade in films and audio-visual products, not simply because this would have swamped their public and private screens with American products, since an American-based (though by now internationally owned and controlled) entertainment industry had re-established a potential world monopoly on the scale of the old Hollywood power. They also, and justly, felt that it was intolerable that pure calculations of comparative costs and profitability should lead to the end of film production in the French language. Whatever the economic arguments, there were things in life which had to be protected. Would any government seriously consider tearing down Chartres Cathedral or the Taj Mahal if it could be shown that building a luxury hotel, shopping mall and conference centre on the site (assuming it were to be sold to private buyers) would make a greater net addition to the country's GNP than could be yielded by the existing tourist traffic? The question has only to be formulated to be answered.

The second is best described as the collective egoism of wealth, and reflected the growing economic disparities within continents, countries and regions. Old fashioned nation-state governments, centralized or federal, as well as supra-national entities like the European Community, had accepted responsibility for developing their entire territories, and therefore, to some extent, for equalizing burdens and benefits across the whole of them. This meant that the poorer and more backward regions were subsidized (via some central distributive mechanism) by the richer and more advanced, or even given preference in investment in order to diminish their lag. The European Community was realistic enough only to admit states to membership whose backwardness and poverty would not put too great a strain on the rest, a realism totally absent from the North American Free Trade Area of 1993 which yoked the U.S.A. and Canada (1990 GNP per capita of about $20,000) with Mexico with one-eighth of this per capita GNP.* The reluctance of rich areas to subsidize poorer ones had long been familiar to students of local government, especially in the U.S.A. The problem of the "inner city," inhabited by the poor, and with a tax-base shrinking because of the flight to the suburbs, was largely due to this. Who wanted to pay for the poor? Rich suburbs in Los Angeles like Santa Monica and Malibu opted out of the city, and in the early 1990s Staten Island voted to secede from New York for the same reason.

Some of the separatist nationalism of the Crisis Decades plainly fed on this collective egoism. The pressure for breaking up Yugoslavia came from "European" Slovenia and Croatia; and for splitting Czechoslovakia from the vociferously "Western" Czech Republic. Catalonia and the Basque country were the wealthiest and most "developed" parts of Spain, and the only signs of significant separatism in Latin America came from the richest state of Brazil, Rio Grande do Sul. The purest example of this phenomenon was the sudden rise in the late 1980s of the Lombard League (later: Northern League) which aimed at the secession of the region centred on Milan, the "economic capital" of Italy, from Rome, the political capital. The rhetoric of the League, with its references to a glorious medieval past and the Lombard dialect, was the usual one of

*The poorest member of the European Union, Portugal, had a 1990 GNP of one-third of the Community's average.

nationalist agitation, but the real issue was the rich region's wish to keep its resources to itself.

The third element was perhaps chiefly a response to the "cultural revolution" of the second half of the century, that extraordinary dissolution of traditional social norms, textures and values, which left so many of the inhabitants of the developed world orphaned and bereft. Never was the word "community" used more indiscriminately and emptily than in the decades when communities in the sociological sense became hard to find in real life—"the intelligence community," "the public relations community," the "gay community." The rise of "identity groups"—human ensembles to which a person could "belong," unequivocally and beyond uncertainty and doubt, was noted from the late 1960s by writers in the always self-observing U.S.A. Most of these, for obvious reasons, appealed to a common "ethnicity," although other groups of people seeking collective separatism used the same nationalist language (as when homosexual activists spoke of "the queer nation").

As the emergence of this phenomenon in the most systematically multi-ethnic of states suggests, the politics of identity groups had no intrinsic connection with the "national self-determination," i.e. the desire to create territorial states, identical with a particular "people," which was the essence of nationalism. Secession made no sense for U.S. Negroes or Italians, nor was it part of their ethnic politics. Ukrainian politics in Canada were not Ukrainian but Canadian.* Indeed, the essence of ethnic or similar politics in urban, i.e. almost by definition heterogeneous societies, was to compete with other such groups for a share of the resources of the non-ethnic state, by using the political leverage of group loyalty. The politicians elected for the New York municipal constituencies, gerrymandered in order to provide specific representation for Latino, Oriental and homosexual voting blocs, wanted more out of New York City, not less.

What ethnic identity politics had in common with *fin-de-siècle* ethnic nationalism was the insistence that one's group identity consisted in some existential, supposedly primordial, unchangeable and therefore permanent personal characteristic shared with other members of the group, and with

---

*At most, local immigrant communities could develop what has been called "long-distance nationalism" on behalf of their original or chosen homelands, generally representing the extremes of nationalist politics in those countries. The North American Irish and Jews were the original pioneers in this field, but the global diasporas created by migration multiplied such organizations, e.g. among Sikh migrants from India. Long-distance nationalism came into its own with the collapse of the socialist world.

no one else. Exclusiveness was all the more essential to it, since the actual differences which marked human communities off from each other were attenuated. Young American Jews searched for their "roots" when the things which stamped them indelibly as Jews were no longer effective markers of Jewry; not least the segregation and discrimination of the years before the Second World War. Though Quebec nationalism insisted on separation because it claimed to be a "distinct society," it actually emerged as a significant force precisely when Quebec ceased to be the "distinct society" it had so patently and unmistakably been until the 1960s (Ignatieff, 1993, pp. 115–17). The very fluidity of ethnicity in urban societies made its choice as the only criterion of the group arbitrary and artificial. In the U.S.A., except for Blacks, Hispanics, and those of English and German origins, at least 60 per cent of American-born women of *all* ethnic origins married outside their group (Lieberson, Waters, 1988, p. 173). Increasingly one's identity had to be constructed by insisting on the non-identity of others. How otherwise could the neo-Nazi skinheads in Germany, wearing the uniforms, hair-styles and musical tastes of the cosmopolitan youth culture, establish their essential Germanness, except by beating up local Turks and Albanians? How, except by eliminating those who did not "belong" could the "essentially" Croat or Serb character of some region be established in which, for most of history, a variety of ethnicities and religions had lived as neighbours?

The tragedy of this exclusionary identity politics, whether or not it set out to establish independent states, was that it could not possibly work. It could only pretend to. The Italian-Americans from Brooklyn, who (perhaps increasingly) insisted on their Italianness and talked to one another in Italian, apologising for their lack of fluency in what they supposed to be their native language,* worked in an American economy to which Italianness as such was irrelevant, except as a key to a relatively modest niche market. The pretence that there was a Black, or Hindu, or Russian, or female truth incomprehensible and therefore essentially incommunicable to those outside the group, could not survive outside institutions whose only function was to encourage such views. Islamic fundamentalists who studied physics did not study Islamic physics; Jewish engineers did not learn Chassidic engineering; even the most culturally nationalist Frenchmen or Germans learned that operating in the global village of the scientists and technical experts who made the world work required

---

*I have overheard such conversations in a New York department store. Their immigrant parents or grandparents had almost certainly not spoken Italian, but Neapolitan, Sicilian or Calabrian.

communication in a single global language analogous to medieval Latin, which happened to be based on English. Even a world divided into theoretically homogeneous ethnic territories by genocide, mass expulsion and "ethnic cleansing" was inevitably heterogenized again by mass movements of people (workers, tourists, businessmen, technicians), of styles and by the tentacles of the global economy. That, after all, is what happened to the countries of Central Europe, "ethnically cleansed" during and after the Second World War. That is what would inevitably happen again in an increasingly urbanized world.

Identity politics and *fin-de-siècle* nationalism were thus not so much programmes, still less effective programmes for dealing with the problems of the late twentieth century, but rather emotional reactions to these problems. And yet, as the century drew to its end, the absence of institutions and mechanisms actually capable of dealing with these problems became increasingly evident. The nation-state was no longer capable of dealing with them. Who or what was?

Various devices had been invented for this purpose since the United Nations had been set up in 1945 on the assumption, immediately disappointed, that the U.S.A. and U.S.S.R. would continue to agree sufficiently to take global decisions. About the best that could be said for this organization is that, unlike its predecessor, the League of Nations, it remained in being throughout the second half of the century, and indeed became a club whose membership, increasingly, proved that a state had been formally accepted as internationally sovereign. It had, by the nature of its constitution, no powers or resources independent of those assigned to it by member-nations, and hence no powers of independent action.

The sheer need for global co-ordination multiplied international organizations faster than ever in the Crisis Decades. By the mid-1980s there were 365 inter-governmental ones and no less than 4,615 non-governmental ones, or more than twice as many as in the early 1970s (Held, 1988, p. 15). Moreover, global action on problems such as conservation and the environment was increasingly recognized to be urgent. However, unfortunately, the only formal procedures for achieving it, namely by international treaties separately signed and ratified by sovereign nation-states, were slow, clumsy and inadequate, as was demonstrated by the efforts to preserve the Antarctic continent and permanently to ban the hunting of whales. The very fact that in the 1980s the government of Iraq killed thousands of its citizens by poison gas, thus breaking one of the few genuinely universal international conventions, the Geneva Protocol of 1925 against the use of chemical warfare, underlined the weakness of available international instruments.

Nevertheless, two ways of securing international action were available, and the Crisis Decades saw both substantially reinforced. One was the voluntary abdication of national power to supra-national authorities by middle-sized states which no longer felt strong enough to stand on their own in the world. The European Economic Community (re-named the European Community in the 1980s and the European Union in the 1990s) doubled its size in the 1970s and prepared to expand it even further in the 1990s, while reinforcing its authority over the affairs of its member-states. The fact of this double extension was unquestionable, though it was to provoke considerable national resistance, both by member-governments and public opinion in their countries. The strength of the Community/Union lay in the fact that its un-elected central authority in Brussels took independent policy initiatives and was virtually immune to the pressures of democratic politics, except very indirectly, through the periodic meetings and negotiations of representatives of its (elected) member-governments. This state of affairs enabled it to function as an effective supra-national authority, subject only to specific vetos.

The other instrument of international action was equally, if not more, protected against nation-states and democracies. This was the authority of the international financial bodies set up in the aftermath of the Second World War, mainly the International Monetary Fund and the World Bank (see pp. 274ff.). Backed by the oligarchy of the major capitalist countries which, under the vague label of the "Group of Seven" became increasingly institutionalized from the 1970s, they acquired increasing authority during the Crisis Decades, as the uncontrollable vagaries of the global exchanges, debt crisis of the Third World and, after 1989, the collapse of the Soviet bloc economies made a growing number of countries dependent on the willingness of the rich world to grant them loans. These loans were increasingly made conditional on the local pursuit of economic policies agreeable to the global banking authorities. The triumph of neo-liberal theology in the 1980s was, in effect, translated into policies of systematic privatization and free-market capitalism which were imposed on governments too bankrupt to resist them, whether they were immediately relevant to their economic problems or not (as in post-Soviet Russia). It is interesting, but, alas, pointless to speculate on what J. M. Keynes and Harry Dexter White would have thought about this transformation of the institutions they had constructed with very different objects in mind, not least the object of full employment in their respective countries.

Still, these were effective international authorities, at all events for the imposition of policies by the rich on the poor countries. At the end of the century it remained to be seen what the consequences of these policies were, and what their effects on world development would be.

Two vast regions of the world were about to test them. One was the region of the U.S.S.R. and its associated European and Asian economies, which, after the fall of the Western communist systems, now lay in ruins. The other was the storehouse of social explosives which filled so much of the Third World. As we shall see in the next chapter, it had, since the 1950s, formed the major element of political instability on the globe.

CHAPTER FIFTEEN

Third World and Revolution

In January 1974 General Beleta Abebe stopped over in the Gode barracks on his way to an inspection . . . The next day an incredible report came to the Palace: the general has been arrested by the soldiers, who are forcing him to eat what they eat. Food so obviously rotten that some fear the general will fall ill and die. The Emperor [of Ethiopia] sends in the airborne unit of his Guard, which liberates the general and takes him to the hospital.

> —Ryszard Kapuściński, *The Emperor* (1983, p. 120)

We killed all the cattle [of the university's experimental farm] that we could. But while we were killing them, the peasant women started to cry: those poor beasts, why are they killing them like that, what have they done? When the ladies (*señoras*) began to cry, oh poor thing, we gave up, but we had already killed about a quarter, like eighty head. We wanted to kill the lot, but we couldn't because the peasant women started to cry.

When we'd been there for a while, a gentleman on his horse, over towards Ayacucho, he'd gone to tell them what had happened. So, the next day, it was on the news on the *La Voz* radio station. Just then we were on the way back, and some comrades had those little radios, so we listened, and, well, that made us feel good, didn't it?

> —A young member of *Sendero Luminoso, Tiempos*
> (1990, p. 198)

I

However we interpret the changes in the Third World and its gradual decomposition and fission, all of it differed from the First World in one fundamental respect. It formed a worldwide zone of revolution—whether just achieved, impending or possible. The First World was, by and large, politically and socially stable when the global Cold War began. Whatever simmered under the surface of the Second World was held down by the lid of party power and potential Soviet military intervention. On the other hand, very few Third World states of any size passed through the period from 1950 (or the date of their foundation) without revolution; military coups to suppress, prevent or advance revolution; or some other form of internal armed conflict. The main exceptions up to the date of writing are India, and a few colonies ruled by long-lived and authoritarian paternalists, like Dr. Banda of Malawi (the former colony of Nyasaland) and the (until 1994) indestructible M. Felix Houphouet-Boigny of the Ivory Coast. This persistent social and political instability of the Third World provided its common denominator.

This instability was equally evident to the U.S.A., protector of the global status quo, which identified it with Soviet communism, or at least regarded it as a permanent and potential asset for the other side in the great global struggle for supremacy. Almost from the start of the Cold War, the U.S.A. set out to combat this danger by all means, from economic aid and ideological propaganda through official and unofficial military subversion to major war; preferably in alliance with a friendly or bought local regime, but if need be without local support. This is what kept the Third World a zone of war, when the First and Second Worlds settled down to the longest era of peace since the nineteenth century. Before the collapse of the Soviet system it was estimated that about nineteen—perhaps even twenty—millions had been killed in over one hundred "major wars and military actions and conflicts" between 1945 and 1983, virtually all in the Third World: over nine millions in East Asia; three-and-a-half millions in Africa; two-and-a-half in South Asia; rather over half a million in the Middle East, without counting the most murderous of its wars, the Iran-Iraq conflict of 1980–88 which had barely begun; and rather less in Latin America (U.N. World Social Situation, 1985, p. 14). The Korean War of 1950–53, whose dead have been estimated at between three and four millions (in a country of thirty millions) (Halliday/Cumings, 1988, pp. 200–1) and the thirty years of Vietnam wars (1945–1975) were much the largest, and the only ones in which American forces themselves were directly engaged on a large scale. In each about fifty thousand Americans were killed. The losses of the Vietnamese and other Indochinese peoples are difficult to estimate, but the most modest estimate runs to two millions. However, some of the indirectly fought anti-communist wars were of comparable barbarity, especially in Africa, where about one million-and-a-half are said to have died between 1980 and 1988 in the wars against the governments of Mozambique and Angola (joint population c. twenty-three millions), with twelve millions displaced from their homes or threatened by hunger (U.N. Africa, 1989, p. 6).

The revolutionary potential of the Third World was equally evident to the communist regimes, if only because, as we have seen, the leaders of colonial liberation tended to see themselves as socialists, engaged on the same sort of project of emancipation, progress and modernization as the Soviet Union, and along the same lines. If educated in the Western style, they might even think of themselves as inspired by Lenin and Marx, though powerful communist parties in the Third World were uncommon, and (outside Mongolia, China and Vietnam) none became the main force in the movements of national liberation. However, several new regimes appreciated the usefulness of the Leninist type of party, and built or borrowed their own, as Sun Yat-sen had done in China after 1920. Some communist parties which acquired particular strength and influence were sidelined (as in Iran and Iraq in the 1950s) or eliminated by massacre, as in Indonesia in 1965, where something like half a million communists or supposed communists were killed after what was said to be a pro-communist military coup—probably the largest political butchery in history.

For several decades the U.S.S.R. took an essentially pragmatic view of its relations with Third World revolutionary, radical and liberation movements, since it neither intended nor expected to enlarge the region under communist government beyond the range of Soviet occupation in the West, or of Chinese intervention (which it could not entirely control) in the East. This did not change even in the Khrushchev period (1956–64), when a number of home-grown revolutions, in which communist parties played no significant part, came to power under their own steam, notably in Cuba (1959) and Algeria (1962). African decolonization also brought to power national leaders who asked for nothing better than the title of anti-imperialist, socialist and friend of the Soviet Union, especially when the latter brought technical and other aid not tainted by the old colonialism: Kwame Nkrumah in Ghana, Sekou Touré in Guinea, Modibo Keita in Mali, and the tragic Patrice Lumumba in the Belgian Congo, whose murder made him a Third World icon and martyr. (The U.S.S.R. renamed the Peoples' Friendship University it established for Third World students in 1960, "Lumumba University.") Moscow sympathized with such new regimes and helped them, though soon abandoning excessive optimism about the new African states. In the ex-Belgian Congo it gave armed support to the Lumumbist side against the clients or puppets of the U.S.A. and the Belgians in the civil war (with interventions by a military force of the United Nations, equally disliked by both superpowers) that followed the precipitate granting of independence to the vast colony. The results were disappointing.* When one of the new regimes, Fidel Castro's in Cuba, actually declared itself to be officially communist, to everyone's surprise, the U.S.S.R. took it under its wing, but not at the risk of permanently jeopardising its relations with the U.S.A. Nevertheless, there is no real evidence that it planned to push forward the frontiers of communism by revolution until the middle 1970s, and even then the evidence suggests that the U.S.S.R. made use of a favourable conjuncture it had not set out to create. Khrushchev's hopes, older readers may recall, were that capitalism would be buried by the economic superiority of socialism.

Indeed, when Soviet leadership of the international communist movement was challenged in 1960 by China, not to mention by various dissident Marxists, in the name of revolution, Moscow's parties in the Third World maintained their chosen policy of studied moderation. Capitalism was not the enemy in such countries, insofar as it existed, but the precapitalism, local interests and the (U.S.) imperialism that supported them. Armed struggle was not the way forward, but a broad popular or national front in which the "national" bourgeoisie or petty-bourgeoisie were allies. In short, Moscow's Third World strategy continued the Comintern line of the 1930s against all denunciations of treason to the cause of the October revolution (see chapter 5). This strategy, which infuriated those who preferred the way of the gun, sometimes looked like winning, as in Brazil and in Indonesia in the early 1960s, and in Chile in 1970. Perhaps not surprisingly, when it got to this point, it was stopped short by military coups followed by terror, as in Brazil after 1964, in Indonesia in 1965 and in Chile in 1973.

Nevertheless, the Third World now became the central pillar of the hope and faith of those who still put their faith in social revolution. It represented the great majority of human beings. It seemed to be a global volcano waiting to erupt, a seismic field whose tremors announced the major earthquakes to come. Even the analyst of what he called "the end of ideology" in the stabilized, liberal, capitalist West of the Golden Age (Bell, 1960) admitted that the age of millennial and revolutionary hope

---

*A brilliant Polish journalist, then reporting from the (theoretically) Lumumbist province, has given the most vivid account of the tragic Congolese anarchy (Kapuściński, 1990).

was not dead there. Nor was the Third World important only to the old revolutionaries of the October tradition, or to romantics, recoiling from the tawdry if prosperous mediocrity of the 1950s. The entire Left, including humanitarian liberals and moderate social democrats, needed something more than social security legislation and rising real wages. The Third World could preserve its ideals; and parties belonging to the great tradition of the Enlightenment need ideals as well as practical politics. They cannot survive without them. How otherwise can we explain the genuine passion for giving aid to Third World countries in those strongholds of non-revolutionary progress, the Scandinavian countries, the Netherlands and the (Protestant) World Council of Churches, which was the late-twentieth-century equivalent of the support of missionary endeavour in the nineteenth? In the later twentieth century it led European liberals to support or sustain Third World revolutionaries and revolutions.

II

What struck both the opponents of revolution and the revolutionaries was that, after 1945, the primary form of revolutionary struggle in the Third World, i.e. anywhere in the world, now seemed to be guerrilla warfare. A "chronology of major guerrilla wars" compiled in the middle 1970s listed thirty-two since the end of the Second World War. All but three (the Greek civil war of the late forties, the Cyprus struggle against Britain in the 1950s and Ulster (1969–), were outside Europe and North America (Laqueur, 1977, p. 442). The list could have been easily prolonged. The image of revolution as emerging exclusively from the hills was not quite accurate. It underestimated the role of Left-wing military coups, which admittedly seemed implausible in Europe until a dramatic example of the species occurred in Portugal in 1974, but which were common enough in the Islamic world and not unexpected in Latin America. The Bolivian revolution of 1952 was made by a conjunction of miners and army insurrectionaries; the most radical reform of Peruvian society by a military regime in the late 1960s and 1970s. It also underestimated the revolutionary potential of old-fashioned urban mass actions, which was to be demonstrated by the Iranian revolution of 1979 and thereafter in Eastern Europe. However, in the third quarter of the century all eyes were on the guerrillas. Their tactics, moreover, were strongly propagated by ideologues on the radical Left, critical of Soviet policy. Mao Tse-tung (after his split with the U.S.S.R.) and, after 1959, Fidel Castro, or rather his comrade, the handsome and peripatetic Che Guevara (1928–67), inspired these activists. The Vietnamese communists, though by far the most formidable and successful practitioners of the guerrilla strategy, and internationally much admired for defeating both the French and the might of the U.S.A., did not encourage their admirers to take sides in the internecine ideological feuds of the Left.

The 1950s were full of Third World guerrilla struggles, practically all in those colonial countries in which, for one reason or another, the former colonial powers or local settlers resisted peaceful decolonization— Malaya, Kenya (the Mau Mau movement) and Cyprus in the dissolving British Empire; the much more serious wars in Algeria and Vietnam in the dissolving French one. Oddly it was a relatively small movement— certainly smaller than the Malayan insurgency (Thomas, 1971, p. 1040)— untypical but successful, which put the guerrilla strategy on the world's front pages: the revolution that took over the Caribbean island of Cuba on 1 January 1959. Fidel Castro (1927–   ) was a not uncharacteristic figure in Latin American politics: a strong and charismatic young man of a good landowning family, whose politics were hazy, but who was determined to demonstrate personal bravery and to be a hero of whatever cause of freedom against tyranny presented itself at a suitable moment. Even his slogans ("Fatherland or Death"—originally "Victory or Death"— and "We shall be victorious") belong to an older era of liberation: admirable but lacking in precision. After an obscure period among the pistol-packing gangs of Havana University student politics, he chose rebellion against the government of General Fulgencio Batista (a familiar and tortuous figure in Cuban politics since his debut in an army coup in 1933 as the then Sergeant Batista), who had taken power again in 1952 and abrogated the Constitution. Fidel's approach was activist: an attack on an army barracks in 1953, jail, exile, and the invasion of Cuba by a guerrilla force which, on its second attempt, established itself in the mountains of the remotest province. The ill-prepared gamble paid off. In purely military terms the challenge was modest. Che Guevara, the Argentinian doctor and highly gifted guerrilla leader, set out to conquer the rest of Cuba with 148 men, rising to 300 by the time he had virtually done so. Fidel's own guerrillas only captured their first town of 1,000 inhabitants in December 1958 (Thomas, 1971, pp. 997, 1020, 1024). The most that he demonstrated by 1958—though that was much—was that an irregular force could control a large "liberated territory" and defend it against an offensive by an admittedly demoralized army. Fidel won because the Batista regime was fragile, lacking all real support, except that motivated by convenience and self-interest, and led by a man grown lazy by long corruption. It collapsed as soon as the opposition of all political classes from the democratic bourgeoisie to the communists united against him and the dictator's own agents, soldiers, policemen and torturers concluded that his time had run out. Fidel proved that it had run out, and, naturally enough, his forces inherited the government. A bad regime which few supported had been overthrown. The victory of the rebel army was genuinely felt by most Cubans as a moment of liberation and infinite promise, embodied in its young commander. Probably no leader in the Short Twentieth Century, an era full of charismatic figures on balconies and before microphones, idolized by the masses, had fewer sceptical or hostile listeners than this large, bearded, unpunctual man in crinkled battle-dress who spoke for hours at a time, sharing his rather unsystematic thoughts with the attentive and unquestioning multitudes (including the present writer). For once revolution was experienced as a collective honeymoon. Where would it lead? It had to be somewhere better.

Latin American rebels in the 1950s inevitably found themselves drawing not only on the rhetoric of their historic liberators, from Bolívar to Cuba's own José Martí, but on the anti-imperialist and social-revolutionary tradition of the post-1917 Left. They were both for "agrarian reform," whatever that meant (see p. 354), and, at least implicitly, against the U.S.A., especially in poor central America, so far from God, so near to the U.S.A., in the phrase of the old Mexican strong-man Porfirio Díaz. Though radical, neither Fidel nor any of his comrades were communists nor (with two exceptions) even claimed to have Marxist sympathies of any kind. In fact, the Cuban Communist Party, the only such mass party in Latin America apart from the Chilean one, was notably unsympathetic until parts of it joined him rather late in his campaign. Relations between them were distinctly frosty. The U.S. diplomats and policy advisers constantly debated whether the movement was or was not pro-communist—if it were, the CIA, which had already overthrown a reforming government in Guatemala in 1954, knew what to do—but clearly concluded that it was not.

However, everything was moving the Fidelist movement in the direction of communism, from the general social-revolutionary ideology of those likely to undertake armed guerrilla insurrections to the passionate anti-communism of the U.S.A. in the decade of Senator McCarthy, which automatically inclined the anti-imperialist Latin rebels to look more kindly on Marx. The global Cold War did the rest. If the new regime antagonized the U.S.A., which it was almost certain to do, if only by threatening American investments, it could rely on the almost guaranteed sympathy and support of the U.S.A.'s great antagonist. Moreover,

Fidel's form of government by informal monologues before the millions, was not a way to run even a small country or a revolution for any length of time. Even populism needs organization. The Communist Party was the only body on the revolutionary side which could provide him with it. The two needed one another and converged. However, by March 1960, well before Fidel had discovered that Cuba was to be socialist and he himself was a communist, though very much in his own manner, the U.S.A. had decided to treat him as such, and the CIA was authorized to arrange for his overthrow (Thomas, 1971, p. 1271). In 1961 they tried by an invasion of exiles at the Bay of Pigs, and failed. A Communist Cuba survived seventy miles from Key West, isolated by the U.S. blockade and increasingly dependent on the U.S.S.R.

No revolution could have been better designed to appeal to the Left of the western hemisphere and the developed countries, at the end of a decade of global conservatism; or to give the guerrilla strategy better publicity. The Cuban revolution had everything: romance, heroism in the mountains, ex-student leaders with the selfless generosity of their youth—the eldest were barely past thirty—a jubilant people, in a tropical tourist paradise pulsing with rumba rhythms. What is more, it could be hailed by all Left revolutionaries.

In fact, it was more likely to be hailed by the critics of Moscow, long dissatisfied with the Soviets' priority for peaceful coexistence between it and capitalism. Fidel's example inspired the militant intellectuals everywhere in Latin America, a continent of ready trigger-fingers and a taste for unselfish bravery, especially in heroic postures. After a while Cuba came to encourage continental insurrection, urged on by Guevara, the champion of pan-Latin American revolution and of the creation of "two, three, many Vietnams." A suitable ideology was provided by a brilliant young French Leftist (who else?) who systematized the idea that, in a continent ripe for revolution, all that was needed was the import of small groups of armed militants into suitable mountains to form "focuses" (*focos*) for mass liberation struggle (Debray, 1965).

All over Latin America enthusiastic groups of young men launched themselves into uniformly doomed guerrilla struggles under the banner of Fidel, or Trotsky or Mao Tse-tung. Except in Central America and Colombia, where there was an old base for peasant support for armed irregulars, most such enterprises collapsed almost immediately, leaving behind the corpses of the famous—Che Guevara himself in Bolivia; the equally handsome and charismatic priest-rebel Father Camilo Torres in Colombia—and the unknown. It was a spectacularly misconceived strategy, all the more so because, given the right conditions, effective and lasting guerrilla movements in many of these countries *were* possible, as the (official communist) FARC (Armed Forces of the Colombian Revolution) proved in Colombia from 1964 to the time of this writing, and the (Maoist) Shining Path movement (*Sendero Luminoso*) proved in Peru in the 1980s.

However, even when peasants took to the guerrilla road, guerrillas were seldom—the Colombian FARC are a rare exception—a peasant movement. They were overwhelmingly carried into the Third World countryside by young intellectuals, initially drawn from their countries' established middle classes, later reinforced by the new generation of student sons and (more rarely) daughters of the rising rural petty-bourgeoisie. This was also true when the guerrilla tactic was transferred from the rural back country to the world of the big cities, as some parts of the revolutionary Third World Left (e.g. in Argentina, Brazil and Uruguay and in Europe) began to do from the late 1960s.* As it happens, urban guerrilla operations are much easier to mount than rural ones, since they need not rely on mass solidarity or connivance, but can exploit the anonymity of the big city plus the purchasing power of money and a minimum of, mostly middle-class, sympathisers. These "urban-guerrilla" or "terrorist" groups found it easier to produce dramatic publicity coups, and spectacular killings (as of Admiral Carrero Blanco, Franco's intended successor, by the Basque ETA in 1973; of the Italian premier Aldo Moro by the Italian Red Brigades in 1978), not to mention money-raising raids, than to revolutionize their countries.

For even in Latin America the major forces for political change were civilian politicians—and armies. The wave of Right-wing military regimes which began to flood large parts of South America in the 1960s—military government had never gone out of fashion in Central America, except for revolutionary Mexico and little Costa Rica, which actually abolished its army after a revolution in 1948—were not primarily responding to armed rebels. In Argentina they overthrew the populist chieftain Juan Domingo Perón (1895–1974) whose force lay in the organization of labour and the mobilization of the poor (1955), after which they found themselves resuming power at intervals, since the Perónist mass movement proved indestructible and no stable civilian

---

*The major exception are the activists of what may be called "ghetto" guerrilla movements, such as the Provisional IRA in Ulster, the short-lived U.S. "Black Panthers" and the Palestinian guerrillas, children of the diaspora of refugee camps, who may come largely or wholly from among the children of the street and not the seminar; especially where the ghettoes contain no significant middle class.

alternative could be constructed. When Perón returned from exile in 1972, this time with much of the local Left hanging to his coat-tails, once again to demonstrate the predominance of his supporters, the military took over again with blood, torture and patriotic rhetoric, until dislodged after the defeat of their armed forces in the brief, pointless but decisive Anglo–Argentinian war of 1982.

The armed forces took over in Brazil in 1964 against a very similar enemy: the heirs of the great Brazilian populist leader Getulio Vargas (1883–1954), moving towards the political Left in the early 1960s and offering democratization, land reform and scepticism about U.S. policy. The small guerrilla attempts of the late 1960s, which provided an excuse for the ruthless repressions of the regime, never represented the slightest real challenge to it; but it must be said that after the early 1970s the regime began to relax and returned the country to civilian rule by 1985. In Chile the enemy was the united Left of socialists, communists and other progressives—what European (and for that matter Chilean) tradition knew as a "popular front" (see chapter 5). Such a front had already won elections in Chile in the 1930s, when Washington was less nervous and Chile was a byword for civilian constitutionalism. Its leader, the socialist Salvador Allende, was elected President in 1970, his government was destabilized and, in 1973, overthrown by a military coup strongly backed, perhaps even organized, by the U.S.A., which introduced Chile to the characteristic features of 1970s military regimes—executions or massacres, official and para-official, systematic torture of prisoners, and the mass exile of political opponents. The military chief General Pinochet remained in power for seventeen years, which he used to impose a policy of economic ultra-liberalism on Chile, thus demonstrating, among other things, that political liberalism and democracy are not natural partners of economic liberalism.

Possibly the military take-over in revolutionary Bolivia after 1964 had some connection with American fears of Cuban influence in that country, where Che Guevara himself died in a half-baked attempt at guerrilla insurrection, but Bolivia is not a place readily controlled for any length of time by any local soldier, however brutal. The military era ended after fifteen years filled with a rapid succession of generals, increasingly eyeing the profits of the drug trade. Though in Uruguay the military took a particularly intelligent and effective "urban guerrilla" movement as an excuse for the usual killings and tortures, it was the rise of a "Broad Left" popular front, competing with the traditional two-party system, that probably explains the military takeover of 1972 in the only South American country which could be described as a genuine lasting democracy. The Uruguayans retained enough of their tradition eventually to vote down the handcuffed constitution offered them by their military rulers and in 1985 returned to civilian rule.

Though it had already achieved, and was likely to achieve more dramatic successes in Latin America, Asia and Africa, in the developed countries the guerrilla road to revolution made little sense. However, it is not surprising that, through its guerrillas, rural and urban, the Third World inspired the growing number of youthful rebels and revolutionaries, or merely the cultural dissidents of the First World. Rock music reporters compared the juvenile masses at the Woodstock music festival (1969) to "an army of peaceful guerrillas" (Chapple and Garofalo, 1977, p. 144). Images of Che Guevara were carried like icons by student demonstrators in Paris and Tokyo, and his bearded, bereted and unquestionably manly features fluttered even non-political hearts in the counter-culture. No name (except that of the philosopher Marcuse) is mentioned more often than his in a well-informed survey of the global "New Left" of 1968 (Katsiaficas, 1987), even if, in practice, the name of the Vietnamese leader Ho-Chi-Minh ("Ho Ho Ho-Chi-Minh") was chanted even more frequently in the demonstrations of the First World Left. For it was support for Third World guerrillas, and, in the U.S.A. after 1965, resistance against being sent to fight against them, which mobilized the Left more than anything else, except hostility to nuclear arms. *The Wretched of the Earth*, written by a Caribbean psychologist who had taken part in the Algerian war of liberation, became an enormously influential text among intellectual activists who were thrilled by its praise of violence as a form of spiritual liberation for the oppressed.

In short, the image of guerrillas with coloured skins amid tropical vegetation was an essential part, perhaps the chief inspiration, of the First World radicalization of the 1960s. "Third Worldism," the belief that the world would be emancipated by means of the liberation of its impoverished and agrarian "periphery," exploited and pressed into "dependency" by the "core countries" of what a growing literature called "the world system," captured much of the theorists of the First World Left. If, as the "world system" theorists implied, the roots of the world's troubles lay not in the rise of modern industrial capitalism, but in the conquest of the Third World by European colonialists in the sixteenth century, then the reversal of this historical process in the twentieth century offered the powerless revolutionaries of the First World a way out of their impotence. No wonder that some of the most powerful arguments to this effect came from American Marxists, who could hardly count on a victory of socialism by forces indigenous to the U.S.A.

III

Nobody in the flourishing countries of industrial capitalism took the classic prospect of social revolution by insurrection and mass action seriously any more. And yet, at the very peak of Western prosperity, at the very core of capitalist society, governments suddenly, unexpectedly and, at first sight, inexplicably found themselves facing something that not only looked like old-fashioned revolution, but also disclosed the weaknesses of apparently firm regimes. In 1968–69 a wave of rebellion swept across all three worlds, or large parts of them, carried essentially by the new social force of students, whose numbers were now counted by the hundreds of thousands in even medium-sized Western countries, and would soon be counted in millions (see chapter 10). Moreover, their numbers were reinforced by three political characteristics which multiplied their political effectiveness. They were easily mobilized in the enormous knowledge-factories which contained them, while leaving them much more free time than workers in giant plants. They were usually to be found in capital cities, under the eyes of politicians and the cameras of the media. And, being members of the educated classes, often children of the established middle class, and—almost everywhere but especially in the Third World—the recruiting ground for the ruling elite of their societies, they were not so easy to shoot down as the lower orders. In Europe, west and east, there were no serious casualties, not even in the vast riots and street-combats of Paris in May 1968. The authorities took care that there should be no martyrs. Where there was a major massacre, as in Mexico City in 1968—the official count was twenty-eight dead and two hundred wounded when the army dispersed a public meeting (González Casanova, 1975, vol. II, p. 564)—the subsequent course of Mexican politics was permanently changed.

The student rebellions were thus disproportionately effective, especially where, as in France in 1968 and in the "hot autumn" of Italy in 1969, they released huge waves of working-class strikes which temporarily paralysed the economy of entire countries. And yet, of course, they were not genuine revolutions nor likely to develop into such. For the workers, where they took part in them, they were merely the opportunity to discover the industrial bargaining-power they had accumulated without noticing over the past twenty years. They were not revolutionaries. The First World students were rarely interested in such trifling matters as overthrowing governments and seizing power, although in fact the French ones came quite close to bringing down General de Gaulle in May 1968 and certainly shortened his reign (he retired a year later), and the American student anti-war protest unseated President L. B. Johnson in the same year. (Third World students were closer to the realities of power: Second World students knew that they were necessarily remote from them.) The Western student rebellion was more of a cultural revolution, a rejection of everything in society represented by "middle-class" parental values, and has been discussed as such in chapters 10 to 11.

Nevertheless, it helped to politicize a substantial number of the rebel student generation, who naturally turned towards the accepted inspirers of radical revolution and total social transformation—Marx, the non-Stalinist icons of the October revolution, and Mao. For the first time since the anti-fascist era, Marxism, no longer confined to Moscow orthodoxy, attracted large numbers of young Western intellectuals. (It had, of course, never ceased to attract them in the Third World.) It was a peculiar seminar-oriented Marxism, combined with a variety of other then-current academic fashions, and sometimes with other ideologies, nationalist or religious, for it came out of the classroom, not the experience of working lives. Indeed, it had little relation to the practical political behaviour of these new disciples of Marx, which usually called for the kind of radical militancy that has no need for analysis. When the utopian expectations of the original rebellion had evaporated, many returned to, or rather turned to, the old parties of the Left, which (like the French Socialist Party, reconstructed at this period, or the Italian Communist Party) were revived partly by the infusion of young enthusiasm. Since the movement was largely one of intellectuals, many were recruited to the academic profession. In the U.S.A., this consequently acquired an unprecedented contingent of politico-cultural radicals. Others saw themselves as revolutionaries in the October tradition and joined or recreated the small, disciplined, preferably clandestine "vanguard" organizations of cadres along Leninist lines, either to infiltrate mass organizations or for terrorist purposes. Here the West converged with the Third World, which was also full of bodies of illegal fighters hoping to offset mass defeat by small-group violence. The various Italian "Red Brigades" of the 1970s were probably the most important among the European groups of Bolshevik provenance. A curious clandestine world of conspiracy emerged in which direct-action groups of nationalist and social revolutionary ideology, sometimes both, were linked in an international network that consisted of various—generally tiny—"Red Armies," Palestinian, Basque insurrectionaries, the IRA and the rest, overlapping with other illegal networks, infiltrated by intelligence services, protected and where necessary assisted by Arab or eastern states.

It was a milieu ideally suited to the writers of secret-service and terror thrillers, for whom the 1970s were a golden age. It was also the darkest era of torture and counter-terror in the history of the West. This was the blackest period so far recorded in the modern history of torture, of nominally unidentifiable "death squadrons" or kidnapping and death gangs in unmarked cars who "disappeared" people, but whom everyone knew to be part of army and police, of armed services, police and intelligence or security services that made themselves virtually independent of government, let alone of democratic control, of unspeakable "dirty wars."* This was observable even in a country of old and powerful traditions of law and constitutional procedure like Great Britain, when the early years of the conflict in Northern Ireland led to some serious abuses, which attracted the attention of Amnesty International's report on torture (1975). It was probably at its worst in Latin America. Though it was not much noticed, the socialist countries were barely affected by this sinister fashion. Their ages of terror were behind them, and they had no terrorist movements in their borders, only tiny groups of public dissidents who knew that, in their circumstances, the pen was mightier than the sword, or rather the typewriter (plus Western public protest) than the bomb.

The student revolt of the late 1960s was the last hurrah of the old world revolution. It was revolutionary in both the ancient utopian sense of seeking a permanent reversal of values, a new and perfect society, and in the operational sense of seeking to achieve it by action on streets and barricades, by bomb and mountain ambush. It was global, not only because the ideology of the revolutionary tradition, from 1789 to 1917, was universal and internationalist—even so exclusively nationalist a movement as the Basque separatist ETA, a typical product of the 1960s, claimed to be in some sense Marxian—but because, for the first time, the world, or at least the world in which student ideologists lived, was genuinely global. The same books appeared, almost simultaneously, in the student bookshops in Buenos Aires, Rome and Hamburg (in 1968 almost certainly including Herbert Marcuse). The same tourists of revolution crossed oceans and continents from Paris to Havana to São Paulo to Bolivia. The first generation of humanity to take rapid and cheap global air travel and telecommunications for granted, the students of the late

---

*The best estimate of the number of people "disappeared" or murdered in the Argentinian "dirty war" of 1976–82 is about ten thousand (Las Cifras, 1988, p. 33).

1960s, had no difficulty in recognizing what happened at the Sorbonne, in Berkeley, in Prague, as part of the same event in the same global village in which, according to the Canadian guru Marshall McLuhan (another fashionable name of the 1960s), we all lived.

And yet this was not the world revolution as the generation of 1917 had understood it, but the dream of something that no longer existed: often enough not much more than the pretence that behaving as though the barricades were up would somehow cause them to rise, by sympathetic magic. The intelligent conservative Raymond Aron even described the "events of May 1968" in Paris, not quite inaccurately, as street theatre or psychodrama.

Nobody any longer expected social revolution in the Western world. Most revolutionaries no longer even regarded the industrial working class, Marx's "gravedigger of capitalism," as fundamentally revolutionary, unless by loyalty to the orthodox doctrine. In the western hemisphere, whether among the theoretically committed ultra-Left of Latin America or among the untheoretical student rebels of North America, the old "proletariat" was even dismissed as an enemy of radicalism, whether as a favoured labour aristocracy or as patriotic supporters of the Vietnam War. The future of revolution lay in the (now rapidly emptying) peasant hinterlands of the Third World, but the very fact that their inhabitants had to be shaken out of their passivity by armed apostles of revolt from far away, led by Castros and Guevaras, suggested a certain flagging in the old belief that historic inevitability guaranteed the "damned of the earth," of whom the Internationale sang, would break their chains alone.

Moreover, even where revolution was a reality, or a probability, was it any longer genuinely worldwide? The movements in which the revolutionaries of the 1960s put their hopes were the opposite of ecumenical. The Vietnamese, the Palestinians, the various guerrilla movements for colonial liberation, were concerned purely with their own national affairs. They were linked to the wider world only insofar as they were led by communists who had such wider commitments, or insofar as the bipolar structure of the Cold War world system automatically made them the friends of their enemy's enemy. How inessential the old ecumenism had become, was demonstrated by Communist China, which, in spite of a rhetoric of global revolution, pursued a relentlessly self-centred national policy that was to take it, in the 1970s and 1980s, into a policy of alignment with the U.S.A. against Communist U.S.S.R. and into actual armed conflict with both the U.S.S.R. and Communist Vietnam. Revolution aiming beyond national borders survived only in the attenuated form of regional movements: pan-African, pan-Arabic and especially pan-Latin American. Such movements had a certain reality, at least for intellectual militants who spoke the same language (Spanish, Arabic) and moved freely from country to country, as exiles or planners of revolt. One could even claim that some of them—notably the Fidelista version—contained genuinely globalist elements. After all, Che Guevara himself fought for a while in the Congo, and Cuba was to send its troops to assist revolutionary regimes in the Horn of Africa and in Angola in the 1970s. And yet, outside the Latin American Left, how many really expected even an all-African or all-Arabic triumph of socialist emancipation? Did not the break-up of the short lived United Arab Republic of Egypt and Syria, with a loosely attached Yemen (1958–61), and the constant frictions between the equally pan-Arab and socialist Ba'ath Party regimes in Syria and Iraq demonstrate the fragility, even the political unreality, of supranational revolutions?

Indeed, the most dramatic proof of the fading of world revolution, was the disintegration of the international movement dedicated to it. After 1956 the U.S.S.R. and the international movement under its leadership, lost their monopoly of the revolutionary appeal, and of the theory and ideology that unified it. There were now many different species of Marxists, several of Marxist-Leninists, and even two or three different brands among those few communist parties which, after 1956, maintained the picture of Joseph Stalin on their banners (the Chinese, the Albanians, the very different C. P. [Marxist] which split from the orthodox Indian Communist Party).

What remained of the Moscow-centred international communist movement disintegrated between 1956 and 1968, as China broke with the U.S.S.R. in 1958–60 and called, with little success, for the secession of states from the Soviet bloc and the formation of rival communist parties, as (mainly Western) communist parties, headed by the Italians, began openly to distance themselves from Moscow, and as even the original "socialist camp" of 1947 was now split into states with varying degrees of loyalty to the U.S.S.R., ranging from the totally committed Bulgarians* to the totally independent Yugoslavia. The Soviet invasion of Czechoslovakia, in 1968, for the purpose of replacing one form of communist policy by another, finally nailed down the coffin of "proletarian internationalism." Thereafter it became normal for even Moscow-aligned communist parties to criticise the U.S.S.R. in public and to adopt policies at variance with those of Moscow ("Eurocommunism"). The end of the international

*It appears that Bulgaria actually asked for incorporation into the U.S.S.R. as a Soviet Republic, but was refused on grounds of international diplomacy

communist movement was also the end of any kind of socialist or social-revolutionary internationalism, for the dissident and anti-Muscovite forces developed no effective international organizations other than rival sectarian synods. The only body which still faintly recalled the tradition of ecumenical liberation was the old, or rather revived, Socialist International (1951), which now represented government and other parties, mostly Western, that had formally abandoned revolution, world-wide or not, and, in most cases, even the belief in the ideas of Marx.

IV

However, if the tradition of social revolution in the mode of October 1917 was exhausted—or even, as some argued, its parent tradition of revolution in the mode of the French Jacobins of 1793—the social and political instability which generated revolutions remained. The volcano had not ceased to be active. As the Golden Age of world capitalism came to an end in the early 1970s, a new wave of revolution swept across large parts of the world, to be followed in the 1980s by the crisis of the Western communist systems, which led to their breakdown in 1989.

Though they occurred overwhelmingly in the Third World, the revolutions of the 1970s formed a geographically and politically ill-assorted ensemble. They began, surprisingly enough, in Europe with the overthrow in April 1974 of the Portuguese regime of the longest-lived Right-wing system of the Continent, and, shortly after, the collapse of a much briefer ultra-Right-wing military dictatorship in Greece (see p. 349). After General Franco's long-awaited death in 1975, the peaceful transition of Spain from authoritarianism to parliamentary government completed this return to constitutional democracy in southern Europe. These transformations could still be considered as the liquidation of unfinished business left over from the era of European fascism and the Second World War.

The coup of radical officers which revolutionized Portugal was engendered in the long and frustrating wars against African colonial liberation guerrillas, which the Portuguese army had been waging since the early 1960s, though without major troubles, except in the small colony of Guinea-Bissau, where perhaps the ablest of all African liberation leaders, Amilcar Cabral, had fought them to a standstill by the end of the 1960s. African guerrilla movements had multiplied in the 1960s, following the Congo conflict and the hardening of South African *apartheid* policy (the creation of the black "homelands"; the Sharpeville massacre), but without significant success, and weakened by both inter-tribal and Soviet–Chinese rivalries. With increasing Soviet help—China was otherwise occupied with the bizarre cataclysm of Mao's "Great Cultural Revolution"—they revived in the early 1970s, but it was the Portuguese revolution that enabled the colonies finally to win their independence in 1975. Mozambique and Angola were soon plunged into a far more murderous civil war again by the joint intervention of South Africa and the U.S.A.

However, as the Portuguese Empire collapsed, a major revolution broke out in the oldest independent African country, the famine-stricken Ethiopia, where the Emperor was overthrown (1974) and eventually replaced by a Leftist military junta strongly aligned with the U.S.S.R., which therefore switched its support in this region from the military dictatorship of Siad Barre in Somalia (1969–91), also then advertising its enthusiasm for Marx and Lenin. Within Ethiopia the new regime was challenged, and was eventually to be overthrown in 1991 by equally Marxist-inclined regional liberation or secession movements.

These changes created a fashion for regimes dedicated, at least on paper, to the cause of socialism. Dahomey declared itself a People's Republic under the usual military leader and changed its name to Benin; the island of Madagascar (Malagasy) declared its commitment to socialism, also in 1975, after the usual military coup; Congo (not to be confused with its giant neighbour, the former Belgian Congo, now renamed Zaire under the sensationally rapacious pro-American militarist Mobutu) stressed its character as a People's Republic, also under the military; and in Southern Rhodesia (Zimbabwe) the eleven-year attempt to establish a white-ruled independent state came to an end in 1976 under growing pressure from two guerrilla movements, divided by tribal identity and political orientation (Russian and Chinese respectively). In 1980 Zimbabwe became independent under one of the guerrilla leaders.

While on paper these movements belonged to the old revolutionary family of 1917, in reality they clearly belonged to a different species, inevitably so given the differences between the societies for which Marx's and Lenin's analyses had been designed, and those of sub-Saharan postcolonial Africa. The only African country in which some of the conditions of such an analysis applied was the economically developed and industrialized settler capitalism of South Africa, where a genuine mass liberation movement crossing tribal and racial frontiers came into existence—the African National Congress—with the help of the organization of a genuine mass trade union movement and an effective Communist Party. After the end of the Cold War even the *apartheid* regime was forced into retreat by it. Still, even here the movement was disproportionately strong among certain African tribes, relatively much weaker among others (e.g.

the Zulus), a situation exploited by the *apartheid* regime to some effect. Everywhere else, except for the small and sometimes tiny cadre of the educated and Westernized urban intellectuals, "national" or other mobilizations were essentially based on tribal loyalties or alliances, a situation which was to enable the imperialists to mobilize other tribes against the new regimes—as notably in Angola. The only relevance of Marxism-Leninism to these countries was a recipe for forming disciplined cadre parties and authoritarian governments.

The U.S. withdrawal from Indochina reinforced the advance of communism. All of Vietnam was now under unchallenged communist government, and similar governments now took over in Laos and Cambodia, in the latter case under the leadership of the "Red Khmer" party, a particularly murderous combination of the Paris café Maoism of their leader Pol Pot (1925–) and the armed backwoods peasantry bent on destroying the degenerate civilization of the cities. The new regime killed its citizens in numbers enormous even by the standards of our century—they cannot have eliminated much less than 20 per cent of the population—until it was driven from power by a Vietnamese invasion which restored a human government in 1978. After this—in one of the more depressing episodes of diplomacy—both China and the U.S. bloc continued to support the remains of the Pol Pot regime on anti-Soviet and anti-Vietnamese grounds.

The late 1970s saw the wave of revolution send its sprays directly over the U.S.A., as Central America and the Caribbean, Washington's unquestioned zone of domination, seemed to veer to the Left. Neither the Nicaraguan revolution of 1979, which overthrew the Somoza family, kingpins of U.S. control in the small republics of the region, nor the growing guerrilla movement in El Salvador, nor even the troublesome General Torrijos, who sat by the Panama Canal, weakened U.S. dominance seriously, any more than the Cuban revolution had done; still less the revolution on the tiny island of Grenada in 1983 against which President Reagan mobilized all his armed might. And yet the success of such movements contrasted strikingly with their failure in the 1960s, and caused an atmosphere little short of hysteria in Washington during the period of President Reagan (1980–88). Nevertheless, these were undoubtedly revolutionary phenomena, though of a familiar Latin American type; the major novelty, both puzzling and troubling to those of the old Left-wing tradition, which had been basically secular and anticlerical, was the appearance of Marxist-Catholic priests who supported or even participated in and led insurrections. The tendency, legitimized by a "theology of liberation" backed by an episcopal conference in Colombia (1968), had emerged after the Cuban Revolution* and found powerful intellectual support in the most unexpected quarter, the Jesuits, and less unexpected opposition in the Vatican.

While the historian sees how far from the October revolution even those revolutions of the 1970s were, which claimed an affinity to it, the governments of the U.S.A. inevitably regarded them essentially as part of a global offensive by the communist superpower. This was partly due to the supposed rule of the zero-sum game of the Cold War. The loss of one player must be the gain of the other, and, since the U.S.A. had aligned itself with the conservative forces in most of the Third World, and more than ever in the 1970s, it found itself on the losing side of revolutions. Moreover, Washington thought it had some cause for nervousness about the progress of the Soviet nuclear armament. In any case, the Golden Age of world capitalism, and the centrality of the dollar in it, was at an end. The position of the U.S. as a superpower was inevitably weakened by the universally predicted defeat in Vietnam, from which the greatest military power on earth was forced finally to withdraw in 1975. Since Goliath had been felled by the slingshot of David, there had not been such a debacle. Is it too much to suppose, especially in the light of the Gulf War against Iraq in 1991, that a more confident U.S.A. would, in 1973, have taken the coup of OPEC so unresistingly? What was OPEC other than a group of mostly Arab states of no political significance apart from their oil wells and not yet armed to the teeth thanks to the high oil prices they could now extort?

The U.S.A. inevitably saw any weakening in its global supremacy as a challenge to it, and as a sign of Soviet thirst for world domination. The revolutions of the 1970s therefore led to what has been called "the Second Cold War" (Halliday, 1983), which was, as usual, fought by proxy between the two sides, mainly in Africa and later in Afghanistan, where the Soviet army itself became involved outside its frontiers for the first time since the Second World War. Yet we cannot dismiss the assertion that the U.S.S.R. itself felt that the new revolutions allowed it to shift the global balance slightly in its favour—or, more precisely, to offset at least part of the major diplomatic loss it suffered in the 1970s by the setbacks in China and Egypt, whose alignments Washington managed to shift. The U.S.S.R. kept out of the Americas, but it intervened elsewhere, especially in Africa, to a far greater extent than before, and with some

---

*The present writer recalls hearing Fidel Castro himself, in one of his great public monologues in Havana, expressing his astonishment at this development, as he urged his listeners to welcome these surprising new allies.

success. The mere fact that the U.S.S.R. allowed or encouraged Fidel Castro's Cuba to send troops to help Ethiopia against the new U.S. client-state Somalia (1977), and Angola against the U.S.-backed rebel movement UNITA and the South African army, speaks for itself. Soviet statements now spoke of "socialist-oriented states" in addition to fully communist ones. Angola, Mozambique, Ethiopia, Nicaragua, South Yemen and Afghanistan attended the funeral of Brezhnev in 1982 under this heading. The U.S.S.R. had neither made these revolutions nor controlled them, but it visibly welcomed them as allies with some alacrity.

Nevertheless, the next succession of regimes to collapse or be overthrown demonstrated that neither Soviet ambition nor the "communist world conspiracy" could be made responsible for these upheavals, if only because, from 1980 on, it was the Soviet system itself that began to be destabilized, and, at the end of the decade, it disintegrated. The fall of "really existing socialism" and the question how far it can be treated as revolutions will be discussed in another chapter. However, even the major revolution which preceded the eastern crises, though a greater blow to the U.S.A. than any of the other changes of regime in the 1970s, had nothing to do with the Cold War.

This was the overthrow of the Shah of Iran in 1979, the greatest by far of the revolutions of the 1970s, and which will enter history as one of the major social revolutions of the twentieth century. It was the response to the programme of lightning modernization and industrialization (not to mention armament) undertaken by the Shah on the basis of the solid support of the U.S.A. and the country's oil-wealth, its value multiplied after 1973 by the OPEC price revolution. No doubt, apart from other signs of the megalomania usual among absolute rulers with a formidable and dreaded secret police, he hoped to become the dominant power in western Asia. Modernization meant agrarian reform as the Shah saw it, which turned large numbers of share-croppers and tenants into large numbers of sub-economic smallholders or unemployed labourers who migrated to the cities. Teheran grew from 1.8 millions (1960) to six millions. The capital-intensive high-tech agribusinesses favoured by the government made more labour surplus, but did not help the per capita production of agriculture, which declined in the 1960s and 1970s. By the late 1970s Iran was importing most of its food from abroad.

Increasingly, therefore, the Shah relied on industrialization financed by oil, and, unable to compete in the world, promoted and protected at home. The combination of a declining agriculture, an inefficient industry, massive foreign imports—not least of arms—and the oil boom produced inflation. It is possible that the standard of living of most Iranians not directly involved in the modern sector of the economy, and or the growing and flourishing urban business classes, actually dipped in the years before the revolution.

The energetic cultural modernization of the Shah also turned against him. His (and the Empress's) genuine support for an improvement in the position of women was unlikely to be popular in a Muslim country, as the Afghan communists also were to discover. And his equally genuine enthusiasm for education increased mass literacy (but about half the population remained illiterate) and produced a large body of revolutionary students and intellectuals. Industrialization strengthened the strategic position of the working-class, especially in the oil industry.

Since the Shah had been put back on the throne in 1953 by a CIA-organized coup against a large popular movement, he did not have much accumulated capital of loyalty and legitimacy to draw on. His very dynasty, the Pahlavis, could look back only to a coup by its founder, Reza Shah, a soldier in the Cossack Brigade, who took the imperial title in 1925. Still, in the 1960s and 1970s the old communist and National opposition was kept down by the secret police, regional and ethnic movements were repressed, as were the usual Leftist guerrilla groups, whether orthodox Marxist or Islamic-Marxist. These could not provide the spark for the explosion, which—a return to the ancient tradition of revolution from Paris in 1789 to Petrograd in 1917—was essentially a movement of the urban masses. The countryside remained quiet.

The spark came from the peculiar speciality of the Iranian scene, the organized and politically active Islamic clergy which occupied a public position that had no real parallel elsewhere in the Muslim world, or even within its Shiite sector. They, with the bazaar merchants and artisans, had in the past formed the activist element in Iranian politics. They now mobilized the new urban plebs, a vast body with more than adequate reasons for opposition.

Their leader, Ayatollah Ruholla Khomeini, aged, eminent and vindictive, had been in exile since the middle 1960s when he had led demonstrations against a proposed referendum on land reform and police repression of clerical activities in the holy city of Qum. Thence he denounced the monarchy as un-Islamic. From the early 1970s he began to preach a total Islamic form of government, the duty of the clergy to rebel against despotic authorities and, in effect, to take power: in short, an Islamic revolution. This was a radical innovation, even for politically activist Shiite clergymen. These sentiments were communicated to the masses by means of the post-Koranic device of tape-cassettes, and the masses listened. The young religious students in the holy city acted in 1978 by demonstrating against an alleged assassination by the secret police, and were shot down. Further demonstrations mourning the martyrs were organized, and these were to be repeated every forty days. They grew, until by the end of the year millions went on the street to demonstrate against the regime. The guerrillas went into action again. The oil workers shut down the oil fields in a crucially effective strike, the bazaars their shops. The country was at a standstill and the army failed or refused to suppress the uprising. On 16 January 1979 the Shah went into exile and the Iranian revolution had won.

The novelty of this revolution was ideological. Virtually all the phenomena commonly recognized as revolutionary up to that date had followed the tradition, ideology and, in general, the vocabulary of Western revolution since 1789; more precisely: of some brand of the secular Left, mainly socialist or communist. The traditional Left was indeed present and active in Iran, and its part in the overthrow of the Shah, e.g. by means of the workers' strikes, was far from insignificant. Yet it was almost immediately eliminated by the new regime. The Iranian revolution was the first made and won under the banner of religious fundamentalism and which replaced the old regime by a populist theocracy whose professed programme was a return to the seventh century A.D., or rather, since we are in an Islamic milieu, the situation after the *hijra* when the Holy Koran was written down. For revolutionaries of the old kind this was as bizarre a development as if Pope Pius IX had taken the lead in the Roman revolution of 1848.

This does not mean that henceforth religious movements were to fuel revolutions, even though from the 1970s on in the Islamic world they undoubtedly became a mass political force among the middle classes and intellectuals of their countries' swelling populations, and took an insurrectionary turn under the influence of the Iranian revolution. Islamic fundamentalists revolted and were savagely put down in Ba'athist Syria, stormed the holiest of shrines in pious Saudi Arabia, and assassinated the President of Egypt (under the leadership of an electrical engineer), all in 1979–82.* No single doctrine of revolution replaced the old revolutionary tradition of 1789/1917, nor any single dominant project for changing the world, as distinct from overthrowing it.

It does not even mean that the old tradition disappeared from the

---

*Other apparently religious movements of violent politics which gained ground in this period lack, and indeed deliberately exclude the universalist appeal, and are best seen as subvarieties of ethnic mobilization, e.g. the militant Buddhism of the Sinhalese in Sri Lanka, and the Hinduist and Sikh extremisms in India.

political scene, or lost all force to overthrow regimes, though the fall of Soviet communism virtually eliminated it as such over a large part of the world. The old ideologies retained substantial influence in Latin America, where the most formidable insurrectionary movement of the 1980s, the Peruvian *Sendero Luminoso*, or Shining Path, flaunted its Maoism. They were alive in Africa and India. Moreover, to the surprise of those brought up on Cold War commonplaces, the "vanguard" ruling parties of the Soviet type survived the fall of the U.S.S.R., especially in backward countries and in the Third World. They won bona fide elections in the southern Balkans, and demonstrated in Cuba and Nicaragua, in Angola, even, after the withdrawal of the Soviet army, in Kabul, that they were more than simple clients of Moscow. Still, even here the old tradition was eroded, and often virtually destroyed from within, as in Serbia, where the Communist Party transformed itself into a party of Greater Serb chauvinism, or in the Palestinian movement, where a leadership of the secular Left was increasingly undermined by the rise of Islamic fundamentalism.

V

The revolutions of the late twentieth century thus had two characteristics: the atrophy of the established tradition of revolution was one; the revival of the masses was another. As we have seen (see chapter 2), few revolutions since 1917–18 had been made at the grass roots. Most had been made by the activist minorities of the committed and organized, or imposed from above, as by army coups or military conquest; which does not mean that they had not, in suitable circumstances, been genuinely popular. Except where they came with foreign conquerors, they could rarely have established themselves otherwise. Yet in the late twentieth century the "masses" returned to the scene in major rather than supporting roles. Minority activism, in the form of rural or urban guerrillas and terrorism, continued, and indeed became endemic in the developed world, and in significant parts of South Asia and the Islamic zone. International terrorist incidents, as counted by the U.S. State Department, rose almost continuously from 125 in 1968 to 831 in 1987, the number of their victims rose from 241 to 2,905 (U.N. World Social Situation, 1989, p. 165).

The list of political assassinations grew longer—Presidents Anwar Sadat of Egypt (1981); Indira Gandhi (1984) and Rajiv Gandhi of India (1991), to name but some. The activities of the Provisional Irish Republican Army in the United Kingdom and of the Basque ETA in Spain are characteristic of this type of small-group violence, which had the advantage that it could be conducted by a few hundred, or even a few dozen activists, with the help of the extremely powerful, cheap and portable explosives and armaments that a flourishing international arms traffic now scattered wholesale over the globe. They were a symptom of the growing barbarization of all three worlds, and added to the pollution by generalized violence and insecurity of the atmosphere which urban humanity at the end of the millennium learned to breathe. However, its contribution to political revolution was small.

Not so, as the Iranian revolution showed, the readiness of people in their millions to come out on the streets. Or, as in East Germany ten years later, the decision of citizens of the German Democratic Republic—unorganized, spontaneous, though decisively facilitated by the decision of Hungary to open its frontiers—to vote against their regime with their feet and cars by migrating to West Germany. Within two months about 130,000 had done so (Umbruch, 1990, pp. 7–10), before the Berlin Wall fell. Or, as in Romania, where television for the first time caught the moment of revolution, in the sagging face of the dictator as the crowd convoked by the regime on the public square began to boo rather than to cheer. Or in the occupied parts of Palestine, when the mass non-cooperation movement of the *intifada*, which began in 1987, demonstrated that henceforth only active repression, not passivity or even tacit acceptance, sustained Israeli occupation. Whatever stimulated hitherto inert populations into action—modern communications like TV and tape-recorders made it hard to insulate even the most secluded from the world's affairs—it was the readiness of the masses to come out that decided matters.

These mass actions did not and could not overthrow regimes by themselves. They might even have been stopped short by coercion and guns, as the mass mobilization for democracy in China was, in 1989, by the massacre of Tiananmen Square in Beijing. (Still, vast though it was, this student and urban movement represented only a modest minority in China and, even so, it was large enough to cause the regime serious hesitation.) What such mobilization of the masses achieved was to demonstrate a regime's loss of legitimacy. In Iran, as in Petrograd 1917, the loss of legitimacy was demonstrated in the most classical fashion by the refusal of army and police to obey orders. In Eastern Europe it convinced old regimes already demoralized by the refusal of Soviet help that their time had run out. It was a textbook demonstration of Lenin's maxim that voting with citizens' feet could be more effective than voting in elections. Of course the mere clump of the massed citizens' feet alone could not make revolutions. They were not armies, but crowds, or statistical aggregates of individuals. They required leaders, political structures or strategies to be effective. What mobilized them in Iran was a campaign of political protest by adversaries of the regime; but what turned that campaign into a revolution was the readiness of the millions to join it. Just so earlier massive examples of such direct mass intervention responded to a political call from above—whether from the Indian National Congress to abstain from cooperation with the British in the 1920s and 1930s (see chapter 7) or from the supporters of President Perón to demand the release of their arrested hero on the famous "Day of Loyalty" in the Plaza de Mayo of Buenos Aires (1945). Moreover, what counted was not sheer numbers, but numbers acting in a situation which made them operationally effective.

We do not yet understand why voting with massed feet became so much more significant a part of politics in the last decades of the century. One reason must be that in this period the gap between rulers and ruled widened almost everywhere, though in states which provided political mechanisms for discovering what their citizens thought, and ways for them to express political preferences from time to time, this was unlikely to produce revolution or complete loss of contact. Demonstrations of almost unanimous non-confidence were most likely to occur in regimes which had either lost or (like Israel in the occupied territories) never had legitimacy, especially when they concealed this from themselves.* Still, massive demonstrations of rejection for existing political or party systems became common enough even in established and stable parliamentary-democratic systems, as witness the Italian political crisis of 1992–93, and the rise of new and large electoral forces in several countries, whose common denominator was simply that they were *not* identified with any of the old parties.

However, there is another reason for the revival of the masses: the urbanization of the globe, and especially the Third World. In the classic era of revolution, from 1789 to 1917, old regimes were overthrown in the great cities, but new ones were made permanent by the inarticulate plebiscites of the countryside. The novelty of the post-1930s phase of revolutions was that they were made in the countryside and, once victorious, imported into the cities. In the late twentieth century, a few retrograde regions apart, revolution once more came from the city, even in the Third World. It had to, both because a majority of the inhabitants

---

*Four months before the collapse of the German Democratic Republic local elections in that state had given the ruling party a vote of 98 85 per cent

of any large state now lived there, or seemed likely to, and because the big city, seat of power, could survive and defend itself against rural challenge, thanks not least to modern technology, so long as its authorities did not lose the loyalty of their populations. The war in Afghanistan (1979–88) demonstrated that a city-based regime could maintain itself in classic guerrilla country, bristling with rural insurrectionaries, supported, financed and equipped with modern high-technology weaponry, even after the withdrawal of the foreign army on which it had relied. The government of President Najibullah, to everyone's surprise, survived some years after the Soviet army left; and when it fell, it was not because Kabul could no longer resist the rural armies, but because a section of its own professional warriors decided to change sides. After the Gulf War of 1991, Saddam Hussein maintained himself in Iraq, against major insurrections in the north and south of his country, and in a state of military weakness, essentially because he did not lose Baghdad. Revolutions in the late twentieth century have to be urban if they are to win.

Will they continue to occur? Will the four great twentieth-century waves of 1917–20, 1944–62, 1974–78 and 1989– be followed by further bouts of breakdown and overthrow? No one who looks back on a century in which no more than a handful of states existing at present have come into being or survived without passing through revolution, armed counter-revolution, military coups or armed civil conflict* would bet much money on the universal triumph of peaceful and constitutional change, as predicted in 1989 by some euphoric believers in liberal democracy. The world which enters the third millennium is not a world of stable states or stable societies.

However, if it is virtually certain that the world, or at least a great part of it, will be full of violent changes, the nature of these changes is obscure. The world at the end of the Short Twentieth Century is in a state of social breakdown rather than revolutionary crisis, though it naturally contains countries in which like Iran in the 1970s, the conditions are present for the overthrow of hated regimes that have lost legitimacy, by popular upsurge under the leadership of forces capable of replacing them: for instance, at the time of writing, Algeria and, before the

---

*Omitting the mini-states of less than half-a-million inhabitants, the only consistently "constitutional" states are the U.S.A., Australia, Canada, New Zealand, Ireland, Sweden, Switzerland and Great Britain (excluding Northern Ireland). States occupied during and after the Second World War have not been classified as enjoying unbroken constitutionality, but, at a pinch, a few ex-colonies or backwaters which never knew military coups or domestic armed challenge could also be regarded as "non-revolutionary"—e.g. Guyana, Bhutan and the United Arab Emirates.

abdication of the apartheid regime, South Africa. (It does not follow that revolutionary conditions potential or actual, will produce successful revolutions.) Nevertheless, this sort of focused discontent with the status quo is today less common than an unfocused rejection of the present, an absence or distrust of political organization, or simply a process of disintegration to which the domestic and international politics of states adjust, as best they can.

It is also full of violence—more violence than in the past—and, what is perhaps equally relevant, full of arms. In the years before Hitler came to power in Germany and Austria, acute though racial tensions and hatreds were, it is difficult to imagine that they would have taken the form of neo-Nazi teenage skinheads burning down a house inhabited by immigrants, killing six members of a Turkish family. Yet in 1993 such an incident shocks but no longer surprises when it occurs in the heart of tranquil Germany, incidentally in a city (Solingen) with one of the oldest traditions of working-class socialism in the country.

Moreover, the accessibility of highly destructive weaponry and explosives today is such that the usual state monopoly of armaments in developed societies can no longer be taken for granted. In the anarchy of poverty and greed which replaced the former Soviet bloc, it was no longer even inconceivable that nuclear arms, or the means of making them, could get into the hands of bodies other than governments.

The world of the third millennium will therefore almost certainly continue to be one of violent politics and violent political changes. The only thing uncertain about them is where they will lead.

CHAPTER SIXTEEN

End of Socialism

[The] health [of revolutionary Russia], however, is subject to one indispensable condition: that never (as one day happened even to the Church) should a black market of power be opened. Should the European correlation of power and money penetrate Russian too, then perhaps not the country, perhaps not even the Party, but Communism in Russia would be lost.

—Walter Benjamin (1979, pp. 195–6)

It is not true any more that a single official creed is the only operative guide to action. More than one ideology, a mixture of modes of thinking and frames of references, coexist and not only in society at large but also inside the Party and inside the leadership . . . A rigid and codified "Marxism-Leninism" could not, except in official rhetoric, respond to the regime's real needs.

—M. Lewin in Kerblay (1983, p. xxvi)

The key to achieving modernization is the development of science and technology . . . Empty talk will get our modernization programme nowhere; we must have knowledge and trained personnel . . . Now it appears that China is fully twenty years behind the developed countries in science, technology and education . . . As early as the Meiji restoration the Japanese began to expend a great deal of effort on science, technology and education. The Meiji Restoration was a kind of modernization drive undertaken by the emerging Japanese bourgeoisie. As proletarians we should, and can, do better.

—Deng Xiaoping, "Respect Knowledge, Respect Trained Personnel," 1977

I

One socialist country in the 1970s was particularly worried by its relative economic backwardness, if only because its neighbour, Japan, was the most spectacularly successful of the capitalist states. Chinese communism cannot be regarded simply as a subvariety of Soviet communism, still less as part of the Soviet satellite system. For one thing, it triumphed in a country with a far larger population than the U.S.S.R., or for that matter any other state. Even allowing for the uncertainties of Chinese demography, something like one out of every five human beings was a Chinese living on mainland China. (There was also a substantial Chinese diaspora in East and South-east Asia.) Moreover, China was not only nationally far more homogeneous than most other countries—about 94 per cent of its population were Han Chinese—but had formed a single, though intermittently disrupted, political unit probably for a minimum of two thousand years. Even more to the point, for most of these two millennia the Chinese Empire, and probably most of its inhabitants who had a view on these matters, had considered China to be the centre and model of world civilization. With minor exceptions *all* other countries in which communist regimes triumphed, from the U.S.S.R. on, were and saw themselves as culturally backward and marginal, relative to some more advanced and paradigmatic centre of civilization. The very stridency with which the U.S.S.R. insisted, in the Stalin years, on its lack of intellectual and technological dependence on the West, and on the indigenous source of all the leading inventions from telephones to aircraft, was a telling symptom of this sense of inferiority.*

Not so China, which, quite correctly, saw its classical civilization, art, script and social value-system as the acknowledged inspiration and model for others—not least for Japan itself. It certainly had no sense whatever of any intellectual and cultural inferiority, either collectively or of individual Chinese compared to any other people. The very fact that China had no neighbouring states which could even faintly threaten her, and, thanks to adopting fire-arms, no longer had any difficulty in fending off the barbarians on its frontier, confirmed the sense

---

*The intellectual and scientific achievements of Russia between *c.* 1830 and 1930 were indeed extraordinary, and included some striking technological innovations, which backwardness rarely allowed to be economically developed. Yet the brilliance and world significance of a few Russians only makes the broad inferiority of Russia to the West more obvious.

of superiority, even as it made the empire unprepared for Western imperial expansion. The technological inferiority of China which became only too evident in the nineteenth century, because it was translated into military inferiority, was not due to technical or educational incapacity, but to the very sense of self-sufficiency and self-confidence of traditional Chinese civilization. This made it reluctant to do what the Japanese did after the Meiji Restoration of 1868: plunge into "modernization" by adopting European models wholesale. This could and would be done only on the ruins of the ancient Chinese Empire, guardian of the old civilization, and through social revolution, which was at the same time a cultural revolution against the Confucian system.

Chinese communism, therefore, was both social and, if the word does not beg questions, national. The social explosive which fuelled communist revolution was the extraordinary poverty and oppression of the Chinese people, initially of the labouring masses in the great coastal cities of central and South China which formed enclaves of foreign imperialist control and sometimes modern industry—Shanghai, Canton, Hong Kong—later of the peasantry which formed 90 per cent of the country's vast population. Its condition was far worse than even the Chinese urban population, whose consumption, per capita, was something like two-and-a-half times higher. The sheer poverty of China is hard for Western readers to imagine. Thus at the time of the communist take-over (1952 data) the average Chinese lived essentially on half a kilogram of rice or grains a day, and consumed rather less than 0.08 kilos of tea *a year*. He or she acquired a new pair of footwear once every five years or so (China Statistics, 1989, Tables 3.1, 15.2, 15.5).

The national element in Chinese communism operated both through the intellectuals of upper- and middle-class origin who provided most of the leadership of all twentieth-century Chinese political movements, and through the feeling, undoubtedly widespread among the Chinese masses, that the barbarian foreigners meant no good to such Chinese individuals as they had dealings with, and to China as a whole. Since China had been attacked, defeated, partitioned and exploited by every foreign state within reach since the middle of the nineteenth century, this assumption was not implausible. Mass anti-imperialist movements with a traditional ideology were already familiar before the end of the Chinese Empire, for instance the so-called Boxer Rising of 1900. There is little doubt that resistance to the Japanese conquest of China is what turned the Chinese communists from a defeated force of social agitators, which they were in the middle 1930s, into the leaders and representatives of the entire Chinese people. That they also called for the social liberation of the Chinese poor made their appeal for national liberation and regeneration sound more convincing to the (mainly rural) masses.

In this they had the advantage over their rivals, the (older) Kuomintang Party, which had attempted to rebuild a single, powerful, Chinese republic out of the scattered warlord-led fragments of the Chinese Empire after its fall in 1911. The short-term objectives of the two parties did not seem incompatible, the political base of both was in the more advanced cities of South China (where the Republic established its capital) and their leadership consisted of very much the same sort of educated elite, allowing for a certain bias towards businessmen in one, peasants and workers in the other. Both, for instance, contained virtually the same percentage of men drawn from the traditional landlords and scholar-gentry, the elites of imperial China, although the communists tended to have more leaders with a higher education of the Western type (North/Pool, 1966, pp. 378–82). Both movements came out of the anti-imperial movement of the 1900s, reinforced by the "May movement," the national upsurge among students and teachers in Peking after 1919. Sun Yat-sen, the Kuomintang leader, was a patriot, democrat and socialist, who relied for advice and support on Soviet Russia—the only revolutionary and anti-imperialist power—and found the Bolshevik model of the single state-party more suited than Western models for his task. In fact, the communists became a major force largely through this Soviet tie-up, which allowed them to be integrated into the official national movement, and, after Sun's death in 1925, to share in the great northern advance by which the Republic extended its influence into the half of China it did not control. Sun's successor, Chiang Kai-shek (1887–1975), never managed to establish complete control over the country, even though in 1927 he broke with the Russians and suppressed the communists, whose main body of mass support at that time was among the small urban working class.

The communists, forced to turn their main attention to the countryside, now waged a peasant-based guerrilla war against the Kuomintang, on the whole—thanks, not least, to their own divisions and confusions and the remoteness of Moscow from Chinese realities—with little success. In 1934 their armies were forced to retreat to a remote corner of the far north-west in the heroic "Long March." These developments made Mao Tse-tung, who had long favoured the rural strategy, into the undisputed leader of the Communist Party in its exile in Yenan, but did not offer any immediate prospects of communist advance. On the contrary, the Kuomintang steadily extended their control over most of the country until the Japanese invasion of 1937.

Yet the Kuomintang's lack of a genuine mass appeal to the Chinese, as well as its abandonment of the revolutionary project, which was at the same time a project of modernization and regeneration, made them no match for their communist rivals. Chiang Kai-shek never became an Ataturk—another head of a modernizing, anti-imperialist, national revolution who found himself making friends with the young Soviet Republic, using the local communists for his own purposes and turning away from them, though less stridently than Chiang. Like Ataturk, he had an army: but it was not an army with national loyalty, let alone the revolutionary morale of the communist armies, but a force recruited from among men for whom, in times of trouble and social collapse, a uniform and a gun are the best way to get by, and officered by men who knew—as did Mao Tse-tung himself—that at such times "power grew from the barrel of a gun," and so did profit and wealth. He had a good deal of urban middle-class support, and perhaps even more support from the wealthy overseas Chinese: but 90 per cent of Chinese, and almost all the country's territory, were outside the cities. They were controlled, if at all, by local notables and men of power, from warlords with their armed men to gentry families and relics of the imperial power-structure, with whom the Kuomintang came to terms. When the Japanese set out to conquer China seriously, the Kuomintang armies could not prevent them from almost immediately overrunning the coastal cities, where its genuine strength lay. In the rest of China, they became what they had always potentially been, another corrupt landlord-warlord regime, resisting the Japanese ineffectively, if at all. Meanwhile the communists effectively mobilized mass resistance to the Japanese in the occupied areas. When they took over China in 1949, having almost contemptuously swept aside the Kuomintang forces in a brief civil war, they were, for all except the fleeing remnants of the Kuomintang power, the legitimate government of China, true successors to the imperial dynasties after a forty-years interregnum. And they were all the more readily accepted as such because, from their experience as a Marxist–Leninist party, they were able to forge a nation-wide disciplined organization capable of bringing government policy from the centre to the remotest villages of the giant country—as, in the mind of most Chinese, a proper empire should do. *Organization*, rather than doctrine, was the chief contribution of Lenin's Bolshevism to changing the world.

Yet, of course, they were more than the empire revived, even though they undoubtedly benefited from the enormous continuities of Chinese history, which established both how ordinary Chinese expected to relate to any government enjoying the "mandate of heaven," and how those who administered China expected to think about their tasks. There is no other country in which political debates within a communist system would have been conducted by reference to what a loyal mandarin said to the Ming Emperor Chia-ching in the sixteenth century.* That is what a hard-nosed old China-watcher—the London *Times* correspondent—meant in the 1950s by the claim, shocking to those who heard it at the time, like the present writer, that there would be no communism left in the twenty-first century, except in China, where it would survive as the national ideology. For most Chinese this was a revolution which was primarily a restoration: of order and peace; of welfare; of a system of government whose civil servants found themselves appealing to precedents from the T'ang dynasty; of the greatness of a great empire and civilization.

And, for the first few years, that is what most Chinese seemed to be getting. Peasants raised their output of food-grains by more than 70 per cent between 1949 and 1956 (China Statistics, 1989, p. 165), presumably because they were not yet interfered with too much, and while China's intervention in the Korean War of 1950–52 created a serious panic, the ability of the Chinese communist army first to defeat, then to hold at bay the mighty U.S.A. could hardly fail to impress. Planning for industrial and educational development began in the early 1950s. Yet very soon the new People's Republic, under the now unchallenged and unchallengeable Mao, began to enter two decades of largely arbitrary catastrophes provoked by the great helmsman. From 1956 the rapidly deteriorating relations with the U.S.S.R., which ended in the clamorous breach between the two communist powers in 1960, led to the withdrawal of the important technical and other material aid from Moscow. However, this complicated rather than caused the calvary of the Chinese people, which was marked by three main stations of the cross: the ultra-rapid collectivization of peasant farming in 1955–57; the "Great Leap Forward" of industry in 1958, followed by the great famine of 1959–61, probably the greatest famine of the twentieth century,† and the ten years of "Cultural Revolution" which ended with Mao's death in 1976.

*Cf. the article "Hai Tui reprimands the Emperor" in the *People's Daily* in 1959. The same author (Wu Han) composed a libretto for a classical Peking opera, *The Dismissal of Hai Tui*, in 1960, which, some years later, provided the occasion that sparked off the "Cultural Revolution" (Leys, 1977, pp. 30, 34).

†According to official Chinese statistics, the country's population in 1959 was 672.07 millions. At the natural growth rate of the preceding seven years, which was

These cataclysmic plunges were, it is generally agreed, due largely to Mao himself, whose policies were often received with reluctance in the party leadership, and sometimes—most notably in the case of the "Great Leap Forward"—with frank opposition, which he overcame only by launching the "Cultural Revolution." Yet they cannot be understood without a sense of the peculiarities of Chinese communism, of which Mao made himself the spokesman. Unlike Russian communism, Chinese communism had virtually no direct relations with Marx and Marxism. It was a post-October movement which came to Marx *via* Lenin, or more precisely Stalin's "Marxism–Leninism." Mao's own knowledge of Marxist theory seems to have been almost entirely derived from the Stalinist *History of the CPSU* [*b*]: *Short Course* of 1939. And yet below the Marxist-Leninist top-dressing, there was—and this is very evident in the case of Mao, who never travelled outside China until he became head of state, and whose intellectual formation was entirely home-grown—a very Chinese utopianism. This naturally had points of contact with Marxism: all social-revolutionary utopias have something in common, and Mao, no doubt in complete sincerity, seized on those aspects of Marx and Lenin which fitted into his vision and used them to justify it. Yet his view of an ideal society united by a total consensus, and in which, it has been said, "the individual's total self-abnegation and total immersion in the collectivity (are) ultimate goods . . . a kind of collectivist mysticism," is the opposite of classical Marxism which, at least in theory and as the ultimate object, envisaged the complete liberation and self-fulfilment of the individual (Schwartz, 1966). The characteristic emphasis on the power of spiritual transformation to bring this about by remoulding man, though it seizes on Lenin's, and later Stalin's belief in consciousness and voluntarism, went far beyond it. With all his belief in the role of political action and decision, Lenin never lost sight of the fact—how could he have done?—that practical circumstances imposed severe constraints on the effectiveness of action, and even Stalin recognized that his power had limits. Yet without the belief that "subjective forces" were all-powerful, that men *could* move mountains and storm heaven if they wanted to, the lunacies of the Great Leap Forward are inconceivable. Experts told you what could and could not be done, but revolutionary fervour alone could

---

at least 20 per thousand per year (actually a mean of 21.7 per 1000), one would have expected the Chinese population in 1961 to have been 699 millions. In fact, it was 658.59 millions or *forty millions* less than might have been expected (China Statistics, 1989, Tables T 3.1 and T 3.2).

overcome all material obstacles, and mind transform matter. Hence to be "Red" was not so much more important than to be expert, but its alternative. A unanimous surge of enthusiasm in 1958 would industrialize China *immediately*, leaping across the ages into the future when communism would *immediately* come into full operation. The countless little low-quality backyard furnaces by which China was to double its steel output within one year—and did actually more than treble it by 1960, before it fell back by 1962 to less than it had been before the Great Leap—represented one side of the transformation. The 24,000 "peoples communes" of farmers, set up in a mere two months of 1958, represented the other side. They were completely communist, not only in that all aspects of peasant life were collectivized, including family life—communal nurseries and mess-halls freeing women from household and child care, and sending them, regimented, into the fields—but the free supply of six basic services were to replace wages and money income. These six services were food, medical care, education, funerals, haircuts and movies. Patently, this did not work. Within months, faced with passive resistance, the extremer aspects of the system were abandoned, though not before it had (like Stalin's collectivization) combined with nature to produce the famine of 1960–61.

In one way this belief in the capacity of willed transformation rested on a more specific Maoist belief in "the people," ready to be transformed and hence to take part, creatively and with all the traditional Chinese intelligence and ingenuity, in the great march forward. It was the essentially romantic view of an artist, though, one gathers from those who can judge the poetry and calligraphy he liked to practice, not a very good one. ("Not as bad as Hitler's painting, but not as good as Churchill's," in the view of the British orientalist Arthur Waley, using painting as an analogy for poetry.) It led him, against the sceptical, and realistic advice of other communist leaders, to call on the intellectuals of the old elite to contribute their gifts freely in the "Hundred Flowers" campaign of 1956–57, on the assumption that the revolution, and perhaps he himself, had already transformed them. ("Let a hundred flowers bloom, let a hundred schools of thought contend.") When, as less inspirational comrades had foreseen, this outburst of free thought proved lacking in unanimous enthusiasm for the new order, Mao's native distrust of intellectuals as such was confirmed. It was to find spectacular expression in the ten years of the Great Cultural Revolution, when higher education virtually came to a complete stop, and such intellectuals as already existed were massively re-generated by compulsory physical labour in the countryside.* Neverthe-

*In 1970 the total number of students in all China's "Institutions of Higher

less, Mao's belief in the peasants, who were urged to solve all the problems of production during the Great Leap on the principle of "letting all schools [i.e. of local experience] contend" remained unaffected. For—and this was yet another aspect of Mao's thought which found support in what he read into the Marxist dialectic—Mao was fundamentally convinced of the importance of struggle, conflict and high tension as something that was not only essential to life but prevented the relapse into the weaknesses of the old Chinese society, whose very insistence on unchanging permanence and harmony had been its weakness. The revolution, communism itself, could only be saved from degeneration into stasis by a constantly renewed struggle. Revolution could never end.

The peculiarity of the Maoist policy was that it was "at once an extreme form of Westernization and a partial reversion to traditional patterns," on which, indeed, it largely relied, for the old Chinese Empire was characterized, at least in the periods when the emperor's power was strong and secure, and therefore legitimate, by the autocracy of the ruler and the acquiescence and obedience of the subjects (Hu, 1966, p. 241). The mere fact that 84 per cent of Chinese peasant households had allowed themselves to be quietly collectivized within a single year (1956), apparently without any of the consequences of Soviet collectivization, speaks for itself. Industrialization, on the heavy-industry-inflected Soviet model, was the unconditional priority. The murderous absurdities of the Great Leap were due primarily to the conviction, which the Chinese regime shared with the Soviet, that agriculture must both supply industrialization and maintain itself without the diversion of resources from industrial to farming investment. Essentially this meant substituting "moral" for "material" incentives, which meant, in practice, the almost unlimited amount of human muscle-power available in China for the technology that was not available. At the same time the countryside remained the foundation of Mao's system, as it had ever since the guerrilla epoch, and, unlike the U.S.S.R., the Great Leap model made it the preferred locus of industrialization also. Unlike the U.S.S.R., China experienced no mass urbanization under Mao. Not until the 1980s did the rural population fall below 80 per cent.

Learning" was 48,000; in the country's technical schools (1969) 23,000; and in its Teachers' Training Colleges (1969) 15,000. The absence of any data about postgraduates suggests that there was no provision for them at all. In 1970 a grand total of 4,260 young persons began to study the natural sciences at Institutions of Higher Learning, and a grand total of ninety began to study the social sciences. This in a country of, at the time, 830 million people (China Statistics, Tables T 17.4, T 17.8, T 17.10).

However much we may be shocked by the record of the twenty Maoist years, a record combining mass inhumanity and obscurantism with the surrealist absurdities of the claims made on behalf of the divine leader's thoughts, we should not allow ourselves to forget that, by the standards of the poverty-stricken Third World, the Chinese people were doing well. At the end of the Mao period the average Chinese food consumption (in calories) ranked just above the median of all countries, above fourteen countries in the Americas, thirty-eight in Africa, and just about in the middle of the Asian ones—well above all South and South-east Asia, except Malaysia and Singapore (Taylor/Jodice, 1983, Table 4.4). The average expectation of life at birth rose from thirty-five years in 1949 to sixty-eight in 1982, mainly owing to a dramatic and—except for the famine years—continuous fall in the mortality rate (Liu, 1986, p. 323–24). Since the Chinese population, even allowing for the great famine, grew from *c*. 540 to *c*. 950 millions between 1949 and Mao's death, it is evident that the economy managed to feed them—a little above the level of the early 1950s—and it slightly improved their supply of clothing (China Statistics, Table T 15.1). Education, even at the elementary level, suffered both from the famine, which cut attendance down by twenty-five millions and from the Cultural Revolution, which reduced it by fifteen millions. Nevertheless, there is no denying that in the year of Mao's death six times as many children went to primary school as when he came to power—i.e. a 96 per cent enrolment rate, compared to less than 50 per cent even in 1952. Admittedly, even in 1987 more than a quarter of the population over the age of twelve remained illiterate and "semi-illiterate"—among women this figure was as high as 38 per cent— but we should not forget that literacy in Chinese is unusually difficult, and only a fairly small proportion of the 34 per cent born before 1949 could have been expected to have acquired it fully (China Statistics, pp. 69, 70–72, 695). In short, while the achievement of the Maoist period might not impress sceptical Western observers—there were many who lacked scepticism—it would certainly have appeared impressive to say, Indian or Indonesian ones, and it might not have looked particularly disappointing to the 80 per cent of rual Chinese, isolated from the world, whose expectations were those of their fathers.

Nevertheless, it was undeniable that internationally China had lost ground since the revolution, and notably in relation to its non-communist neighbours. Its rate of economic growth per capita, though impressive in the Mao years (1960–75), was less than that of Japan, Hong Kong, Singapore, South Korea and Taiwan—to name the East Asian countries which Chinese observers would certainly keep an eye on. Vast though it was, its total GNP was just about the same size as Canada's, less than Italy's, and a mere quarter of Japan's (Taylor/Jordice, Tables 3.5, 3.6). The disastrous zigzag course steered by the Great Helmsman since the middle 1950s had continued only because Mao, in 1965, with military backing, launched an anarchic, initially student, movement of young "Red Guards" against the party leadership which had quietly sidelined him, and intellectuals of any kind. This was the Great Cultural Revolution which devastated China for some time, until Mao called in the army to restore order, and in any case found himself obliged to restore some kind of party control. Since he was plainly on his last legs, and Maoism without him had very little real support, it did not survive his death in 1976, and the almost immediate arrest of the "Gang of Four" ultra-Maoists, headed by the leader's widow, Jiang Quing. The new course, under the pragmatical Deng Xiaoping, began immediately.

II

Deng's new course in China was the frankest public recognition that dramatic changes in the structure of "really existing socialism" were needed, but as the 1970s turned into the 1980s it was increasingly evident that something was seriously wrong with all socialist systems that claimed to have come into being. The slowing-down of the Soviet economy was palpable: the rate of growth of almost everything that counted, and could be counted in it, fell steadily from one five-year period to the next after 1970: gross domestic product, industrial output, farming output, capital investment, productivity of labour, real income per head. If not actually regressing, the economy was advancing at the pace of an increasingly tired ox. Moreover, so far from becoming one of the industrial giants of world trade, the U.S.S.R. appeared to be internationally regressing. In 1960 its major exports had been machinery, equipment, means of transport, and metals or metal articles, but in 1985 it relied for its exports primarily (53 per cent) on energy (i.e. oil and gas). Conversely, almost 60 per cent of its imports consisted of machinery, metals, etc. and industrial consumer articles (SSSR, 1987, pp. 15–17, 32–33). It had become something like an energy-producing colony of more advanced industrial economies—i.e. in practice largely its own Western satellites, notably Czechoslovakia and the German Democratic Republic, whose industries could rely on the unlimited and undemanding market of the U.S.S.R. without doing much to improve their own deficiencies.*

*"It seemed to the economic policy-makers at that time that the Soviet market was

In fact, by the 1970s it was clear that not only economic growth was lagging, but even the basic social indicators such as mortality were ceasing to improve. This undermined confidence in socialism perhaps more than anything else, since its ability to improve the lives of ordinary people through greater social justice did not depend primarily on its ability to generate greater wealth. That the average expectation of life at birth in the U.S.S.R., Poland and Hungary remained virtually unchanged during the last twenty years before the collapse of communism—indeed from time to time it actually dipped—was cause for serious worry, for in most other countries it continued to rise (including, it ought to be said, in Cuba and the Asian communist countries about which we have data). In 1969 Austrians, Finns and Poles could expect to die at the same average age (70.1 years), but in 1989 Poles had a life expectancy about four years shorter than Austrians and Finns. This may have made people healthier, as demographers suggested, but only because in socialist countries people died who might have been kept alive in capitalist ones (Riley, 1991). Reformers in the U.S.S.R. and elsewhere did not fail to observe these trends with growing anxiety (World Bank Atlas, 1990, pp. 6–9 and World Tables, 1991, passim).

About this time another symptom of recognized decline in the U.S.S.R. is reflected in the rise of the term *nomenklatura* (it appears to have reached the West via dissident writings). Until then the officer-corps of party *cadres*, which constituted the command system of the Leninist states, had been regarded abroad with respect and a reluctant admiration, although defeated oppositionists at home, like the Trotskyites and—in Yugoslavia—Milovan Djilas (Djilas, 1957), had pointed out its potential for bureaucratic degeneration and personal corruption. Indeed, in the 1950s, even into the 1960s, the general tone of Western, and especially U.S. comment had been that here—in the organizational system of the communist parties and its body of monolithic, selfless cadres, loyally (if brutally) carrying out "the line"—was the secret of communism's global advance (Fainsod, 1956; Brzezinski, 1962; Duverger, 1972).

On the other hand, the term *nomenklatura*, practically unknown before 1980, except as part of CPSU administrative jargon, came to suggest precisely the weaknesses of the self-serving party bureaucracy of the Brezhnev era: a combination of incompetence and corruption. And,

---

inexhaustible and that the Soviet Union could secure the necessary quantity of energy and raw materials for a continuous extensive economic growth" (D. Rosati and K. Mizsei, 1989, p. 10).

indeed, it became increasingly evident that the U.S.S.R. itself operated primarily through a system of patronage, nepotism and payment.

With the exception of Hungary, serious attempts to reform the socialist economies in Europe had been, in effect, abandoned in despair after the Prague Spring. As for the occasional attempts to revert to the old command economies, in a Stalinist form (as in Ceauşescu's Romania), or in the Maoist form which substituted voluntarism and putative moral zeal for economics (as with Fidel Castro), the less said about them the better. The Brezhnev years were to be called the "era of stagnation" by the reformers, essentially because the regime had stopped trying to do anything serious about a visibly declining economy. Buying wheat on the world market was easier than trying to cure the apparently growing inability of Soviet agriculture to feed the people of the U.S.S.R. Lubricating the rusty engine of the economy by means of a universal and omnipresent system of bribery and corruption was easier than to clean and re-tune, let alone to replace it. Who knew what would happen in the long run? In the short run it seemed more important to keep the consumers happy, or, at any rate to keep their discontent within limits. Hence probably in the first half of the 1970s most inhabitants of the U.S.S.R. were and felt better off than at any other time within living memory.

The trouble for "really existing socialism" in Europe was that, unlike the inter-war U.S.S.R., which was virtually outside the world economy and therefore immune to the Great Slump, now socialism was increasingly involved in it, and therefore not immune to the shocks of the 1970s. It is an irony of history that the "real socialist" economies of Europe and the U.S.S.R., as well as parts of the Third World, became the real victims of the post-Golden Age crisis of the global capitalist economy, whereas the "developed market economies," though shaken, made their way through the difficult years without major trouble, at least until the early 1990s. Until then some, indeed, like Germany and Japan, barely faltered in their forward march. "Real socialism," however, now confronted not only its own increasingly insoluble systemic problems, but also those of a changing and problematic world economy into which it was increasingly integrated. This may be illustrated by the ambiguous example of the international oil crisis which transformed the world energy market after 1973: ambiguous because its effects were potentially both negative and positive. Under pressure from the global oil-producers' cartel, OPEC (the Organization of Petrol-Exporting Countries), the oil price, low and, in real terms actually falling since the war, more or less quadrupled in 1973 and more or less trebled again at the end of the 1970s, in the aftermath of the Iranian Revolution. Indeed, the actual range of fluctuations was even more dramatic: in 1970 oil was selling at an average price of $2.53 a barrel, but in late 1980 a barrel was worth about $41.

The oil crisis had two apparently fortunate consequences. For oil producers, of whom the U.S.S.R. happened to be one of the most important, it turned black liquid into gold. It was like a guaranteed weekly winning ticket to the lottery. The millions simply rolled in without effort, postponing the need for economic reform and, incidentally, enabling the U.S.S.R. to pay for its rapidly growing imports from the capitalist West with exported energy. Between 1970 and 1980 Soviet exports to the "developed market economies" rose from just under 19 per cent of total exports to 32 per cent (SSSR, 1987, p. 32). It has been suggested that it was this enormous and unforeseen bonanza that tempted Brezhnev's regime into a more active international policy of competing with the U.S.A. in the middle 1970s, as revolutionary unrest once again swept the Third World (see chapter 15), and into the suicidal course of trying to match American arms superiority (Maksimenko, 1991).

The other apparently fortunate consequence of the oil crises was the flood of dollars which now spurted from multi-billionaire OPEC states, often with tiny populations, and which was distributed by the international banking system in the form of loans to anyone who wanted to borrow. Few developing countries resisted the temptation to take the millions thus shovelled into their pockets, and which were to provoke the world debt crisis of the early 1980s. For the socialist countries which succumbed to it—notably Poland and Hungary—loans seemed a providential way of simultaneously paying for investment in accelerating growth and raising their people's standard of living.

This only made the crisis of the 1980s more acute, for the socialist economies—and notably the free-spending Polish one—were too inflexible to utilize the influx of resources productively. The mere fact that oil consumption in Western Europe (1973–85) fell by 40 per cent in response to the rise in prices, but in the U.S.S.R. and Eastern Europe by only little more than 20 per cent in the same period, speaks for itself (Kollo, 1990, p. 39). That Soviet production costs increased sharply, while the Romanian oil fields dried up, makes the failure to economize energy even more striking. By the early 1980s Eastern Europe was in an acute energy crisis. This in turn produced shortages of food and manufactured goods (except where, as in Hungary, the country plunged even more heavily into debt, accelerating inflation and lowering real wages). This was the situation in which "really existing socialism" in Europe entered what proved to be its final decade. The only immediate effective way of dealing with such a crisis was the traditional Stalinist recourse to strict central orders and restrictions, at least where central planning was still operational (as it no longer quite was in Hungary and Poland). It worked, between 1981 and 1984. Debt fell by 35–70 per cent (except in these two countries). This even encouraged illusory hopes of a return to dynamic economic growth without basic reforms, which "brought about a Great Leap Back to the debt crisis and further deterioration of economic perspectives" (Köllö, p. 41). This was the moment when Mikhail Sergeyevitch Gorbachev became the leader of the U.S.S.R.

III

At this point we must revert from the economics to the politics of "really existing socialism," since politics, both high and low, were to bring about the Euro–Soviet collapse of 1989–1991.

Politically, Eastern Europe was the Achilles heel of the Soviet system, and Poland (plus, to a lesser extent, Hungary) its most vulnerable spot. After the Prague Spring it was clear, as we have seen, that the satellite communist regimes had lost all legitimacy as such in most of the region.* They were maintained in being by state coercion, backed by the threat of Soviet intervention, or, at best—as in Hungary—by giving the citizenry material conditions and relative freedom far superior to the Eastern European average, but which the economic crisis made it impossible to maintain. However, with one exception, no serious form of organized political or other public opposition was possible. In Poland the conjunction of three factors produced this possibility. The country's public opinion was overwhelmingly united not only by a dislike of the regime but by an anti-Russian (and anti-Jewish) and consciously Roman Catholic, Polish nationalism; the Church retained independent nationwide organization; and its working class had demonstrated its political power by massive strikes at intervals since the middle 1950s. The regime had long resigned itself to tacit toleration or even retreat—as when the strikes of 1970 forced the abdication of the then communist leader—so long as opposition was unorganized, though its room for manoeuvre shrank dangerously. But from the middle of the 1970s it had to face both a politically organized labour movement backed by a brains trust of politically sophisticated

*The less developed parts of the Balkan peninsula—Albania, southern Yugoslavia, Bulgaria—may be an exception, since communists still won the first multi-party elections after 1989. However, even here the weakness of the system soon became patent.

dissident intellectuals, mainly ex-Marxists, and also by an increasingly aggressive Church, encouraged in 1978 by the election of the first Polish pope in history, Karol Wojtyla (John Paul II).

In 1980 the triumph of the trade union movement Solidarity as, in effect, a national public opposition movement armed with the weapon of the mass strike, demonstrated two things: that the Communist Party regime in Poland was at the end of its tether; but also that it could not be overthrown by mass agitation. In 1981 Church and State quietly agreed to pre-empt the danger of armed Soviet intervention (which was seriously considered), by a few years of martial law under the commander of the armed forces, which could plausibly claim both communist and national legitimacy. Order was re-established with little trouble by the police rather than by the army, but in effect the government, as helpless as ever to cope with the economic problems, had nothing to set against an opposition which remained in being as the organized expression of the nation's public opinion. Either the Russians decided to intervene, or, sooner rather than later, the regime had to abandon the key position of communist regimes, the one-party system under the "leading role" of the state party, i.e. to abdicate. But, as the rest of the satellite governments nervously watched the unfolding of this scenario while mostly and vainly trying to stop their people from also doing so, it became increasingly evident that the Soviets were no longer prepared to intervene.

In 1985 a passionate reformer, Mikhail Gorbachev, came to power as General Secretary of the Soviet Communist Party. This was no accident. Indeed, but for the death of the desperately ill General Secretary and former chief of the Security apparatus, Yuri Andropov (1914–84) who had actually made the decisive break with the Brezhnev era in 1983, the era of change would have begun a year or two earlier. It was entirely evident to all other communist governments, in and out of the Soviet orbit, that major transformations were at hand, though quite unclear, even to the new General Secretary, what they would bring.

The "era of stagnation" (*zastoi*) which Gorbachev denounced had, in fact, been an era of acute political and cultural ferment among the Soviet elite. This included not only the relatively tiny group of self-co-opted Communist Party chieftains at the top of the Union hierarchy, the only place where real political decisions were, or could be, made, but the relatively vast group of educated and technically trained middle classes as well as the economic managers who actually kept the country going: academics, technical intelligentsia, experts and executives of various kinds. In some ways Gorbachev himself represented this new educated cadre generation—he studied law, whereas the classical way up for the old Stalinist cadre had been (and still surprisingly often remained) from the factory floor via an engineering or agronomical degree into the apparatus. The depth of this ferment is not to be measured by the size of the actual group of public dissidents which now appeared—a few hundreds at most. Banned or semi-legalized (through the influence of brave editors like that of the famous "thick journal" *Novy Mir*), criticism and self-criticism pervaded the cultural milieu of the metropolitan U.S.S.R. under Brezhnev, including important sectors of party and state, notably in the security and foreign services. The enormous and sudden response to Gorbachev's call for *glasnost* ("openness" or "transparency") can hardly be explained otherwise.

Yet the response of the political and intellectual strata must not be taken as the response of the mass of Soviet peoples. For these, unlike the peoples of most European communist states, the Soviet regime was legitimate and entirely accepted, if only because they knew no other and could have known no other (except under German occupation in 1941–44, which was hardly attractive). Every Hungarian over the age of sixty in 1990 had some adolescent or adult memory of the pre-communist era, but no inhabitant of the original U.S.S.R. under the age of eighty-eight could have had such first-hand experience. And if the government of the Soviet state had an unbroken continuity stretching back to the end of the Civil War, the country itself had an unbroken, or virtually unbroken, continuity stretching back even longer, except for the territories along the western border acquired or re-acquired in 1939–40. It was the old Tsarist Empire under new management. That, incidentally, is why before the late 1980s there was no sign of serious political separatism anywhere except in the Baltic countries (which had been independent states from 1918 to 1940), in the western Ukraine (which had been part of the Habsburg and not the Russian Empire before 1918), and perhaps in Bessarabia (Moldavia), which had been part of Romania from 1918 to 1940. Even in the Baltic States there was little more open dissidence than in Russia (Lieven, 1993).

Moreover, the Soviet regime was not merely home-grown and domestically rooted—as time went on even the party, originally much stronger among Great Russians than other nationalities, recruited much the same percentage of inhabitants in the European and Transcaucasian republics—but the people itself, in ways difficult to specify, fitted themselves into it, as the regime adjusted to them. As the dissident satirist Zinoviev pointed out, there really was a "new Soviet man," even if he corresponded to his (or, insofar as she was considered, which was hardly at all, her) official public image no more than anything else did in the U.S.S.R. He/she was at ease in the system (Zinoviev, 1979). It provided a guaranteed livelihood and comprehensive social security at a modest but real level, a socially and economically egalitarian society and at least one of the traditional aspirations of socialism, Paul Lafargue's "Right to Idleness" (Lafargue, 1883). Moreover, for most Soviet citizens the Brezhnev era spelled not "stagnation" but the best times they and their parents, or even grandparents, had ever known.

Small wonder that radical reformers found themselves up against Soviet humanity as well as Soviet bureaucracy. In the characteristic tone of irritated anti-plebeian elitism, one reformer wrote:

> Our system has generated a category of individuals supported by society, and more interested in taking than in giving. This is the consequence of a policy of so-called egalitarianism which has . . . totally invaded Soviet society . . . That society is divided into two parts, those who decide and distribute and those who are commanded and who receive, constitutes one of the major brakes on the development of our society. *Homo sovieticus* . . . is both ballast and brake. On the one hand, he is opposed to reform, on the other he constitutes the base of support for the existing system (Afanassiev, 1991, pp. 13–14).

Socially and politically, most of the U.S.S.R. was a stable society, no doubt partly by virtue of ignorance of other countries maintained by authority and censorship, but by no means only for this reason. Is it an accident that there had been no equivalent of the 1968 student rebellion in the U.S.S.R., unlike Poland, Czechoslovakia and Hungary? That even under Gorbachev the reform movement did not mobilize the young to any great extent (outside some Western nationalist regions)? That it was, as the saying went, "a rebellion of the thirty- and forty-year-olds," i.e. of the generation born after the end of the war but before the not uncomfortable torpor of the Brezhnev years? Wherever the pressure to change came from in the U.S.S.R., it was not from the grass-roots.

In fact it came, as it had to come, from the top. Precisely how an obviously passionate and sincere communist reformer came to be Stalin's successor at the head of the Soviet CP on 15 March 1985 still remains unclear, and will remain so until Soviet history in the last decades becomes a subject for history rather than accusation and self-exculpation. In any case, what matters are not the ins and outs of politics in the Kremlin, but the two conditions which allowed someone like Gorbachev to come to power. First, the growing, and increasingly unconcealed, corruption of the Communist Party leadership in the Brezhnev era could not but outrage that section of the party which still believed in its ideology, in however oblique a fashion. And a Communist Party, however degenerate, without some leaders who are socialists is no more likely than a Catholic Church without some bishops and cardinals who are Christians, both being based on genuine systems of belief. Second, the educated and technically competent strata which actually kept the Soviet economy running were keenly aware that without drastic, indeed fundamental change it would inevitably founder sooner or later, not only because of the built-in inefficiency and inflexibility of the system, but because its weaknesses were compounded by the demands of a status as a military superpower, which a declining economy simply could not support. The military strain on the economy had actually increased dangerously since 1980 when, for the first time in many years, the Soviet armed forces found themselves involved directly in a war. They sent a force into Afghanistan to establish some sort of stability in that country, which since 1978 had been governed by a local communist People's Democratic Party, split into conflicting factions, both of which antagonized local landlords, Muslim clergy and other believers in the status quo by such godless activities as land reform and rights for women. The country had been quietly in the Soviet sphere of influence since the early 1950s, without raising Western blood-pressure noticeably. However, the U.S.A. chose or purported to regard the Soviet move as a major military offensive directed against the "free world." It therefore (via Pakistan) poured money and advanced armaments without limits into the hands of fundamentalist Muslim mountain warriors. As was to be expected, the Afghan government with heavy Soviet support, had little trouble in holding the major cities of the country, but the cost to the U.S.S.R. was inordinately high. Afghanistan became—as some people in Washington undoubtedly intended it to be—the Soviet Union's Vietnam.

But what could the new Soviet leader do to change the situation in the U.S.S.R., other than to end, as soon as possible, the Second Cold War confrontation with the U.S.A. which was haemorrhaging the economy? This, of course, was Gorbachev's immediate objective, and his greatest success, for, within a surprisingly short period, he convinced even sceptical Western governments that this was indeed the Soviet intention. It won him a huge and lasting popularity in the West, which contrasted strikingly with the growing lack of enthusiasm for him in the U.S.S.R., to which he eventually fell victim in 1991. If any single man ended some forty years of global cold war it was he.

The aims of communist economic reformers since the 1950s had been to make the centrally planned command economies more rational and flexible by the introduction of market pricing and calculations of profit and loss in enterprises. The Hungarian reformers had gone some way in this direction, and, but for the Soviet occupation of 1968, the Czech reformers would have gone even further: both hoping that this would also make it easier to liberalize and democratize the political system. This was also Gorbachev's position* which he naturally saw as a way of restoring or establishing a better socialism than the "really existing" one. It is possible, but very unlikely that any influential reformer in the U.S.S.R. envisaged the abandonment of socialism, if only because this seemed quite impracticable politically, although elsewhere trained economists who had been associated with reform began to conclude that the system, whose defects were first systematically analysed in public from within in the 1980s, could not be reformed from within.†

IV

Gorbachev launched his campaign to transform Soviet socialism with the two slogans of *perestroika*, or restructuring (of both economy and political structure), and *glasnost*, or freedom of information.‡

There was what turned out to be an insoluble conflict between them. The only thing that made the Soviet system work, and could conceivably transform it, was the command structure of party/state inherited from the Stalinist days. This was a familiar situation in Russian history even in the days of the Tsars. Reform came from the top. But the party/state structure was at the same time the chief obstacle to transforming a system which it had created, to which it had adjusted, in which it had a large vested interest, and to which it found it hard to conceive an alternative.§

*He had publicly identified himself with the extremely "broad" and virtually social-democratic position of the Italian Communist Party even before his official election (Montagni, 1989, p. 85).

†The crucial texts here are by the Hungarian Janos Kornai, notably *The Economics of Shortage* (Amsterdam, 1980).

‡It is an interesting sign of the interpenetration of official reformers and dissident thinking in the Brezhnev years, that *glasnost* was what the writer Alexander Solzhenitsyn had called for in his open letter to the Congress of the Union of Soviet Writers in 1967, before his expulsion from the U.S.S.R.

§As a Chinese communist bureaucrat told the writer in 1984 in the midst of a similar "restructuring": "We are reintroducing elements of capitalism into our system, but how can we know what we are letting ourselves in for? Since 1949 nobody in China, except perhaps some old men in Shanghai, has had any experience of what capitalism is."

It was far from the only obstacle, and reformers, not only in Russia, have always been tempted to blame "the bureaucracy" for the failure of their country and people to respond to their initiatives, but it is undeniable that large parts of the party/state apparatus greeted any major reform with inertia concealing hostility. *Glasnost* was intended to mobilize support within and outside the apparatus against such resistance. But its logical consequence was to undermine the only force which could act. As has been suggested above, the structure of the Soviet system and its *modus operandi* were essentially military. Democratizing armies does not improve their efficiency. On the other hand, if a military system is not wanted, care must be taken that a civilian alternative is available before it is destroyed, otherwise reform produces not reconstruction but collapse. The U.S.S.R. under Gorbachev fell into this widening chasm between *glasnost* and *perestroika*.

What made the situation worse was that in the minds of the reformers, *glasnost* was a far more specific programme than *perestroika*. It meant the introduction, or re-introduction, of a constitutional and democratic state based on the rule of law and the enjoyment of civil liberties as commonly understood. This implied the separation of party and state, and (contrary to all development since the rise of Stalin) the shift of the locus of effective government from party to state. This in turn implied the end of the single-party system, and of the party's "leading role." It also, obviously, meant the revival of the Soviets at all levels, in the form of genuinely elected representative assemblies, culminating in a Supreme Soviet which would be a genuinely sovereign legislative assembly, granting power to, but capable of controlling a strong executive. That, at least, was the theory.

In fact, the new constitutional system was eventually installed. The new economic system of *perestroika* was barely sketched out in 1987–88 by the half-hearted legalization of petty private enterprise ("cooperatives")—i.e. of much of the "second economy"—and by the decision in principle to allow permanently loss-making state enterprises to go bankrupt. In fact, the gap between the rhetoric of economic reform and the reality of an economy visibly running down widened day by day.

This was desperately dangerous. For constitutional reform merely dismantled one set of political mechanisms and replaced it with another. It left open the question of what the new institutions would do, though the processes of decision would presumably be more cumbersome in a democracy than in a military command system. For most people the difference would merely be that, in one case, they had a genuine electoral choice every so often and had the choice in between of listening to opposition politicians criticizing the government. On the other hand, the criterion of *perestroika* was and had to be not how the economy was run in principle but how it performed every day, in ways that could easily be specified and measured. It could only be judged by results. For most Soviet citizens this meant by what happened to their real incomes, to the effort needed to earn them, to the quantity and range of the goods and services within their reach, and the ease with which they could acquire them. But while it was very clear what the economic reformers were against and wished to abolish, their positive alternative, a "socialist market economy" of autonomous and economically viable enterprises, public, private and cooperative, macro-economically steered by "the centre of economic decision-making," was little more than a phrase. It simply meant that the reformers wished to have the advantages of capitalism without losing those of socialism. Nobody had the slightest idea of how, in practice, the transition from a centralized state command economy to the new system was to be made and—equally to the point—how what would inevitably remain a dual state and non-state economy for the foreseeable future would actually work. The appeal of the ultra-radical Thatcherite or Reaganite free-market ideology to young intellectual reformers was that it promised to provide a drastic but also an *automatic* solution for these problems. (As might have been foreseen, it did not.)

Probably the nearest thing to a model of transition for the Gorbachev reformers was the vague historical memory of the New Economic Policy of 1921–28. This had, after all, "yielded spectacular results in revitalizing agriculture, trade, industry, finances, for several years after 1921" and had restored a collapsed economy to health because it "relied on market forces" (Vernikov, 1989, p. 13). Moreover, a very similar policy of market liberalization and decentralization had, since the end of Maoism, produced dramatic results in China, whose rate of GNP growth in the 1980s, surpassed only by South Korea, averaged almost 10 per cent per annum (World Bank Atlas, 1990). Yet there was no comparison between the desperately poor, technologically backward and overwhelmingly rural Russia of the 1920s and the highly urbanized and industrialized U.S.S.R. of the 1980s, whose most advanced industrial sector, the military-industrial-scientific complex (including the space programme), in any case depended on a market consisting of a single customer. It is safe to say that *perestroika* would have worked rather better if Russia in 1980 had still been (like China at that date) a country of 80 per cent villagers, whose idea of wealth beyond the dreams of avarice would be a television set. (Even in the early 1970s some 70 per cent of the Soviet population watched television for an average of one-and-a-half hours a day) (Kerblay, pp. 140–41).

Nevertheless, the contrast between Soviet and Chinese *perestroika* is not entirely explained by such time-lags, nor even by the obvious fact that the Chinese were careful to keep their central command system intact. How far they benefited from the cultural traditions of the Far East, which turned out to favour economic growth irrespective of social systems, must be left for twenty-first-century historians to investigate.

Did anyone in 1985 seriously suppose that, six years later, the U.S.S.R. and its Communist Party, would have ceased to exist, and indeed that all other communist regimes in Europe would have disappeared? To judge by the complete lack of preparation of Western governments for the sudden collapse of 1989–91, the predictions of the imminent demise of the West's ideological enemy were no more than the small change of public rhetoric. What drove the Soviet Union with accelerating speed towards the precipice, was the combination of *glasnost* that amounted to the disintegration of authority, with a *perestroika* that amounted to the destruction of the old mechanisms that made the economy work, without providing any alternative; and consequently the increasingly dramatic collapse of the citizens' standard of living. The country moved towards a pluralist electoral politics at the very moment that it subsided into economic anarchy: for the first time since the inception of planning, Russia in 1989 no longer had a Five-Year Plan (Di Leo, 1992, p. 100 n). It was an explosive combination, for it undermined the shallow foundations of the U.S.S.R.'s economic and political unity.

For the U.S.S.R. had increasingly evolved towards a structural decentralization, its elements held together primarily by the all-Union institutions of party, army, security forces and the central plan, and never more rapidly than in the long Brezhnev years. *De facto* much of the Soviet Union was a system of autonomous feudal lordships. Its local chieftains—the Party Secretaries of the Union republics with their subordinate territorial commanders, and the managers of the great and lesser production units, who kept the economy in operation—were united by little more than their dependency on the central party apparatus in Moscow, which nominated, transferred, deposed and coopted, and by the need to "fulfil the plan" elaborated in Moscow. Within these very broad limits the territorial chieftains had considerable independence. Indeed the economy would not have functioned at all but for the development, by those who actually had to run institutions with real functions, of a network of lateral relations independent of the centre. This system of deals, barter arrangements and exchanges of favours with other cadres in similar positions was another "second economy" within the nominally planned whole. One might add that, as the U.S.S.R. became a more complex industrial and urban society, the cadres in charge of the actual production, distribution, and general care of the citizenry had diminished sympathy for the ministries and the purely party figures who were their superiors, but whose concrete functions were no longer clear, apart from that of feathering their nests, as many of them did in the Brezhnev period, often in the most spectacular manner. Revulsion against the increasingly monumental and all-pervasive corruption of the *nomenklatura* was the initial fuel for the process of reform, and Gorbachev had fairly solid support for *perestroika* from the economic cadres, especially those from the military-industrial complex, who genuinely wanted to improve the management of a stagnant and, in scientific and technical terms, paralytic economy. No one knew better than they how bad things really had become. Moreover, they did not need the party to carry on their activities. If the party bureaucracy were to disappear, they would still be there. They were indispensable, it was not. Indeed, they *were* still there after the collapse of the U.S.S.R., now organized as a pressure group in the new (1990) "Industrial-Scientific Union" (NPS) and its successors, after the end of communism, as the (potentially) legal owners of the enterprises which they had commanded without legal property rights before.

Nevertheless, corrupt, inefficient and largely parasitic as the party command system had been, it remained essential in an economy based on command. The alternative to party authority was not the constitutional and democratic authority, but, in the short run, no authority. This is indeed what happened. Gorbachev, like his successor, Yeltsin, shifted his power-base from party to state, and, as constitutional president, legally accumulated powers to rule by decree, in some instances powers greater in theory than any earlier Soviet leader had formally enjoyed, even Stalin (Di Leo, 1992, p. 111). Nobody took any notice, outside the newly established democratic, or rather constitutional-public assemblies, the People's Congress and the Supreme Soviet (1989). Nobody governed or, rather, obeyed in the Soviet Union any more.

Like a crippled giant tanker moving towards the reefs, a rudderless Soviet Union therefore drifted towards disintegration. The lines along which it was to fracture were already drawn: on the one hand the system of territorial power-autonomy largely embodied in the state's federal structure, on the other the autonomous economic complexes. Since the official theory on which the Union had been constructed was one of territorial autonomy for national groups, both in the fifteen Union Republics and in the autonomous regions and areas within each,* national-

---

*In addition to the RSFSR (Russian Federation), by far the largest territorially

ist fracture was potentially built into the system, although, with the exception of the three small Baltic States, separatism was not even thought
of before 1988, when the first nationalist "fronts" or campaign organizations were founded in response to *glasnost* (in Estonia, Latvia, Lithuania
and Armenia). However, at this stage, even in the Baltic States, they were
directed not so much against the centre as against the insufficiently Gor-
bachevist local communist parties, or, as in Armenia, against neighbouring Azerbaijan. The object was not yet independence, although
nationalism was rapidly radicalized in 1989–90 under the impact of the
rush into electoral politics, and the struggle between radical reformers
and the organized resistance of the old party establishment in the new assemblies, as well as the frictions between Gorbachev and his resentful
victim, rival and eventual successor, Boris Yeltsin.

Essentially the radical reformers looked for support against the entrenched party hierarchies to the nationalists in the republics and, in
doing so, strengthened these. In Russia itself, the appeal to Russian interests against the peripheral republics, subsidized by Russia and increasingly felt to be better off than Russia, was a powerful weapon in the
radicals' struggle to eject the party bureaucracy, entrenched in the central
state apparatus. For Boris Yeltsin, an old party boss from the command
society, who combined the gifts of getting on in the old politics (toughness and cunning) with the gifts for getting on in the new (demagogy,
joviality and a sense of the media), the way to the top lay through the
capture of the Russian Federation, thus allowing him to by-pass the institutions of Gorbachev's Union. Hitherto, in effect, the Union and its
chief component, the RSFSR, had not been clearly distinct. In transforming Russia into a Republic like the others, Yeltsin *de facto* favoured
the disintegration of the Union, which a Russia under his control would
in effect supplant. This is, indeed, what happened in 1991.

Economic disintegration helped to advance political disintegration,
and was nourished by it. With the end of the Plan, and of party orders
from the centre, there was no effective *national* economy, but a rush, by
any community, territory, or other unit that could manage it, into self-
protection and self-sufficiency, or bilateral exchanges. The commanders
of the great provincial company towns, always used to such arrangements,
bartered industrial products for foodstuffs with the heads of the regional
collective farms, as—a dramatic example—the Leningrad Party chief,

---

and demographically, there were also Armenia, Azerbaijan, Byelorussia, Estonia,
Georgia, Kazakhstan, Kyrghyzstan, Latvia, Lithuania, Moldavia, Tadjikistan, Turk-
menistan, Ukraine and Uzbekistan.

Gidaspov, dealt with an acute grain shortage in his city by a phone-call to Nazarbayev, the Kazakhstan Party boss, who arranged a swap of cereals for footwear and steel (Yu Boldyrev, 1990). But even this kind of transaction between two of the top figures in the old party hierarchy in effect treated the national system of distribution as irrelevant. "Particularisms, autarchies, relapses into primitive practices seemed to be the real results of the laws which had liberalized local economic forces" (Di Leo, p. 101).

The point of no return was reached in the second half of 1989, bicentenary of the outbreak of the French Revolution, whose non-existence or irrelevance to twentieth-century politics French "revisionist" historians were busy trying to demonstrate at the time. The political breakdown followed (as in eighteenth century France) the calling of the new democratic, or largely democratic assemblies in the summer of that year. The economic breakdown became irreversible in the course of a few crucial months between October 1989 and May 1990. However, the eyes of the world at this time were fixed on a related, but secondary phenomenon: the sudden, and once again unpredicted, dissolution of the satellite communist regimes in Europe. Between August 1989 and the end of that year communist power abdicated or ceased to exist in Poland, Czechoslovakia, Hungary, Romania, Bulgaria and the German Democratic Republic— without so much as a shot being fired, except in Romania. Shortly thereafter the two Balkan states which were not Soviet satellites, Yugoslavia and Albania, also ceased to be communist regimes. The German Democratic Republic was soon to be annexed to West Germany, and Yugoslavia was soon to break up into civil war. The process was watched not only on the television screens of the Western world, but also, with great care, by the communist regimes in other continents. Though they ranged from the radically reformist (at least in economic matters), as in China, to the implacably old-style centralist, as in Cuba (chapter 15), all presumably had doubts about the Soviet plunge into unrestricted *glasnost*, and the weakening of authority. When the movement for liberalization and democracy spread from the U.S.S.R. to China, the Beijing government decided, in mid-1989, after some obvious hesitations and lacerating internal disagreements, to re-establish its authority in the most unambiguous manner, by what Napoleon, who also used the army to suppress public agitation during the French Revolution, had called "a whiff of grapeshot." The troops cleared a mass student demonstration from the capital's main square, at a heavy cost in lives, probably—though no reliable data were available at the time of writing—several hundreds. The massacre of Tiananmen Square horrified Western public opinion, and undoubtedly lost the Chinese Communist Party most of what little legitimacy it may still have had among the younger generations of Chinese intellectuals, including party members, but it left the Chinese regime free to continue the policy of successful economic liberalization without immediate political problems. The collapse of communism after 1989 was confined to the U.S.S.R. and the states in its orbit (including Outer Mongolia, which had chosen Soviet protection over Chinese domination between the world wars). The three surviving Asian communist regimes (China, North Korea and Vietnam) as well as remote and isolated Cuba, were not immediately affected.

V

It seemed natural, particularly in the bicentenary year of 1789, to describe the changes of 1989–90 as the Eastern European revolutions, and, insofar as events which lead to the complete overthrow of regimes are revolutionary, the word is apposite, but misleading. For none of the regimes in Eastern Europe were *over-thrown*. None, except Poland, contained any internal force, organized or not, which constituted a serious threat to them, and the fact that Poland contained a powerful political opposition actually guaranteed that the system there was not destroyed from one day to the next, but replaced by a negotiated process of compromise and reform, not unlike the way in which Spain made the transition to democracy after the death of General Franco in 1975. The most immediate threat to those in the Soviet orbit came from Moscow, which made it clear that it would no longer rescue them by military intervention, as in 1956 and 1968, if only because the end of the Cold War made them strategically less necessary to the U.S.S.R. If they wanted to survive, in Moscow's opinion, they would be well advised to follow the line of liberalization, reform and flexibility of the Polish and Hungarian communists, but, by the same token, Moscow would not compel the hardliners in Berlin and Prague. They were on their own.

The very withdrawal of the U.S.S.R. underlined their bankruptcy. They remained in power merely by virtue of the void they had created around them, which had left no alternative to the status quo except (where this was possible) emigration or (for a few) the formation of marginal dissident groups of intellectuals. The bulk of the citizens had accepted things as they were, because they had no alternative. People of energy, talent and ambition worked within the system, since any position requiring these things, and indeed any public expression of talent, was within the system or by its permission, even in entirely non-political fields like pole-vaulting and chess. This applied even to the licensed opposition, mainly in the arts, which was allowed to develop in the decline of the systems, as dissident writers who had chosen not to emigrate, discovered to their cost after the fall of communism, when they were treated as collaborators.* No wonder that most people opted for the quiet life, which included the formal gestures of support for a system nobody except primary school-children believed in, such as voting or demonstrating, even when the penalties for dissidence were no longer terrifying. One of the reasons why the old regime was denounced with such fury after its fall, especially in hardline countries like Czechoslovakia and the ex-GDR, was that

> the great majority voted in the sham elections to avoid unpleasant consequences, though not very serious ones; they took part in the obligatory marches ... The police informers were easily recruited, won over by miserable privileges, often agreeing to serve as the result of very mild pressure (Kolakowski, 1992, pp. 55–56).

Yet hardly anyone believed in the system or felt any loyalty to it, not even those who governed it. They were no doubt surprised when the masses finally abandoned their passivity and demonstrated their dissidence—the moment of amazement has been caught forever on the videotape of President Ceauşescu, in December 1989, confronting a crowd that booed instead of loyally applauding—but they were surprised, not by the dissidence, only by the action. At that moment of truth, no Eastern European government ordered its forces to fire. All abdicated quietly, except in Romania, and even there resistance was brief. Perhaps they could not have regained control, but nobody even tried. No groups of communist ultras anywhere prepared to die in the bunker for their faith, or even for the far-from-unimpressive record of forty years' communist rule in a number of these states. What should they have defended? Economic systems whose inferiority to their Western neighbours leaped to the eye, which were running down, and which had proved to be unreformable, even where serious and intelligent efforts at reform had been made? Systems which had plainly lost the justification that had sustained their communist cadres in the past, namely that socialism was superior to capitalism and destined to replace it? Who could any longer believe that, though it had not looked implausible in the 1940s or even

---

*Even so passionate an opponent of communism as the Russian writer Alexander Solzhenitsyn had his career as a writer established through the system, which permitted/encouraged the publication of his first novels for reformist purposes

1950s? Since communist states were no longer even united, and sometimes actually fought each other with arms (e.g. China and Vietnam in the early 1980s), one could no longer even speak of a single "socialist camp." All that remained of the old hopes was the fact that the U.S.S.R., the country of the October revolution, was one of the two global superpowers. Except perhaps for China, all communist governments, and a good many communist parties and states or movements in the Third World, knew well enough how much they owed to the existence of this counterweight to the economic and strategic predominance of the other side. But the U.S.S.R. was visibly shedding a politico-military burden it could no longer carry, and even communist states which were in no sense dependencies of Moscow (Yugoslavia, Albania) could not but realize how profoundly its disappearance would weaken them.

In any case, in Europe as in the U.S.S.R., the communists, who had once been sustained by the old convictions, were now a generation of the past. In 1989 few under sixty could have shared the experience that linked communism and patriotism in several countries, namely the Second World War and Resistance, and few under fifty could even have firsthand memories of that time. The legitimizing principle of states was, for most people, official rhetoric or senior citizens' anecdotage.* Even party members among the less-than-elderly were likely to be not communists in the old sense, but men and women (alas, far too few women) who made careers in countries that happened to be under communist rule. When times changed, and if they were allowed to, they were ready at a moment's notice to change their coats. In short, those who ran the Soviet satellite regimes had lost their faith in their own systems, or had never had it. While the systems were operational, they operated them. When it became clear that the U.S.S.R. itself was cutting them adrift, the reformers (as in Poland and Hungary) tried to negotiate a peaceful transition, the hardliners (as in Czechoslovakia and the GDR) to stand pat until it became evident that the citizens no longer obeyed, even if the army and police still did. In both cases they went quietly when they realized that their time was up, thus taking an unconscious revenge on the propagandists of the West who had argued that this was precisely what "totalitarian" regimes could never conceivably do.

They were replaced, briefly, by the men and (once again, far too rarely) women who had represented dissidence or opposition, and who

---

*This was obviously not the case in Third-World communist states like Vietnam, where liberation struggles had continued until the middle 1970s, but there the civil divisions of the liberation wars were probably also more vivid in people's minds.

had organized, or perhaps better, successfully called for the mass demonstrations which gave the signal for the old regimes' peaceful abdication. Except in Poland, where Church and the trade unions formed the backbone of opposition, they consisted of a few often very brave intellectuals, a stage-army of leaders which briefly found itself at the head of peoples: often, as in the 1848 revolutions which come to the historian's mind, academics or from the world of the arts. For a moment dissident philosophers (Hungary) or medieval historians (Poland) were considered as presidents or prime ministers, and a dramatist, Vaclav Havel, actually became President of Czechoslovakia, surrounded by an eccentric body of advisers ranging from a scandal-loving American rock musician to a member of the Habsburg high aristocracy (Prince Schwarzenberg). There was a tidal wave of talk about "civil society," i.e. the ensemble of voluntary citizens' organizations or private activities, taking the place of authoritarian states, and about the return to the principles of revolutions before Bolshevism had distorted them.* Alas, as in 1848, the moment of freedom and truth did not last. Politics, and those who ran the affairs of state reverted to those who usually occupy such functions. The *ad hoc* "fronts" or "civic movements" crumbled as rapidly as they had risen.

This also proved to be the case in the U.S.S.R., where the collapse of party and state proceeded more slowly until August 1991. The failure of *perestroika* and the consequent rejection of Gorbachev by the citizenry were increasingly obvious, though not appreciated in the West, where his popularity remained justifiably high. It reduced the leader of the U.S.S.R. to a series of backstairs manoeuvres and shifting alliances with the political groups and power groups that had emerged from the parliamentarization of Soviet politics, which made him equally distrusted by the reformers who had initially rallied round him—whom he had indeed made into a state-changing force—and the fragmented party bloc whose power he had broken. He was and will go into history as a tragic figure, a communist "Tsar-Liberator" like Alexander II (1855–81) who destroyed what he wanted to reform and was destroyed in the process.†

*The author recalls one of those discussions at a Washington conference in 1991, brought down to earth by the Spanish ambassador to the U.S.A., who remembered the young (at that time mainly liberal communist) students and ex-students feeling much the same after General Franco's death in 1975 "Civil society," he thought, merely meant that young ideologues who actually found themselves, for a moment, speaking for the whole people, were tempted to see this as a permanent situation.

†Alexander II (1855–81) freed the serfs and undertook a number of other reforms, but was assassinated by members of the revolutionary movement, which for the first time became a force in his reign.

Charming, sincere, intelligent and genuinely moved by the ideals of a communism which he saw corrupted since the rise of Stalin, Gorbachev was, paradoxically, too much of an organization man for the hurly-burly of democratic politics he created; too much of a committee man for decisive action; too remote from the experiences of urban and industrial Russia, which he had never managed, to have the old party boss' sense of grass-roots realities. His trouble was not so much that he had no effective strategy for reforming the economy—nobody had even after his fall—as that he was remote from the everyday experience of his country.

The contrast with another of the post-war generation of leading Soviet communists in their fifties is instructive. Nursultan Nazarbayev, who took charge of the Asian republic of Kazakhstan in 1984 as part of the reform drive, had (like many other Soviet politicians, and unlike Gorbachev and practically any statesmen in non-socialist countries) come into full-time public life from the factory floor. He shifted from party to state, becoming President of his Republic, pushed forward the required reforms, including decentralization and the market, and survived both the fall of Gorbachev, of the party of the Union, none of which he welcomed. After the fall he remained one of the most powerful men in the shadowy "Community of Independent States." But Nazarbayev, always the pragmatist, had systematically pursued a policy of optimising the position of his fief (and its population), and had taken the utmost care that market reforms should not be socially disruptive. Markets yes, uncontrolled price-rises decidedly no. His own preferred strategy was bilateral trade deals with other Soviet (or ex-Soviet) republics—he favoured a Central Asian Soviet common market—and joint ventures with foreign capital. He had no objection to radical economists, for he hired some from Russia, or even non-communist ones, for he brought in one of the brains of the South Korean economic miracle, which showed a realistic sense of how really successful post-Second World War capitalist economies actually worked. The road to survival and perhaps to success was paved less with good intentions than with the hard cobbles of realism.

The last years of the Soviet Union were a slow-motion catastrophe. The fall of the European satellites in 1989, and Moscow's reluctant acceptance of German reunification, demonstrated the collapse of the Soviet Union as an international power, let alone as a superpower. Its utter inability to play any role in the Persian Gulf crisis of 1990–91 merely underlined this. Internationally speaking, the U.S.S.R. was like a country comprehensively defeated, as after a major war—only without a war. Nevertheless, it retained the armed forces and the military-industrial complex of the former superpower, a situation that imposed severe limits on its politics. However, though the international debacle encouraged secessionism in the republics where nationalist sentiment was strong, notably the Baltic States and Georgia—Lithuania tested the waters with a provocative declaration of total independence in March 1990*—the disintegration of the Union was not due to nationalist forces.

It was due essentially to the disintegration of central authority, which forced every region or sub-unit of the country to look after itself, and, not least, to save what it could from the ruins of an economy sliding into chaos. Hunger and shortage lie behind everything that happened in the last two years of the U.S.S.R. Despairing reformers, mainly from among the academics who had been such obvious beneficiaries of *glasnost*, were pushed into an apocalyptic extremism: nothing could be done until the old system and everything about it was destroyed utterly. In economic terms, the system must be completely pulverized by total privatization and the introduction of a 100 per cent free market immediately and at whatever cost. Dramatic plans for doing this in a matter of weeks or months (there was a "programme of five hundred days") were proposed. These policies were not based on any knowledge of free markets or capitalist economies, though they were vigorously recommended by visiting American and British economists and financial experts, whose opinions were not, in turn, based on any knowledge of what actually went on in the Soviet economy. Both were correct in supposing that the existing system, or rather, while it existed, the command economy, was far inferior to economies based primarily on private property and private enterprise, and that the old system, even in a modified form, was doomed. Yet both failed to confront the real problem of how a centrally planned command economy was, in practice, to be transformed into some version or another of a market-dynamized economy. Instead they repeated first-year-economics-course demonstrations of the virtues of the market in the abstract. It would, they argued, automatically fill the shelves of shops with goods withheld by producers at affordable prices, once supply and demand were allowed free play. Most of the long-suffering citizens of the U.S.S.R. knew that this would not happen, and when, after it ceased to exist, the shock liberation treatment was briefly applied, it did not. Moreover, no serious observer of the country believed that in the year

*Armenian nationalism, though provoking the breakdown of the Union by reclaiming the region of Mountain Karabakh from Azerbaijan, was not crazy enough to *desire* the disappearance of the U.S.S.R., but for whose existence there would be no Armenia.

2000 the state and public sector of the Soviet economy would not still be substantial. The disciples of Friedrich Hayek and Milton Friedman condemned the very idea of such a mixed economy. They had no advice to offer about how it was to be operated, or transformed.

Yet, when it came, the final crisis was not economic but political. For virtually the entire Establishment of the U.S.S.R., from the party, the planners and scientists, the state, to the armed forces, the security apparatus and the sporting authorities, the idea of a total break-up of the U.S.S.R. was unacceptable. Whether it was desired, or even conceived of by any large body of Soviet citizens outside the Baltic States, even after 1989, we cannot tell, but it is not likely: whatever reservations we have about the figures, 76 per cent of voters in a referendum of March 1991 voted for maintaining the U.S.S.R., "as a renovated Federation of sovereign and equal Republics, in which the rights and liberty of every person of whatever nationality are fully safeguarded" (*Pravda*, 25/1/91). It was certainly not officially part of any major Union politician's policy. Yet the dissolution of the centre seemed inevitably to strengthen the centrifugal forces and to make the break-up inevitable, not least because of the policy of Boris Yeltsin, whose star rose as Gorbachev's waned. By now the Union was a shadow, the republics the only reality. At the end of April, Gorbachev, supported by the nine major republics,* negotiated a "Treaty of Union" which, somewhat in the manner of the Austro-Hungarian Compromise of 1867, was intended to preserve the existence of a central federal power (with a directly elected federal president), in charge of the armed forces, foreign policy, the coordination of financial policy and of economic relations with the rest of the world. The Treaty was to come into force on 20 August.

For most of the old party and Soviet establishment, this treaty was yet another of Gorbachev's paper formulas, doomed like all the others. Hence they regarded it as the gravestone of the Union. Two days before the Treaty was due to come into force, virtually all the heavyweights of the Union, ministers of defence and interior, head of the KGB, vice-president and prime minister of the U.S.S.R. and pillars of the party, proclaimed that an Emergency Committee would take over power in the absence of the President and General Secretary (under house arrest on vacation). It was not so much a coup—nobody was arrested in Moscow, not even the broadcasting stations were taken over—as a proclamation that the machinery of real power was once again in operation, in the

---

*I e. all except the three Baltic states, Moldavia and Georgia, as well as, for obscure reasons, Kyrghyzstan.

confident hope that the citizenry would welcome, or at least quietly accept, the return to order and government. It was not defeated by a revolution or rising of the people either, for the population of Moscow remained quiet, and the call for a strike against the coup went unheeded. As in so much of Soviet history, it was a drama played by a small body of actors over the heads of the long-suffering people.

But not quite. Thirty, even ten years earlier, the mere proclamation of where power really lay would have been enough. Even as it was, most citizens of the U.S.S.R. kept their heads down: 48 per cent of the people (according to a poll) and—less surprisingly—70 per cent of party committees, supported the "coup" (Di Leo, 1992, pp. 141, 143n). Equally to the point, more governments abroad than cared to admit it, expected the coup to succeed.* Yet the old-style reassertion of the power of party/ state relied on universal and automatic assent rather than counting heads. By 1991 there was neither central power nor universal obedience. A genuine coup might well have succeeded over most of the territory and population of the U.S.S.R., and, whatever the divisions and uncertainties within the armed forces and security apparatus, enough reliable troops for a successful *putsch* in the capital could probably have been found. But the symbolic reassertion of authority was no longer enough. Gorbachev was right: *perestroika* had defeated the conspirators by changing society. It had also defeated him.

A symbolic coup could be defeated by a symbolic resistance, for the last thing the plotters were prepared for or wanted was a civil war. Indeed, their gesture was intended to stop what most people feared: a slide into such a conflict. So, while the shadowy institutions of the U.S.S.R. fell into line with the plotters, the barely less shadowy institutions of the Russian Republic under Boris Yeltsin, just elected as its President by a substantial majority of voters, did not. The plotters had nothing to do except throw in their hand, after Yeltsin, surrounded by some thousands of supporters come to defend his headquarters, defied the embarrassed tanks camped in front of it, for the benefit of the world's television screens. Bravely, but also safely, Yeltsin, whose political gifts and capacity for decision contrasted dramatically with Gorbachev's style, immediately seized his opportunity to dissolve and expropriate the Communist Party and take over for the Russian Republic what remained of

---

*On the first day of the "coup" the Finnish government's official news digest reported the news of President Gorbachev's arrest briefly without comment halfway down page 3 of a four-page bulletin. It only began to express opinions when the attempt had evidently failed.

the assets of the U.S.S.R., which was formally ended a few months later. Gorbachev himself was pushed into oblivion. The world, which had been ready to accept the coup, now accepted the much more effective counter-coup of Yeltsin, and treated Russia as the natural successor to the dead U.S.S.R. in the United Nations and elsewhere. The attempt to save the old structure of the Soviet Union had destroyed it more suddenly and irrevocably than anyone had expected.

However, it had solved none of the problems of economy, state and society. In one respect it had made them worse, for the other republics were now afraid of their big brother Russia as they had not been of the non-national U.S.S.R., especially since Russian nationalism was the best card Yeltsin could play to conciliate the armed forces, whose core had always been among the Great Russians. Since most of the republics contained large minorities of ethnic Russians, Yeltsin's hint that the frontiers between the republics might have to be renegotiated, accelerated the rush to total separation: the Ukraine immediately declared its independence. For the first time populations used to the impartial oppression of all (including Great Russians) by central authority had cause to fear oppression from Moscow in the interests of one nation. In fact, this paid to the hope of maintaining even a semblance of union, for the shadowy "Commonwealth of Independent States" which succeeded the U.S.S.R. soon lost all reality, and even the last survivor of the Union, the (extremely successful) United Team which competed at the 1992 Olympic Games, beating the United States, did not seem destined for a long life. Thus the destruction of the U.S.S.R. achieved the reversal of almost four hundred years of Russian history, and the return of the country to something like the dimensions and international standing of the era before Peter the Great (1672–1725). Since Russia, whether under the Tsars or as the U.S.S.R., had been a great power since the middle of the eighteenth century, its disintegration left an international void between Trieste and Vladivostok, which had not previously existed in modern world history, except briefly during the Civil War of 1918–20: a vast zone of disorder, conflict and potential catastrophe. This was the agenda for the world's diplomats and military men at the end of the millennium.

VI

Two observations may conclude this survey. The first is to note how superficial the hold of communism proved to be over the enormous area it had conquered more rapidly than any other ideology since Islam in its first century. Though a simplistic version of Marxism–Leninism became the dogmatic (secular) orthodoxy for all citizens between the Elbe and the China Seas, it disappeared from one day to the next with the political regimes that had imposed it. Two reasons may be suggested for this historically rather startling phenomenon. Communism was not based on mass conversion, but was a faith of cadres or (in Lenin's terms) "vanguards." Even Mao's famous phrase about successful guerrillas moving among the peasantry like fish in water, implies the distinction between the active element (the fish) and the passive (the water). Unofficial labour and socialist movements (including some mass communist parties) might be coextensive with their community or constituency, as in coalmining villages. On the other hand, all ruling communist parties were, by choice and definition, minority elites. The assent to communism of "the masses" depended not on their ideological or other convictions but on how they judged what life under communist regimes did for them, and how they compared their situation with others'. Once it ceased to be possible to insulate populations from contact with, or even knowledge about, other countries, these judgments were sceptical. Again, communism was essentially an instrumental faith: the present having value purely as a means of reaching an undefined future. Except in rare cases—for instance patriotic wars, where victory justifies present sacrifices—such a set of beliefs is better suited to sects or elites than to universal churches, whose field of operation, whatever their promise of ultimate salvation, is and must be the everyday range of human life. Even the cadres of communist parties began to concentrate on the ordinary satisfactions of life once the millennial aim of earthly salvation, to which they had dedicated their lives, moved into an undefined future. And—typically enough—when this happened, the party provided no guidance for their behaviour. In short, by the nature of its ideology communism asked to be judged by success, and had no reserves against failure.

But why did it fail, or rather break down? It is the paradox of the U.S.S.R. that, in its death, it provided one of the strongest arguments for the analysis of Karl Marx, which it had claimed to exemplify. Marx wrote in 1859:

> In the social production of their means of existence human beings enter into definite, necessary relations independent of their will, productive relationships which correspond to a definite stage in the development of their material productive forces ... At a certain stage of their development the material productive forces of society come into contradiction with the existing productive relationships,

or, what is but a legal expression for these, with the property relationships within which they had moved before. From forms of development of the productive forces these relationships are transformed
into their fetters. We then enter an era of social revolution.

Rarely has there been a clearer example of Marx's forces of production
coming into conflict with the social, institutional and ideological super-
structure which had transformed backward agrarian economies into advanced industrial ones—up to the point where they turn from forces into
fetters of production. The first result of the "era of social revolution"
thus initiated was the disintegration of the old system.

But what would replace it? Here we can no longer follow the nineteenth-century optimism of Marx, who argued that the overthrow of the
old system must lead to a better one, because "mankind always sets itself
only such problems as it can solve." The problems which "mankind," or
rather the Bolsheviks, set themselves in 1917 were not soluble in the circumstances of their time and place, or only very incompletely soluble.
And today it would take a high degree of confidence to argue that in the
foreseeable future a solution is visible for the problems arising out of the
collapse of Soviet communism, or that any solution that may arise within
the next generation will strike the inhabitants of the former U.S.S.R. and
the communist Balkans as an obvious improvement.

With the collapse of the U.S.S.R. the experiment of "really existing socialism" came to an end. For, even where communist regimes survived
and succeeded, as in China, they abandoned the original ideal of a single,
centrally controlled and state-planned economy based on a completely
collectivized state—or cooperatively owned economy virtually without a
market. Will this experiment ever be renewed? Clearly not in the form
developed in the U.S.S.R., or probably in any form, except in conditions of
something like a total war economy, or some other analogous emergency.

This is because the Soviet experiment was designed not as a global alternative to capitalism, but as a specific set of responses to the particular
situation of a vast and spectacularly backward country at a particular and
unrepeatable historical conjuncture. The failure of revolution elsewhere
left the U.S.S.R. committed to build socialism alone, in a country in
which, by the universal consensus of Marxists in 1917, including the
Russian ones, the conditions for doing so were simply not present. The
attempt to do so produced remarkable achievements—not least the ability
to defeat Germany in the Second World War—but at quite enormous and
intolerable human cost, and at the cost of what proved eventually to be a
dead-end economy and a political system for which there was nothing to

be said. (Had not George Plekhanov, the "father of Russian Marxism," predicted that the October revolution could lead at best to a "Chinese Empire coloured red"?) The other "really existing" socialism, emerging under the wings of the Soviet Union, operated under the same disadvantages, though to a lesser extent, and with—compared to the U.S.S.R.—far less human suffering. A revival or rebirth of this pattern of socialism is neither possible, desirable, nor—even assuming conditions were to favour it—necessary.

How far the failure of the Soviet experiment throws doubt on the entire project of traditional socialism, an economy essentially based on the social ownership and planned management of the means of production, distribution and exchange, is another question. That such a project is economically rational in theory has been accepted by economists since before the First World War, though, curiously enough, the theory was worked out not by socialists but by non-socialist pure economists. That it would have practical drawbacks, if only through bureaucratization, was obvious. That it had to work, at least partly, through *prices*, both market pricing and realistic "accounting prices," was also clear if socialism was to take account of the wishes of consumers rather than telling them what was good for them. In fact, socialist economists in the West who thought about these matters in the 1930s, when the subject was naturally much debated, assumed a combination of planning, preferably decentralized, with prices. To demonstrate the feasibility of such a socialist economy is not, of course, to demonstrate its necessary superiority to, say, some socially juster version of the Golden Age mixed economy, still less, that people would prefer it. It is merely to separate the question of socialism in general from that of the specific experience of "really existing socialism." The failure of Soviet socialism does not reflect on the possibility of other kinds of socialism. Indeed, the very inability of the dead-end economy of Soviet-type central command-planning to reform itself into "market socialism," as it wanted to, demonstrates the gap between the two kinds of development.

The tragedy of the October revolution was precisely that it could only produce its kind of ruthless, brutal, command socialism. One of the most sophisticated socialist economists of the 1930s, Oskar Lange, returned from the U.S.A. to his native Poland to build socialism, until he came to a London hospital to die. On his death-bed he talked to the friends and admirers who came to visit him, including myself. This, as I recall, is what he said:

If I had been in Russia in the 1920s, I would have been a

Bukharinite gradualist. If I had advised on Soviet industrialization, I would have recommended a more flexible and limited set of targets, as indeed the able Russian planners did. And yet, as I think back, I ask myself, again and again: was there an alternative to the indiscriminate, brutal, basically unplanned rush forward of the first Five-Year Plan? I wish I could say there was, but I cannot. I cannot find an answer.

CHAPTER SEVENTEEN

The Avant-garde Dies—
The Arts After 1950

Art as an investment is a conception scarcely older than the early 1950s.

—G. Reitlinger, *The Economics of Taste*, vol. 2 (1982, p. 14)

The great big white goods, the things that keep our economy going—refrigerators, stoves, all the things that used to be porcelain and white—they're now tinted. This is new. There's pop art that goes along with them. Very nice. Mandrake the Magician coming off the wall at you as you open your refrigerator to get your orange juice.

—Studs Terkel, *Division Street: America* (1967, p. 217)

I

It is the practice of historians—including this one—to treat the development of the arts, however obvious and profound their roots in society, as in some way separable from their contemporary context, as a branch or type of human activity subject to its own rules, and capable of being judged accordingly. Yet in the era of the most revolutionary transformations of human life so far recorded, even this ancient and convenient principle of structuring a historical survey becomes increasingly unreal. Not only because the boundary between what is and is not classifiable as "art," "creation" or artifice became increasingly hazy, or even disappeared altogether, or because an influential school of literary critics at the *fin de siècle* thought it impossible, irrelevant and undemocratic to decide whether Shakespeare's *Macbeth* was better or worse than *Batman*. It was also because the forces determining what happened within the arts, or what old-fashioned observers would have called by that name, were overwhelmingly exogenous. As might have been expected in an era of extraordinary techno-scientific revolution, they were predominantly technological.

Technology revolutionized the arts most obviously by making them omnipresent. Radio had already brought sounds—words and music—into most households in the developed world, and continued its penetration of the backward world. But what made it universal was the transistor, which made it both small and portable, and the long-life electric battery which made it independent of official (i.e. mainly urban) networks of electric power. The gramophone or record-player was already ancient, and, though technically improved, remained comparatively cumbersome. The long-playing record (1948), which established itself rapidly in the 1950s (Guiness, 1984, p. 193) benefited the lovers of classical music, whose compositions, unlike those of popular music, had rarely tried to keep within the three-or five-minute limit of the 78 rpm disc, but what made self-chosen music genuinely transportable was the tape-cassette, playable on the increasingly small and portable and battery-powered recorder/players, which swept the world in the 1970s and had the additional advantage of being readily copied. By the 1980s music could be everywhere: privately accompanying every possible activity through earphones attached to pocket-sized devices pioneered (as so often) by the Japanese, or projected only too publicly from the large portable "ghetto-blasters" (for loudspeakers had not yet been successfully miniaturized). This technological revolution had political as well as cultural consequences. In 1961 President de Gaulle appealed successfully to French conscripts against their commanders' military coup, because soldiers could hear him on portable radios. In the 1970s the speeches of Ayatollah Khomeini, exiled leader of the future Iranian revolution, were readily transported into Iran, copied and diffused.

Television never became as readily portable as radio—or at least it lost far more by reduction than sound—but it domesticated the moving image. Moreover, while a TV set remained a far more expensive and physically clumsy device than a radio set, it soon became almost universally and constantly accessible even to the poor in some backward countries, wherever an urban infrastructure existed. In the 1980s some 80 per cent of the population of a country like Brazil had access to television. This is more surprising than that in the U.S.A. the new medium replaced both radio and films as the standard form of popular entertainment in the 1950s, and in prosperous Britain in the 1960s. The mass demand for it was overwhelming. In the advanced countries it began (via the video-cassette player, which still remained a rather expensive device) to bring the whole range of the filmed image into the domestic small screen. While the repertoire produced for the big screen generally suffered from being miniaturized, the VCR had the advantage of giving the viewer a theoretically almost unlimited choice of what to see and when to see it. With the spread of domestic computers, the small screen seemed about to become the individual's major visual link with the outside world.

Yet technology not only made the arts omnipresent, but transformed their perception. It is barely possible for someone who has been brought up in the age when electronic and mechanically generated music is the standard sound heard on live and recorded pop music, when any child can freeze frames, and repeat a sound or visual passage as once only textual passages could be re-read, when theatrical illusion is as nothing to what technology can do in television commercials, including telling a dramatic narrative in thirty seconds, to recapture simple linearity or sequentiality of perception in the days before modern high-tech made it possible to move within seconds through the full range of available television channels. Technology transformed the world of the arts, though that of the popular arts and entertainments earlier and more completely than that of the "high arts," especially the more traditional ones.

II

But what had happened to these?

At first sight the most striking thing about the development of the high arts in the world after the Age of Catastrophe was a marked geographical shift away from the traditional (European) centres of elite culture, and—given the era of unprecedented global prosperity—an enormous rise in the financial resources available to support them. Closer scrutiny, as we shall see, was to prove less encouraging.

That "Europe" (by which most people in the West between 1947 and 1989 meant "Western Europe") was no longer the major home of the high arts became a commonplace observation. New York prided itself on having replaced Paris as the centre of the visual arts, by which it meant the art market or the place where living artists became the highest-priced commodities. More significantly, the jury of the Nobel Prize for literature, a body whose sense of politics is usually more interesting than its literary judgments, began to take non-European literature seriously from the 1960s on, having previously neglected it almost completely, except for North America (which got prizes regularly from 1930, when Sinclair Lewis became its first laureate). No serious reader of novels could, by the

1970s, fail to have made contact with the brilliant school of Latin American writers. No serious film-buff could fail to admire, or at least to talk as though he or she admired the great Japanese film directors who, starting with Akira Kurosawa (1910–) in the 1950s, conquered the international film festivals, or the Bengali Satyadjit Ray (1921–92). Nobody was surprised when in 1986 the first sub-Saharan African, the Nigerian Wole Soyinka (1934–), got a Nobel Prize.

The shift away from Europe was even more obvious in the most visually insistent art, namely architecture. As we have already seen, the modern movement in architecture had actually built very little between the wars. After the war, when it came into its own, the "international style" achieved both its largest and most numerous monuments in the U.S.A., which developed it further and eventually, mainly via the American-owned networks of hotels which settled on the world from the 1970s on like spiderwebs, exported a peculiar form of dream-palace for travelling business executives and prosperous tourists. In their most characteristic versions they were easily recognizable by a sort of central nave or giant conservatory, generally with indoor trees, plants and fountains; transparent elevators visibly gliding up the insides or outsides of walls; glass everywhere and theatrical lighting. They were to be for late twentieth-century bourgeois society what the standard opera house had been for its nineteenth-century predecessor. But the modern movement created equally prominent monuments elsewhere: Le Corbusier (1887–1965) constructed an entire capital city in India (Chandigarh); Oscar Niemeyer (1907–) much of another in Brazil (Brasilia); while perhaps the most beautiful of the great products of the modern movement—also built by public commission rather than private patronage or profit—is to be found in Mexico City, the National Museum of Anthropology (1964).

It seemed equally evident that the old European centres of the arts were showing signs of battle-fatigue, with the possible exception of Italy, where the mood of anti-fascist self-liberation, largely under communist leadership, inspired a decade or so of cultural renaissance which made its main international impact through the Italian "neo-realist" films. The French visual arts did not maintain the reputation of the inter-war school of Paris, which was in itself little more than an afterglow of the era before 1914. The major reputations of French fiction writers were intellectual rather than literary: as inventors of gimmicks (like the "*nouveau roman*" of the 1950s and 1960s) or as non-fiction writers (like J.-P. Sartre), rather than for their creative work. Had any post-1945 "serious" French novelist established any international reputation as such by the 1970s? Probably not. The British artistic scene had been considerably livelier, not least because London after 1950 transformed itself into one of the world's major centres for musical and theatrical performance, and also produced a handful of avant-garde architects whose adventurous projects gained them more fame abroad—in Paris or Stuttgart—than at home. Nevertheless, if post-Second World War Britain occupied a less marginal place in the Western European arts than between the wars, its record in the field where the country had always been strong, literature, was not particularly impressive. In poetry, the post-war writers of little Ireland could more than hold their own against the U.K. As for Federal Germany, the contrast between that country's resources and achievements, and indeed between its glorious Weimar past and its Bonn present, was striking. It was not entirely explained by the disastrous effects and after-effects of the twelve Hitler years. It is significant that in the fifty post-war years several of the best talents active in West German literature were not natives but immigrants from further east (Celan, Grass and various incomers from the GDR).

Germany, of course, was divided between 1945 and 1990. The contrast between the two parts—one militantly democratic-liberal, market-oriented and Western, the other a textbook version of communist central-ization—illustrates a curious aspect of the migration of high culture: its relative flowering under communism, at least at certain periods. This plainly does not apply to all arts, nor, of course, to states under the iron heel of a genuinely murderous dictatorship, like Stalin's and Mao's, or of lesser megalomaniac tyrannies, like Ceauşescu's in Romania (1961–89) or Kim Il Sung's in North Korea (1945–1994).

Moreover, insofar as arts depended upon public, i.e. central government, patronage, the standard dictatorial preference for pompous gigantism reduced the artists' choice, as did the official insistence on a sort of upbeat sentimental mythology known as "socialist realism." It is possible that the wide open spaces lined with neo-Victorian towers so characteristic of the 1950s may one day find admirers—one thinks of Smolensk Square in Moscow—but the discovery of their architectural merits must be left to the future. On the other hand it must be admitted that, where communist governments did not insist on telling artists exactly what to do, their generosity in subsidising cultural activities (or, as others might put it, their defective sense of accountancy) was helpful. It is presumably not an accident that the West imported the typical avant-garde opera producer of the 1980s from East Berlin.

The U.S.S.R. remained culturally fallow, at least in comparison with its pre-1917 glories and even the ferment of the 1920s, except perhaps for the writing of poetry, the art most capable of being practised in private and the one where the great twentieth-century Russian tradition maintained its continuity best after 1917—Akhmatova (1889–1966), Tsvetayeva (1892–1941), Pasternak (1890–1960), Blok (1880–1921), Mayakovsky (1893–1930), Brodsky (1940–), Voznesensky (1933–), Akhmadulina (1937–). Its visual arts suffered particularly from the combination of a rigid orthodoxy, both ideological, aesthetic and institutional, and total isolation from the rest of the world. The passionate cultural nationalism which began to emerge in parts of the U.S.S.R. during the Brezhnev period—orthodox and Slavophil in Russia (Solzhenitsyn (1918–), mythical-medievalist in Armenia (e.g. in the films of Sergei Paradjanov (1924–)—derived largely from the fact that those who rejected anything recommended by the system and the party, as so many intellectuals did, had no other traditions to draw on but the local conservative ones. Moreover, the intellectuals in the U.S.S.R. were spectacularly isolated not only from the system of government but also from the bulk of ordinary Soviet citizens who, in some obscure way, accepted its legitimacy and adjusted to the only life they knew, and which, in the 1960s and 1970s, was actually improving quite noticeably. They hated the rulers and despised the ruled, even when (like the neo-Slavophils) they idealized the Russian soul in the shape of a Russian peasant who no longer existed. It was not a good atmosphere for the creative artist, and the dissolution of the apparatus of intellectual coercion, paradoxically, turned talents from creation to agitation. The Solzhenitsyn who is likely to survive as a major twentieth-century writer is the one who still had to preach by writing novels (*A Day in the Life of Ivan Denisovich, The Cancer Ward*) because he as yet lacked the freedom to write sermons and historical denunciations.

The situation in Communist China until the late 1970s was dominated by ruthless repression, underlined by rare momentary relaxation ("let a hundred flowers bloom") which served to identify the victims of the next purges. The regime of Mao Tse-tung reached its climax in the "Cultural Revolution" of 1966–76, a campaign against culture, education and intelligence without parallel in twentieth-century history. It virtually shut down secondary and university education for ten years, brought the practice of (Western) classical and other music to a halt, where necessary by destroying its instruments, and reduced the national repertoire of stage and film to half-a-dozen politically correct pieces (as judged by the Great Helmsman's wife, once a second-rank Shanghai film actress), which were endlessly repeated. Given both this experience and the ancient Chinese tradition of imposing orthodoxy, which was modified but not abandoned in the post-Mao era, the light shining out of Communist China in the arts remained dim.

On the other hand, creativity flourished under the communist regimes of Eastern Europe, at least once orthodoxy was even slightly relaxed, as happened during de-Stalinization. The film industry in Poland, Czechoslovakia and Hungary, hitherto not much heard of even locally, burst into unexpected bloom from the late fifties on, and for a while became one of the most distinguished sources of interesting movies anywhere. Until the collapse of communism, which also entailed the collapse of the mechanisms for cultural production in the countries concerned, even the revival of repression (after 1968 in Czechoslovakia, after 1980 in Poland) did not halt it, though the rather promising start of the East German film industry in the early 1950s had been brought to a stop by political authority. That an art so dependent on heavy state investment should have flourished artistically under communist regimes is more surprising than that creative literature should, for, after all, even under intolerant governments, books can be written "for the bottom drawer" or for circles of friends.* However narrow the public for which they originally wrote, several of the writers won international admiration—the East Germans, who produced substantially more interesting talent than the prosperous Federal Republic, and the Czechs of the 1960s whose writings only reached the West via internal and external emigration after 1968.

What all these talents had in common was something that few writers and film-makers in the developed market-economies enjoyed, and Western theatre folk (a group given to uncharacteristic political radicalism dating back, in the U.S.A. and Britain, to the 1930s) dreamed about: the sense of being needed by their public. Indeed, in the absence of real politics and a free press, practitioners of the arts were the *only* ones who spoke for what their people, or at least the educated among them, thought and felt. These feelings were not confined to artists in communist regimes, but in other regimes where intellectuals were at odds with the prevalent political system, and, though not totally unrestricted, were free enough to express themselves in public. Apartheid in South Africa inspired its adversaries to more good literature than had come out of that subcontinent before. That most Latin American intellectuals south of Mexico between the 1950s and the 1990s were likely, at some point in their lives, to be political refugees, is not irrelevant to the cultural achievements of that part of the Western hemisphere. The same was true of Turkish intellectuals.

---

*However, the processes of copying remained incredibly laborious, since no technology later than the manual typewriter and carbon paper were available. For political reasons the pre-*perestroika* communist world did not use the Xerox.

Nevertheless, there was more to the ambiguous flowering of some arts in Eastern Europe than their function as a tolerated opposition. Most of their younger practitioners had been inspired by the hope that their countries, even under unsatisfactory regimes, would in some way enter a new era after the horrors of wartime; some, more than cared to be reminded of it, had actually felt the wind of utopia in the sails of youth, at least in the first few post-war years. A few continued to be inspired by their times: Ismail Kadaré (1930–   ), perhaps the first Albanian novelist to make a mark on the outside world, became the mouth-piece not so much of Enver Hoxha's hardline regime as of a small mountain country which, under communism, won a place in the world for the first time (he emigrated in 1990). Most of the others sooner or later moved into varying degrees of opposition—yet, often enough, rejecting the only alternative offered to them (whether across the West German border or by Radio Free Europe), in a world of binary and mutually exclusive opposites. And even where, as in Poland, rejection of the existing regime became total, all but the youngest knew enough about their country's history since 1945 to pick shades of grey as well as the propagandist's black and white. That is what gives a tragic dimension to the films of Andrzej Wajda (1926–   ), their ambiguity to the Czech film-makers of the 1960s, then in their thirties, and the writers of the GDR—Christa Wolf (1929–   ), Heiner Müller (1929–   )—disillusioned but not oblivious of their dreams.

Paradoxically, artists and intellectuals in both the (socialist) Second World and the various parts of the Third World enjoyed both prestige and relative prosperity and privilege, at least between bouts of persecution. In the socialist world they might be among the richest citizens and enjoy that rarest of all freedoms in those collective prison-houses, the right to travel abroad, or even to have access to foreign literature. Under socialism their political influence was zero, but in the various third worlds (and, after the fall of communism, briefly in the former world of "really existing socialism") being an intellectual or even an artist was a public asset. In Latin America leading writers, almost irrespective of their political opinions, could expect diplomatic posts, preferably in Paris, where the location of UNESCO gave each country that wanted to several chances to place citizens in the neighbourhood of Left Bank cafés. Professors had always expected spells as cabinet ministers, preferably of economics, but the fashion of the late 1980s for persons connected with the arts to stand as presidential candidates (as a good novelist did in Peru), or actually to become presidents (as in post-communist Czechoslovakia and Lithuania) seemed new, though it had precedents in earlier times among new states, both European and African, which were likely to give prominence to those few of their citizens who were known abroad, i.e. most likely concert pianists, as in 1918 Poland, French poets, as in Senegal, or dancers, as in Guinea. Still, novelists, dramatists, poets and musicians were political non-starters in most developed Western countries under any circumstances, even in intellectually-minded ones, except perhaps as potential Ministers of Culture (André Malraux in France, Jorge Semprún in Spain).

The public and private resources devoted to the arts were inevitably far greater than before in an era of unprecedented prosperity. Thus even the British government, never in the forefront of public patronage, spent well over £1 billion sterling on the arts in the late 1980s, whereas in 1939 it had been £900,000 (*Britain: An Official Handbook*, 1961, p. 222; 1990, p. 426). Private patronage was less important, except in the U.S.A., where billionaires, encouraged by suitable fiscal concessions, supported education, learning and culture on a more munificent scale than anywhere else, partly out of a genuine appreciation of the higher things in life, especially among first-generation tycoons; partly because, in the absence of a formal social hierarchy, what might be called Medici-status was the next best thing. Increasingly the big spenders did not merely donate their collections to national or civic galleries (as in the past), but insisted on founding their own museums named after themselves, or at least their own wings or sectors of museums in which their own collections were presented in the form laid down by their owners and donors.

As for the art market, from the 1950s on it discovered that almost half a century of depression was lifting. Prices, especially of French Impressionists, post-Impressionists and the most eminent Parisian early modernists, rose into the sky, until in the 1970s the international art market, whose location shifted first to London and then to New York, had equalled the all-time records (in real terms) of the Age of Empire, and in the mad bull market of the 1980s soared beyond them. The price of Impressionists and post-Impressionists multiplied twenty-three-fold between 1975 and 1989 (Sotheby, 1992). However, comparisons with earlier periods were henceforth impossible. True, the rich still collected—old money, as a rule, preferring old masters, new money going for novelty—but increasingly art-purchasers bought for investment, as once men had bought speculative gold mining shares. The British Rail Pensions Fund, which (on the best advice) made a lot of money out of art, cannot be thought of as an art lover, and the ideal-typical art transaction of the late 1980s was one in which a Western Australian instant tycoon bought a Van Gogh for £31 million, a large part of which had been lent him by the auctioneers, both presumably hoping for further price rises which would make the picture a more valuable collateral for bank loans, and raise the dealer's future profits. As it happens, both were disappointed: Mr. Bond of Perth went bankrupt and the speculative art boom collapsed in the early 1990s.

The relation between money and the arts is always ambiguous. It is far from clear that the major achievements of the arts in the second half of the century owed much to it; except in architecture, where, on the whole, big is beautiful, or, at any rate, more likely to get into the guidebooks. On the other hand, another kind of economic development unquestionably affected most of the arts profoundly; their integration into academic life, in the institutions of superior education whose extraordinary expansion we have noticed elsewhere (chapter 10). This development was both general and specific. Speaking generally, the decisive development of twentieth-century culture, the rise of a revolutionary popular entertainment industry geared to the mass market, reduced the traditional forms of high art to elite ghettoes, and from the middle of the century their inhabitants were essentially people who had enjoyed a higher education. The public of theatre and opera, the readers of their country's literary classics and the sort of poetry and prose taken seriously by the critics, the visitors to museums and art galleries belonged overwhelmingly to those who had at least completed secondary education—except in the socialist world where the profit-maximizing entertainment industry was kept at bay—until, after its fall, it was no longer kept at bay. The common culture of any late twentieth-century urbanized country was based on the mass entertainment industry—cinema, radio, television, pop music—in which the elite shared, certainly from the triumph of rock music onwards, and to which intellectuals no doubt gave a highbrow twist to make it suitable for elite taste. Beyond this, segregation was increasingly complete, for the bulk of the public to which the mass market industry appealed only encountered by occasional accident, the genres that high-culture buffs raved about, as when a Puccini aria sung by Pavarotti found itself associated with the World Soccer Cup in 1990, or when brief themes from Handel or Bach appeared incognito in television commercials. If one did not want to join the middle classes one did not bother about seeing Shakespeare plays. Conversely, if one did, the most obvious means being to pass the requisite exams at secondary school, one could not avoid seeing them: they were the subject of examinations. In extreme cases, of which class-divided Britain was a notable example, newspapers addressed respectively to the educated and the uneducated virtually inhabited different universes.

More specifically, the extraordinary expansion of higher education increasingly provided employment, and constituted the market for men and women with inadequate commercial appeal. This was most dramatically exemplified in literature. Poets taught, or at least were resident at colleges. In some countries the occupation of novelist and professor overlapped to such an extent that an entirely new genre appeared in the 1960s and, since vast numbers of potential readers were familiar with the milieu, flourished: the campus novel which, apart from the usual subject-matter of fiction, the relation between the sexes, dealt with matters of more esoteric interest, such as academic exchanges, international colloquia, university gossip and the peculiarities of students. More dangerously, academic demand encouraged the production of creative writing that lent itself to seminar dissection, and therefore benefited by complexity, if not incomprehensibility, following the example of the great James Joyce, whose later work had as many commentators as genuine readers. Poets wrote for other poets, or for students expected to discuss their works. Protected by academic salaries, grants and obligatory reading lists, the non-commercial creative arts could hope, if not necessarily to flourish, then at least to survive in comfort. Alas, another by-product of the growth of academia undermined their position, for the glossators and scholiasts made themselves independent of their subject by claiming that the text was only what the reader made of it. The critic who interpreted Flaubert, they argued, was as much the creator of Madame Bovary as the author, perhaps—since that novel survived only through others' readings, mainly for academic purposes—even more than the author. This theory had long been hailed by avant-garde theatrical producers (anticipated by the actor-managers and film-moguls of old) for whom Shakespeare or Verdi were basically raw material for their own adventurous and preferably provocative interpretations. Triumphant though these sometimes were, they actually underlined the growing esotericism of the highbrow arts, for they were themselves commentaries upon and critiques of earlier interpretations, and not fully comprehensible except to initiates. The fashion spread even to the populist genre of films, where sophisticated directors advertised their cinematic erudition to the elite which understood their allusions while keeping the masses (and hopefully the box office) happy with blood and sperm.*

Is it possible to guess how the cultural histories of the twenty-first cen-

---

*Thus Brian de Palma's *The Untouchables* (1987), ostensibly a rousing cops-and-robbers film about Al Capone's Chicago (though actually a pastiche of the original genre), contains a literal quote from Eisenstein's *Battleship Potemkin*, incomprehensible to all who had not seen the famous passage of the pram careering down the Odessa steps.

tury will assess the artistic achievements of the high arts of the second half of the twentieth? Obviously not, but they will hardly fail to notice the decline, at least regionally, of characteristic genres that had flourished greatly in the nineteenth century, and survived into the first half of the twentieth. Sculpture is an example that springs to mind, if only because the main expression of this art, the public monument, virtually died out after the First World War, except in dictatorial countries, where, by general consent, quality did not equal quantity. It is impossible to avoid the impression that painting was not what it had been even between the wars. At all events it would be difficult to draw up a list of painters of 1950–1990 who would be accepted as major figures (e.g. worthy of inclusion in museums other than the artist's own country) comparable to such a list for the inter-war period. That, we may remind ourselves, would have included at the very least Picasso (1881–1973), Matisse (1869–1954), Soutine (1894–1943), Chagall (1889–1985) and Rouault (1871–1958) from the École de Paris; Klee (1879–1940), perhaps two or three Russians and Germans, and one or two Spaniards and Mexicans. How would a later twentieth-century list compare with these, even if it included several leaders of the New York School of "abstract expressionists," Francis Bacon and a couple of Germans?

In classical music, once again, the decline in the old genres was concealed by the enormous increase in their performance, but mainly in the form of a repertoire of dead classics. How many new operas, written after 1950, had established themselves in the international, or even any national, repertoires, which endlessly recycled the products of composers of whom the youngest had been born in 1860? Except for Germany and Britain (Henze, Britten and at best two or three others), very few composers even created grand operas. The Americans (e.g. Leonard Bernstein, 1918–90) preferred the less formal genre of the musical. How many composers other than the Russians any longer wrote symphonies, regarded as the crown of instrumental achievement in the nineteenth century?* Musical talent, which continued in plentiful and distinguished supply, simply tended to abandon the traditional forms of expression, even though these overwhelmingly dominated the high-art market.

A similar retreat from the nineteenth-century genre is obvious in the novel. Naturally it continued to be written in vast quantities, bought and read. Yet if we look for the great novels and the great novelists of the second half of the century, the ones which took an entire society or

---

*Prokofiev wrote seven and Shostakovich fifteen, and even Stravinsky wrote three: but all these belonged, or had been formed in the first part of the century.

historical era as their subject, we find them outside the central regions of Western culture—except, once again, for Russia, where the novel re-surfaced, with the early Solzhenitsyn, as the major creative mode of coming to terms with the experience of Stalinism. We may find novels of the great tradition in Sicily (Lampedusa's *The Leopard*), in Yugoslavia (Ivo Andrić, Miroslav Krleža) and Turkey. We shall certainly find them in Latin America, whose fiction, hitherto unknown outside the countries concerned, captured the literary world from the 1950s on. The novel most unhesitatingly and instantly recognized as a masterpiece all over the globe came from Colombia, a country that most educated people in the developed world had trouble even identifying on a map before it became identified with cocaine: Gabriel García Márquez's *A Hundred Years of Solitude*. Perhaps the remarkable rise of the Jewish novel in several countries, notably the U.S.A. and Israel, reflects the exceptional trauma of its people's experience under Hitler, with which, directly or indirectly, Jewish writers felt they had to come to terms.

The decline of the classical genres of high art and literature was certainly not due to any shortage of talent. For even if we know little about the distribution of exceptional gifts among human beings and its variation, it is safer to assume that there are rapid changes in the incentives to express them, or in the outlets for expressing them, or in the encouragement to do so in some particular manner, rather than in the quantity of available talent. There is no good reason to assume that Tuscans today are less talented, or even have a less developed aesthetic sense than in the century of the Florentine Renaissance. Talent in the arts abandoned the old ways of seeking expression because new ways were available or attractive, or rewarding, as when, even between the wars, young avant-garde composers might be tempted, like Auric and Britten, to write soundtracks for films rather than string quarters. A great deal of routine painting and drawing was replaced by the triumph of the camera, which, to take one example, took over the representation of fashion almost completely. The serial novel, already a dying breed between the wars, gave way in the age of television to the screen serial. The film, which allowed far greater scope for individual creative talent after the collapse of the Hollywood studio system of factory production, and as the mass cinema audience melted into its homes to watch television and later video, took the place once occupied by both novel and drama. For every culture-lover who could fit two plays to the names of even five living playwrights, there were fifty who could reel off all the leading movies of a dozen or more film-directors. Nothing was more natural than this. Only the social status associated with old-fashioned "high culture" prevented an even more rapid decline of its traditional genres.*

However, there were two even more important factors which now undermined classical high culture. The first was the universal triumph of the society of mass consumption. From the 1960s on the images which accompanied human beings in the Western world—and increasingly in the urbanized Third World—from birth to death were those advertising or embodying consumption or dedicated to commercial mass entertainment. The sounds which accompanied urban life, in and outdoors, were those of commercial pop music. Compared to these the impact of the "high arts" on even the most "cultured" was occasional at best, especially since the technology-based triumph of sound and image put severe pressure on what had been the major medium for the continuous experience of high culture, namely the printed word. Except for light entertainment—mainly love-stories for women, thrillers of various kinds for men and perhaps, in the era of liberalization, some erotica or pornography—people who read books seriously for other than professional, educational or other instructional purposes, were a smallish minority. Though the educational revolution expanded their numbers absolutely, ease of reading declined in countries of theoretically universal literacy, when print ceased to be the main gate to the world beyond mouth-to-ear communication. After the 1950s even the children of the educated classes in the rich Western world did not take to reading as spontaneously as their parents had done.

The words which dominated Western consumer societies were no longer the words of holy books, let alone of secular writers, but the brand-names of goods or whatever else could be bought. They were printed on T-shirts, attached to other garments like magical charms by means of which the wearer acquired the spiritual merit of the (generally youthful) life-style which these names symbolized and promised. The images that became the icons of such societies were those of mass entertainment and mass consumption: stars and cans. It is not surprising that in the 1950s, in the heartland of consumer democracy, the leading school of painters abdicated before image-makers so much more powerful than old-fashioned art. "Pop Art" (Warhol, Lichtenstein, Rauschenberg, Oldenburg), spent its time reproducing, with as much accuracy and insensitivity as possible, the visual trappings of American commercialism: soup cans, flags, Coca-Cola bottles, Marilyn Monroe.

---

*A brilliant French sociologist analysed the use of culture as a class-marker in a book entitled *La Distinction* (Bourdieu, 1979).

Negligible as art (in the nineteenth-century sense of the word), this fashion nevertheless recognized that the triumph of the mass market was, in some profound ways, based on satisfying the spiritual as well as the material needs of consumers, a fact of which advertising agencies had long been vaguely aware when they geared their campaigns to selling "not the steak but the sizzle," not soap but the dream of beauty, not tins of soup but family happiness. What became increasingly clear in the 1950s was that this had what could be called an aesthetic dimension, a grass-roots creativity, occasionally active but mainly passive, which producers had to compete to supply. The baroque excesses of 1950s Detroit automobile design had exactly this in view; and in the 1960s a few intelligent critics began to investigate what had previously been overwhelmingly dismissed and rejected as "commercial" or just aesthetically null, namely what actually attracted men and women on the street (Banham, 1971). The older intellectuals, now increasingly described as "elitist" (a word adopted with enthusiasm by the new radicalism of the 1960s), had looked down on the masses whom they saw as passive recipients of what big business wanted them to buy. Yet the 1950s demonstrated most dramatically through the triumph of rock-and-roll, an adolescents' idiom derived from the self-made urban blues of North American black ghettoes, that the masses themselves knew, or at least recognized what they liked. The recording industry, which made its fortunes from rock music, did not create let alone plan it, but took it over from the amateurs and small street-corner operators who discovered it. No doubt rock music was corrupted in the process. "Art" (if that was the right word) was seen to come from the soil rather than from exceptional flowers growing out of it. Moreover, as the populism shared by both the market and anti-elitist radicalism held, the important thing about it was not to distinguish between good and bad, elaborate and simple, but at most between what appealed to more and fewer people. This did not leave much space for the old-fashioned concept of the arts.

Yet an even more powerful force undermined the high arts: the death of "modernism" which had, since the late nineteenth century, legitimated the practice of non-utilitarian artistic creation and certainly had provided the justification for the artists' claim to freedom from all constraints. Innovation had been its core. On the analogy of science and technology, "Modernity" tacitly assumed that art was progressive and therefore today's style was superior to yesterday's. It had been, by definition, the art of the *avant-garde*, a term which entered critical vocabulary in the 1880s, i.e. of minorities which in theory looked forward one day to capturing the majority, but in practice were happy as yet not to have done so.

Whatever its specific form, "modernism" rested on the rejection of nineteenth-century bourgeois-liberal conventions in both society and art, and on the perceived need to create an art in some way suited to the technologically and socially revolutionary twentieth century, to which the arts and lifestyles of Queen Victoria, the Emperor William and President Theodore Roosevelt were so plainly unsuited (see *Age of Empire*, chapter 9). Ideally the two objectives went together: Cubism was both a rejection and critique of Victorian representative painting and an alternative to it, as well as a collection of "works of art" by "artists" in its and their own right. In practice they did not have to coincide, as the (deliberate) artistic nihilism of Marcel Duchamp's urinal and Dada had demonstrated long ago. These were not intended to be any kind of art, but anti-art. Again, ideally the social values which "modernist" artists looked for in the twentieth century and the ways of expressing these in word, sound, image and shape should melt into each other, as they very largely did in modernist architecture, which was essentially a style for building social utopias in forms allegedly suited to it. Once again, in practice form and substance were not logically connected. Why, for instance, should Le Corbusier's "radiant city" (*cité radieuse*) consist of high-rise buildings with flat roofs rather than pitched ones?

Nevertheless, as we have seen, in the first half of the century "modernism" worked, the feebleness of its theoretical foundations unnoticed, the short distance to the limits of development permitted by its formulas (e.g. twelve-tone music or abstract art) not yet quite traversed, its fabric uncracked as yet by inner contradictions or potential fissures. Formal avant-garde innovation and social hope were still welded together by the experience of world war, world crisis and potential world revolution. The era of anti-fascism postponed reflection. Modernism still belonged to avant-garde and opposition, except among the industrial designers and advertising agencies. It had not won.

Except in the socialist regimes it shared the victory over Hitler. Modernism in art and architecture conquered the U.S.A., filling the galleries and prestige corporation offices with "abstract expressionists," and the business districts of American cities with the symbols of the "international style"—elongated rectangular boxes standing on end, not so much scraping the sky as flattening their roofs against it: with great elegance, as in Mies van der Rohe's Seagram building, or just very high, like the World Trade Center (both in New York). On the old Continent, to some extent following the American trend, which now inclined to associate modernism with "Western values," abstraction ("non-figurative art") in the visual arts and modernism in architecture became part, sometimes the dominant part, of the established cultural scene, even reviving in countries like Britain, where it had seemed to stagnate.

Yet from the end of the 1960s a marked reaction against it became increasingly manifest and, in the 1980s, fashionable under such labels as "postmodernism." It was not so much a "movement" as a denial of any pre-established criteria of judgment and value in the arts, or indeed of the possibility of such judgments. In architecture, where this reaction first and most visibly made itself felt, it surmounted skyscrapers with Chippendale pediments, all the more provocative for having been built by the very co-inventor of the term "international style," Philip Johnson (1906–). Critics for whom the spontaneously shaped Manhattan skyline had once been the model of the modern city-scape, discovered the virtues of the totally unstructured Los Angeles, a desert of detail without shape, the paradise (or hell) of those who "did their own thing." Irrational though they were, aesthetic-moral rules had governed modern architecture, but henceforth anything went.

The achievement of the modern movement in architecture had been impressive. It had, since 1945, built the airports that bound the world together, its factories, its office buildings and such public buildings as still needed to be erected—capital cities in the Third World, museums, universities and theatres in the First. It had presided over the massive and global rebuilding of cities in the 1960s, for even in the socialist world its technical innovations, which lent themselves to cheap and rapid construction of mass housing, left their mark. It had, without serious doubt, produced a substantial number of very beautiful buildings or even masterpieces, though also a number of ugly ones and very many more faceless and inhuman ant-boxes. The achievements of post-war modernist painting and sculpture were incomparably less and usually much inferior to their inter-war predecessors, as a comparison of Parisian art in the 1950s with that of the 1920s immediately demonstrates. It consisted largely of a series of increasingly desperate gimmicks by which artists sought to give their work an immediately recognizable individual trademark, a succession of manifestos of despair or abdication in the face of the floods of non-art which submerged the old-style artist (pop art, Dubuffet's *art brut* and the like), the assimilation of doodles and other bits and pieces, or of gestures reducing the sort of art which was primarily bought for investment and its collectors *ad absurdum*, as by adding an individual's name to piles of brick or soil ("minimal art") or by preventing it from becoming such a commodity through making it too short-lived to be permanent ("performance art").

The smell of impending death rose from these avant-gardes. The future was no longer theirs, though nobody knew whose it was. More than ever, they knew themselves to be on the margin. Compared to the real revolution in perception and representation achieved via technology by the money-makers, the formal innovations of studio bohemians had always been child's play. What were the Futurists' imitations of speed on canvas compared to real speed, or even to mounting a film camera on a locomotive footplate, which anyone could do? What were concert experiments with electronic sound in modernist compositions, which every impresario knew to be box office poison, compared to rock music which made electronic sound into the music of the millions? If all "high arts" were segregated in ghettos, could the avant-gardes fail to observe that their own sections of the ghetto were tiny and diminishing, as any comparison of the sales of Chopin and Schönberg confirmed? With the rise of pop art, even the major rampart of modernism in the visual arts, abstraction, lost its hegemony. Representation once again became legitimate.

"Postmodernism" therefore attacked both self-confident and exhausted styles, or rather the ways of conducting both activities which had to go on, in one style or another, like building and public works, and those which were not in themselves indispensable, like the artisan production of easel paintings to be sold singly. Hence it would be misleading to analyse it primarily as a trend within the arts, like the development of the earlier avant-gardes. Actually, we know that the term "postmodernism" spread to all manner of fields that had nothing to do with the arts. By the 1990s there were "postmodern" philosophers, social scientists, anthropologists, historians and other practitioners of disciplines that had not previously tended to borrow their terminology from the arts avant-garde, even when they happened to be associated with them. Literary criticism, of course, adopted it with enthusiasm. In fact "postmodern" fashions, pioneered under various names ("deconstruction," "post-structuralism," etc.) among the French-speaking intelligentsia, made their way into (U.S.) departments of literature and thence into the rest of the humanities and social sciences.

All "postmodernisms" had in common an essential scepticism about the existence of an objective reality, and/or the possibility of arriving at an agreed understanding of it by rational means. All tended to a radical relativism. All, therefore, challenged the essence of a world that rested on the opposite assumptions, namely the world transformed by science and the technology based upon it, and the ideology of progress which reflected it. We shall consider the development of this strange, yet not unexpected contradiction in the next chapter. Within the more restricted field of the high arts, the contradiction was not so extreme since, as we have seen (*Age of Empire*, chapter 9), the modernist avant-gardes had already extended the limits of what could claim to be "art" (or, at any rate, yield products that could be sold or leased or otherwise profitably separated from their creators as "art") almost to infinity. What "postmodernism" produced was rather a (largely generational) gap between those who were repelled by what they saw as the nihilist frivolity of the new mode and those who thought taking the arts "seriously" was just one more relic of the obsolete past. What, they argued, was wrong with "the refuse dumps of civilization . . . camouflaged with plastic" which so outraged the social philosopher Jürgen Habermas, last outpost of the famous Frankfurt School? (Hughes, 1988, p. 146).

"Postmodernism" was therefore not confined to the arts. Nevertheless, there were probably good reasons why the term should have first emerged from the art scene. For the very essence of the avant-garde arts was the search for ways of expressing what could not possibly be expressed in terms of the past, namely the reality of the twentieth century. This was one of the two branches of that century's great dream, the other being the search for the radical transformation of that reality. Both were revolutionary in different senses of the word, but both were about the same world. Both coincided to some extent in the 1880s and 1890s, and again between 1914 and the defeat of fascism, when creative talents were so often revolutionary, or at least radical, in both senses—usually but by no means always on the Left. Both were to fail, although in fact both have modified the world of 2000 so profoundly that their marks cannot conceivably be effaced.

In retrospect it is clear that the project of avant-garde revolution was doomed to failure from the outset, both by virtue of its intellectual arbitrariness and by the nature of the mode of production the creative arts represented in a liberal bourgeois society. Almost any of the numerous manifestos by means of which avant-garde artists have announced their intentions in the course of the past hundred years demonstrate the lack of coherence between ends and means, the object and the methods of achieving it. A particular version of novelty is not the necessary consequence of choosing to reject the old. Music which deliberately avoids tonality is not necessarily Schönberg's serial music, based on the permutations of the twelve notes of the chromatic scale; nor is this the only basis for serial music; nor is serial music necessarily atonal. Cubism, however attractive, had no theoretical rationale whatever. Indeed, the very decision to abandon traditional procedures and rules for new ones may be as arbitrary as the choice of particular novelties. The equivalent of "modernism" in chess, the so-called "hyper-modern" school of players of the 1920s

(Réti, Grünfeld, Nimzowitsch, et al.) did not propose to change the rules of the game, as some did. They merely reacted against convention (the "classical" school of Tarrasch) by exploiting paradox—choosing unconventional openings ("After 1, P-K4 White's game is in the last throes") and observing rather than occupying the centre. Most writers, and certainly most poets, in practice did the same. They went on accepting the traditional procedures, e.g. rhymed and metred verse where it seemed appropriate, and broke with convention in other ways. Kafka was not less "modern" than Joyce because his prose was less adventurous. Moreover, where modernist style claimed to have an intellectual rationale, e.g. as expressing the era of the machine or of (later) the computer, the connection was purely metaphorical. In any case, the attempt to assimilate "the work of art in the era of its technical reproducibility" (Benjamin, 1961) to the old model of the individual creative artist recognizing only his personal inspiration was bound to fail. Creation was now essentially cooperative rather than individual, technological rather than manual. The young French film critics who, in the 1950s, developed a theory of film as the work of a single creative *auteur*, the director, on the basis, of all things, of a passion for the Hollywood B-movies of the 1930s and 1940s, were absurd because coordinated cooperation and division of labour was and is the essence of those whose business is to fill the evenings on public and private screens, or to produce some other regular succession of works for mental consumption, such as newspapers or magazines. The talents that went into the characteristic forms of twentieth-century creation, which were mainly products for, or by-products of the mass market, were not inferior to those of the classic nineteenth-century bourgeois model, but they could no longer afford the classical artist's role of the loner. Their only direct link with their classic predecessors was through that limited sector of the classic "high arts" which had always operated through collectives: the stage. If Akira Kurosawa (1910–), Luchino Visconti (1906–76) or Sergei Eisenstein (1898–1948)—to name only three unquestionably very great artists of the century, all with a theatrical background—had wished to create in the manner of Flaubert, Courbet or even Dickens, none of them would have got very far.

Yet, as Walter Benjamin observed, the era of "technical reproducibility" transformed not only the way in which creation took place—thus making the film, and all that derived from it (television, video) into the central art of the century—but also the way in which human beings perceived reality and experienced creative works. This was no longer by means of those acts of secular worship and prayer for which the museums, galleries, concert halls and public theatres, that were so typical of nineteenth-century bourgeois civilization, provided the churches. Tourism, which now filled these establishments with foreigners rather than natives, and education were the last strongholds of this sort of art-consumption. The numbers undergoing these experiences were, of course, enormously larger than ever before, but even most of these who, after elbowing themselves to within sight of the *Primavera* in the Florence Uffizi, stood in silent awe, or who were moved as they read Shakespeare as part of the examination syllabus, usually lived in a different multifarious and motley universe of perception. Sense impressions, even ideas, were apt to reach them simultaneously from all sides—through the combination of headlines and pictures, text and advertisement on the newspaper page, the sound in the earphone as the eye scanned the page, through the juxtaposition of image, voice, print and sound—all, as like as not, taken in peripherally, unless, for a moment, something concentrated attention. This had long been the way in which city people experienced the street, in which popular fairground and circus entertainment operated, familiar to artists and critics since the days of the Romantics. The novelty was that technology had drenched everyday life in private as well as in public with art. Never had it been harder to avoid aesthetic experience. The "work of art" was lost in the flow of words, of sounds, of images, in the universal environment of what would once have been called art.

Could it still be so called? For those who cared for such things, great and lasting works could still be identified, though in the developed parts of the world the works exclusively created by a single individual and identifiable only with him or her became increasingly marginal. And so, with the exception of buildings, did single works of creation or construction that were not designed for reproduction. Could it still be judged and graded by the standards which had governed the assessment of these matters in the great days of bourgeois civilization? Yes and no. Measuring merit by chronology had never suited the arts: creative works had never been better merely because they were old, as was thought in the Renaissance, or because they were more recent than others, as the avant-gardes held. The latter criterion became absurd in the later twentieth century, when it merged with the economic interests of consumer industries, which made their profits out of a short fashion-cycle, and instant mass sales of articles for intensive but brief use.

On the other hand it was still both possible and necessary to apply the distinction between what was serious and what was trivial, between good and bad, professional and amateur in the arts, and all the more necessary because a number of interested parties denied such distinctions, on the grounds that the only measure of merit was the sales figure, or that they were elitist, or that, as postmodernism argued, no objective distinctions could be made at all. Indeed, only the ideologists and salesmen held such absurd views in public, and in their private capacity even most of these knew that they distinguished between good and bad. In 1991 a highly successful British mass market jeweller created a scandal by telling a conference of businessmen that his profits came from selling crap to people who had no taste for anything better. He, unlike postmodern theorists, knew that judgments of quality were part of life.

But if such judgments were still possible, were they still relevant to the world in which, for most urban citizens, the spheres of life and art, of emotion generated from within and emotion generated from without, or work and leisure, were increasingly indistinguishable? Or rather, were they still relevant outside the specialized enclosures of school and academia in which so much of the traditional arts were seeking refuge? It is difficult to say, because the very attempt to answer or to formulate such a question may beg it. It is quite easy to write the history of jazz or to discuss its achievements in terms quite similar to those applicable to classical music, allowing for the considerable difference in the social milieu, and the public and the economics of this form of art. It is by no means clear that such a procedure makes any sense for rock music, even though this is also derived from American black music. What the achievements of Louis Armstrong or Charlie Parker are, and their superiority over other contemporaries is or can be made clear. On the other hand it seems far more difficult for someone who has not fused a particular sound with his or her life, to pick out this or that rock group from the huge flood of sound which has swept down the valley of this music for the past forty years. Billie Holiday has (at least, until the time of writing) been able to communicate with listeners who were born many years after she died. Can anyone who was not a contemporary of the Rolling Stones develop anything like the passionate enthusiasm which this group aroused in the middle 1960s? How much of the passion for some sound or image today is based on association: not because the song is admirable but because "this is our song"? We cannot tell. The role, or even the survival, of living arts in the twenty-first century are obscure until we can.

This is not the case with the roles of the sciences.

CHAPTER EIGHTEEN

Sorcerers and Apprentices—
The Natural Sciences

Do you think there is a place for philosophy in today's world?

Of, course, but only if it is based on the current state of scientific knowledge and achievement . . . Philosophers cannot insulate themselves against science. Not only has it enlarged and transformed our vision of life and the universe enormously: it has also revolutionized the rules by which the intellect operates.

—Claude Lévi-Strauss (1988)

The standard text in gas dynamics written by its author while on a Guggenheim Fellowship has been described by him as having had its form dictated by the needs of industry. Within this framework, confirming Einstein's theory of general relativity came to be seen as a critical step toward improving "ballistic missille accuracy by accounting for minute gravitational effects." Increasingly post-war physics narrowed its concentration into those areas thought to have military applications.

—Margaret Jacob (1993, pp. 66–7)

I

No period in history has been more penetrated by and more dependent on the natural sciences than the twentieth century. Yet no period, since Galileo's recantation, has been less at ease with it. This is the paradox with which the historian of the century must grapple. But before I try to do so, the dimensions of the phenomenon must be recognized.

In 1910 all the German and British physicists and chemists put together amounted to perhaps eight thousand people. In the late 1980s the number of scientists and engineers actually engaged in research and experimental development in the world was estimated at about five *millions*, of whom almost one million were in the U.S.A., the leading scientific power, and a slightly larger number in the states of Europe.* Though scientists continued to form a tiny fraction of the population, even in the developed countries, their numbers continued to rise quite dramatically, more or less doubling in the twenty years after 1970, even in the most advanced economies. However, by the late 1980s they formed the tip of a much larger iceberg of what could be called potential scientific and technological manpower, which essentially reflected the educational revolution of the second half of the century (see chapter 10). It represented perhaps 2 per cent of the global population, and perhaps 5 per cent of the North American population (UNESCO, 1991, Table 5.1). The actual scientists were increasingly selected by means of an advanced "doctoral thesis" which became the ticket of entry to the profession. In the 1980s the typical advanced Western country generated something like the 130–140 such science doctorates per year for each million of its inhabitants (Observatoire, 1991). Such countries also spent, mainly from public funds—even in the most capitalist countries—quite astronomic sums on such activities. Indeed, the most expensive forms of "big science" were beyond the scope of any single country except (until the 1990s) the U.S.A.

There was, however, one major novelty. In spite of the fact that 90 per cent of scientific papers (whose numbers doubled every ten years) appeared in four languages (English, Russian, French and German), Eurocentric science ended in the twentieth century. The Age of Catastrophe, and especially the temporary triumph of fascism, transferred its centre of gravity to the U.S.A., where it has remained. Between 1900 and 1933 only seven science Nobel prizes were awarded to the U.S.A., but between 1933 and 1970 seventy-seven. The other countries of European settlement also established themselves as independent centres of research—Canada, Australia, the often under-rated Argentina†—though some, for reasons of size or politics, exported most of their major scientists (New Zealand, South Africa). At the same time the rise of non-European scientists, especially those from East Asia and the Indian subcontinent, was striking. Before the end of the Second World War only one Asian had won a science Nobel prize (C. Raman in physics, 1930); since 1946 such prizes

---

*The even larger number in the then U.S.S.R. (about 1.5 millions) was probably not entirely comparable (UNESCO, 1991, Tables 5.2, 5.4, 5.16).

†Three Nobel prizes, all since 1947.

have been awarded to more than ten workers with obviously Japanese, Chinese, Indian and Pakistani names, and this clearly under-estimates the rise of Asian science as much as the pre-1933 record under-estimated the rise of U.S. science. However, at the end of the century there were still parts of the world which generated notably few scientists in absolute terms and even more markedly in relative terms, e.g. most of Africa and Latin America.

Yet it is a striking fact that (at least) a third of the Asian laureates do not appear under their own country of origin, but as U.S. scientists. (Indeed, of the U.S. laureates twenty-seven are first-generation immigrants.) For, in an increasingly globalized world, the very fact that the natural sciences speak a single universal language and operate under a single methodology has paradoxically helped to concentrate them in the relatively few centres with adequate resources for their development, i.e. in a few highly developed rich states, and above all in the U.S.A. The brains of the world, which in the Age of Catastrophe fled from Europe for political reasons, have since 1945 drained from poorer to richer countries mainly for economic ones.* This is natural, since in the 1970s and 1980s the developed capitalist countries spent almost three-quarters of all the world's outlays on research and development, whereas the poor countries ("developing") spent no more than 2–3 per cent (U.N. World Social Situation 1989, p. 103).

Yet, even within the developed world, science gradually lost dispersion, partly because of the concentration of people and resources—for reasons of efficiency—partly because the enormous growth in higher education inevitably created a hierarchy or, rather, an oligarchy among its institutes. In the 1950s and 1960s half the doctorates in the United States came from the fifteen most prestigious university graduate schools, to which the ablest young scientists consequently flocked. In a democratic and populist world, scientists were an elite, concentrated in a relatively few subsidized centres. As a species, they occurred in groups, for communication ("someone to talk to") was central to their activities. As time went on, these activities became ever more incomprehensible to nonscientists, though laymen tried desperately to understand, with the help of a large literature of popularization, sometimes written by the best scientists themselves. Indeed, as specialization grew, even scientists increasingly

---

*A small temporary drain out of the U.S.A. during the McCarthyite years may be noted, and larger occasional political flights from the Soviet region (Hungary 1956, Poland and Czechoslovakia 1968, China and the U.S.S.R. at the end of the 1980s), as well as a steady drain from the German Democratic Republic to West Germany

required journals to explain to each other what was happening outside their own field.

That the twentieth century depended on science hardly needs proof. "Advanced" science, that is to say, the kind of knowledge which could neither be acquired by everyday experience, nor practised nor even understood without many years of schooling, culminating in esoteric postgraduate training, had only a comparatively narrow range of practical applications until the end of the nineteenth century. The physics and mathematics of the seventeenth century governed the engineers, while, by the middle of Victoria's reign, chemical and electrical discoveries of the late eighteenth and early nineteenth centuries were already essential to industry and communications, and the explorations of professional scientific researchers were recognized as the necessary spearhead of even technological advance. In short, science-based technology was already at the core of the nineteenth-century bourgeois world, even though practical people did not quite know what to do with the triumphs of scientific theory except, in suitable cases, to turn them into ideology: as the eighteenth century had done with Newton and the late nineteenth century did with Darwin. Nevertheless, vast areas of human life continued to be ruled by little more than experience, experiment, skill, trained common sense and, at most, the systematic diffusion of knowledge about the best available practices and techniques. This was plainly the case in farming, building and medicine, and indeed over a vast range of activities which supplied human beings with their needs and luxuries.

Some time in the last third of the century this had begun to change. In the Age of Empire not only do the outlines of modern high technology begin to be visible—one has only to think of automobiles, aviation, radio and film—but so do those of modern scientific theory: relativity, the quantum, genetics. Moreover, the most esoteric and revolutionary discoveries of science were now seen to have immediate technological potential, from wireless telegraphy to the medical use of X-rays, both based on discoveries of the 1890s. Nevertheless, while the high science of the Short Twentieth Century was already visible before 1914, and while the high technology of the later century was already implicit in it, high science was not yet something without which everyday life *everywhere* on the globe was inconceivable.

This is the case as the millennium draws to its close. As we have seen (see chapter 9), technology based on advanced scientific theory and research, dominated the economic boom of the second half of the twentieth century, and no longer only in the developed world. Without state-of-the-art genetics India and Indonesia could not have produced enough food for their exploding populations, and by the end of the century biotechnology had become a significant element in both agriculture and medicine. The point about such technologies is that they were based on discoveries and theories so far from the world of the ordinary inhabitant of even the most sophisticated of developed countries that barely a few dozen or, at most, a few hundred persons in the world could initially grasp that they had practical implications. When the German physicist Otto Hahn discovered nuclear fission in 1937 even some of the scientists most active in the field, such as the great Niels Bohr (1885–1962), doubted that it had practical applications in peace or war, at all events for the foreseeable future. And if the physicists who understood its potential had not told their generals and politicians, these would certainly have remained in ignorance, unless they were themselves postgraduate physicists, which was very unlikely. Again, Alan Turing's celebrated paper of 1935, which was to provide the foundation of modern computer theory, was originally written as a speculative exploration for mathematical logicians. The war gave him and others the occasion to translate theory into the beginnings of practice for the purpose of code-breaking, but when it appeared nobody except a handful of mathematicians even read, let alone took notice of Turing's paper. Even in his own college this clumsy-looking pale-faced genius, then a junior fellow with a taste for jogging, who posthumously became a sort of icon among homosexuals, was not a figure of any prominence; at least I do not remember him as such.* Even when scientists were plainly engaged in trying to solve problems of acknowledged capital importance, only a small huddle of brains in an isolated intellectual corner recognized what they were up to. Thus the present author was a Fellow of a Cambridge college at the very time when Crick and Watson were preparing their triumphant discovery of the structure of DNA (the "Double Helix"), immediately recognized as

_____

*Turing committed suicide in 1954, after having been convicted of homosexual behaviour, then officially a crime, and believed to be a medically or psychologically curable pathological condition. He could not stand the compulsory "cure" imposed on him. He was not so much a victim of the criminalization of (male) homosexuality in Britain before the 1960s as of his own failure to recognize it. His sexual proclivities had raised no problem whatever in the milieu of boarding school, King's College, Cambridge, and among the notorious collection of anomalies and eccentrics in the wartime code-breaking establishment at Bletchley, in which he had passed his life before going to Manchester after the war. Only a man who did not quite recognize the world most people lived in would have gone to the police to complain that a (temporary) boy-friend had robbed his apartment, thus giving the police the opportunity to catch two legal delinquents at the same time.

one of the crucial breakthroughs of the century. Yet, though I even recall meeting Crick socially at the time, most of us were simply not aware that these extraordinary developments were being hatched within a few tens of yards of my college gates, in laboratories we passed regularly and pubs where we drank. It was not that we took no interest in such matters. Those who pursued them simply saw no point in telling us about them, since we could not have contributed to their work, or probably even understood exactly what their difficulties were.

Nevertheless, however esoteric and incomprehensible the innovations of science, once made they were almost immediately translated into practical technologies. Thus transistors emerged as a by-product of researches in solid-state physics, i.e. the electro-magnetic properties of slightly imperfect crystals in 1948 (their inventors were given Nobel prizes within eight years), as did lasers (1960), which came not from optical studies but from work to make molecules vibrate in resonance with an electric field (Bernal, 1967, p. 563). Their inventors were also quickly recognized by Nobel prizes, as was—belatedly—the Cambridge and Soviet physicist Peter Kapitsa (1978) for work in low-temperature physics which produced superconductors. The experience of wartime research in 1939–46, which demonstrated—at least to the Anglo-Americans—that an overwhelming concentration of resources could solve the most difficult technological problems within an improbably short time,* encouraged technological pioneering regardless of cost, for purposes of war or national prestige (e.g. the exploration of cosmic space). This, in turn, accelerated the transformation of laboratory science into technology, some of which proved to have a wide potential for everyday use. Lasers are an example of this speed. First seen in the laboratory in 1960, they had by the early 1980s reached the consumer in the form of the compact disc. Biotechnology was even quicker off the mark. Recombinant DNA techniques, i.e. techniques for combining genes from one species with those of another, were first recognized as adequately practicable in 1973. Less than twenty years later biotechnology was a staple of medical and agricultural investment.

Moreover, thanks largely to the astonishing explosion of information

---

*Essentially it is now clear that Nazi Germany failed to make a nuclear bomb not because German scientists did not know how it could be made, or try to make it, with different degrees of reluctance, but because the German war-machine was unwilling or unable to devote the necessary resources to it. They abandoned the effort and switched to what seemed the more cost-effective concentration on rocketry, which promised quicker returns.

theory and practice, new scientific advances were translated, with ever-diminishing time-lags, into a technology that required no understanding whatever by the end-users. The ideal result was an entirely idiot-proof set of buttons or a keyboard which only required pressing in the right places to activate a self-acting, self-correcting and, so far as possible, decision-taking procedure which required no further inputs from the limited and unreliable skills and intelligence of the average human being. Indeed, ideally the procedure could be programmed to do without human intervention entirely, except when something went wrong. The supermarket check-out of the 1990s typified this elimination of the human element. It required no more of the human operator than to recognize the notes and coins of the local currency and to key in the quantity offered by the customer. An automatic scanner translated the bar-code on the purchase into a price, added up all the purchase prices, deducted the total from the amount offered by the customer and told the operator how much change to give. The procedure for ensuring the performance of all these activities is extraordinarily complex, resting as it does on a combination of enormously sophisticated hardware and very elaborate programming. Yet, unless or until something went wrong, such miracles of late twentieth-century scientific technology required no more of the operators than the recognition of the cardinal numbers, a minimal attention span and a rather greater capacity for concentrated tolerance of boredom. It did not even require literacy. So far as most operators were concerned, the forces which told them to inform the customer that he or she had to pay £2.15 and instructed them to offer £7.85 as change for a £10 note, were as irrelevant as they were incomprehensible. They did not have to understand anything about them to operate them. The sorcerer's apprentice no longer had to worry about his or her lack of knowledge.

For practical purposes the situation of the supermarket check-out operator represented the human norm of the late twentieth century; the operation of miracles of avant-garde scientific technology which we do not need to understand or modify, even if we know, or think we know, what is going on. Someone else will do or has done it for us. For, even if we suppose ourselves to be experts in one special field or another—i.e. the sort of person who could put the device right if it went wrong, or could design or construct it—faced with most of the other everyday products of science and technology, we are ignorant and uncomprehending laymen and lay women. And even if we were not, our understanding of what makes the thing we use work, and of the principles behind it, is largely irrelevant knowledge, as the technical process for manufacturing playing cards is to the (honest) poker-player. Fax machines are designed to be used by people who have no idea why the machine in London reproduces a text fed into it in Los Angeles. They do not function better when operated by professors of electronics.

Thus science, through the technology-saturated fabric of human life, demonstrates its miracles daily to the late twentieth-century world. It is as indispensable and omnipresent—for even the remoter corners of humanity know the transistor radio and the electronic calculator—as Allah is to the pious Muslim. We may debate when this capacity of certain human activities to produce superhuman results became part of the common consciousness, at least in the urban parts of "developed" industrial societies. It certainly did so after the explosion of the first nuclear bomb in 1945. However, there can be no doubt that the twentieth century was the one in which science transformed both the world and our knowledge of it.

We should have expected the ideologies of the twentieth century to glory in the triumphs of science, which are the triumphs of the human mind, as the secular ideologies of the nineteenth century had done. Indeed, we should have expected even the resistance of traditional religious ideologies, the great redoubts of nineteenth-century resistance to science, to weaken. For not only did the hold of traditional religions slacken over most of the century, as we shall see, but religion itself became as dependent on high-science-based technology as any other human activity in the developed world. At a pinch, a bishop or imam or holy man in the 1900s could have conducted his activities as though Galileo, Newton, Faraday or Lavoisier had not existed, i.e. on the basis of fifteenth-century technology, and such nineteenth-century technology has raised no problems of compatability with theology or holy texts. It became far harder to overlook the conflict between science and holy writ in an age when the Vatican was obliged to communicate by satellite and to test the authenticity of the Turin shroud by radio-carbon dating: when the Ayatollah Khomeini spread his words from abroad into Iran by means of tape-cassettes, and when states dedicated to the laws of the Koran were also engaged in trying to equip themselves with nuclear weapons. The *de facto* acceptance of the most sophisticated contemporary science, via the technology which depended on it, was such that in *fin-de-siècle* New York the sales of super-high-tech electronic and photographic goods became largely the specialty of Chassidim, a brand of eastern messianic Judaism chiefly known, apart from their extreme ritualism and insistence on wearing a version of eighteenth-century Polish costume, by a preference for ecstatic emotion over intellectual enquiry. In some ways the superiority of "science" was even accepted officially. The Protestant fundamentalists in the U.S.A. who rejected the theory of evolution as unscriptural (the world having been created in its present version in six days) demanded that Darwin's teaching should be replaced, or at least countered by the teaching of what they described as "creation science."

And yet, the twentieth century was not at ease with the science which was its most extraordinary achievement, and on which it depended. The progress of the natural sciences took place against a background glow of suspicion and fear, occasionally flaring up into flames of hatred and rejection of reason and all its products. And in the undefined space between science and anti-science, among the searchers for ultimate truth by absurdity and the prophets of a world composed exclusively of fictions, we increasingly find that characteristic and largely Anglo-American product of the century, and especially of its second half, "science fiction." The genre, anticipated by Jules Verne (1828–1905) was initiated by H. G. Wells (1866–1946) at the very end of the nineteenth century. While its more juvenile forms, such as the familiar TV and wide-screen space-westerns with cosmic capsules as horses and death-rays as six-shooters, continued the old tradition of fantastic adventures with high-tech gadgets, in the second half of the century the more serious contributions to the genre veered towards a gloomy or at least an ambiguous view of the human condition and its prospects.

The suspicion and fear of science was fuelled by four feelings: that science was incomprehensible; that both its practical and moral consequences were unpredictable and probably catastrophic; and that it underlined the helplessness of the individual, and undermined authority. Nor should we overlook the sentiment that, to the extent that science interfered with the natural order of things, it was inherently dangerous. The first two feelings were shared by both scientists and laymen, the last two belonged mainly to outsiders. Lay individuals could only react against their sense of impotence by seeking out things which "science could not explain" along the lines of Hamlet's "There are more things in heaven and earth . . . than are dreamt of in your philosophy," by refusing to believe that they could ever be explained by "official science," by hungering to believe in the inexplicable *because* it seemed absurd. At least in an unknown and unknowable world everyone would be equally powerless. The greater the palpable triumphs of science, the greater the hunger to seek the inexplicable. Shortly after the Second World War, which culminated in the atom bomb, Americans (1947), later followed as usual by their cultural followers the British, took to observing the mass arrival of "unidentified flying objects," plainly inspired by science fiction. These, it was firmly believed, came from extra-terrestrial civilizations different from and superior to ours. The more enthusiastic observers had actually seen their strangely shaped denizens emerging from these "flying saucers," and one or two even claimed to have been given rides by them. The phenomenon became world-wide, although a distribution-map of the landings of these extra-terrestrials would show a heavy preference for landing on or circling over Anglo-Saxon territories. Any scepticism about UFOs was put down to the jealousy of narrow-minded scientists helpless to explain phenomena beyond their narrow horizons, perhaps even to a conspiracy of those who kept the common man in intellectual bondage to conceal superior wisdom from him.

These were not the beliefs in magic and miracles of traditional societies, for which such interventions in reality were part of very incompletely controllable lives, and much less amazing than, say, the sight of an airplane or the experience of speaking into a telephone. Nor were they part of the universal and permanent fascination of human beings with the monstrous, the freakish and the marvellous to which popular literature bears witness since the invention of printing, from broadsheet woodcut to U.S. supermarket check-out magazine. They were a rejection of the claims and the rule of science, sometimes consciously so, as in the extraordinary (and once again U.S.-centred) rebellion of fringe groups against the practice of putting fluoride into the water supply after it had been discovered that an intake of this element would dramatically reduce dental decay in modern urban populations. It was passionately resisted not merely in the name of the freedom to choose caries but (by its more extreme opponents) as a dastardly plot to enfeeble human beings by compulsory poisoning. And in this reaction, vividly brought to life in Stanley Kubrik's film *Dr. Strangelove* (1963), suspicion of science as such merged with fear of its practical consequences.

The built-in valetudinarianism of North American culture also spread such fears, as life was increasingly submerged by modern technology, including medical technology, with its risks. The unusual fondness of the U.S.A. for letting litigation answer all matters in human dispute, allows us to monitor these fears (Huber, 1990, pp. 97–118). Did spermicides cause birth defects? Did electric power-lines cause medical harm to people who lived near them? The gap between experts, who had some criterion for judgment, and lay persons, who had only hope or fear, was widened by the difference between dispassionate assessment, which might well judge a small degree of risk to be a price worth paying for a large degree of benefit, and individuals who, understandably, desired zero risk (at least in theory).*

---

*The difference between theory and practice in this area is enormous, since people who are prepared to run quite significant risks in practice (e.g. being in a car

In effect, such fears were the fears of the unknown menace of science by men and women who only knew that they lived under its dominion; fears whose intensity and focus differed according to the nature of their views, and fears about contemporary society (Fischhof et al., 1978, pp. 127–52).*

However, in the first half of the century, the major hazards to science came not from those who felt humbled by its unlimited and uncontrollable powers but from those who thought they could control them. The only two types of political regimes (apart from the then rare reversions to religious fundamentalism) which interfered with scientific research *on principle* were both deeply committed to technical progress without limit and, in one case, to an ideology which identified it with "science" and hailed the conquest of the world by reason and experiment. Yet in different ways both Stalinism and German National Socialism rejected science even as they used it for technological purposes. What they objected to was its challenge to world-views and values expressed in *a priori* truths.

Thus neither regime felt at ease with post-Einsteinian physics. The Nazis rejected it as "Jewish" and the Soviet ideologists as insufficiently "materialist" in Lenin's sense of the word, though both tolerated it in practice, since modern states could not do without the physicists who were post-Einsteinians to a man or woman. The National Socialists, however, deprived themselves of the flower of continental Europe's physical talent by driving Jews and ideological opponents into exile, incidentally destroying the early twentieth-century German scientific supremacy in the process. Between 1900 and 1933 twenty-five out of sixty-six Nobel prizes in Physics and Chemistry had gone to Germany, but since 1933 only about one in ten. Neither regime was in tune with the biological sciences either. Nazi Germany's racial policies horrified serious geneticists, who—largely because of racists' enthusiasm for eugenics—had begun after the First World War to put some distance between themselves and policies of human genetic selection and breeding

---

on a motorway or using the subway in New York) may insist on avoiding aspirin on the grounds that it has side-effects in some rather rare cases.

*Participants rated the risks and benefits of twenty-five technologies: refrigerators, photocopy machines, contraceptives, suspension bridges, nuclear power, electronic games, diagnostic X-rays, nuclear weapons, computers, vaccinations, water fluoridation, roof-top solar collectors, lasers, tranquillizers, Polaroid photographs, fossil electric power, motor vehicles, movie special effects, pesticides, opiates, food preservatives, open-heart surgery, commercial aviation, genetic engineering and windmills (also Wildavsky, 1990, pp. 41–60).

(which included the killing of the "unfit"), although it must be sadly admitted that there was a good deal of support for National Socialist racism among German biologists and medical men (Proctor, 1988). The Soviet regime, under Stalin, found itself at odds with genetics both for ideological reasons and because state policy was committed to the principle that, with sufficient effort, *any* change was achievable, whereas science pointed out that, in the field of evolution in general and agriculture in particular this was not the case. In other circumstances the controversy among evolutionary biologists between the followers of Darwin (for whom inheritance was genetic) and those of Lamarck (who had believed in the inheritance of characteristics acquired and practised during a creature's lifetime) would have been left to be settled in seminars and laboratories. Indeed, it was regarded by most scientists as settled in favour of Darwin, if only because no satisfactory evidence for the inheritance of acquired characteristics had ever been found. Under Stalin, a fringe biologist, Trofim Denisovich Lysenko (1898–1976), won the support of the political authorities with the argument that farm output could be multiplied by Lamarckian procedures which short-circuited the relatively slow processes of orthodox plant- and animal-breedings. In those days it was unwise to disagree with authority. Academician Nikolai Ivanovich Vavilov (1885–1943), the most famous of Soviet geneticists, died in a labour camp for disagreeing with Lysenko (a view shared by the rest of serious Soviet geneticists), though it was not until after the Second World War that Soviet biology was officially committed to the obligatory rejection of genetics, as understood in the rest of the world, at least until after the dictator's demise. The effect of such policies on Soviet science was, predictably, disastrous.

Regimes of the National Socialist and Soviet communist type, utterly different as they were in many respects, shared the belief that their citizens were supposed to assent to a "true doctrine," but one formulated and imposed by the secular politico/ideological authorities. Hence the ambiguity and uneasiness about science, which was felt in so many societies, found *official* expression in such states, unlike in political regimes which were agnostic about their citizens' individual beliefs, as secular governments had learned to be during the long nineteenth century. In fact, the rise of regimes of secular orthodoxy was, as we have seen (see chapters 4 and 13), a by-product of the Age of Catastrophe, and they did not last. In any case, the attempt to force science into ideological straitjackets was plainly counter-productive, where it was seriously made (as in Soviet biology), or ridiculous, where science was left to go its own way, while the superiority of ideology was merely asserted (as in both German and Soviet physics).* The official imposition of criteria for scientific theory in the later twentieth century was once again left to regimes based on religious fundamentalism. Nevertheless, the uneasiness persisted, not least because science itself became increasingly incredible and uncertain. But until the second half of the century it was not due to fear of the practical results of science.

True, scientists themselves knew better and earlier than anyone else what the potential consequences of their discoveries might be. Ever since the time the first atom bomb became operational (1945) some of them had warned their masters in government of the destructive forces the world now had at its disposal. Yet the idea that science equals potential catastrophe essentially belonged to the second half of the century: in its first phase—the nightmare of nuclear war—to the era of superpower confrontation after 1945; in its later and more universal phase, to the era of crisis that opened in the 1970s. However, the Age of Catastrophe, perhaps because it strikingly slowed down world economic growth, was still one of scientific complacency about man's ability to control the powers of nature, or, at worst, about nature's ability to adjust to the worst that man could do.† On the other hand, what made scientists themselves uneasy then was their own uncertainty about what to make of their theories and findings.

II

Some time during the Age of Empire the links had snapped between the findings of scientists and the reality based on, or imaginable by sense experience; and so did the links between science and the sort of logic based on, or imaginable by common sense. The two breaks reinforced one another, since the progress of the natural sciences became increasingly dependent on people writing equations (i.e. mathematical sentences) on pads of paper, rather than experimenting in laboratories. The twentieth century was to be the century of the theoreticians telling the practitioners what they were to look for and should find in the light of their theories; in other words, the century of the mathematicians. Molecular biology, in

*Thus in Nazi Germany Werner Heisenberg was allowed to teach relativity, but on the condition that the name of Einstein should not be mentioned (Peierls, 1992, p. 44).

†"One may sleep in peace with the consciousness that the Creator has put some foolproof elements into his handiwork, and that man is powerless to do it any titanic damage," wrote Robert Millikan of Caltech (Nobel Prize, 1923) in 1930.

which, good authority informs me, there is as yet very little theory, is an exception. Not that observation and experiment were secondary. On the contrary, their technology was more profoundly revolutionized than at any time since the seventeenth century by new devices and new techniques, several of which were to be given the ultimate scientific accolade of Nobel prizes.* To give only one example, the limitations of merely optical magnification were overcome by the electron microscope (1937) and the radio telescope (1957), with the result that a far deeper observational penetration into the molecular and even atomic realm and into the remotenesses of the universe became possible. In recent decades the automation of routine, and increasingly more complex forms of laboratory activity and calculation, as by computers, has further and enormously raised the powers of experimenters, observers, and increasingly of the model-building theorists. In some fields, notably in astronomy, this led to the making of discoveries, sometimes by accident, which subsequently compelled theoretical innovation. Modern cosmology is at bottom the result of two such discoveries: Hubble's observation that the universe must be expanding, based on the analysis of the spectra of galaxies (1929); and Penzias' and Wilson's discovery of the cosmic background radiation (radio noise) in 1965. Nevertheless, while science is and must be a collaboration between theorists and practitioners, in the Short Twentieth Century the theorists were in the driving seat.

For the scientists themselves, the break with sense experience and common sense meant a break with the traditional certainties of their field and its methodology. Its consequences can be most vividly illustrated by following the unquestioned queen of sciences in the first half of the century, physics. Indeed, inasmuch as this discipline is still the one concerned both with the smallest elements of all matter, live or dead, and with the constitution and structure of the largest ensemble of matter, namely the universe, physics remained the central pillar of the natural sciences even at the end of the century, though in the second half it had increasing competition from the life sciences, transformed after the 1950s by the revolution in molecular biology.

No field of the sciences seemed more firm, coherent, and methodologically certain than the Newtonian physics whose foundations were undermined by the theories of Planck and Einstein and the transformation of atomic theory that followed on the discovery of radioactivity in the 1890s.

---

*Well over twenty Nobel prizes in Physics and Chemistry since the First World War have been given wholly or partly for new research methods, devices and techniques.

It was objective, i.e. it could be adequately observed, subject to technical limitations in the observing apparatus (e.g. of the optical microscope or telescope). It was unambiguous: an object or phenomenon was either one thing or something else, and the distinction between these was clear. Its laws were universal, equally valid at the cosmic and the microcosmic level. The mechanism linking phenomena were understandable (i.e. capable of being expressed as "cause and effect"). Consequently, the entire system was in principle determinist, and the purpose of the laboratory experiment was to demonstrate this determinacy by eliminating, so far as possible, the complex muddle of ordinary life which concealed it. Only a fool or a child would claim that the flight of birds and butterflies negated the laws of gravitation. Scientists knew quite well that there were "non-scientific" statements, but these were not their concern as scientists.

All these characteristics were put into question between 1895 and 1914. Was light a continuous wave motion or an emission of discrete particles (photons) as Einstein held, following Planck? Sometimes it was best to treat it as one, sometimes as the other, but how, if at all, were they connected? What was light "really"? As the great Einstein himself stated, twenty years after having created the puzzle: "We now have two theories of light, both indispensable, but, it must be admitted, without any logical connection between them, despite twenty years of colossal effort by theoretical physicists" (Holton, 1970, p. 1017). What was happening inside the atom, which was now seen to be not (as its original Greek name implied) the smallest possible, and therefore indivisible, unit of matter, but a complex system consisting of a variety of even more elementary particles? The first assumption, after Rutherford's great discovery of the atomic nucleus in 1911 in Manchester—a triumph of the experimental imagination and the foundation of modern nuclear physics and of what eventually became "big science"—was that electrons circulated in orbits round this nucleus in the manner of a miniaturized solar system. Yet when the structure of individual atoms was investigated, notably that of hydrogen by Niels Bohr, who knew about Max Planck's "quanta," in 1912–13, the results showed, once again, a profound conflict between what his electrons did and—his own words—"the admirably coherent group of conceptions which have been rightly termed the classical theory of electrodynamics" (Holton, 1970, p. 1028). Bohr's model worked, i.e. it had brilliant explanatory and predictive force, but it was "quite irrational and absurd" from the point of view of classical Newtonian mechanics, and in any case disclaimed any idea of what actually happened inside the atom as the electron "leaped" or otherwise got from one orbit to another, or what happened between the moment when it was discovered in one and when it appeared in another.

What, indeed, happened to the certainties of science itself, as it became clear that the very process of observing phenomena at the sub-atomic level actually changes them: for this reason the more precisely we want to know the position of a sub-atomic particle, the more uncertain must be its velocity. It has been said of any means of detailed observation to find out where an electron "really" is: "To look at it means to knock it out" (Weisskopf, 1980, p. 37). This was the paradox which a brilliant young German physicist, Werner Heisenberg, in 1927 generalized into the famous "uncertainty principle" that bears his name. The very fact that the name concentrates on *uncertainty* is significant, since it indicates what was worrying the explorers of the new scientific universe as they left the certainties of the old one behind them. It was not that they themselves were uncertain or produced doubtful results. On the contrary, their theoretical predictions, however implausible and bizarre, were verified by humdrum observation and experiment, from the time Einstein's theory of general relativity (1915) appeared to be verified in 1919 by a British eclipse expedition which found that light from some distant stars was deflected towards the sun, as predicted by the theory. For practical purposes particle physics was as subject to regularity and as predictable as Newtonian physics, though in a different way; and in any case at the supra-atomic level Newton and Galileo remained completely valid. What made scientists nervous was that they did not know how to fit the old and the new together.

Between 1924 and 1927 the dualities which so troubled physicists in the first quarter of the century were eliminated, or rather side-stepped, by a brilliant coup of mathematical physics, the construction of "quantum mechanics," almost simultaneously devised in a number of countries. The true "reality" within the atom was not wave or particle, but indivisible "quantum states" which were potentially manifested as either or both. It was pointless to regard it as continuous or discontinuous movement, because we cannot, now or ever, follow the path of the electron step by step. Classical physical concepts such as position, velocity or momentum simply do not apply beyond certain points, marked out by Heisenberg's "uncertainty principle." But, of course, beyond these points other concepts apply, which produce far from uncertain results. These arise from the specific patterns produced by the "waves" or vibrations of (negatively charged) electrons, kept within the confined space of the atom near the (positive) nucleus. Successive "quantum states" within this confined space produce well-defined patterns of different frequencies which, as Schrödinger showed in 1926, could be calculated, as could the energy corresponding to each ("wave mechanics"). These electron patterns had quite remarkable predictive and explanatory power. Thus many years later, when plutonium was first produced in nuclear reactions at Los Alamos, on the way to constructing the first atomic bomb, the quantities were so small that its properties could not be observed. However, from the number of electrons in the atom of this element, and from the patterns of these ninety-four electrons vibrating round the nucleus, *and from nothing else*, scientists predicted (correctly) that plutonium would turn out to be a brown metal with a specific mass of about twenty grams per cubic centimetre, and possess a certain electric and thermal conductivity and elasticity. Quantum mechanics also explained why atoms (and the molecules and higher combinations based on them) remain stable, or rather what extra input of energy would be necessary to change them. Indeed it has been said that

> even the phenomena of life—the shape of DNA and the fact that different nucleotides are resistant to thermal motion at room temperature—are based on those primal patterns. The fact that every spring the same flowers emerge is based on the stability of the patterns of the different nucleotides (Weisskopf, 1980, pp. 35–38).

Yet this great and astonishingly fruitful advance in the exploration of nature was achieved on the ruins of all that had been considered certain and adequate in scientific theory, and by a willed suspension of disbelief, which not only the older scientists found troublesome. Consider the "antimatter" which Paul Dirac proposed from Cambridge, after he discovered (1928) that his equations had solutions corresponding to electron states with an energy *less* than the zero energy of empty space. The concept of "antimatter," meaningless in everyday terms, was happily manipulated by physicists thereafter (Steven Weinberg, 1977, pp. 23–4). The mere word itself implied a deliberate refusal to allow the progress of theoretical calculation to be diverted by any preconceived notion of reality: whatever reality turned out to be, it would catch up with the equations. And yet, it was not easy to accept this, even for scientists who had long put behind them the great Rutherford's view that no physics could be good unless it could be explained to a barmaid.

There were pioneers of the new science who simply found it impossible to accept the end of the old certainties, not least its founders, Max Planck and Albert Einstein himself, who expressed his suspicion of purely probabilistic laws rather than determinist causality in a well-known phrase: "God does not play dice." He had no valid arguments, but "an inner voice tells me that Quantum mechanics is not the real truth" (cited in M. Jammer, 1966, p. 358). More than one of the quantum revolutionaries themselves had dreamed of eliminating the contradictions by subsuming one side under the other: Schrödinger hoped his "wave mechanics" had dissolved the supposed "jumps" of electrons from one atomic orbit to another, into the *continuous* process of energy change, and, in doing so, preserved classical space, time and causality. Reluctant pioneer revolutionaries, notably Planck and Einstein, sighed with relief, but in vain. The ball-game was new. The old rules no longer held good.

Could physicists learn to live with permanent contradiction? Niels Bohr thought they could and must. There was no way of expressing the wholeness of nature in a single description, given the nature of human language. There could be no single, directly comprehensive model. The only way of seizing reality was by reporting it in different ways, and putting them all together to complement each other in an "exhaustive overlay of different descriptions that incorporate apparently contradictory notions" (Holton, 1970, p. 1018). This was Bohr's principle of "complementarity," a metaphysical concept akin to relativity which he derived from writers far removed from physics, and regarded as having universal applicability. Bohr's "complementarity" was not intended to advance the research of the atomic scientists, but rather to comfort them by justifying their confusions. Its appeal lies outside the field of reason. For while we all, and not least intelligent scientists, know that there are different ways of perceiving the same reality, sometimes non-comparable or even contradictory, but all needed to grasp it in its totality, we still have no idea how we connect them. The effect of a Beethoven sonata can be analysed physically, physiologically and psychologically, and it can also be absorbed by listening to it: but how are these modes of understanding connected? Nobody knows.

Nevertheless, the uneasiness remained. On the one hand there was the mid-1920s synthesis of the new physics, which provided an extraordinarily effective way of breaking into the bank-vaults of nature. The basic concepts of the quantum revolution were still being applied in the late twentieth century. Unless we follow those who see the non-linear analysis, made possible by computing, as a radically new departure, there has been no revolution in physics since 1900–27, but only vast evolutionary advances within the same conceptual framework. On the other hand, there was generalized incoherence. In 1931 that incoherence was extended to the ultimate redoubt of certainty, mathematics. An Austrian mathematical logician, Kurt Gödel, proved that a system of axioms can never be based on itself. If it is to be shown as being consistent, statements from outside the system must be used. In the light of "Gödel's theorem," a non-contradictory internally consistent world could not even be thought of.

Such was the "crisis in physics," to cite the title of a book by a young British Marxist autodidactic intellectual who was killed in Spain, Christopher Caudwell (1907–37). It was not only a "crisis of the foundations," as the period 1900–30 has been called in mathematics (see *Age of Empire*, chapter 10) but also of the scientists' general world picture. Indeed, as the physicists learned to shrug their shoulders about philosophical questions, while they plunged into the new territory opening before them, the second aspect of the crisis became ever more obtrusive. For in the 1930s and 1940s the structure of the atom became more complicated year by year. Gone was the simple duality of positive nucleus and negative electron(s). Atoms were now inhabited by a growing fauna and flora of elementary particles, some of them very strange indeed. Chadwick of Cambridge discovered the first of these in 1932, the electrically neutral neutrons—though others, such as the massless and electrically neutral neutrino, had already been predicted on theoretical grounds. These subatomic particles, almost all shortlived and fleeting, multiplied, particularly under the bombardment of the high-energy accelerators of "big science" which became available after the Second World War. By the end of the 1950s there were more than a hundred of them, and no end was in sight. The picture was still further complicated, from the early 1930s, by the discovery of two unknown and obscure forces at work within the atom, in addition to the electrical ones that bonded nucleus and electrons together. The so-called "strong force" bonded neutron and positively charged proton together in the atomic nucleus, and the so-called "weak force" was responsible for certain kinds of particle decay.

Now in the conceptual debris on which the twentieth-century sciences were built, one basic and essentially aesthetic assumption was not challenged. Indeed, as uncertainty clouded all the others, it became increasingly central to scientists. Like the poet Keats, they believed that "Beauty is truth, truth beauty," though their criterion of beauty was not his. A beautiful theory, which was in itself a presumption of truth, must be elegant, economical and general. It must unify and simplify, as the great triumphs of scientific theory had hitherto done. The scientific revolution of Galileo and Newton's time had shown that the same laws govern heaven and earth. Chemical revolution had reduced the endless variety of forms in which matter appeared to ninety-two systematically connected elements. The triumph of nineteenth-century physics had been to show that electricity, magnetism and optical phenomena had the same roots.

Yet the new revolution in science produced not simplification but complication. Einstein's marvellous relativity theory, which described gravitation as a manifestation of the curvature of spacetime, actually introduced a troubling duality into nature: "on the one hand was the stage—the curved spacetime, gravity; on the other hand the actors—the electrons, the protons, the electromagnetic fields—and there was no link between them" (Steven Weinberg, 1979, p. 43). For the last forty years of his life Einstein, the Newton of the twentieth century, laboured to produce a "unified field theory" which would unify electromagnetism with gravitation, but he failed—and now there were two more apparently unconnected classes of force in nature with no apparent relations with electromagnetism and gravitation. The multiplication of subatomic particles, however exciting, could only be a temporary, a preliminary truth because, however pretty in detail, there was no beauty in the new atom as there had once been in the old. Even the pure pragmatist of the era for which the only criterion of a hypothesis was that it worked, had at least sometimes to dream of a noble, beautiful and general "theory of everything" (to use the phrase of a Cambridge physicist, Stephen Hawking). But it appeared to recede into the distance, although from the 1960s on physicists began, once again, to discern the possibility of such a synthesis. Indeed, by the 1990s there was a widespread belief among physicists that they were nearly down to some really basic level, and that the multiplicity of elementary particles could be reduced to a relatively simple and coherent grouping.

At the same time on the undefined borders between such widely disparate subjects as meteorology, ecology, non-nuclear physics, astronomy, fluid dynamics and various branches of mathematics independently pioneered in the Soviet Union and (slightly later) in the West, and aided by the extraordinary development of computers as an analytical tool and a visual inspiration, a new branch of synthesis was emerging—or re-emerging—under the somewhat misleading name of "chaos theory." For what it revealed was not so much the unpredictable results of perfectly determinist scientific procedures, but the extraordinary universality of the shapes and patterns of nature in its most disparate and apparently unconnected manifestations.* Chaos theory helped to put a new spin, as it were, on old causality. It broke the links between causality and predictability, for its essence was not that events were fortuitous but

---

*The development of "chaos theory" in the 1970s and 1980s has something in common with the emergence in the early nineteenth century of a "romantic" school of science, mainly centred in Germany ("*Naturphilosophie*") in reaction against the "classical" mainstream, centred in France and Britain. It is interesting that two

that the effects which followed specifiable causes could not be predicted. It reinforced another development, pioneered among palaeontologists, and of considerable interest to historians. This suggests that chains of historical or evolutionary development are perfectly coherent and capable of explanation *after* the fact, but that eventual results cannot be predicted from the outset, because, if the same course was set again, any early change, however slight and without apparent importance at the time, "and evolution cascades into a radically different channel" (Gould, 1989, p. 51). The political, economic and social consequences of this approach may be far-reaching.

Furthermore, there was the sheer absurdity of much of the new physicists' world. So long as it was confined within the atom, it did not directly affect ordinary life, which even scientists live, but at least one new and unassimilated discovery could not be so quarantined. This was the extraordinary fact, predicted by some on the basis of relativity theory, but observed by the American astronomer E. Hubble in 1929, that the entire universe appeared to be expanding at a dizzying rate. This expansion, which even many scientists found hard to swallow, some devising alternative "steady state" theories of the cosmos, was verified by other astronomical data in the 1960s. It was impossible not to speculate where this expansion was taking it (and us), when and how it began, and therefore about the history of the universe, starting with the initial "Big Bang." This produced the flourishing field of cosmology, the part of twentieth-century science most readily turned into bestsellers. It also enormously increased the element of history in natural sciences hitherto (except for geology and its by-products) proudly uninterested in it, and incidentally diminished the identification of "hard" science with experiment, i.e. with reproduction of natural phenomena. For how could events unrepeatable by definition be repeated? The expanding universe thus added to the confusion of both scientists and lay persons.

This confusion confirmed those who lived through the Age of Catastrophe, and knew or thought about such matters, in their conviction that an old world had ended, or, at the very least, was in terminal upheaval, but that the contours of the new one were not yet clearly discernible. The great Max Planck had no doubt of the link between the crisis in science and in outside life:

---

eminent pioneers of the new research (Feigenbaum, Libchaber—see Gleick, pp. 163, 197) were actually inspired by reading Goethe's passionately anti-Newtonian theory of colours, and his treatise on *The Transformation of Plants*, which may be regarded as a prospectively anti-Darwinian/evolutionary theory (For *Naturphilosophie*, see *Age of Revolution*, chapter 15).

We are living in a very singular moment of history. It is a moment of crisis in the literal sense of that word. In every branch of our spiritual and material civilization we seem to have arrived at a critical turning point. This spirit shows itself not only in the actual state of public affairs, but also in the general attitude towards fundamental values in personal and social life . . . Now the iconoclast has invaded the temple of science. There is scarcely a scientific axiom that is not nowadays denied by somebody. And at the same time almost any nonsensical theory would be almost sure to find believers and disciples somewhere or other (Planck, 1933, p. 64).

Nothing was more natural than that a middle-class German brought up in the nineteenth century certainties should express such sentiments in the days of the Great Slump, and Hitler's rise to power.

Nevertheless, gloom was the opposite of what most scientists felt. They agreed with Rutherford who told the British Association (1923) that "we are living in the heroic age of physics" (Howarth, 1978, p. 92). Every issue of the scientific journals, every colloquium—for most scientists loved, more than ever, to combine cooperation and competition—brought new, exciting and profound advances. The scientific community was still small enough, at least in spearhead subjects like nuclear physics and crystallography, to offer almost every young researcher the prospect of stardom. To be a scientist was to be envied. Certainly those of us who were students in Cambridge, which produced most of the thirty British Nobel prizes of the first half of the century—which, for practical purposes, *was* British science at this time—knew what we would have wanted to study, if our mathematics had been good enough.

Indeed, the natural sciences could look forward to nothing except further triumph and intellectual advance, which made the patchiness, the imperfections and improvisations of current theory tolerable, since they were bound to be only temporary. Why should people who got Nobel prizes for work done in their mid-twenties lack confidence about the future?* And yet, how could even the men (and the occasional rare woman) who continued to prove the reality of the shaken idea of "progress" in their field of human activity remain immune to the epoch of crisis and catastrophe in which they lived?

They could not and did not. The Age of Catastrophe was therefore

---

*The physics revolution of 1924–28 was made by men born in 1900–2 (Heisenberg, Pauli, Dirac, Fermi, Joliot). Schrödinger, de Broglie and Max Born were in their thirties.

also one of the comparatively rare ages of politicized scientists, and not only because the mass migration of racially and ideologically unacceptable scientists from large zones of Europe demonstrated that scientists could not take their personal immunity for granted. At all events, the typical British scientist of the 1930s was a member of the (Left-wing) Cambridge Scientists' Anti-War Group, confirmed in his or her radicalism by the undisguised radical sympathies of their seniors, whose distinction ranged from the Royal Society to the Nobel prize: Bernal (crystallography), Haldane (genetics), Needham (chemical embryology),* Blackett (physics), Dirac (physics) and the mathematician G. H. Hardy, who considered that only two others in the twentieth century were in the class of his Australian cricketing hero Don Bradman: Lenin and Einstein. The typical young American physicist of the 1930s was more than likely to be in political trouble in the post-war years of the Cold War for his pre-war or continuing radical sympathies, like Robert Oppenheimer (1904–67), the chief architect of the atom bomb, and Linus Pauling the chemist, (1901–   ) who won two Nobel prizes, including one for Peace and a Lenin prize. The typical French scientist was a sympathiser with the Popular Front of the 1930s and an active supporter of the Resistance during the war; not many Frenchmen were the latter. The typical refugee scientist from central Europe could hardly not be hostile to fascism, however uninterested in public affairs. Scientists who stayed in or were prevented from leaving fascist countries or the U.S.S.R. could not avoid their government's politics either, whether or not they sympathised with them, if only because public gestures were imposed on them, like the Hitler salute in Germany, which the great physicist Max von Laue (1897–1960) avoided by carrying something in both hands whenever he left his house. Unlike the social or human sciences, such politicization was unusual in the natural sciences, whose subject does not require or (except in parts of the life sciences) even suggest views about human affairs, though it often suggests views about God.

However, scientists were more directly politicized by their well-founded belief that laymen, including politicians, had no idea of the extraordinary potential that modern science, properly used, put at the disposal of human society. Both the collapse of the world economy and the rise of Hitler seemed to confirm this in different ways. (Conversely, the official Marxist devotion of the Soviet Union and its ideology to the natural sciences, misled many Western scientists at this time into seeing it as a regime suited to realizing this potential.) Technocracy and radicalism

*He later became the eminent historian of science in China.

converged, because at this point it was the political Left, with its ideological commitment to science, rationalism and progress (lampooned by conservatives with the new term "scientism")* which naturally represented adequate recognition and support for "The Social Function of Science," to cite the title of a highly influential book-cum-manifesto of the time (Bernal, 1939) characteristically written by a brilliant and militantly Marxist physicist. It was equally characteristic that the French Popular Front government of 1936–39 established the first Undersecretaryship for Scientific Research (occupied by the Nobel Laureate Irène Joliot-Curie), and developed what is still the main mechanism for funding French research, the CNRS (*Centre National de la Recherche Scientifique*). Indeed, it became increasingly obvious, at least to scientists, that not only public funding but publicly organized research was needed. British government scientific services, which in 1930 employed a grand total of 743 scientists, could not be adequate—thirty years later it employed over seven thousand (Bernal, 1967, p. 931).

The era of politicized science reached its climax in the Second World War, the first conflict since the Jacobin era of the French revolution when scientists were systematically and *centrally* mobilized for military purposes; probably more effectively on the side of the Allies than of Germany, Italy and Japan, because they never expected to win rapidly with immediately available resources and methods (see chapter 1). Tragically, nuclear warfare itself was the child of anti-fascism. A mere war between nation-states would almost certainly not have moved the spearhead nuclear physicists, themselves largely refugees or exiles from fascism, to urge the British and American governments to build an atom bomb. And the very horror of these scientists at their achievement, their desperate last-minute struggles to prevent the politicians and generals from actually using the bomb, and later to resist the construction of a hydrogen bomb, bears witness to the strength of *political* passions. Indeed, insofar as antinuclear campaigns after the Second World War had weighty support in the scientific community, it was among the members of the politicized anti-fascist generations.

At the same time the war finally convinced governments that the commitment of hitherto unimaginable resources to scientific research was both practicable and, in future, essential. No economy except that of the U.S.A.'s could have found the two billion dollars (wartime value) to build the atom bomb during the war; but it is also true that no government at all would, before 1940, have dreamed of spending even a small fraction of

*The word appears for the first time in 1936 in France (Guerlac, 1951, pp. 93–4).

this money on a speculative project based on some incomprehensible calculations by wild-haired academics. After the war the sky, or rather the size of the economy alone, became the limit on government scientific outlays and employment. In the 1970s the U.S. government funded two-thirds of the basic research costs in that country, which then ran at almost five billion dollars *a year*, and it employed something like one million scientists and engineers (Holton, 1978, pp. 227–28).

III

The political temperature of science dropped after the Second World War. Radicalism in the laboratories receded rapidly in 1947–49 when views regarded as baseless and bizarre elsewhere became mandatory for scientists in the U.S.S.R. Even most hitherto loyal communists found Lysenkoism (see p. 533) impossible to swallow. Moreover, it became increasingly evident that the regimes modelled on the Soviet system were neither materially nor morally attractive, at least to most scientists. On the other hand, in spite of much propaganda, the Cold War between the West and the Soviet bloc never generated anything like the political passions once roused among scientists by fascism. Perhaps because of the traditional affinity between liberal and Marxist rationalism, perhaps because the U.S.S.R., unlike Nazi Germany, never looked as though it were in a position to conquer the West, even if it had wanted to, which there was good reason to doubt. For most Western scientists the U.S.S.R., its satellites and Communist China were bad states whose scientists were to be pitied, rather than evil empires calling for a crusade.

In the developed West the natural sciences remained politically and ideologically quiescent for a generation, enjoying their intellectual triumphs and the vastly expanded resources now available for their researches. In fact, the munificent patronage of governments and large corporations encouraged a breed of researchers who took their paymasters' policies for granted and preferred not to think about the wider implications of their work, especially when these were military. At most, the scientists in such sectors protested against not being allowed to publish their research results. Indeed, most members of what was now a very large army of Ph.Ds, employed in the National Aeronautics and Space Administration (NASA), which was established to face the Soviet challenge in 1958, had no more interest in querying the rationale of their activities than members of any other army. In the later 1940s men and women still agonized over the question whether to join government establishments specialising in chemical and biological war research.* There is no evidence that subsequently such establishments had any trouble in recruiting their staff.

Somewhat unexpectedly, it was in the Soviet region of the globe that science became, if anything, more political as the second half of the century advanced. It was no accident that the major national (and international) spokesman for dissidence in the U.S.S.R. was to be a scientist, Andrei Sakharov (1921–89), the physicist who had been chiefly responsible in the late 1940s for the construction of the Soviet hydrogen bomb. Scientists were members *par excellence* of that new, large, educated and technically trained professional middle class, which was the main achievement of the Soviet system, but at the same time the class most directly aware of its weaknesses and limitations. They were more essential to it than their opposite numbers in the West, since they and they alone enabled an otherwise backward economy to face the U.S.A. as a superpower. Indeed, they demonstrated their indispensability by allowing the U.S.S.R. for a short time to overtake the West in the highest of technologies, that of outer space. The first man-made satellite (Sputnik, 1957), the first manned space flight by man and woman (1961, 1963), and the first space-walks were all Russian. Concentrated in research institutes or special "science cities," articulate, necessarily conciliated and allowed some degree of freedom by the post-Stalin regime, it is not surprising that critical opinions were generated in the milieu of research, whose social prestige was in any case higher than that of any other Soviet occupation.

IV

Can it be said that these fluctuations in political and ideological temperature affected the progress of the natural sciences? Plainly far less than was the case in the social and human sciences, let alone the ideologies and philosophies. The natural sciences could reflect the century scientists lived in only within the confines of the empiricist methodology that necessarily became standard in an era of epistemological uncertainty: that of hypotheses verifiable—or, in the terms of Karl Popper (1902–   ), which many scientists made their own, falsifiable—by practical tests. This imposed limits on ideologizing. Economics, though subject to the requirements

*I recall the embarrassment at this time of a (formerly pacifist, later communist) biochemist friend who had taken such a post in the relevant British establishment.

of logic and consistency, has flourished as a form of theology—probably, in the Western world, as the most influential branch of secular theology—because it can be, and usually is, so formulated as to lack this control. Physics cannot. So, while it is easy to show that the conflicting schools and changing fashions in economic thought directly reflect contemporary experience and ideological debate, this is not so in cosmology.

Yet science did echo its times, even though it is undeniable that some important movements in science are endogenous. Thus it was almost inevitable that the disordered multiplication of sub-atomic particles, particularly after it accelerated in the 1950s, should lead theorists to seek for simplification. The (initially) arbitrary nature of the new and hypothetical "ultimate" particle, of which protons, electrons, neutrons and the rest were now said to be composed, is indicated by its very name, taken from James Joyce's *Finnegan's Wake*: the *quark* (1963). It was soon divided into three or four sub-species (with their "anti-quarks"), described as "up," "down," "sideways" or "strange," and quarks with "charm," each of them endowed with a property called "colour." None of these words had anything like their usual meanings. As usual, successful predictions on the basis of this theory were made, thus concealing the fact that no experimental evidence for the existence of quarks of any kind had been found by the 1990s.* Whether these new developments constituted a simplification of the sub-atomic maze or an additional layer of complexity, must be left to suitably qualified physicists to judge. However, the sceptical, if admiring, lay observer may sometimes be reminded of the titanic labours of intelligence and ingenuity expended at the end of the nineteenth century to maintain scientific belief in the "aether" before the work of Planck and Einstein banished it into the museum of pseudo-theories together with the "phlogiston" (see *Age of Empire*, chapter 10).

The very lack of contact of such theoretical constructs with the reality they set out to explain (except as falsifiable hypotheses) opened them to influences from the outside world. Was it not natural that, in a century so dominated by technology, mechanical analogies should help to shape them again, though in the form of the techniques of communication and control in both animals and machines, which from 1940 on generated a body of theory known under various names (cybernetics, general systems theory, information theory, etc.)? Electronic computers, which developed

---

*John Maddox comments that it depends what one means by "found." Particular effects of quarks have been identified, but, it appears, they are not found "bare" but only as pairs or triples. What puzzles physicists is not whether quarks are there, but why they are never alone.

at a dizzying speed after the Second World War, especially after the discovery of the transistor, had an enormous capacity for simulation, which made it far easier than before to evolve mechanical models of what had hitherto been regarded as the physical and mental operations of organisms, including the human. Late twentieth century scientists talked about the brain as though it were essentially an elaborate information processing system, and one of the familiar philosophical debates of the second half of the century was whether, and, if so, how, human intelligence could be distinguished from "artificial intelligence," i.e. what, if anything, in the human mind was not theoretically programmable in a computer. That such technological models have advanced research is not in question. Where would the study of the nervous system (i.e. the study of the electric nerve impulses) be without that of electronics? Yet at bottom these are reductionist analogies, which may well some day look as dated as the eighteenth century description of human movement in terms of a system of levers.

Such analogies were useful in the formulation of particular models. Yet beyond these, the life experience of scientists could not but affect their way of looking at nature. Ours has been a century when, to quote one scientist reviewing another, "the conflict between gradualists and catastrophism pervades human experience" (Steve Jones, 1992, p. 12). And so, not surprisingly, it came to pervade science.

In the nineteenth century of bourgeois improvement and progress, continuity and gradualism dominated the paradigms of science. Whatever nature's mode of locomotion, it was not allowed to jump. Geological change and the evolution of life on earth had proceeded without catastrophes and by tiny increments. Even the foreseeable end of the universe in some remote future would be gradual, by the insensible but inevitable transformation of energy into heat, according to the second law of thermodynamics (the "heat death of the universe"). Twentieth-century science has developed a very different image of the world.

Our universe was born, fifteen million years ago, in a massive super-explosion and according to the cosmological speculations at the time of writing may end in an equally dramatic manner. Within it the life history of stars, and hence of their planets, is, like the universe, full of cataclysms: novas, supernovas, red giants, dwarfs, black holes and the rest—none recognized or regarded as more than peripheral astronomic phenomena before the 1920s. Most geologists long resisted the idea of large lateral displacements, such as the continents shifting all over the globe in the course of the earth's history, though the evidence for it was really rather strong. They did so on grounds which were largely ideological, to judge

by the extraordinary bitterness of the controversy against the main proponent of "continental drift," Alfred Wegener. At all events, the argument that it could not be true because no geophysical mechanism to
bring about such movements was known was no more convincing *a priori*
in view of the evidence than Lord Kelvin's nineteenth-century argument
that the timescale then postulated by geologists must be wrong, because
physics, as then understood, made the earth much younger than geology
required. Yet since the 1960s the previously unthinkable has become the
everyday orthodoxy of geology: a globe of shifting, sometimes rapidly
shifting giant plates ("plate tectonics").*

Perhaps even more to the point is the return of direct catastrophism to
both geology and evolutionary theory via palaeontology, since the 1960s.
Once again the *prima facie* evidence has long been familiar: every child
knows about the extinction of dinosaurs at the end of the Cretaceous period. Such was the force of the Darwinian belief that evolution was *not*
the result of catastrophes (or creation) but of slow and tiny changes operating throughout geological history, that this apparent biological cataclysm attracted little attention. Geological time was simply regarded as
long enough to allow for any observed evolutionary changes. Is it surprising, in an era when human history was so plainly cataclysmic, that evolutionary discontinuities should attract attention again? One might even go
further. The mechanism most favoured by both geological and palaeonto-
logical catastrophists at the time of writing is bombardment from outer
space, i.e. the collision of the earth with one or more very large mete-
orites. According to some calculations an asteroid large enough to destroy
civilization, i.e. the equivalent to eight million Hiroshimas, is likely to ar-
rive every three hundred thousand years. Such scenarios have always
been part of fringe pre-history, but would any serious scientist before
the epoch of nuclear war have thought in such terms? Such theories of
evolution as slow change interrupted from time to time by relatively
sudden change ("punctuated equilibrium") remained controversial in
the 1990s, but now they were part of a debate *within* the scientific community. Again, the lay observer cannot but notice the emergence, within
the field of thought remotest from flesh-and-blood human life, of two
mathematical sub-fields known respectively as "catastrophe theory"

---

*The *prima facie* evidence consisted mainly of a) the "fit" of the coastlines of remote continents—notably the west coasts of Africa and the east coasts of South
America; b) the similarity of the geological strata in such cases; and c) the geographical distribution of certain types of land animals and plants. I can remember my surprise at the total refusal of a geophysical colleague in the 1950s—shortly before the
breakthrough of plate tectonics—even to consider that this needed explaining

(from the 1960s) and "chaos theory" (1980s) (see pp. 541ff.). The one, a development of topology pioneered in France in the 1960s, claimed to investigate the situations when gradual change produced sudden ruptures, i.e. the interrelation between continuous and discontinuous change; the other (of American origin) modelled the uncertainty and unpredictability of situations in which apparently tiny events (the fluttering of a butterfly's wings) could be shown to lead to huge results elsewhere (a hurricane). Those who lived through the later decades of the century had no difficulty in understanding why such images as chaos and catastrophe should come into the minds of scientists and mathematicians also.

V

However, from the 1970s on, the outside world began to impinge on the laboratories and seminar rooms more indirectly, but also more powerfully, through the discovery that science-based technology, its power multiplied by global economic explosion, looked like producing fundamental and perhaps irreversible changes to the planet Earth, or at least to the Earth as a habitat for living organisms. This was even more disquieting than the prospect of the man-induced catastrophe of nuclear war which haunted imaginations and consciences during the long Cold War; for a Soviet-U.S. world nuclear war was avoidable and, as it turned out, was avoided. It was not so easy to escape by-products of science-linked economic growth. Thus in 1973 two chemists, Rowland and Molina, first noticed that fluorocarbons (widely used in refrigeration and the newly popular aerosols) depleted the ozone in the earth's atmosphere. It could hardly have been noticed much earlier, since the release of such chemicals (CFC 11 and CFC 12) had not totalled forty thousand tons before the early 1950s. But between 1960 and 1972 over 3.6 million tons of them had entered the atmosphere.* Yet by the early 1990s the existence of large "ozone holes" in the atmosphere was layman's knowledge, and the only question was how rapidly the depletion of the ozone layer would proceed, and how soon it would go beyond the earth's powers of natural recuperation. If CFCs were got rid of, nobody doubts that it would reappear. The "greenhouse effect," i.e. the uncontrollable warming of the global temperature through the release of man-produced gases, which began to be seriously discussed around 1970, became a major preoccupation of

*World Resources, 1986, Table 11.1, p. 319.

both specialists and politicians in the 1980s (Smil, 1990); the danger was real, though sometimes much exaggerated.

At about the same time the word "ecology," coined in 1873 for the branch of biology that dealt with the interrelationships of organisms and their environment, acquired its now familiar quasi-political meaning (E. M. Nicholson, 1970).* These were the natural consequences of the secular economic superboom (see chapter 9).

These worries would be enough to explain why politics and ideology began, once again, to surround the natural sciences in the 1970s. However, they began to penetrate even parts of the sciences themselves in the form of debates about the need for practical and moral limitations on scientific enquiry.

Never since the end of theological hegemony had such issues been seriously raised. Not surprisingly, they emerged from that part of the natural sciences which had always had, or seemed to have, direct implications for human affairs: genetics and evolutionary biology. For within ten years of the Second World War, the life sciences were revolutionized by the astonishing advances of molecular biology, which revealed the universal mechanism of inheritance, the "genetic code."

The revolution in molecular biology was not unexpected. After 1914 it could be taken for granted that life had to be, and could be, explained in terms of physics and chemistry and not in terms of some essence peculiar to living beings.† Indeed, biochemical models of the possible origin of life on earth, starting with sunlight, methane, ammonia and water, were first suggested in the 1920s (largely with anti-religious intentions) in Soviet Russia and Britain, and put the subject on the serious scientific agenda. Hostility to religion, by the way, continued to animate researchers in this field: both Crick and Linus Pauling are cases in point (Olby, 1970, p. 943). The major thrust of biological research had for decades been biochemical, and increasingly physical, since the recognition that protein molecules could be crystallized, and therefore analysed crystallographically. It was known that one substance, deoxyribonucleic acid (DNA) played a central, possibly the central role in heredity: it seemed to be the

---

*"Ecology . . is also the main intellectual discipline and tool which enables us to hope that human evolution can be mutated, can be shifted on to a new course, so that man will cease to knock hell out of the environment on which his own future depends."

†"How can the events in space and time which take place within the spatial boundary of a living organism be accounted for by physics and chemistry?" (E. Schrodinger, 1944, p. 2).

basic component of the gene, the unit of inheritance. The problem of how the gene "cause(d) the synthesis of another structure like itself, in which even the mutations of the original gene are copied" (Muller, 1951, p. 95), i.e. how heredity operated, was already under serious investigation in the late 1930s. After the war it was clear that, in Crick's words, "great things were just around the corner." The brilliance of Crick and Watson's discovery of the double-helical structure of DNA and of the way it explained "gene copying" by an elegant chemico-mechanical model is not diminished by the fact that several workers were converging on the same result in the early 1950s.

The DNA revolution, "the greatest single discovery in biology" (J. D. Bernal), which dominated the life-sciences in the second half of the century, was essentially about genetics and, since twentieth-century Darwinism is exclusively genetic, about evolution.* Both these are notoriously touchy subjects, both because scientific models are themselves frequently ideological in such fields—we remember Darwin's debt to Malthus (Desmond/Moore, chapter 18)—and because they frequently feed back into politics ("social Darwinism"). The concept of "race" illustrates this interplay. The memory of Nazi racial policies made it virtually unthinkable for liberal intellectuals (which included most scientists) to operate with this concept. Indeed, many doubted that it was legitimate even to enquire systematically into the genetically determined differences between human groups, for fear that the results might provide encouragement for racist opinions. More generally, in the Western countries the post-fascist ideology of democracy and equality revived the old debates of "nature v. nurture," or heredity v. environment. Plainly the human individual was shaped both by heredity and environment, by genes and culture. Yet conservatives were only too willing to accept a society of irremovable, i.e. genetically determined inequalities, while the Left, committed to equality, naturally held that all inequalities could be removed by social action: they were at bottom environmentally determined. The controversy flared up over the question of human intelligence, which (because of its implications for selective or universal schooling) was highly political. It raised far wider issues than those of race, though it bore on these also. How wide they were, emerged with the revival

---

*It was also "about" the essentially mathematical-mechanical variant of experimental science, which is perhaps why it has met with less than 100 per cent enthusiasm in some less readily quantifiable or experimental life sciences, such as zoology and palaeontology. (See R. C. Lewontin, *The Genetic Basis of Evolutionary Change.*)

of the feminist movement (see chapter 10), several of whose ideologists came close to claiming that *all* mental differences between men and women were essentially culture-determined, i.e. environmental. Indeed, the fashionable substitution of the term "gender" for "sex" implied the belief that "woman" was not so much a biological category as a social role. A scientist who tried to investigate such sensitive subjects knew himself to be in a political minefield. Even those who entered it deliberately, like E. O. Wilson of Harvard (b. 1929), the champion of "sociobiology," shied away from plain speech.*

What made the atmosphere more explosive, was that scientists themselves, especially on the more obviously social wing of the life sciences— evolutionary theory, ecology, ethology or the study of animal social behaviour and the like—were only too apt to use anthropomorphic metaphors or draw human conclusions. Sociobiologists, or those who popularized their findings, suggested that the (male) traits inherited from the millennia during which primitive man had been selected to adapt, as a hunter, to a more predatory existence in open habitats (Wilson, ibid.) still dominated our social existence. Not only women but also historians were irritated. Evolutionary theorists analysed natural selection, in the light of the great biological revolution, as the struggle for existence of "The Selfish Gene" (Dawkins, 1976). Even some who sympathised with the hard version of Darwinism wondered what real bearing genetic selection had on debates about human egoism, competition and cooperation. Science was once more beleaguered by critics, though—significantly—it was no longer seriously under fire from traditional religion, apart from intellectually negligible fundamentalist groups. The clergy now accepted the hegemony of the laboratory, drawing what theological comfort it could from scientific cosmology, whose "Big Bang" theories could, with

---

*"My overall impression of the available information is that *Homo Sapiens* is a typical animal species with reference to the quality and magnitude of the genetic diversity affecting behavior. If the comparison is correct, the psychic unity of humankind has been reduced in status from a dogma to a testable hypothesis. This is not an easy thing to say in the present political ambience of the United States, and it is regarded as punishable heresy in some sectors of the academic community. But the idea needs to be faced squarely if the social sciences are to be entirely honest . . It will be better for scientists to study the subject of genetic behavioral diversity than to maintain a conspiracy of silence out of good intentions" (Wilson, 1977, "Biology and the Social Sciences," p. 133).

The plain meaning of this convoluted passage is: there are races and for genetic reasons they are permanently unequal in certain specifiable respects.

the eye of faith, be presented as proof that a God had created the world. On the other hand the Western cultural revolution of the 1960s and 1970s produced a strong neo-romantic and irrationalist attack on the scientific view of the world, which could readily shift from a radical to a reactionary key.

Unlike the outlying trenches of the life-sciences, the main fortress of pure research in the "hard" sciences was little disturbed by such snipings until it became evident by the 1970s that research could not be divorced from the social consequences of the technologies it now, and almost immediately, generated. It was the prospect of "genetic engineering"—logically of humans as well as other forms of life—which really raised the immediate question of whether limits on scientific research should be envisaged. For the first time such opinions were heard among scientists themselves, notably in the biological field, for by now some of the essential elements of the Frankensteinian technologies were not separable from pure research and subsequent to it, but—as in the Genome project, the plan to map all the genes in human heredity—they *were* the basic research. These criticisms undermined what all scientists had hitherto regarded, and most scientists continued to regard as the basic principle of science, namely that, with the most marginal concessions to the moral beliefs of society,* science should pursue truth wherever that pursuit led them. They had no responsibility for what non-scientists did with their results. That, as one American scientist observed in 1992, "no prominent molecular biologist of my acquaintance is without a financial stake in the biotechnology business" (Lewontin, 1992, p. 37; pp. 31–40); that—to cite another—"the issue (of ownership) is at the heart of everything we do" (ibid, p. 38), made the claim of purity even more dubious.

What was now at issue was not the pursuit of truth, but the impossibility of separating it from its conditions and consequences. At the same time the debate was essentially between pessimists and optimists about the human race. For the basic assumption of those who envisaged restraints or self-limitation on scientific enquiry was that humanity, as at present organized, was not capable of handling the earth-transforming powers it had, or even of recognizing the risks it was running. For even those sorcerers who resisted all limits on their enquiries did not trust their apprentices. The arguments for unlimited enquiry "pertain to basic scientific research, not to the technological applications of science, some of which ought to be restrained" (Baltimore, 1978).

And yet, such arguments were beside the point. For, as all scientists

---

*Such as, notably, the restriction of experiment on human beings.

knew, scientific research was *not* unlimited and free, if only because it required resources which were in limited supply. The question was not whether anyone should tell researchers what to do or not to do, but who imposed such limits and directions, and by what criteria. For most scientists, whose institutions were directly or indirectly paid for out of public funds, these controllers of research were governments, whose criteria, however sincere their devotion to the values of free enquiry, were not those of a Planck or a Rutherford or an Einstein.

Theirs were, by definition, not the priorities of "pure" research, especially when that research was expensive; and, after the end of the great global boom, even the richest governments, their revenue no longer climbing ahead of their expenditure, had to budget. Nor were they, or could they be, the priorities of "applied" research, which employed the great majority of scientists, for these were set not in terms of the "advance of knowledge" in general (though this might well result), but by the need to achieve certain practical results—for instance a cure for cancer or AIDS. Researchers in these fields pursued not necessarily what interested them, but what was socially useful or economically profitable, or at least what money was available for, even when they hoped it would lead them back to the path of fundamental research. Under the circumstances it was windy rhetoric to claim that restraints on research were intolerable because man was by nature a species that needed "to satisfy our curiosity, exploration and experimentation" (Lewis Thomas in Baltimore, p. 44) or that the peaks of knowledge must be climbed, in the classic mountaineer's phrase, "because they are there."

The truth is that "science" (by which most people meant the "hard" natural sciences) was too big, too powerful, too indispensable to society in general and its paymasters in particular to be left to its own devices. The paradox of its situation was that, in the last analysis, the huge powerhouse of twentieth-century technology, and the economy it made possible, increasingly depended on a relatively minuscule community of people for whom these titanic consequences of their activities were secondary, and often trivial. For them the ability of men to travel to the moon or to bounce the images of a Brazilian soccer match off a satellite so that it could be watched on a screen in Düsseldorf, was far less interesting than the discovery of some cosmic background noise which was identified during the search for phenomena that troubled communication, but confirmed a theory about the origins of the universe. Yet, like the ancient Greek mathematician Archimedes, they knew that they lived in and helped to shape a world that could not understand and did not care about what they did. Their call for the freedom of research was like Archimedes' *cri-de-coeur* to the invading soldiers, against whom he had devised military engines for his city of Syracuse, and who took no notice of them as they killed him: "For God's sake, don't ruin my diagrams." It was understandable, but not necessarily realistic.

Only the world-changing powers to which they had the key protected them, for these appeared to depend on allowing an otherwise incomprehensible and privileged elite—incomprehensible, until late in the century, even in its relative lack of interest in the external signs of wealth and power—to go its own way. All twentieth-century states which had done otherwise had cause to regret it. All states therefore supported science, which, unlike the arts and most of the humanities, could not effectively function without such support, while avoiding interference so far as possible. But governments are not concerned with ultimate truth (except those of ideology or religion) but with instrumental truth. At most they may foster "pure" (i.e. at the moment useless) research because it might one day yield something useful, or for reasons of national prestige, in which the pursuit of Nobel prizes preceded that of Olympic medals and still remains more highly valued. Such were the foundations on which the triumphant structures of scientific research and theory were erected, by which the twentieth century will be remembered as an age of human progress and not primarily of human tragedy.

CHAPTER NINETEEN

Towards the Millennium

We are at the beginning of a new era, characterised by great insecurity, permanent crisis and the absence of any kind of *status quo* . . . We must realise, that we find ourselves in one of those crises of world history which Jakob Burckhardt described. It is no less significant than the one after 1945, even if the initial conditions for surmounting it seem better today. There are no victors and no defeated powers today, not even in Eastern Europe.

—M. Stürmer in Bergedorf (1993, p. 59)

Although the earthly ideal of Socialism-Communism has collapsed, the problems it purported to solve remain: the brazen use of social advantage and the inordinate power of money, which often direct the very course of events. And if the global lesson of the twentieth century does not serve as a healing inoculation, then the vast red whirlwind may repeat itself in entirety.

—Alexander Solzhenitsyn in *New York Times*, 28 November 1993

It is a privilege for a writer to have experienced the end of three states: the Weimar republic, the fascist state and the GDR. I don't suppose I'll live long enough to see the end of the Federal Republic.

—Heiner Müller (1992, p. 361)

I

The Short Twentieth Century ended in problems, for which nobody had, or even claimed to have, solutions. As the citizens of the *fin de siècle* tapped their way through the global fog that surrounded them, into the third millennium, all they knew for certain was that an era of history had ended. They knew very little else.

Thus, for the first time in two centuries, the world of the 1990s entirely lacked any international system or structure. The very fact that, after 1989, dozens of new territorial states appeared without any independent mechanism for determining their borders—without even third parties accepted as sufficiently impartial to act as general mediators—speaks for itself. Where was the consortium of great powers which had once established, or at least formally ratified disputed frontiers? Where were the victors of the First World War who supervised the re-drawing of the map of Europe and the world, fixing a borderline here, insisting on a plebiscite there? (Where, indeed, were those working international conferences so familiar to the diplomats of the past, so different from the brief public-relations and photo-exercise summits which had now taken their place?)

What, indeed, were international powers, old or new, at the end of the millennium? The only state left that would have been recognized as a great power, in the sense in which the word had been used in 1914, was the U.S.A. What this meant in practice was quite obscure. Russia had been reduced to the size it had been in the mid-seventeenth century. Never since Peter the Great had it been so negligible. Britain and France had been reduced to purely regional status, which was not concealed by the possession of nuclear arms. Germany and Japan were certainly economic "great powers," but neither had seen the need to back their enormous economic resources with military muscle, in the traditional manner, even when they became free to do so, though nobody knew what they might want to do in the unknown future. What was the international political status of the new European Union, which aspired to a common political policy but proved spectacularly incapable of even pretending to have one, unlike in economic matters? It was not even clear whether all but a few states, large or small, old or young, would exist in their present form by the time the twenty-first century reached its first quarter.

If the nature of the players on the international scene was unclear, so was the nature of the dangers that confronted the world. The Short Twentieth Century had been one of world wars, hot or cold, conducted by great powers and their allies with increasingly apocalyptic scenarios of mass destruction, culminating in the, fortunately avoided, nuclear holocaust of the superpowers. This danger had clearly disappeared. Whatever the future would bring, the very disappearance or transformation of all but one of the old actors in the world drama, meant that a Third World War of the old kind was among the least likely prospects.

Patently this did not mean that the age of wars was at an end. The 1980s had already demonstrated by means of the British–Argentinian war of 1983 and the Iran–Iraq war of 1980–88 that wars which had nothing to do with the global superpower confrontation were a permanent possibility. The years after 1989 saw more military operations in more parts of Europe, Asia and Africa than anyone could remember, though not all of them were officially classified as wars: in Liberia, Angola, the Sudan and the Horn of Africa, in ex-Yugoslavia, in Moldova, in several countries of the Caucasus and Transcaucasus, in the ever-explosive Middle East, in ex-Soviet Central Asia and Afghanistan. Since it was often not clear who was fighting whom and why in the increasingly frequent situations of national breakdown and disintegration, these activities did not readily fit under any of the classic headings of "war," international or civil. Yet the inhabitants of the region concerned could hardly feel themselves to be living in times of peace, especially when, as in Bosnia, Tadzhikistan or Liberia, they had been living in unquestionable times of peace not so long ago. Besides, as the Balkans in the early 1990s demonstrated, there was no sharp line between regional internecine struggles and a more recognizable war of the old type, into which they could quite easily turn. In short, the global danger of war had not disappeared. It had merely changed.

No doubt the inhabitants of stable, strong and favoured states (the European Union as distinct from the adjoining zone of troubles; Scandinavia as distinct from the ex-Soviet shores of the Baltic Sea) might think themselves immune to such insecurity and carnage in the unhappy parts of the Third World and the ex-socialist world, but, if they did so, they were mistaken. The crisis in the affairs of the traditional nation-states was enough to make them vulnerable. Quite apart from the possibility that some states might in turn split or break up, a major, and not often recognized innovation of the second half of the century weakened them, if only by depriving them of the monopoly of effective force, which had been the criterion of state power in all regions of permanent settlement. This was the democratization or privatization of the means of destruction, which transformed the prospect of violence and wreckage *anywhere* on the globe.

It was now possible for quite small groups of political or other dissidents to disrupt and destroy anywhere, as the mainland activities of the IRA in Britain and the attempt to blow up the World Trade Center in New York (1993) showed. Up to the end of the Short Twentieth Century, the costs of these activities, except to the insurance companies, were modest, since non-state terrorism, contrary to common assumptions, was much less indiscriminate than the bombardments of official warfare, if only because its aim (where it had one) was mainly political rather than military. Moreover, except for explosive charges, it usually operated with hand-held arms more suitable for small-scale killing than for mass murder. However, there was no reason why even nuclear arms, and the material and know-how for their manufacture, all widely available on the world market, could not be adapted for small-group use.

Moreover, the democratization of the means of destruction raised the costs of keeping unofficial violence under control quite dramatically. Thus the British government, faced with actual combatant forces among the Catholic and Protestant para-militaries of Northern Ireland of no more than a few hundreds, maintained itself in being in the province by the constant presence of something like twenty thousand trained troops, eight thousand armed police and an expenditure of £3 billion a year. What was true of small rebellions or other forms of domestic violence was even more true of small conflicts outside a country's borders. There were not many international situations in which even quite rich states would be prepared to incur such costs without limit.

Several situations in the immediate aftermath of the Cold War dramatized this unsuspected limitation on state power, notably Bosnia and Somalia. They also threw light on what looked like becoming perhaps the major cause of international tension in the new millennium, namely that which arose out of the rapidly widening gap between the rich and the poor parts of the world. Each resented the other. The rise of Islamic fundamentalism was patently a movement not only against the ideology of modernization by Westernization, but against the "West" itself. Not by accident did the activists of such movements pursue their ends by disrupting the visits of Western tourists, as in Egypt, or murdering local Western residents in substantial numbers, as in Algeria. Conversely, the most jagged edge of popular xenophobia in the rich countries was directed against foreigners from the Third World, and the European Union dammed its borders against the flood of the Third World's labour-seeking poor. Even within the U.S.A., signs of serious opposition to that country's *de facto* tolerance of unlimited immigration began to appear.

And yet, politically and in military terms, each side lay beyond the power of the other. In almost any conceivable open conflict between states of the North and South, the overwhelming technical superiority and wealth of the North was bound to win, as the Gulf War of 1991 demonstrated conclusively. Even the possession of a few nuclear missiles by some Third World country—assuming it also had the means of maintaining and delivering them—was most unlikely to be an effective deterrent, since Western states, as Israel and the Gulf War coalition proved in Iraq, were both ready and able to undertake pre-emptive strikes against potential enemies too weak to be really threatening as yet. From a military point of view the First World could safely treat the Third as what Mao had called a "paper tiger."

Yet it had become increasingly clear over the last half of the Short Twentieth Century that the First World could win battles but not wars against the Third, or rather that winning wars, even if possible, could not guarantee control of such territories. The major asset of imperialism had disappeared, namely the readiness of colonial populations, once conquered, to let themselves be quietly administered by a handful of occupiers. Ruling Bosnia-Hercegovina had been no problem for the Habsburg Empire, but in the early 1990s all governments were advised by their military advisers that the pacification of that unhappy war-torn country would require the presence, for an indefinite period, of several hundreds of thousands of troops, i.e. a mobilization comparable to that of a major war. Somaliland had always been a difficult colony, and had once even briefly required the intervention of a British force headed by a Major-General, and yet it had not crossed the minds of London or Rome that even Muhammad ben Abdallah, the celebrated "Mad Mullah," raised permanently unmanageable problems for the British and Italian colonial governments. Yet in the early 1990s the U.S.A. and the rest of the U.N. forces of occupation of several tens of thousands withdrew ignominiously when confronted with the option of an indefinite occupation without clear ends. Even the might of the great U.S.A. blenched when faced in neighbouring Haiti—a traditional satellite and dependent of Washington—by a local general, heading the local, American-armed and shaped army, who refused to allow an elected and (reluctantly) American-backed president to return, and challenged the U.S.A. to occupy Haiti. The U.S.A. refused to occupy Haiti once again, as it had done from 1915 until 1934, not because the one thousand or so uniformed thugs of the Haitian army constituted a serious military problem, but because it simply did not know any longer how to settle the Haitian problem by outside force.

In short, the century ended in a global disorder whose nature was unclear, and without an obvious mechanism for either ending it or keeping it under control.

II

The reason for this impotence lay not only in the genuine profundity and complexity of the world's crises, but also in the apparent failure of all programmes, old and new, for managing or improving the affairs of the human race.

The Short Twentieth Century had been an era of religious wars, though the most militant and bloodthirsty of its religious were secular ideologies of nineteenth-century vintage, such as socialism and nationalism, whose god-equivalents were either abstractions or politicians venerated in the manner of divinities. Probably the extremes of such secular devotion were already in decline even before the end of the Cold War, including the various political cults of personality, or, rather, they had been reduced from universal churches to a scattering of rival sects. Nevertheless, their strength had lain not so much in their ability to mobilize emotions akin to those of traditional religion—ideological liberalism hardly even tried—but in their promise to provide lasting solutions to the problems of a world in crisis. Yet just this was what they now failed to provide as the century ended.

The collapse of the U.S.S.R. naturally drew attention primarily to the failure of Soviet communism, that is to say, of the attempt to base an entire economy on universal state-ownership of the means of production and all-encompassing central planning, without any effective recourse to market or pricing mechanisms. All other historic forms of the socialist ideal had assumed an economy based on the social ownership of all means of production, distribution and exchange (though not necessarily central state ownership), and the elimination of private enterprise and resource allocation by a competitive market. Hence this failure also undermined the aspirations of non-communist socialism, Marxist or otherwise, even though no such regimes or governments had actually claimed to establish socialist economies. Whether, or in which of its forms, Marxism, the intellectual justification and inspiration of communism, would continue remained a matter of debate. However, clearly, if Marx would live on as a major thinker, which could hardly be doubted, none of the versions of Marxism formulated since the 1890s as doctrines of political action and aspiration for socialist movements were likely to do so in their original forms.

On the other hand, the counter-utopia to the Soviet one was also demonstrably bankrupt. This was the theological faith in an economy in which resources were allocated *entirely* by the totally unrestricted market, under conditions of unlimited competition, a state of affairs believed to produce not only the maximum of goods and services, but also the maximum of happiness and the only kind of society deserving the name of "freedom." No such purely *laissez-faire* society had ever existed. Unlike the Soviet utopia, fortunately no attempt to institute the ultra-liberal utopia in practice had been made before the 1980s. It had survived most of the Short Twentieth Century as a principle for criticizing both the inefficiencies of existing economies and the growth of state power and bureaucracy. The most consistent attempt to do so in the West, Mrs. Thatcher's regime in Britain, whose economic failure was generally admitted by the time of her overthrow, had to operate with a certain gradualism. However, when attempts were made to institute such *laissez-faire* economies to replace the former Soviet-socialist economies at short notice by means of the "shock therapies" recommended by Western advisers, the results were economically dreadful and both socially and politically disastrous. The theories on which the neo-liberal theology was based, while elegant, had little relation to reality.

The failure of the Soviet model confirmed supporters of capitalism in their conviction that no economy without a stock exchange could work; the failure of the ultra-liberal model confirmed socialists in the more justified belief that human affairs, including the economy, were too important to be left to the market. It also supported the supposition of sceptical economists that there was no visible correlation between a country's economic success or failure and the distinction of its economic theorists.* However, it may well be that the debate which confronted capitalism and socialism as mutually exclusive and polar opposites will be seen by future generations as a relic of the twentieth-century ideological Cold Wars of Religion. It may turn out to be as irrelevant to the third millennium as the debate between Catholics and various reformers in the sixteenth and seventeenth centuries on what constituted true Christianity proved to be in the eighteenth and nineteenth.

More serious than the evident breakdown of the two polar extremes was the disorientation of what might be called the intermediate or mixed

---

*If anything, it might even suggest an inverse correlation. Austria was not a byword for economic success in the days (before 1938) when it possessed one of the most distinguished schools of economic theorists; it became one after the Second World War when it was hard to think of any economist resident in that country with a reputation outside it. Germany, which refused even to recognize the internationally recognized brand of economic theory in its universities, did not appear to suffer. How many Korean or Japanese economists are cited in the average issue of the *American Economic Review*? However, Scandinavia, social-democratic, prosperous and full of the most internationally respected economic theorists since the late nineteenth century, could be cited on the other side of the argument.

programmes and policies which had presided over the most impressive economic miracles of the century. These had pragmatically combined public and private, market and planning, state and business, as the occasion and local ideology warranted. The problem here lay not in the application of some intellectually attractive or impressive theory, whether or not this was defensible in the abstract, for the strength of these programmes had been practical success rather than intellectual coherence. It was the erosion of that practical success. The Crisis Decades demonstrated the limitations of the various Golden Age policies, but without—as yet—generating convincing alternatives. They also revealed the unpredicted but dramatic social and cultural consequences of the era of economic world revolution since 1945, as well as their potentially catastrophic ecological consequences. In short, they revealed that human collective institutions had lost control over the collective consequences of human action. Indeed, one of the intellectual attractions which helps to explain the brief vogue for the neo-liberal utopia was precisely that it purported to by-pass collective human decisions. Let every individual pursue his or her satisfaction without restraint, and, whatever the result was, it was the best that could be achieved. Any alternative course it was implausibly argued, was worse.

If the programmatic ideologies born of the Age of Revolution and the nineteenth century found themselves at a loss at the end of the twentieth century, the most ancient guides to the perplexed of this world, the traditional religions, provided no plausible alternative. The Western ones were in disarray, even in the few countries—headed by that strange anomaly, the U.S.A.—where membership of churches and frequent attendance at religious rituals were still habitual (Kosmin, Lachmann, 1993). The decline of the various Protestant denominations accelerated. Churches and chapels, constructed at the beginning of the century, stood empty at its end, or were sold to be used for some other purpose, even in countries like Wales, where they had helped to shape the national identity. From the 1960s on, as we have seen, the decline of Roman Catholicism became precipitous. Even in the ex-communist countries, where the Church had enjoyed the advantage of symbolizing opposition to deeply unpopular regimes, the post-communist Catholic sheep showed the same tendency to stray from their shepherd as elsewhere. Religious observers sometimes believed they could detect a return to religion in the post-Soviet region of Orthodox Christianity, but at the end of the century the evidence for this unlikely, though not impossible development was not strong. A diminishing number of men and women listened to the various doctrines of these Christian denominations, whatever their merits.

The decline and fall of the traditional religions was not compensated, at least in the urban society of the developed world, by the growth of militantly sectarian religion, or by the rise of novel cults and cult communities, still less by the evident desire of so many men and women to take refuge from a world they could neither understand nor control in a variety of beliefs whose very irrationality constituted their strength. The public visibility of such sects, cults and beliefs should not distract attention from the relative weakness of their support. Not more than 3–4 per cent of British Jews belonged to any of the ultra-orthodox sects or groups. Not more than 5 per cent of the U.S. adult population belonged to the militant and missionary sects (Kosmin, Lachmann, 1993, pp. 15–16).*

In the Third World and on its fringes the situation was indeed different, always excepting the vast population of the Far East, whom the Confucian tradition had kept immune to official religion for some millennia, though not to unofficial cults. Here, indeed, one might have expected the religious traditions which constituted popular ways of thinking about the world to become prominent on the public scene, as the common people became established actors on that scene. This is what happened in the last decades of the century, as the secularized and modernizing elite minorities who had led their countries into the modern world were marginalized (see chapter 12). The appeal of politicized religion was all the greater because the old religions were, almost by definition, enemies to the Western civilization which was the agent of social disruption, and to the rich and godless countries that looked, more than ever, like the exploiters of the poor world's poverty. That the local targets of such movements were the Westernized rich with their Mercedes and emancipated women, added a tinge of class struggle to such movements. They became familiarly (but misleadingly) known as "fundamentalism" in the West. Whatever the fashionable name, such movements looked back, as it were *ex officio*, to some simpler and stabler and more comprehensible age of the imagined past. Since there was no way back to such an era, and since these ideologies could have nothing of relevance to say about the actual problems of societies utterly unlike those of, say, pastoral nomads in the ancient Middle East, they provided no guidance to these problems. They were symptoms of what the Viennese wit Karl Kraus called psychoanalysis: "the disease of which they purport to be the cure."

*I have counted in those describing themselves as Pentecostal, Churches of Christ, Jehovah's Witnesses, Seventh Day Adventists, Assemblies of God, Holiness Churches, "Born Again" and "Charismatic."

This was also the case of the amalgam of slogans and emotions—it can hardly be called an ideology—which flourished on the ruins of the old institutions and ideologies, much in the way weeds had colonized the bombed ruins of European cities after the Second World War bombs fell. This was xenophobia and identity politics. To reject an unacceptable present is not necessarily to formulate, let alone to provide a solution to its problems (see chapter 14/v). Indeed, the closest thing to a political programme reflecting such an approach, the Wilsonian–Leninist "right to national self-determination" for supposedly homogeneous ethnic-linguistic-cultural "nations," was patently being reduced to a savage and tragic absurdity as the new millennium approached. In the early 1990s, perhaps for the first time, rational observers irrespective of politics (other than those of some specific group of nationalist activism) began publicly to propose the abandonment of the "right of self-determination."*

Not for the first time, the combination of intellectual nullity with strong, even desperate, mass emotion, was politically powerful in times of crisis, insecurity, and—over large parts of the globe—disintegrating states and institutions. Like the movements of inter-war resentment which had generated fascism, the religio-political protests of the Third World and the hunger for a secure identity and social order in a disintegrating world (the call for "community" was habitually joined with the call for "law and order") provided the humus in which effective political forces could grow. These in turn could overthrow old regimes and become new ones. However, they were no more likely to produce solutions for the new millennium than fascism had been to produce solutions for the Age of Catastrophe. At the end of the Short Twentieth Century it was not even clear whether they were capable of generating organized national mass movements of the kind which had made some fascisms politically formidable even before they acquired the decisive weapon of state power. Their major asset was probably an immunity to academic economics and the anti-state rhetoric of a liberalism identified

*Cf. the 1949 forecast of an exiled anti-communist Russian, Ivan Ilyin (1882–1954), who predicted the consequences of attempting an impossible "rigorous ethnic and territorial sub-division" of post-Bolshevik Russia. "On the most modest assumptions we would have a score of separate 'states,' none with an uncontested territory, nor governments with authority, nor laws, nor tribunals, nor army, nor an ethnically defined population. A score of empty labels. And slowly, in the course of the following decades, new states would form, by separation or disintegration. Each of them would wage a long struggle with its neighbours for territory and population, in what would amount to an endless series of civil wars within Russia" (cited in Chiesa, 1993, pp. 34, 36–37).

with the free market. If politics were to dictate re-nationalizing an industry, they would not be put off by arguments to the contrary, especially when they could not understand them. And yet, if they were ready to do anything, they knew no more than anyone else what should be done.

III

Neither, of course, does the author of this book. And yet, some long-term tendencies of development were so plain that they allow us to sketch both an agenda of some of the world's major problems, and at least some of the conditions for their solution.

The two central, and, in the long run, decisive, problems were demographic and ecological. The world's population, exploding in size since the middle of the twentieth century, was generally expected to stabilize at about ten billion human beings, or five times its 1950 numbers, some time around 2030, essentially by a decline in the Third World's birthrate. If this forecast were to prove wrong, all bets on the future would be off. Even if it proved roughly realistic, it would raise the problem, not hitherto ever faced on a global scale, of how to maintain a stable world population or, more likely, a world population fluctuating round a level or slightly rising (or falling) trend. (A dramatic fall in the global population, improbable but not inconceivable, would introduce yet further complexities.) However, stable or not, the predictable movements of the world's population were certain to increase the disequilibria among its different regions. On the whole, as in the Short Twentieth Century, the rich and developed countries would be those whose population would be the first to stabilize, or even no longer to reproduce itself, as several such countries in the 1990s no longer did.

Surrounded by poor countries with vast armies of the young, clamouring for the modest jobs in the rich world which make men and women rich by the standards of El Salvador or Morocco, these countries of many senior citizens and few children would face the choice of allowing massive immigration (which produced political troubles at home), barricading themselves against the immigrants whom they needed (which might be impracticable in the long run), or finding some other formula. The most likely was to permit temporary and conditional immigration, which did not give the foreigners the social and political rights of citizens, i.e. to create essentially inegalitarian societies. These could range from the societies of frank *apartheid* like those of South Africa and Israel (declining in some parts of the world but by no means excluded in others), to the informal toleration of immigrants who made no claims on the receiving country, because they saw it simply as a place in which to earn money from time to time, while basically remaining rooted in their own homeland. Later twentieth-century transport and communications, as well as the enormous gap between the incomes that could be earned in rich and poor countries, made this sort of dual existence more possible than before. Whether it could in the long or even the medium run, render the frictions between natives and foreigners less incendiary, remains in dispute between the eternal optimists and the illusionless sceptics.

There can be little doubt that these frictions will be a major factor in the politics, national or global, of the next decades.

The ecological problems, though in the long run decisive, were not so immediately explosive. This is not to underestimate them, even though, from the time they entered public consciousness and public debate in the 1970s, they tended to be mistakenly discussed in terms of an imminent apocalypse. However, the fact that the "greenhouse effect" may not cause the average sea-level to rise high enough by the year 2000 to drown all of Bangladesh and the Netherlands, or that the loss of an unknown number of species every day is not unprecedented, was no cause for complacency. A rate of economic growth like that of the second half of the Short Twentieth Century, if maintained indefinitely (assuming this to be possible), must have irreversible and catastrophic consequences for the natural environment of this planet, including the human race which is part of it. It will not destroy the planet or make it absolutely uninhabitable, but it will certainly change the pattern of life on the biosphere, and may well make it uninhabitable by the human species as we know it in anything like its present numbers. Moreover, the rate at which modern technology has increased the capacity of our species to transform the environment is such that, even if we assume that it does not accelerate, the time available to deal with the problem must be measured in decades rather than centuries.

About the answer to this approaching ecological crisis only three things can be said with reasonable certainty. First, that it must be global rather than local, even though clearly more time would be gained if the greatest single source of global pollution, the 4 per cent of the world's population who inhabit the U.S.A., were to be charged a realistic price for the petrol they consume. Second, that the objective of ecological policy must be both radical and realistic. Market solutions, i.e. including the costs of environmental externalities in the price consumers pay for their goods and services, are neither. As the example of the U.S.A. shows, even a modest attempt to raise an energy tax in that country can raise insuperable political difficulties. The record of oil prices since 1973 proves that, in a free market society, the effect of multiplying energy costs twelve-to fifteenfold in six years, was not to diminish energy use but to make it more efficient, while encouraging massive investment in new and environmentally dubious sources of irreplaceable fossil fuel. These in turn would lower the price again and encourage more wasteful use. On the other hand, proposals like a world of zero growth, let alone fantasies like a return to the alleged primitive symbiosis between man and nature, while radical, were completely impracticable. Zero growth under existing conditions would freeze the present inequalities between the world's countries, a situation more tolerable to the average inhabitant of Switzerland than to the average inhabitant of India. It is no accident that the main support for ecological policies comes from the rich countries and from the comfortable rich and middle classes in all countries (except for businessmen who hope to make money by polluting activities). The poor, multiplying and under-employed, wanted more "development" not less.

Yet, rich or not, the supporters of ecological policies were right. The rate of development must be reduced to what was "sustainable" in the medium run—the term was conveniently meaningless—and, in the long run, a balance would have to be struck between humanity, the (renewable) resources it consumed and the effect of its activities on the environment. Nobody knew and few dared to speculate how this was to be done, and at what level of population, technology and consumption such a permanent balance would be possible. Scientific expertise could no doubt establish what needed to be done to avoid an irreversible crisis, but the problem of establishing such a balance was not one of science and technology, but political and social. One thing, however, was undeniable. It would be incompatible with a world economy based on the unlimited pursuit of profit by economic enterprises dedicated, by definition, to this object and competing with each other in a global free market. From the environmental point of view, if humanity was to have a future, the capitalism of the Crisis Decades could have none.

IV

Considered in isolation, the problems of the world economy were, with one exception, less serious. Even left to itself, it would continue to grow. If there was anything in the Kondratiev periodicity (see p. 87), it was due to enter another era of prosperous expansion before the end of the millennium, although this might be hampered for a while by the after-effects of the disintegration of Soviet socialism, by the collapse of parts of the world into anarchy and warfare, and perhaps by an excessive dedication to global free trade, about which economists tend to be more starry-eyed than economic historians. Nevertheless, the scope for expansion was enormous. The Golden Age, as we have seen, was primarily the great leap forward of the "developed market economies," perhaps twenty countries inhabited by about six hundred millions (1960). Globalization and the international redistribution of production would continue to bring most of the rest of the world's six thousand million into the global economy. Even congenital pessimists had to admit that this was an encouraging prospect for business.

The major exception was the, apparently irreversible, widening of the chasm between the rich and poor countries of the world, a process somewhat accelerated by the disastrous impact of the 1980s in much of the Third World, and the pauperization of many ex-socialist countries. Short of a spectacular fall in the growth-rate of the Third World population, the gap looked like continuing to widen. The belief, following neoclassical economics, that unrestricted international trade would allow the poorer countries to come closer to the rich, runs counter to historical experience as well as common sense.* A world economy developing by the generation of such growing inequalities was, almost inevitably, accumulating future troubles.

However, in any case economic activities do not and cannot exist in isolation from their context and consequences. As we have seen, three aspects of the late twentieth-century world economy gave cause for alarm. First, technology continued to squeeze human labour out of the production of goods and services, without providing either enough work of the same kind for those it jettisoned, or the guarantee of a rate of economic growth sufficient to absorb them. Very few observers seriously expected even a temporary return to the full employment of the Golden Age in the West. Second, while labour remained a major factor of production, the globalization of the economy shifted industry from its old centres in the rich countries with high-cost labour to countries whose main advantage, other things being equal, was cheap hands and heads.

---

*The examples of successful export-led Third World industrialization usually quoted—Hong Kong, Singapore, Taiwan and South Korea—represent less than 2 per cent of the Third World population.

One or both of two consequences must follow: the transfer of jobs from high-wage to low-wage regions and (on free-market principles) the fall of wages in high-wage regions under the pressure of global wage competition. Old industrial countries like Britain could therefore move in the direction of becoming cheap-labour economies themselves, though with socially explosive results and unlikely to compete on this basis with the NICs. Historically such pressures had been countered by state action— e.g. by protectionism. However, and this was the third worrying aspect of the *fin-de-siècle* world economy, its triumph and that of a pure free market ideology, weakened, or even removed most instruments for managing the social effects of economic upheavals. The world economy was an increasingly powerful and uncontrolled engine. Could it be controlled, and, if so, by whom?

This raised both economic and social problems, though obviously far more immediately troubling ones in some countries (e.g. Britain) than in others (e.g. South Korea).

The economic miracles of the Golden Age had rested on rising real incomes in the "developed market economies," for mass-consumption economies need mass consumers with enough income for high-technology consumer durables.* Most of these incomes had been earned as wages in high-wage labour markets. These were now at risk, though mass consumers were more essential to the economy than ever. Of course, in the rich countries the mass market had been stabilized by the shift of labour from industry to tertiary occupations, which had, in general, much stabler employment, and by the vast growth in transfer incomes (mostly social security and welfare). These represented something like 30 per cent of the joint GNP of the Western developed countries in the late 1980s. In the 1920s they had probably stood at less than 4 per cent of GNP (Bairoch, 1993, p. 174). This may well explain why the Wall Street stock exchange collapse of 1987, the largest since 1929, did not lead to a world capitalist slump like that of the 1930s.

However, precisely these two stabilizers were now being undermined. As the Short Twentieth Century ended, Western governments and economic orthodoxy agreed that the cost of public social security and welfare was too high and must be reduced, and mass reduction of employment in the hitherto stablest sectors of tertiary occupations—

---

*It is not widely realized that all developed countries except the U.S.A sent a *smaller* share of their exports to the Third World in 1990 than in 1938. The Western ones (including the U.S.A.) sent less than one fifth of their exports there in 1990 (Bairoch, 1993, Table 6.1, p. 75).

public employment, banking and finance, the technologically redundant mass office-work—became common. These were not immediate dangers to the global economy, so long as the relative decline in the old markets was compensated by expansion in the rest of the world or, so long as the global number of those with rising real incomes grew faster than the rest. To put it brutally, if the global economy could discard a minority of poor countries as economically uninteresting and irrelevant, it could also do so with the very poor within the borders of any and all its countries, so long as the number of potentially interesting consumers was sufficiently large. Seen from the impersonal heights from which business economists and corporate accountants survey the scene, who needed the 10 per cent of the U.S. population whose real hourly earnings since 1979 had *fallen* by up to 16 per cent?

Again, taking the global perspective which is implicit in the model of economic liberalism, inequalities of development are irrelevant unless it can be shown that they produce globally more negative than positive results.* From this point of view there is no economic reason why, if comparative costs say so, France should not shut down its entire agriculture and import all its foodstuffs, or why, if this were technically possible, as well as cost-effective, all the world's TV programmes should not be made in Mexico City. However, this is not a view that can be held without reservations by those who live in the national economy, as well as in the global one; that is to say, by all national governments and most of the inhabitants of their countries. Not least, because we cannot avoid the social and political consequences of worldwide upheavals.

Whatever the nature of these problems, an unrestricted and uncontrolled global free-market economy could provide no solution for them. If anything, it was likely to make developments such as the growth of permanent unemployment and underemployment worse, since the rational choice of profit-making businesses was a) to cut down the number of its employees as much as possible, human beings being more expensive than computers, and b) to cut down social security (or any other) taxes as far as possible. Nor was there any good reason to suppose that the global free-market economy would solve them. Until the 1970s national and world capitalism had never operated under such conditions or, if they had, had not necessarily benefited. For the nineteenth century it is at least arguable that "contrary to the classical model, free trade coincided with and was probably the main cause of depression and protectionism

---

*As a matter of fact, this can often be shown.

was probably the main cause of development for most of today's developed countries" (Bairoch, 1993, p. 164). As for the twentieth century, its economic miracles were not achieved by *laissez-faire* but against it.

It was therefore likely that the fashion for economic liberalization and "marketization," which had dominated the 1980s, and reached a peak of ideological complacency after the collapse of the Soviet system, would not last long. The combination of the world crisis of the early 1990s, and the spectacular failure of such policies when applied as "shock therapy" in the ex-socialist countries, already caused second thoughts among some former enthusiasts—who would have expected economic consultants in 1993 to announce "Perhaps Marx was right after all"? However, two major obstacles stood in the way of a return to realism. The first was the absence of a credible political threat to the system, such as communism and the existence of the U.S.S.R., or—in a different way—the Nazi conquest of Germany had once seemed to be. These, as this book has tried to show, had provided the incentive for capitalism to reform itself. The collapse of the U.S.S.R., the decline and fragmentation of the working class and its movements, the military insignificance in conventional war of the Third World, the reduction of the really poor in the developed countries to a minority "underclass"—all these diminished the incentive for reform. Nevertheless, the rise of movements of the ultra-Right, and the unexpected revival of support for the heirs of the old regime in the ex-communist countries, were warning signals, and, by the early 1990s, once again seen to be such. The second was the very process of globalization, reinforced by the dismantling of the national mechanisms for protecting the victims of the free global economy from the social costs of what was proudly described as "the system of wealth creation . . . now everywhere regarded as the most effective that humanity has yet devised."

For, as the same editorial of the *Financial Times* (24/12/93) admitted

It remains, however, an imperfect force . . . About two thirds of the world's population have gained little or no substantial advantage from rapid economic growth. In the developed world, the lowest quartile of income earners have witnessed trickle-up rather than trickle-down.

As the millennium approached, it became increasingly evident that the central task of the time was not to gloat over the corpse of Soviet communism, but to consider, once again, the built-in defects of capitalism. What changes in the system would their removal require? Would it still be the same system after their removal? For, as Joseph Schumpeter

had observed, apropos of the cyclical fluctuations of the capitalist economy, they "are not, like tonsils, separate things that can be treated by
themselves, but are, like the beat of the heart, of the essence of the organism that displays them" (Schumpeter, 1939, I, v).

V

The immediate reaction of Western commentators to the collapse of the
Soviet system was that it ratified the permanent triumph of both capitalism and liberal democracy, two concepts which the less sophisticated of
North American world-watchers tended to confuse. Though capitalism
was certainly not in the best of shape at the end of the Short Twentieth
Century, Soviet-type communism was unquestionably dead, and quite
unlikely to revive. On the other hand, no serious observer in the early
1990s could be as sanguine about liberal democracy as about capitalism.
The most that could be predicted with some confidence (except, perhaps,
for the more divinely inspired fundamentalist regimes) was that practically all states would continue to declare their profound attachment to
democracy, organize elections of some kind, with some toleration for a
sometimes notional opposition, while putting their own gloss on the
meaning of the term.*

Indeed, the most obvious thing about the political situation of the
world's states was its instability. In most of them the chances of survival
for the existing regime over the next ten or fifteen years were, on the
most optimistic calculation, not good. Even where countries had a relatively predictable system of government, as, for instance, Canada, Belgium or Spain, their existence as single states in ten or fifteen years might
be uncertain, and, consequently, so would be the nature of their possible
successor regimes, if any. In short, politics was not a field that encouraged
futurology.

Nevertheless, some features of the global political landscape stood out.
The first, as already noted, was the weakening of the nation-state, the
central institution of politics since the Age of Revolution, both by virtue
of its monopoly of public power and law, and because it constituted the

---

*Thus a Singaporean diplomat argued that developing countries might benefit
from a "postponement" of democracy, but that, when it arrived, it would be less
permissive than the Western type; more authoritarian, stressing the common good
rather than individual rights; often with a single dominant party; and nearly always
a centralized bureaucracy and "strong state."

effective field of political action for most purposes. The nation-state was eroded in two ways, from above and below. It was rapidly losing power and function to various supra-national entities, and, indeed, absolutely, inasmuch as the disintegration of large states and empires produced a multiplicity of smaller ones, too weak to defend themselves in an era of international anarchy. It was also, as we have seen, losing its monopoly of effective power and its historic privileges within its borders, as witness the rise of private security or protection and the rise of private courier services to compete with the post, hitherto virtually everywhere managed by a state ministry.

These developments did not make the state either redundant or ineffective. Indeed, in some respects its capacity to monitor and control the affairs of its citizens was reinforced by technology, since virtually all their financial and administrative transactions (other than small cash payments) were now likely to be recorded by some computer, and all their communications (except for most face-to-face conversations in the open air) could now be intercepted and recorded. And yet, its posture had changed. From the eighteenth century until the second half of the twentieth, the nation-state had extended its range, powers and functions almost continuously. This was an essential aspect of "modernization." Whether governments were liberal, conservative, social-democratic, fascist or communist, at the peak of this trend, the parameters of citizens' lives in "modern" states were almost exclusively determined (except during inter-state conflict) by the activities or inactivities of that state. Even the impact of global forces, such as world economic booms and slumps, came to them filtered through their state's policy and institutions.* By the end of the century the nation-state was on the defensive against a world economy it could not control; against the institutions it had constructed to remedy its own international weakness, such as the European Union; against its apparent financial incapacity to maintain the services to its citizens so confidently undertaken a few decades ago; against its real incapacity to maintain what, by its own criteria, was its major function: the maintenance of public law and order. The very fact that, during the era of its rise, the state had taken over and centralized so many functions,

---

*Thus Bairoch suggests that the reason why the Swiss GNP per capita fell in the 1930s while that of the Swedes rose—in spite of the fact that the Great Slump had been much less severe in Switzerland—is "largely explained by the wide range of socio-economic measures taken by the Swedish government and the lack of intervention by the Swiss federal authorities" (Bairoch, 1993, p. 9).

and set itself such ambitious standards of public order and control, made its inability to maintain them doubly painful.

And yet, the state, or some other form of public authority representing the public interest, was more indispensable than ever if the social and environmental iniquities of the market economy were to be countered, or even—as the reform of capitalism in the 1940s had shown—if the economic system was to operate satisfactorily. Without some state allocation and redistribution of the national income, what, for instance, would happen to the peoples of the old developed countries, whose economy rested on a relatively shrinking foundation of income earners, squeezed between the rising numbers of those not needed for labour by the high-tech economy, and a swelling proportion of the non-earning old? It was absurd to argue that the citizens of the European Community, whose per capita share of the joint national income had increased by 80 per cent from 1970 to 1990, could not "afford" the level of income and welfare in 1990 that had been taken for granted in 1970 (World Tables, 1991, pp. 8–9). But these could not exist without the state. Suppose—the scenario is not utterly fantastic—present trends continued, and led to economies in which one quarter of the population worked gainfully, and three quarters did not, but after twenty years the economy produced a national income per capital twice as large as before. Who, except public authority, would and could ensure a minimum of income and welfare for all? Who could counter the tendencies to inequality so strikingly visible in the Crisis Decades? To judge by the experience of the 1970s and 1980s, not the free market. If these decades proved anything it was that the major political problem of the world, and certainly of the developed world, was not how to multiply the wealth of nations, but how to distribute it for the benefit of their inhabitants. This was so even in poor "developing" countries which needed more economic growth. Brazil, a monument to social neglect, had a GNP per capita almost two-and-a-half times as large as Sri Lanka in 1939, and over six times as large at the end of the 1980s. In Sri Lanka, which had subsidized basic foodstuffs and given free education and health care until the later 1970s, the average newborn could expect to live several years longer than the average Brazilian, and to die as an infant at about half the Brazilian rate in 1969, at a third of the Brazilian rate in 1989 (World Tables, pp. 144–47, 524–27). The percentage of illiteracy in 1989 was almost twice as great in Brazil as on the Asian island.

Social distribution and not growth would dominate the politics of the new millennium. Non-market allocation of resources, or, at least, a ruthless limitation of market allocation, was essential to head off the impending ecological crisis. One way or another, the fate of humanity in the new millennium would depend on the restoration of public authorities.

VI

This leaves us with a double problem. What would be the nature and scope of the decision-making authorities—supranational, national, subnational and global, alone or in combination? What would be their relation to the people about whom these decisions are made?

The first was, in a sense, a technical question, since the authorities were already in existence, and in principle—though by no means in practice—so were models of the relationship between them. The expanding European Union provided plenty of relevant material, even if every specific proposal for dividing labour between global, supranational, national and subnational authorities was likely to be bitterly resented by someone or other. The existing global authorities were no doubt too specialized in their functions, though they tried to extend their range by imposing political and ecological policies on countries that needed to borrow money. The European Union stood alone, and, being the child of a specific and probably unrepeatable historical conjuncture, was likely to remain alone, unless something similar was to be reconstituted from fragments of the former U.S.S.R. The pace at which supranational decision-making would advance, could not be predicted. Nevertheless, it would certainly advance, and one could see how it might operate. It operated already, through the global bank-managers of the great international lending-agencies, representing the joint resources of the oligarchy of the richest countries, which also happened to include the most powerful ones. As the gap between the rich and poor grew, the scope for exercising such global power looked like increasing. The trouble was that, since the 1970s, the World Bank and the International Monetary Fund, politically backed by the U.S.A., had pursued a policy systematically favouring free-market orthodoxy, private enterprise and global free trade, which suited the late twentieth-century U.S. economy as well as it had the mid-nineteenth-century British one, but not necessarily the world. If global decision-making was to realize its potential, such policies would have to be changed. This did not look an immediate prospect.

The second problem was not technical at all. It arose out of the dilemma of a world committed, at the end of the century, to a particular brand of political democracy, but also faced with policy problems, to which the election of presidents and pluri-party assemblies were irrelevant, even when it did not complicate their solutions. More generally, it was the dilemma of the role of the common people in what had been called, correctly, at least by pre-feminist standards, "the century of the common man." It was the dilemma of an age when government could—some would say: must—be "of the people" and "for the people," but could not in any operational sense be "by the people," or even by representative assemblies elected among those who competed for its vote. The dilemma was not new. The difficulties of democratic politics (discussed for the inter-war years in an earlier chapter) had been familiar to political scientists and satirists since the politics of universal suffrage became more than a peculiarity of the U.S.A.

The democratic predicament was more acute now, both because public opinion, monitored by polls, magnified by the omnipresent media, was now constantly inescapable, and because public authorities had to make far more decisions to which public opinion was no sort of guide. Often they might have to be decisions which might well be opposed by the majority of the electorate, each voter disliking their prospective effect on his or her private affairs, though perhaps believing them to be desirable in the general interest. Thus at the end of the century politicians in some democratic countries had come to the conclusion that any proposal to raise taxes for any purpose meant electoral suicide. Elections therefore became contests in fiscal perjury. At the same time voters and parliaments were constantly faced with decisions on matters about which non-experts—that is to say, the vast majority both of the electors and the elected—had no qualifications to express an opinion, for instance the future of the nuclear industry.

There had been moments, even in democratic states, when the citizen body was so identified with the purposes of a government enjoying legitimacy and public trust that a sense of the common interest prevailed, as in Britain during the Second World War. There had been other situations which made possible a basic consensus between the main political rivals, once again leaving governments free to pursue the general aims of policies, about which there was no major disagreement. As we have seen, this was the case in a number of Western countries during the Golden Age. Governments had also, often enough, been able to rely on a consensus of peer judgment among their technical and scientific advisers, indispensable to administrations of laymen. When they spoke with the same voice, or, at any rate, their consensus overrode dissidents, policy controversy narrowed. It is when they do not, that lay decision-makers grope through darkness, like juries faced with rival psychologists called by prosecution and defence, neither of whom there is strong reason to believe.

But, as we have seen, the Crisis Decades had undermined political consensus and generally accepted truths in intellectual matters, especially in fields with a bearing on policy. As for undivided peoples firmly identified with their governments (or the other way round), they were thin on the ground in the 1990s. True, there were still many countries whose citizens accepted the idea of a strong, active and socially responsible state that deserved some freedom of action, because it served the common welfare. Unfortunately the actual governments of the *fin de siècle* rarely looked like this ideal. As for the countries in which government as such was suspect, they were those which modelled themselves on the U.S.A.'s pattern of individualist anarchism, tempered by litigation and pork-barrel politics, and the much more numerous ones where the state was so weak or so corrupt that citizens did not expect it to produce any public good at all. These were common in parts of the Third World, but, as Italy in the 1980s showed, not unknown in the First.

Hence the most untroubled decision-makers were those who escaped democratic politics altogether: private corporations, supranational authorities and, of course, non-democratic regimes. Within democratic systems it was not so easy to shelter decision-making from politicians, although central banks were removed from their grasp in some countries and conventional wisdom wanted this example followed elsewhere. Increasingly, however, governments took to by-passing both the electorate and its representative assemblies, if possible, or at least to taking decisions first and then challenging both to reverse a *fait accompli*, relying on the volatility, divisions or inertness of public opinion. Politics increasingly became an exercise in evasion, as politicians were afraid to tell voters what they did not want to hear. After the end of the Cold War, unavowable actions were no longer so easily hidden behind the iron curtain of "national security." Almost certainly this strategy of evasion would continue to gain ground. Even in democratic countries more and more decision-making bodies would be withdrawn from electoral control, except in the most indirect sense that the governments which appointed such bodies had themselves, at one time, been elected. Centralizing governments, such as those of Britain in the 1980s and early 1990s, were particularly inclined to multiply such *ad hoc* authorities not answering to an electorate and nicknamed "quangos." Even countries without an effective division of powers found this tacit demotion of democracy convenient. In countries like the U.S.A. it was indispensable, since the built-in conflict between executive and legislature made it almost impossible to take decisions under normal circumstances, except behind the scenes.

By the century's end large numbers of citizens were withdrawing from politics, leaving the affairs of state to the "political class"—the phrase seems to have originated in Italy—who read each others' speeches and editorials, a special-interest group of professional politicians, journalists, lobbyists and others whose occupations ranked at the bottom of the scale of trustworthiness in sociological enquiries. For many people the political process was irrelevant, or merely something that affected their personal lives favourably or not. On the one hand, wealth, the privatization of life and entertainment, and consumer egoism, made politics less important and less attractive. On the other hand, those who reckoned to get little out of elections, turned their backs on them. Between 1960 and 1988 the proportion of blue-collar workers who cast their vote in American presidential elections, fell by one third (Leighly, Naylor, 1992, p. 731). The decline of the organized mass parties, class-based, ideological or both, eliminated the major social engine for turning men and women into politically active citizens. For most people even the collective identification with their country now came more easily through the national sports, teams and non-political symbols than through the institutions of the state.

One might have supposed that de-politicization would leave the authorities freer to take decisions. In fact, it had the opposite effect. The minorities which went on campaigning, sometimes for specific issues of public interest, more often for some sectional interest, could interfere with the smooth processes of government just as effectively, perhaps even more effectively, than all-purpose political parties, since, unlike these, each pressure group could concentrate its energy on pursuing a single objective. Moreover, the increasingly systematic tendency of governments to sidestep the electoral process, magnified the political function of the mass media, which now reached into every household, providing by far the most powerful means of communication from the public sphere to the private men, women and children. Their capacity to discover and publish what authority wished to keep quiet, and to give expression to public feelings which were not, or could no longer be, articulated by the formal mechanisms of democracy, made them into major actors on the public scene. Politicians used them and were frightened of them. Technical progress made them increasingly difficult to control, even in highly authoritarian countries. The decline of state power made them harder to monopolize in non-authoritarian ones. As the century ended it became evident that the media were a more important component of the political process than parties and electoral systems, and likely to remain so—

unless politics took a sharp turn away from democracy. However, while they were enormously powerful as a counterweight to government secrecy, they were in no sense a means of democratic government.

Neither the media, nor assemblies elected by the politics of universal suffrage, nor "the people" itself could actually govern in any realistic sense of the word. On the other hand, government, or any analogous form of public decision-making, could no longer govern against the people or even without it, any more than "the people" could live without or against government. For better or worse, in the twentieth century the common people entered history as actors in their own collective right. Every regime except theocracy now derived its authority from them, even those who terrorized and killed their citizens on a large scale. The very concept of what it was once fashionable to call "totalitarianism" implied populism, for if it did not matter what "the people" thought about those who ruled in its name, why bother to make them think the thoughts deemed appropriate by their rulers? Governments which derived their authority from the unquestioning obedience to some divinity, to tradition, or from the deference of lower to higher ranks in a hierarchical society, were on the way out. Even Islamic "fundamentalism," the most flourishing brand of theocracy, advanced not by the will of Allah, but by the mass mobilization of the common people against unpopular governments. Whether "the people" had the right to elect its government or not, its interventions in public affairs, active or passive, were decisive.

Indeed, just because the twentieth century had plenty of examples of incomparably ruthless regimes, and those seeking to impose minority power on majorities by force—as in *apartheid* South Africa—it demonstrated the limits of sheer coercive power. Even the most ruthless and brutal rulers were well aware that unlimited power alone could not supplant the political assets and skills of authority: a public sense of the regime's legitimacy, a degree of active popular support, the ability to divide and rule, and—especially in times of crisis—the citizens' willing obedience. When, as in 1989, this obedience was visibly withdrawn from Eastern European regimes, these regimes abdicated, even though they still had the full backing of their civil functionaries, armed forces and security services. In short, contrary to appearances, the twentieth century showed that one can rule against all the people for some of the time, some of the people all the time, but not all the people all the time. Admittedly, this was no comfort to permanently oppressed minorities or to peoples who suffered during a generation or more of virtually universal oppression.

Yet all this did not answer the question of what the relation between decision-makers and peoples should be. It merely underlined the difficulty of the answer. The policies of authorities had to take account of what people, or at least majorities of citizens, wanted or did not want, even if it was not their purpose to reflect popular wishes. At the same time they could not govern simply on the basis of asking them. Moreover, unpopular decisions were harder to impose on masses than on power-groups. It was far easier to impose mandatory standards of emission on a few giant auto-producers than to persuade millions of motorists to halve their petrol consumption. Every European government discovered that the results of leaving the future of the European Community to popular votes were unfavourable, or at best unpredictable. Every serious observer knew that many of the policy decisions that would have to be taken in the early twenty-first century, would be unpopular. Perhaps another tension-relaxing era of general prosperity and improvement, like the Golden Age, would soften the citizens' mood, but neither a return to the 1960s nor a relaxation of the social and cultural insecurities and tensions of the Crisis Decades was to be expected.

If voting by universal suffrage remained the general rule—as was probable—there seemed to be two main options. Where decision-making was not already outside politics, it would increasingly side-step the electoral process, or rather the constant monitoring of government inseparable from it. Authorities which had themselves to be elected would also, increasingly, hide, octopus-like, behind clouds of obfuscation to confuse their electorates. The other option was to recreate the sort of consensus which allowed authorities substantial freedom of action, at least so long as the bulk of citizens did not feel too much cause for discontent. An old-established political model for this had been available since Napoleon III in the mid-nineteenth century: the democratic election of a saviour of the people or a nation-saving regime—i.e. "plebiscitary democracy." Such a regime might or might not have come to power constitutionally, but, if ratified by a reasonably honest election with a choice of rival candidates, and some voice for an opposition, it satisfied the *fin-de-siècle* criteria of democratic legitimacy. But it offered no encouraging prospect for the future of parliamentary democracy of the liberal kind.

VII

What I have written cannot tell us whether and how humanity can solve problems it faces at the end of the millennium. Perhaps it can help us understand what these problems are, and what the conditions for their solution must be, but not how far these conditions are present, or in the process of coming into being. It can tell us how little we know, and how extraordinarily poor has been the understanding of men and women who took the major public decisions in the century; how little of what happened, especially in the second half of that century, was expected and still less predicted by them. It can confirm what many have always suspected, that history—among many other and more important things—is the record of the crimes and follies of mankind. It is no help to prophesy.

So it would be foolish to end this book with predictions of what a landscape will look like which has already been left unrecognizable by the tectonic upheavals of the Short Twentieth Century, and will be left even more unrecognizable by those which are even now taking place. There is less reason to feel hopeful about the future than in the middle 1980s, when the present author concluded his trilogy on the history of the "long nineteenth century" (1789–1914) with the words:

> The evidence that the world in the twenty-first century will be better is not negligible. If the world succeeds in not destroying itself [i.e. by nuclear war], the probability will be quite strong.

Nevertheless, even a historian whose age precludes him from expecting dramatic changes for the better in what remains of his lifetime, cannot reasonably deny the possibility that in another quarter- or half-century things may look more promising. In any case it is highly likely that the present phase of post-Cold War breakdown will be temporary, even though it already looks like lasting rather longer than the phases of breakdown and disruption which followed the two "hot" world wars. However, hopes or fears are not predictions. We know that behind the opaque cloud of our ignorance and the uncertainty of detailed outcomes, the historical forces that shaped the century, are continuing to operate. We live in a world captured, uprooted and transformed by the titanic economic and techno-scientific process of the development of capitalism, which has dominated the past two or three centuries. We know, or at least it is reasonable to suppose, that it cannot go on *ad infinitum*. The future cannot be a continuation of the past, and there are signs, both externally, and, as it were, internally, that we have reached a point of historic crisis. The forces generated by the techno-scientific economy are now great enough to destroy the environment, that is to say, the material foundations of human life. The structures of human societies themselves, including even some of the social foundations of the capitalist economy, are on the point of being destroyed by the erosion of what we have inherited from the human past. Our world risks both explosion and implosion. It must change.

We do not know where we are going. We only know that history has brought us to this point and—if readers share the argument of this book—why. However, one thing is plain. If humanity is to have a recognizable future, it cannot be by prolonging the past or the present. If we try to build the third millennium on that basis, we shall fail. And the price of failure, that is to say, the alternative to a changed society, is darkness.

References

Abrams, 1945: Mark Abrams, *The Condition of the British People, 1911–1945* (London, 1945)

Acheson, 1970: Dean Acheson, *Present at the Creation: My Years in the State Department* (New York, 1970)

Afanassiev, 1991: Juri Afanassiev, in M. Paquet ed. *Le court vingtième siècle, preface* d'Alexandre Adler (La Tour d'Aigues, 1991)

Agosti/Borgese, 1992: Paola Agosti, Giovanna Borgese, *Mi pare un secolo: Ritratti e parole di centosei protagonisti del Novecento* (Turin, 1992)

Albers/Goldschmidt/Oehlke, 1971: *Klassenkämpfe in Westeuropa* (Hamburg, 1971)

Alexeev, 1990: M. Alexeev, book review in *Journal of Comparative Economics* vol.14, pp. 171–73 (1990)

Allen, 1968: D. Elliston Allen, *British Tastes: An enquiry into the likes and dislikes of the regional consumer* (London, 1968)

Amnesty, 1975: Amnesty International, *Report on Torture* (New York, 1975)

Andrić, 1990: Ivo Andrić, *Conversation with Goya: Bridges, Signs* (London, 1990)

Andrew, 1985: Christopher Andrew, *Secret Service: The Making of the British Intelligence Community* (London, 1985)

Andrew/Gordievsky, 1991: Christopher Andrew and Oleg Gordievsky, *KGB: The Inside Story of its Foreign Operations from Lenin to Gorbachev* (London, 1991)

Anuario, 1989: *Comisión Economica para America Latina y el Caribe, Anuario Estadístico de America Latina y el Caribe: Edición 1989* (Santiago de Chile, 1990)

Arlacchi, 1983: Pino Arlacchi, *Mafia Business* (London, 1983)

Armstrong, Glyn, Harrison: Philip Armstrong, Andrew Glyn, John Harrison, *Capitalism Since 1945* (Oxford, 1991 edn.)

Arndt, 1944: H. W. Arndt, *The Economic Lessons of the 1930s* (London, 1944)

Asbeck, 1939: Baron F. M. van Asbeck, *The Netherlands Indies' Foreign Relations* (Amsterdam, 1939)

Atlas, 1992: A. Fréron, R. Hérin, J. July eds, *Atlas de la France Universitaire* (Paris, 1992)

Auden: W. H. Auden, *Spain* (London, 1937)

Babel, 1923: Isaac Babel, *Konarmiya* (Moscow, 1923); *Red Cavalry* (London, 1929)

Bairoch, 1985: Paul Bairoch, *De Jéricho à Mexico: villes et économie dans l'histoire* (Paris, 1985)

Bairoch, 1988: Paul Bairoch, *Two major shifts in Western European Labour Force: the Decline of the Manufacturing Industries and of the Working Class* (Geneva, 1988 mimeo)

Bairoch, 1993: Paul Bairoch, *Economics and World History: Myths and Paradoxes* (Hemel Hempstead, 1993)

Ball, 1992: George W. Ball, "JFK's Big Moment" in *New York Review of Books*, 13 February 1992, pp. 16–20

Ball 1993: George W. Ball, "The Rationalist in Power" in *New York Review of Books*, 22 April 1993, pp. 30–36

Baltimore, 1978: David Baltimore, "Limiting Science: A Biologist's Perspective" in *Daedalus* 107/2 spring 1978, pp. 37–46

Banham, 1971: Reyner Banham, *Los Angeles* (Harmondsworth, 1973)

Banham, 1975: Reyner Banham, in C. W. E. Bigsby ed. *Superculture: American Popular Culture and Europe*, pp. 69–82 (London, 1975)

Banks, 1971: A. S. Banks, *Cross-Polity Time Series Data* (Cambridge, MA and London, 1971)

Barghava/Singh Gill, 1988: Motilal Barghava and Americk Singh Gill, *Indian National Army Secret Service* (New Delhi, 1988)

Barnet, 1981: Richard Barnet, *Real Security* (New York, 1981)

Becker, 1985: J. J. Becker, *The Great War and the French People* (Leamington Spa, 1985)

Bédarida, 1992: François Bédarida, *Le génocide et la nazisme: Histoire et témoignages* (Paris, 1992)

Beinart, 1984: William Beinart, "Soil erosion, conservationism and ideas about development: A Southern African exploration, 1900–1960" in *Journal of Southern African Studies* 11, 1984, pp. 52–83

Bell, 1960: Daniel Bell, *The End of Ideology* (Glencoe, 1960)

Bell, 1976: Daniel Bell, *The Cultural Contradictions of Capitalism* (New York, 1976)

Benjamin, 1961: Walter Benjamin, "*Das Kunstwerk im Zeitalter seiner Reproduzierbarkeit*" in *Illuminationen: Ausgewählte Schriften*, pp. 148–184 (Frankfurt, 1961)

Benjamin, 1971: Walter Benjamin, *Zur Kritik der Gewalt und andere Aufsätze*, pp. 84–85 (Frankfurt 1971)

Benjamin, 1979: Walter Benjamin, *One-Way Street, and Other Writings* (London, 1979)

Bergson/Levine, 1983: A. Bergson and H. S. Levine eds. *The Soviet Economy: Towards the Year 2000* (London, 1983)

Berman: Paul Berman, "The Face of Downtown" in *Dissent* autumn 1987, pp. 569–73

Bernal, 1939: J. D. Bernal, *The Social Function of Science* (London, 1939)

Bernal, 1967: J. D. Bernal, *Science in History* (London, 1967)

Bernier/Boily: Gérard Bernier, Robert Boily et al., *Le Québec en chiffres de 1850 à nos jours*, p. 228 (Montreal, 1986)

Bernstorff, 1970: Dagmar Bernstorff, "Candidates for the 1967 General Election in Hyderabad" in E. Leach and S. N. Mukhejee eds, *Elites in South Asia* (Cambridge, 1970)

Beschloss, 1991: Michael R. Beschloss, *The Crisis Years: Kennedy and Khrushchev 1960–1963* (New York, 1991)

Beyer, 1981: Gunther Beyer, "The Political Refugee: 35 Years Later" in *International Migration Review* vol. XV, pp. 1–219

Block, 1977: Fred L. Block, *The Origins of International Economic Disorder: A Study of United States International Monetary Policy from World War II to the Present* (Berkeley, 1977)

Bobinska/Pilch 1975: Celina Bobinska, Andrzej Pilch, *Employment-seeking Emigrations of the Poles World-Wide XIX and XX C* (Cracow, 1975)

Bocca, 1966: Giorgio Bocca, *Storia dell'Italia Partigiana Settembre 1943–Maggio 1945* (Bari, 1966)

Bokhari, 1993: Farhan Bokhari, "Afghan border focus of region's woes" in *Financial Times*, 12 August 1993

Boldyrev, 1990: Yu Boldyrev in *Literaturnaya Gazeta*, 19 December 1990, cited in Di Leo, 1992

Bolotin, 1987: B. Bolotin in *World Economy and International Relations* No. 11, 1987, pp. 148–52 (in Russian)

Bourdieu, 1979: Pierre Bourdieu, *La Distinction: Critique Sociale du Jugement* (Paris, 1979), English trs: *Distinction: A Social Critique of the Judgment of Taste* (Cambridge, MA, 1984)

Bourdieu, 1994: Pierre Bourdieu, Hans Haacke, *Libre-Echange* (Paris, 1994)

Brecht, 1964: Bertolt Brecht, *Über Lyrik* (Frankfurt, 1964)

Brecht, 1976: Bertolt Brecht, *Gesammelte Gedichte*, 4 vols (Frankfurt, 1976)

Britain: *Britain: An Official Handbook* 1961, 1990 eds. (London, Central Office for Information)

Briggs, 1961: Asa Briggs, *The History of Broadcasting in the United Kingdom* vol. 1 (London, 1961); vol.2 (1965); vol.3 (1970); vol.4 (1979)

Brown, 1963: Michael Barratt Brown, *After Imperialism* (London, Melbourne, Toronto, 1963)

Brzezinski 1962: Z. Brzezinski, *Ideology and Power in Soviet Politics* (New York, 1962)

Brzezinski, 1993: Z. Brzezinski, *Out of Control: Global Turmoil on the Eve of the Twenty-first Century* (New York, 1993)

Burks, 1961: R. V. Burks, *The Dynamics of Communism in Eastern Europe* (Princeton, 1961)

Burlatsky, 1992: Fedor Burlatsky, "The Lessons of Personal Diplomacy" in *Problems of Communism*, vol. XVI (41), 1992

Burloiu, 1983: Petre Burloiu, *Higher Education and Economic Development in Europe 1975–80* (UNESCO, Bucharest, 1983)

Butterfield 1991: Fox Butterfield, "Experts Explore Rise in Mass Murder" in *New York Times* 19 October 1991, p. 6

Calvocoressi, 1989: Peter Calvocoressi, *World Politics Since 1945* (London, 1989 edn.)

Carritt, 1985: Michael Carritt, *A Mole in the Crown* (Hove, 1980)

Carr-Saunders, 1958: A. M. Carr-Saunders, D. Caradog Jones, C. A. Moser, *A Survey of Social Conditions in England and Wales* (Oxford, 1958)

Catholic: *The Official Catholic Directory* (New York, annual)

Chamberlin, 1933: W. Chamberlin, *The Theory of Monopolistic Competition* (Cambridge, MA, 1933)

Chamberlin, 1965: W. H. Chamberlin, *The Russian Revolution, 1917–1921*, 2 vols (New York, 1965 edn).

Chandler, 1977: Alfred D. Chandler Jr., *The Visible Hand: The Managerial Revolution in American Business* (Cambridge, MA, 1977)

Chapple/Garofalo, 1977: S. Chapple and R. Garofalo, *Rock'n Roll Is Here to Pay* (Chicago, 1977)

Chiesa, 1993: Giulietta Chiesa, *"Era una fine inevitabile?"* in *Il Passagio: rivista di dibattito politico e culturale*, VI, July-October, pp. 27–37

Childers, 1983: Thomas Childers, *The Nazi Voter: The Social Foundations of Fascism in Germany, 1919–1933* (Chapel Hill, 1983)

Childers, 1991: "The *Sonderweg* controversy and the Rise of German Fascism" in (unpublished conference papers) *Germany and Russia in the 20th Century in Comparative Perspective*, pp. 8, 14–15 (Philadelphia, 1991)

China Statistics, 1989: State Statistical Bureau of the People's Republic of China, *China Statistical Yearbook 1989* (New York, 1990)

Ciconte, 1992: Enzo Ciconte, *"Ndrangheta dall" Unita a oggi* (Barri, 1992)

Cmd 1586, 1992: British Parliamentary Papers cmd 1586: *East India (Non-Cooperation)*, XVI, p. 579, 1922 (Telegraphic Correspondence regarding the situation in India)

Considine, 1982. Douglas M. Considine and Glenn Considine, *Food and Food Production Encyclopedia* (New York, Cincinnati, etc., 1982). Article in "meat," section, "Formed, Fabricated and Restructured Meat Products"

Crosland, 1957: Anthony Crosland, *The Future of Socialism* (London, 1957)

Dawkins, 1976: Richard Dawkins, *The Selfish Gene* (Oxford, 1976)

Deakin/Storry, 1966: F. W. Deakin and G.R. Storry, *The Case of Richard Sorge* (London, 1966)

Debray, 1965: Régis Debray, *La révolution dans la révolution* (Paris, 1965)

Debray, 1994: Régis Debray, *Charles de Gaulle: Futurist of the Nation* (London, 1994)

Degler, 1987: Carl N. Degler, "On re-reading 'The Woman in America' " in *Daedalus*, autumn 1987

Delgado, 1992: Manuel Delgado, *La Ira Sagrada: Anticlericalismo, iconoclastia y antirritualismo en la España contemporanea* (Barcelona, 1992)

Delzell, 1970: Charles F. Delzell ed., *Mediterranean Fascism, 1919–1945* (New York, 1970)

Deng, 1984 Deng Xiaoping, *Selected Works of Deng Xiaoping (1975–1984)* (Beijing, 1984)

Desmond/Moore: Adrian Desmond and James Moore, *Darwin* (London, 1991)

Destabilization, 1989: United Nations Inter-Agency Task Force, Africa Recovery Programme/Economic Commission for Africa, *South African Destabilization: The Economic Cost of Frontline Resistance to Apartheid* (New York, 1989)

Deux Ans, 1990: *Ministère de l'Education Nationale:Enseignement Supérieur*, Deux Ans d'Action, 1988–1990 (Paris, 1990)

Di Leo, 1992: Rita di Leo, *Vecchi quadri e nuovi politici: Chi commanda davvero nell'ex-Urss?* (Bologna, 1992)

Din, 1989: Kadir Din, "Islam and Tourism" in *Annals of Tourism Research*, vol. 16/4, 1989, pp. 542 ff.

Djilas, 1957: Milovan Djilas, *The New Class* (London, 1957)

Djilas, 1962: Milovan Djilas, *Conversations with Stalin* (London, 1962)

Djilas, 1977: Milovan Djilas, *Wartime* (New York, 1977)

Drell, 1977: Sidney D. Drell, "Elementary Particle Physics" in *Daedalus* 106/3, summer 1977, pp. 15–32

Duberman et al., 1989: M. Duberman, M. Vicinus and G. Chauncey, *Hidden From History: Reclaiming the Gay and Lesbian Past* (New York, 1989)

Dutt, 1945: Kalpana Dutt, *Chittagong Armoury Raiders: Reminiscences* (Bombay, 1945)

Duverger, 1972: Maurice Duverger, *Party Politics and Pressure Groups: A Comparative Introduction* (New York, 1972)

Dyker, 1985: D. A. Dyker, *The Future of the Soviet Economic Planning System* (London, 1985)

Echenberg, 1992: Myron Echenberg, *Colonial Conscripts: The* Tirailleurs Sénégalais *in French West Africa, 1857–1960* (London, 1992)

EIB Papers, 1992: European Investment Bank, Cahiers BEI/EIB Papers, J. Girard, *De la recession à la reprise en Europe Centrale et Orientale,* pp. 9–22, (Luxemburg, 1992)

Encyclopedia Britannica, article "war" (11th edn., 1911).

Ercoli, 1936: Ercoli, *On the Peculiarity of the Spanish Revolution* (New York, 1936); reprinted in Palmiro Togliatti, *Opere* IV/i, pp. 139–54 (Rome, 1979)

Esman, 1990: Aaron H. Esman, *Adolescence and Culture* (New York, 1990)

Estrin/Holmes, 1990: Saul Estrin and Peter Holmes, "Indicative Planning in Developed Economies" in *Journal of Comparative Economics* 14/4 December 1990, pp. 531–54

Eurostat: *Eurostat. Basic Statistics of the Community* (Office for the Official Publications of the European Community, Luxemburg, annual since 1957)

Evans, 1989: Richard Evans, *In Hitler's Shadow: West German Historians and the Attempt to Escape from the Nazi Past* (New York, 1989)

Fainsod, 1956: Merle Fainsod, *How Russia Is Ruled* (Cambridge, MA, 1956)

FAO, 1989: FAO (U.N. Food and Agriculture Organization), *The State of Food and Agriculture: World and Regional Reviews, Sustainable Development and Natural Resource Management* (Rome, 1989)

FAO Production: FAO *Production Yearbook,* 1986

FAO Trade: FAO *Trade Yearbook* vol. 40, 1986

Fitzpatrick, 1994: Sheila Fitzpatrick, *Stalin's Peasants* (Oxford, 1994)

Firth, 1954: Raymond Firth, "Money, Work and Social Change in Indo-Pacific Economic Systems" in *International Social Science Bulletin,* vol. 6, 1954, pp. 400–410

Fischhof et al., 1978: B. Fischhof, P. Slovic, Sarah Lichtenstein, S. Read, Barbara Coombs, "How Safe is Safe Enough? A Psychometric Study of Attitudes towards Technological Risks and Benefits" in *Policy Sciences 9,* 1978, pp. 127–52

Flora, 1983: Peter Flora et al., *State, Economy and Society in Western Europe 1815–1975: A Data Handbook in Two Volumes* (Frankfurt, London, Chicago, 1983)

Floud et al., 1990: Roderick Floud, Annabel Gregory, Kenneth Wachter, *Height, Health and History: Nutritional Status in the United Kingdom 1750–1980* (Cambridge, 1990)

Fontana, 1977: Alan Bullock and Oliver Stallybrass eds., *The Fontana Dictionary of Modern Ideas* (London, 1977 edn.)

Foot, 1976: M. R. D. Foot, *Resistance: An Analysis of European Resistance to Nazism 1940–1945* (London, 1976)

Francia, Muzzioli, 1984: Mauro Francia, Giuliano Muzzioli, *Cent'anni di cooperazione: La cooperazione di consumo modenese aderente alla Lega dalle origini all'unificazione* (Bologna, 1984)

Frazier, 1957: Franklin Frazier, *The Negro in the United States* (New York, 1957 edn.)

Freedman, 1959: Maurice Freedman, "The Handling of Money: A Note on the Background to the Economic Sophistication of the Overseas Chinese" in *Man*, vol. 59, April 1959, pp. 64–65

Friedan, 1963: Betty Friedan, *The Feminine Mystique* (New York, 1963)

Friedman 1968: Milton Friedman, "The Role of Monetary Policy" in *American Economic Review*, vol. LVIII, no. 1, March 1968, pp. 1–17

Frobel, Heinrichs, Kreye, 1986: Folker Frobel, Jürgen Heinrichs, Otto Kreye, *Umbruch in der Weltwirtschaft* (Hamburg, 1986)

Galbraith, 1974: J. K. Galbraith, *The New Industrial State* (2nd edn., Harmondsworth, 1974)

Gallagher, 1971: M. D. Gallagher, "Léon Blum and the Spanish Civil War" in *Journal of Contemporary History*, vol. 6, no. 3, 1971, pp. 56–64

Garton Ash, 1990: Timothy Garton Ash, *The Uses of Adversity: Essays on the Fate of Central Europe* (New York, 1990)

Gatrell/Harrison, 1993: Peter Gatrell and Mark Harrison, "The Russian and Soviet Economies in Two World Wars: A Comparative View" in *Economic History Review* XLVI, 3, 1993, pp. 424–52

Giedion, 1948: S. Giedion, *Mechanisation Takes Command* (New York, 1948)

Gillis, 1974: John R. Gillis, *Youth and History* (New York, 1974)

Gillis, 1985: John R. Gillis, *For Better, For Worse:British Marriages 1600 to the Present* (New York, 1985)

Gillois, 1973: André Gillois, *Histoire Secrète des Français à Londres de 1940 à 1944* (Paris, 1973)

Gimpel, 1992: "Prediction or Forecast? Jean Gimpel interviewed by Sanda Miller" in *The New European*, vol. 5/2, 1992, pp. 7–12

Ginneken/Heuven, 1989: Wouter van Ginneken and Rolph van der Heuven, "Industrialisation, employment and earnings (1950–87): An international survey" in *International Labour Review*, vol. 128, 1989/5, pp. 571–99

Gleick, 1988: James Gleick, *Chaos: Making a New Science* (London, 1988)

Glenny 1992: Misha Glenny, *The Fall of Yugoslavia: The Third Balkan War* (London, 1992)

Glyn, Hughes, Lipietz, Singh, 1990: Andrew Glyn, Alan Hughes, Alan Lipietz, Ajit Singh, *The Rise and Fall of the Golden Age* in Marglin and Schor, 1990, pp. 39–125

Gómez Rodríguez, 1977: Juan de la Cruz Gómez Rodríguez, *"Comunidades de pastores y reforma agraria en la sierra sur peruana"* in Jorge A. Flores Ochoa, *Pastores de puna* (Lima, 1977)

González Casanova 1975: Pablo González Casanova, coord. *Cronología de la violencia política en América Latina (1945–1970)*, 2 vols (Mexico DF, 1975)

Goody, 1968: Jack Goody, "Kinship: descent groups" in *International Encyclopedia of Social Sciences*, vol. 8, pp. 402–3 (New York, 1968)

Goody, 1990: Jack Goody, *The Oriental, the Ancient and the Primitive:Systems of Marriage and the Family in the Pre-Industrial Societies of Eurasia* (Cambridge, 1990)

Gopal, 1979: Sarvepalli Gopal, *Jawaharlal Nehru: A Biography, vol. II, 1947–1956* (London, 1979)

Gould, 1989: Stephen Jay Gould, *Wonderful Life: The Burgess Shale and the Nature of History* (London, 1990)

Graves/Hodge, 1941: Robert Graves, and Alan Hodge, *The Long Week-End: A Social History of Great Britain 1918–1939* (London, 1941)

Gray, 1970: Hugh Gray, "The landed gentry of Telengana" in E. Leach and S. N. Mukherjee eds. *Elites in South Asia* (Cambridge, 1970)

Guerlac, 1951: Henry E. Guerlac, "Science and French National Strength" in Edward Meade Earle ed., *Modern France: Problems of the Third and Fourth Republics* (Princeton, 1951)

Guidetti/Stahl, 1977: M. Guidetti and Paul M. Stahl eds., *Il sangue e la terra: Comunità di villagio e comunità familiari nell Europea dell 800* (Milano, 1977)

Guinness, 1984: Robert and Celia Dearling, *The Guinness Book of Recorded Sound* (Enfield, 1984)

Haimson, 1964/5: Leopold Haimson, "The Problem of Social Stability in Urban Russia 1905–1917" in *Slavic Review*, December 1964, pp. 619–64; March 1965, pp. 1–22

Halliday, 1983: Fred Halliday, *The Making of the Second Cold War* (London, 1983)

Halliday/Cumings, 1988: Jon Halliday and Bruce Cumings, *Korea: The Unknown War* (London, 1988)

Halliwell, 1988: *Leslie Halliwell's Filmgoers' Guide Companion* 9th edn., 1988, p. 321

Hànak, 1970: *"Die Volksmeinung wahrend des letzten Kriegsjahres in Österreich-Ungarn"* in *Die Auflosung des Habsburgerreiches. Zusammenbruch und Neuorientierung im Donauraum, Schriftenreihe des osterreichischen Ost- und Südosteuropainstituts* vol. III, pp. 58–66 (Vienna, 1970)

Harden, 1990: Blaine Harden, *Africa, Despatches from a Fragile Continent* (New York, 1990)

Harff/Gurr, 1988: Barbara Harff and Ted Robert Gurr, "Victims of the State: Genocides, Politicides and Group Repression since 1945" in *International Review of Victimology*, I, 1989, pp. 23–41

Harff/Gurr, 1989: Barbara Harff and Ted Robert Gurr, "Toward Empirical Theory of Genocides and Politicides: Identification and Measurement of Cases since 1945," *International Studies Quarterly*, 32, 1988, pp. 359–71

Harris, 1987: Nigel Harris, *The End of the Third World* (Harmondsworth, 1987)

Hayek, 1944: Friedrich von Hayek, *The Road to Serfdom* (London, 1944)

Heilbroner, 1993: Robert Heilbroner, *Twenty-first Century Capitalism* (New York, 1993)

Hilberg 1985: Raul Hilberg, *The Destruction of the European Jews* (New York, 1985)

Hilgerdt: See League of Nations, 1945

Hill, 1988: Kim Quaile Hill, *Democracies in Crisis: Public Policy Responses to the Great Depression* (Boulder and London, 1988)

Hirschfeld, 1986: G. Hirschfeld ed., *The Policies of Genocide: Jews and Soviet Prisoners of War in Nazi Germany* (Boston, 1986)

Historical Statistics of the United States: Colonial Times to 1970, part 1c, 89–101, p. 105 (Washington DC, 1975)

Hobbes: Thomas Hobbes, *Leviathan* (London, 1651)

Hobsbawm 1974: E. J. Hobsbawm, "Peasant Land Occupations" in *Past & Present*, 62, February 1974, pp. 120–52

Hobsbawm, 1986: E. J. Hobsbawm, "The Moscow Line and international Communist policy 1933–47" in Chris Wrigley ed. *Warfare, Diplomacy and Politics: Essays in Honour of A. J. P. Taylor*, pp. 163–88 (London, 1986)

Hobsbawm, 1987: E. J. Hobsbawm, *The Age of Empire 1870–1914* (London, 1987)

Hobsbawm, 1990: E. J. Hobsbawm, *Nations and Nationalism Since 1780: Programme, Myth, Reality* (Cambridge, 1990)

Hobsbawm, 1993: E. J. Hobsbawm, *The Jazz Scene* (New York, 1993)

Hodgkin, 1961: Thomas Hodgkin, *African Political Parties: An Introductory Guide* (Harmondsworth, 1961)

Hoggart, 1958: Richard Hoggart, *The Uses of Literacy* (Harmondsworth, 1958)

Holborn, 1968: Louise W. Holborn, "Refugees I: World Problems" in *International Encyclopedia of the Social Sciences* vol. XIII, p. 363

Holland, R.F., 1985: R. F. Holland, *European Decolonization 1918–1981: An Introductory Survey* (Basingstoke, 1985)

Holman, 1993: Michael Holman, "New Group Targets the Roots of Corruption" in *Financial Times*, 5 May 1993

Holton, 1970: G. Holton, "The Roots of Complementarity" in *Daedalus*, autumn 1978, p.1017

Holton, 1972: Gerald Holton ed., *The Twentieth-Century Sciences: Studies in the Biography of Ideas* (New York, 1972)

Horne, 1989: Alistair Horne, *Macmillan*, 2 vols (London, 1989)

Housman, 1988: A. E. Housman, *Collected Poems and Selected Prose* edited and with an introduction and notes by Christopher Ricks (London, 1988)

Howarth, 1978: T .E. B. Howarth, *Cambridge Between Two Wars* (London, 1978)

Hu, 1966: C. T. Hu, "Communist Education: Theory and Practice" in R. Mac-Farquhar ed., *China Under Mao: Politics Takes Command* (Cambridge, MA, 1966)

Huber, 1990: Peter W. Huber, "Pathological Science in Court" in *Daedalus*, vol. 119, no. 4, autumn 1990, pp. 97–118

Hughes, 1969: H. Stuart Hughes, "The second year of the Cold War: A Memoir and an Anticipation" in *Commentary*, August 1969

Hughes 1983: H. Stuart Hughes, *Prisoners of Hope: The Silver Age of the Italian Jews 1924–1947* (Cambridge, MA, 1983)

Hughes, 1988: H. Stuart Hughes, *Sophisticated Rebels* (Cambridge and London, 1988)

Human Development: United Nations Development Programme (UNDP) *Human Development Report,* (New York, 1990, 1991, 1992)

Hutt, 1935: Allen Hutt, *This Final Crisis* (London, 1935)

Ignatieff, 1993: Michael Ignatieff, *Blood and Belonging: Journeys into the New Nationalism* (London, 1993)

ILO, 1990: *ILO Yearbook of Labour Statistics: Retrospective edition on Population Censuses 1945–1989* (Geneva, 1990)

IMF, 1990: International Monetary Fund, Washington: *World Economic Outlook: A Survey by the Staff of the International Monetary Fund,* Table 18: Selected Macro-economic Indicators 1950–1988 (IMF, Washington, May 1990)

Investing: *Investing in Europe's Future* ed. Arnold Heertje for the European Investment Bank (Oxford, 1983)

Isola, 1990: Gianni Isola, *Abbassa la tua radio, per favore. Storia dell'ascolto radiofonico nell'Italia fascista* (Firenze, 1990)

Jacobmeyer, 1985: Wolfgang Jacobmeyer, *Vom Zwangsarbeiter zum heimatlosen Auslander* (Gottingen, 1985)

Jacob, 1993: Margaret C. Jacob, "Hubris about Science" in *Contention*, vol. 2, no. 3 (Spring 1993)

Jammer, 1966: M. Jammer, *The Conceptual Development of Quantum Mechanics* (New York, 1966)

Jayawardena, 1993: Lal Jayawardena, *The Potential of Development Contracts and Towards Sustainable Development Contracts, UNU/WIDER: Research for Action* (Helsinki, 1993)

Jensen, 1991: K. M. Jensen ed., *Origins of the Cold War: The Novikov, Kennan and Roberts "Long Telegrams" of 1946,* United States Institute of Peace (Washington, DC, 1991)

Johansson/Percy 1990: Warren Johansson and William A. Percy ed., *Encyclopedia of Homosexuality,* 2 vols (New York and London, 1990)

Johnson, 1972: Harry G. Johnson, *Inflation and the Monetarist Controversy* (Amsterdam, 1972)

Jon, 1993: Jon Byong-Je, *Culture and Development: South Korean Experience*, International Inter-Agency Forum on Culture and Development, September 20–22 1993, Seoul

Jones, 1992: Steve Jones, review of David Raup, *Extinction: Bad Genes or Bad Luck?* in *London Review of Books*, 23 April 1992

Jowitt, 1991: Ken Jowitt, "The Leninist Extinction" in Daniel Chirot ed., *The Crisis of Leninism and the Decline of the Left* (Seattle, 1991)

Julca, 1993: Alex Julca, *From the Highlands to the City* (unpublished paper, 1993)

Kakwani, 1980: Nanak Kakwani, *Income Inequality and Poverty* (Cambridge, 1980)

Kapuściński, 1983: Ryszard Kapuściński, *The Emperor* (London, 1983)

Kapuściński, 1990: Ryszard Kapuściński, *The Soccer War* (London, 1990)

Kater, 1985: Michael Kater, *"Professoren und Studenten im dritten Reich"* in *Archiv f. Kulturgeschichte* 67/1985, no. 2, p. 467

Katsiaficas, 1987: George Katsiaficas, *The Imagination of the New Left: A Global Analysis of 1968* (Boston, 1987)

Kedward, 1971: R. H. Kedward, *Fascism in Western Europe 1900–1945* (New York, 1971)

Keene, 1984: Donald Keene, *Japanese Literature of the Modern Era* (New York, 1984)

Kelley, 1988: Allen C. Kelley, "Economic Consequences of Population Change in the Third World" in *Journal of Economic Literature*, XXVI, December 1988, pp.1685–1728

Kennedy, 1987: Paul Kennedy, *The Rise and Fall of the Great Powers* (New York, 1987)

Kerblay, 1983: Basile Kerblay, *Modern Soviet Society* (New York, 1983)

Kershaw, 1983: Ian Kershaw, *Popular Opinion and Political Dissent in the Third Reich: Bavaria 1933–1945* (Oxford, 1983)

Kershaw, 1993: Ian Kershaw, *The Nazi Dictatorship: Perspectives of Interpretation*, 3rd edn. (London, 1993)

Khrushchev, 1990: Sergei Khrushchev, *Khrushchev on Khrushchev: An Inside Account of the Man and His Era* (Boston, 1990)

Kidron/Segal, 1991: Michael Kidron and Ronald Segal, *The New State of the World Atlas*, 4th edn (London, 1991)

Kindleberger, 1973: Charles P. Kindleberger, *The World in Depression 1919–1939* (London and New York, 1973)

Koivisto, 1983: Peter Koivisto, "The Decline of the Finnish–American Left 1925–1945" in *International Migration Review*, XVII, 1, 1983

Kolakowski, 1992: Leszek Kolakowski, "Amidst Moving Ruins" in *Daedalus* 121/2, spring 1992

Kolko, 1969: Gabriel Kolko, *The Politics of War: Allied Diplomacy and the World Crisis of 1943–45* (London, 1969)

Kollo, 1990: János Kollö, "After a dark golden age—Eastern Europe" in *WIDER Working Papers* (duplicated), Helsinki, 1990

Kornai: János Kornai, *The Economics of Shortage* (Amsterdam, 1980)

Kosinski, 1987: L. A. Kosinski, review of Robert Conquest, *The Harvest of Sorrow: Soviet Collectivisation and the Terror Famine* in *Population and Development Review*, vol. 13, no. 1, 1987

Kosmin/Lachman, 1993: Barry A. Kosmin and Seymour P. Lachman, *One Nation Under God: Religion in Contemporary American Society* (New York, 1993)

Kraus, 1922: Karl Kraus, *Die letzten Tage der Menschheit: Tragodie in fünf Akten mit Vorspiel und Epilog* (Wien-Leipzig, 1922)

Kulischer, 1948: Eugene M. Kulischer *Europe on the Move: War and Population Changes 1917–1947* (New York, 1948)

Kuttner, 1991: Robert Kuttner, *The End of Laissez-Faire: National Purpose and the Global Economy after the Cold War* (New York, 1991)

Kuznets, 1956: Simon Kuznets, "Quantitative Aspects of the Economic Growth of Nations" in *Economic Development and Culture Change*, vol. 5, no. 1, 1956, pp. 5–94

Kyle, 1990: Keith Kyle, *Suez* (London, 1990)

Ladurie, 1982: Emmanuel Le Roy Ladurie, *Paris–Montpellier: PC-PSU 1945–1963* (Paris, 1982)

Lafargue: Paul Lafargue, *Le droit à la paresse* (Paris, 1883); *The Right to Be Lazy and Other Studies* (Chicago, 1907)

Land Reform: Philip M. Raup, "Land Reform" in art. "Land Tenure," *International Encyclopedia of Social Sciences*, vol. 8, pp. 571–75 (New York, 1968)

Lapidus, 1988: Ira Lapidus, *A History of Islamic Societies* (Cambridge, 1988)

Laqueur, 1977: Walter Laqueur, *Guerrilla: A Historical and Critical Study* (London, 1977)

Larkin, 1988: Philip Larkin, *Collected Poems* ed. and with an introduction by Anthony Thwaite (London, 1988)

Larsen E., 1978: Egon Larsen, *A Flame in Barbed Wire: The Story of Amnesty International* (London, 1978)

Larsen S. et al., 1980· Stein Ugevik Larsen, Bernt Hagtvet, Jan Petter, My Klebost et al., *Who Were the Fascists?* (Bergen–Oslo–Tromso, 1980)

Lary, 1943: Hal B. Lary and Associates, *The United States in the World Economy: The International Transactions of the United States during the Interwar Period*, U.S. Dept. of Commerce (Washington, DC, 1943)

Las Cifras, 1988: *Asamblea Permanente para los Derechos Humanos, La Cifras de la Guerra Sucia* (Buenos Aires, 1988)

Latham, 1981: A. J. H. Latham, *The Depression and the Developing World, 1914–1939* (London and Totowa NJ, 1981)

League of Nations, 1931: *The Course and Phases of the World Depression* (Geneva, 1931; reprinted 1972)

League of Nations, 1945: *Industrialisation and Foreign Trade* (Geneva, 1945)

Leaman, 1988: Jeremy Leaman, *The Political Economy of West Germany 1945–1985* (London, 1988)

Leighly, Naylor, 1992: J. E. Leighly and J. Naylor, "Socioeconomic Class Bias in Turnout 1964–1988: the voters remain the same" in *American Political Science Review*, 86/3 September, 1992, pp. 725–36

Lenin, 1970: V. I. Lenin, *Selected Works in 3 Volumes* (Moscow, 1970: "Letter to the Central Committee, the Moscow and Petrograd Committees and the Bolshevik Members of the Petrograd and Moscow Soviets," October 1/14 1917, V.I. Lenin op. cit, vol. 2, p. 435; Draft Resolution for the Extraordinary All-Russia Congress of Soviets of Peasant Deputies, November 14/27, 1917, V. I. Lenin, loc. cit, p. 496; Report on the activities of the Council of People's Commissars, January 12/24 1918, loc. cit., p. 546

Leontiev, 1977: Wassily Leontiev, "The Significance of Marxian Economics for Present-Day Economic Theory" in *Amer. Econ. Rev. Supplement* vol. XXVIII, 1 March 1938, republished in *Essays in Economics: Theories and Theorizing*, vol. 1, p. 78 (White Plains, 1977)

Lettere: P. Malvezzi and G. Pirelli eds. *Lettere di Condannati a morte della Resistenza europea*, p. 306 (Turin, 1954)

Lévi-Strauss: Claude Lévi-Strauss, Didier Eribon, *De Près et de Loin* (Paris, 1988)

Lewin, 1991: Moshe Lewin, "Bureaucracy and the Stalinist State" unpublished paper in *Germany and Russia in the 20th Century in Comparative Perspective* (Philadelphia, 1991)

Lewis, 1981: Arthur Lewis, "The Rate of Growth of World Trade 1830–1973" in Sven Grassman and Erik Lundberg eds., *The World Economic Order:Past and Prospects* (London, 1981)

Lewis, 1938: Cleona Lewis, *America's Stake in International Investments* (Brookings Institution, Washington, DC,1938)

Lewis, 1935: Sinclair Lewis, *It Can't Happen Here* (New York, 1935)

Lewontin, 1973: R. C. Lewontin, *The Genetic Basis of Evolutionary Change* (New York, 1973)

Lewontin, 1992: R. C. Lewontin, "The Dream of the Human Genome" in *New York Review of Books*, 28 May 1992, pp. 32–40

Leys,1977: Simon Leys, *The Chairman's New Clothes: Mao and the Cultural Revolution* (New York, 1977)

Lieberson, Waters, 1988: Stanley Lieberson and Mary C. Waters, *From Many Strands: Ethnic and Racial Groups in Contemporary America* (New York, 1988)

Liebman/Walker/Glazer: Arthur Liebman, Kenneth Walker, Myron Glazer, *Latin American University Students: A Six-nation Study* (Cambridge, MA, 1972)

Lieven, 1993: Anatol Lieven, *The Baltic Revolution: Estonia, Latvia, Lithuania and the Path to Independence* (New Haven and London, 1993)

Linz, 1975: Juan J. Linz, "Totalitarian and Authoritarian Regimes" in Fred J. Greenstein and Nelson W. Polsby eds., *Handbook of Political Science*, vol. 3, *Macropolitical Theory* (Reading, MA, 1975)

Liu, 1986: Alan P. L. Liu, *How China Is Ruled* (Englewood Cliffs, 1986)

Loth, 1988: Wilfried Loth, *The Division of the World 1941–1955* (London, 1988)

Lu Hsün: as cited in Victor Nee and James Peck eds., *China's Uninterrupted Revolution: From 1840 to the Present*, p. 23 (New York, 1975)

Lynch, 1990: Nicolas Lynch Gamero, *Los jovenes rojos de San Marcos: El radicalismo universitario de los años setenta* (Lima, 1990)

McCracken, 1977: Paul McCracken et al., *Towards Full Employment and Price Stability* (Paris, OECD 1977)

Macluhan, 1962: Marshall Macluhan, *The Gutenberg Galaxy* (New York, 1962)

Macluhan, 1967: Marshall Macluhan and Quentin Fiore, *The Medium is the Massage* (New York, 1967)

McNeill, 1982: William H. McNeill, *The Pursuit of Power: Technology, Armed Force and Society since AD 1000* (Chicago, 1982)

Maddison, 1969: Angus Maddison, *Economic Growth in Japan and the U.S.S.R.* (London, 1969)

Maddison, 1982: Angus Maddison, *Phases of Capitalist Economic Development* (Oxford, 1982)

Maddison, 1987: Angus Maddison, "Growth and Slowdown in Advanced Capitalist Economies: Techniques of Quantitative Assessment" in *Journal of Economic Literature*, vol. XXV, June 1987

Maier, 1987: Charles S. Maier, *In Search of Stability: Explorations in Historical Political Economy* (Cambridge, 1987)

Maksimenko, 1991: V. I. Maksimenko, "Stalinism without Stalin: the mechanism of '*zastoi*'" unpublished paper in *Germany and Russia in the 20th Century in Comparative Perspective* (Philadelphia, 1991)

Mangin, 1970: William Mangin ed., *Peasants in Cities: Readings in the Anthropology of Urbanization* (Boston, 1970)

Manuel, 1988: Peter Manuel, *Popular Musics of the Non-Western World: An Introductory Survey* (Oxford, 1988)

Marglin and Schor, 1990: S. Marglin and J. Schor eds, *The Golden Age of Capitalism* (Oxford, 1990)

Marrus, 1985: Michael R. Marrus, *European Refugees in the Twentieth Century* (Oxford, 1985)

Martins Rodrigues, 1984: "*O PCB: os dirigentes e a organização*" in *O Brasil Republicano*, vol. X, *tomo* III of Sergio Buarque de Holanda ed., *Historia Geral da Civilizacão Brasileira* pp. 390–97 (Saõ Paulo, 1960–84)

Mencken, 1959: Alistair Cooke ed. *The Viking Mencken* (New York, 1959)

Jean A. Meyer, *La Cristiada*, 3 vols (Mexico D.F., 1973–79); English: *The Cristero*

Rebellion: The Mexican People between Church and State 1926–1929 (Cambridge, 1976)

Meyer-Leviné, 1973: Rosa Meyer-Leviné, *Leviné: The Life of a Revolutionary* (London, 1973)

Miles et al., 1991: M. Miles, E. Malizia, Marc A. Weiss, G. Behrens, G. Travis, *Real Estate Development: Principles and Process* (Washington, DC, 1991)

Miller, 1989: James Edward Miller, "Roughhouse diplomacy: the United States confronts Italian Communism 1945–1958" in *Storia delle relazioni internazionali*, V/1989/2, pp. 279–312

Millikan, 1930: R. A. Millikan, "Alleged Sins of Science, in *Scribners Magazine* 87(2), 1930, pp. 119–30

Milward, 1979: Alan Milward, *War, Economy and Society 1939–45* (London, 1979)

Milward, 1984: Alan Milward, *The Reconstruction of Western Europe 1945–51* (London, 1984)

Minault, 1982: Gail Minault, *The Khilafat Movement: Religious Symbolism and Political Mobilization in India* (New York, 1982)

Misra, 1961: B. B. Misra, *The Indian Middle Classes: Their Growth in Modern Times* (London, 1961)

Mitchell/Jones: B. R. Mitchell and H. G. Jones *Second Abstract of British Historical Statistics* (Cambridge, 1971)

Mitchell, 1975: B. R. Mitchell, *European Historical Statistics* (London, 1975)

Moisí, 1981: D. Moisí ed., *Crises et guerres au XXe siècle* (Paris, 1981)

Molano, 1988: Alfredo Molano, *"Violencia y colonización"* in *Revista Foro: Fundación Foro Nacional por Colombia*, 6 June 1988 pp. 25–37

Montagni, 1989: Gianni Montagni, *Effetto Gorbaciov: La politica internazionale degli anni ottanta. Storia di quattro vertici da Ginevra a Mosca* (Bari, 1989)

Morawetz, 1977: David Morawetz, *Twenty-five Years of Economic Development 1950–1975* (Johns Hopkins, for the World Bank, 1977)

Mortimer, 1925: Raymond Mortimer, *"Les Matelots"* in *New Statesman*, 4 July 1925, p. 338

Muller, 1951: H. J. Muller in L. C. Dunn ed. *Genetics in the 20th Century: Essays on the Progress of Genetics During the First Fifty Years* (New York, 1951)

Müller, 1992: Heiner Müller, *Krieg ohne Schlacht: Leben in zwei Diktaturen* (Cologne, 1992)

Muzzioli, 1993: Giuliano Muzzioli, *Modena* (Bari, 1993)

Nehru, 1936: Jawaharlal Nehru, *An Autobiography, with musings on recent events in India* (London, 1936)

Nicholson, 1970: E. M. Nicholson cited in *Fontana Dictionary of Modern Thought:* "Ecology" (London, 1977)

Noelle/Neumann, 1967: Elisabeth Noelle and Erich Peter Neumann eds., *The Germans: Public Opinion Polls 1947–1966* p. 196 (Allensbach and Bonn, 1967)

Nolte, 1987: Ernst Nolte, *Der europäische Burgerkrieg, 1917–1945: Nationalsozialismus und Bolschewismus* (Stuttgart, 1987)

North/Pool, 1966: Robert North and Ithiel de Sola Pool, "Kuomintang and Chinese Communist Elites" in Harold D. Lasswell and Daniel Lerner eds., *World Revolutionary Elites: Studies in Coercive Ideological Movements* (Cambridge, MA, 1966)

Nove, 1969: Alec Nove, *An Economic History of the U.S.S.R.* (London, 1969)

Nwoga, 1970: Donatus I. Nwoga, "Onitsha Market Literature" in *Mangin*, 1970

Observatoire, 1991: *Comité Scientifique auprès du Ministère de l'Education Nationale*, unpublished paper, *Observatoire des Thèses* (Paris, 1991)

OECD Impact: OECD: *The Impact of the Newly Industrializing Countries on Production and Trade in Manufactures: Report by the Secretary-General* (Paris, 1979)

OECD National Accounts: *OECD National Accounts 1960–1991*, vol. 1 (Paris, 1993)

Ofer, 1987: Gur Ofer, "Soviet Economic Growth, 1928-1985" in *Journal of Economic Literature*, XXV/4, December 1987, p. 1778

Ohlin, 1931: Bertil Ohlin, for the League of Nations, *The Course and Phases of the World Depression* (1931; reprinted Arno Press, New York, 1972)

Olby, 1970: Robert Olby, "Francis Crick, DNA, and the Central Dogma" in Holton 1972, pp. 227–80

Orbach, 1978: Susie Orbach, *Fat is a Feminist Issue: The Anti-diet Guide to Permanent Weight Loss* (New York and London, 1978)

Ory, 1976: Pascal Ory, *Les Collaborateurs: 1940–1945* (Paris, 1976)

Paucker, 1991: Arnold Paucker, *Jewish Resistance in Germany: The Facts and the Problems* (Gedenkstaette Deutscher Widerstand, Berlin, 1991)

Pavone, 1991: Claudio Pavone, *Una guerra civile: Saggio storico sulla moralità nella Resistenza* (Milan, 1991)

Peierls, 1992: Peierls, Review of D.C. Cassidy, *Uncertainty: The Life of Werner Heisenberg* in *New York Review of Books*, 23 April 1992, p. 44

People's Daily, 1959: "Hai Jui reprimands the Emperor" in *People's Daily* Beijing, 1959, cited in Leys, 1977

Perrault, 1987: Gilles Perrault, *A Man Apart: The Life of Henri Curiel* (London, 1987)

Peters, 1985: Edward Peters, *Torture* (New York, 1985)

Petersen, 1986: W. and R. Petersen, *Dictionary of Demography*, vol. 2, art: "War" (New York–Westport–London, 1986)

Piel, 1992: Gerard Piel, *Only One World: Our Own To Make And To Keep* (New York, 1992)

Planck, 1933: Max Planck, *Where Is Science Going?* with a preface by Albert Einstein; translated and edited by James Murphy (New York, 1933)

Polanyi, 1945: Karl Polanyi, *The Great Transformation* (London, 1945)

Pons Prades, 1975: E. Pons Prades, *Republicanos Españoles en la 2a Guerra Mundial* (Barcelona, 1975)

Population, 1984: U.N. Dept of International Economic and Social Affairs: *Population Distribution, Migration and Development. Proceedings of the Expert Group, Hammamet (Tunisia) 21–25 March 1983* (New York, 1984)

Potts, 1990: Lydia Potts, *The World Labour Market: A History of Migration* (London and New Jersey, 1990)

Pravda, 25 January 1991.

Proctor, 1988. Robert N. Proctor, *Racial Hygiene: Medicine Under the Nazis* (Cambridge, MA, 1988)

Programma 2000: PSOE (Spanish Socialist Party), *Manifesto of Programme: Draft for Discussion*, January 1990 (Madrid, 1990)

Prost: A. Prost, *"Frontières et espaces du privé"* in *Histoire de la Vie Privée de la Première Guerre Mondiale à nos Jours* vol. 5, pp.13–153 Paris, 1987

Rado, 1962: A. Rado ed., *Welthandbuch: internationaler politischer und wirtschaftlicher Almanach 1962* (Budapest, 1962)

Ranki, 1971: George Ranki in Peter F. Sugar ed., *Native Fascism in the Successor States: 1918–1945* (Santa Barbara, 1971)

Ransome, 1919: Arthur Ransome, *Six Weeks in Russia in 1919* (London, 1919)

Rate-China, 1973: Manfred Hinz ed., *Rate-China: Dokumente der chinesischen Revolution* (1927–31) (Berlin, 1973)

Raw, Page, Hodgson 1972: Charles Raw, Bruce Page, Godfrey Hodgson, *Do You Sincerely Want To Be Rich?* (London, 1972)

Reale, 1954: Eugenio Reale, *Avec Jacques Duclos au Banc des Accusés à la Réunion Constitutive du Cominform* (Paris, 1958)

Reed, 1919: John Reed, *Ten Days That Shook The World* (New York, 1919 and numerous editions)

Reinhard et al., 1968: M. Reinhard, A. Armengaud, J. Dupaquier, *Histoire Générale de la population mondiale*, 3rd edn. (Paris, 1968)

Reitlinger, 1982: Gerald Reitlinger, *The Economics of Taste: The Rise and Fall of Picture Prices 1760–1960* 3 vols (New York, 1982)

Riley, 1991: C. Riley, "The Prevalence of Chronic Disease During Mortality Increase: Hungary in the 1980s" in *Population Studies*, 45/3 November 1991, pp. 489–97

Riordan, 1991: J. Riordan, *Life After Communism*, inaugural lecture, University of Surrey (Guildford, 1991)

Ripken/Wellmer, 1978: Peter Ripken and Gottfried Wellmer, *"Bantustans und ihre Funktion für das südafrikanische Herrschaftssystem"* in Peter Ripken,

Sudliches Afrika: Geschichte, Wirtschaft, politische Zukunft, pp. 194–203, Berlin, 1978

Roberts, 1991: Frank Roberts, *Dealing with the Dictators: The Destruction and Revival of Europe 1930–1970* (London, 1991)

Rosati/Mizsei, 1989: Darius Rosati and Kalman Mizsei, *Adjustment through opening of socialist economies* in UNU/WIDER, Working Paper 52 (Helsinki, 1989)

Rostow, 1978: W. W. Rostow, *The World Economy:History and Prospect* (Austin, 1978)

Russell Pasha, 1949: Sir Thomas Russell Pasha, *Egyptian Service, 1902–1946* (London, 1949)

Samuelson, 1943: Paul Samuelson, "Full employment after the war" in S. Harris ed., *Post-war Economic Problems* (New York, 1943), pp. 27–53

Sareen, 1988: T.R. Sareen, *Select Documents on Indian National Army* (New Delhi, 1988)

Sassoon, 1947: Siegfried Sassoon, *Collected Poems* (London, 1947)

Schatz, 1983: Ronald W. Schatz, *The Electrical Workers: A History of Labor at General Electric and Westinghouse* (University of Illinois Press, 1983)

Schell, 1993: Jonathan Schell, "A Foreign Policy of Buy and Sell" (*New York Newsday*, 21 November 1993)

Schram, 1966: Stuart Schram, *Mao Tse Tung* (Baltimore, 1966))

Schrodinger, 1944: Erwin Schrodinger, *What Is Life: The Physical Aspects of the Living Cell* (Cambridge, 1944)

Schumpeter, 1939: Joseph A. Schumpeter, *Business Cycles: A Theoretical, Historical and Statistical Analysis of the Capitalist Process*, 2 vols. (New York, 1939)

Schumpeter, 1954: Joseph A. Schumpeter, *History of Economic Analysis* (New York, 1954)

Schwartz, 1966: Benjamin Schwartz, "Modernisation and the Maoist Vision" in Roderick MacFarquhar ed., *China Under Mao: Politics Takes Command* (Cambridge, MA, 1966)

Scott, 1985. James C. Scott, *Weapons of the Weak: Everyday Forms of Peasant Resistance* (New Haven and London, 1985)

Seal, 1968: Anil Seal, *The Emergence of Indian Nationalism: Competition and Collaboration in the later Nineteenth Century* (Cambridge, 1968)

Sinclair, 1982: Stuart Sinclair, *The World Economic Handbook* (London, 1982)

Singer, 1972: J. David Singer, *The Wages of War 1816–1965: A Statistical Handbook* (New York, London, Sydney, Toronto, 1972)

Smil, 1990: Vaclav Smil, "Planetary Warming: Realities and Responses" in *Population and Development Review*, vol. 16, no.1, March 1990

Smith, 1989: Gavin Alderson Smith, *Livelihood and Resistance: Peasants and the Politics of the Land in Peru* (Berkeley, 1989)

Snyder, 1940: R. C. Snyder, "Commercial policy as reflected in Treaties from 1931 to 1939" in *American Economic Review*, 30, 1940, pp. 782–802

Social Trends: UK Central Statistical Office, *Social Trends 1980* (London, annual)

Solzhenitsyn, 1993: Alexander Solzhenitsyn in *New York Times* 28 November 1993

Somary, 1929: Felix Somary, *Wandlungen der Weltwirtschaft seit dem Kriege* (Tubingen, 1929)

Sotheby: *Art Market Bulletin*, A Sotheby's Research Department Publication, End of season review, 1992

Spencer, 1990: Jonathan Spencer, *A Sinhala Village in Time of Trouble: Politics and Change in Rural Sri Lanka* (New Delhi, 1990)

Spero, 1977: Joan Edelman Spero, *The Politics of International Economic Relations* (New York, 1977)

Spriano, 1969: Paolo Spriano, *Storia del Partito Comunista Italiano* Vol. II (Turin, 1969)

Spriano, 1983: Paolo Spriano, *I comunisti europei e Stalin* (Turin, 1983)

S.S.S.R., 1987: *S.S.S.R. v. Tsifrakh v. 1987*, pp. 15–17, 32–33

Staley, 1939: Eugene Staley, *The World Economy in Transition* (New York, 1939)

Stalin, 1952: J. V. Stalin, *Economic Problems of Socialism in the U.S.S.R.* (Moscow, 1952)

Starobin, 1972: Joseph Starobin, *American Communism in Crisis* (Cambridge, MA, 1972)

Starr, 1983: Frederick Starr, *Red and Hot: The Fate of Jazz in the Soviet Union 1917–1980* (New York, 1983)

Stat. Jahrbuch: Federal Republic Germany, Bundesamt für Statistik, *Statistisches Jahrbuch für das Ausland* (Bonn, 1990)

Steinberg, 1990: Jonathan Steinberg, *All or Nothing: The Axis and the Holocaust 1941–43* (London, 1990)

Stevenson, 1984: John Stevenson, *British Society 1914–1945* (Harmondsworth, 1984)

Stoll, 1990: David Stoll, *Is Latin America Turning Protestant: The Politics of Evangelical Growth* (Berkeley, Los Angeles, Oxford, 1992)

Stouffer/Lazarsfeld, 1937: S. Stouffer and P. Lazarsfeld, *Research Memorandum on the Family in the Depression*, Social Science Research Council (New York, 1937)

Stürmer, 1993: Michael Stürmer in *"Orientierungskrise in Politik und Gesellschaft? Perspektiven der Demokratie an der Schwelle zum 21. Jahrhundert"* in *Bergedorfer Gesprächskreis, Protokoll Nr 98* (Hamburg-Bergedorf, 1993)

Stürmer, 1993: Michael Stürmer, *99 Bergedorfer Gesprächskreis* (22–23 May, Ditchley Park): *Wird der Westen den Zerfall des Ostens überleben? Politische und okonomische Herausforderungen für Amerika und Europa* (Hamburg, 1993)

Tanner, 1962: J. M. Tanner, *Growth at Adolescence*, 2nd edn. (Oxford, 1962)

Taylor/Jodice, 1983: C. L. Taylor and D. A. Jodice, *World Handbook of Political and Social Indicators*, 3rd edn. (New Haven and London, 1983)

Taylor, 1990: Trevor Taylor, "Defence industries in international relations" in *Rev. Internat.Studies* 16, 1990, pp. 59–73

Technology, 1986: U.S. Congress, Office of Technology Assessment, *Technology and Structural Unemployment: Reemploying Displaced Adults* (Washington, DC, 1986)

Temin, 1993: Peter Temin, "Transmission of the Great Depression" in *Journal of Economic Perspectives*, vol. 7/2, spring 1993, pp. 87–102

Terkel, 1967: Studs Terkel, *Division Street: America* (New York, 1967)

Terkel, 1970: Studs Terkel, *Hard Times: An Oral History of the Great Depression* (New York, 1970)

Therborn, 1984: Goran Therborn, "Classes and States, Welfare State Developments 1881–1981" in *Studies in Political Economy: A Socialist Review*, no. 13, spring 1984, pp. 7–41

Therborn, 1985: Göran Therborn, "Leaving the Post Office Behind" in M. Nikolic ed., *Socialism in the Twenty-first Century* pp. 225–51 (London, 1985)

Thomas 1971: Hugh Thomas, *Cuba or the Pursuit of Freedom* (London 1971)

Thomas, 1977: Hugh Thomas, *The Spanish Civil War* (Harmondsworth, 1977 edition)

Tiempos, 1990: Carlos Ivan Degregori, Marfil Francke, José López Ricci, Nelson Manrique, Gonzalo Portocarrero, Patricia Ruíz Bravo, Abelardo Sánchez León, Antonio Zapata, *Tiempos de Ira y Amor: Nuevos Actores para viejos problemas*, DESCO (Lima, 1990)

Tilly/Scott, 1987: Louise Tilly and Joan W. Scott, *Women, Work and Family* (second edition, London, 1987)

Titmuss: Richard Titmuss, *The Gift Relationship: From Human Blood to Social Policy* (London, 1970)

Tomlinson, 1976: B. R. Tomlinson, *The Indian National Congress and the Raj 1929–1942: The Penultimate Phase* (London, 1976)

Touchard, 1977: Jean Touchard, *La gauche en France* (Paris, 1977)

Townshend, 1986: Charles Townshend, "Civilization and Frightfulness: Air Control in the Middle East Between the Wars" in C. Wrigley ed. (see Hobsbawm, 1986)

Trofimov/Djangava, 1993: Dmitry Trofimov and Gia Djangava, *Some reflections on current geopolitical situation in the North Caucasus* (London, 1993, mimeo)

Tuma, 1965: Elias H. Tuma, *Twenty-six Centuries of Agrarian Reform: A Comparative Analysis* (Berkeley and Los Angeles, 1965)

Umbruch: See Fröbel, Heinrichs, Kreye, 1986

Umbruch, 1990: Federal Republic of Germany: *Umbruch in Europa: Die Ereignisse im 2. Halbjahr 1989. Eine Dokumentation, herausgegeben vom Auswärtigen Amt* (Bonn, 1990)

U.N. Africa, 1989: U.N. Economic Commission for Africa, Inter-Agency Task Force, Africa Recovery Programme, *South African Destabilization: The Economic Cost of Frontline Resistance to Apartheid* (New York, 1989)

U.N. Dept. of International Economic and Social Affairs, 1984: See Population, 1984

U.N. International Trade: U.N. *International Trade Statistics Yearbook*, 1983

U.N. Statistical Yearbook (annual)

U.N. Transnational, 1988: United Nations Centre on Transnational Corporations, *Transnational Corporations in World Development: Trends and Prospects* (New York, 1988)

U.N. World Social Situation, 1970: U.N. Department of Economic and Social Affairs, *1970 Report on the World Social Situation* (New York, 1971)

U.N. World Social Situation 1985: U.N. Dept. of International Economic and Social Affairs: *1985 Report on the World Social Situation* (New York, 1985)

U.N. World Social Situation 1989: U.N. Dept of International Economic and Social Affairs: *1989 Report on the World Social Situation* (New York, 1989)

U.N. World's Women: U.N. Social Statistics and Indicators Series K no. 8: *The World's Women 1970–1990: Trends and Statistics* (New York, 1991)

UNCTAD: UNCTAD (U.N. Commission for Trade and Development) *Statistical Pocket Book 1989* (New York, 1989)

UNESCO: UNESCO *Statistical Yearbook*, for the years concerned.

U.S. Historical Statistics: U.S. Dept of Commerce. Bureau of the Census, *Historical Statistics of the United States: Colonial Times to 1970*, 3 vols (Washington, DC, 1975)

Van der Linden, 1993: "Forced labour and non-capitalist industrialization: the case of Stalinism" in Tom Brass, Marcel van der Linden, Jan Lucassen, *Free and Unfree Labour* (IISH, Amsterdam, 1993)

Van der Wee: Herman Van der Wee, *Prosperity and Upheaval: The World Economy 1945–1980* (Harmondsworth, 1987)

Veillon 1992: Dominique Veillon, *"Le quotidien" in Ecrire l'histoire du temps présent. En hommage á Francois Bédarida: Actes de la journée d études de l'IHTP*, pp. 315–28 (Paris CNRS, 1993)

Vernikov, 1989: Andrei Vernikov, "Reforming Process and Consolidation in the Soviet Economy," *WIDER Working Papers WP 53* (Helsinki, 1989)

Walker, 1988: Martin Walker, "Russian Diary" in the *Guardian*, 21 March 1988, p. 19

Walker, 1991: Martin Walker, "Sentencing system blights land of the free" in the *Guardian*, 19 June 1991, p. 11

Walker, 1993: Martin Walker, *The Cold War: And the Making of the Modern World* (London, 1993)

Ward, 1976: Benjamin Ward, "National Economic Planning and Politics" in Carlo Cipolla ed., *Fontana Economic History of Europe: The Twentieth Century*, vol. 6/1 (London, 1976)

Watt, 1989: D.C. Watt, *How War Came* (London, 1989)

Weber, 1969: Hermann Weber, *Die Wandlung des deutschen Kommunismus: Die Stalinisierung der KPD in der Weimarer Republik* 2 vols (Frankfurt, 1969)

Weinberg, 1977: Steven Weinberg, "The Search for Unity: Notes for a History of Quantum Field Theory" in *Daedalus*, autumn 1977

Weinberg, 1979: Steven Weinberg, "Einstein and Spacetime Then and Now" in *Bulletin, American Academy of Arts and Sciences*, xxxiii. 2 November 1979

Weisskopf, 1980: V. Weisskopf, "What Is Quantum Mechanics?" in *Bulletin, American Academy of Arts and Sciences*, vol. xxxiii, April 1980

Wiener, 1984: Jon Wiener, *Come Together: John Lennon in his Time* (New York, 1984)

Wildavsky, 1990: Aaron Wildavsky and Karl Dake, "Theories of Risk Perception: Who Fears What and Why?" in *Daedalus*, vol. 119, no. 4, autumn 1990, pp. 41–60

Willett, 1978: John Willett, *The New Sobriety: Art and Politics in the Weimar Period* (London, 1978)

Wilson, 1977: E. O. Wilson, "Biology and the Social Sciences" in *Daedalus* 106/4, autumn 1977, pp. 127–40

Winter, 1986: Jay Winter, *War and the British People* (London, 1986)

"Woman," 1964: "The Woman in America" in *Daedalus* 1964

The World Almanac (New York, 1964, 1993)

World Bank Atlas: *The World Bank Atlas 1990* (Washington, 1990)

World Development: World Bank: *World Development Report* (New York, annual)

World Economic Survey, 1989: U.N. Dept. of International Economic and Social Affairs, *World Economic Survey 1989: Current Trends and Policies in the World Economy* (New York, 1989)

World Labour, 1989: International Labour Office (ILO), *World Labour Report 1989* (Geneva, 1989)

World Resources, 1986: *A Report by the World Resources Institute and the International Institute for Environment and Development* (New York, 1986)

World Tables, 1991: The World Bank: *World Tables 1991* (Baltimore and Washington, DC, 1991)

World's Women: see U.N. World's Women

Zetkin, 1968: Clara Zetkin, "Reminiscences of Lenin" in *They Knew Lenin: Reminiscences of Foreign Contemporaries* (Moscow, 1968)

Ziebura, 1990: Gilbert Ziebura, *World Economy and World Politics 1924–1931: From Reconstruction to Collapse* (Oxford, New York, Munich, 1990)

Zinoviev, 1979: Aleksandr Zinoviev, *The Yawning Heights* (Harmondsworth, 1979)

Further Reading

Here are some suggestions for non-historians who want to know more.

The basic facts of twentieth-century world history can be found in a good college textbook, such as R. R. Palmer and Joel Colton, *A History of the Modern World* (6th edn., 1983 or later), which has the advantage of excellent bibliographies. There are good single-volume surveys of some regions and continents, but not of others. Ira Lapidus, *A History of Islamic Societies* (1988), Jack Gray, *Rebellions and Revolutions: China from the 1800s to the 1980s* (1990), Roland Oliver and Anthony Atmore, *Africa since 1800* (1981) and James Joll, *Europe since 1870* (the most recent edition) are useful. Peter Calvocoressi, *World Politics since 1945* (6th edn., 1991) is quite excellent for its period. It should be read against the background of Paul Kennedy, *The Rise and Fall of the Great Powers* (1987) and Charles Tilly, *Coercion, Capital and European States AD 900-1990* (1990).

Still within the compass of single volumes, W. W. Rostow, *The World Economy: History and Prospect* (1978), though debatable and far from bedside reading, provides a vast stock of information. Much to the point is Paul Bairoch, *The Economic Development of the Third World Since 1900* (1975), as is David Landes, *The Unbound Prometheus* (1969) on the development of technology and industry.

Several works of reference are listed in the reference notes. Among statistical compendia, note the *Historical Statistics of the United States: Colonial Times to 1970* (3 vols., 1975), B. R. Mitchells's *European Historical Statistics* (1980), his *International Historical Statistics* (1986) and P. Flora, *State, Economy and Society in Western Europe 1815-1975* (2 vols., 1983). Chambers' *Biographical Dictionary* is wide-ranging and convenient. For those who like maps, information is available in the imaginative *Times Atlas of World History* (1978), the brilliantly devised Michael Kidron and Ronald Segal, *The New State of the World Atlas* (4th edn., 1991) and the (economic and social) *World Bank Atlas*, annually since 1968. Among the numerous other map compendia, note Andrew Wheatcroft, *The World Atlas of Revolution* (1983), Colin McEvedy & R. Jones, *An Atlas of World Population History* (1982 edn.) and Martin Gilbert, *Atlas of the Holocaust* (1972).

Maps are perhaps even more useful for the historical study of particular regions, among them G. Blake, John Dewdney, Jonathan Mitchell, *The*

Cambridge Atlas of the Middle East and North Africa (1987), Joseph E. Schwarzberg, *A Historical Atlas of South Asia* (1978), J. F. Adeadjayi and M. Crowder, *Historical Atlas of Africa* (1985) and Martin Gilbert, *Russian History Atlas* (1993 edn.). There are good, up-to-date multi-volume histories of several of the world's regions and continents, but, oddly enough, not (in English) of Europe, nor of the world—except in economic history. The Penguin *History of the World Economy in the Twentieth Century* in five volumes is of remarkably high quality: Gerd Hardach, *The First World War 1914–1918;* Derek Aldcroft, *From Versailles to Wall Street, 1919–1929;* Charles Kindleberger, *The World in Depression 1929–1939;* Alan Milward's superb *War, Economy and Society, 1939–45;* and Herman Van der Wee, *Prosperity and Upheaval: The World Economy 1945–1980.*

Of the regional works, the twentieth-century volumes of the *Cambridge Histories of Africa* (vols. 7–8), of *China* (vols. 10–13) and of (Leslie Bethell ed.) *Latin America* (vols. 6–9) are state-of-the art historiography, though for sampling rather than continuous reading. The enterprising *New Cambridge History of India* is unfortunately not sufficiently advanced as yet.

Marc Ferro, *The Great War* (1973) and Jay Winter, *The Experience of World War I* (1989) can guide readers into the First World War; Peter Calvocoressi, *Total War* (1989 edn.), Gerhard L. Weinberg, *A World at Arms: a Global History of World War II* (1994) and Alan Milward's book into the Second World War. Gabriel Kolko, *Century of War. Politics, Conflict and Society since 1914* (1994) covers both wars and their revolutionary aftermath. For the world revolution, John Dunn, *Modern Revolutions* (2nd edn., 1989) and Eric Wolf, *Peasant Wars of the Twentieth Century* (1969) cover the whole range—or almost—including Third World revolutions. See also William Rosenberg and Marilyn Young, *Transforming Russia and China: Revolutionary Struggle in the Twentieth Century* (1982). E. J. Hobsbawm, *Revolutionaries* (1973), especially chapters 1–8, introduces the history of revolutionary movements.

The Russian revolution, drowned in monographs, as yet lacks the bird's-eye syntheses available for the French revolution. It continues to be rewritten. Leon Trotsky, *A History of The Russian Revolution* (1932) is the view from the (Marxist) top; W. H. Chamberlin, *The Russian Revolution 1917–21* (2 vols., 1965 reprint) from the contemporary observer. Marc Ferro, *The Russian Revolution of February 1917* (1972) and *October 1917* (1979) are a fine introduction. The numerous volumes of E. H. Carr's monumental *History of Soviet Russia* (1950–78) are best used for reference. They only reach 1929. Alec Nove, *An Economic History of the U.S.S.R.* (1972) and *The Economics of Feasible Socialism* (1983) are good introductions to the operations of "really existing socialism." Basile Kerblay, *Modern Soviet Society* (1983) is as close to a dispassionate survey of its results in the U.S.S.R. as we have so far got. F. Fejto has written contemporary histories of the "people's democracies." For China, Stuart Schram, *Mao Tsetung* (1967) and John K. Fairbank, *The Great Chinese Revolution 1800–1985* (1986); see also Jack Gray, already cited.

The world economy is covered by the Penguin History series already cited, P. Armstrong, A. Glyn and J. Harrison, *Capitalism since 1945* (1991) and S. Marglin and J. Schor eds., *The Golden Age of Capitalism* (1990). For the period before 1945 the publications of the League of Nations, and for the period since 1960 those of the World Bank, OECD and IMF, are indispensable.

For the politics of inter-war and the crisis of liberal institutions one might suggest Charles S. Maier, *Recasting Bourgeois Europe* (1975), F. L. Carsten, *The Rise of Fascism* (1967), H. Rogger and E. Weber eds., *The European Right: a Historical Profile* (1965) and Ian Kershaw, *The Nazi Dictatorship: Problems and Perspectives* (1985). For the spirit of anti-fascism, P. Stansky and W. Abrahams, *Journey to the Frontier: Julian Bell and John Cornford* (1966). For the outbreak of war, Donald Cameron Watt, *How War Came* (1989). The best conspectus of the Cold War so far is Martin Walker, *The Cold War and the Making of the Modern World* (1993) and the clearest introduction to its later phases, F. Halliday, *The Making of the Second Cold War* (2nd edn., 1986). See also J. L. Gaddis, *The Long Peace: Inquiries into the History of the Cold War* (1987). For the reshaping of Europe, Alan Milward, *The Reconstruction of Western Europe 1945–51* (1984). For consensus politics and the welfare state, P. Flora and A. J. Heidenheimer eds., *Development of Welfare States in America and Europe* (1981) and D. W. Urwin, *Western Europe since 1945: a Short Political History* (revised edn., 1989). See also J. Goldthorpe ed., *Order and Conflict in Contemporary Capitalism* (1984). For the U.S.A., W. Leuchtenberg, *A Troubled Feast: American Society since 1945* (1973).

For the end of empires, Rudolf von Albertini, *Decolonization: the Administration and Future of Colonies, 1919–1960* (1961) and the excellent R. F. Holland, *European Decolonization 1918–1981* (1985). The best way to point readers in the direction of Third World history is to name a handful of otherwise unrelated works about it. Eric Wolf's *Europe and the People without History* (1983) is fundamental, though it only deals marginally with our century. So, in a different way, both about capitalism and communism, is Philip C. C. Huang, *The Peasant Family and Rural Development in the Yangzi Delta, 1350–1988* (1990), to which Robin Blackburn has drawn my attention. It may be compared with Clifford Geertz's classic *Agricultural Involution* (1963), which is about Indonesia. On the urbanization of the Third World, part 4 of Paul Bairoch, *Cities and Economic Development* (1988) is essential. On politics, Joel S. Migdal, *Strong Societies and Weak States* (1988) is full of examples and ideas, some of them convincing.

For the sciences, Gerald Holton ed., *The Twentieth-Century Sciences* (1972) is a starting-point; for intellectual developments in general, George Lichtheim, *Europe in the Twentieth Century* (1972). A fine introduction to the avant-garde arts is John Willett, *Art and Politics in the Weimar Period: The New Sobriety, 1917–1933* (1978).

There are as yet no properly historical treatments of the social and cultural revolutions of the second half of the century, though the mass of comment and documentation is vast, and sufficiently accessible to let many of us form our own opinions (see the reference notes). Readers should not be misled by the confident tone of the literature (including my own observations) into confusing opinion with established truth.

Index

624   *Index*